READINGS IN
Russian History

VOLUME II

From Alexander II
to the Soviet Period

Readings in Russian History
IN TWO VOLUMES

Volume I: From Ancient Times to Nicholas I

Volume II: From Alexander II to the Soviet Period

Among other works by Warren B. Walsh are:

The Development of Western Civilization, 1940
Readers' Guide to Russia, 1945
Russia under Tsars and Commissars, 1946
Russia and the Soviet Union: A Modern History, 1958
Perspectives and Patterns: Discourses on History, 1962

READINGS IN
Russian History

From Ancient Times to the Post-Stalin Era

VOLUME II
From Alexander II
to the Soviet Period

Compiled and edited by

WARREN B. WALSH

Professor of Russian History, Chairman of
the Department of History, and former
Chairman of the Board of Russian Studies
at Syracuse University

FOURTH EDITION
Extensively Revised

SYRACUSE UNIVERSITY PRESS . . . 1963

To
Elizabeth Cantril Walsh

Library of Congress
Catalog Card: 63–14771

FOURTH EDITION

*Manufactured in the United States of America
by Kingsport Press, Inc., Kingsport, Tennessee*

Contents

* indicates primary source

Part VII: THE ROAD TO REVOLUTION

* indicates primary source

Part VIII: THE SOVIET PERIOD

* indicates primary source

* indicates primary source

* indicates primary source

A Note on Translations, Transliterations, and Spellings

The originals of the selections which comprise this anthology range in age from a few years to seven centuries. The language of the originals ranges from Old Slavonic and Latin to modern Russian and French, and some of the translations were made many years ago. All translations which are not the work of the editor are attributed to the translators of record. Styles in translation vary from generation to generation, as well as from country to country, and no attempt to achieve uniformity has been made. Variations in translation, however, are less likely to be troublesome than differences in transliteration and in spelling.

There has never been any uniformly accepted system for the transliteration of Russian personal and place names, and none exists today. At least seven major systems of transliteration were in use in the United States and the United Kingdom in 1962. The French have been wont to transliterate in one fashion, the Germans in a second, the British in a third, and so on; and some of the fashions, moreover, have changed from time to time. National habits, changing styles, accepted conventions (such as the use of Moscow instead of Moskva), and personal idiosyncracies—not to mention errors in writing and in typography—have combined to produce a multiplicity which can be puzzling. The same general comments apply to spellings of English words. To have achieved uniform, consistent transliterations and spellings would have required numerous alterations in almost every selection of this anthology. This seemed neither feasible nor desirable, so—to the dismay of compositors, proofreaders, and copy editors—the transliterations and spellings of the originals have not been changed. Only by pronouncing them to himself will the beginning reader learn that the following pairs, for example, are not different objects or persons, but only variant transliterations: boyar, boiar; vieche, veche; mir, meer; czar, tsar; Lwoff, Lvov; Kluchevsky, Klyuchevskii; and even Rus and Russe.

Preface

This anthology originated in a series of mimeographed "Readings" produced for students in my courses in Russian history. When it became apparent that the need for such supplementary materials was not confined to one campus I prepared the first edition of *Readings in Russian History* (1948). Its chronological scope was from very early times to the February/March Revolution in 1917. Critics soon pointed out that the collection would be more useful if it contained materials on the Soviet period. Selections dealing with the development of the Leninist program and with events after 1917 were added in the second edition (1950).

In the third edition (1959) the coverage of the Soviet period was more than doubled. Other changes included the elimination of those selections which had proved least useful, the addition of new material, and a reorganization of the last part of the book.

The chronological coverage in the fourth edition is now from prehistory to the post-Stalin era. This edition is also different from its predecessors in other ways, but the original emphasis on primary sources continues. There are, in all, 205 selections—many of them having several parts—and over two-thirds of the total are from primary sources. Sitxy-one selections are new, twenty-five of these having been translated from Russian specifically for this book. An additional twenty-six items, selected from secondary sources, are of Russian or Soviet origin. All the editorial notes have been reviewed, and many have been revised. The Table of Contents has been expanded to facilitate the finding of specific items, additional suggestions for further reading have been made, and the general organization has been altered to accommodate the new material and to improve the balance among the eight sections into which the book is now divided.

All these changes stem from experience—either firsthand or generously shared with me by students and colleagues throughout the country. I am grateful for their criticisms, their suggestions, and their advice. I am regretful that it was not always feasible to accept or to implement their counsel. The final choice as to what to print and what to omit obviously had to be mine. I was guided by three specific criteria as well as by my general philosophy of history.

History is, to me, primarily the study of people; or, to put it a little more formally, it is the study of the continuous interactions of multiple and shifting variables, the most important of which are people. I have therefore sought out reports concerning the ways in which people lived, the manner and content of their thinking, their habits of action, their customs, their social norms, and their value judgments—in short, their reality worlds. "People" includes the rulers as well as the ruled, and in an autocracy the characteristics of the autocrat and his associates affect the lives of all. I have therefore included materials which reveal some aspects of the rulers' personalities and policies.

Since social, political, economic, and other institutions also form a part of a society's norm and value pattern, some selections deal with the origins and development of such institutions. Not all institutions nor all aspects of Russian and Soviet history have equal coverage. Legal and military history and the arts, for example, receive relatively little attention. Descriptions of Soviet norms and values are comparatively limited, not because these are unimportant but simply because materials dealing with them are generally available.

Probable availability, or, more accurately, probable unavailability was one of the three specific criteria. Except in a few instances, I have not included selections from materials which seem likely to be readily available. This criterion alone ruled out many basic documents of the Soviet period, such as the constitutions and the Communist party programs and statutes, which have been printed and distributed in large quantities and many forms. The second specific criterion was that an item be of intrinsic interest; the third, that it make a particular contribution toward an increased understanding of some aspect of Russian and Soviet history.

The general organization and the mechanics are essentially the same as in the preceding editions. Each selection is introduced by an editorial note which identifies the source, establishes the relation of the selection to the whole, or comments on the subject or the source. Suggestions for further reading are made at the end of each part under the title, "Where to Find More Information." Emphasis is on items likely to be found in institutional and personal libraries. To assist teachers and students, I have included page or chapter references to textbooks and some other standard sources. Additional bibliographical information is available in many of the books listed, including my *Russia and the Soviet Union* which contains extensive "Bibliographical Notes."

All copyrighted material is used by agreement with the copyright owners to whom I here express my appreciation. I am the author or the translator of all material not specifically accredited to others.

WARREN B. WALSH

Syracuse, New York
21 December, 1962

Part VI

Reforms and Reactions, Alexander II and Alexander III

"The Crimean Defeat and Reform"

When Sir Donald Mackenzie Wallace first sought a publisher for his scholarly study of Russia he met only rebuffs. No one, they told him, would be interested in such a work; that it combined careful research with years of firsthand investigation seemed almost to count against it. Sir Donald perforce bowed to the publishers' judgment and rewrote the entire book, sugar-coating facts with anecdotes. This version was accepted and was first published in 1877. Revised editions were published in 1905 and 1912. All the selections from Wallace's work which appear in this anthology were taken from the first edition in order to show how Russia looked to a very talented and careful observer in the 1870's. (Some of the judgments set forth in this first edition were revised and modified in the later editions.) The first edition of Wallace's *Russia* is both a primary and a secondary source—primary when it records his personal observations, secondary when it rests on the reports of others. The order of the selections has been changed to accord with the pattern of the anthology and to facilitate comparisons between Wallace's findings and other sources.

The source is: D. M. Wallace, *Russia*. London, 1877. Pp. 445–448.

Under the sting of the great national humiliation the upper classes awoke from their optimistic resignation. They had borne patiently the oppression of a semi-military administration, and for this! The system of Nicholas had been put to a crucial test, and found wanting. The policy which had sacrificed all to increase the military power of the Empire was seen to be a fatal error, and the worthlessness of the drill-sergeant régime was proved by bitter experience. Those administrative fetters which for more than a quarter of a century cramped every spontaneous movement had failed to fulfill even

367

the narrow purpose for which they had been forged. They had, indeed, secured a certain external tranquility during those troublous times when Europe was convulsed by revolutionary agitation; but this tranquility was not that of healthy normal action, but of death—and underneath the surface lay secret and rapidly-spreading corruption. The army still possessed that dashing gallantry which it had displayed in the campaigns of Suvórof, that dogged, stoical bravery which had checked the advance of Napoleon on the field of Borodino, and that wondrous power of endurance which had often redeemed the negligence of generals and the defects of the commissariat; but the result was now not victory, but defeat. How could this be explained except by the radical defects of that system which had been long practiced with such inflexible perseverance? The Government had imagined that it could do everything by its own wisdom and energy, and in reality it had done nothing, or worse than nothing. The higher officers had learned only too well to be mere automatons; the ameliorations in the military organization, on which Nicholas had always bestowed special attention, were found to exist for the most part only in the official reports; the shameful exploits of the commissariat department were such as to excite the indignation of those who had long lived in an atmosphere of official jobbery and peculation; and the finances, which people had generally supposed to be in a highly-satisfactory condition, had become seriously crippled by the first great effort.

This deep and wide-spread dissatisfaction was not allowed to appear in the press, but it found very free expression in the manuscript literature and in conversation. In almost every house—I mean, of course, among the educated classes—words were spoken which a few months before would have seemed treasonable, if not blasphemous. Philippics and satires in prose and verse were written by the dozen, and circulated in hundreds of copies. A pasquil on the Commander-in-chief, or a tirade against the Government, was sure to be eagerly read and warmly approved of. As a specimen of this kind of literature, and an illustration of the public opinion of the time, I may translate here one of these metrical tirades. Though it was never printed, it obtained a wide circulation:—

" 'God has placed me over Russia,' said the Tsar to us, 'and you must bow down before me, for my throne is His altar. Trouble not yourselves with public affairs, for I think for you and watch over you every hour. My watchful eye detects internal evils and the machination of foreign enemies; and I have no need of counsel, for God inspires me with wisdom. Be proud, therefore, of being my slaves, O Russians, and regard my will as your law.'

"We listened to these words with deep reverence, and gave a tacit consent; and what was the result? Under mountains of official papers real interests were forgotten. The letter of the law was observed, but negligence and crime were allowed to go unpunished. While groveling in the dust before ministers and directors of departments, in the hope of receiving *Tchins* and decorations, the officials stole unblushingly; and theft became so common that he who stole the most was the most respected. The merits of officers were decided at reviews; and he who obtained the rank of General was supposed capable of becoming at once an able governor, an excellent engineer, or a most wise senator. Those who were appointed governors were for the most part genuine satraps, the scourges of the provinces intrusted to their care. The other offices were filled up with as little attention to the merits of the candidates. A stable-boy became Press-censor! an Imperial fool became admiral!! Kleinmichel became a count!!! In a word, the country was handed over to the tender mercies of a band of robbers.

"And what did we Russians do all this time?

"We Russians slept! With groans the peasant paid his yearly dues; with groans the proprietor mortgaged the second half of his estate; groaning, we all paid our heavy tribute to the officials. Occasionally, with a grave shaking of the head, we remarked in a whisper that it was a shame and a disgrace—that there was no justice in the courts—that millions were squandered on Imperial tours, kiosks, and pavilions—that everything was wrong; and then, with an easy conscience, we sat down to our rubber, praised Rachel, criticised the singing of Frezzolini, bowed low to venal magnates, and squabbled with each other for advancement in the very service which we so severely condemned. If we did not obtain the place we wished we retired to our ancestral estates, where we talked of the crops, fattened in indolence and gluttony, and lived a genuine animal life. If any one, amidst the general lethargy, suddenly called upon us to rise and fight for the truth and for Russia, how ridiculous did he appear! How cleverly the Pharisaical official ridiculed him, and how quickly the friends of yesterday showed him the cold shoulder! Under the anathema of public opinion, in some distant Siberian mine he recognized what a heinous sin it was to disturb the heavy sleep of apathetic slaves. Soon he was forgotten, or remembered as an unfortunate madman; and the few who said, 'Perhaps after all he was right,' hastened to add, 'but that is none of our business.'

"But amidst all this we had at least one consolation, one thing to be proud of—the might of Russia in the assembly of kings. 'What need we care,' we said, 'for the reproaches of foreign nations? We are stronger than those who reproach us.' And when at great reviews the stately regiments marched past with waving standards, glittering helmets, and sparkling bayonets, when we heard the loud hurrah with which the troops greeted the Emperor, then our hearts swelled with patriotic pride, and we were ready to repeat the words of the poet—

'Strong is our native country, and great the Russian Tsar.'

Then British statesmen, in company with the crowned conspirator of France, and with treacherous Austria, raised Western Europe against us, but we laughed scornfully at the coming storm. 'Let the nations rave,' we said; 'we have no cause to be afraid. The Tsar doubtless foresaw all, and has long since made the necessary preparations.' Boldly we went forth to fight, and confidently awaited the moment of the struggle.

"And lo! after all our boasting we were taken by surprise, and caught unawares, as by a robber in the dark. The sleep of innate stupidity blinded our Ambassadors, and our Foreign Minister sold us to our enemies. Where were our millions of soldiers? Where was the well-considered plan of defense? One courier brought the order to advance; another brought the order to retreat; and the army wandered about without definite aim or purpose. With loss and shame we retreated from the forts of Silistria, and the pride of Russia was humbled before the Hapsburg eagle. The soldiers fought well, but the parade-admiral (Menshikof)—the amphibious hero of lost battles —did not know the geography of his own country, and sent his troops to certain destruction.

"Awake, O Russia! Devoured by foreign enemies, crushed by slavery, shamefully oppressed by stupid authorities and spies, awaken from your long sleep of ignorance and apathy! You have been long enough held in bondage by the successors of the Tartar Khan. Stand forward calmly before the throne of the despot, and demand from him an account of the national disaster. Say to him boldly that his throne is not the altar of God, and that God did not condemn us to be slaves. Russia intrusted to you, O Tsar, the supreme power, and you were as a God upon earth. And what have you done? Blinded by ignorance and passion you have lusted after power and have forgotten Russia. You have spent your life in reviewing troops, in modifying uniforms, and in appending your signature to the legislative projects of ignorant charlatans. You created the despicable race of Press-censors, in order to sleep in peace—in order not to know the wants and not to hear the groans of the people—in order not to listen to Truth. You buried Truth, rolled a great stone to the door of the sepulcher, placed a strong guard over it, and said in the pride of your heart: For her there is no resurrection! But the third day has dawned, and Truth has arisen from the dead.

"Stand forward, O Tsar, before the judgment-seat of history and of God! You have mercilessly trampled Truth under foot, you have denied Freedom, you have been the slave of your own passions. By your pride and obstinacy you have exhausted Russia and raised the world in arms against us. Bow down before your brethren and humble yourself in the dust! Crave pardon and ask advice! Throw yourself into the arms of the people! There is now no other salvation!"

The innumerable tirades of which the above is a fair specimen were not very remarkable for literary merit or political wisdom. For the most part they were simply bits of bombastic rhetoric couched in doggerel rhyme, and they have consequently been long since consigned to well-merited oblivion —so completely that it is now difficult to obtain copies of them. They have, however, an historical interest, because they express in a more or less exaggerated form the public opinion and prevalent ideas of the educated classes at that moment. In order to comprehend their real significance, we must remember that the writers and readers were not a band of conspirators, but ordinary, respectable, well-intentioned people, who never for a moment dreamed of embarking on revolutionary designs. It was the same society that had been a few months before so indifferent to all political questions, and even now there was no intention of putting the loud-sounding phrases into action. We can imagine the comical discomfiture of those who read and listened to these appeals, if the "despot" had obeyed their summons, and suddenly appeared before them. How they would have instantly changed their tone, and assured the august accused that they had no intention of curbing his power, that they had merely given way to a momentary impulse of patriotic indignation, that they were perfectly loyal subjects, and that they did not really intend to do anything contrary to his will!

Was the movement, then, merely an outburst of childish petulance? Certainly not. The public were really and seriously convinced that things were all wrong, and they were seriously and enthusiastically desirous that a new and better order of things should be introduced. It must be said to their honor that they did not content themselves with accusing and lampooning the individuals who were supposed to be the chief culprits. On the contrary, they looked reality boldly in the face, made a public confession of their past sins, sought conscientiously the causes which had produced the recent disasters, and endeavored to find means by which such calamities might be prevented in the future. The public feeling and aspirations were not strong enough to conquer the traditional respect for the Imperial will and create an open opposition to the autocratic power, but they were strong enough to do great things by aiding the Government, if the Emperor voluntarily undertook a series of radical reforms.

Serfs and Peasants

Wallace's descriptions of the serfs prior to emancipation were based upon study, as was the preceding selection, rather than upon personal observation. Originally published under the two subtitles, "Serfs and Peasants," and "The Serfs," the material is here combined under a single heading. The source is: Wallace, *Russia*, pp. 105–110, 472–484.

During all my travels in Russia, one of the objects which I constantly kept in view was the collection of materials for a History of the Emancipation of the Serfs—a great reform, which has always seemed to me one of the most interesting events of modern history. It was natural, therefore, that I should gather in this northern region as much information as possible regarding the life of the peasantry and their relation to the landed proprietors during the time of serfage; and I think that a little of this information will be not un acceptable to the reader.

In this, as in other parts of Russia, a very large portion of the land— perhaps as much as one-half—belonged to the State. The peasants living on this land had no masters, and were governed by a special branch of the Imperial Administration. In a certain sense they were serfs, for they were not allowed to change their official domicile, but practically they enjoyed a very large amount of liberty. By paying a small sum for a passport they could leave their villages for an indefinite length of time, and so long as they paid regularly their taxes and dues they were in little danger of being molested. Many of them, though officially inscribed in their native villages, lived permanently in the towns, and not a few of them succeeded in amassing large fortunes.

Of the remaining land, a considerable portion belonged to rich nobles, who rarely or never visited their estates, and left the management of them either to the serfs themselves or to a steward, who acted according to a code of instructions. On these estates the position of the serfs was very similar to that of the State peasants. They had their Communal land, which they distributed among themselves as they thought fit, and enjoyed the remainder of the arable land in return for a fixed yearly rent.

Some proprietors, however, lived on their estates and farmed on their own account, and here the condition of the serfs was somewhat different. A considerable number of these, perhaps as many as ten per cent. were, properly speaking, not serfs at all, but rather domestic slaves, who fulfilled the functions of coachmen, grooms, gardeners, gamekeepers, cooks, lackeys, and the like. Their wives and daughters acted as nurses, domestic servants, ladies' maids, and seamstresses. If the master organized a private theater or orchestra, the actors or musicians were drawn from this class. These serfs lived in the mansion or the immediate vicinity, possessed no land, except perhaps a little plot for a kitchen-garden, and were fed and clothed by the master. Their number was generally out of all proportion to the amount of work they had to perform, and consequently they were always imbued with an hereditary spirit of indolence, and performed lazily and carelessly what they had to do. On the other hand, they were often sincerely attached to the family they served, and occasionally proved by acts their fidelity and attachment. Here is an instance out of the many for which I can vouch. An old nurse, whose mistress was dangerously ill, vowed that, in the event of the patient's recovery, she would make a pilgrimage first to Kief, the Holy City on the Dnieper, and afterwards to Solovetsk, a much-revered monastery on an island in the White Sea. The patient recovered, and the old woman walked in fulfillment of her vow more than two thousand miles!

I have called this class of serfs "domestic slaves," because I cannot find any more appropriate term, but I must warn the reader that he ought not to use this phrase in presence of a Russian. On this point Russians are extremely sensitive. Serfage, they say indignantly, was something quite different from slavery; and slavery never existed in Russia!

This assertion, which I have heard scores of times from educated Russians, cannot be accepted unreservedly. The first part of it is perfectly true; the second, perfectly false. In old times slavery was a recognized institution in Russia, as in other countries. It is almost impossible to read a few pages of the old native chronicles without stumbling on references to slaves; and I distinctly remember—though I cannot at this moment give chapter and verse—that there was one Russian Prince who was so valiant and so successful in his wars, that during his reign a slave might be bought for a few coppers. How the distinction between serfs and slaves gradually disappeared, and how the latter term fell into disuse, I need not here relate; but I must assert, in the interests of truth, that the class of serfs above mentioned, though they were officially and popularly called *dvorovuiye lyudi*—that is to say, courtyard people—were to all intents and purposes domestic slaves. Down to the commencement of the present century the Russian newspapers contained advertisements of this kind—I take the examples almost at random from the *Moscow Gazette* of 1801: "TO BE SOLD, three coachmen, well-trained and handsome; and two girls, the one eighteen and the other fifteen years of age, both of them good-looking and well acquainted with various kinds of handiwork. In the same house there are for sale two hair-dressers: the one twenty-one years of age can read, write, play on a musical instrument, and act as huntsman; the other can dress ladies' and gentle-men's hair. In the same house are sold pianos and organs." A little further on, a first-rate clerk, a carver, and a lackey are offered for sale, and the reason assigned is super-abundance of the articles in question (*za izlisheston*). In some instances it seems as if the serfs and the cattle were intentionally put in the same category, as in the following: "In this house one can buy a coachman, and a Dutch cow about to calve." The style of these advertisements and the frequent recurrence of the same address show plainly that there was at that time a regular class of slave-dealers.

The humane Alexander I. prohibited public advertisements of this kind, but he did not put down the custom which they represented; and his successor, Nicholas, took no active measures for its repression. Thus until the commencement of the present reign—that is to say, until about twenty years ago—the practice was continued under a more or less disguised form. Middle-aged people have often told me that in their youth they knew proprietors who habitually caused young domestic serfs to be taught trades, in order afterwards to sell them or let them out for hire. It was from such proprietors that the theaters obtained a large number of their best actors.

Very different was the position of the serfs properly so-called. They lived in villages, possessed houses and gardens of their own, tilled the Communal land for their own benefit, enjoyed a certain amount of self-government, of which I shall speak presently, and were rarely sold except as part of the estate. They might, indeed, be sold to a landed proprietor, and transferred to his estates; but such transactions rarely took place. The ordinary relations which existed between serfs and the proprietor may be best explained by one or two examples. Let us take first Ivánofka.

Though the proprietor's house was situated, as I have said, close to the village, the manor land and the Communal land had always been kept clearly separate, and might almost be said to form two independent estates. The proprietor who reigned in Ivánofka during the last years of serfage was keenly alive to his own interests, and always desirous of increasing his revenue; but he was, at the same time, a just and intelligent man, who was never guilty of extortion or cruelty. Though he had the welfare of his serfs really at heart, he rarely interfered in their domestic or Communal arrangements, because he believed that men in general, and Russian peasants in particular, are the best administrators of their own affairs. He did not, indeed, always carry out this principle to its logical consequences, for he was not by any means a thorough doctrinaire. Thus, for example, he insisted on being consulted when a Village Elder was to be elected, or any important matter decided; and when circumstances seemed to demand his interference, he usually showed the peasants that he could be dictator if he chose. These were, however, exceptional incidents. In the ordinary course of affairs he treated the Commune almost as a respected farmer or trusted steward. In return for the land which he ceded to it, and which it was free to distribute among its members as it thought fit, he demanded a certain amount of labor and dues; but he never determined what particular laborers should be sent to him, or in what way the dues should be levied.

The amount of the labor-dues was determined in this way. The tyagló, or labor-unit, was composed of a man, a woman, and a horse; and each tyagló owed to the proprietor three days' labor every week. If a household contained two tyágla, one of them might work for the proprietor six days in the week, and thereby liberate the other from its obligation. In this way one-half of a large family could labor constantly for the household, whilst the other half fulfilled all the obligations towards the proprietor. The other dues consisted of lambs, chickens, eggs, and linen-cloth, together with a certain sum of money, which was contributed by those peasants who were allowed to go away and work in the towns.

At a short distance from Ivánofka was an estate, which had been managed in the time of serfage on entirely different principles. The proprietor was a man who had likewise the welfare of his serfs at heart, because he knew that on their welfare depended his own revenues, but he did not believe in the principle of allowing them to manage their own affairs. The Russian peasant, he was wont to say, is a child—a foolish, imprudent, indolent child, who inevitably ruins himself when not properly looked after. In accordance with this principle the proprietor sought to regulate not merely the Communal, but also the domestic concerns of his serfs. Not only did he always nominate the Village Elder and decide all matters touching the communal welfare, but he at the same time arranged the marriages, decided who was to seek work in the towns and who was to stay at home, paid frequent visits of inspection to the peasants' houses, prohibited the heads of families from selling their grain without his permission, and exercised in various other ways a system of minute supervision. In return for all this paternal solicitude he was able to extract a wonderfully large revenue from his estate, though his fields were by no means more fertile or better cultivated than those of his neighbors. The additional revenue was derived not from the land, but from the serfs. Knowing intimately the domestic affairs of each family, he could lay on them the heaviest possible burdens without adding that last hair which is said to break the camel's back. And many of the expedients he employed did more credit to his ingenuity than to his moral character. Thus, for instance, if he discovered that a family had saved a little money, he would propose that one of the daughters should marry some one of whom, he knew, her father would certainly disapprove, or he would express his intention of giving one of the sons as a recruit. In either case a ransom was pretty sure to be paid in order to ward off the threatened danger.

All the proprietors who lived on their estates approached more or less nearly to one of these two types; but here in the northern regions the latter type was not very often met with. Partly from the prevailing absenteeism among the landlords, and partly from the peasants' old-established habit of wandering about the country and going to the towns in search of work, these peasants of the north are more energetic, more intelligent, more independent, and consequently less docile and pliable than those of the fertile central provinces. They have, too, more education. A large proportion of them can read and write, and occasionally one meets among them men who have a keen desire for knowledge. Several times I encountered peasants in this region who had a small collection of books, and twice I found in such collections, much to my astonishment, a Russian translation of Buckle's "History of Civilization"!

. . .

If we compare the development of serfage in Russia and in Western Europe, we find very many points in common, but in Russia the movement had certain peculiarities. One of the most important of these was caused by the rapid development of the autocratic power. In feudal Europe, where there was no strong central authority to control the noblesse, the free Communes entirely, or almost entirely, disappeared. They were either appropriated by the nobles or voluntarily submitted to powerful landed proprietors or to monasteries, and in this way the whole of the reclaimed land, with a few rare exceptions, became the property of the nobles or of the church. In Russia we find the same movement, but it was arrested by the Imperial power before all the land had been appropriated. The nobles could reduce to serfage the peasants settled on their estates, but they could not take possession of the free Communes, because such an appropriation would have infringed the rights and diminished the revenues of the Tsar. Down to the commencement of the present century, it is true, large grants of land with serfs were made to favored individuals among the noblesse, and in the reign of Paul (1796–1801), a considerable number of estates were affected to the use of the Imperial family under the name of appanages (*Udyélniya iméniya*); but, on the other hand, the extensive church-lands, when secularized by Catherine II., were not distributed among the nobles, as in many other countries, but were transformed into State Demesnes. Thus, at the date of the Emancipation (1861), by far the greater part of the territory belonged to the State, and one-half of the rural population were so-called State Peasants (*Gosudárstvennie krestyané*).

Regarding the condition of these State Peasants, or Peasants of the Demesnes, as they are sometimes called, I may say briefly that they were, in a certain sense, serfs, being attached to the soil like the others; but their condition was, as a rule, somewhat better than the serfs in the narrower acceptation of the term. They had to suffer much from the tyranny and extortion of the special administration under which they lived, but they had more land and more liberty than was commonly enjoyed on the estates of resident proprietors, and their position was much less precarious. It is often asserted that the officials of the Demesnes were worse than the serf-owners, because they had not the same interest in the prosperity of the peasantry; but this *á priori* reasoning does not stand the test of experience.

It is not a little interesting to observe the numerical proportion and geographical distribution of these two rural classes. In European Russia, as a whole, about three-eighths of the population were composed of serfs belonging to the nobles; but if we take the provinces separately we find great variations from this average. In five provinces the serfs were less than three per cent., whilst in others they formed more than seventy per cent. of the population! This is not an accidental phenomenon. In the geographical distribution of serfage we can see reflected the origin and history of the institution.

If we were to construct a map showing the geographical distribution of the serf population, we should at once perceive that serfage radiated from Moscow. Starting from that city as a center and traveling in any direction towards the confines of the Empire, we find that, after making allowance for a few disturbing local influences, the proportion of serfs regularly declines in the successive provinces traversed. In the region representing the old Muscovite Tsardom they form considerably more than a half of the peasantry. Immediately to the south and east of this, in the territory that was gradually annexed during the seventeenth and first half of the eighteenth century, the proportion varies from twenty-five to fifty per cent., and in the more recently annexed provinces it steadily decreases till it almost reaches zero.

We may perceive, too, that the percentage of serfs decreases toward the north much more rapidly than toward the east and south. This points to the essentially agricultural nature of serfage in its infancy. In the south and east there was abundance of rich "black earth" celebrated for its fertility, and the nobles in quest of estates naturally preferred this region to the inhospitable north, with its poor soil and severe climate.

A more careful examination of the supposed map would bring out other interesting facts. Let me notice one by way of illustration. Had serfage been the result of conquest we should have found the Slavonic race settled on the State Demesnes, and the Finnish and Tartar tribes supplying the serfs of the nobles. In reality we find quite the reverse; the Finns and Tartars were nearly all State Peasants, and the serfs of the proprietors were nearly all of Slavonic race. This is to be accounted for by the fact that the Finnish and Tartar tribes inhabit chiefly the outlying regions, in which serfage never attained such dimensions as in the center of the Empire.

The dues paid by the serfs were of three kinds: labor, money, and farm produce. The last-named is so unimportant that it may be dismissed in a few words. It consisted chiefly of eggs, chickens, lambs, mushrooms, wild berries, and linen cloth. The amount of these various products depended entirely on the will of the master. The other two kinds of dues, as more important, we must examine more closely.

When a proprietor had abundance of fertile land and wished to farm on his own account, he commonly demanded from his serfs as much labor as possible. Under such a master the serfs were probably entirely free from money dues, and fulfilled their obligations to him by laboring in his fields in summer and transporting his grain to market in winter. When, on the contrary, a land-owner had more serf labor at his disposal than he required for the cultivation of his fields, he put the superfluous serfs "on *obrók*"—that is to say, he allowed them to go and work where they pleased on condition of paying him a fixed yearly sum. Sometimes the proprietor did not farm at all on his own account, in which case he put all the serfs "on *obrók*," and generally gave to the Commune in usufruct the whole of the arable land and pasturage. In this way the *Mir* played the part of a tenant.

We have here the basis for a simple and important classification of estates in the time of serfage: (1) Estates on which the dues were exclusively in labor; (2) Estates on which the dues were partly in labor and partly in money; and (3) Estates on which the dues were exclusively in money.

In the manner of exacting the labor dues there was considerable variety. According to the famous manifesto of Paul I., the peasant could not be compelled to work more than three days in the week; but this law was by no means universally observed, and those who did observe it had various methods of applying it. A few took it literally, and laid down a rule that the serfs should work for them three definite days in the week—for example, every Monday, Tuesday, and Wednesday—but this was an extremely inconvenient method, for it prevented the field labor from being carried on regularly. A much more rational system was that according to which one-half of the serfs worked the first three days of the week, and the other half the remaining three. In this way there was, without any contravention of the law, a regular and constant supply of labor. It seems, however, that the great majority of the proprietors followed no strict method, and paid no attention whatever to Paul's manifesto, which gave to the peasant no legal means of making formal complaints. They simply summoned daily as many laborers as they required. The evil consequences of this for the peasants' crops were in part counteracted by making the peasants sow their own grain a little later than that of the proprietor, so that the master's harvest-work was finished, or nearly finished, before their grain was ripe. This combination did not, however, always succeed, and in cases where there was a conflict of interests, the serf was, of course, the losing party. All that remained for him to do in such cases was to work a little in his own fields before six o'clock in the morning and after nine o'clock at night, and in order to render this possible, he economized his strength, and worked as little as possible in his master's fields during the day.

It has frequently been remarked, and with much truth—though the indiscriminate application of the principle has often led to unjustifiable legislative inactivity—that the practical result of institutions depends less on the intrinsic abstract nature of the institutions themselves than on the character of those who work them. So it was with serfage. When a proprietor habitually acted towards his serfs in an enlightened, rational, humane way, they had little reason to complain of their position, and their life was much easier than that of many men who live in a state of complete individual freedom and unlimited, unrestricted competition. When I say that the condition of many free men is worse than was the condition of many Russian serfs, the reader must not imagine that I am thinking of some barbarous tribe among whom freedom means an utter absence of law and an unrestricted right of pillage. On the contrary, I am thinking of a class of men who have the good fortune to live under the beneficent protection of British law, not in some distant, inhospitable colony, but between St. George's Channel and the North Sea. However paradoxical the statement may seem to those who are in the habit of regarding all forms of slavery from the sentimental point of view, it is unquestionable that the condition of serfs under such a proprietor as I have supposed was much more enviable than that of the majority of English agricultural laborers. Each family had a house of its own, with a cabbage-garden, one or more horses, one or two cows, several sheep, poultry, agricultural implements, a share of the Communal land, and everything else necessary for carrying on its small farming operations; and in return for this it had to supply the proprietor with an amount of labor which was by no means oppressive. If, for instance, a serf had three adult sons—and the households, as I have said, were at that time generally numerous—two of them might work for the proprietor, whilst he himself and the remaining son could attend exclusively to the family affairs. From those events which used to be called "the visitations of God" he had no fear of being permanently ruined. If his house was burnt, or his cattle died from the plague, or a series of "bad years" left him without seed for his fields, he could always count upon temporary assistance from his master. He was protected, too, against all oppression and exactions on the part of the officials; for the police, when there was any cause for its interference, applied to the proprietor, who was to a certain extent responsible for his serfs. Thus the serf might live a tranquil, contented life, and die at a ripe old age, without ever having been conscious that serfage was a burden.

If all the serfs had lived in this way we might, perhaps, regret that the Emancipation was ever undertaken. In reality there was, as the French say, *le revers de la médaille,* and serfage generally appeared under a form very different from that which I have just depicted. The proprietors were, unfortunately, not all of the enlightened, humane type. Amongst them were many who demanded from their serfs a most inordinate amount of labor, and treated them in a most inhuman fashion.

These oppressors of their serfs may be divided into four categories. First, there were the proprietors who managed their own estates, and oppressed simply for the purpose of increasing their revenues. Secondly, there were a number of retired officers, who wished to establish a certain order and discipline on their estates, and who employed for this purpose the barbarous measures which were until lately used in the army, believing that merciless corporal punishment was the only means of curing laziness, disorderliness, and other vices. Thirdly, there were the absentees who lived beyond their means, and demanded from their steward, under pain of giving him or his son as a recruit, a much greater yearly sum than the estate could be reasonably expected to yield. Lastly, in the latter years of serfage, there were a number of men who bought estates as a mercantile speculation, and endeavored to make as much money out of them as possible in the shortest possible space of time.

Of all hard masters, the last-named were the most terrible. Utterly indifferent to the welfare of the serfs and the ultimate fate of the property, they cut down the timber, sold the cattle, exacted heavy money dues under threats of giving the serfs or their children as recruits, presented to the military authorities a number of conscripts greater than was required by law— selling the conscription receipts (*zatchétniya kvitántsii*) to the merchants and burghers who were liable to the conscription but did not wish to serve— compelled some of the richer serfs to buy their liberty at an enormous price, and, in a word, used every means, legal and illegal, for extracting money. By this system of management they ruined the estate completely in the course of a few years; but by that time they had realized probably the whole sum paid, with a very fair profit from the operation; and this profit could be considerably augmented by selling a number of peasant families for transportation to another estate (*na svoz*), or by mortgaging the property in the Opekúnski Sovêt—a Government institution which lent money on landed property without examining carefully the nature of the security.

As to the means which the proprietors possessed of oppressing their peasants, we must distinguish between the legal and the actual. The legal were almost as complete as any one could desire. "The proprietor," it is said in the Laws (Vol. IX., 1045, ed. an. 1857), "may impose on his serfs every kind of labor, may take from them money dues (obrók) and demand from them personal service, with this one restriction, that they should not be thereby ruined, and that the number of days fixed by law should be left to them for their own work." Besides this, he had the right to transform peasants into domestic servants, and might, instead of employing them in his own service, hire them out to others who had the rights and privileges of noblesse (1047–48). For all offenses committed against himself or against any one under his jurisdiction he could subject the guilty ones to corporal punishment not exceeding forty lashes with the birch or fifteen blows with the stick (1052); and if he considered any of his serfs as incorrigible he could present them to the authorities to be drafted into the army or transported to Siberia as he might desire (1053–55). In cases of insubordination, where the ordinary domestic means of discipline did not suffice, he could call in the police and the military to support his authority.

Such were the legal means by which the proprietor might oppress his peasants, and it will be readily understood that they were very considerable and very elastic. By law he had the power to impose any dues in labor or money which he might think fit, and in all cases the serfs were ordered to be docile and obedient (1027). Corporal punishment, though restricted by law, he could in reality apply to any extent. Certainly none of the serfs, and very few of the proprietors, were aware that the law placed any restriction on this right. All the proprietors were in the habit of using corporal punishment as they thought proper, and unless a proprietor became notorious for inhuman cruelty, the authorities never thought of interfering. But in the eyes of the peasants corporal punishment was not the worst. What they feared infinitely more than the birch or the stick was the proprietor's power of giving them or their sons as recruits. The law assumed that this extreme means would be employed only against those serfs who showed themselves incorrigibly vicious or insubordinate; but the authorities accepted those presented without making any investigations, and consequently the proprietor might use this power as an effective means of extortion.

Against these means of extortion and oppression the serfs had no legal protection. The law provided them with no means of resisting any injustice to which they might be subjected, or of bringing to punishment the master who oppressed and ruined them. The Government, notwithstanding its sincere desire to protect them from inordinate burdens and cruel treatment, rarely interfered between the master and his serfs, being afraid of thereby undermining the authority of the proprietors, and awakening among the peasantry a spirit of insubordination. The serfs were left, therefore, to their own resources, and had to defend themselves as they best could. The simplest way was open mutiny; but this was rarely employed, for they knew by experience that any attempt of the kind would be at once put down by the military and mercilessly punished. Much more favorite and efficient methods were passive resistance, flight, and fire-raising or murder.

We might naturally suppose that an unscrupulous proprietor, armed with the enormous legal and actual power which I have just described, could very easily extort from his peasants anything he desired. In reality, however, the process of extortion, when it exceeded a certain measure, was a very difficult operation. The Russian peasant has a capacity of patient endurance that would do honor to a martyr, and a power of continued, dogged, passive resistance such as is possessed, I believe, by no other class of men in Europe; and these qualities formed a very powerful barrier against the rapacity of unconscientious proprietors. As soon as the serfs remarked in their master a tendency to rapacity and extortion, they at once took measures to defend themselves. Their first step was to sell secretly all the cattle which they did not actually require, and all the movable property which they possessed, except the few articles necessary for everyday use; and the little capital that they thus realized was carefully hidden somewhere in or near the house. When this had been effected, the proprietor might threaten and punish as he liked, but he rarely succeeded in unearthing the hidden treasure. Many a peasant, under such circumstances, bore patiently the most cruel punishment, and saw his sons taken away as recruits, and yet he persisted in declaring that he had no money to ransom himself and his children. A spectator in such a case would probably have advised him to give up his little store of money, and thereby liberate himself from persecution; but the peasants reasoned otherwise. They were convinced, and not without reason, that the sacrifice of their little capital would merely put off the evil day, and that the persecution would very soon recommence. In this way they would have to suffer as before, and have the additional mortification of feeling that they had spent to no purpose the little that they possessed. Their fatalistic belief in the "perhaps" (avos') came here to their aid. Perhaps the proprietor might become weary of his efforts when he saw that they led to no result, or perhaps something might happen which would remove the persecutor.

It always happened, however, that when a proprietor treated his serfs with extreme injustice and cruelty, some of them lost patience, and sought refuge in flight. As the estates lay perfectly open on all sides, and it was utterly impossible to exercise a strict supervision, nothing was easier than to run away, and the fugitive might be a hundred miles off before his absence was noticed. Why then did not all run away as soon as the master began to oppress them? There were several reasons which made the peasant bear much, rather than adopt this resource. In the first place, he had almost always a wife and family, and he could not possibly take them with him; flight, therefore, was expatriation for life in its most terrible form. Besides this, the life of a fugitive serf was by no means enviable. He was liable at any moment to fall into the hands of the police, and to be put in prison or sent back to his master. So little charm indeed did this life present that not unfrequently after a few months or a few years the fugitive returned of his own accord to his former domicile.

Regarding fugitives or passportless wanderers in general, I may here remark parenthetically that there were two kinds. In the first place, there was the young, able-bodied peasant, who fled from the oppression of his master or from the conscription. Such a fugitive almost always sought out for himself a new domicile—generally in the southern provinces, where there was a great scarcity of laborers, and where many proprietors habitually welcomed all peasants who presented themselves, without making any inquiries as to passports. In the second place, there were those who chose fugitivism as a permanent mode of life. These were, for the most part, men or women of a certain age—widowers or widows—who had no close family ties, and who were too infirm or too lazy to work. The majority of these assumed the character of pilgrims. As such they could always find enough to eat, and could generally collect a few roubles with which to grease the palm of any zealous police-officer who should arrest them. For a life of this kind Russia presented, and still presents, peculiar facilities. There are abundance of monasteries, where all comers may live for three days without any questions being asked, and where those who are willing to do a little work for the patron saint may live for a much longer period. Then there are the towns, where the rich merchants consider almsgiving as very profitable for salvation. And, lastly, there are the villages, where a professing pilgrim is sure to be hospitably received and entertained so long as he refrains from stealing and other acts too grossly inconsistent with his assumed character. For those who contented themselves with simple fare, and did not seek to avoid the usual privations of a wanderer's life, these ordinary means of subsistence were amply sufficient. Those who were more ambitious and more cunning often employed their talents with great success in the world of the Old Ritualists and Sectarians.

The last and most desperate means of defense which the serfs possessed were fire-raising and murder. With regard to the amount of fire-raising there are no trustworthy statistics. With regard to the number of agrarian murders I possessed some interesting statistical data, but have, unfortunately, lost them. I may say, however, that these cases were not very numerous. This is to be explained in part by the patient, long-suffering character of the peasantry, and in part by the fact that the great majority of the proprietors were by no means such inhuman taskmasters as is sometimes supposed. When a case did occur, the Administration always made a strict investigation—punishing the guilty with exemplary severity, and taking no account of the provocation to which they had been subjected. The peasantry, on the contrary—at least, when the act was not the result of mere personal vengeance—secretly sympathized with "the unfortunates," and long cherished their memory as that of men who had suffered for the Mir.

In speaking of the serfs I have hitherto confined my attention to the members of the Mir, or rural Commune—that is to say, the peasants in the narrower sense of the terms; but besides these there were the Dvoróvuié, or domestic servants, and of these I must add a word or two.

The Dvoróvuié were domestic slaves rather than serfs in the proper sense of the word. Let us, however, avoid wounding unnecessarily Russian sensibilities by the use of the ill-sounding word. We may call the class in question "domestics"—remembering, of course, that they were not quite domestic servants in the ordinary sense. They received no wages, were not at liberty to change masters, possessed almost no legal rights, and might be punished, hired out, or sold by their owners with any infraction of the written law.

These "domestics" were very numerous—out of all proportion to the work to be performed—and could consequently lead a very lazy life; but the peasant considered it a great misfortune to be transferred to their ranks, for he thereby lost his share of the Communal land and the little independence which he enjoyed. It very rarely happened, however, that the proprietor took an able-bodied peasant as domestic. The class generally kept up its numbers by the legitimate and illegitimate method of natural increase; and involuntary additions were occasionally made when orphans were left without near relative, and no other family wished to adopt them. To this class belonged the lackeys, servant-girls, cooks, coachmen, stable-boys, gardeners, and a large number of nondescript old men and women who had no very clearly-defined functions. Those of them who were married and had children occupied a position intermediate between the ordinary domestic servant and the peasant. On the one hand they received from the master a monthly allowance of food and a yearly allowance of clothes, and they were obliged to live in the immediate vicinity of the mansion-house, but on the other hand they had each a separate house or apartment, with a little cabbage-garden, and commonly a small plot of flax. The unmarried ones lived in all respects like ordinary domestic servants.

Of the whole number of serfs belonging to the proprietors, the domestics formed, according to the last census, no less than 6¾ per cent. (6.79), and their numbers were evidently rapidly increasing, for in the preceding census they represented only 4.79 per cent. of the whole. This fact seems all the more remarkable when we observe that during this period the number of peasant serfs had diminished from 20,576,229 to 20,158,231.

I must now bring this long chapter to an end, though I feel that I have been able to do little more than sketch roughly in outline the subject which I desired to describe. I have endeavored to represent serfage in its normal, ordinary forms rather than in its occasional monstrous manifestations. Of these latter I have a collection containing ample materials for a whole series of sensational novels, but I refrain from quoting them, because I do not believe that the criminal annals of a country give a fair representation of its real condition. Imagine an author describing family life in England by the chronicles of the Divorce Court! The method would, of course, seem to all men incredibly absurd, and yet it would not be much more unjust than that of an author who should describe serfage in Russia by those cases of reckless oppression and inhuman cruelty which certainly did sometimes occur, but which as certainly were exceptional. Most foreigners are already, I believe, only too disposed to exaggerate the oppression and cruelty to which serfage gave rise, so that in quoting a number of striking examples I should simply be pandering to that taste for the horrible and the sensational which is for the present in need of no stimulus.

It must not, however, be supposed that in refraining from all description of those abuses of authority which the proprietors sometimes practiced I am actuated by any desire to whitewash serfage or attenuate its evil consequences. No great body of men could long wield such enormous uncontrolled power without abusing it, and no great body of men could long live under such power without suffering morally and materially from its pernicious influence. And it must be remembered that this pernicious influence affected not only the serfs, but also the proprietors. If serfage did not create that moral apathy and intellectual lethargy which formed, as it were, the atmosphere of Russian provincial life, it did much at least to preserve it. In short, serfage was the chief barrier to all material and moral progress, and it was, therefore, natural that in a time of moral awakening such as that which I have described in the preceding chapter the question of Serf Emancipation at once came to the front.

Serfs and Serfowners: Data from the Tenth Revision

Today's demographers warn that none of the revisions [censuses] taken in the Russian Empire prior to 1897 were accurate. The time factor alone introduced errors. The Tenth Revision, for example, begun in June, 1857, was not completed until 1859 by which time natural changes had rendered the first-made counts obsolete. Other methodological faults included lack of uniformity in categorization, enumeration, and calculation. The results must therefore be considered as only approximations or orders of magnitude.

The data which follow were processed and published by a Russian statistician, A. G. Troinitskii, immediately after the collection was completed. The original souce is: A. Troinitskii, *Krepostnoe naselenie v Rossii po 10-i narodnoi perepisi. Statisticheskoe issledovanie. Izdanie statisticheskogo otdela tsentral'nogo statisticheskogo komiteta* (*The serf population of Russia according to the 10th population census. Statistical research. Published by the Statistical Department of the Central Statistics Committee*). St. Petersburg, 1861. The excerpts below have been translated from: S. S. Dmitriev (Compiler), *Khrestomatiya po istorii SSSR* (*Anthology for the History of the USSR*). Volume III. Moscow, 1952. Pp. 7–15. Abridged.

Serf Population, 1857–1859

	Males	Females	Total
European Russia and Siberia	10,974,944	11,588,142	22,563,086
Transcaucasian area	269,969	236,576	506,545
Total	11,244,913	11,824,718	23,069,631

Serf Distribution by Category (*European Russia and Siberia only*)

As the following table shows, the overwhelming majority of serfs in European Russia and Siberia (almost 22,000,000) are owned by the *dvorianstvo*. The remainder (less than 600,000), who are attached to private factories or to various departments, constitute only one thirty-seventh of the total of *dvorianstvo* serfs. The "Conditional Serf Law" applied to serfs on estates in the western *gubernia* which had once been part of Lithuania and Poland. The position of serfs under the Conditional Serf Law differed in almost no way from the position of those under the general serf law.

	Total serfs	Percentage of the total	Percentage of *dvorianstvo* serfs
Dvorianstvo serfs under the general law	21,625,609		98.34
Dvorianstvo serfs under the conditional law	354,324		1.66
Total *dvorianstvo* serfs	21,979,33	97.42	100.00
Attached to private factories	542,599	2.40	—
Attached to departments	40,554	.18	—
Total	22,563,086	100.00	—

Relationship of "Settled Serfs" and "Manor Serfs"

The total number of *dvorianstvo* serfs decreased by 465,500 between the Eighth and the Ninth Revisions [censuses], but increased by 13,500 between the Ninth and Tenth Revisions. The number of settled serfs [*i.e.,* those attached to the land] steadily decreased, and the number of manor serfs [*i.e.,* landless serfs] steadily increased. There were almost 587,000 fewer settled serfs at the time of the Ninth Revision than at the time of the Eighth; 418,000 less at the time of Tenth than at the time of the Ninth—a total decrease in twenty-two years of a million. The number of manor serfs increased by over 650,000 during this same period; an increase of 121,500 between the Eighth and Ninth, and of 431,500 between the Ninth and Tenth Revisions.

	Settled Serfs	Manor Serfs	Percentage Ratio
Eighth Revision	21,163,099	914,524	96:4
Ninth Revision	20,576,229	1,035,924	95:5
Tenth Revision	20,158,231	1,467,378	93:7

The most significant increases in the number of manor serfs between the Ninth and Tenth Revisions took place in the following *gubernia* (listed in descending order): Kharkov, Poltava, Kursk, Kherson, Ekaterinoslav, Chernigov, Kostrom, Voronezh, Tambov, Orlov, and Minsk. The causes are obscure. It is probably not significant that the population in most of these *gubernia* is predominantly Malorussian [Ukrainian] or a mixture of Malorussian and Velikorussian [Great Russian]. A more plausible explanation is that rumors were spread during the taking of the Tenth Revision to the effect that manor serfs would be bought by the government when the peasant reform took place. It was natural in regions where there were many petty proprietors and where the [fertile] black earth made land values high for the proprietors to try to limit in advance the number of peasants [or the amount of land] which might be allotted to peasants by the reform.

Serfs and Serfowners

The official records of the numbers of serfs owned by individuals do not include female serfs because females are not taxed. It is probable that the figures are somewhat inflated as to the number of serfs due to duplications, but that the actual number of owners may be somewhat less than shown. According to the Tenth Revision, there are about 700,000 serfowners in European Russia and Siberia. The number of landless serfowners is 3.46 per cent of the total number of serfowners, and they own 0.11 per cent of the total number of serfs. This works out on the basis of numerical averages that each landless owner possesses 3.32 male serfs. The heaviest concentration of such owners is in the three Malorussian *gubernia* of Poltava, Kharkov, and Chernigov—each of which had over two hundred landless owners. The *gubernia* of Orenburg, St. Petersburg, Kiev, Voronezh, Ekaterinoslav, Mogilov, Moscow, Saratov, Tambov, and Podol each have over a hundred. There are less than ten in each of the four Siberian *gubernia*. The Tenth Revision revealed the following data:

Category of owners	Number of owners	Number of male serfs owned	Average number of serfs per owner
Up to 21 serfs	42,978	339,586	7.90
21–100 serfs	36,193	1,697,914	46.91
101–500 serfs	20,165	3,974,629	197.11
501–1000 serfs	2,462	1,597,691	648.94
More than 1000 serfs	1,396	3,074,033	2,202.03

Slightly over 3,800 serfowners, constituting 3.7 per cent of the total number of owners, possess 43.7 per cent of all male serfs; over 20,000 serfowners, or 19.5 per cent, possess 37.20 per cent; and approximately 79,000 serfowners, or 76.7 per cent of the owners as a class, possess only 19 per cent of the total number of serfs. In other words, at the taking of the Tenth Revision, approximately 23 per cent of the serfowners possessed 80 per cent of the male serfs.

Total Population and Serf Population (Tenth Revision)

	Total Population	Serf Population	Serfs per 100 of population
European Russia	60,143,478	22,558,748	37.5
Siberia	4,239,534	4,338	0.1
Transcaucasia	2,688,173	506,545	18.8
Possessions of the Russian North American Company	9,982	—	—
Totals	67,081,167	23,069,631	34.4

Geographic Distribution of Serfs

The serf population was not equally distributed throughout the Empire. The highest concentration was in the gubernia of Kiev where there were over 1,121,000 serfs of both sexes, comprising about 58 per cent of the total population. Podol had over a million serfs (about 60 per cent of the total population); six regions had between 750,000 and a million serfs; sixteen, between 500,000 and 750,000; eighteen, from 100,000 to 250,000; six, from 10,000 to 100,000; and four, less than ten thousand. In seventeen gubernia and oblasts, the serf population was greater than 50 per cent of the total, and in twenty-five others it ranged from 10 per cent to 50 per cent.

Estates, Debts, and Mortgaged Serfs, 1859 (European Russia only)

Number of estates	103,158	
Number of serfs	10,682,400	
Number of endebted estates	44,166	(43%)
Number of serfs pledged as collateral for loans	7,107,185	(67%)
Total of loans in silver rubles	425,503,061*	

* An increase over 1856 of approximately 600,000 serfs and 27,500,000 silver rubles.

Three Views on Emancipation

Tsar Alexander II's announcement of the Peace of Paris (1856) which marked the end of the Crimean War concluded with a promise of domestic reforms. Soon thereafter, the tsar declared it "better to abolish serfdom from above than to wait until it begins to abolish itself from below," and adjured the landowners "to think of the proper way in which this can be done." After a number of special secret committees had discussed the problem, Alexander created, in January of 1857, a group known variously as the Main Committee and as the Emperor's Private Committee. Several of its members, including the chairman, Orlov, were extreme conservatives; and it was partly to offset their influence that the tsar added to the committee his brother, the liberal Grand Duke Constantine Nicholaevich. The tsar also solicited the advice of Count P. D. Kisilev, then the Russian ambassador to France, but previously an active member of Nicholas I's secret committees on the peasant problem.

Serf emancipation and its many ramifications—land settlement, compensation, and repayments, among others—involved many conflicts of interest and evoked many opinions. The three selections below illustrate some of these interests and opinions. The first, which is in question and answer form, consists of excerpts from a letter sent to the Grand Duke Constantine by Kisilev in September, 1857. Kisilev argues in favor of giving land to the peasants, compensating the landowners, and retaining communal ownership under the mir. The second selection is from a memorandum sent to the tsar in the fall of 1857 by M. P. Posen, a rich landowner from Poltava who was a member of the Main Committee. Posen, a spokesman for the conservative landowners of *barshchina* estates in the black-earth belt, proposed, in effect, that the landowners and the peasants be left to work out their own arrangements. The third selection is taken from a memorandum presented to Alexander II by A. M. Unkovskii, a liberal landowner from Tver, in December, 1857. He presents a view common to owners of less fertile lands whose profits derived mainly from the rents and fees paid by their peasantry.

All three selections have been translated from the previously cited *Khrestomatiya,* vol. III, pp. 58–59, 62–63, 65–66. Slightly adapted.

Q. If it is decided to proceed with common measures, then it is necessary in this regard (a) to reserve to the landowner the right of full ownership of the land, (b) or to give to the serfs the land which they are using, (c) or only the farm and vegetable land [garden plot]; and should this be with or without compensation to the landowner?

A. "I have always proposed, and propose now, that the peasant land should remain in the full and inalienable possession of the peasants with compensation to the landowner. I consider this the most important condition in regard to the liberation of the peasants. It is the chief guarantee of a peaceful achievement of the desired goal. The peasants will not understand emancipation without their own land; and if an improvement in their situation pleases the serfs, then the taking away of the land will alter this first impression and turn the affair upside down.

"Granting garden plots with houses in return for payment is a hidden redemption charge. If this proves necessary, it would be better to raise the price of all the serf land than to make this redemption a charge upon one private farmstead. Emancipation with land is, in my opinion, a necessary condition not only economically, but also politically. In France, the landowners, who number seven million, constitute a group who are peaceful and are devoted to the government as the defender of their property. They form a majority over the proletariat, and do not allow the latter to spread their false notions. . . ."

Q. . . . Must the communal principle be continued in the control and use of the peasants' land, or should this be abolished and replaced with personal and separate use by each peasant?

A. "The question of the abolition of the communal principle [*i.e.,* ownership and control of the land by the *mir*] is important; until now it has not seemed necessary to raise it. Actually, the communal principle has both good and bad sides, but the right of equal use of the land has been so rooted among our people that it would be imprudent to change this centuries-old tradition by force of law. I had experience with this in Samarsk province where I offered rich grain fields to those peasants who wanted them on the one condition that they be divided into hereditary, family plots. I found little sympathy for this; on the contrary, there was a continual striving against private allotments. It must be admitted that although communal ownership has obvious shortcomings in its economic aspects and the advancement of agriculture, all other aspects outweigh this."

* * * * *

. . . The main points of the manifesto should be as follows.

1. Equality of all civil rights and identical obligations to the government for all classes of peasants.

2. Individual serf law abolished forever, and not to exist under such form.

3. Peasants to be the owners of the lands on which they are now settled. Those settled on their own lands to hold under general ownership—gratis; those settled on land not their own to pay quit-rent in either work or cash to the appanage princes, if on appanage estates; to the Treasury, if on fiscal [government] estates; to the landlord, if on landlords' estates. . . .

6. In allotting the land, the determination of the annual payment and the value of work is established for one general period by the whole state.

7. The present relationship between landlords and peasants is preserved until the expiration of this period. . . .

8. Any responsibility on the part of the landlords for the payment of taxes and for provisioning the peasants ceases upon the termination of the allotting and the establishment of land values and work fees. The lands are divided and allotted not separately to each person, but to the whole peasant commune which distributes plots among its members according to their ability to till the plots, and assesses the payment according to value in cash or in labor.

9. Paying for the lands is, therefore, the responsibility of the entire commune. . . .

11. On *obrok* estates, the amount of quit-rent for each estate will

remain as established by the Imperial Manifesto; any decrease in quit-rent may always be made by the owner of the land, but any increase must have special authorization by the gubernia committees. [Posen proposed that gubernia committees should be elected by the local land and serf owners from among their own number.]

12. On *barshchina* estates, the annual payment for the land is calculated in cash, but is produced by the peasants in the form of evaluated labor. . . .

13. The gubernia committees establish minimum allotments for each person, but the land is allotted to the peasants in such amount as the owner deems possible. It is obligatory for the landowner to give and for the peasant to accept the minimum allotment; any increase above this minimum depends on a mutual agreement between the landowner and the peasant.

14. In addition to the work days which peasants on *barshchina* estates give to the landowners in payment of quit-rent for the land, the gubernia committees fix for every season of the year several special work days which the peasants must also give to the landowner. The committees, however, in arranging this, see to it that the total of usual and special work days does not exceed the existing three days per week. . . .

* * * * *

At the time of the freeing of the peasants from the land and from their relation with the landowners, that is, upon the abolition of all kinds of mutually binding relations, serf freedom, even despite greater or lesser ties to the land, is incontestable. The landowner has received a substantial remuneration in cash or obligations for the peasant and the land, and the obligation of the peasants for the land given into their possession is guaranteed by the government. This is the only true way of liberating the peasants; not by word but by deed; not gradually but immediately, at one time and in all places; not transgressing against anyone's rights nor giving rise to discontent on any side nor threatening Russia's future.

Justice demands that, at the time of such freeing of the peasants, the landowners be compensated for the land which is taken from their possession and for the peasants who are emancipated. . . .

. . . the value of settled estates existing under serfdom consists not only of the land but also of the people for whom the owner should be compensated just as for the land. Moreover, in certain localities, land without people has no value at all. Of course, the liberated peasants should themselves pay for the land awarded them, but who should compensate the owners for the persons of the freed peasants and household serfs? It cannot possibly be assumed in this case that the value of the people was identical with the value of the land, nor that the very same people whose freedom was taken away in the name of governmental necessity should pay for their own bondage! They themselves are the least responsible of all for the existence of serfdom, having been sacrificed to the common state benefit. . . .

We see in the Russian serfs people deprived of their personal liberty and transformed into things through the decree of the government of the Russian land. . . . We see that serfdom was established by the government itself, for which action all the government hierarchy must answer equally. We see, moreover, that the governmental edict on this subject was certainly in accord with the needs, opinions, and wishes of the whole people, and that serf emancipation constitutes an interest of the whole state. . . .

. . . Compensation to the landowners for loss should comprise two elements: remuneration for the land and ransom for the people removed from their ownership. The latter should be a charge upon the state; the former, upon the emancipated peasants themselves. In our judgement, this remuneration should be made only in negotiable capital and should be paid to the landowners in the form of fully guaranteed, interest-bearing obligations. Such capital payments are necessary to support the land-owning economy and its adaptation to operation by hired labor. Therefore remuneration in the form of annual, continuing rents is inconvenient; and all other kinds of non-monetary remuneration—such as obligatory labor, agricultural products, etc.—can have no place in this case and are not in accord with the concepts of freedom; otherwise there will be no room for freedom, and serfdom will be replaced by some eternal bondage, intolerable for the people and providing no security for the landowner.

Drafting the Great Reform

The ways in which various proposals and projects for serf emancipation were solicited, discussed and coordinated, drafted into laws and edicts, and issued to the country are schematically represented below. The diagram is based on a chart published with N. P. Eroshkin, *Ocherki istorii gosudarstvennyikh uchrezdenii dorevolyutsionnoi Rossii* (*An Outline History of State Institutions in Prerevolutionary Russia*). Moscow, 1960.

THE STATE APPARATUS FOR
IMPLEMENTING THE PEASANT REFORM

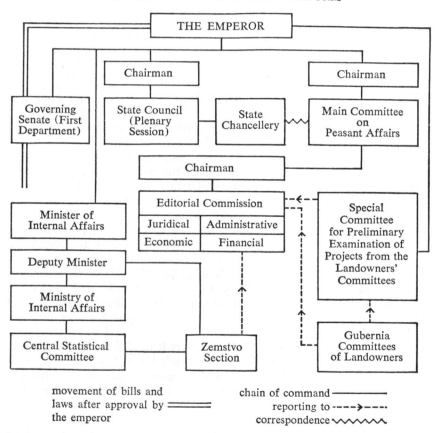

Two Analyses of Peasant Reactions to Emancipation

> The first of the analyses which follow was written by Wallace, who has already been identified as a foreign student (in his case, a British student) of Russia. The source is Wallace, *Russia,* pp. 500–505.
>
> The second analysis was written by a very different sort of person. S. M. Kravchinski, who used the pen-name of Stepniak, was a Russian revolutionary—a member, in fact, of the Land and Liberty Party. Kravchinski fled his native land after committing a political murder, and found refuge in Great Britain. He wrote several books which were published both in that country and in the United States. This selection from his work serves several purposes. It analyzes peasant attitudes, gives an account of a curious peasant reaction to the emancipation, illustrates one aspect of the position of the early socialist opponents of the autocracy, and exemplifies the campaign which they conducted in exile. The source is: Stepniak (S. M. Kravchinski), *The Russian Peasantry. Their Agrarian Conditions, Social Life and Religion.* New edition. London: George Routledge and Sons, 1905. Pp. 620–630.

It might be reasonably supposed that the serfs received with boundless gratitude and delight the Manifesto proclaiming these principles. Here at last was the realization of their long-cherished hopes. Liberty was accorded to them, and not only liberty, but a goodly portion of the soil— more than a half of all the arable land possessed by the proprietors.

In reality the Manifesto created among the peasantry a feeling of disappointment rather than delight. To understand this strange fact we must endeavor to place ourselves at the peasant's point of view.

In the first place it must be remarked that all vague, rhetorical phrases about free labor, human dignity, national progress, and the like, which may readily produce among educated men a certain amount of temporary enthusiasm, fall on the ears of the Russian peasant like drops of rain on a granite rock. The fashionable rhetoric of philosophical liberalism is as incomprehensible to him as the flowery circumlocutionary style of an Oriental scribe would be to a keen city merchant. The idea of liberty in the abstract and the mention of rights which lie beyond the sphere of his ordinary everyday life awaken no enthusiasm in his breast. And for mere names he has a profound indifference. What matters it to him that he is officially called, not a "serf," but a "free village inhabitant," if the change in official terminology is not accompanied by some immediate material advantage? What he wants is a house to live in, food to eat, and raiment wherewithal to be clothed, and to gain these first necessaries of life with as little labor as possible. If, therefore, the Government would make a law by which his share of the Communal land would be increased, or his share of the Communal burdens diminished, he would in return willingly consent to be therein designated by the most ugly name that learned ingenuity could devise. Thus the sentimental considerations which had such an important influence on the educated classes had no hold whatever on the mind of the peasants. They looked at the question exclusively from two points of view —that of historical right and that of material advantage—and from both of these tne Emancipation Law seemed to offer no satisfactory solution of the question.

On the subject of historical right the peasantry had their own traditional conceptions, which were completely at variance with the written law. According to the positive legislation the Communal land formed part of the estate, and consequently belonged to the proprietor; but according to the conceptions of the peasantry it belonged to the Commune, and the right of the proprietor consisted merely in that personal authority over the serfs which had been conferred on him by the Tsar. The peasants could not, of course, put these conceptions into a strict legal form, but they often expressed them in their own homely laconic way of saying to their master. "Mui vashi no zemlyá nasha"—that is to say, "We are yours, but the land is ours." And it must be admitted that this view, though legally untenable, had a certain historical justification. In old times the nobles had held their land by feudal tenure, and were liable to be ejected as soon as they did not fulfill their obligations to the State. These obligations had been long since abolished, and the feudal tenure transformed into an unconditional right of property, but the peasants clung to the old ideas in a way that strikingly illustrates the vitality of deep-rooted popular conceptions. In their minds the proprietors were merely temporary occupants, who were allowed by the Tsar to exact labor and dues from the serfs. What then was Emancipation? Certainly the abolition of all obligatory labor and money dues, and perhaps the complete ejectment of the proprietors. On this latter point there was a difference of opinion. All assumed, as a matter of course, that the Communal land would remain the property of the Commune, but it was not so clear what would be done with the rest of the estate. Some thought that it would be retained by the proprietor, but very many believed that the nobles would receive salaries from the Tsar, and that *all* the land would be given to the Communes. In this way the Emancipation would be in accordance with historical right and with the material advantage of the peasantry, for whose exclusive benefit, it was assumed, the reform had been undertaken.

Instead of this the peasants found that they were still to pay dues, even for the Communal land which they regarded as unquestionably their own! So at least said the expounders of the law. But the thing was incredible. Either the proprietors must be concealing or misinterpreting the law, or this was merely a preparatory measure, which would be followed by the real Emancipation. Thus were awakened among the peasantry a spirit of mistrust and suspicion and a widespread belief that there would be a second Emancipation, by which all the land would be divided and all the dues abolished.

On the nobles the Manifesto made a very different impression. The fact that they were to be intrusted with the putting of the law into execution, and the flattering allusions made to the spirit of generous self-sacrifice which they had exhibited, kindled amongst them enthusiasm enough to make them forget for a time their just grievances and their hostility toward.

the bureaucracy. They found that the conditions on which the Emancipation was effected were by no means so ruinous as they had anticipated; and the Emperor's appeal to their generosity and patriotism made many of them throw themselves with ardor into the important task confided to them.

Unfortunately they could not at once begin the work. The law had been so hurried through the last stages that the preparations for putting it into execution were by no means complete when the Manifesto was published. The task of regulating the future relations between the proprietors and the peasantry was intrusted to local proprietors in each district, who were to be called Arbiters of the Peace (*Mirovuié Posrédniki*); but three months elapsed before these Arbiters could be appointed. During that time there was no one to explain the law to the peasants and settle the disputes between them and the proprietors; and the consequence of this was that many cases of insubordination and disorder occurred. The peasants naturally imagined that, as soon as the Tsar said they were free, they were no longer obliged to work for their old masters—that all obligatory labor ceased as soon as the Manifesto was read. In vain the proprietors endeavoured to convince them that, in regard to labor, the old relations must continue, as the law enjoined, until a new arrangement had been made. To all explanations and exhortations the peasants turned a deaf ear, and to the efforts of the rural police they too often opposed a dogged, passive resistance. In many cases the simple appearance of the authorities sufficed to restore order, for the presence of one of the Tsar's servants convinced many that the order to work for the present as formerly was not a mere invention of the proprietors. But not unfrequently the birch had to be applied. Indeed, I am inclined to believe, from the numerous descriptions of this time which I have received from eye-witnesses, that rarely, if ever, had the serfs seen and experienced so much flogging as during these first three months after their liberation. Sometimes even the troops had to be called out, and on three occasions they fired on the peasants with ball cartridge. In the most serious case, where a young peasant had set up for a prophet and declared that the Emancipation Law was a forgery, fifty-one peasants were killed and seventy-seven were more or less seriously wounded. But in spite of these lamentable incidents, there was nothing which even the most violent alarmist could dignify with the name of an insurrection. Nowhere was there anything that could be called organized resistance. Even in the case above alluded to, the 3,000 peasants on whom the troops fired were entirely unarmed, made no attempt to resist, and dispersed in the utmost haste as soon as they discovered that they were being shot down. Had the military authorities shown a little more judgment, tact, and patience, the history of the Emancipation would not have been stained even with those three solitary cases of unnecessary bloodshed.

This interregnum between the reigns of serfage and liberty was brought to an end by the appointment of the Arbiters of the Peace. Their first duty was to explain the law, and to organize the new self-government of the peasantry. The lowest instance or primary organ of this self-government, the rural Commune, already existed, and at once recovered much of its ancient vitality as soon as the authority and interference of the proprietors were removed. The second instance, the Vólost—a territorial administrative unit comprising several contiguous Communes—had to be created, for nothing of the kind had previously existed on the estates of the nobles. It had existed, however, for nearly a quarter of a century among the peasants of the Demesnes, and it was therefore necessary merely to copy an already existing model.

As soon as all the Vólosts in his district had been thus organized, the Arbiter had to undertake the much more arduous task of regulating the agrarian relations between the proprietors and the Communes—with the individual peasants, be it remembered, the proprietors had no direct relations whatever. It had been enacted by the law that the future agrarian relations between the two parties should be left, as far as possible, to voluntary contract; and accordingly each proprietor was invited to come to an agreement with the Commune or Communes on his estate. On the ground of this agreement a statute-charter (*ustávnaya grámota*) was prepared, specifying the number of male serfs, the quantity of land actually enjoyed by them, any proposed changes in this amount, the dues proposed to be levied, and other details. If the Arbiter found that the conditions were in accordance with the law and clearly understood by the peasants, he confirmed the charter, and the arrangement was complete. When the two parties could not come to an agreement within a year, he prepared a charter according to his own judgment, and presented it for confirmation to the higher authorities.

The dissolution of partnership, if it be allowed to use such a term, between the proprietor and his serfs was sometimes very easy and sometimes very difficult. On many estates the charter did little more than legalize the existing arrangements, but in many instances it was necessary to add to, or subtract from, the amount of Communal land, and sometimes it was even necessary to remove the village to another part of the estate. In all cases there were, of course, conflicting interests and complicated questions, so that the Arbiter had always abundance of difficult work. Besides this, he had to act as mediator in those differences which naturally arose during the transition period, when the authority of the proprietor had been abolished but the separation of the two classes had not yet been effected. The unlimited patriarchial authority which had been formerly wielded by the proprietor or his steward now passed with certain restrictions into the hands of the Arbiters, and these peacemakers had to spend a great part of their time in driving about from one estate to another to put an end to alleged cases of insubordination—some of which, it must be admitted, existed only in the imagination of the proprietors.

At first the work of amicable settlement proceeded slowly. The proprietors generally showed a spirit of concession, and some of them generously proposed conditions much more favorable to the peasants than the law demanded; but the peasants were filled with vague suspicions, and feared to commit themselves by "putting pen to paper." Even the highly-respected proprietors, who imagined that they possessed the unbounded confidence of the peasantry, were suspected like the others, and their generous offers were regarded as well-baited traps. Often I have heard old men, sometimes with tears in their eyes, describe the distrust and ingratitude of the peasantry at this time. Many peasants believed that the proprietors were hiding the real Emancipation Law, and imaginative or ill-intentioned persons fostered this belief by professing to know what the real law contained. The most absurd rumors were afloat, and whole villages sometimes acted upon them. In the province of Moscow, for instance, one Commune sent a deputation to the proprietor to inform him that, as he had always been a good master, the *Mir* would allow him to retain his house and garden during his lifetime. In another locality it was rumored that the Tsar sat daily on a golden throne in the Crimea, receiving all peasants who came to him, and giving them as much land as they desired; and in order to take advantage of the Imperial liberality a large body of peasants set out for the place indicated, and advanced quickly till they were stopped by the military!

As an illustration of the illusions in which the peasantry indulged at this time, I may introduce here one of the many characteristic incidents related to me by gentlemen who had served as Arbiters of the Peace.

In the province of Riazán there was one Commune which had acquired a certain local notoriety for the obstinacy with which it refused all arrangements with the proprietor. My informant, who was Arbiter for the locality, was at last obliged to make a statute-charter for it without its consent. He wished, however, that the peasants should voluntarily accept the arrangement he proposed, and accordingly called them together to talk with them on the subject. After explaining fully the part of the law which related to their case, he asked them what objection that had to make a fair contract with their old master. For some time he received no answer, but gradually by questioning individuals he discovered the cause of their obstinacy: they were firmly convinced that not only the Communal land, but also the rest of the estate, belonged to them. To eradicate this false idea he set himself to reason with them, and the following characteristic dialogue ensued:—

Arbiter. "If the Tsar gave all the land to the peasantry, what compensation could he give to the proprietors to whom the land belongs?"

Peasant. "The Tsar will give them salaries according to their service."

Arbiter. "In order to pay these salaries he would require a great deal more money. Where could he get that money? He would have to increase the taxes, and in that way you would have to pay all the same."

Peasant. "The Tsar can make as much money as he likes."

Arbiter. "If the Tsar can make as much money as he likes, why does he make you pay the poll-tax every year?"

Peasant. "It is not the Tsar that receives the taxes we pay."

Arbiter. "Who then receives them?"

Peasant (after a little hesitation, and with a knowing smile). "The officials, of course!"

Gradually, through the efforts of the Arbiters, the peasants came to know better their real position, and the work began to advance more rapidly. But soon it was checked by another influence. By the end of the first year the "liberal," patriotic enthusiasm of the nobles had cooled. All the sentimental idyllic tendencies had melted away at the first touch of reality, and those who had imagined that liberty would have an immediately salutary effect on the moral character of the serfs confessed themselves disappointed.

The work of conciliating and regulating was thus extremely difficult, but the great majority of the Arbiters showed themselves equal to the task, and displayed an impartiality, tact, and patience beyond all praise.

* * * * *

As for our *moujiks,* who in their *mir* had before them a tangible embodiment of this patriarchal idea of government, they performed a curious psychological operation. They mentally transferred to the Tzar the whole of the functions performed by the *mir,* thus giving to his authority a remarkably precise and clear definition. The Tzar's authority is the *mir's* authority, magnified so as to suit the requirements of the State, without being in the smallest degree changed in its most characteristic attributes. The Tzar is the common Father of the country, its Protector, and the supreme dispenser of impartial justice to all, defending the weaker members of the community from the stronger. The Tzar "pities" everybody like the *mir.* The whole of the nation's riches "belong to the Tzar" exactly in the same sense as the land and meadows and forests within the boundaries of the commune belong to the *mir.* The most important function the peasant's imagination imposes on the Tzar is that of *universal leveller—* not, however, of movable property. The Tzar, like the *mir,* has the right to impose taxes on whomsoever he chooses, and on whatever he chooses, but he is expected not to interfere with what the people regard as the private property of each household, *i.e.,* movable capital. On the contrary, the Tzar is in duty bound to step in and to equitably redistribute the natural riches of the country, especially the land, whenever this is needed in the common interest.

All these restrictions and obligations are purely moral. The people repose implicit confidence in the Tzar's wisdom and justice. He is absolute master of the life and property of every man within his dominions, and no exception may be taken to his orders. The occasional blunders made by the Tzar, however heavy they may be, must be borne with patience, as they can be only temporary; the Tzar will redress the evil as soon as he is better informed on the matter.

Nobody would accuse us, I suppose, of unfairness in defining the popular legend of the autocracy, though we are not really sure to what extent it represents the past, and how far the present views of our peasantry as a body. Since the Emancipation many new influences have been at work in an opposite direction, in addition to which it must also be remembered that the two pillars of our patriarchism—the *mir* and the family—have changed vastly during the last twenty years, the *mir* for the worse, the family for the better.

Before the Emancipation, and for from ten to fifteen years afterwards, these institutions were in their full vigour, and so was the superstitious belief in the monarchy. It seemed to be something immutable, and so frightfully earnest that it overwhelmed and crushed the hopes of many noble Russian hearts. Thus a melody, which we dismiss as flat and commonplace when sung by a single voice, becomes strikingly solemn and impressive when taken up by an enormous crowd. During the three reigns which preceded the present one, to oppose autocracy seemed an act of madness. Yet all the thinking men of the day, in whom pusillanimity did not obscure judgment, could see that the Tzars were less capable than ever of playing the part of people's Tribunes.

A century ago, many years before any opposition was dreamt of in Russia, namely, after the outbreak of the French Revolution, autocracy lost the most essential element of a patriarchal Government, i.e., full confidence in its own immutability. Abject fear took possession of the hearts of the autocrats—fear of the surging Democracy that they were expected to champion. The Tzars were no longer sure of their position, or even of their personal security, and they wanted to protect themselves by making common cause with the privileged classes. They ceased to be the representatives of the State as a whole, with no vested interests in any particular party. Prior to the Emancipation the Tzars were pleased to parade their title of "first nobleman (dvorianin) of Russia"; but after the Emancipation they might well have assumed the name of "first broker of the Empire."

The sentimental, liberal Alexander I., and the tory-democrat Nicholas I., both so intensely worshipped by the poor moujiks, kept them enslaved because they feared a revolution. The Emperor Alexander II. had the courage to break the spell and to cancel this terrible injustice, but he wanted to remain an autocrat at all costs, and only grew the more obstinate the more the new needs pressed upon him. He was inevitably driven to the fatal course of re-establishing with his left hand, abuses which he had overthrown with his right. Instead of inaugurating a new and brilliant era of progress for the nation, and securing a happy reign for himself, he merely introduced the last phase in the terrible struggle between the people and their Government.

The enemy is now at their door. If our people at the present crisis lose the battle, they will never again have anything of their own to lose. With a nation of hereditary husbandmen, the land question is the question of life and death. It is silly and cruel to consider the problem as in any way solved by the inquiry as to whether the peasants themselves would or would not prefer a return to their former state of serfdom. Certainly they would not; but they would prefer yet more, to be free without the danger of starvation.

They received the announcement of their liberation with transports of joy, but they were utterly disappointed by the details of the new agrarian regulations. Their secular superstition gave rise to some very curious phenomena of social psychology.

To begin with, they declined to believe in the authenticity of the Emancipation Act. To their candid, unsophisticated minds it seemed utterly incredible that their Tzar should have "wronged" them so bitterly as to the land. They obstinately repeated that their "freedom," *i.e.,* the Emancipation Act, had been tampered with by the nobility, who had concealed the Tzar's real "freedom," which had been quite a different thing. The most emphatic declarations made before the peasants' deputies and elders by the Emperor's ministers and by the Emperor in person could not disabuse them. They persisted in believing against belief. There were hundreds of peasants' rebellions in all parts of the empire, owing to this misunderstanding, especially during the first years which followed the Act of Emancipation. They subsided at last. After ten years of incessant persuasion through the medium of speeches, *ukazes,* floggings, and an occasional shooting, this superstition began to give way. It did not disappear, however,—it only changed its shape.

Since 1870 or thereabouts we hear no more of the peasants' doubts as to the authenticity of the agrarian arrangements of 1861. They have ended by admitting that it was really the work of the Tzar's own hands, but the whole of our peasantry have made up their minds, and expect a *new* agrarian arrangement from the Tzar, which will rectify the blunders of the old regulations. Rumours as to the coming agrarian *ravnenie* or "redistribution," which is to take place next spring, next summer, and so forth, now and then spread like wildfire over whole provinces and regions. It is not uncommon for them to give rise to "disorderly" and illegal conduct, such as refusal to pay rent due to the landlords, or the arbitrary appropriation of his fields by the peasants. The authorities of course intervene, and the central Government, which ascribes all things to the Nihilist propaganda, makes strenuous efforts to dissipate these dangerous rumours.

Up to the present time official and Imperial declarations have not opened the peasants' eyes. The *moujiks* see in them either a new trick of the nobles (landlords), or by some strange aberration of intellect understand the plainest statements in an exactly inverse sense to the real one. We know, for instance, cases where peasants' deputies, expressly summoned before a Governor-General to be instructed in the right views on the agrarian question, have on their return to their villages emphatically affirmed that "His Excellency has positively charged them to be reassured, because the Tzar will ere long effect an agrarian 'redistribution.' " They have doubtless been spoken to "about the land," and then probably the General has indulged in some vapouring about the Tzar's solicitude and benevolence. The two things when put together could for them mean nothing but "agrarian redistribution."

In 1878–79, after the enormous strain of the Turkish war, rumours relating to this supposed coming agrarian "redistribution" assumed particular definiteness and enlargement. They penetrated everywhere, and even into the ranks of the army; people openly discussed the coming rearrangements at the village meetings, in the presence of the rural authorities, who, as peasants, fully shared in the common expectations.

General Makov, then Minister of the Interior, issued a circular letter, to be publicly read in all villages, and affixed to the walls in all communal houses. This circular contradicted these rumours, and declared positively that there would be no "redistribution," and that the landlords would retain their own property. It produced no effect. Professor Engelhardt, who wrote one of his Letters from a Village at the time of this fit of popular hopefulness, says that the *moujiks* who heard Makov's circular understood it in the following sense:—"It is requested that people shall, for a time, abstain from gossiping at random about the 'redistribution.'" As to the ministerial warnings against the evil-intentioned disseminators of false reports, and the orders to apprehend them, they produced the most amusing bewilderment. The superior and the inferior agents of the administration could not understand each other's language. The superior officers, the gentlemen, as Engelhardt calls them, by "evil-intentioned people" meant to imply the Nihilists, the advocates and partisans of agrarian "redistribution;" whilst according to the Elders and other village authorities the "evil-intentioned" were those who opposed this movement.

The year 1880, which was almost a year of famine, gave new zest to the popular expectations. "There is no bread in the country," they said, "the *moujiks* are so pressed that they cannot move on their little patches of land, and the landlords have no end of land lying waste." A universal conviction grew up among the peasants that in the course of the next spring (1881) the Tzar's surveyor would come and start upon the work of general readjustment.

Wallace's Observations

The next ten selections deal with various norms and values of Russia as these appeared to Sir Donald during his years of residency and travel there. For the most part, therefore, they constitute firsthand reporting. The source is: Wallace, *Russia*, pp. 57–58, 79–80, 88–92, 95–97.

Priests and the People

Since that time I have frequently spoken on this subject with competent authorities, and nearly all have admitted that the present condition of the clergy is highly unsatisfactory, and that the parish priest rarely enjoys the respect of his parishioners. In a semi-official report, which I once accidentally stumbled upon when searching for material of a different kind, the facts are stated in the following plain language: "The people"—I seek to translate as literally as possible—"do not respect the clergy, but persecute them with derision and reproaches, and feel them to be a burden. In nearly all the popular comic stories, the priest, his wife, or his laborer is held up to ridicule, and in all the proverbs and popular sayings where the clergy are mentioned it is always with derision. The people shun the clergy, and have recourse to them not from the inner impulse of conscience, but from necessity. . . . And why do the people not respect the clergy? Because it forms a class apart; because, having received a false kind of education, it does not introduce into the life of the people the teaching of the Spirit, but remains in the mere dead forms of outward ceremonial, at the same time despising these forms even to blasphemy; because the clergy itself continually presents examples of want of respect to religion, and transforms the service of God into a profitable trade. Can the people respect the clergy when they hear how one priest stole money from below the pillow of a dying man at the moment of confession, how another was publicly dragged out of a house of ill fame, how a third christened a dog, how a fourth whilst officiating at the Easter service was dragged by the hair from the altar by the deacon? Is it possible for the people to respect priests who spend their time in the gin-shop, write fraudulent petitions, fight with the cross in their hands, and abuse each other in bad language at the altar? One might fill several pages with examples of this kind—in each instance naming the time and place—without overstepping the boundaries of the province of Nizhni-Novgorod. Is it possible for the people to respect the clergy when they see that truth has disappeared from it, and that the consistories, guided in their decisions not by rules, but by personal friendship and bribery, destroy in it the last remains of truthfulness? If we add to all this the false certificates which the clergy give to those who do not wish to partake of the Eucharist, the dues illegally extracted from the Old Ritualists, the conversion of the altar into a source of revenue, the giving of churches to priests' daughters as a dowry, and similar phenomena, the question as to whether the people can respect the clergy requires no answer."

As these words were written by an orthodox Russian, celebrated for his extensive and intimate knowledge of Russian provincial life, and were addressed in all seriousness to a member of the Imperial family, we may safely assume that they contain a considerable amount of truth. The reader must not, however, imagine that all Russian priests are of the kind above referred to. Many of them are honest, respectable, well-intentioned men, who conscientiously fulfill their humble duties, and strive hard to procure a good education for their children.

Peasant Credulity

The most amusing instance of credulity . . . was . . . related to me by a peasant-woman who came from the village in question. One day in winter, about the time of sunset, a peasant-family was startled by the entrance of a strange visitor—a female figure, dressed as St. Barbara is commonly represented in the religious pictures. All present were very much astonished by this apparition; but the figure told them, in a low, soft voice, to be of good cheer, for she was St. Barbara, and had come to honor them with a visit as a reward for their piety. The peasant thus favored was not remarkable for his piety, but he did not consider it necessary to correct the mistake of his saintly visitor, and requested her to be seated. With perfect readiness she accepted the invitation, and began at once to discourse in an edifying way. Meanwhile the news of this wonderful apparition spread like wildfire, and all the inhabitants of the village, as well as those of a neighboring village about a mile distant, collected in and around the house of the favored family. Whether the priest was among those who came my informant did not know. Many of those who had come could not get within hearing, but those at the outskirts of the crowd hoped that the saint might come out before disappearing. Their hopes were gratified. About midnight the mysterious visitor announced that she would go and bring St. Nicholas, the miracle-worker, and requested all to remain perfectly still during her absence. The crowd respectfully made way for her, and she passed out into the darkness. With breathless expectation all awaited the arrival of St. Nicholas, who is the favorite saint of the Russian peasantry; but hours passed, and he did not appear. At last, towards sunrise, some of the less zealous spectators began to return home, and those of them who had come from the neighboring village discovered to their horror that during their absence their horses had been stolen! At once they raised the hue-and-cry; and the peasants scoured the country in all directions in search of the *soi-disant* St. Barbara and her accomplices, but they never recovered the stolen property. "And serve them right, the blockheads!" added my informant, who had herself escaped falling into the trap by being absent from the village at the time.

An Old-Fashioned Peasant Family

Ivan's household was a good specimen of the Russian peasant family of the old type. Previous to the Emancipation in 1861, there were many households of this kind, containing the representatives of three generations. All the members, young and old, lived together in patriarchal fashion under the direction and authority of the Head of the House, called usually *Khozaïn,* that is to say, the Administrator; or, in some districts, Bolshák, which means literally "the Big One." Generally speaking, this important position was occupied by the grandfather, or, if he was dead, by the eldest brother, but this rule was not very strictly observed. If, for instance, the grandfather became infirm, or if the eldest brother was incapacitated by disorderly habits or other cause, the place of authority was taken by some other member—it might be by a woman—who was a good manager, and possessed the greatest moral influence. The relations between the Head of the Household and the other members depended on custom and personal character, and they consequently varied greatly in different families. If the Big One was an intelligent man, of decided, energetic character, like my friend Ivan, there was probably perfect discipline in the house, except perhaps in the matter of female tongues, which do not readily submit to the authority even of their owners; but very often it happened that the Big One was not thoroughly well fitted for his post, and in that case endless quarrels and bickerings inevitably took place. Those quarrels were generally caused and fomented by the female members of the household—a fact which will not seem strange if we try to realize how difficult it must be for several sisters-in-law to live together, with their children and a mother-in-law, within the narrow limits of a peasant's house. The complaints of the young bride, who finds that her mother-in-law puts all the hard work on her shoulders, form a favorite motive in the popular poetry.

The house, with its appurtenances, the cattle, the agricultural implements, the grain and other products, the money gained from the sale of these products—in a word, the house and nearly everything it contained—was the joint-property of the family. Hence, nothing was bought or sold by any member—not even by the Big One himself, unless he possessed an unusual amount of authority—without the express or tacit consent of the other grown-up males, and all the money that was earned was put into the common purse. When one of the sons left home to work elsewhere, he was expected to bring or send home all his earnings, except what he required for food, lodgings, and other *necessary* expenses; and if he understood the word "necessary" in too lax a sense, he had to listen to very plain-spoken reproaches when he returned. During his absence, which might last for a whole year or several years, his wife and children remained in the house as before, and the money which he earned was probably devoted to the payment of the family taxes.

The peasant household of the old type is thus a primitive labor association, of which the members have all things in common, and it is not a little remarkable that the peasant conceives it as such rather than as a family. This is shown by the customary terminology and by the law of inheritance. The Head of the Household is not called by any word corresponding to Paterfamilias, but is termed, as I have said, Khozaïn, or Administrator —a word that is applied equally to a farmer, a shopkeeper, or the head of an industrial undertaking, and does not at all convey the idea of blood-relationship.

The law of inheritance is likewise based on this conception. When a household is broken up, the degree of blood-relationship is not taken into consideration in the distribution of the property. All the adult male members share equally. Illegitimate and adopted sons, if they have contributed their share of labor, have the same rights as the sons born in lawful wedlock. The married daughter, on the contrary—being regarded as belonging to her husband's family—and the son who has previously separated himself from the household, are excluded from the succession. Strictly speaking, there is no succession or inheritance whatever, except as regards the wearing apparel and any little personal effects of a similar kind. The house and all that it contains belong not to the Khozaïn, but to the little household community; and, consequently, when the Khozaïn dies and the community is broken up, the members do not inherit, but merely appropriate individually what they had hitherto possessed collectively. Thus there is properly no inheritance or succession, but simply liquidation and distribution of the property among the members. The written law of inheritance, founded on the conception of personal property, is quite unknown to the peasantry, and quite inapplicable to their mode of life. In this way a large and most important section of the Code remains a dead letter for about four-fifths of the population!

This predominance of practical economic consideration is likewise exemplified by the way in which marriages are arranged in these large families.

In all respects the Russian peasantry are, as a class, extremely practical and matter-of-fact in their conceptions and habits, and are not at all prone to indulge in sublime, ethereal sentiments of any kind. They have little or nothing of what may be roughly termed the Hermann-and-Dorothea element in their composition, and consequently they know very little about those sentimental, romantic ideas which we habitually associate with the preliminary steps to matrimony. This fact is so patent to all who have studied the Russian peasantry, that even those who have endeavored to idealize peasant life have rarely ventured to make their story turn on a sentimental love affair. These general remarks I insert here parenthetically, in order that the reader may more clearly understand what I have to say regarding peasant marriages.

In the primitive system of agriculture usually practiced in Russia, the natural labor-unit—if it be allowed to use such a term—comprises a man, a woman, and a horse. As soon, therefore, as a boy becomes an able-bodied laborer he ought to be provided with the two accessories necessary for the completion of the labor-unit. To procure a horse, either by purchase or by rearing a foal, is the duty of the Head of the House; to procure a wife for the youth is the duty of "the female Big One" (bolshúkha). And the chief consideration in determining the choice is in both cases the same. Prudent domestic administrators are not to be tempted by showy horses or beautiful brides; what they seek is not beauty, but physical strength and capacity for work. When the youth reaches the age of eighteen he is informed that he ought to marry at once, and as soon as he gives his consent negotiations are opened with the parents of some eligible young person. In the larger villages the negotiations are sometimes facilitated by certain old women called *svakhi,* who occupy themselves specially with this kind of mediation; but very often the affair is arranged directly by, or through the agency of, some common friend of the two houses. Care must of course be taken that there is no legal obstacle to the marriage, and these obstacles are not always easily avoided in a small village, the inhabitants of which have been long in the habit of intermarrying. According to Russian ecclesiastical law, not only is marriage between first-cousins illegal, but affinity is considered as equivalent to consanguinity—that is to say, a mother-in-law and a sister-in-law are regarded as a mother and a sister— and even the fictitious relationship created by standing together at the baptismal font as godfather and godmother is legally recognized. If all the preliminary negotiations are successful, the marriage takes place, and the bridegroom brings his bride home to the house of which he is a member. She brings nothing with her as a dowry except her trousseau, but she brings a pair of good strong arms, and thereby enriches her adopted family. Of course it happens occasionally—for human nature is everywhere essentially the same—that a young peasant falls in love with one of his former playmates, and brings his little romance to a happy conclusion at the altar;

but such cases are very rare, and as a rule it may be said that the marriages of the Russian peasantry are arranged under the influence of economic rather than sentimental considerations.

The custom of living in large families has many decided economic advantages. We all know the edifying fable of the dying man who showed to his sons by means of a piece of wicker-work the advantages of living together and mutually assisting each other. In ordinary times the necessary expenses of a large household of ten members are considerably less than the combined expenses of two households comprising five members each, and when a "black day" comes, a large family can bear temporary adversity much more successfully than a small one. These are principles of world-wide application, and in the life of the Russian peasantry they have a peculiar force. Each adult peasant possesses, as I shall hereafter explain, a share of the Communal land, but this share is not sufficient to occupy all his time and working power. One married pair can easily cultivate two shares—at least in all provinces where land is not very abundant. Now if a family is composed of two married couples, one of the men can go elsewhere and earn money, whilst the other, with his wife and sister-in-law, can cultivate the two combined shares of land. If, on the contrary, a family consists merely of one pair with their children, the man must either remain at home, in which case he may have difficulty in finding work for the whole of his time, or he must leave home, and intrust the cultivation of his share of the land to his wife, whose time must be in great part devoted to domestic affairs.

In the time of serfage the proprietors clearly perceived these and similar advantages, and compelled their serfs to live together in large families. No family could be broken up without the proprietor's consent, and this consent was not easily obtained unless the family had assumed quite abnormal proportions, and was permanently disturbed by domestic dissension. In the matrimonial affairs of the serfs, too, the majority of the proprietors systematically exercised a certain supervision, not necessarily from any paltry, meddling spirit, but because their material interests were thereby affected. A proprietor would not, for instance, allow the daughter of one of his serfs to marry a serf belonging to another proprietor—because he would thereby lose a female laborer—unless some compensation were offered. The compensation might be a sum of money, or the affair might be arranged on the principle of reciprocity, by the master of the bridegroom allowing one of his female serfs to marry a serf belonging to the master of the bride.

However advantageous the custom of living in large families may appear when regarded from the economic point of view, it has very serious defects, both theoretical and practical.

That families connected by the ties of blood-relationship and marriage can easily live together in harmony is one of those social axioms which are accepted universally and believed by nobody. We all know by our own experience, or by that of others, that the friendly relations of two such families are greatly endangered by proximity of habitation. To live in the same street is not advisable; to occupy adjoining houses is positively dangerous; and to live under the same roof is certainly fatal to prolonged amity. . . . Neither affinities, affection, nor good intentions can withstand the constant friction which ensues.

Communal Agriculture

Ivánofka may be taken as a fair specimen of the villages in the northern half of the country, and a brief description of its inhabitants will convey a tolerably correct notion of the northern peasantry in general.

Nearly the whole of the female population, and about one-half of the male inhabitants, are habitually engaged in cultivating the Communal land, which comprises about two thousand acres of a light sandy soil. The arable part of this land is divided into three large fields, each of which is cut up into long narrow strips. The first field is reserved for the winter grain—that is to say, rye, which forms, in the shape of black bread, the principal food of the peasantry. In the second are raised oats for the horses, and buckwheat, which is largely used for food. The third lies fallow, and is used in the summer as pasturage for the cattle.

All the villagers in this part of the country divide the arable land in this way, in order to suit the triennial rotation of crops. This triennial system is extremely simple. The field which is used this year for raising winter grain will be used next year for raising summer grain, and in the following year will lie fallow. Before being sown with winter grain it ought to receive a certain amount of manure. Every family possesses in each of the two fields under cultivation one or more of the long, narrow strips or belts into which they are divided.

The annual life of the peasantry is that of simple husbandmen, inhabiting a country where the winter is long and severe. The agricultural year begins in April with the melting of the snow. Nature has been lying dormant for some months. Awakening now from her long sleep, and throwing off her white mantle, she strives to make up for lost time. No sooner has the snow disappeared than the fresh young grass begins to shoot up, and very soon afterwards the shrubs and trees begin to bud. The rapidity of this transition from winter to spring astonishes the inhabitants of more temperate climes.

On St. George's Day (April 23rd), the cattle are brought out for the first time and sprinkled with holy water by the priest. The cattle of the Russian peasantry are never very fat, but at this period of the year their appearance is truly lamentable. During the winter they have been cooped up in small unventilated cow-houses, and fed almost exclusively on straw; now, when they are released from their imprisonment, they look like the ghosts of their former emaciated selves. All are lean and weak, many are lame, and some cannot rise to their feet without assistance.

Meanwhile the peasants are impatient to begin the field labor. An old proverb which they all know says: "Sow in mud and you will be a prince;" and they always act in accordance with this dictate of traditional wisdom. As soon as it is possible to plow they begin to prepare the land for the summer grain, and this labor occupies them probably till the end of May. Then comes the work of carting out manure and preparing the fallow field for the winter grain, which will last probably till about St. Peter's Day (June 29th), when the hay-making generally begins. After the hay-making comes the harvest, by far the busiest time of the year. From the middle of July—especially from St. Elijah's Day (July 20th), when the saint is usually heard rumbling along the heavens in his chariot of fire—until the end of August, the peasant may work day and night, and yet he will find that he has barely time to get all his work done. In little more than a month he has to reap and stack his grain—rye, oats, and whatever else he may have sown either in spring or in the preceding autumn—and to sow the winter grain for next year. To add to his troubles, it sometimes happens that the rye and the oats ripen almost simultaneously, and his position is then still more difficult than usual.

Whether the seasons favor him or not, the peasant has at this time a hard task, for he can rarely afford to hire the requisite number of laborers, and has generally the assistance merely of his wife and family; but he can at this season work for a short time at high pressure, for he has the prospect of soon obtaining a good rest and an abundance of food. About the end of September the field labor is finished, and on the 1st day of October the harvest festival begins—a joyous season, during which the parish fêtes are commonly celebrated.

The Mir

On my arrival at Ivánofka, my knowledge of the institution was of that vague, superficial kind which is commonly derived from men who are fonder of sweeping generalizations and rhetorical declamation than of serious, patient study of phenomena. I knew that the chief personage in a Russian village is the *Selski starosta,* or the Village Elder, and that all important communal affairs are regulated by the *Selski Skhod,* or Village Assembly. Further, I was aware that the land in the vicinity of the village belongs to the Commune, and is distributed periodically among the members in such a way that every able-bodied peasant possesses a share sufficient, or nearly sufficient, for his maintenance. Beyond this elementary information I knew little or nothing.

My first attempt at extending my knowledge was not very successful. Hoping that my friend Ivan might be able to assist me, and knowing that the popular name for the Commune is *Mir,* which means also "the world," I put to him the direct, simple question, "What is the Mir?"

Ivan was not easily disconcerted, but for once he looked puzzled, and stared at me vacantly. When I endeavored to explain to him my question, he simply knitted his brows and scratched the back of his head. This latter movement is the Russian peasant's method of accelerating cerebral action; but in the present instance it had no practical result. In spite of his efforts, Ivan could not get much further than the "Kak vam skatzat'?" that is to say, "How am I to tell you?"

It was not difficult to perceive that I had adopted an utterly false method of investigation, and a moment's reflection sufficed to show me the absurdity of my question. I had asked from an uneducated man a philosophical definition, instead of extracting from him material in the form of concrete facts, and constructing therefrom a definition for myself. These concrete facts, Ivan was both able and willing to supply; and as soon as I adopted a rational mode of questioning, I received an abundant supply of most interesting information. This information, together with the results of much subsequent conversation and reading, I now propose to present to the reader in my own words.

The peasant family of the old type is, as we have just seen, a kind of primitive association, in which the members have nearly all things in common. The village may be roughly described as a primitive association on a larger scale.

Between these two social units there are many points of analogy. In both there are common interests and common responsibilities. In both there is a principal personage, who is in a certain sense ruler within, and representative as regards the outside world: in the one case called Khozaïn, or Head of the Household, and in the other Starosta, or Village Elder. In both the authority of the ruler is limited; in the one case by the adult members of the family, and in the other by the heads of households. In both there is a certain amount of common property: in the one case the house and nearly all that it contains, and in the other the arable land and pasturage. In both cases there is a certain amount of common responsibility: in the one case for all of the debts, and in the other for all the taxes and Communal obligations. And both are protected to a certain extent against the ordinary legal consequences of insolvency, for the family cannot be deprived of its house or necessary agricultural implements, and the Commune cannot be deprived of its land, by importunate creditors.

On the other hand, there are many important points of contrast. The Commune is, of course, much larger than the family, and the mutual relations of its members are by no means so closely interwoven. The members of a family all farm together, and those of them who earn money from other sources are expected to put their savings into the common purse; whilst the households composing a Commune farm independently, and pay into the common treasury only a certain fixed sum.

From these brief remarks the reader will at once perceive that a Russian village is something very different from a village in our sense of the term, and that the villagers are bound together by ties quite unknown to the English rural population. A family living in an English village has little reason to take an interest in the affairs of its neighbors. The isolation of the individual families may not be quite perfect, for man, being a social animal, takes, and ought to take, a certain interest in the affairs of those around him, and this social duty is sometimes fulfilled by the weaker sex with more zeal than is absolutely indispensable for the public welfare; but families may live for many years in the same village without ever becoming conscious of common interests. So long as the Jones family do not commit any culpable breach of public order, such as putting obstructions on the highway or habitually setting their house on fire, their neighbor Brown takes probably no interest in their affairs, and has no ground for interfering with their perfect liberty of action. Jones may be a drunkard and hopelessly insolvent, and he may some night decamp clandestinely with his whole family and never more be heard of; but all these things do not affect the interests of Brown, unless he has been imprudent enough to entertain with the delinquent more than simply neighborly relations. Now, amongst the families composing a Russian village, such a state of isolation is impossible. The Heads of Households must often meet together and consult in the Village Assembly, and their daily occupations must be influenced by the Communal decrees. They cannot begin to mow the hay or plow the fallow field until the Village Assembly has passed a resolution on the subject. If a peasant becomes a drunkard, or takes some equally efficient means to become insolvent, every family in the village has a right to complain, not merely in the interests of public morality, but from selfish motives, because all the families are collectively responsible for his taxes. For the same reason no peasant can permanently leave the village without the consent of the Commune, and this consent will not be granted if all his actual and future liabilities are not met. If a peasant wishes to go away for a short time, in order to work elsewhere, he must obtain a written permission, which serves him as a passport during his absence; and he may be recalled at any moment by a Communal decree. In reality he is rarely recalled so long as he sends home regularly the full amount of his taxes—including the dues which he has to pay for the temporary passport—but sometimes the Commune uses the power of recall for the purpose of extorting money from the absent member. If it becomes known, for instance, that an absent member receives a good salary in one of the towns, he may one day receive a formal order to return at once to his native village, and be informed at the same time, unofficially, that his presence will be dispensed with if he will send to the commune a certain amount of money. The money thus sent is generally used by the commune for convivial purposes. Whether this method of extortion is frequently used by the Communes, I cannot confidently say, but I suspect that it is by no means rare, for one or two cases have accidentally come under my own observation, and I know that the police of St. Petersburg have been recently ordered not to send back any peasants to their native villages until some proof is given that the ground of recall is not a mere pretext.

In order to understand the Russian village system, the reader must bear in mind these two important facts: the arable land and the pasturage belong not to the individual houses, but to the Commune, and all the households are collectively and individually responsible for the entire sum which the Commune has to pay annually into the Imperial Treasury.

In all countries the theory of government and administration differs considerably from the actual practice. Nowhere is this difference greater than in Russia, and in no Russian institution is it greater than in the Village Commune. It is necessary, therefore, to know both theory and practice; and it is well to begin with the former, because it is the simpler of the two.

When we have once thoroughly mastered the theory, it is easy to understand the deviations that are made to suit peculiar local conditions.

According, then, to theory, all male peasants in every part of the Empire are inscribed in census lists, which form the basis of the direct taxation. These lists are revised at irregular intervals, and all males alive at the time of the "revision," from the newborn babe to the centenarian, are duly inscribed. Each Commune has a list of this kind, and pays to the Government an annual sum proportionate to the number of names which the list contains, or, in popular language, according to the number of "revision souls." During the intervals between the revisions the financial authorities take no notice of the births and deaths. A Commune which has a hundred male members at the time of the revision may have in a few years considerably more or considerably less than that number, but it has to pay taxes for a hundred members all the same until a new revision is made for the whole Empire.

Now in Russia, so far at least as the rural population is concerned, the payment of taxes is inseparably connected with the possession of land. Every peasant who pays taxes is supposed to have a share of the arable land and pasturage belonging to the Commune. If the Communal revision lists contain a hundred names, the Communal land ought to be divided into a hundred shares, and each "revision soul" should enjoy his share in return for the taxes which he pays.

The reader who has followed my explanations up to this point may naturally conclude that the taxes paid by the peasants are in reality a species of rent for the land which they enjoy. So it seems, and so it is sometimes represented, but so in reality it is not. When a man rents a bit of land he acts according to his own judgment, and makes a voluntary contract with the proprietor; but the Russian peasant is obliged to pay his taxes whether he desires to enjoy land or not. The theory, therefore, that the taxes are simply the rent of the land, will not bear even superficial examination. Equally untenable is the theory that they are a species of land-tax. In any reasonable system of land-dues the yearly sum imposed bears some kind of proportion to the quantity and quality of the land enjoyed; but in Russia it may be that the members of one Commune possess six acres, and the members of the neighboring Commune seven acres, and yet the taxes in both cases are the same. The truth is that the taxes are personal, and are calculated according to the number of male "souls," and the Government does not take the trouble to inquire how the Communal land is distributed. The commune has to pay into the Imperial Treasury a fixed yearly sum, according to the number of its "revision souls," and distributes the land among its members as it thinks fit.

How, then, does the Commune distribute the land? To this question it is impossible to give a definite general reply, because each Commune acts as it pleases. Some act strictly according to the theory. These divide their land at the time of the revision into a number of portions or shares corresponding to the number of revision souls, and give to each family a number of shares corresponding to the number of revision souls which it contains.

This is from the administrative point of view by far the simplest system. The census list determines how much land each family will enjoy, and the existing tenures are disturbed only by the revisions which take place at irregular intervals. Since 1719 only ten revisions have been made, so that the average length of these intervals has been about fifteen years—a term which may be regarded as a tolerably long lease. But, on the other hand, this system has serious defects. The revision list represents merely the numerical strength of the families, and the numerical strength is often not at all in proportion to the working power. Let us suppose, for example, two families, each containing at the time of the revision five male members. According to the census list these two families are equal, and ought to receive equal shares of the land; but in reality it may happen that the one contains a father in the prime of life and four able-bodied sons, whilst the other contains a widow and five little boys. The wants and working power of these two families are of course very different; and if the above system of distribution be applied, the man with four sons and a goodly supply of grandchildren will probably find that he has too little land, whilst the widow with her five little boys will find it difficult to cultivate the five shares allotted to her, and utterly impossible to pay the corresponding amount of taxation—for in all cases, it must be remembered, the Communal burdens are distributed in the same proportion as the land.

But why, it may be said, should the widow not accept provisionally the five shares, and let to others the part which she does not require? The balance of rent after payment of the taxes might help her to bring up her young family.

So it seems to one acquainted only with the rural economy of England, where land is scarce, and always gives a revenue more than sufficient to defray the taxes. But in Russia the possession of a share of Communal land is often not a privilege, but a burden. In some Communes the land is so poor and abundant that it cannot be let at any price. Witness, for instance, many villages in the province of Smolensk, where the traveler may see numerous uncultivated strips in the communal fields. In others the soil will repay cultivation, but a fair rent will not suffice to pay the taxes and dues.

To obviate these inconvenient results of the simpler system, some communes have adopted the expedient of allotting the land, not according to the number of revision souls, but according to the working power of the families. Thus, in the instance above supposed, the widow would receive perhaps two shares, and the large household, containing five workers, would receive perhaps seven or eight. Since the breaking-up of the large families, such inequality as I have supposed is, of course, rare; but inequality of a less extreme kind does still occur, and justifies a departure from the system of allotment according to the revision lists.

Even if the allotment be fair and equitable at the time of the revision, it may soon become unfair and burdensome by the natural fluctuations of the population. Births and deaths may in the course of a very few years entirely alter the relative working power of the various families. The sons of the widow may grow up to manhood, whilst two or three able-bodied members of the other family may be cut off by an epidemic. Thus, long before a new revision takes place, the distribution of the land may be no longer in accordance with the wants and capacities of the various families composing the Commune. To correct this, various expedients are employed. Some Communes transfer particular lots from one family to another, as circumstances demand; whilst others make from time to time, during the intervals between the revisions, a complete re-distribution and re-allotment of the land.

The system of allotment adopted depends entirely on the will of the particular Commune. In this respect the Communes enjoy the most complete autonomy, and no peasant ever dreams of appealing against a Communal decree. The higher authorities not only abstain from all interference in the allotment of the Communal lands, but remain in profound ignorance as to which system the Communes habitually adopt. Though the Imperial Administration has a most voracious appetite for symmetrically-constructed statistical tables—many of them formed chiefly out of materials supplied by the mysterious inner consciousness of the subordinate officials—no attempt has yet been made to collect statistical data which might throw light on this important subject. In spite of the systematic and persistent efforts of the centralized bureaucracy to regulate minutely all departments of the national life, the rural Communes, which contain above five-sixths of the population, remain in many respects entirely beyond its influence, and even beyond its sphere of vision! But let not the reader be astonished overmuch. He will learn in time that Russia is the land of paradoxes; and meanwhile he is about to receive a still more startling bit of information—a statement that should be heralded in by a flourish of trumpets. In "the great stronghold of Cæsarian despotism and centralized bureaucracy," these Village Communes, containing about five-sixths of the population, are capital specimens of representative Constitutional government of the extreme democratic type!

When I say that the rural Commune is a good specimen of Constitutional government, I use the phrase in the English, and not in the continental sense. In the continental languages a Constitutional government means a government which possesses a long, formal document, composed of many successive paragraphs, in which the functions of the various institutions, the powers of the various authorities, and all the possible methods of procedure are carefully defined. Such a document was never heard of in Russian Village Communes. Their Constitution is of the English type—a body of unwritten, traditional conceptions, which have grown up and modified themselves under the influence of ever-changing practical necessity. If the functions and mutual relations of the Village Elder and the Village Assembly have ever been defined, neither the Elders nor the members of the Assembly know anything of such definitions; and yet every peasant knows, as if by instinct, what each of these authorities can do and cannot do. The Commune is, in fact, a living institution, whose spontaneous vitality enables it to dispense with the assistance and guidance of the written law.

As to its thoroughly democratic character there can be no possible doubt. The Elder represents merely the executive power. All the real authority resides in the Assembly, of which all Heads of Households are members.

The simple procedure, or rather the absence of all formal procedure, at the Assemblies, illustrates admirably the essentially practical character of the institution. The meetings are held in the open air, because in the village there is no building—except the church, which can be used only for religious purposes—large enough to contain all the members; and they almost always take place on Sundays or holidays, when the peasants have plenty of leisure. Any open space, where there is sufficient room and little mud, serves as a Forum. The discussions are occasionally very animated, but there is rarely any attempt at speech-making. If any young member should show an inclination to indulge in oratory, he is sure to be unceremoniously interrupted by some of the older members, who have never any sympathy with fine talking. The whole assemblage has the appearance of a crowd of people who have accidentally come together, and are discussing in little groups subjects of local interest. Gradually some one group, containing two or three peasants who have more moral influence than their fellows, attracts the others, and the discussion becomes general. Two or more peasants may speak at a time, and interrupt each other freely—using plain, unvarnished language, not at all parliamentary—and the discussion may become for a few moments a confused, unintelligible noise, "a din to fright a monster's ear"; but at the moment when the spectator imagines that the consultation is about to be transformed into a promiscuous fight, the tumult spontaneously subsides, or perhaps a general roar of laughter announces that some one has been successfully hit by a strong *argumentum ad hominem,* or biting personal remark. In any case there is no danger of the disputants coming to blows. No class of men in the world is more good-natured and pacific than the Russian peasantry. When sober they never fight, and even when under the influence of alcohol they are more likely to be violently affectionate than disagreeably quarrelsome. If two of them take to drinking together, the probability is that in a few minutes, though they may never have seen each other before, they will be expressing in very strong terms their mutual regard and affection, confirming their words with an occasional friendly embrace.

Theoretically speaking, the Village Parliament has a Speaker, in the person of the Village Elder. The word Speaker is etymologically less objectionable than the term President, for the personage in question never sits down, but mingles in the crowd like the ordinary members. Objection may be taken to the word on the ground that the Elder speaks much less than many other members, but this may likewise be said of the Speaker of the House of Commons. Whatever we may call him, the Elder is officially the principal personage in the crowd, and wears the insignia of office in the form of a small medal suspended from his neck by a thin brass chain. His duties, however, are extremely light. To call to order those who interrupt the discussion is no part of his functions. If he calls an honorable member Durák (blockhead), or interrupts an orator with a laconic "Moltchi!" (hold your tongue!), he does so in virtue of no special prerogative, but simply in accordance with a time-honored privilege, which is equally enjoyed by all present, and may be employed with impunity against himself. Indeed, it may be said in general that the phraseology and the procedure are not subjected to any strict rules. The Elder comes prominently forward only when it is necessary to take the sense of the meeting. On such occasions he may stand back a little from the crowd and say, "Well, orthodox, have you decided so?" and the crowd will probably shout, "Ladno! ladno!" that is to say, "Agreed! agreed!"

Communal measures are generally carried in this way by acclamation; but it sometimes happens that there is such a decided diversity of opinion that it is difficult to tell which of the two parties has a majority. In this case the Elder requests the one part to stand to the right and the other to the left. The two groups are then counted, and the minority submits, for no one ever dreams of opposing openly the will of the "Mir."

Nearly half a century ago an attempt was made to regulate by the written law the procedure of Village Assemblies amongst the peasantry of the State Demesnes, and among other reforms voting by ballot was introduced; but the new custom never struck root. The peasants did not regard with favor the new method, and persisted in calling it, contemptuously, "playing at marbles." Here, again, we have one of these wonderful and apparently anomalous facts which frequently meet the student of Russian affairs: the Emperor Nicholas, the Incarnation of Autocracy and the Champion of the Reactionary Party throughout Europe, forces the ballot-box, the ingenious invention of extreme radicals, on several millions of his subjects!

In the crowd may generally be seen, especially in the northern provinces, where a considerable portion of the male population is always absent from the village, a certain number of female peasants. These are women who, on account of the absence or death of their husbands, happen to be for the moment Heads of Households. As such they are entitled to be present, and their right to take part in the deliberations is never called in question. In matters affecting the general welfare of the Commune they rarely speak, and if they do venture to enounce an opinion on such occasions they have little chance of commanding attention, for the Russian peasantry are as yet little imbued with the modern doctrines of female equality, and express their opinion of female intelligence by the homely adage: "The hair is long, but the mind is short." According to one proverb, seven women have collectively but one soul, and according to a still more ungallant popular saying, women have no souls at all, but only a vapor. Woman, therefore, as woman, is not deserving of much consideration, but a particular woman, as head of a household is entitled to speak on all questions directly affecting the household under her care. If, for instance, it be proposed to increase or diminish her household's share of the land and the burdens, she will be allowed to speak freely on the subject, and even to indulge in a little personal invective against her male opponents. She thereby exposes herself, it is true, to uncomplimentary remarks; but any which she happens to receive she will probably repay with interest—referring, perhaps, with pertinent virulence to the domestic affairs of those who attack her. And when argument and invective fail, she is pretty sure to try the effect of pathetic appeal, supported by copious tears—a method of persuasion to which the Russian peasant is singularly insensible.

As the Village Assembly is really a representative institution, in the full sense of the term, it reflects faithfully the good and the bad qualities of the rural population. Its decisions are therefore usually characterized by plain, practical common sense, but it is subject to occasional unfortunate aberrations in consequence of pernicious influences, chiefly of an alcoholic kind. An instance of this fact occurred during my sojourn at Ivánofka. The question under discussion was whether a *kabák,* or gin-shop, should be established in the village. A trader from the district town desired to establish one, and offered to pay to the Commune a yearly sum for the necessary permission. The more industrious, respectable members of the Commune, backed by the whole female population of the locality, were strongly opposed to the project, knowing fell well that a kabák would certainly lead to the ruin of more than one household; but the enterprising trader had strong arguments wherewith to seduce a large number of the members, and succeeded in obtaining a decision in his favor.

The Assembly discusses all matters affecting the Communal welfare, and, as these matters have never been legally defined, and there is no means of appealing against its decisions, its recognized competence is very wide. It fixes the time for making the hay, and the day for commencing the plowing of the fallow field; it decrees what measures shall be employed against those who do not punctually pay their taxes; it decides whether a new member shall be admitted into the Commune, and whether an old member shall be allowed to change his domicile; it gives or withholds permission to erect new buildings on the Communal land; it prepares and signs all contracts which the Commune makes with one of its own members or with a stranger; it interferes, whenever it thinks necessary, in the domestic affairs of its members; it elects the Elder—as well as the Communal tax-collector, and watchman, where such offices exist—and the Communal herd-boy; above all, it divides and allots the Communal land among the members as it thinks fit.

Of all these various proceedings, the English reader may naturally assume that the elections are the most noisy and exciting. In reality this is a mistake. The elections produce little excitement, for the simple reason that, as a rule, no one desires to be elected. Once, it is said, a peasant who had been guilty of some misdemeanor was informed by an Arbiter of the Peace —a species of official of which I shall have much to say in the sequel—that he would be no longer capable of filling any Communal office; and instead of regretting this diminution of his civil rights, he bowed very low, and respectfully expressed his thanks for the new privilege which he had acquired. This anecdote may not be true, but it illustrates the undoubted fact that the Russian peasant regards office as a burden rather than as an honor. There is no civic ambition in those little rural Commonwealths, whilst the privilege of wearing a bronze medal, which commands no respect, and the reception of a few roubles as salary, afford no adequate compensation for the trouble, annoyance, and responsibility which a Village Elder has to bear. The elections are therefore generally very tame and uninteresting. The following descriptions may serve as an illustration.

It is a Sunday afternoon. The peasants, male and female, have turned out in Sunday attire, and the bright costumes of the women help the sunshine to put a little rich color into the scene, which is at ordinary times monotonously gray. Slowly the crowd collects on the open space at the side of the church. All classes of the population are represented. On the extreme outskirts are a band of fair-haired, merry children—some of them standing or lying on the grass and gazing attentively at the proceedings, and others running about and playing at tag. Close to these stand a group of young girls, convulsed with half-suppressed laughter. The cause of their merriment is a youth of some seventeen summers, evidently the wag of the village, who stands beside them with an accordion in his hand, and relates to them in a half-whisper how he is about to be elected Elder, and what mad pranks he will play in that capacity. When one of the girls happens to laugh outright, the matrons who are standing near turn round and scowl; and one of them, stepping forward, orders the offender, in a tone of authority, to go home at once if she cannot behave herself. Crest-fallen, the culprit retires, and the youth who is the cause of the merriment makes the incident the subject of a new joke. Meanwhile the deliberations have begun. The majority of the members are chatting together, or looking at a little group composed of three peasants and a woman, who are standing a little apart from the others. Here alone the matter in hand is being really discussed. The woman is explaining, with tears in her eyes, and with a vast amount of useless repetition, that her "old man," who is Elder for the time being, is very ill, and cannot fulfill his duties.

"But he has not yet served a year, and he'll get better," remarks one peasant, evidently the youngest of the little group.

"Who knows?" replies the woman, sobbing. "It is the will of God, but I don't believe that he'll ever put his foot to the ground again. The Feldsher has been four times to see him, and the doctor himself came once, and said that he must be brought to the hospital."

"And why has he not been taken there?"

"How could he be taken? Who is to carry him? Do you think he's a baby? The hospital is forty versts off. If you put him in a cart he would die before he had gone a verst. And then, who knows what they do with people in the hospital?" This last question contained probably the true reason why the doctor's orders had been disobeyed.

"Very well; that's enough; hold your tongue," says the gray beard of the little group to the woman; and then, turning to the other peasants, remarks, "There is nothing to be done. The Stanovoi (officer of rural police) will be here one of these days, and will make a row again if we don't elect a new Elder. Whom shall we choose?"

As soon as this question is asked, several peasants look down to the ground, or try in some other way to avoid attracting attention, lest their names should be suggested. When the silence has continued a minute or two, the gray beard says, "There is Alexei Ivánof; he has not served yet!"

"Yes, yes, Alexei Ivánof!" shout half a dozen voices, belonging probably to peasants who fear they may be elected.

Alexei protests in the strongest terms. He cannot say that he is ill, because his big ruddy face would give him the lie direct, but he finds half a dozen other reasons why he should not be chosen, and accordingly requests to be excused. But his protestations are not listened to, and the proceedings terminate. A new Village Elder has been duly elected.

Far more important than the elections, is the redistribution of the Communal land. It can matter but little to the Head of a Household how the elections go, provided he himself is not chosen. He can accept with perfect equanimity Alexei, or Ivan, or Nikolaï, because the office-bearers have very little influence in communal affairs. But he cannot remain a passive, indifferent spectator, when the division and allotment of the land come to be discussed, for the material welfare of every household depends to a great extent on the amount of land and of burdens which it receives.

In the southern provinces, where the soil is fertile, and the taxes do not exceed the normal rent, the process of division and allotment is comparatively simple. Here each peasant desires to get as much land as possible, and consequently each household demands all the land to which it is entitled—that is to say, a number of shares equal to the number of its members inscribed in the last revision list. The Assembly has, therefore, no difficult questions to decide. The Communal revision list determines the number of shares to be allotted to each family. The only difficulty likely to arise is as to which particular shares a particular family shall receive, and this difficulty is commonly obviated by the custom of casting lots. There may be, it is true, some difference of opinion as to when a re-distribution should be made, but this question is easily decided by a simple vote of the Assembly.

Very different is the process of division and allotment in many Communes of the northern provinces. Here the soil is often very unfertile, and the taxes exceed the normal rent, and consequently it may happen that the peasants strive to have as little land as possible. In these cases such scenes as the following may occur.

Ivan is being asked how many shares of the Communal land he will take, and replies in a slow, contemplative way, "I have two sons, and there is myself, so I'll take three shares, or somewhat less if it is your pleasure."

"Less!" exclaims a middle-aged peasant, who is not the Village Elder, but merely an influential member, and takes the leading part in the proceedings. "You talk nonsense. Your two sons are already old enough to help you, and soon they may get married, and so bring you two new female laborers."

"My eldest son," explains Ivan, "always works in Moscow, and the other often leaves me in summer."

"But they both send or bring home money, and when they get married, the wives will remain with you."

"God knows what will be," replies Ivan, passing over in silence the first part of his opponent's remark. "Who knows if they will marry?"

"You can easily arrange that!"

"That I cannot do. The times are changed now. The young people do as they wish, and when they do get married they all wish to have houses of their own. Three shares will be heavy enough for me!"

"No, no. If they wish to separate from you, they will take some land from you. You must take at least four. The old wives there who have little children cannot take shares according to the number of souls."

"He is a rich Muzhík!" (peasant), says a voice in the crowd. "Lay on him five souls!" (that is to say, give him five shares of the land and of the burdens).

"Five souls I cannot! By God, I cannot!"

"Very well, you shall have four," says the leading spirit to Ivan; and then, turning to the crowd, inquires, "Shall it be so?"

"Four! four!" murmurs the crowd; and the question is settled.

Next comes one of the old wives just referred to. Her husband is a permanent invalid, and she has three little boys, only one of whom is old enough for field labor. If the revision list were taken strictly as the basis of distribution, she would receive four shares; but she would never be able to pay four shares of the Communal burdens. She must therefore receive less than that amount. When asked how many she will take, she replies with downcast eyes, "As the Mir decides, so be it!"

"Then you must take three."

"What do you say, little father?" cries the woman, throwing off suddenly her air of subservient obedience. "Do you hear that, ye orthodox?" They want to lay upon me three souls! Was such a thing ever heard of? Since St. Peter's Day my husband has been bed ridden—bewitched, it seems, for nothing does him good. He cannot put a foot to the ground—all the same as if he were dead; only he eats bread!"

"You talk nonsense," says a neighbor; "he was in the kabák (gin-shop) last week."

"And you!" retorts the woman, wandering from the subject in hand, "what did *you* do last parish fête? Was it not you who got drunk and beat your wife till she roused the whole village with her shrieking? And no further gone than last Sunday—pfu!"

"Listen!" says the old man sternly, cutting short the torrent of invective. "You must take at least two shares and a half. If you cannot manage it yourself, you can get some one to help you."

"How can that be? Where am I to get the money to pay a laborer?" asks the woman, with much wailing and a flood of tears. "Have pity, ye orthodox, on the poor orphans! God will reward you;" and so on, and so on.

I need not weary the reader with a further description of these scenes, which are always very long and sometimes violent. All present are deeply interested, for the allotment of the land is by far the most important event in Russian peasant life, and the arrangement cannot be made without endless talking and discussion. After the number of shares for each family has been decided, the distribution of the lots gives rise to new difficulties. The families who have manured plentifully their land strive to get back their old lots, and the Commune respects their claims so far as these are consistent with the new arrangement; but often it happens that it is impossible to conciliate private rights and Communal interests, and in such cases the former are sacrificed in a way that would not be tolerated by men of Anglo-Saxon race. This leads, however, to no serious consequences. The peasants are accustomed to work together in this way, to make concessions for the Communal welfare, and to bow unreservedly to the will of the Mir. I know of many instances where the peasants have set at defiance the authority of the police, of the provincial governor, and of the central Government itself, but I have never heard of any instance where the will of the Mir was openly opposed by one of its members.

In the preceding pages I have repeatedly spoken about "shares of the Communal land." To prevent misconception, I must explain carefully what this expression means. A share does not mean simply a plot or parcel of land; on the contrary, it always contains at least four, and may contain a large number of distinct plots. We have here a new point of difference between the Russian village and the villages of Western Europe.

Communal land in Russia is of three kinds: the land on which the village is built, the arable land, and the meadow or hay-field. On the first of these each family possesses a house and garden, which are the hereditary property of the family, and are never affected by the periodical re-distributions. The other two kinds are both subject to re-distribution, but on somewhat different principles.

The whole of the Communal arable land is first of all divided into three fields, to suit the triennial rotation of crops already described, and each field is divided into a number of long narrow strips—corresponding to the number of male members in the Commune—as nearly as possible equal to each other in area and quality. Sometimes it is necessary to divide the field into several portions, according to the quality of the soil, and then to subdivide each of these portions into the requisite number of strips. Thus in all cases every household possesses at least one strip in each field; and in those cases where subdivision is necessary, every household possesses a strip in each of the portions into which the field is subdivided. This complicated process of division and subdivision is accomplished by the peasants themselves, with the aid of simple measuring-rods, and the accuracy of the result is truly marvelous.

The meadow, which is reserved for the production of hay, is divided into the same number of shares as the arable land. There, however, the division and distribution take place not at irregular intervals, but annually. Every year, on a day fixed by the Assembly, the villagers proceed in a body to this part of their property, and divide it into the requisite number of portions. Lots are then cast, and each family at once mows the portion allotted to it. In some Communes the meadow is mown by all the peasants in common, and the hay afterwards distributed by lot among the families; but this system is by no means so frequently used.

As the whole of the Communal land thus resembles to some extent a big farm, it is necessary to make certain rules concerning cultivation. A family may sow what it likes in the land allotted to it, but all families must at least conform to the accepted system of rotation. In like manner, a family cannot begin the autumn plowing before the appointed time, because it would thereby interfere with the rights of the other families, who use the fallow field as pasturage.

It is not a little strange that this primitive system of land tenure should have succeeded in living into the nineteenth century, and still more remarkable that the institution of which it forms an essential part should be regarded by many intelligent people as one of the great institutions of the future, and almost as a panacea for social and political evils.

Proprietors of the Old School

Of all the foreign countries in which I have traveled Russia certainly bears off the palm in all that regards hospitality. Every spring I found myself in possession of a large number of invitations from landed proprietors in different parts of the country—far more than I could possibly accept—and a great part of the summer was generally spent in wandering about from one country-house to another. I have no intention of asking the reader to accompany me in these expeditions—for, though pleasant in reality, they might be tedious in description—but I wish to convey to him some idea of the Russian landed proprietors, and shall therefore single out for description a few typical specimens of the class.

Among the Russian landed proprietors are to be found nearly all ranks and conditions of men, from the rich magnate, surrounded with all the refined luxury of West-European civilization, to the poor, ill-clad, ignorant owner of a few acres which barely supply him with the necessaries of life. Let us take, first of all, a few specimens from the middle ranks.

In one of the central provinces, near the bank of a sluggish, meandering stream, stands an irregular group of wooden constructions—old, unpainted, blackened by time, and surmounted by high, sloping roofs of moss-covered planks. The principal building is a long, one-storied dwelling-house, constructed at right angles to the road. At the front of the house is a spacious, ill-kept yard, and at the back an equally spacious shady garden, in which art carries on a feeble conflict with encroaching nature. At the other side of the yard, and facing the front door—or rather the front doors, for there are two—stand the stables, hay-shed, and granary, and near to that end of the house which is furthest from the road are two smaller houses, one of which is the kitchen, and the other the Lyudskáya, or servants' apartments. Beyond these we can perceive, through a single row of lime-trees, another group of time-blackened wooden constructions in a still more dilapidated condition. That is the farm-yard.

There is certainly not much symmetry in the disposition of these buildings, but there is nevertheless a certain order and meaning in the apparent chaos. All the buildings which do not require stoves are built at a considerable distance from the dwelling-house and kitchen, which are more liable to take fire; and the kitchen stands by itself, because the odor of cookery where oil is used is by no means agreeable, even for those whose olfactory nerves are not very sensitive. The plan of the house is likewise not without a certain meaning. The rigorous separation of the sexes, which formed a characteristic trait of old Russian society, has long since disappeared, but its influence may still be traced in houses built on the old model. The house in question is one of these, and consequently it is composed of three sections— at the one end the male apartments, at the other the female apartments, and in the middle the neutral territory, comprising the dining-room and the sa- lon. This arrangement has its conveniences, and explains the fact that the house has two front doors. At the back is a third door, which opens from the neutral territory into a spacious veranda overlooking the garden.

Here lives and has lived for many years Ivanovitch K......, a gentle- man of the old school, and a very worthy man of his kind. If we look at him as he sits in his comfortable arm-chair, with his capacious dressing-gown hanging loosely about him, and his long Turkish pipe in his hand, we shall be able to read at a glance something of his character. Nature endowed him with large bones and broad shoulders, and evidently intended him to be a man of great muscular power, but he has contrived to frustrate this benevo- lent intention, and has now more fat than muscle. His close-cropped head is round as a bullet, and his features are massive and heavy, but the heaviness is relieved by an expression of calm contentment and imperturbable good- nature, which occasionally blossoms into a broad grin. His face is one of those on which no amount of histrionic talent could produce a look of care and anxiety, and for this it is not to blame, for such an expression has never been demanded of it. Like other mortals he experiences sometimes little an- noyances, and on such occasions his small gray eyes sparkle and his face be- comes suffused with a crimson glow that suggests apoplexy; but ill-fortune has never been able to get sufficiently firm hold of him to make him under- stand what such words as care and anxiety mean. Of struggle, disappoint- ment, hope, and all the other feelings which give to human life a dramatic interest, he knows little by hearsay and nothing by experience. He has, in fact, always lived outside of that struggle for existence which modern phi- losophers declare to be the law of Nature.

Somewhere about sixty years ago Ivan Ivan'itch was born in the house where he still lives. His first lessons he received from the parish priest, and afterward he was taught by a deacon's son, who had studied in the ecclesi- astical seminary to so little purpose that he was unable to pass the final ex- amination. By both of these teachers he was treated with extreme leniency, and was allowed to learn as little as he chose. His father wished him to study hard, but his mother was afraid that study might injure his health, and accordingly gave him several holidays every week. Under these circum- stances his progress was naturally not very rapid, and he was still very slightly acquainted with the elementary rules of arithmetic, when his father one day declared that he was already eighteen years of age, and must at once enter the service. But what kind of service? Ivan had no natural incli- nation for any kind of activity. The project of entering him as a "Junker" in a cavalry regiment, the colonel of which was an old friend of his father's, did not at all please him. He had no love for military service, and positively disliked the prospect of an examination. Whilst seeming, therefore, to bow implicitly to the paternal authority, he induced his mother to oppose the scheme.

The dilemma in which Ivan found himself was this: in deference to his father he wished to be in the service and gain that official rank which every Russian noble desires to possess, and at the same time, in deference to his mother and his own tastes, he wished to remain at home and continue his indolent mode of life. The Marshall of Noblesse, who happened to call one day, helped him out of the difficulty by offering to inscribe him as secretary in the *Dvoryánskaya Opéka,* a bureau which acts as curator for the estates of minors. All the duties of this office could be fulfilled by a paid secretary, and the nominal occupant would be periodically promoted as if he were an active official. This was precisely what Ivan required. He accepted eagerly the proposal, and obtained, in the course of seven years, without any effort on his part, the rank of "collegiate secretary," corresponding to the "capitaine-en-second" of the military hierarchy. To mount higher he would have had to seek some place where he could not have fulfilled his duty by proxy, so he determined to rest on his easily-won laurels, and sent in his resignation.

Immediately after the termination of his official life his married life began. Before his resignation had been accepted he suddenly found himself one morning on the high road to matrimony. Here again there was no effort on his part. The course of true love, which is said never to run smooth for ordinary mortals, ran smooth for him. He never had even the trouble of proposing. The whole affair was arranged by his parents, who chose as bride for their son the only daughter of their nearest neighbor. The young lady was only about sixteen years of age, and was not remarkable for beauty, talent, or any other peculiarity, but she had one very important qualification—she was the daughter of a man who had an estate contiguous to their own, and who might give as a dowry a certain bit of land which they had long desired to add to their own property. The negotiations, being of a delicate nature, were intrusted to an old lady who had a great reputation for diplomatic skill in such matters, and she accomplished her mission with such success, that in the course of a few weeks the preliminaries were arranged and the day fixed for the wedding. Thus Ivan Ivan'itch won his bride as easily as he had won his Tchin of "collegiate secretary."

Though the bridegroom had received rather than taken to himself a wife and did not imagine for a moment that he was in love, he had no reason to regret the choice that was made for him. Maria Petrovna was exactly suited by character and education to be the wife of a man like Ivan Ivan'itch. She had grown up at home in the society of nurses and servant-maids, and had never learned anything more than could be obtained from the parish priest and from "Ma'mselle," a personage occupying a position midway between a servant-maid and a governess. The first events of her life were the announcement that she was to be married and the preparations for the wedding. All her life afterwards she remembered the delight which the purchase of her trousseau afforded her, and kept in her memory a full catalogue of the articles bought. The first years of her married life were not very happy, for she was treated by her mother-in-law as a naughty child who required to be frequently snubbed and lectured; but she bore the discipline with exemplary patience, and in due time became her own mistress and autocratic ruler in all domestic affairs. From that time she lived an active, uneventful life. Between her and her husband there is as much mutual attachment as can reasonably be expected in phlegmatic natures after thirty years of matrimony. She devotes all her energies to satisfying his simple material wants—of intellectual wants he has none—and securing his comfort in every possible way. Under this fostering care he has, as he is wont to say, "effeminated himself" (obábilsya). His love of hunting and shooting has died out, he cares less and less to visit his neighbors, and each successive year he spends more and more time in his comfortable arm-chair.

The daily life of this worthy couple is singularly regular and monotonous, varying only with the changing seasons. In summer Ivan Ivan'itch gets up about seven o'clock, and puts on, with the assistance of his *valet de chambre,* a simple costume, consisting chiefly of a faded, plentifully-stained dressing-gown. Having nothing particular to do, he sits down at the open window and looks into the yard. As the servants pass he stops and questions them, and then gives them orders, or scolds them, as circumstances demand. Toward nine o'clock tea is announced, and he goes into the dining-room—a long, narrow apartment with bare wooden floor and no furniture but a table and chairs, all in a more or less rickety condition. Here he finds his wife with the tea-urn before her. In a few minutes the younger children come in, kiss their papa's hand, and take their places round the table. As this morning meal consists merely of bread and tea, it does not last long; and all disperse to their several occupations. The head of the house begins the labors of the day by resuming his seat at the open window and having his Turkish pipe filled and lighted by a boy whose special function is to keep his master's pipes in order. When he has smoked two or three pipes and indulged in a proportionate amount of silent contemplation, he goes out with the intention of visiting the stables and farmyard, but generally before he has crossed the court he finds the heat unbearable, and returns to his former position by the open window. Here he sits tranquilly till the sun has so far moved round that the veranda at the back of the house is completely in the shade, when he has his arm-chair removed thither, and sits there till dinner-time.

Maria Petrovna spends her morning in a more active way. As soon as the breakfast-table has been cleared, she goes to the larder, takes stock of the provisions, arranges the *menu du jour,* and gives to the cook the necessary materials, with detailed instructions as to how they are to be prepared. The rest of the morning she devotes to her other household duties.

Towards one o'clock dinner is announced, and Ivan Ivan'itch prepares his appetite by swallowing at a gulp a wine-glassful of home-made bitters. Dinner is the great event of the day. The food is abundant and of good quality, but mushrooms, onions, and fat play a rather too important part in the repast, and the whole is prepared with very little attention to the recognized principles of culinary hygiene. Many of the dishes, indeed, would make a British valetudinarian stand aghast, but they seem to produce no bad effect on those Russian organisms which have never been weakened by town life, nervous excitement, or intellectual exertion.

No sooner has the last dish been removed than a deathlike stillness falls upon the house; it is the time of the after-dinner siesta. The young folks go into the garden, and all the other members of the household give way to the drowsiness naturally engendered by a heavy meal on a hot summer day. Ivan Ivan'itch retires to his own room, from which the flies have been carefully expelled by his pipe-bearer. Maria Petrovna dozes in an arm-chair in the sitting-room, with a pocket-handkerchief spread over her face. The servants snore in the corridors, the garret, or the hayshed; and even the old watch-dog in the corner of the yard stretches himself out at full length on the shady side of his kennel.

In about two hours the house gradually re-awakens. Doors begin to creak; the names of various servants are bawled out in all tones, from base to falsetto; and footsteps are heard in the yard. Soon a man-servant issues from the kitchen, bearing an enormous tea-urn, which puffs like a little steam-engine. The family assemble for tea. In Russia, as elsewhere, sleep after a heavy meal produces thirst, so that the tea and other beverages are very acceptable. Then some little delicacies are served—such as fruit and wild berries, or cucumbers with honey, or something else of the kind, and the family again disperses. Ivan Ivan'itch takes a turn in the fields on his *begovuiya droshki*—an extremely light vehicle, composed of two pairs of wheels joined together by a single board, on which the driver sits stride-legged; and Maria Petrovna probably receives a visit from the Popadyá (the priest's wife), who is the chief gossipmonger of the neighborhood. There is not much scandal in the district, but what little there is the Popadyá carefully collects, and distributes among her acquaintances with undiscriminating generosity.

In the evening it often happens that a little group of peasants come into the court, and ask to see the "master." The master goes to the door, and generally finds that they have some favor to request. In reply to his question, "Well, children, what do you want?" they tell their story in a confused, rambling way, several of them speaking at a time, and he has to question and cross-question them before he comes to understand clearly what they desire. If he tells them he cannot grant it, they probably do not accept a first refusal, but endeavor by means of supplication to make him reconsider his decision. Stepping forward a little, and bowing low, one of the group begins in a half-respectful, half-familiar, caressing tone—"Little father, Ivan Ivan'itch, be gracious; you are our father, and we are your children"—and so on. Ivan Ivan'itch good-naturedly listens, and again explains that he cannot grant what they ask, but they have still hopes of gaining their point by entreaty, and continue their supplications till at last his patience is exhausted and he says to them in a paternal tone, "Now, enough! enough! you are blockheads—blockheads all round! there's no use talking, it can't be done." And with these words he enters the house, so as to prevent all further discussion.

A regular part of the evening's occupation is the interview with the steward. The work that has just been done, and the programme for the morrow, are always discussed at great length; and much time is spent in speculating as to the weather during the next few days. On this latter point the calendar is always carefully consulted, and great confidence is placed in its predictions, though past experience has often shown that they are not to be implicitly trusted. The conversation drags on till supper is announced, and immediately after that meal, which is an abridged repetition of dinner, all retire for the night.

Thus pass the days, and weeks, and months, in the house of Ivan Ivan'-itch, and rarely is there any deviation from the ordinary programme. The climate necessitates, of course, some slight modifications. When it is cold, the doors and windows have to be kept shut, and after heavy rains, those who do not like to wade in mud have to remain in the house or garden. In the long winter evenings the family assemble in the sitting-room, and all kill time as they best can. Ivan Ivan'itch smokes his long pipe, and meditates, or listens to the barrel-organ played by one of the children. Maria Petrovna knits a stocking. The old aunt, who commonly spends the winter with them, plays Patience, and sometimes draws from the game conclusions as to the future. Her favorite predictions are that a stranger will arrive, or that a marriage will take place, and she can determine the sex of the stranger and the color of the bridegroom's hair; but beyond this her art does not go, and she cannot satisfy the young ladies' curiosity as to further details.

Books and newspapers are rarely seen in the sitting-room, but for those who wish to read, there is a book-case full of miscellaneous literature, which gives some idea of the literary tastes of the family during several generations. The oldest volumes were bought by Ivan Ivan'itch's grandfather—a man who, according to the family traditions, enjoyed the confidence of the great Catherine. Though wholly overlooked by recent historians, he was evidently a man who had some pretensions to culture. He had his portrait painted by a foreign artist of considerable talent—it still hangs in the sitting-room—and he bought several pieces of Sévres ware, the last of which stands on a commode in the corner and contrasts strangely with the rude home-made furniture and squalid appearance of the apartment. Among the books which bear his name are the tragedies of Sumarókof, who imagined himself to be "the Russian Voltaire;" the amusing comedies of Von-Wisin, some of which still keep the stage; the loud-sounding odes of the courtly Derzhávin; two or three books containing the mystic wisdom of Freemasonry as interpreted by Schwarz and Novikoff; Russian translations of Richardson's "Pamela," "Sir Charles Grandison" and "Clarissa Harlowe;" Rousseau's "Nouvelle Héloise," in Russian garb; and three or four volumes of Voltaire in the original. Among the works collected at a somewhat later period are translations of Ann Radcliffe, of Scott's early novels, and of Ducray Duménil, whose stories, "Lolotte et Fanfan" and "Victor" once enjoyed a great reputation. At this point the literary tastes of the family appear to have died out, for the succeeding literature is represented exclusively by Kryloff's Fables, a farmer's manual, a hand-book of family medicine, and a series of calendars. There are, however, some signs of a revival, for on the lowest shelf stand recent editions of Pushkin, Lérmontof, and Gógol, and a few works by living authors.

Sometimes the monotony of the winter is broken by visiting neighbors and receiving visitors in return, or in a more decided way by a visit of a few days to the capital of the province. In the latter case Maria Petrovna spends nearly all her time in shopping, and brings home a large collection of miscellaneous articles. The inspection of these by the assembled family forms an important domestic event, which completely throws into the shade the occasional visits of peddlers and colporteurs. Then there are the festivities at Christmas and Easter, and occasionally little incidents of a less agreeable kind. It may be that there is a heavy fall of snow, so that it is necessary to cut roads to the kitchen and stables; or wolves enter the courtyard at night and have a fight with the watch-dogs; or the news is brought that a peasant who had been drinking in a neighboring village has been found frozen to death on the road.

Altogether the family live a very isolated life, but they have one bond of connection with the great outer world. Two of the sons are officers in the army, and both of them write home occasionally to their mother and sisters. To these two youths is devoted all the little stock of sentimentality which Maria Petrovna possesses. She can talk of them by the hour to any one who will listen to her, and has related to the Popadyá a hundred times every trivial incident of their lives. Though they have never given her much cause for anxiety, she lives in constant fear that some evil may befall them. What she most fears is that they may be sent on a campaign or may fall in love with actresses. War and actresses are in fact the two bugbears of her existence, and whenever she has a disquieting dream she asks the priest to offer up a *molében* for the safety of her absent ones. Sometimes she ventures to express her anxiety to her husband, and recommends him to write to them; but he considers writing a letter a very serious bit of work, and always replies, evasively, "Well, well, we must think about it."

During the Crimean War—though the two sons were not yet in the army—Ivan Ivan'itch half awoke from his habitual lethargy, and read occasionally the meagre official reports published by the Government. He was a little surprised that no great victories were reported, and that the army did not at once advance on Constantinople. As to causes he never speculated. Some of his neighbors told him that the army was disorganized, and the whole system of Nicholas had been proved to be utterly worthless. That might all be very true, but he did not understand military and political matters. No doubt it would all come right in the end. All did come right, after a fashion, and he again gave up reading newspapers; but ere long he was startled by reports much more alarming than any rumors of war. People began to talk about the peasant question, and to say openly that the serfs must soon be emancipated. For once in his life Ivan Ivan'itch asked explanations. Finding one of his neighbors, who had always been a respectable, sensible man, and a severe disciplinarian, talking in this way, he took him aside and asked what it all meant. The neighbor explained that the old order of things

had shown itself bankrupt, and was doomed, that a new epoch was opening, that everything was to be reformed, and that the Emperor, in accordance with a secret clause of the Treaty with the Allies, was about to grant a
Constitution! Ivan Ivan'itch listened for a little in silence, and then, with
a gesture of impatience, interrupted the speaker: "Polno durátchitsya!
enough of fun and tomfoolery. Vassili Petrovitch, tell me seriously what
you mean."

When Vassili Petrovitch vowed that he spoke in all seriousness, his
friend gazed at him with a look of intense compassion, and remarked, as he
turned away, "So you, too, have gone out of your mind!"

The utterances of Vassili Petrovitch, which his lethargic, soberminded
friend regarded as indicating temporary insanity in the speaker, represented fairly the mental condition of very many Russian nobles at that time,
and were not without a certain foundation. The idea about a secret clause
in the Treaty of Paris was purely imaginary, but it was quite true that the
country was entering on an epoch of great reforms, among which the Emancipation question occupied the chief place. Of this even the skeptical Ivan
Ivan'itch was soon convinced. The Emperor formally declared to the noblesse of the province of Moscow that the actual state of things could not
continue for ever, and called on the landed proprietors to consider by what
means the condition of their serfs might be ameliorated. Provincial committees were formed for the purpose of preparing definite projects, and gradually it became apparent that the Emancipation of the serfs was really at
hand.

Ivan Ivan'itch was somewhat alarmed at the prospect of losing his authority over his serfs. Though he had never been a cruel task-master, he
had not spared the rod when he considered it necessary, and he believed
birch-twigs to be a necessary instrument in the Russian system of agriculture. For some time he drew consolation from the thought that peasants
were not birds of the air, that they must under all circumstances require
food and clothing, and that they would be ready to serve him as agricultural
laborers; but when he learned that they were to receive a large part of the
estate for their own use, his hopes fell, and he greatly feared that he would
be inevitably ruined.

These dark forebodings have not been by any means realized. His serfs
have been emancipated and have received about a half of the estate, but in
return for the land ceded they pay him annually a considerable sum, and
they are always ready to cultivate his fields for a fair remuneration. The
yearly outlay is now considerably greater, but the price of grain has risen,
and this quite counterbalances the additional yearly expenditure. The administration of the estate is much less patriarchal; much that was formerly
left to custom and tacit understanding is now regulated by express agreement on purely commercial principles; a great deal more money is paid out
and a great deal more received; there is much less authority in the hands of
the master, and his responsibilities are proportionately diminished; but in
spite of all these changes, Ivan Ivan'itch would have great difficulty in deciding whether he is a richer or a poorer man. He has fewer horses and

fewer servants, but he has still more than he requires, and his mode of life has undergone no perceptible alteration. Maria Petrovna complains that she is no longer supplied with eggs, chickens, and home-spun linen by the peasants, and everything is three times as dear as it used to be; but somehow the larder is still full, and abundance reigns in the house as of old.

Proprietors of the Modern School

In the district in which Nikolai Petróvitch lives the resident landed-proprietors are, for the most part, as I have said, men of the old school, decidedly rustic in their manners and conceptions. But there are a few exceptions, and among the most conspicuous of these is Victor Alexandr'itch L....... As we approach his house we can at once perceive that he differs from the majority of his neighbors. The gate is painted and moves easily on its hinges, the fence is in good repair, the short avenue leading up to the front door is well kept, and in the garden we can perceive at a glance that more attention is paid to flowers than to vegetables. The house is of wood, and not large, but it has some architectural pretensions in the form of a great, pseudo-Doric wooden portico that covers three-fourths of the façade. In the interior we remark everywhere the influence of Western civilization. Victor Alexandr'itch is by no means richer than Ivan Ivan'itch, but his rooms are much more luxuriously furnished. The furniture is of a lighter model, more comfortable, and in a much better state of preservation. Instead of the bare, scantily furnished sitting-room, with the old-fashioned barrel-organ which played only six airs, we find an elegant drawing-room, with a piano by one of the most approved makers, and numerous articles of foreign manufacture, comprising a small buhl table and two bits of genuine old wedgewood. The servants are clean, and dressed in European costume. The master, too, is very different in appearance. He pays great attention to his toilet, wearing a dressing-gown only in the early morning, and a fashionable lounging coat during the rest of the day. The Turkish pipes which his grandfather loved he holds in abhorence, and habitually smokes cigarettes. With his wife and daughters he always speaks French, and calls them by French or English names. But the part of the house which most strikingly illustrates the difference between the old and new styles is "le cabinet de monsieur." In the cabinet of Ivan Ivan'itch the furniture consists of a broad sofa which serves as a bed, a few deal chairs, a long range of pipes, and a clumsy deal table, on which are generally to be found a bundle of greasy papers, an old chipped ink-bottle, a pen, and a calendar. The cabinet of Victor Alexandr'itch has an entirely different appearance. It is small, but at once comfortable and elegant. The principal objects which it contains are a library-table, with ink-stand, presse-papier, paper-cutters, and other articles in keeping, and in the opposite corner a large bookcase. The collection of books is remarkable, not from the number of volumes or the presence of rare editions, but from the variety of the subjects. History, art, fiction, the drama, political economy, and agriculture are represented in about equal proportions. Some of the works are in Russian, others in German, a large number in French, and a few in Italian. The collection illustrates the former life and present occupations of the owner.

The father of Victor Alexandr'itch was a landed proprietor, who had made a successful career in the civil service, and desired that his son should follow the same profession. For this purpose Victor was first carefully trained at home, and then sent to the University of Moscow, where he spent four years as a student of law. From the University he passed to the Ministry of the Interior in St. Petersburg, but he found the monotonous routine of official life not at all suited to his taste, and very soon sent in his resignation. The death of his father had made him proprietor of an estate, and thither he retired, hoping to find there plenty of occupation more congenial than the writing of official papers.

At the University of Moscow he had attended the lectures of the famous Granófski, and had got through a large amount of desultory reading. The chief result of his studies was the acquisition of many ill-digested general principles, and certain vague, generous, humanitarian aspirations. With this intellectual capital he hoped to lead a useful life in the country. When he had repaired and furnished the house he set himself to improve the estate. In the course of his promiscuous reading he had stumbled on some descriptions of English and Tuscan agriculture, and had there learned what wonders might be effected by a rational system of farming. Why should not Russia follow the example of England and Tuscany? By proper drainage, plentiful manure, good plows, and the cultivation of artificial grasses, the production might be multiplied tenfold; and by the introduction of agricultural machines the manual labor might be greatly diminished. All this seemed simple as a sum in arithmetic, and Victor Alexandr'itch, "more scholarium rei familiaris ignarus," without a moment's hesitation expended his ready money in procuring from England a threshing-machine, plows, harrows, and other implements of the newest model.

The arrival of these was an event that was long remembered. The peasants examined them with attention, not unmixed with wonder, but said nothing. When the master explained to them the advantages of the new instruments, they still remained silent. Only one old man, gazing at the threshing-machine, remarked, in an audible "aside," "A cunning people these Germans!" On being asked for their opinion, they replied vaguely, "How should we know? It *ought* to be so." But when their master had retired, and was explaining to his wife and the French governess that the chief obstacle to progress in Russia was the apathetic indolence and conservative spirit of the peasantry, they expressed their opinions more freely. "These may be all very well for the Germans, but they won't do for us. How are our little horses to drag these big plows and harrows? And as for that"—the threshing-machine—"it's of no use." Further examination and reflection confirmed this first impression, and it was unanimously decided that no good would come of the new-fangled inventions.

These apprehensions proved to be only too well-founded. The plows and harrows were much too heavy for the peasants' small horses, and the threshing-machine broke down at the first attempt to use it. For the purchase of lighter implements or stronger horses there was no ready money, and for the repairing of the threshing-machine there was not an engineer within a radius of a hundred and fifty miles. The experiment was, in short, a complete failure, and the new purchases were put away out of sight.

For some weeks after this incident Victor Alexandr'itch felt very despondent, and spoke more than usual about the apathy and stupidity of the peasantry. His faith in infallible science was somewhat shaken, and his benevolent aspirations were for a time laid aside. But this eclipse of faith was not of long duration. Gradually he recovered his normal condition, and began to form new schemes. From the study of certain works on political economy he learned that the system of communal property was ruinous to the fertility of the soil, and that free labor was always more productive than serfage. By the light of these principles he discovered why the peasantry in Russia were so poor, and by what means their condition could be ameliorated. The communal land should be divided into family lots, and the serfs, instead of being forced to work for the proprietor, should pay a yearly sum as rent. The advantages of this change he perceived clearly—as clearly as he had formerly perceived the advantages of English agricultural implements—and he determined to make the experiment on his own estate.

His first step was to call together the more intelligent and influential of his serfs, and to explain to them his project; but his efforts at explanation were eminently unsuccessful. Even with regard to ordinary current affairs he could not express himself in that simple, homely language with which alone the peasants are familiar, and when he spoke on abstract subjects he naturally became quite unintelligible to his uneducated audience. The serfs listened attentively, but understood nothing. He might as well have spoken to them, as he often did in another kind of society, about the comparative excellence of Italian and German music. At a second attempt he was rather more successful. The peasants came to understand that what he wished was to break up the "Mir," or rural commune, and to put them all "on Obrok" —that is to say, make them pay a yearly sum instead of giving him a certain amount of agricultural labor. Much to his astonishment, his scheme did not meet with any sympathy. As to being put "on Obrok," the serfs did not much object, though they preferred to remain as they were; but his proposal to break up the "Mir" fairly astonished and bewildered them. They regarded it as a sea-captain might regard the proposal of a scientific wise-acre to knock a hole in the ship's bottom in order to make her sail faster. Though they did not say much, he was intelligent enough to see that they would offer a strenuous, passive opposition, and as he did not wish to act tyrannically, he let the matter drop. Thus a second benevolent scheme was shipwrecked. Many other schemes had a similar fate, and Victor Alexandr'itch began to perceive that it was very difficult to do good in this world, especially when the persons to be benefited were the Russian peasants.

In reality the fault lay less with the serfs than with their master. Victor Alexandr'itch was by no means a stupid man. On the contrary, he had more than average talents. Few men were more capable of grasping a new idea

and forming a scheme for its realization, and few men could play more dexterously with abstract principles. What he wanted was the power of dealing
with concrete facts. The principles which he had acquired from University
lectures and desultory reading were far too vague and abstract for practical
use. He had studied abstract science without gaining any technical knowledge of details, and consequently when he stood face to face with real life
he was like a student who, having studied mechanics in text-books, is suddenly placed in a workshop and ordered to construct a machine. Only there
was one difference: Victor Alexandr'itch was not ordered to do anything.
Voluntarily, without any apparent necessity, he set himself to work with
tools which he could not handle. It was this that chiefly puzzled the peasants. Why should he trouble himself with these new schemes, when he
might live comfortably as he was? In some of his projects they could detect
a desire to increase the revenue, but in others they could discover no such
motive. In these latter they attributed his conduct to pure caprice, and put
it into the same category as those mad pranks in which proprietors of jovial
humor sometimes indulged.

In the last years of serfage there were a good many landed proprietors
like Victor Alexandr'itch—men who wished to do something beneficent,
and did not know how to do it. When serfage was being abolished the majority of these men took an active part in the great work and rendered valuable service to their country. Victor Alexandr'itch acted otherwise. At first
he sympathized warmly with the proposed emancipation and wrote several
articles on the advantages of free labor, but when the Government took the
matter into its own hands he declared that the officials had deceived and
slighted the noblesse, and he went over to the opposition. Before the Imperial Edict was signed he went abroad, and traveled for three years in Germany, France, and Italy. Shortly after his return he married a pretty,
accomplished young lady, the daughter of an eminent official in St. Petersburg, and since that time he has lived in his country-house.

Though a man of education and culture, Victor Alexandr'itch spends
his time in almost as indolent a way as the men of the old school. He rises
somewhat later, and instead of sitting by the open window and gazing into
the courtyard, he turns over the pages of a book or periodical. Instead of
dining at mid-day and supping at nine o'clock, he takes déjeûner at twelve
and dines at five. He spends less time in sitting in the veranda and pacing
up and down with his hands behind his back, for he can vary the operation
of time-killing by occasionally writing a letter, or by standing behind his
wife at the piano while she plays selections from Mozart and Beethoven.
But these peculiarities are merely variations in detail. If there is any essential difference between the lives of Victor Alexandr'itch and of Ivan Ivan'-
itch, it is in the fact that the former never goes into the fields to see how the
work is done, and never troubles himself with the state of the weather, the
condition of the crops, and cognate subjects. He leaves the management of
his estate entirely to his steward, and refers to that personage all peasants
who come to him with complaints or petitions. Though he takes a deep interest in the peasant as an impersonal, abstract entity, and loves to contem-

plate concrete examples of the genus in the works of certain popular authors, he does not like to have any direct relations with peasants in the flesh.
If he has to speak with them he always feels awkward, and suffers from the
odor of their sheepskins. Ivan Ivan'itch is ever ready to talk with the peasants, and give them sound, practical advice, or severe admonitions; and in
the old times he was apt, in moments of irritation, to supplement his admonitions by a free use of his fists. Victor Alexandr'itch, on the contrary, never
could give any advice except vague common-place, and as to using his fist,
he would have shrunk from that, not only from respect to humanitarian
principles, but also from motives which belong to the region of esthetic sen-
sitiveness.

This difference between the two men has an important influence on their
pecuniary affairs. The stewards of both steal from their masters, but that of
Ivan Ivan'itch steals with difficulty, and to a very limited extent, whereas
that of Victor Alexandr'itch steals regularly and methodically, and counts
his gains, not by kopeks, but by roubles. Though the two estates are of
about the same size and value, they give a very different revenue. The
rough, practical man has a much larger income than his elegant, well-
educated neighbor, and at the same time spends very much less. The consequences of this, if not at present visible, must soon become painfully
apparent. Ivan Ivan'itch will doubtless leave to his children an unen-
cumbered estate and a certain amount of capital. The children of Victor
Alexandr'itch have a different prospect. He has already begun to mortgage
his property and to cut down timber, and he always finds a deficit at the
end of the year. What will become of his wife and children when the
estate comes to be sold for payment of the mortgage, it is difficult to predict.
He thinks very little of that eventuality, and when his thoughts happen to
wander in that direction, he consoles himself with the thought that before
the crash comes he will have inherited a fortune from a rich uncle who has
no children. He knows very well—or at least might know, if he took the
trouble to think—that this calculation is founded on mere possibilities.
The uncle may still marry, and have children, or he may choose some
other nephew as his heir, or he may simply live on and enjoy his fortune
for thirty years to come. The chances, therefore, are very uncertain; but
Victor Alexandr'itch, like other improvident people, likes to think that
there must be somewhere behind the scenes a beneficent *Deus ex machina,*
that will doubtless appear at the proper moment, and miraculously rescue
him from the natural consequences of his folly.

The proprietors of the old school lead the same uniform, monotonous
life year after year, with very little variation. Victor Alexandr'itch, on the
contrary, feels the need of a periodical return to "civilized society," and
accordingly spends a few weeks every winter in St. Petersburg. During the
summer months he has the society of his brother—*un homme tout-à-fait
civilisé*—who possesses an estate a few miles off.

The Nobility

Certainly the Noblesse as a whole cannot be called an aristocracy. If the term is to be used at all, it must be applied to a group of families which cluster around the Court and form the highest ranks of the Noblesse. This social aristocracy contains many old families, but its real basis is official rank and general culture rather than pedigree or blood. The feudal conceptions of noble birth, good family, and the like have been adopted by some of its members, but do not form one of its conspicuous features. Though habitually practicing a certain exclusiveness, it has none of those characteristics of a caste which we find in the German *Adel,* and is utterly unable to understand such institutions as *Tafelfähigkeit,* by which a man who has not a pedigree of a certain length is considered unworthy to sit down at a royal table. It takes rather the English aristocracy as its model, and harbors the secret hope of one day obtaining a social and political position similar to that of the nobility and gentry of England. Though it has no peculiar legal privileges, its actual position in the Administration and at Court gives its members great facilities for advancement in the public service. On the other hand, its semi-bureaucratic character, together with the law and custom of dividing landed property among the children at the death of their parents, deprives it of stability. New men force their way into it by official distinction, whilst many of the old families are compelled by poverty to retire from its ranks. The son of a small proprietor or even of a parish priest may rise to the highest offices of State, whilst the descendants of the half-mythical Rurik may descend to the rank of peasants. It is said that not long ago a certain Prince Krapotkin gained his living as a cabman in St. Petersburg!

It is evident then, that this social aristocracy must not be confounded with the titled families. Titles do not possess the same value in Russia as in Western Europe. They are very common—because the titled families are numerous, and all the children bear the titles of the parents even while the parents are still alive—and they are by no means always associated with official rank, wealth, social position, or distinction of any kind. There are hundreds of princes and princesses who have not the right to appear at Court, and who would not be admitted into what is called in St. Petersburg "la société," or indeed into refined society in any country.

The only genuine Russian title is Knyaz, commonly translated "Prince." It is borne by the descendants of Rurik, of the Lithuanian Prince Ghedimin, and of the Tartar Khans and Murzi officially recognized by the Tsars. Besides these, there are fourteen families who have adopted it by Imperial command during the last two centuries. The titles of count and baron are modern importations, beginning with the time of Peter the Great. From Peter and his successors sixty-seven families have received the title of count and ten that of baron. The latter are all, with two exceptions, of foreign extraction, and are mostly descended from Court Bankers.

There is a very common idea that Russian nobles are as a rule enormously rich. This is a mistake. The majority of them are poor. At the time of the Emancipation, in 1861, there were 100,247 landed proprietors, and of these, more than 41,000 were possessors of less than twenty-one male serfs—that is to say, were in a condition of poverty. A proprietor who was owner of 500 serfs was not considered as by any means very rich, and yet there were only 3,803 proprietors belonging to that category. There were a few, indeed, whose possessions were enormous. Count Sheremetief, for instance, possessed more than 150,000 male serfs, or in other words more than 300,000 souls; and at the present day Count Orloff-Davydof owns considerably more than half a million of acres. The Demídof family derive colossal revenues from their mines, and the Strógonofs have estates which, if put together, would be sufficient in extent to form a good-sized independent state in Western Europe. The very rich families, however, are not numerous. The lavish expenditure in which Russian nobles often indulge indicates too frequently not large fortune, but simply foolish ostentation and reckless improvidence. Of the present economic position of the proprietors I shall have more to say when I come to speak of serf-emancipation and its consequences.

Social Classes

What are social classes in the Russian sense of the term? It may be well, therefore, before going further, to answer this question.

If the question were put to a Russian it is not at all unlikely that he would reply somewhat in this fashion: "In Russia there are no social classes, and there never have been any. That fact constitutes one of the most striking peculiarities of her historical development, and one of the surest foundations of her future greatness. We know nothing, and have never known anything, of those class-distinctions and class-enmities which in Western Europe have often shaken society to its basis, and imperil its existence in the future."

This statement will not be readily accepted by the traveler who visits Russia with no preconceived ideas and forms his opinions from his own observations. To him it seems that class distinctions form one of the most prominent characteristics of Russian society. In a few days he learns to distinguish the various classes by their outward appearance. He easily recognizes the French-speaking nobles in West-European costume; the burly, bearded merchant in black cloth cap and long, shiny, double-breasted coat; the priest with his uncut hair and flowing robes; the peasant with his full, fair beard and unsavory, greasy sheep-skin. Meeting everywhere those well-marked types, he naturally assumes that Russian society is composed of exclusive castes; and this first impression will be fully confirmed by a glance at the Code. Of the fifteen volumes which form the codified legislation, he finds that an entire volume—and by no means the smallest—is devoted to the rights and obligations of the various classes. From this he concludes that the classes have a legal as well as an actual existence. To make assurance doubly sure he turns to official statistics, and there he finds the following table:—

Hereditary nobles	652,887
Personal nobles	374,367
Clerical classes	695,905
Town classes	7,196,005
Rural classes	63,840,291
Military classes	4,767,703
Foreigners	153,135
	77,680,293

Armed with these materials, the traveler goes to his Russian friends who have assured him that their country knows nothing of social classes. He is confident of being able to convince them that they have been laboring under a strange delusion, but he will be disappointed. They will tell him that these laws and statistics prove nothing, and that the classes therein mentioned are mere administrative fictions.

This apparent contradiction is to be explained by the equivocal meaning of the Russian terms Sosloviya and Sostoyaniya, which are commonly translated "social classes." If by these terms are meant "castes" in the Oriental sense, then it may be confidently asserted that such do not exist in Russia. Between the nobles, the clergy, the burghers, and the peasants there is no distinction of race and no impassable barriers. The peasant often becomes a merchant, and there are many cases on record of peasants and sons of parish priests becoming nobles. Until very recently the parish clergy composed, as we have seen, a peculiar and exclusive class, with many of the characteristics of a caste; but this has been changed, and it may now be said that in Russia there are no castes in the Oriental sense.

If the word Soslovié be taken to mean an organized political unit with an *esprit de corps* and a clearly-conceived political aim, it may likewise be admitted that there are none in Russia. As there has been for centuries no political life among the subjects of the Tsars, there have been no political parties.

On the other hand, however, it is a piece of exaggeration to say that social classes have never existed in Russia, and that the categories which appear in the legislation and in the official statistics are mere administrative fictions.

Towns and Townsmen

At about eighty miles from St. Petersburg the Moscow railway crosses the Volkhof, a rapid, muddy river, which connects Lake Ilmen with Lake Ladoga. At the point of intersection I got on board a small steamer, and sailed up the river for about fifty miles. The journey was tedious, for the country is flat and monotonous, and the steamer did not make more than nine knots an hour. Towards sunset Novgorod appeared on the horizon. Seen thus, in the soft twilight, the town appears decidedly picturesque. On the western bank of the river stands the kremlin, a slightly-elevated piece of ground surrounded by high brick walls, over which peep the painted cupolas of the cathedral. On the opposite bank stands the larger part of the town, the sky-line of which is agreeably broken by the green roofs and pear-shaped cupolas of many churches. Here and there a bit of foliage indicates the existence of gardens. Spanning the river between the kremlin and the town on the opposite bank is a long stone bridge, half hidden by a high temporary wooden bridge, which does duty—or at least did duty at that time—for the older structure. Many people asserted then that the temporary structure was destined to become permanent, because it yielded a comfortable revenue to the officials whose duty it was to keep it in repair; but whether this uncharitable prediction has been realized, I know not.

Those who wish to enjoy the illusions produced by scene-painting and stage-decorations should never go behind the scenes. In like manner he who wishes to preserve the delusion that Russian towns are picturesque should never enter them, but content himself with viewing them from a distance. A walk through the streets inevitably dispels the illusion, and proves satisfactorily that irregularity, even when combined with squalor, is not necessarily picturesque.

However imposing Russian towns may look when seen from the outside, they will generally be found on closer inspection to be little more than villages in disguise. If they have not a positively rustic, they have at least a suburban, appearance. The streets are straight and wide, and are either miserably paved or not paved at all. *Trottoirs* are not considered indispensable. The houses are built of wood or stone, generally one-storied, and separated from each other by spacious yards. Many of them do not condescend to turn their façades to the street. The general impression produced is that the majority of the burghers have come from the country, and have brought their country houses with them. There are few or no shops with merchandise tastefully arranged in the window to tempt the passer-by. If you wish to make purchases you must go to the Gostinny Dvor, or Bazaar, which consists of long symmetrical rows of low-roofed, dimly-lighted stores, with a colonnade in front. This is the place where merchants most do congregate, but it presents nothing of that bustle and activity which we are accustomed to associate with commercial life. The shopkeepers stand at their doors or loiter about in the immediate vicinity waiting for customers. From the scarcity of these latter I should say that when sales are effected the profits must be enormous. In the other parts of the town the air of solitude and languor is still more conspicuous. In the great square, or by the side of the promenade—if the town is fortunate enough to have one—cows or horses may be seen grazing tranquilly, without being at all conscious of the incongruity of their position. And, indeed, it would be strange if they had any such consciousness, for it does not exist in the minds either of the police or of the inhabitants. At night the streets are not lighted at all, or are supplied merely with a few oil-lamps, which do little more than render the darkness visible, so that cautious citizens returning home late often arm themselves with lanterns. A few years ago an honorable town-councilor of Moscow opposed a project for lighting the city with gas, and maintained that those who chose to go out at night should carry their lamps with them. The objection was over-ruled, and Moscow was supplied with gas-lamps, but very few of the provincial towns have as yet followed the example of the ancient capital.

This description does not apply to St. Petersburg and Odessa, but these cities may for the present be left out of consideration, for they have a distinctly foreign character. The genuine Russian towns—and Moscow may still almost be included in the number—have a semi-rustic air, or at least the appearance of those retired suburbs of a large city which are still free from the jurisdiction of the municipal authorities.

The scarcity of towns in Russia is not less remarkable than their rustic appearance. I use the word here in the popular and not in the official sense. In official language a town means a collection of houses, containing certain organs of administration, and hence the term is sometimes applied to petty villages. Let us avoid, then, the official list of the towns, and turn to the statistics of population. It may be presumed, I suppose, that no town is worthy of the name unless it contains at least 10,000 inhabitants. Now, if we apply this test, we shall find that in the whole of European Russia in the narrower sense of the term—excluding Finland, the Baltic provinces, Lithuania, Poland, and the Caucausus, which are politically but not socially parts of Russia—there are only 127 towns. Of these, only twenty-five contain more than 25,000, and only eleven contain more than 50,000 inhabitants.

These facts indicate plainly that in Russia, as compared with Western Europe, the urban element in the population is relatively small; and this conclusion is borne out by statistical data. In Russia the urban element composes only a tenth part of the entire population, whereas in Great Britain more than one-half of the inhabitants are dwellers in towns. A serious effort to discover the causes of this would certainly bring out some striking peculiarities in the past history and present condition of the Russian Empire. I have myself made the attempt, and I propose now to communicate a few results of the investigation.

The chief cause is that Russia is much less densely populated than Western Europe. Towards the East she has never had a natural frontier, but always a wide expanse of fertile, uncultivated land, offering a tempting field for emigration; and the peasantry have ever shown themselves ready to take advantage of their geographical position. Instead of improving their primitive system of agriculture, which requires an enormous area and rapidly exhausts the soil, they have always found it easier and more profitable to emigrate and take possession of the virgin land to the eastward. Thus the territory—sometimes with the aid of, and sometimes in spite of, the Government—has constantly expanded, and has already reached Behring's Straits and the northern offshoots of the Himalayas. The little district around the sources of the Dnieper has grown into a great empire forty times as large as France, and in all this vast area there are only about eighty millions of inhabitants. Prolific as the Russian race is, its powers of reproduction could not keep pace with its power of territorial expansion, and consequently the country is still very thinly peopled. If we take European Russia as a whole, we find that the population is only about fourteen to the square verst, whilst in Great Britain, for a similar area, the average density is about 114. Even the most densely-populated region—the northern part of the Black-earth zone—has only about forty to the square verst. A people that has such an abundance of land, and can support itself by agriculture, is not likely to devote itself to industry, and not likely to congregate in towns.

The second cause which hindered the formation of towns was serfage. Serfage, and the administrative system of which it formed a part, hemmed the natural movements of the population. The nobles habitually lived on their estates, and taught a portion of their serfs to supply them with nearly everything they required; and the peasants who might desire to settle as artisans in the towns were not free to do so, because they were attached to the soil. Thus arose those curious village industries of which I have already spoken.

The insignificance of the Russian towns is in part explained by these two causes. The abundance of land tended to prevent the development of industry, and the little industry which did exist was prevented by serfage from collecting in the towns. But this explanation is evidently incomplete. The same causes existed during the Middle Ages in Central Europe, and yet, in spite of them, flourishing cities grew up and played an important part in the social and political history of Germany. In these cities collected traders and artisans, forming a distinct social class, distinguished from the nobles on the one hand, and the surrounding peasantry on the other, by peculiar occupations, peculiar aims, peculiar intellectual physiognomy, and peculiar moral code.

According to Catherine's legislation, which remained in full force down to the present reign, and still exists in its main features, towns are of three kinds: (1) "Government towns" (gubernskie gorodá)—that is to say, the chief towns of provinces, or "Governments" (gubernii)—in which are concentrated the various organs of provincial administration; (2) District towns (uyezdnie gorodá), in which resides the administration of the districts (uyezdi) into which the provinces are divided; and (3) Supernumerary towns (zashtatnie gorodá), which have no particular significance in the territorial administration. . . .

In all these the municipal organization is the same. Leaving out of consideration those persons who happen to reside in the towns but in reality belong to the noblesse, the clergy, or the lower ranks of officials, we may say that the town population is composed of three groups: the merchants (kuptsi), the burghers in the narrower sense of the term (meshtchayne), and the artisans (tsekhoviye). Those categories are not hereditary castes, like the nobles, the clergy, and the peasantry. A noble may become a merchant, or a man may be one year a burgher, the next year an artisan, and the third year a merchant, if he changes his occupation and pays the necessary dues. But the categories form, for the time being, distinct corporations, each possessing a peculiar organization and peculiar privileges and obligations.

Of these three groups the first in the scale of dignity is that of the merchants. It is chiefly recruited from the burghers and the peasantry. Any one who wishes to engage in commerce inscribes himself in one of the three guilds, according to the amount of his capital and the nature of the operations in which he wishes to embark, and as soon as he has paid the required dues, he becomes officially a merchant. As soon as he ceases to pay these dues he ceases to be a merchant in the legal sense of the term, and returns to the class to which he formerly belonged. There are some families whose members have belonged to the merchant class for several generations, and the law speaks about a certain "velvet-book" (barkhatnaya kniga) in which their names should be inscribed, but in reality they do not form a distinct category, and they descend at once from their privileged position as soon as they cease to pay the annual guild dues.

The artisans form the connecting link between the town population and the peasantry, for peasants often enroll themselves in the trades corporations, or Tsekhi, without severing their connection with the rural communes to which they belong. Each trade or handicraft constitutes a Tsekh, at the head of which stands an elder and two assistants, elected by the members; and all the Tsekhi together form a corporation under an elected head (Remeslenny Golová), assisted by a council composed of the elders of the various Tsekhi. It is the duty of this council and its president to regulate all matters connected with the Tsekhi, and to see that the multifarious regulations regarding masters, journeymen, and apprentices are duly observed.

The nondescript class, composed of those who are inscribed as permanent inhabitants of the towns but who do not belong to any guild or Tsekh, constitutes what is called the burghers in the narrower sense of the term. Like the other two categories, they form a separate corporation with an elder and an administrative bureau.

Some idea of the relative numerical strength of these three categories may be obtained from the following figures. In European Russia the merchant class (including wives and children) numbers about 466,000, the burghers about 4,033,000, and the artisans about 260,000.

The link of connection between these three categories is the Town Council (Gorodskaya Dûma), the central and highest organ of the municipal administration, with its president the Mayor (Gorodskoi Golová). A few years ago this body was thoroughly re-organized according to the most recent theories of municipal administration; and now all house-proprietors, to whatever class they belong, may take part in its proceedings, and serve as its office-bearers. The consequence of this has been that many towns have now a noble as mayor, but it cannot be said that the spirit of the institution has radically changed. Very few seek election, and those who are elected display very little zeal in the discharge of their duties. Not long ago it was proposed, in the Town Council of St. Petersburg, to insure the presence of a quorum by imposing fines for non-attendance! This fact speaks volumes for the low vitality of these institutions. When such an incident occurs in the capital, we can readily imagine what takes place in the provincial towns.

Oblomovism

One of the figures of the "inner liberation" of Nicholas' reign was the writer, I. A. Goncharov. His most important work, however, was published in the reign of Alexander II. This novel, entitled *Oblomov* after its hero, so effectively depicted the good-natured indolence and ineffectiveness of many Russians that the word "oblomovism" entered the language as a synonym for lazy carelessness. The following description of oblomovism was written by N. A. Dobrolyubov, a follower of Belinsky and a contemporary of Goncharov. The excerpt below is reprinted from Wiener, *Anthology,* vol. 2, pp. 278–280.

All these people have this in common: they have no work in life as their vital necessity, as their heart's holiness, their religion, that might organically grow up with them so that to deprive them of it would mean to take their life away. Everything is external with them, nothing has any roots in their natures. They may be doing something if compelled by outward necessity. . . . But they have not their souls in the work which accident imposes upon them. If they were offered gratis all the external comforts which their labour gives them, they would gladly turn away from their work. By dint of his Oblomovism, the Oblomov official will stop going to his office, if that would not interfere with getting salary and his promotions. The warrior will make a vow not to touch his arms, if he is offered the same conditions, provided they permit also to keep his beautiful uniform which is very useful on certain occasions. The professor will abandon his lecture, the student his studies, the writer his authorship, the actor will not appear on the stage, the artist will break his chisel or his palette, to express myself in eloquent style, if they can see their way of obtaining for nothing that which they now get by work.

They talk of higher aims, of the consciousness of moral obligations, of being imbued with the interests of society,—but investigate it all, and you will find that it is nothing but words and words. Their sincerest, most heartfelt aim is their aim for rest, for the morning gown, and the very activity in nothing else but *an honorable morning gown* (the expression does not belong to me), with which they cover their inanity and apathy. Even the most cultivated people, such as possess a vivid nature and a warm heart, in practical life very easily depart from their ideas and plans, very readily make their peace with the reality that surrounds them, though they do not cease speaking of it as low and contemptible. This means that everything of which they speak and dream is, in their case, foreign and external; but in the depth of their soul is rooted one dream, one ideal,—a most undisturbed rest, quietism, Oblomovism. Many go even so far as not to be able to imagine a man working for the love of it, from predilection—

—If I now see a landed proprietor discussing the rights of humanity and the necessity for the development of the individual,—I know from his first words that he is an Oblomov. If I meet an official who complains of the intricacy and laboriousness of the official routine,—he is an Oblomov. If I hear from an officer tirades on the weariness of parades and bold discussions of the uselessness of slow steps, etc., I have no doubt that he is an Oblomov. When I read in the periodicals liberalizing sallies against malfeasance, and expressions of joy that at last that which we have been hoping and wishing for has been done,—I think that these must be correspondences from Oblomovka. When I am in a circle of cultivated people who feel warmly for the needs of humanity and who for a series of years have with undiminished zeal been telling the same anecdotes, or at times even new ones, about bribe-takers, about oppressions, about illegalities of all kinds,—I involuntarily feel that I am transferred to old Oblomovka.

Stop these people in their noisy disputations and say to them: "You say that so and so is wrong; well, what is to be done?" They do not know. Propose the simplest means to them, and they will say: "But pray, why so suddenly?" You may be sure they will say that, because Oblomovs cannot speak otherwise. Continue your conversation with them and ask them: "What do you intend to do?" They will give you the same answer . . . : "What is to be done? Of course, submit to fate. What is to be done? I know too well how bitter, how hard and intolerable it is, but judge yourself"— and so forth. You will get nothing else out of them, because upon all of them is the stamp of Oblomovism.

Who will, at last, stir them from the spot with the almighty word "Forward!" of which Gogol has dreamed so much and for which Russia has been waiting so long and so yearningly? So far there is no answer to this question, neither in society, nor in literature. Goncharov, who knew how to grasp and represent to us our Oblomovism, could not help paying his tribute to the universal delusion which still holds strong sway over our society; he decided to bury Oblomovism and to hold a funeral sermon over it. "Farewell, old Oblomovka, you have lived your day," he says . . . but he tells an untruth. All Russia that has read or will read *Oblomov* will not agree with it. No, Oblomovka is our real country; its owners are our educators, its three hundred Zakhars are ever ready for our services. In every one of us there is a goodly part of Oblomov, and it is still too early to write the inscription on our tomb.

The Imperial Administration

The following description was written by Wallace, *Russia*, pp. 197–208.

In its present form the Russian administration seems at first sight a very imposing edifice. At the top of the pyramid stands the Emperor, "the autocratic monarch," as Peter the Great described him, "who has to give an account of his acts to no one on earth, but has a power and authority to rule his states and lands as a Christian sovereign according to his own will and judgment." Immediately below the Emperor we see the Council of

State, the Committee of Ministers, and the Senate, which represent respectively the legislative, the administrative, and the judicial power. An Englishman glancing over the first volume of the Code might imagine that the Council of State is a kind of parliament, and the Committee of Ministers a ministry in our sense of the term, but in reality both institutions are simply incarnations of the autocratic power. Though the Council is intrusted by law with many important functions—such as examining and criticising the annual budget, declaring war, concluding peace, and performing other important duties—it has merely a consultative character, and the Emperor is not in any way bound by its decisions. The Committee is not at all a ministry as we understand the word. The ministers are all directly and individually responsible to the Emperor, and therefore the Committee has no common responsibility or other cohesive force. As to the Senate, it has descended from its high estate. It was originally intrusted with the supreme power during the absence or minority of the monarch, and was intended to exercise a controlling influence in all sections of the administration, but now its activity is restricted to judicial matters, and it is little more than a supreme court of appeal.

Immediately below these three institutions stand the Ministries, ten in number. They are the central points, in which converge the various kinds of territorial administration, and from which radiates the Imperial will all over the Empire.

For the purposes of territorial administration Russia Proper—that is to say, European Russia, exclusive of Poland, the Baltic Provinces, Finland, and the Caucasus, each of which has a peculiar administration of its own—is divided into forty-six provinces, or "Governments" (*gubernii*) and each Government is subdivided into districts (*uyezdi*). The average area of a province is about the size of Portugal, but some are as small as Belgium, whilst one at least is twenty-five times as big. The population, however, does not correspond to the amount of territory. In the largest province, that of Archangel, there are less than 300,000 inhabitants, whilst in some of the smaller ones there are over two millions. The districts likewise vary greatly in size. Some are smaller than Oxfordshire or Buckingham, and others are much bigger than the whole of the United Kingdom.

Over each province is placed a Governor, who is assisted in his duties by a Vice-Governor and a small council. According to the legislation of Catherine II., which still appears in the Code and has only been partially repealed, the Governor is termed "the steward of the province," and is intrusted with so many and such delicate duties, that in order to obtain men qualified for the post, it would be necessary to realize the great Empress's design of creating, by education, "a new race of people." Down to very recent times the Governors understood the term "stewards" in a very literal sense, and ruled in a most arbitrary, high-handed style, often exercising an important influence on the civil and criminal tribunals. These extensive and vaguely-defined powers have now been very much curtailed, partly by positive legislation, and partly by increased publicity and improved means of communication. All judicial matters have been placed completely beyond the Governor's control, and many of his former functions are now fulfilled by the Zemstvo—the new organ of local self-government, of which I shall have more to say presently. Besides this, all ordinary current affairs are regulated by an already big and ever-growing body of instructions, in the form of Imperial orders and ministerial circulars, and as soon as anything not provided for by the instructions happens to occur, the minister is consulted through the post-office or by telegraph. Even within the sphere of their lawful authority the Governors have now a certain respect for public opinion, and occasionally a very wholesome dread of casual newspaper correspondents. Thus the men who were formerly described by the satirists as "little satraps," have sunk to the level of very subordinate officials. I can confidently say that many (I believe the majority) of them are honest, upright men, who are perhaps not endowed with any unusual administrative capacities, but who perform their duties faithfully according to their lights. Certainly, M. Lerche, who was Governor of Novgorod during my sojourn there, was a most honorable, conscientious, and intelligent man, who had gained golden opinions from all classes of the people. If any representatives of the old "satraps" still exist, they must be sought for in the outlying Asiatic provinces.

Independent of the Governor, who is the local representative of the Ministry of the Interior, are a number of resident officials, who represent the other ministries, and each of them has a bureau, with the requisite number of assistants, secretaries, and scribes.

To keep this vast and complex bureaucratic machine in motion it is necessary to have a large and well-drilled army of officials. These are drawn chiefly from the ranks of the noblesse and the clergy, and form a peculiar social class called Tchinovniks, or men with "Tchins." As the Tchin plays an important part in Russia not only in the official world, but also to some extent in social life, it may be well to explain its significance.

All offices, civil and military, are, according to a scheme invented by Peter the Great, arranged in fourteen classes or ranks, and to each class or rank a particular name is attached. As promotion is supposed to be given according to personal merit, a man who enters the public service for the first time must, whatever be his social position, begin in the lower ranks, and work his way upwards. Educational certificates may exempt him from the necessity of passing through the lowest classes, and the Imperial will may disregard the restrictions laid down by law, but as a general rule a man must begin at or near the bottom of the official ladder, and he must remain on each step a certain specified time. The step on which he is for the moment standing, or, in other words, the official rank or Tchin which he possesses, determines what offices he is competent to hold. Thus rank or tchin is a necessary condition for receiving an appointment, but it does not designate any actual office, and the names of the different ranks are extremely apt to mislead a foreigner.

We must always bear this in mind when we meet with those imposing titles which Russian tourists sometimes put on the visiting-cards, such as "Conseiller de Cour," "Conseiller d'État," "Conseiller privé de S. M. l'Empereur de toutes les Russies." It would be uncharitable to suppose that these titles are used with the intention of misleading, but that they do sometimes mislead there cannot be the least doubt. I shall never forget the look of intense disgust which I once saw on the face of an American who had invited to dinner a "Conseiller de Cour," on the assumption that he would have a court dignitary as his guest, and who casually discovered that the personage in question was simply an insignificant official in one of the public offices. No doubt other people have had similar experiences. The unwary foreigner who has heard that there is in Russia a very important institution called the "Conseil d'État," naturally supposes that a "Conseiller d'État" is a member of that venerable body; and if he meets "Son Excellence le Conseiller privé," he is pretty sure to assume—especially if the word "actuel" has been affixed—that he sees a real living member of the Russian Privy Council. When to the title is added, "de S. M. l'Empereur de toutes les Russies," a boundless field is opened up to the non-Russian imagination. In reality these titles are not nearly so important as they seem. The *soi-disant* "Conseiller de Cour" has probably nothing to do with the court. The Conseiller d'État is so far from being a member of the Conseil d'État that he cannot possibly become a member till he receives a higher Tchin. As to the Privy Counsellor, it is sufficient to say that the Privy Council, which had a very odious reputation in its lifetime, died more than a century ago, and has not since been resuscitated. The explanation of these anomalies is to be found in the fact that the Russian Tchins, like the German honorary titles—Hofrath, Staatsrath, Geheimrath—of which they are a literal translation, indicate not actual office, but simply official rank. Formerly the appointment to an office generally depended on the Tchin; now there is a tendency to reverse the old order of things and make the Tchin depend upon the office actually held.

The reader of practical mind who is in the habit of considering results rather than forms and formalities desires probably no further description of the Russian bureaucracy, but wishes to know simply how it works in practice. What has it done for Russia in the past, and what is it doing in the present?

At the present day, when faith in despotic civilizers and paternal government has been rudely shaken, and the advantages of a free, spontaneous national development are fully recognized, centralized bureaucracies have everywhere fallen into bad odor. In Russia the dislike to them is particularly strong, because it has there something more than a purely theoretical basis. The recollection of the reign of Nicholas, with its stern military régime, and minute, pedantic formalism, makes many Russians condemn in no measured terms the administration under which they live, and most Englishmen will feel inclined to indorse this condemnation. Before passing sentence, however, we ought to know that the system has at least an historical justification, and we must not allow our love of constitutional liberty and local self-government to bind us to the distinction between theoretical and historical possibility. What seems to political philosophers abstractly the best possible government may be utterly inapplicable in certain concrete cases. We need not attempt to decide whether it is better for humanity that Russia should exist as a nation, but we may boldly assert that without a strongly centralized administration Russia would never have become one of the great European powers. Until comparatively recent times the part of the world which is known as the Russian Empire was a conglomeration of independent or semi-independent political units, animated with centrifugal as well as centripetal forces; and even at the present day it is far from being a compact homogeneous State. In many respects it resembles our Indian Empire more closely than a European country, and we all know what India would become if the strong cohesive power of the administration were withdrawn. It was the autocratic power, with the centralized administration as its necessary complement, that first created Russia, then saved her from dismemberment and political annihilation, and ultimately secured for her a place among European nations by introducing Western civilization. Theoretically it would have been better that the various units should have united spontaneously, and the European civilization should have been voluntarily adopted by all classes of the inhabitants, but historically such a phenomenon was impossible.

Whilst thus recognizing clearly that autocracy and a strongly centralized administration were necessary first for the creation and afterwards for the preservation of national independence, we must not shut our eyes to the evil consequences which resulted from this unfortunate necessity. It was in the nature of things that the Government, aiming at the realization of designs which its subject neither sympathized with nor clearly understood, should have become separated from the nation; and the reckless haste and violence with which it attempted to carry out its schemes aroused a spirit of positive opposition among the people. A considerable section of the people long looked on the reforming Tsars as incarnations of the spirit of evil, and the Tsars in their turn looked upon the people as a passive instrument for the carrying out of their political designs. This peculiar relation between the nation and the Government has given the key-note to the whole system of administration. The Government has always treated the people as minors, utterly incapable of understanding its political designs, and only very partially competent to look after their own local affairs. The officials have naturally acted in the same spirit. Looking for direction and approbation merely to their superiors, they have systematically treated those over whom they were placed, as a conquered or inferior race. The State has thus come to be regarded as an abstract entity, with interests entirely different from those of the human beings composing it; and in all matters in which State interests are supposed to be involved, the rights of individuals are ruthlessly sacrificed.

If we remember that the difficulties of centralized administrations are always in direct proportion to the extent and territorial variety of the country to be governed, we may readily understand how slowly and imperfectly the administrative machine necessarily works in Russia. The whole of the vast region stretching from the Polar Ocean to the Caspian, and from the shores of the Baltic to the confines of the Celestial Empire, is administered from St. Petersburg. The genuine bureaucrat has a wholesome dread of formal responsibility, and generally tries to avoid it by taking all matters out of the hands of his subordinates, and passing them on to the higher authorities. As soon, therefore, as affairs are caught up by the administrative machine they begin to ascend, and probably arrive some day at the cabinet of the minister. Thus the ministries are flooded with papers—many of the most trivial import—from all parts of the Empire; and the higher officials, even if they had the eyes of an Argus and the heads of a Briareus, could not possibly fulfill conscientiously the duties imposed on them. In reality the Russian administrators of the higher ranks recall neither Argus nor Briareus. They commonly show neither an extensive nor a profound knowledge of the country which they are supposed to govern, and seem always to have a fair amount of leisure time at their disposal.

Besides the unavoidable evils of excessive centralization, russia has had to suffer much from the jobbery, venality, and extortion of the officials. When Peter the Great one day prepared to hang every man who should steal as much as would buy a rope, his Procurator-General frankly replied that if his Majesty put his project into execution there would be no officials left. "We all steal," added the worthy official; "the only difference is that some of us steal larger amounts and more openly than others." Since these words were spoken more than a century and a half has passed, and during all that time Russia has steadily made progress in many respects, but until the commencement of the present reign little change took place in the moral character of the administration. The elder half of the present generation can still remember the time when they could have repeated, without much exaggeration, the confession of Peter's Procurator-General.

To appreciate aright this ugly phenomenon we must distinguish two kinds of venality. On the one hand there was the habit of exacting what are vulgarly termed "tips" for services performed, and on the other there were the various kinds of positive dishonesty. Though it might not be always easy to draw a clear line between the two categories, the distinction was fully recognized in the moral consciousness of the time, and many an official who received regularly "sinless revenues" (*bezgreshniye dokhodi*), as the tips were sometimes called, would have been very indignant had he been stigmatized as a dishonest man. The practice was, in fact, universal, and could be, to a certain extent, justified by the smallness of the official salaries. In some departments there was a recognized tariff. The "brandy farmers," for example, paid regularly, a fixed sum to every official, from the governor to the policeman, according to his rank. I know of one case where an official, on receiving a larger sum than was customary, conscientiously handed back the change! The other and more heinous offences were by no means so common, but were still fearfully frequent. Many high officials and important dignitaries were known to receive large revenues, to which the term "sinless" could not by any means be applied, and yet they retained their position, and were received in society with respectful deference. That undeniable fact speaks volumes for the moral atmosphere of the official world at that time.

The sovereigns were always perfectly aware of the abuses, and all strove more or less to root them out, but the success which attended their efforts does not give us a very exalted idea of the practical omnipotence of autocracy. In a centralized bureaucratic administration, in which each official is to a certain extent responsible for the sins of his subordinates, it is always extremely difficult to bring an official culprit to justice, for he is sure to be protected by his superiors; and when the superiors are themselves habitually guilty of malpractices, the culprit is quite safe from exposure and punishment. The Tsar, indeed, might do much towards exposing and punishing offenders, if he could venture to call in public opinion to his assistance, but in reality he is very apt to become a party to the system of hushing up official delinquencies. He is himself the first official in the realm, and he knows that the abuse of power by a subordinate has a tendency to produce hostility towards the fountain of all official power. Frequent punishment of officials might, it is thought, diminish public respect for the Government, and undermine that social discipline which is necessary for the public tranquility. It is therefore considered expedient to give to official delinquencies as little publicity as possible. Besides this, strange as it may seem, a Government which rests on the arbitrary will of a single individual is, notwithstanding occasional outbursts of severity, much less systematically and invariably severe than authority founded on free public opinion. When delinquencies occur in very high places the Tsar is almost sure to display a leniency approaching to tenderness. If it be necessary to make a sacrifice to justice, the sacrificial operation is likely to be made as painless as may be, and illustrious scape-goats are not allowed to die of starvation in the wilderness—the wilderness being generally Paris or Baden-Baden. This fact may seem strange to those who are in the habit of associating autocracy with Neapolitan dungeons and the mines of Siberia, but it is not difficult to explain. No individual, even though he should be the Autocrat of all the Russias, can so case himself in the armor of official dignity as to be completely proof against personal influences. The severity of autocrats is reserved for political offenders, against whom they naturally harbor a feeling of personal resentment. It is so much easier for us to be lenient and charitable towards a man who sins against public morality, than towards one who sins against our own interests!

In justice to the bureaucratic reformers in Russia, it must be said that they have preferred prevention to cure. Refraining from all Draconian legislation, they have put their faith in a system of ingenious checks and a complicated formal procedure. When we examine the complicated formalities and labryrinthine procedure by which the administration is controlled, our first impression is that administrative abuses must be almost impossible. Every possible act of every official seems to have been foreseen, and every possible outlet from the narrow path of honesty seems to have been carefully walled up. As the English reader has probably no conception of formal procedure in a highly centralized bureaucracy, let me give an instance by way of illustration.

In the residence of a Governor-General one of the stoves is in need of repairs. An ordinary mortal may assume that a man with the rank of Governor-General may be trusted to expend a few shillings conscientiously, and that consequently his Excellency will at once order the repairs to be made and the payment to be put down among the petty expenses. To the bureaucratic mind the case appears in a very different light. All possible contingencies must be carefully provided for. As a Governor-General may possibly be possessed with a mania for making useless alterations, the necessity of the repairs ought to be verified; and as wisdom and honesty are more likely to reside in an assembly than in an individual, it is well to intrust the verification to a council. A council of three or four members accordingly certifies that the repairs are necessary. This is pretty strong authority, but it is not enough. Councils are composed of mere human beings, liable to error and subject to be intimidated by the Governor-General. It is prudent, therefore, to demand that the decision of the council be confirmed by the Procureur, who is directly subordinated to the Minister of Justice. When this double confirmation has been obtained, an architect examines the stove, and makes an estimate. But it would be dangerous to give *carte blanche* to an architect, and therefore the estimate has to be confirmed, first by the aforesaid council and afterwards by the Procureur. When all these formalities—which require sixteen days and ten sheets of paper—have been duly observed, his Excellency is informed that the contemplated repairs will cost two roubles and forty kopeks, or about five shillings of our money. Even here the formalities do not stop, for the Government must have the assurance that the architect who made the estimate and superintended the repairs has not been guilty of negligence. A second architect is therefore sent to examine the work, and his report, like the estimate, requires to be confirmed by the council and the Procureur. The whole correspondence lasts thirty days, and requires no less than thirty sheets of paper! Had the person who desired the repairs been not a Governor-General but an ordinary mortal, it is impossible to say how long the procedure might have lasted.

It might naturally be supposed that this circuitous and complicated method, with its registers, ledgers, and minutes of proceeding, must at least prevent pilfering; but this *á priori* conclusion has been emphatically belied by experience. Every new ingenious device had merely the effect of producing a still more ingenious means of avoiding it. The system did not restrain those who wished to pilfer, and it had a deleterious effect on honest officials, by making them feel that the Government reposed no confidence in them. Besides this, it produced among all officials, honest and dishonest alike, the habit of systematic falsification. As it was impossible for even the most pedantic of men—and pedantry, be it remarked, is a rare quality among Russians—to fulfill conscientiously all the prescribed formalities, it became customary to observe the forms merely on paper. Officials certified facts which they never dreamed of examining, and secretaries gravely wrote the minutes of meetings that had never been held! Thus, in the case above cited, the repairs were in reality begun and ended long before the architect was officially authorized to begin the work. The comedy was nevertheless gravely played out to the end, so that any one afterwards revising the documents would have found that everything had been done in perfect order.

Perhaps the most ingenious means for preventing administrative abuses was devised by the Emperor Nicholas. Fully aware that he was regularly and systematically deceived by the ordinary officials, he formed a body of well-paid officers, called the "Gendarmerie," who were scattered over the country, and ordered to report directly to his Majesty whatever seemed to them worthy of attention. Bureaucratic minds considered this an admirable expedient; and the Tsar confidently expected that he would, by means of these official observers who had no interest in concealing the truth, be able to know everything, and to correct all official abuses. In reality the institution produced a few good results, and in some respects had a very pernicious influence. Though picked men and provided with good salaries, these officers were all more or less permeated with the prevailing spirit. They could not but feel that they were regarded as spies and informers—a humiliating conviction, little calculated to develop that feeling of self-respect which is the main foundation of uprightness—and that all their efforts could do but little good. They were, in fact, in pretty much the same position as Peter's Procurator-General, and with that *bonhomie* which is a prominent trait of the Russian character, they disliked ruining individuals who were no worse than the majority of their fellows. Besides this, according to the received code of official morality, insubordination was a more heinous sin than dishonesty, and political offenses were regarded as the blackest of all. The Gendarmerie shut their eyes, therefore, to the prevailing abuses, which were believed to be incurable, and directed their attention to real or imaginary political delinquencies. Oppression and extortion remained unnoticed, whilst an incautious word or a foolish joke at the expense of the Government was too often magnified into an act of high treason.

This force still exists, and has at least one representative in every important town. It serves as a kind of supplement to the ordinary police, and is generally employed in all matters in which secrecy is required. Unfortunately it is not bound by those legal restrictions which protect the public against the arbitrary will of the ordinary authorities. It has a vaguely-defined roving commission, to watch and arrest all persons who seem to it in any way dangerous or *suspects,* and it may keep such in confinement for an indefinite time, or remove them to some distant and inhospitable part of the Empire, without making them undergo a regular trial. It is, in short, the ordinary instrument for punishing political dreamers, suppressing secret societies, counteracting political agitations, and in general executing the extra-legal orders of the Government.

The Imperial Bureaucracy

The graded officials of the Russian bureaucracy (chinoviki) were thoroughly hated by all revolutionaries and many liberals. From the time of Gogol's *The Revisor,* the bureaucrats were traditionally and often deservedly the targets of many Russian writers. Stepniak (Kravchinski), who wrote this biting description of the chinoviki, was an ardent revolutionary and the avowed enemy of the tsarist regime. The source is: Stepniak, *Peasantry,* pp. 155, 158, 159, 163–166.

What is a *tchinovnik?* It is a man convinced that were it not for his "prescriptions," "instructions," and "enjoinments" the world would go all askew, and the people would suddenly begin to drink ink instead of water, to put their breeches on their heads instead of on their legs, and to commit all sorts of other incongruities. As all his life is passed from his most tender youth upward in offices, amidst heaps of scribbled papers, in complete isolation from any touch with real life, the *tchinovnik* understands nothing, has faith in nothing but these papers. He is as desperately sceptical as regards human nature as a monk, and does not trust one atom to men's virtue, honesty, or truthfulness. There is nothing in the world which can be relied upon but scribbled papers, and he is their votary. . . .

Now, in modifying the system of rural self-government the St. Petersburg *tchinovniks* were inspired to transform this very modest and humble village elder into a diminutive *tchinovnik,* created in their own image and likeness. The task was not without its difficulties. The elder was as a rule deficient in the most essential qualification for his profession—he could not write! It was therefore necessary that he should be provided with a secretary, who could inscribe the paper to which he should affix his seal or his cross. This important person, the clerk, was generally a perfect stranger to the village, a man picked up from the streets. As the law must needs give him extensive powers, it was all the more desirable that he should be easily controlled.

Our legislators proved equal to their task; for they blessed our villagers with a system of lawcourt proceedings which would do honour to much bigger places. To give some idea of their method, suffice it to say that the clerk of the *volost* is bound to supply his office with no less than sixty-five different registers, wherein to keep a record of the sixty-five various papers he has to issue daily, monthly, or quarterly. This was pushing their solicitude for the welfare of the countrymen rather too far, and taxing the clerk's powers rather too highly. In some of the larger *volosts* one man does not suffice for the task, and the peasants are compelled to maintain two, nay, even three clerks. It is needless to add that such a complication of legal business can in no way keep an adroit clerk in check nor prevent the abuse of his power. The opposite is rather the case. The figure cut by the *pissar* or clerk in the annals of our new rural local government is a most unseemly one indeed. In its earlier period it was decidedly its blackest point.

The Government has undoubtedly had a hand in making the *pissar* such a disreputable character, by expressly prohibiting the engagement for this office of men of good education,—for fear of a revolution. All who have completed their studies at a gymnasium (college), much more those who have attended a high school, are precluded from filling this post. Only the more ignorant, those who have been expelled from college or who have never passed farther than through a primary school, have been trusted to approach the peasantry at such close quarters. Being generally self-seekers, and not particularly high-minded, they easily turned the peculiar position in which they were placed to their own advantage. The *pissar*, the interpreter of the law, and, more often than not, the only literate man in the district, could practically do whatever he chose. The elder, his nominal chief, in whom the word law inspired the same panic that it did in the breast of every peasant, and who was quite bewildered by the bureaucratic complication of his new administrative duties, was absolutely helpless in the *pissar's* hands. . . .

Local village government had as yet to be linked in hierarchical order with the whole of the administrative machine of the State. After having created, in the midst of the once democratic villages, a sort of *tchin*, it was necessary to discover another *tchin* to which to subject the newly-founded one.

The government, in the honeymoon of its liberalism, acted with sense and discretion in entrusting this function to the *mediators*, officers nominated conjointly by the ministry and by the election of the citizens. These *mediators*, elected from among the liberal and really well-intentioned part of the nobility, exercised their authority with moderation and wisdom, not so much as regarded subjection to the control of the *mir*, which was perfectly equal to its task, but to protect it from the abuses and malversations of the local police and its *pissars*.

Since 1863, the year of the Polish Insurrection, which marks the point at which our Government adopted a policy of reaction, the state of things has changed considerably. The Government then threw all the weight of its authority into the scale with the party of the "planters," as the obdurate advocates of serfdom were, in 1861, christened. The whole administration changed sides, and Russia has since seen *mediators* who have used their powers in order to compel the peasants to gratuitously do all sorts of work on their estates; who have publicly flogged the elders— mocking at the law, which exempted them from corporal punishment, by first degrading them from their office, and then restoring to them the attributes of their dignity after they have been flogged.

The regular bondage of the *mir* began, however, a few years later. From 1868 down to 1874, when the office of the *mediators* was entirely suppressed, the mir gradually passed under the supreme command of the *ispravnik, i.e.,* the superintendents of the local police.

The peasants' bitterest enemy could not have made a worse choice.

A police officer—we are speaking now of the common police, charged with the general maintenance of order and the putting down of common offenders—is a *tchin* in the administrative hierarchy like all the others. But between him and a paper-scribbling *tchin* of the innumerable Government offices, there is as wide a difference as between a decent, peaceful Chinese, votary of his ten thousand commandments, and a brutal and fierce Mogul of Jenghiz—though both have beardless faces and oblique eyes. A police *tchin* is our man of action. With him the instrument of command is not the pen, but the fist, the rod, and the stick. He breaks more teeth and flays more backs than he issues papers. As regards other people's property, *tchins* of all denominations hold the same somewhat strange views. But whilst the scribbling *tchin* cheat and swindle, the police *tchin* ransack and extort like Oriental pachas.

In the villages, amongst the *moujiks,* who will suffer to the uttermost before "going to law," the police can afford to go to any extreme short of open homicide and arson. The function of tax collector alone, which, after the Emancipation, was entrusted to the police, offered a vast field for interference, abuse, and oppression, and of these the early *zemstvos* often complain. When the *ispravniks* were charged with the chief control of the rural administration, and could at their pleasure, and by way of disciplinary punishment, indict, fine, and imprison both the district and communal elders, self-government by the peasants, as such, was practically abolished. It could exist only as far and in so much as the police chose to tolerate it. "The *ispravniks,* thanks to the powers they have received, have transformed the elected officers of the rural government, the elders, into their submissive servants, who are more dependent on them than are even the soldiers of the police-stations,"—that is the statement made by the most competent authorities on the subject, the members of the *zemstvos.* (*Russian Courier,* Nov. 8th, 1844.)

The village communes have become for the country police a permanent source of income, often levied in a way which reminds one forcibly of the good old days of serfdom. Thus, in the circular issued by the Minister of the Interior on March 29th, 1880, we find the significant confession that, "according to the reports accumulated in the offices of the ministry," the country police officers, profiting by their right to have *one* orderly to run their errands, were in the habit of taking from forty to fifty such orderlies from the communes under their command, *whom they used as their house and field labourers.* In some cases the communes, instead of this tribute of gratuitous labour, paid a regular tribute of money (called *obrok* by former serfs), amounting in some provinces, according to the same authority, to from forty thousand to sixty thousand roubles a year per province.

Local Government

> This description of local government in Russia was written by one of the outstanding Russian scholars of the early twentieth century, Paul Vinogradoff. Deprived of his position as Professor of History in the University of Moscow because of his opposition to tsarist autocracy, Professor Vinogradoff went into voluntary exile in Great Britain where he achieved the distinction of becoming Corpus Professor of Jurisprudence at Oxford. The source is: P. Vinogradoff, *Self Government in Russia*. London: Constable and Co., Ltd., 1915. Pp. 42–43, 52–56.

Provinces and districts were formed on lines which have more or less endured up to now: the province was assigned a territory with approximately 300–400,000 heads of population, and the district (uyezd) one with 30,000. Governors remained at the heads of provinces and captains (ispravniks) exercised similar functions in a greatly limited manner in the district. Judicial authority was separated from administration and from fiscal affairs. The main point was that in all the tribunals and collegiate institutions assessors elected by the gentry and, in the lower instances, also by merchants or craft guilds and by the free peasantry, were called upon to play a prominent part. The gentry in particular was organised in corporations according to provinces. Its members met once in three years to elect marshals and the assessors of different courts, to audit accounts, to receive reports, to draw up petitions and statements of claims, etc.

.   .   .

In fact, the beginning of local government reform had to be made in connection with the very statute of emancipation, because an administrative machinery had to be set up to replace the authority of the lords abolished by the statute. Certain principles were laid down in this respect in 1861 and developed in detail in 1866. The main point was the organisation of the civil parish (volost) for administrative and judiciary purposes. This unit was not a new one: it had existed all through ancient Russia at a time when the free peasantry had not been subjected to secular and ecclesiastical lords. It lingered on in the North and East, where the black, i.e. the free, population had kept its ground. It was resorted to on the domains of the Imperial family and of the State in the reigns of Paul and Nicholas I.

In the 'sixties the civil parish, consisting of several neighbouring villages with a normal area formed by a radius of some 9 miles and a population ranging from some 700 to 5000, was used as the pivot of local administration in rural districts.

1. Its institutions were: (i) an assembly of representatives of the component villages for the principal purpose of electing the officers of the volost; (ii) an executive consisting of a volost elder, assessors and a parish clerk; and (iii) a court with elective judges. These are the three parts of the

volost machinery. There was a good deal of election, as you see, and those who framed the arrangement meant it undoubtedly to form the basis of popular self-government. It was, however, vitiated by substantial drawbacks which made themselves felt from the very beginning. The organisation came into being as an institution devised for a particular class and designed to keep up the isolation of the latter from the rest of the people. The civil parish is exclusively composed of members belonging to the peasant order or of persons of other orders who have joined the volost under special conditions: the gentry, the clergy, merchants, members of liberal professions do not participate in its work, although their interests as landowners or occupiers of rural holdings are materially affected by it.

2. As regards the peasant class itself, the unit which displays the greatest vitality is not the volost, but the township or village. Business transactions, questions as to education, etc., are usually settled by the officers and the assembly of the township, especially in districts where the communal system still prevails. Yet the township unit is considered in the light of a private law corporation, and it is the volost which plays the part of the lowest administrative subdivision.

3. While the volost is thus not very active for the promotion of its own interests, it is overburdened with tasks of police and finance imposed on it by the Government, with the result that it represents everything irksome and onerous in rural practice and that the best men try in every way to avoid it.

4. The judicial activity of the volost court is confused and devoid of authority. The judges are supposed to administer customary law, but in truth they are bewildered by the variety and complexity of relations created by the movement of legislations and of economic practice, and their jurisdiction in civil and petty criminal matters is at best a kind of shifting equity tempered by corruption. The clerk of the parish is too often a crafty promoter of the latter. Lastly, this whole cumbersome system of rural administration is under the meddlesome and by no means disinterested supervision of Government officials and of nominees of the local gentry, who even exercise the power to subject the luckless parish officers to fines and imprisonment. All these features have proved a great handicap in the development of rural self-government.

This short sketch of peasant administration discloses the characteristic and unfortunate dualism of the reform legislation in the 'sixties. It was a compromise between liberal ideals and bureaucratic limitations: sometimes the latter actually succeeded in distorting the progressive intentions of the reformers, in most cases they at least hampered them.

One of the results of the situation was that while the peasants were presented with local self-government of a kind, the gentry and other upper classes of rural districts were left without any. Their affairs and interests were diverted in the direction of *provincial* institutions. A committee for the reorganisation of the counties was created immediately after the completion of the emancipation statute. It was initiated by Nicholas Milutine with a view of endowing Russia with a network of efficient self-governing provinces, but it was intercepted at the start by the reactionaries, smarting from the effects of emancipation and apprehensive of further inroads at the hands of the "revolutionary" Milutine. The great reformer was traduced and ousted in a manner which will be an ever-memorable example of political ingratitude. D. Valuieff, a clever time-server, took his place, and the proceedings were conducted in a spirit of duplicity which deprived the provincial reform of a great deal of its significance. Enough was achieved, however, by the public spirit of the age to make the Zemstvo reform of 1864 a landmark in the history of Russia.

The Zemstva and Their Development

> Professor Vinogradoff, writing at a much later date and from quite a different viewpoint, presents a somewhat different description of the Zemstva than the one given by Wallace in the next selection. The source is: Vinogradoff, *Self Government*, pp. 57–70.

The "Zemstvo Statute" of January 1, 1864, created two sets of institutions —assemblies and executive boards. Each district (uyezd) elected representatives for the district assembly, meeting once a year for some ten days, according to a certain system which will be described presently, and an executive board (uprava) transacting business under the direction and the supervision of the assembly and a board acted in the province or government comprising several districts, the members of the assembly in this case being elected at the district meetings. The electoral system in the district, from which all the authorities were derived either directly or indirectly, was characterised by high franchise qualifications and by the splitting up of the electorate into colleges. Of these there were three: the first was composed of landowners possessed of real estate of the value of 15,000 Rb. (about £ 1500 at the rate of exchange before the war), or of owners of factories and other business undertakings of a similar value or of 6000 Rb. yearly turnover. Smaller owners were not disenfranchised, but had to club together and meet previously in order to elect representatives according to the above rates. The second college comprised townspeople with analogous franchise qualifications. The third consisted of representatives of the peasantry by volosts. The economic importance of the gentry in the rural districts assured it of a very great share in the ultimate electoral results: about 43 percent of the deputies in the early Zemstvos belonged to the gentry class; the peasants sent 38 percent, while all other professions were represented by about 18 percent. Another feature designed to secure the predominance of the gentry was the fact that the assemblies were to be presided over by the provincial and district marshals, although the executive boards were granted elective chairmen. It was intended to restrict the Zemstvos to the management of economic interests, while administrative affairs were to be reserved to functionaries appointed by the Government; the class group of the gentry or hereditary *noblesse* retained corporate existence and the right of presenting petitions as to political questions. As a matter of fact it was impossible to draw a definite line between administration and economic functions, as may be gathered even from a simple enumeration of the departments of Zemstvo activity: (1) imposition and collection of provincial and district rates and services in kind; (2) the management of property belonging to the Zemstvos; (3) taking care of a sufficiency of food and other supplies and measures of relief in case of shortage; (4) the construction and keeping in good order of roads, canals, quays and other means of communication; (5) arrangements as to the mutual insurance of local bodies; (6) the rearrangement of hospitals, charity organisations, asylums, relief of the poor and of the sick; (7) measures of public health, of veterinary supervision and treatment; (8) the prevention and suppression of fires; (9) the spread of popular education and participation in the management of schools and other institutions of enlightenment; (10) assistance to industry and commerce, measures for checking the ravages of insects and diseases of plants; (11) the performance of obligations imposed on localities for the benefit of the military and civil administration, e.g. the provision of barracks or the quartering of soldiers.

To mention one example of the inevitable overlapping of attributions—as regards popular education the Zemstvos were invited to open schools, to provide them with equipment, to pay teachers, in fact to maintain the schools in a state of efficiency, and yet the appointment of the teachers and the supervision of the instruction was put in the hands of a school board in which Crown officials and representatives of the *noblesse* and of the clergy were in the majority. However, the saying that he who pays the piper orders the tune held good in this as in other cases. As the Zemstvos provided the means they acquired the actual management of this important branch of local administration—not without much friction and obstruction. Another point in which the distrust of the Government as regards the newly created bodies found vent was the absence of compulsory power. In all cases when force was required to put by-laws into execution, to collect rates, to seize goods, etc., the Zemstvos could not act by themselves but had to apply for help to the general police, which was often very remiss in assisting the new organisations and in any case regarded their requirements as of secondary importance. Lastly, the acts of the Zemstvos, both as to decrees or by-laws and as to appointments of all kinds, were subjected to constant and suspicious supervision by governors and other agents of the Central Authority; when the trend of general policy pointed towards reaction, as it often did, the Zemstvos were hampered and harassed under the slightest pretexts. This was not a fortunate situation: many strong liberals were driven away from Zemstvo work and did not spare bitter criticism of such incomplete and stunted institutions.

Yet it would be not only wrong, but absurd to disparage the immense work achieved by the Zemstvos in an exceedingly short space of time. The wonder is not that they were hampered and distracted, but that they achieved so much. It is not an exaggeration to say that a new age was initiated by their activity in Russia. Such bodies as, for example, the Moscow provincial Zemstvo, under the leadership of Dmitry Shipoff, would have done honour to any country, and it is not their fault that they were not able to carry out their plans in their entirety. An estimate of the activity of the Zemstvos and of the rate of their progress may be obtained by glancing at the movement of receipts and expenditure in the years 1865–1912. In 1865 the Zemstvo provinces started with a modest income of 5 millions Rb. In 1912 it had reached 220 millions in the original thirty-four Zemstvo provinces and 250 together with the receipts of the western provinces placed under a special régime: in other words, the original figure has been multiplied fifty times. As to expenditure, a considerable share has to be assigned to cover duties imposed by the State, e.g., the construction of barracks or the maintenance of prisons. Productive Zemstvo expenditure develops outside such necessary, imposed payments. Now, in 1871, 43 percent of the expenditure budget could be devoted to voluntary requirements, while in 1910 80 percent was allotted to them. The repartition of expenditure under various heads is very characteristic. In 1895 nearly 13½ millions or 20.5 percent were contributed for the needs of the central government; the service of loans and the formation of reserve capitals swallowed somewhat over 10 millions, or rather more than 15 percent; the cost of Zemstvo administration amounted to somewhat over 6 millions (9.5 percent); popular education was represented by 9.3 millions (14 percent); charitable purposes by 1 million (1.5 percent); roads about 4 millions (6 percent; medicine and sanitation 17.8 millions (27 percent); veterinary department 1 million (1.5 percent); measures for economic assistance 0.7 (1 percent); various sundries 1.5 million (3.5 percent). The same items work out in the following manner in 1912:—

Government requirements	10½ mill.	(5%)
Zemstvo administration	15½ mill.	(7%)
Loans and reserve capitals	27 mill.	(11%)
Roads, etc.	15 mill.	(7%)
Education	66½ mill.	(30%)
Charities and poor relief	3½ mill.	(1.7%)
Medicine and sanitation	57½ mill.	(26%)
Veterinary service	6 mill.	(2.8%)
Economic measures	14 mill.	(6.3%)

In the budget of the six western governments with modified Zemstvo organisation, expenditure on schools and on medical arrangements figured in each case with 7 millions Rb., corresponding to 23 percent of the whole. We shall have occasion to consider in detail the remarkable progress achieved by the Zemstvos in the field of popular education, and the history of this department may be taken as typical of the aspirations and methods of Russian self-government. A reference to the above tables will show that not less momentous progress was marked by the activity of the Zemstvos in connection with medical help and sanitation. Measures of economic policy have been taken up energetically of late years by the more progressive Zemstvos in other ways: the acquisition of agricultural machinery, the spread of agronomic education, improved methods of cultivation, insurance against fires and bad harvests, etc.

Particularly striking results have been obtained by organising statistical work on an extensive scale. A singular gap is noticeable under the head of poor relief and charities. The explanation of this strange fact is certainly not to be sought in callous indifference for destitution. The charitable disposition and the sensitive pity of the Russians is proverbial. The scanty column of expenditure under this head is explained partly by lack of a comprehensive poor law and partly by the fact that the burden of supporting the poor falls principally on village communities and on towns, while the Church and private individuals are very lavish of alms—an attitude condemned by political economists but connected with deeply rooted habits of mind. This is in any case a side of Zemstvo activity in which there is evidently most room for improvement.

Taken as a whole, the services rendered to Russia by the Zemstvos have been immense. The new factor of self-government introduced into the life of the country by the reforms of 1864 has brilliantly justified its right to existence and development. And yet its very success has called forth bitter opposition from the forces of the half-defeated old *régime*. It is my painful duty to call attention to the stages of a campaign of persecution which, though it has not achieved its end, has materially curtailed the beneficial effects of the organisation. The honour of carrying on the war against the most promising force of modern Russia appertains to the reaction which set in after the murder of Alexander II, and has been going on with some interruptions until now. It has been engineered and encouraged in the highest spheres of Petersburg bureaucracy, and it is not for lack of official sanction that it has been unable to carry out its main purpose. As the rise of provincial self-government was preceded by the local reorganisation of the volost, even so the reactionary measures affecting provincial self-government have to be considered in connection with a far-reaching scheme for subjecting the peasantry to the strong government of officials representing the class interests of the gentry, and deriving their power from administrative centralisation. An attempt in this direction was made by the institution of "land-captains" (*Zemskie natchalniki*) under the law of June 12, 1889.

"The new officer was, on the one hand, made the centre of all the administrative affairs of his district—sanitary measures, relief of the poor, relief in cases of agricultural distress, supervision as to all materials and moral interests of the population. On the other, he was to be judge in the first instance in minor civil and criminal cases. Thirdly, he was to act more especially as a guardian and controller in all cases which concerned the peasantry. As one of these land-captains pointedly expressed it, they were to act as nurses to the peasantry. The punishing power of these nurses is very extensive. They have the right of sentencing village elders and judges to prison, and are even provided with discretionary power to put a peasant into prison without any form of trial and without any possibility of appeal, simply for supposed disobedience."

". . . a guarantee seems provided by the right of the inhabitants to appeal from the decision of land-captains to sessions, composed of the same magistrates under the chairmanship of the marshal of the district and with the adjunct of a few trained lawyers. This minority of jurists, exerting some beneficial influence on the lawless practices of the board, are themselves subject to be overruled by the board of the province, in which the legal element is all but absent, and there the procedure stops. The department of this peculiar arbitrary justice is not in direct communication with the Senate, which towers over all other courts of law."

Simultaneously with this measure, designed to revive squirearchy in a new shape, a new statute was enacted for the Zemstvos. The arch-reactionary Minister of the Interior, Count Dmitry Tolstoy, had planned to subordinate the Zemstvos completely to the Crown officials and to turn them into boards for carrying out the orders of centralised bureaucracy. The Count died, however, without having put this delightful scheme into operation. The new statute of 1890 turned out to be only a corrected edition of that of 1864—corrected, to be sure, in a characteristic manner. The gist of the change is disclosed by the altered franchise. Instead of the three colleges of 1864 arranged mainly on property qualifications, the electoral groups were formed frankly on class lines. The first college is composed of members of the gentry (*noblesse*), the second of persons belonging to all other classes except the peasantry and the clergy. A third group is formed by the peasants, who have to elect their representatives not in colleges, but in the volosts, the lists of these representatives being submitted for confirmation to the governor of the province. This is explicit enough, and the character of the change is further emphasised by the proportional distribution of the deputies among the orders; 57 per cent of the seats fall to the gentry, 13 per cent to intermediate classes, about 30 per cent to the peasantry. The clergy do not take part in the representation. This reorganisation undoubtedly poured a good deal of water into the wine of Zemstvo workers. The policy both of the Home Office and of provincial governors kept on a level with the reactionary tendency initiated by the statute of 1890. For instance, after agrarian troubles in the South in 1902, statistical work carried on by the Zemstvos was stopped in twelve provinces because the statisticians were accused of carrying on revolutionary agitation. And yet, strange to say, even these energetic counter-attacks did not succeed in stifling the progressive spirit of the self-governing provinces. The latter could not be prevented from spending money on schools and hospitals, on roads and statistics. In 1900 the magician of the Ministry of Finance, Witte, himself entered the lists against the obnoxious counties. The law of June 12, 1900, enacted that—

"No province is to increase rates by more than three per cent of the previous year."

It has been pointed out that this method of holding expenditure and self-imposition chained to the budget of previous years is entirely lacking in a rational basis. It just falls as a block on schemes of development, and the greatest sufferers are those who for one reason or the other had held back with their imposition and requirements.

Moreover, the late Count Witte presented a secret memoir to the Emperor in which he drew an elaborate comparison between bureaucracy and self-government, and sought to prove that the further progress of the latter would inevitably lead to the downfall of autocratic monarchy. Some of his arguments are so characteristic that I cannot refrain from referring to them at some length.

They amount to this, that self-government, even local or provincial, is in its essence a political arrangement and as such opposed to absolute monarchy. If self-government is to live and to act rationally it has to develop into a constitution. If it cannot be allowed to do so, it has to be replaced by a centralised bureaucracy. After granting that such a bureaucracy leads to arbitrary power and dead formalism, and quoting the contemptuous remarks of Stein as to official writing machines, Count Witte nevertheless assumes that Russian bureaucracy will produce a new political type, unknown to history, that it will in fact turn out to be an aristocracy of work and enlightenment. . . . This government will somehow abstain from arbitrary measures, arrests, exceptional tribunals and other kinds of oppression, it will guarantee freedom of labour, thought and conscience. As for society, it must be left to follow private interests and in them to seek an outlet for its energies. Nothing is more apt to ruin the prestige of authority than a frequent and extensive employment of repression. Measures of repression are dangerous, and when they get to be continuous, they either lead to an explosion or else turn the people into a casual throng, into human dust.

As you see, the most prominent among Russian bureaucrats, Witte, boldly challenged self-government on behalf of an all-powerful bureaucracy. The trial by battle might have been decided in favour of the latter if the opponents had been left to fight out their duel in a "stricken field." But the contest was not waged on these lines: it assumed the shape of a competition for the production of masterpieces. In other words, self-government was able to produce some very creditable results in spite of difficulties. Bureaucracy had also to show what it could do for the people. And its achievements were far from brilliant at the very time when it was especially overbearing and oppressive.

The Zemstva as Wallace Saw Them

> The following description of the zemstva is presented to provide a comparison with the analytical description by Vinogradoff. The source is: Wallace, *Russia*, pp. 213–218.

Very soon after my arrival in Novgorod I made the acquaintance of a gentleman, who was described to me as "the president of the provincial Zemstvo-bureau," and finding him amiable and communicative I suggested that he might give me some information regarding the institution of which he was the chief representative. With the utmost readiness he prepared to be my Mentor with regard to the Zemstvo, at once introduced me to his colleagues, and invited me to come and see him at his office as often as I felt inclined. Of this invitation I made abundant use. At first my visits were discreetly few and short, but when I found that my friend and his colleagues really wished to instruct me in all the details of Zemstvo administration, and had arranged a special table for my convenience, I became a regular attendant, and spent daily several hours in the bureau, studying the current affairs, and noting down the interesting bits of statistical and other information which came before the members, as if I had been one of their number. When they went to inspect the hospital, the lunatic asylum, the seminary for the preparation of village schoolmasters, or any other Zemstvo institution, they invariably invited me to accompany them, and made no attempt to conceal from me the defects which they happened to discover.

I mention these facts because they illustrate well the extreme readiness of the Russians to afford every possible facility to a foreigner who wishes seriously to study their country. They believe that they have long been misunderstood and systematically calumniated by foreigners, and they are extremely desirous that all misconceptions regarding their country should be removed. It must be said to their honor that they have little or none of that false patriotism which seeks to conceal national defects; and in judging themselves and their institutions they are inclined to be over-severe rather than unduly lenient. In the time of Nicholas those who desired to stand well with the Government proclaimed loudly that they lived in the happiest and best governed country of the world, but this shallow official optimism has long since gone out of fashion. During the six years which I spent in Russia I found everywhere the utmost readiness to assist me in my investigations, and very rarely noticed that habit of "throwing dust in the eyes of foreigners," of which some writers have spoken so much.

The Zemstvo is a kind of local administration which supplements the action of the rural communes, and takes cognizance of those higher public wants which individual communes cannot possibly satisfy. Its principal duties are to keep the roads and bridges in proper repair, to provide means of conveyance for the rural police and other officials, to elect the justices of peace, to look after primary education and sanitary affairs, to watch the state of the crops and take measures against approaching famine, and in short to undertake, within certain clearly-defined limits, whatever seems likely to increase the material and moral well-being of the population. In form the institution is parliamentary—that is to say, it consists of an assembly of deputies which meets at least once a year, and of a permanent executive bureau elected by the assembly from among its members. If the assembly be regarded as a local parliament, the bureau corresponds to the ministry. In accordance with this analogy my friend the president was sometimes jocularly termed the prime minister. Once every three years the deputies are elected in certain fixed proportions by the landed proprietors, the rural communes, and the municipal corporations. Every province (*guberniya*) and each of the districts (*uyezdi*) into which the province is subdivided has such an assembly and such a bureau.

Not long after my arrival in Novgorod I had the opportunity of being present at a District Assembly. In the ball-room of the "Club de la Noblesse" I found thirty or forty men seated round a long table covered with green cloth. Before each member lay sheets of paper for the purpose of taking notes, and before the president—the Marshal of Noblesse for the district—stood a small hand-bell, which he rang vigorously at the commencement of the proceedings and on all occasions when he wished to obtain silence. To the right and left of the president sat the members of the executive bureau (uprava), armed with piles of written and printed documents, from which they read long and tedious extracts, till the majority of the audience took to yawning and one or two of the members positively went to sleep. At the close of each of these reports the president rang his bell—presumably for the purpose of awakening the sleepers—and inquired whether any one had remarks to make on what had just been read. Generally some one had remarks to make, and not unfrequently a discussion ensued. When any decided difference of opinion appeared, a vote was taken by handing round a sheet of paper, or by the simpler method of requesting the Ayes to stand up and the Noes to sit still.

What surprised me most in this assembly was that it was composed partly of nobles and partly of peasants—the latter being decidedly in the majority—and that no trace of antagonism seemed to exist between the two classes. Landed proprietors and their *ci-devant* serfs evidently met for the moment on a footing of equality. The discussions were always carried on by the nobles, but on more than one occasion peasant members rose to speak, and their remarks, always clear, practical, and to the point, were invariably listened to with respectful attention by all present. Instead of that violent antagonism which might have been expected considering the constitution of the assembly, there was a great deal too much unanimity—a fact indicating plainly that the majority of the members did not take a very deep interest in the matters presented to them.

This assembly was held in the month of September. At the beginning of December the Assembly for the Province met, and during nearly three weeks I was daily present at its deliberations. In general character and mode of procedure it resembled closely the District Assembly. Its chief peculiarities were that its members were chosen, not by the primary electors, but by the assemblies of the ten Districts which compose the Province, and that it took cognizance merely of those matters which concerned more than one District. Besides this, the peasant deputies were very few in number—a fact which somewhat surprised me, because I was aware that, according to the law, the peasant members of the District Assemblies were eligible, like those of the other classes. The explanation is that the District Assemblies choose their most active members to represent them in the Provincial Assemblies, and consequently the choice generally falls on landed proprietors. To this arrangement the peasants make no objection, for attendance at the Provincial Assemblies demands a considerable pecuniary outlay, and payment to the deputies is expressly prohibited by law.

To give the reader an idea of the elements composing this assembly, let me introduce him to a few of the members. A considerable section of them may be described in a single sentence. They are commonplace men, who have spent part of their youth in the public service as officers in the army, or officials in the civil administration, and have since retired to their estates, where they gain a modest competence by farming. Some of them add to their agricultural revenues by acting as justices of the peace. A few may be described more particularly.

You see there, for instance, that fine-looking old general in uniform, with the St. George's Cross at his button-hole—an order given only for bravery in the field. That is Prince S......, a grandson of one of Russia's greatest men. He has filled high posts in the administration without ever tarnishing his name by a dishonest or dishonorable action, and has spent a great part of his life at Court without ceasing to be frank, generous, and truthful. Though he has no intimate knowledge of current affairs, and sometimes gives way a little to drowsiness, his sympathies in disputed points are always on the right side, and when he gets to his feet he speaks in a clear soldier-like fashion.

The tall gaunt man, somewhat over middle age, who sits a little to the left is Prince W....... He, too, has an historical name, but he cherishes above all things personal independence, and has consequently always kept aloof from the Administration and the Court. The leisure thus acquired he has devoted to study, and he has produced several very valuable works on political and social science. An enthusiastic but at the same time cool-headed abolitionist at the time of the Emancipation, he has since constantly striven to ameliorate the condition of the peasantry by advocating the spread of primary education, the establishment of rural credit associations in the villages, the preservation of the communal institutions, and numerous important reforms in the financial system. Both of these gentlemen, it is said, generously gave to their peasants more land than they were obliged to give by the Emancipation law. In the Assembly Prince W...... speaks frequently, and always commands attention; and in all important committees he is a leading member. Though a warm defender of the Zemstvo institutions, he thinks that their activity ought to be confined to a comparatively narrow field, and thereby he differs from some of his colleagues, who are ready to embark in hazardous, not to say fanciful, schemes for developing the natural resources of the province. His neighbor, Mr. P......, is one of the most able and energetic members of the assembly. He is president of the executive bureau in one of the Districts, where he has founded many primary schools, and created several rural credit associations on the model of those which bear the name of Schultze-Delitsch in Germany. Mr. S......, who sits besides him, was for some years an arbitrator between the proprietors and emancipated serfs, then a member of the Provincial Executive Bureau, and is now director of a bank in St. Petersburg.

To the right and left of the president—who is Marshal of Noblesse for the province—sit the members of the bureau. The gentleman who reads the long reports is my friend "the prime minister," who began life as a cavalry officer, and after a few years of military service retired to his estate; he is an intelligent, able administrator, and a man of considerable literary culture. His colleague, who assists him in reading the reports, is a merchant, and director of the municipal bank. His neighbor is also a merchant, and in some respects the most remarkable man in the room. Though born a serf, he is already, at middle age, an important personage in the Russian commercial world. Rumor says that he laid the foundation of his fortune by one day purchasing a copper caldron in a village through which he was passing on his way to St. Petersburg, where he hoped to gain a little money by the sale of some calves. In the course of a few years he amassed an enormous fortune; but the cautious people think that he is too fond of hazardous speculations, and prophesy that he will end life as poor as he began it.

All these men belong to what may be called the party of progress, which anxiously supports all proposals recognized as "liberal," and especially all measures likely to improve the condition of the peasantry. Their chief opponent is that little man with close-cropped, bullet-shaped head and small piercing eyes, who may be called the leader of the opposition. That gentleman opposes many of the proposed schemes, on the ground that the province is already overtaxed, and that the expenditure ought therefore to be reduced to the smallest possible figure. In the District Assembly he preaches this doctrine with considerable success, for there the peasantry form the majority, and he knows how to use that terse, homely language, interspersed with proverbs, which has far more influence on the rustic mind than scientific principles and logical reasoning; but here, in the Provincial Assembly, his following composes only a respectable minority, and he confines himself to a policy of obstruction.

The Zemstvo of Novgorod has—or at least had at that time—the reputation of being one of the most enlightened and energetic, and I must say that in the assembly of 1870 the proceedings were conducted in a business-like, satisfactory way. The reports were carefully considered, and each article of the annual budget was submitted to minute scrutiny and criticism. In several of the provinces which I afterwards visited I found that affairs were conducted in a very different fashion: quorums were formed with extreme difficulty, and the proceedings, when they at last commenced, were treated as mere formalities and dispatched as speedily as possible. The character of the assembly depends of course on the amount of interest taken in local public affairs. In some districts this interest is considerable; in others it is very near zero.

Railroads and Zemstvamen

The Russian Empire, like other countries, had a boom in railroad building during the last half of the nineteenth century. There were in Russia in 1857 only 663 miles of railroad lines. By 1865, there were

2,320 miles; by 1871, 6,762 miles; and by 1881, 13,987 miles. Private joint-stock companies invested some 698 million rubles in railroad construction between 1861 and 1870, and up to 1877, the government had loaned 1,833 million rubles for railroads. Such large amounts of money, and the various advantages anticipated from the new railroads, attracted the venal and the greedy in Russia as in other countries. The following excerpts from the memoirs of B. N. Chicherin make specific charges of corruption. The source is the previously cited *Khrestomatiya*, vol. III, pp. 220–221.

It was the time of the railroad fever. There began to arise societies for railroad construction as soon as a wide field for private enterprise in such matters opened up at the very beginning of the reign of Alexander II. The first private society to be formed received the concession for a line from Moscow to Saratov. The affair went badly from the start, however, and Mark, the Moscow banker who was the chief shareholder, ruined himself in the enterprise which then passed into the hands of von Derviz who reversed the downward trend. Von Derviz not only built the Moscow-Ryazan section (to which lack of means had limited the former company), but also undertook the concession for the next section from Ryazan to Kozlov, and made millions on this. . . .

Many others followed his lead, and the Zemstva got into the act by vying to bring the route into their own gubernia. A real market opened in St. Petersburg. Those who had money and/or influential connections received concessions. Although the old sore of bribery in the provinces was increasingly healed, bribery developed very greatly in the highest spheres of the bureaucracy. The temptation for people who were greedy for money was great. "There you sit all your life," a man named Sadomets said to me, "you work like an ox and finally accumulate some ten or twenty thousand rubles. When you arrive in Petersburg, they say to you, 'What are these trifles?' It is possible to acquire a hundred thousand rubles in a few days; you have only to arrange the affair." And many Zemstvo members fell into temptation. The first example Sadomets gave was Sheremetov, a leader in the Orlov gubernium. Using his connections, he obtained a concession for the Orlov Zemstvo. On the payment of a million to the Zemstvo, and almost as much to Sheremetov, the concession was assigned to one Gubonin.

The construction of the Tambov-Koslov road took place at the same time. The main figure in this was Gortskin, the Koslov district leader, and he made his fortune out of it. Then Bashmakov, leader of the Tambov gubernium, obtained for himself the concession for a proposed line from Ryazh to Morshansk and on to Sirzran—this time with a government guarantee. Tamashov, Minister of Internal Affairs, needed a market for the products of his huge estate in the gubernium of Orenburg. Naturally, the government considered this road to be very important.

The State Council and the Peasant Land Bank

The original proposal for a Peasant Land Bank had envisioned an institution for the purpose of helping "middle" and "poor" peasants to acquire small plots of land. The majority of the State Council proved unwilling, however, to restrict loans to these peasant groups. The majority's line of reasoning, as given in *a Report of the State Council for 1882*, was as follows. The source is: *Khrestomatiya*, vol. III, p. 446.

It is necessary for the government to act with extreme care in this case because of the existing convictions among the people concerning the lack of land and the hopes cherished by them that the plots will eventually be increased. One must try to eradicate such hopes in a way useful to the people: by a general, practical measure, fully and easily understood by everyone—the establishment of the possibility for all peasants, without regard to their possession of land, to obtain [additional] land by voluntary agreements with the landowners and with the help of credit.

No one denies, of course, that the Russian people are sensible and will understand perfectly the full significance of the measure undertaken by the government. In spite of the rumors of free grants of land, spread by disloyal persons, the Russian people will see that it is impossible to expect the Tsar alone to protect the equal rights of peasants and landlords. It is therefore necessary to abandon these dreams which have been upsetting the villagers, and to recognize that any increase of an allotment must be done by purchase of additional land with the aid of the bank which is established for this purpose, thanks to the great solicitude of the Sovereign. It is true that this bank will make loans only to those peasants who can cover part of the purchase price with their own resources, but this will have a very important educational effect. The people will see that the government, for the most part, helps those who help themselves; that greater achievements can be expected only by those who work, save, and do not squander their lives in laziness, inactivity, and drunkenness. The lands acquired by the peasants by payments from their own resources, by the earnings of the individual's sweat, will also have an important political influence: having gotten the land by his own efforts, the peasant will respect others' property as well as his own. He will defend his own property and, most important of all, will oppose any kind of repartitioning of the land.

Land Prices and the Peasant Bank

There was an almost steady increase in land prices after the establishment of the Peasant Bank in 1883, and some attributed the rising prices to the bank's policy of inflating land costs in order to favor the landlords. Some of the figures on which this charge was based were compiled from the accounts of the bank by A. N. Zak, *Krest'yanskii pozemel'nyi bank* (*The Peasant Land Bank*). Moscow, 1911. The figures reproduced here are from the *Khrestomatiya*, vol. III, p. 447.

LAND PRICES, 1883–1895, STATED AS PRICE IN RUBLES
per Desyatin [2.7 acres]

Year	Land Purchased Through the Bank	All Land Purchased
1883	52.38	27.52
1884	52.49	31.79
1885	52.00	29.37
1886	45.55	33.29
1887	41.73	34.27
1888	34.14	38.05
1889	31.57	42.86
1890	35.93	40.52
1891	38.89	38.19
1892	44.89	41.83
1893	50.14	41.44
1894	48.78	41.81
1895	52.10	41.91

The general land price did increase (by 150 per cent), but prices paid for land purchased through the bank in 1895 were almost identical with the prices in 1883, and between those years the price of land bought with the aid of the Peasant Bank had declined both absolutely and in relation to general land prices. If the bank prices controlled the general prices, as is alleged, why did the latter rise from 1886 through 1890 while the former were declining? An obvious conclusion is that other factors must have also been involved.

The Nobles' Land Bank

Having established a Peasant Land Bank, the government of Alexander III next created a State Land Bank for Nobles. Something of the nature of this institution may be inferred from the provisions of the statute which established it. Seven articles of the statute are reprinted below. They are translated from the *Khrestomatiya*, vol. III, pp. 454–455.

1. The State Land Bank for Nobles is established to issue long-term loans to the hereditary, land-owning nobility, secured by real property belonging to them. (The Regulations of the Nobles' Land Bank, published on 12 June, 1890, were even more specific in stating the Bank's purpose: "The Purpose of the Nobles' Land Bank is to support the hereditary, land-owning nobility by granting personal, cash loans secured by land belonging to them.")

4. The management of the Bank and the supervision of its operations rests with the Manager (Governor) and the Council of the Bank.

8. The Council of the Bank, under the chairmanship of the Manager, consists of not more than seven members nominated by the Manager and appointed by the Minister of Finance, and not more than four members annually invited by the Minister of Finance from the list of members of the Departments of the Bank who are elected by the Landowners' Assemblies.

9. It is the business of the Council of the Bank: 1) to verify and establish the values of mortgaged estates as assessed by the departments; 2) to decide on the making of loans; 3) to issue mortgages; 4) to determine the value of estates offered for sale; 5) to consider and rule upon petitions presented by borrowers.

12. Each Department of the Bank consists of a manager, member-appraisers, and members from the land-owning nobility. The managers and member-appraisers are appointed by the Minister of Finance from those nominated by the Manager of the Bank. The number of member-appraisers in each Department is determined in the same manner. The members for the land-owning nobility [*i.e.,* representing the land-owning nobility] are chosen triennially for each Department by the Gubernia committees of the Nobility on the basis of two from each gubernium. They participate in the discussion and decision of matters of concern to the gubernium from which they were chosen.

31. Loans cannot be issued on estates which have an appraised value of less than one thousand rubles.

47. On loans made by the Bank, borrowers are required to pay, semiannually throughout the life of the loan, 2½ per cent interest [this was reduced in 1890 to 2¼ per cent]; upon paying off 48-year loans, ¼ per cent—on 36-year loans, ½ per cent [the maximum term for loans was raised from 48 to 67 years in 1890]; on expenditure directed by the Bank, or for additional capital, ⅛ per cent. [This worked out to an annual interest rate of from 5.75 per cent to 6.25 per cent. In contrast, borrowers from the Peasant Land Bank paid from 7.5 per cent to 8.5 per cent.]

A Revolutionary Manifesto

The use of terrorism as a regular weapon of the revolutionaries dates from 1878, when Vera Zasulich sought to murder Trepov, Chief of Police in St. Petersburg. During the following summer the revolutionaries split into a right wing which sought to continue the old "V Narod" program and a left wing which took the name "Narodnaya Volya" (The People's Will). The latter was avowedly terroristic. Its formal program was set forth in the manifesto printed below. The source is: George Kennan, *Siberia and the Exile System.* Two volumes. New York: The Century Co., 1891. Vol. 2, pp. 495–499. Slightly adapted.

By fundamental conviction we are socialists and men of the people. We are sure that only through socialistic principles can the human race acquire liberty, equality, and fraternity; secure the full and harmonious development of the individual as well as the material prosperity of all; and thus make progress. We are convinced that all social forms must rest upon the sanction of the people themselves, and that popular development is permanent only when it proceeds freely and independently, and when every idea that is to be embodied in the people's life has first passed through the people's consciousness and has been acted upon by the people's will. The welfare of the people and the will of the people are our two most sacred and most inseparable principles.

A

1. If we look at the environment in which the Russian people are forced to live and act, we see that they are, economically and politically, in a state of absolute slavery. As laborers they work only to feed and support the parasitic classes; and as citizens they are deprived of all rights. Not only does the actual state of things fail to answer to their will, but they dare not even express and formulate their will; they cannot even think what is good and what is bad for them; the very thought that they can have a will is regarded as a crime against the State. Enmeshed on all sides, they are being reduced to a state of physical degeneration, intellectual stolidity, and general inferiority.

2. Around the enchained people we see a class of exploiters whom the state creates and protects. The state itself is the greatest capitalistic power in the land, it constitutes the sole oppressor of the people, and only through its aid and support can the lesser robbers exist. This bourgeois excrescence in the form of a government sustains itself by mere brute force—by means of its military, police, and bureaucratic organization—in precisely the same way that the Mongols of Genghis Khan sustained themselves in Russia. It is not sanctioned by the people, it rules by arbitrary violence, and it adopts and enforces governmental and economical forms and principles that have nothing whatever in common with the people's wishes and ideals.

3. In the nation we can see, crushed but still living, its old traditional principles, such as the right of the people to the land, communal and local self-government, freedom of speech and of conscience, and the rudiments of federal organization. These principles would develop broadly, and would give an entirely different and a more popular direction to our whole history, if the nation could live and organize itself in accordance with its own wishes and its own tendencies.

B

1. We are of opinion, therefore, that it is our first duty, as socialists and men of the people, to free the people from the oppression of the present Government, and bring about a political revolution, in order to transfer the supreme power to the nation. By means of this revolution we shall afford the people an opportunity to develop, henceforth, independently, and shall cause to be recognized and supported, in Russian life,

many purely socialistic principles that are common to us and to the Russian people.

2. We think that the will of the people would be sufficiently well expressed and executed by a national organizing Assembly, elected freely by a general vote, and acting under the instructions of the voters. This, of course, would fall far short of an ideal manifestation of the people's will; but is the only one that is practicable at present, and we therefore think best to adopt it. Our plan is to take away the power from the existing Government, and give it to an Organizing Assembly, elected in the manner above described, whose duty it will be to make an examination of all our social and governmental institutions, and remodel them in accordance with instructions from the electors.

C

Although we are ready to submit wholly to the popular will, we regard it as none the less our duty, as a party, to appear before the people with our program. This program we shall use as a means of propaganda until the revolution comes, we shall advocate it during the election campaign, and we shall support it before the Organizing Assembly. It is as follows:

1. Perpetual popular representation, constituted as above described and having full power to act in all national questions.

2. General local self-government, secured by the election of all officers, and the economic independence of the people.

3. The self-controlled village commune as the economic and administrative unit.

4. Ownership of the land by the people.

5. A system of measures having for their object the turning over to the laborers of all mining works and factories.

6. Complete freedom of conscience, speech, association, public meeting, and electioneering activity.

7. Universal right of franchise, without any class or property limitation.

8. The substitution of a territorial militia for the army.

We shall follow this program, and we believe that all of its parts are so interdependent as to be impracticable one without the other, and that only as a whole will the program insure political and economic freedom and the harmonious development of the people.

D

In view of the stated aim of the party its operations may be classified as follows:

1. *Propaganda and agitation.* Our propaganda has for its object the popularization, in all social classes, of the idea of a political and popular revolution as a means of social reform, as well as popularization of the party's own program. Its essential features are criticism of the existing order of things, and a statement and explanation of revolutionary methods.

The aim of agitation should be to incite the people to protest, as generally as possible against the present state of affairs, to demand such reforms as are in harmony with the party's purposes, and, especially, to demand the summoning of an Organizing Assembly. The popular protest may take the form of meetings, demonstrations, petitions, leading addresses, refusals to pay taxes, etc.

2. *Destructive and terroristic activity.* Terroristic activity consists in the destruction of the most harmful persons in the Government, the protection of the party from spies, and the punishment of official lawlessless and violence in all the more prominent and important cases in which such lawlessness and violence are manifested. The aim of such activity is to break down the prestige of Governmental power, to furnish continuous proof of the possibility of carrying on a contest with the Government, to raise in that way the revolutionary spirit of the people and inspire belief in the practicability of revolution, and, finally, to form a body suited and accustomed to warfare.

3. *The organization of secret societies and the arrangement of them in connected groups around a single center.* The organization of small secret societies with all sorts of revolutionary aims is indispensable, both as a means of executing the numerous functions of the party and of finishing the political training of its members. In order, however, that the work may be carried on harmoniously, it is necessary that these small bodies should be grouped about one common center, upon the principle either of complete identification or of federal union.

4. *The acquirement of ties, and an influential position in the administration, in the army, in society, and among the people.* The administration and the army are particularly important in connection with a revolution, and serious attention should also be devoted to the people. The principal object of the party, so far as the people are concerned, is to prepare them to coöperate with the revolution, and to carry on a successful electioneering contest after the revolution—a contest that shall have for its object the election of popularly chosen delegates to the Organizing Assembly. The party should enlist acknowledged partizans among the more prominent classes of the peasantry and should prearrange for the active coöperation of the masses at the more important points and among the more sympathetic portions of the population. In view of this, every member of the party who is in contact with the people must strive to take a position that will enable him to defend the interests of the peasants, give them aid when they need it, and acquire celebrity among them as an honest man and a man who wishes them well. In this way he must keep up the reputation of the party and support its ideas and aims.

5. *The organization and consummation of the revolution.* In view of the oppressed and cowed condition of the people, and of the fact that the Government, by means of partial concessions and pacifications, may retard for a long time a general revolutionary movement, the party should take the initiative, and not wait until the people are able to do the work without its aid.

6. *The electioneering canvass before the summoning of the Organizing*

Assembly. However the revolution may be brought about—as the result of an open revolution, or with the aid of a conspiracy—the duty of the party will be to aid in the immediate summoning of an Organizing Assembly, to which shall be transferred the powers of the Provisional Government created by the revolution or the conspiracy. During the election canvass the party should oppose, in every way, the candidacy of *kuláks* of all sorts, and strive to promote the candidacy of purely communal people.

The Law on Political Offenses

The terroristic actions of the Narodnaya Volya culminated in the murder of Alexander II. Naturally enough the government of his son and successor, Alexander III, vigorously prosecuted and persecuted all suspects, and took stringent measures to prevent the recurrence of such acts. The following selections from the "Rules relating to measures for the preservation of national order and public tranquility" will show the nature of the government's reaction. The source is: Kennan, *Siberia,* vol. 2, pp. 507–509.

Section 5. (a) When public tranquility in any locality shall be disturbed by criminal attempts against the existing imperial form of government, or against the security of private persons and their property, or by preparations for such attempts, so that, for the preservation of order, a resort to the existing permanent laws seems to be insufficient, then that locality may be declared in a state of reinforced safeguard.

(b) When by reason of such attempts the population of a certain place shall be thrown into a state of alarm which creates a necessity for the adoption of exceptional measures to immediately reëstablish order, then the said place may be declared in a state of extraordinary safeguard.

Section 15. Within the limits of such places (places declared to be in a state of reinforced safeguard) governors-general, governors, and municipal chiefs of police may (a) issue obligatory ordinances relating to matters connected with the preservation of public tranquility and the security of the Empire, and (b) punish by fine and imprisonment violations of such ordinances.

Section 16. Governors-general, governors, and municipal chiefs of police are authorized also (a) to settle by administrative process cases involving violation of the obligatory ordinances issued by them; (b) to prohibit all popular, social, and even private meetings; (c) to close temporarily, or for the whole term of reinforced safeguard, all commercial and industrial establishments; and (d) to prohibit particular persons from residing in places declared to be in a state of reinforced safeguard. (Remark.—Banishment to a specified place, even to one's native place, with obligatory residence there, will be allowed only after communication with the Minister of the Interior. Rules for such banishment are set forth in Sections 32–36.)

Section 32. The banishment of a private person by administrative process to any particular locality in European or Asiatic Russia, with obligatory residence there for a specified time, may not take place otherwise than with an observance of the following rules:

Section 33. The proper authority, upon becoming convinced of the necessity for the banishment of a private person, shall make a statement to that effect to the Minister of the Interior, with a detailed explanation of the reasons for the adoption of this measure, and also a proposition with regard to the period of banishment. (Remark.—The preliminary imprisonment of a person thus presented for exile to a specified place may be extended, by authority of the Minister of the Interior, until such time as a decision shall be reached in his case.)

Section 34. Presentations of this kind will be considered by a special council in the Ministry of the Interior, under the presidency of one of the Minister's associates, such council to consist of two members from the Ministry of the Interior and two members from the Ministry of Justice. The decisions of this council shall be submitted to the Minister of the Interior for confirmation.

Section 35. While considering presentations for exile the above-mentioned council may call for supplemental information or explanations, and, in case of necessity, may summon for personal examination the individual nominated for banishment.

Section 36. A period of from one to five years shall be designated as the term for continuous residence in the assigned place of exile. (Remark.—The term of banishment may be shortened or lengthened, in the manner prescribed in Section 34, within the limits set by Section 36.)

The following are the sections of the Russian penal code under which political offenders are prosecuted when brought before the courts:

Section 245. All persons found guilty of composing and circulating written or printed documents, books, or representations calculated to create disrespect for the Supreme Authority, or for the personal character of the Gossudar (the Tsar), or for the Government of his Empire, shall be condemned, as insulters of Majesty, to deprivation of all civil rights, and to from ten to twelve years of penal servitude. (This punishment carries with it exile in Siberia for what remains of life after the expiration of the hard-labor sentence.)

Section 249. All persons who shall engage in rebellion against the Supreme Authority—that is, who shall take part in collective and conspirative insurrection against the Gossudar and the Empire; and also all persons who shall plan the overthrow of the Government in the Empire as a whole, or in any part thereof; or who shall intend to change the existing form of government, or the order of succession to the throne established by law; all persons who, for the attainment of these ends, shall organize or take part in a conspiracy, either actively and with knowledge of its object, or by participation in a conspirative meeting, or by storing or distributing weapons, or by other preparations for insurrection—all such persons, including not only those most guilty, but their associates, instigators, prompters, helpers, and concealers, shall be deprived of all civil rights and be put to death.

Those who have knowledge of such evil intentions, and of preparations to carry them into execution, and who, having power to inform the Government thereof, do not fulfill that duty, shall be subjected to the same punishment.

Section 250. If the guilty persons have not manifested an intention to resort to violence, but have organized a society or association intended to attain, at a more or less remote time in the future, the objects set forth in Section 249, or have joined such an association, they shall be sentenced, according to the degree of their criminality, either to from four to six years of penal servitude, with deprivation of all civil rights (including exile to Siberia for life) . . . or to colonization in Siberia (without penal servitude), or to imprisonment in a fortress from one year and four months to four years.

Exile by Administrative Process

The general tone of the following indictment of the Russian police state is such that except for the very much smaller numbers of persons involved, one might imagine that it was a report of the Stalin era. George Kennan, who wrote the material, first visited Russia in connection with the abortive scheme of connecting America with Europe by telegraph via Siberia. Later Mr. Kennan lived for some time in Russia and traveled very extensively throughout the empire. Siberia and the exile system greatly interested him and in 1885 he went to Russia as a special correspondent of *The Century Magazine* to make a study of these things. His published report created a sensation in the West and even forced the Russian government to reform some of the worst abuses of the system. The system itself, however, was continued. The source is: Kennan, *Siberia,* vol. 1, pp. 242 ff. Condensed.

Exile by administrative process means the banishment of an obnoxious person from one part of the empire to another without the observance of any of the legal formalities that, in most civilized countries, precede the deprivation of rights and the restriction of personal liberty. The obnoxious person may not be guilty of any crime, and may not have rendered himself amenable in any way to the laws of the state, but if, in the opinion of the local authorities, his presence in a particular place is "prejudicial to public order," or "incompatible with public tranquillity," he may be arrested without a warrant, may be held from two weeks to two years in prison, and may then be removed by force to any other place within the limits of the empire and there be put under police surveillance for a period of from one year to ten years. He may or may not be informed of the reasons for this summary proceeding, but in either case he is perfectly helpless. He cannot examine the witnesses upon whose testimony his presence is declared to be "prejudicial to public order." He cannot summon friends to prove his loyalty and good character, without great risk of bringing upon them the same calamity that has befallen him. He has no right to demand a trial, or even a hearing. He cannot sue out a writ of habeas corpus. He cannot appeal to his fellow-citizens through the press.

His communications with the world are so suddenly severed that some-times even his own relatives do not know what has happened to him. He is literally and absolutely without any means whatever of self-defense. To show the nature of the evidence upon which certain classes of Russians are banished to Siberia, and to illustrate the working of the system generally, I will give a few cases of administrative exile from the large number re-corded in my note-books.

* * *

In the year 1880 the well-known and gifted Russian novelist Vladimir Korolenko, two of whose books have recently been translated into English, was exiled to Eastern Siberia as a result of what the Government itself finally admitted to be an official mistake. Through the influence of Prince Imeretinski, Mr. Korolenko succeeded in getting this mistake corrected before he reached his ultimate destination and was released in the West Siberian city of Tomsk. Hardly had he returned, however, to European Russia, when he was called upon to take the oath of allegiance to Alexan-der III, and to swear that he would betray every one of his friends or acquaintances whom he knew to be engaged in revolutionary or anti-Government work. No honorable and self-respecting man could take such an oath as that, and of course Mr. Korolenko declined to do so. He was thereupon exiled by administrative process to the East Siberian territory of Yakutsk, where, in a wretched native *ulus,* he lived for about three years.

* * *

Mr. Borodin, another Russian author, was banished to the territory of Yakutsk on account of the alleged "dangerous" and "pernicious" charac-ter of a certain manuscript found in his house by the police during a search. This manuscript was the spare copy of an article upon the economic condi-tion of the province of Viatka, which Mr. Borodin had written but which had not been published. The author went to Eastern Siberia in a convict's grey overcoat with a yellow ace of diamonds on his back, and three or four months after his arrival in Yakutsk he had the pleasure of reading in a magazine the very same article for which he had been exiled. The Minister of the Interior had sent him to Siberia merely for having in his possession what the police called a "dangerous" and "pernicious" manuscript, and then the St. Petersburg committee of censorship had certified that another copy of the same manuscript was perfectly harmless, and had allowed it to be published, without the change of a line, in one of the most popular and widely circulated magazines of the empire.

A gentleman named Achkin, in Moscow, was exiled to Siberia by administrative process in 1885 merely because, to adopt the language of the order that was issued for his arrest, he was "suspected of the intention to put himself into an illegal situation." The high crime which Mr. Achkin was "suspected of an intention" to commit was the taking of a fictitious name in the place of his own. Upon what ground he was "suspected of an intention" to do this terrible thing he never knew.

Another exile of my acquaintance, Mr. Y, was banished merely because he was a friend of Mr. Z., who was awaiting trial on the charge of political conspiracy. When Mr. Z's case came to a judicial investigation he was found to be innocent and was acquitted; but in the meantime Mr. Y., merely for being a friend of this innocent man, had gone to Siberia by administrative process. . . .

Exile by administrative process is not a new thing in Russia, nor was it first resorted to by the Russian Government as an extraordinary or exceptional measure of self-defense in the struggle with the revolutionists. It is older than nihilism, it is older than the modern revolutionary movement, it is older than the imperial house of Romanof. It has been practiced for centuries as a short and easy method of dealing with people who happen to be obnoxious or in the way, but who cannot conveniently be tried or convicted in a court of justice. Administrative exile has been not only a recognized but a well established method of dealing with certain classes of offenders ever since the seventeeth century. In the reign of the Emperor Nicholas, for example, nihilism had not been so much as heard of—the very word was unknown—and yet men and women were being exiled to Siberia by administrative process, not in hundreds merely, but in thousands, and not only by the order of the Tsar, but by order of the administrative authorities, by order of the ecclesiastical authorities, by order of the village communes, and even by the order of private landowners. Most of them, it is true, were not political offenders; but they were nonetheless entitled to a trial, and they were all victims of the system. . . .

Between 1827 and 1846 there was not a year in which the number of persons sent to Siberia by administrative process fell below three thousand, and it reached a maximum, for a single year, of more than six thousand. The aggregate number for the twenty year period is 79,909. . . .

In the latter part of the reign of Alexander II, and particularly between the years 1870 and 1880, administrative exile was resorted to, in political cases, upon a scale never before known, and with a recklessness and cynical indifference to personal rights that were almost unparalleled. In Odessa, General Todleben, by virtue of the unlimited discretionary power given him in the Imperial ukaz of April 17, 1879, proceeded to banish, without inquiry or discrimination, the whole "politically untrustworthy" class—that is, to exile every person whose loyalty to the existing Government was even doubtful. The mere fact that a man had been registered as a suspect in the books of the secret police, or had been accused, even anonymously, of political disaffection, was a sufficient reason for his deportation to the remotest part of the empire. Parents who had never had a disloyal thought were exiled because their children had become revolutionists; school-boys who happened to be acquainted with political offenders were exiled because they had betrayed the latter to the police; members of the provincial assemblies were exiled because they insisted upon their right to petition the crown for the redress of grievances; and university students who had been tried for political crime and duly acquitted by the courts were immediately rearrested and exiled by administrative process. . . .

The grotesque injustice, the heedless cruelty, and the preposterous "mistakes" and "misunderstandings" that make the history of administrative exile in Russia seem to an American like the recital of a wild nightmare are due to the complete absence, in the Russian form of government, of checks upon the executive power, and the almost equally complete absence of official responsibility for unjust or illegal action. The Minister of the Interior, in dealing with politicals, is almost wholly unrestrained by law; and as it is utterly impossible for him personally to examine all of the immense number of political cases that come to him for final decision, he is virtually forced to delegate a part of his irresponsible power to chiefs of police, chiefs of gendarmes, governors of provinces, and subordinates in his own administration. They in turn are compelled, for similar reasons, to intrust a part of their authority and discretion to officers of still lower grade; and the latter, who often are stupid, ignorant, or unscrupulous men, are the persons who really make the investigations, the searches, and the examinations upon which the life or liberty of an accused citizen may depend. Theoretically the Minister of the Interior, aided by a council composed of three of his own subordinates and two officers from the Ministry of Justice, reviews and reexamines the cases of all political offenders who are dealt with by administrative process; but practically he does nothing of the kind, and it is impossible that he should do anything of the kind for the very simple reason that he has not the time.

The Character of Political Exiles

There was a quite general impression that all Russian revolutionaries were dangerous desperadoes of the toughest sort. Some of them were dangerous and fanatically ruthless, but most of them did not resemble the stereotype of the bomb-throwing radical. Mr. Kennan's account of them was based upon interviews with many of them as well as upon his study of the general problem. The source is: Kennan, *Siberia*, vol. 2, pp. 436–440, 448–456. Slightly abridged.

For the purposes of this chapter I shall divide Russian political exiles into three classes as follows.

1. THE LIBERALS. In this class are included the cool-headed men of moderate opinions, who believe in the gradual extension of the principles of popular self-government; who favor greater freedom of speech and of the press; who strive to restrict the power of bureaucracy; who deprecate the persecution of religious dissenters and of the Jews; who promote in every possible way the education and the moral up-lifting of the peasants; who struggle constantly against official indifference and caprice; who insist pertinaciously upon "due process of law"; who are prominent in all good works; but who regard a complete overthrow of the existing form of government as impracticable at present even if desirable.

2. THE REVOLUTIONISTS. In this class are comprised the Russian socialists, the so-called "peasantists" (*naródniki*), "people's-willists"

(*narodovóltsi*), and all reformers who regard the overthrow of the autocracy as a matter of such immediate and vital importance as to justify
conspiracy and armed rebellion. They differ from the terrorists chiefly in
their unwillingness to adopt the methods of the highwayman and the blood-
avenger. If they can see a prospect of organizing a formidable insurrection,
and of crushing the autocracy by a series of open blows, fairly delivered,
they are ready to attempt it, even at the peril of death on the scaffold; but
they do not regard it as wise or honorable to shoot a chief of police from
ambush; to wreck an Imperial railroad train; to rob a Government sub-
treasury; or to incite peasants to revolt by means of a forged manifesto in
the name of the Tsar. The objects which they seek to attain are the same
that the liberals have in view, but they would attain them by quicker and
more direct methods, and they would carry the work of reform to greater
extremes. The socialistic revolutionists for example, would attempt to bring
about a redistribution of the land and a more equitable division of the results of labor, and would probably encourage a further development of the
principle of association, as distinguished from competition, which is so
marked a feature of Russian economic life.

3. THE TERRORISTS. The only difference between the terrorists and the
revolutionists is a difference in methods. So far as principles and aims are
concerned the two classes are identical; but the revolutionists recognize
and obey the rules of civilized warfare, while the terrorists resort to any
and every measure that they think likely to injure or intimidate their adversaries. A terrorist, in fact, is nothing more than an embittered revolutionist, who has found it impossible to unite and organize the disaffected
elements of society in the face of a cloud of spies, an immense body of
police, and a standing army; who has been exasperated to the last degree
by cruel, unjust, and lawless treatment of himself, his family, or his friends;
who has been smitten in the face every time he has opened his lips to explain or expostulate, and who, at last, has been seized with the Berserker
madness, and has become, in the words of the St. Petersburg *Gólos,* "a
wild beast capable of anything."

In point of numerical strength these three classes follow one another in
the order in which I have placed them. The liberals, who are the most
numerous, probably comprise three-fourths of all the university graduates
in the Empire outside of the bureaucracy. The revolutionists, who come
next, undoubtedly number tens of thousands, but, under existing circumstances, it is impossible to make a trustworthy estimate of their strength,
and all that I feel safe in saying is that, numerically, they fall far short of
the liberals. The terrorists never were more than a meager handful in comparison with the population of the country, and they constituted only a
fraction even of the anti-Government party; but they were resolute and
daring men and women, and they attracted more attention abroad, of
course, than a thousand times as many liberals, simply on account of the
tragic nature of the roles that they played on the stage of Russian public
life. The liberals, who were limited by the censorship and the police on one
side, and by their own renunciation of violence on the other, could do very

little to attract the attention of foreign observers; but the terrorists, who defied all restrictions, who carried their lives constantly in their hands, and who waged war with dagger, pistol, and pyroxylin bomb, acquired a notoriety that was out of all proportion to their numerical strength.

I met among the political exiles in Siberia representatives of all the classes above described, and I have tried, in the earlier chapters of this work, to convey to the reader the impressions that they made upon me in personal intercourse. I desire now to state, as briefly as I can, my conclusions with regard to their character.

1. THE LIBERALS. So far as I know, it is not pretended by anybody that the Russian liberals are bad men or bad citizens. The Government, it is true, keeps them under strict restraint, prohibits them from making public speeches, drives them out of the universities, forbids them to sit as delegates in provincial assemblies, expels them from St. Petersburg, suppresses the periodicals that they edit, puts them under police surveillance and sends them to Siberia; but, notwithstanding all this, it does not accuse them of criminality, nor even of criminal intent. It merely asserts that they are "politically untrustworthy"; that the "tendency" of their social activity is "pernicious"; or that, from an official point of view, their presence in a particular place is "prejudicial to public tranquillity." These vague assertions mean, simply, that the liberals are in the way of the officials, and prevent the latter, to some extent, from doing what they want to do with the bodies, the souls, or the property of the Russian people. . . .

It seems to me foolish and impolitic for Russian Government officials to try to make it appear that the revolutionists, as a class, are despicable in point of intellectual ability, or morally depraved. They are neither the one nor the other. So far as education is concerned they are far superior to any equal number of Russian officials with whom, in the course of five years' residence in the Russian Empire, I have been brought in contact. In the face of difficulties and discouragements that would crush most men— in financial distress, in terrible anxiety, in prison, in exile, and in the straitjacket of the press censorship—they not only "keep their grip," but they fairly distinguish themselves in literature, in science, and in every field of activity that is open to them. Much of the best scientific work that has been done in Siberia has been done by political exiles. Mikhaiélis in Semipalátinsk was an accomplished naturalist; Andréief in Minusínsk was a skilled botanist and made an exhaustive study of the flora of central Siberia and the Altái; Kléments in Minusínsk was a geologist and an archæologist of whom his country ought to have been proud; Alexander Kropótkin, who committed suicide in Tomsk, was an astronomer and meteorologist who made and recorded scientific observations for the Russian Meteorological Bureau almost up to the time of his death; Belokónski, in Minusínsk, continued these observations, and was a frequent contributor, moreover, to the best Russian magazines and reviews; Chudnófski, in Tomsk, was engaged for many years in active work for the West-Siberian section of the Imperial Russian Geographical Society, and is the author of a dozen or more books and monographs; Leóntief and Dr. Dolgopólof, in Semipalátinsk, made valuable anthropological researches among the Kírghis, and the work of the former has recently been published by the Semipalátinsk Statistical Committee under the title "Materials for the Study of the Legal Customs of the Kírghis"; Lesévich, who was in exile in Yeniséisk, is one of the best-known writers in Russia upon philosophy, morals, and the history and influence of Buddhism; Hoúrwitch, who was in exile in Tiukalínsk, but who is now in New York City, is the author of a monograph on "Emigration to Siberia" which was published in the "Proceedings of the Imperial Geographical Society," and is also the author of the excellent article upon the treatment of the Jews in Russia which was published in the *Forum* for August, 1891; and, finally, the novels, stories, and sketches of the political exiles Korolénko, Máchtet, Staniukóvich, Mámin (Sibiriák), and Petropávlovski are known to every cultivated Russian from the White Sea to the Caspian and from Poland to the Pacific.

Morally, the Russian revolutionists whom I met in Siberia would compare favorably with any body of men and women of equal numerical strength that I could collect from the circle of my own acquaintances. I do not share the opinions of all of them; some of them seem to me to entertain visionary and over-sanguine hopes and plans for the future of their country; some of them have made terrible and fatal mistakes of judgment; and some of them have proved weak or unworthy in the hour of trial; but it is my deliberate conviction, nevertheless, that, tested by any moral standard of which I have knowledge, such political exiles as Volkhófski, Chudnofski, Blok, Leontief, Lobonofski, Kropotkin, Kohan-Bérnstein, Belokónski, Prisédski, Lázaref, Charúshin, Kléments, Shishkó, Nathalie Armfeldt, Heléne Máchtet, Sophie Bárdina, Anna Pávlovna Korbá, and many others whom I have not space to name, represent the flower of Russian young manhood and young womanhood. General Strélnikof may call them "fanatics" and "robbers," and Mr. Gálkine Wrásskoy may describe them as "wretched men and women . . . whose social depravity is so great that it would shock the English people if translated into proper English equivalents," but among these men and women, nevertheless, are some of the best, bravest, and most generous types of manhood and womanhood that I have ever known. I am linked to them only by the ties of sympathy, humanity, or friendship; but I wish that I were bound to them by the tie of kindred blood. I should be proud of them if they were my brothers and sisters, and so long as any of them live they may count upon me for any service that a brother can render.

The last of the three classes into which I have divided the anti-Government party in Russia comprises the terrorists. A recent writer in the Russian historical magazine *Rússkaya Stariná,* in a very instructive paragraph, describes them, and the attitude of the Russian people towards them, as follows:

We have been present at a strange spectacle. Before our eyes there has taken place something like a duel between the mightiest Power on earth armed with all the attributes of authority on one side, and an insignificant gang of discharged telegraph operators, half-educated seminarists, high-school boys and University students, miserable little Jews and loose women on the other; and in this apparently unequal contest success was far from being on the side of strength. Meanwhile the immense mass of the people who without doubt spontaneously loved the serene (*svétloi*) personality of the Tsar, and were sincerely devoted to law and order, and to the embodiment of law and order in the form of monarchical institutions, stood aside and watched this duel in the capacity of uninterested, if not indifferent, observers. We have called this a "strange spectacle," but it ought, with more justice, to be characterized as a shameful spectacle. It was only necessary for the great mass of the Russian people to move—to "shake its shoulders," as the saying is—and the ulcer that had appeared on the body of the social organism would have vanished as completely as if it never had existed. Why this saving movement was not made we shall not attempt to ascertain, since the inquiry would carry us too far from the modest task that we have set for ourselves. We merely state the fact, without explanation, and, in the interest of historical truth, refer, in passing, to one extremely distressing phase of it. The repetition, one after another, of terrible crimes, each of which deeply shocked the social organism, inevitably led, by virtue of the natural law of reaction, to exhaustion. There was danger, therefore, that a continuance of persistent activity in this direction would fatally weaken the organism and extinguish all of its self-preservative energies. . . . Ominous forewarnings of such symptoms had begun already to make their appearance. . . .

According to the statements of this writer the terrorists of 1879–81 were nothing but "an insignificant gang of discharged telegraph-operators, half-educated school-boys, miserable little Jews, and loose women"; but this heterogeneous organization, notwithstanding its insignificance, almost succeeded in overthrowing "the mightiest power on earth, armed with all the attributes of authority." To a simple-minded reader there seems to be an extraordinary disproportion here between cause and effect. So far as I know there is not another instance in history where a gang of telegraph-operators, school-boys, Jews, and loose women have been able to paralyze the energies of a great empire, and almost to overthrow long-established "monarchical institutions" to which a hundred millions of people were "sincerely devoted." If the statements of Count Lóris-Mélikof's biographer are to be accepted as true, Russian telegraph-operators, Russian school-boys, Russian Jews, and Russian loose women must be regarded as new and extraordinary types of the well-known classes to which they nominally belong. There are no telegraph-operators and loose women, I believe, outside of Russia, who are capable of engaging in a "duel" with the "mightiest power on earth" and of "extinguishing all the self-preservative energies" of so tough an "organism" as the Russian bureaucracy. It would be interesting to know how this combative—not to say heroic—strain of telegraphers, school-boys and loose women was produced, and why they should have directed their tremendous energies against the "serene personality" that was so universally and so "spontaneously" beloved, and against the "monarchical institutions" to which all Russians, except telegraphers, school-boys, Jews, and loose women, were so "sincerely devoted." But it is unnecessary to press the inquiry. Every thoughtful student of human affairs must see the absurdity of the supposition that a few telegraph-operators, school-boys, Jews, and loose women could seriously imperil the existence of a government like that of Russia.

As a matter of fact the Russian terrorists were men and women of extraordinary ability, courage, and fortitude; of essentially noble nature; and of limitless capacity for heroic self-sacrifice.

Most of the Russian terrorists were nothing more, at first, than moderate liberals, or, at worst, peaceful socialistic propagandists; and they were gradually transformed into revolutionists, and then into terrorists, by injustice, cruelty, illegality, and contemptuous disregard, by the Government, of all their rights and feelings. I have not a word to say in defense of their crimes. I do not believe in such methods of warfare as assassination, the wrecking of railway trains on which one's enemies are riding, the robbing of Government sub-treasuries, and the blowing up of palaces; but I can fully understand, nevertheless, how an essentially good and noble-natured man may become a terrorist when, as in Russia, he is subjected to absolutely intolerable outrages and indignities and has no peaceful or legal means of redress. It is true, as the Russian Government contends, that after 1878 the terrorists acted in defiance of all the generally accepted principles of civilized combat; but it must not be forgotten that in life and in warfare, as in chess, you cannot disregard all the rules of the game yourself and then expect your adversary to observe them. The Government first set the example of lawlessness in Russia by arresting without warrant; by punishing without trial; by cynically disregarding the judgments of its own courts when such judgments were in favor of politicals; by confiscating the money and property of private citizens whom it merely suspected of sympathy with the revolutionary movement; by sending fourteen-year-old boys and girls to Siberia; by kidnapping the children of "politically untrustworthy" people and exiles and putting them into state asylums; by driving men and women to insanity and suicide in rigorous solitary confinement without giving them a trial; by burying secretly at night the bodies of the people whom it had thus done to death in its dungeons; and by treating as a criminal, *in posse* if not *in esse,* every citizen who dared to ask why or wherefore. A man is not necessarily a ferocious, blood-thirsty fanatic, if, under such provocation, and in the absence of all means of redress, he strikes back with the weapons that lie nearest his hand. It is not my purpose to justify the policy of the terrorists, nor to approve, even by implication, the resort to murder as a means of tempering despotism; but it is my purpose to explain, so far as I can, certain morbid social phenomena; and in making such explanation circumstances seem to lay upon me the duty of saying to the world for the Russian revolutionists and terrorists all that they might fairly say for themselves if the lips of the dead had not already moldered into dust, and if the voices of the living were not lost in the distance or stifled by prison walls. The Russian Government has its own press and its own representatives abroad; it can explain, if it chooses, its methods and measures. The Russian revolutionists, buried alive in remote Siberian solitudes, can only tell their story to an occasional traveler from a freer country, and ask him to lay it before the world for judgment.

Press Censorship

Mr. Kennan's record of censorship, from which these excerpts were taken, fills ten pages of his book. These are random samples. The source is: Kennan, *Siberia,* vol. 2, pp. 484, 485, 491.

Below will be found a list of cases in which Russian periodicals have been punished, or wholly suppressed, for giving voice to ideas and sentiments regarded as objectionable by the ruling class. I have made this list from my own reading of Russian newspapers and magazines, and I am well aware that it probably does not comprise more than a fractional part— perhaps not more than one-tenth—of all the "warnings," "suspensions," and "suppressions" that have been dealt out to the Russian press in the course of the last decade.

1881.	July 7.	The *Odéssa Listók* is suspended for four months.
1882.	Jan. 17.	The *Moscow Telegraph* receives a first warning.
	Jan. 19.	The St. Petersburg *Gólos* reappears, after a suspension of six months.
	Jan. 22.	The newspaper *Poriádok* is suspended for six weeks.
	Jan. 31.	The *Moscow Telegraph* receives a second warning.
	Feb. 11.	The St. Petersburg *Gólos* receives a first warning, with the prohibition of its street sales.
	March 26.	The *Moscow Telegraph* is suspended for four months.
	April 8.	Application for permission to publish a new newspaper in St. Petersburg is denied.
	April 15.	The *Poriádok* gives up the struggle with the censorship and goes into liquidation.
	April 15.	The April number of the magazine *Russian Thought* is seized and suppressed.
	May 27.	Application for permission to publish a new newspaper in Ekaterínburg is denied.
	June 17.	The *Riga Véstnik* publishes the following in lieu of a leading editorial: "In to-day's issue it was our intention to have had a leading editorial, urging the Esthonians to unite more closely among themselves, and with the Russians, and to work with manly energy for the Fatherland; but we have not been allowed to print it."
	July 1.	The humorous illustrated newspaper *Guslá* is seized by order of the censor, and its 24th number is suppressed, for making fun of an irrigation scheme in which the censor is interested.

July 1. Application for permission to publish a new news-paper, to be called the *Donskói Pchéla,* on the Don is denied.

July 15. The *Zémstvo,* the organ of the provincial assemblies, gives up the struggle with the censorship and goes into liquidation, after an existence of a year and a half.

Aug. 19. The *Vostók* receives a first warning for criticism of the higher clergy.

1886. Feb. 19. The Moscow *Rússkia Védomosti,* having been for-bidden to refer editorially to the emancipation of the serfs on the twenty-fifth anniversary of that event, does not appear on that day at all, and thus commem-orates it by voluntary silence.

April 3. An application for leave to publish a newspaper in the East-Siberian town of Nérchinsk is denied.

April 3. Street sales of the Moscow *Rússkia Védomosti* are forbidden.

April 10. Street sales of the *Sovrémmenia Izvéstia* are forbid-den.

April 24. A correspondent of the Irkútsk newspaper *Sibír* is ar-rested by order of a Siberian *isprávnik,* kept two days in prison without food, flogged, put into leg-fetters, and sent back to his place of residence by étape in a temperature of thirty-five degrees below zero (Réaum.) He is not charged with any other crime than furnishing his paper with news.

May 6. The editor of the St. Petersburg *Police Gazette,* a purely official Government organ, is arrested and im-prisoned because, in an article in his paper referring to a "requiem for Alexander II.," there was a typo-graphical error which made it read "a requiem for Alexander III."

Universities in the 1870's

Another aspect of Russian life was rather bitterly described by S. M. Kravchinski, the non-Marxian socialist and revolutionary who wrote under the name of Stepniak. The source is: Stepniak (S. M. Kravchin-ski), *Russia Under the Tzars.* (Authorized ed.) New York: Charles Scribner's Sons, 1885. Pp. 240–243, *passim.*

It is well to observe at the outset that Russian universities occupy a position altogether peculiar and exceptional. . . . [They] are the *foci* of the most intense and ardent political life, and in the higher spheres of the Imperial administration the name of student is identified, not with something young, noble, and aspiring, but with a dark and dangerous power inimical to the laws and institutions of the land. And this impression is so far justified that, as recent political trials abundantly prove, the great majority of the young men who throw themselves into the struggle for liberty are under thirty, and belong either to the class of undergraduates or to those whose academic honors are newly won. This, though it may surprise Englishmen, is neither unprecedented nor unnatural. When a government in possession of despotic power punishes as a crime the least show of opposition to its will, nearly all whom age has made cautious or wealth selfish, or who have given hostages to fortune, shun the strife. It is then that the leaders of the forlorn hope turn to the young, who, though they may lack knowledge and experience, are rarely wanting either in courage or devotion. . . . If the transfer of the center of political gravity to the young is more marked in Russia than it has been elsewhere, it is that the determining causes have been more powerful in their action and more prolonged in their duration. One of the most potent of these causes is the conduct of the Government, whose ill-judged measures of repression exasperate the youth of our universities and convert latent discontent into flat rebellion. . . .

Towards the end of 1878 there occurred among the students of St. Petersburg University some so-called "disorders." They were not serious, and in ordinary circumstances would have been punished by sending a few score of young fellows to waste the rest of their lives in some obscure village of the far north, and neither the Ministry nor the University Council would have given the matter further thought. But this time there was a new departure. After passing judgment on the rioters, the Council appointed a commission of twelve, among whom were some of the best professors of the university, to institute a searching inquiry into the cause of these troubles, which recur with periodical regularity. [Charging that the commission's report had been suppressed, Kravchinski presents extracts from a copy "printed in the clandestine office of *Zemlia i Volia*."]

"Of all departments of the administration the one with which students most come in contact is the Department of Police. By its proceedings they naturally form their opinion of the character of the Government. It is, therefore, in their interest, and that of the State, that the conduct of the police towards the members of our universities should be kind, considerate, and reasonable. But what we see is precisely the reverse. For most young men intercourse with comrades and friends is an absolute necessity. To satisfy this necessity there exists in all other European universities (as also in those of Finland and the Baltic provinces, which enjoy considerable local liberties) special institutions, such as clubs, corporations, and unions. At St. Petersburg there is nothing of the sort, although the great majority of the students, being from the country, have no friends in the city with whom they can associate. Private reunions might, in some measure, make up for deprivations of other opportunities of social intercourse were it not that police interference renders the one almost as impossible as the other. A meeting of several students in the room of one of their number draws immediate attention and gives rise to exaggerated fears. The porters, and even the proprietors of the rooms, are bound on their peril to give prompt information to the police, by whom such meetings are often dispersed. Besides being practically forbidden to enjoy each other's society, students, even in the privacy of their own chambers, are not free from annoyance. Although they may lead studious lives, meddle with nobody, and receive and make few visits, they are nonetheless submitted to a rigorous oversight. . . .

" 'How does he pass his time?' 'Whom does he associate with?' 'What time does he generally come home?' 'What does he read?' 'What does he write?' are among the questions put by the police to porters and lodging-house keepers, people generally of little or no education, who carry out their instructions with scant regard for the feelings of impressionable youth." This is the testimony of the heads of the University of St. Petersburg, speaking in confidence to the Ministers of the Tzar.

"The Cooks' Children"

> I. D. Delyanov, then Minister of Public Education, won an immortality of sorts by a circular issued in June, 1887 to the Moscow school district. The essence of the circular is paraphrased below. The source is the *Khrestomatiya,* vol. III, pp. 467–468.

I find it necessary, in order to improve the student body of the gymnasia, to admit to these institutions only those children who have adequate guidance and supervision at home. The strict application of this rule will free the gymnasia and progymnasia from enrolment in them of the children of coachmen, lackies, cooks, laundresses, petty shopkeepers, and similar persons. Except for the unusually gifted, children of such persons cannot rise above the surroundings to which they belong. Many years of experience show that attempts to educate such children cause them to neglect their parents, to become discontented with their way of life, and arouse in them an animosity against the existing and naturally inevitable disparities in wealth.

Before enrolling children, or even admitting them to entrance examinations, headmasters should question the applicants and make careful inquiries about the material position and the condition of the family. If these do not meet the standards set above, the applications should be firmly denied, and attention should be directed to less demanding educational institutions which are more in keeping with their status and in which the children might advantageously be placed.

Students already enrolled, who subsequently prove to be a bad influence on their classmates because of the domestic situation of their parents or relatives, must be summarily dismissed, any other rules to the contrary notwithstanding. Progymnasia and gymnasia are educational institutions which open opportunities to enter universities and to go on to higher places in government and society. They must therefore educate only well-behaved, fully well-bred young persons concerning whose future trustworthiness in all relations the schools' masters must accept responsibility.

Church and State

This selection and the one immediately following deal with quite different aspects of Russian religious life, but both lay stress on the particular church-state relationships in the Russian Empire. The selection below is from Wallace, *Russia,* pp. 424–431.

The Russian Patriarchate came to an end in the time of Peter the Great. Peter wished among other things to reform the ecclesiastical administration, and to introduce into his country many novelties which the majority of the clergy and of the people regarded as heretical; and he clearly perceived that a bigoted, energetic Patriarch might throw considerable obstacles in his way, and cause him infinite annoyance. Though such a Patriarch might be deposed without any flagrant violation of the canonical formalities, the operation would necessarily be attended with great trouble and loss of time. Peter was no friend of roundabout tortuous methods, and preferred to remove the difficulty in his usual thorough violent fashion. When the Patriarch Adrian died, the customary short interregnum was prolonged for twenty years, and when the people had thus become accustomed to having no Patriarch, it was announced that no more Patriarchs would be elected. Their place was supplied by an ecclesiastical council or Synod, in which, as a contemporary explained, "the mainspring was Peter's power, and the pendulum his understanding." The great autocrat justly considered that such a council could be much more easily managed than a stubborn Patriarch, and the wisdom of the measure has been duly appreciated by succeeding sovereigns. Though the idea of re-establishing the Patriarchate has more than once been raised, it has never been carried into execution. The Holy Synod remains, and is likely to remain, the highest ecclesiastical authority.

But the Emperor? What is his relation to the Synod and to the Church in general?

This is a question about which zealous Orthodox Russians are extremely sensitive. If a foreigner ventures to hint in their presence that the Emperor seems to have a considerable influence in the Church, he may inadvertently produce a little outburst of patriotic warmth and virtuous indignation. The truth is that many Russians have a pet theory on this subject, and have at the same time a dim consciousness that the theory is not quite in accordance with reality. They hold theoretically that the Orthodox Church has no "Head" but Christ, and is in some peculiar, undefined sense entirely independent of all terrestrial authority. In this respect it is often compared with the Anglican Church, and the comparison is made a theme for semi-religious, semi-patriotic exultation, which finds expression not only in conversation, but also in the literature. Khomiakóf, for instance, in one of his most vigorous poems, predicts that God will one day take the destiny of the world out of the hands of England in order to give it to Russia, and he adduces as one of the reasons for this transfer the fact that England "has chained, with sacrilegious hand, the Church of God to the pedestal of the vain earthly power." So far the theory. As to the facts, it is unquestionable that the Church enjoys much more liberty in England than in Russia, and that the Tsar exercises a much greater influence in ecclesiastical affairs than the Queen and Parliament. All who know the internal history of Russia are aware that the Government does not draw a clear line of distinction between the temporal and the spiritual, and that it occasionally uses the ecclesiastical organization for political purposes.

What then are the relations between Church and State?

To avoid confusion, we must carefully distinguish between the Eastern Orthodox Church as a whole and that section of it which is known as the Russian Church.

The Eastern Orthodox Church is, properly speaking, a confederation of independent churches without any central authority—a unity founded on the possession of a common dogma and on the theoretical but now unrealizable possibility of holding Ecumenical Councils. The Russian National Church is one of the members of this ecclesiastical confederation. In matters of faith, it is bound by the decisions of the ancient Ecumenical Councils, but in all other respects it enjoys complete independence and autonomy.

In relation to the Orthodox Church as a whole, the Emperor of Russia is nothing more than a simple member, and can no more interfere with its dogmas or ceremonial than a King of Italy or an Emperor of the French could modify Roman Catholic theology; but in relation to the Russian National Church his position is peculiar. He is described in one of the fundamental laws as "the supreme defender and preserver of the dogmas of the dominant faith," and immediately afterwards it is said, "the autocratic power acts in the ecclesiastical administration by means of the most Holy Governing Synod, created by it." This describes very fairly the relations between the Emperor and the Church. He is merely the defender of the dogmas, and cannot in the least modify them; but he is at the same time the chief administrator, and uses the Synod as an instrument.

Some ingenious people who wish to prove that the creation of the Synod was not an innovation, represent the institution as a resuscitation of the ancient Local Council; but this view is utterly untenable. The Synod is not a council of deputies from various sections of the Church, but a permanent college, or ecclesiastical senate, the members of which are appointed and dismissed by the Emperor as he thinks fit. It has no independent legislative authority, for its legislative projects do not become law till they have received the Imperial sanction; and they are always published, not in the name of the Church, but in the name of the Supreme Power. Even in matters of simple administration it is not independent, for all its resolutions require the consent of the Procureur, a layman nominated by his Majesty. In theory this functionary protests only against those resolutions which are not in accordance with the civil law of the country; but as he alone has the right to address the Emperor directly on ecclesiastical concerns, and as all communications between the Emperor and the Synod must pass through his hands, he possesses in reality considerable power. Besides this, he can always influence the individual members by holding out prospects of advancement and decorations, and if this device fails, he can make the refractory members retire, and fill up their places with men of more pliable disposition. A council constituted in this way cannot, of course, display much independence of thought or action, especially in a country like Russia, where no one ventures to oppose openly the Imperial will.

It must not, however, be supposed that the Russian ecclesiastics regard the Imperial authority with jealousy or dislike. They are all most loyal subjects, and warm adherents of autocracy. Those ideas of ecclesiastical independence which are so common in Western Europe, and that spirit of opposition to the civil power which animates the Roman Catholic clergy, are entirely foreign to their minds. If a bishop sometimes complains to an intimate friend that he has been brought to St. Petersburg and made a member of the Synod, merely to append his signature to official papers and to give his consent to foregone conclusions, his displeasure is directed, not against the Emperor, but aginst the Procureur. He is full of loyalty and devotion to the Tsar, and has no desire to see his Majesty excluded from all influence in ecclesiastical affairs; but he feels saddened and humiliated when he finds that the whole government of the Church is in the hands of a lay functionary, who may be a military man, and who certainly looks at all matters from a layman's point of view.

A foreigner who hears ecclesiastics grumble or laymen express dissatisfaction with the existing state of things is apt to imagine that a secret struggle is going on between Church and State, and that a party favorable to Disestablishment is at present being formed. In reality there is no such struggle and no such party. I have heard Russians propose and discuss every conceivable kind of political and social reforms, but I have never heard any of them speak about disestablishing the Church. Indeed, I do not know how the idea could be expressed in Russian, except by a lengthy circumlocution. So long as the autocratic power exists, no kind of administration can be exempted from Imperial control.

This close connection between Church and State and the thoroughly national character of the Russian Church is well illustrated by the history of the local ecclesiastical administration. The civil and the ecclesiastical administration have always had the same character and have always been modified by the same influences. The terrorism which was largely used by the Muscovite Tsars and brought to a climax by Peter the Great appeared equally in both. In the episcopal circulars, as in the Imperial ukazes, we find frequent mention of "most cruel corporal punishment," "cruel punishment with whips, so that the delinquent and others may not acquire the habit of practicing such insolence," and much more of the same kind. And these terribly severe measures were sometimes directed against very venial offenses. The Bishop of Vologda, for instance, in 1748 decrees "cruel corporal punishment" against priests who wear coarse and ragged clothes, and the records of the Consistorial courts contain abundant proof that such decrees were rigorously executed. When Catherine II. introduced a more humane spirit into the civil administration, corporal punishment was at once abolished in the Consistorial courts, and the procedure was modified according to the accepted maxims of civil jurisprudence. But I must not weary the reader with tiresome historical details. Suffice it to say that, from the time of Peter the Great downwards, the character of all the more energetic sovereigns is reflected in the history of the ecclesiastical administration.

Each province, or "government," forms a diocese, and the bishop, like the civil governor, has a council which theoretically controls his power, but practically has no controlling influence whatever. The Consistorial council, which has in the theory of ecclesiastical procedure a very imposing appearance, is in reality the bishop's *chancellerie,* and its members are little more than secretaries, whose chief object is to make themselves agreeable to their superior. And it must be confessed that so long as they remain what they are, the less power they possess, the better it will be for those who have the misfortune to be under their jurisdiction. The higher dignitaries have at least larger aims and a certain consciousness of the dignity of their position, but the lower officials, who have no such healthy restraints and receive ridiculously small salaries, grossly misuse the little authority which they possess, and habitually pilfer and extort in the most shameless manner. The consistories are in fact what the public offices were in the time of Nicholas.

The ecclesiastical administration is entirely in the hands of the monks, or "Black Clergy," as they are commonly termed, who form a large and influential class.

The monks who first settled in Russia were, like those who first visited North-Western Europe, men of the earnest, ascetic, missionary type. Filled with zeal for the glory of God and the salvation of souls, they took little or no thought for the morrow, and devoutly believed that their Heavenly Father, without whose knowledge no sparrow falls to the ground, would provide for their humble wants. Poor, clad in rags, eating the most simple fare, and ever ready to share what they had with any one poorer than themselves, they performed faithfully and earnestly the work which their Master had given them to do. But this ideal of monastic life soon gave way in Russia, as in the West, to practices less simple and severe. By the liberal donations and bequests of the faithful the monasteries became rich in gold, in silver, in precious stones, and above all in land and serfs. Troitsa, for instance, possessed at one time 120,000 serfs and a proportionate amount of land, and it is said that at the beginning of last century more than a fourth of the entire population had fallen under the jurisdiction of the Church. Many of the monasteries engaged in commerce, and the monks were, if we may credit Fletcher, who visited Russia in 1588, the most intelligent merchants of the country.

During the last century the Church lands were secularized, and the serfs of the Church became serfs of the State. This was a severe blow for the monasteries, but it did not prove fatal, as many people predicted. Some monasteries were abolished and others were reduced to extreme poverty, but many survived and prospered. These could no longer possess serfs, but they had still three sources of revenue: a limited amount of real property, Government subsidies, and the voluntary offerings of the faithful. At present there are about 500 monastic establishments, and the great majority of them, though not wealthy, have revenues more than sufficient to satisfy all the requirements of an ascetic life.

Thus in Russia, as in Western Europe, the history of monastic institutions is composed of three chapters, which may be briefly entitled: asceticism and missionary enterprise; wealth, luxury, and corruption; secularization of property and decline. But between Eastern and Western monasticism there is at least one marked difference. The monasticism of the West made at various epochs of its history a vigorous, spontaneous effort at self-regeneration, which found expression in the foundation of separate Orders, each of which proposed to itself some special aim—some special sphere of usefulness. In Russia we find no similar phenomenon. Here the monasteries never deviated from the rules of St. Basil, which restrict the members to religious ceremonies, prayer, and contemplation. From time to time a solitary individual raised his voice against the prevailing abuses, or retired from his monastery to spend the remainder of his days in ascetic solitude; but neither in the monastic population as a whole, nor in any particular monastery, do we find at any time a spontaneous, vigorous movement toward reform. During the last two hundred years reforms have certainly been effected, but they have all been the work of the civil power, and in the realization of them the monks have shown little more than the virtue of resignation. Here, as elsewhere, we have evidence of that inertness, apathy, and want of spontaneous vigor which form one of the most characteristic traits of Russian national life. In this, as in other departments of national activity, the spring of action has lain not in the people but in the Government.

My personal acquaintance with the Russian monasteries is too slight to enable me to speak with authority regarding their actual condition, but I may say that during casual visits to some of them I have always been disagreeably impressed by the vulgar, commercial spirit which seemed to reign in the place. Several of them have appeared to me little better than houses of refuge for the indolent, and I have had on more than one occasion good grounds for concluding that among monks, as among ordinary mortals, indolence leads to drunkenness and other vices.

The Raskolniki in the Nineteenth Century

The schism (*raskol*) in the Orthodox Church which began in the seventeenth century persisted despite the efforts of the church and the government to suppress it. The numbers of the schismatics (*raskolniki*) increased in spite of persecutions which varied from time to time in intensity, but which continued beyond the life of the Romanov dynasty. Official reports of the number of the *raskolniki* were manifestly inaccurate and wildly contradictory. Scholars have estimated, however, that there were nine million to ten million *raskolniki* in the 1850's, twelve million to thirteen million in the 1880's, twenty million in 1900, and twenty-five million in 1917.

The following summary of the legal position of the *raskolniki* between 1825 and 1903 is reprinted by permission of the publisher from Frederick Cornwallis Conybeare, *The Russian Dissenters*. Cambridge, Mass.: Harvard University Press, 1921. Pp. 233–236.

We have already seen how the accession in 1825 of Nicholas I, a bigot and martinet, was marked by a return to the system of persecution. Raskol communities were placed afresh outside the law, their members denied the right of will and testament, no churches or schools were allowed to be put up, no hospitals or rest-houses. The title of *Raskolnik* had been expugned from official documents: it was now revived, and all public offices and employments were closed afresh to them. No dissenter might engage in trade or become a merchant of the first or second *guilds* or categories. New oratories, of course, or chapels were disallowed, and it was forbidden to repair those which already existed. Most of their charitable institutions were closed or pulled down. The dissenters were also obliged by ukase to take their children to an orthodox priest for baptism; their marriages were declared invalid. The object of such legislation was to allow members of the sect to live on as such till death overtook them, but prevent their ranks from being recruited either by inheritance or by propaganda. To facilitate the project Nicholas had a list made of the names of all living Raskolniks, with an inventory of all their churches, monasteries and sketes so called, between the years 1840 and 1853. Everywhere the police were set on to see that all these oppressive regulations were carried out, and garrisons were located in the chief Raskol centres. In 1847 a special police was created to exact the extra taxes levied upon dissenters.

Any system which reposes on policemen, especially in Russia, is insecure, for they are generally no less venal than unobservant. In spite of Nicholas' campaign therefore the Raskolniks went on building their chapels and increasing their numbers. When an extraordinary inquisition was to be made in any centre, the people were always forewarned. Now and again, as at Semenov, sketes were destroyed, but the inmates were regarded as martyrs and the hatred of the Orthodox oppressors waxed more intense. The exiled and transported managed to correspond with their coreligionists and inflame what Ivanovski calls their fanaticism. The mockery to which church consistories condemned them served, he says, to harden their hearts, and, if they repented, it was only in semblance.

In 1855 Nicholas I was succeeded by Alexander II Nikolaevich, a man of more liberal tendencies. The question of the best way to deal with the Raskol was laid before him in 1858, and he was at first in favour of applying the law as it stood, but impartially and equally all around; for a member of the Raskol never knew beforehand how a court of first instance would decide his case, and was the victim of all sorts of caprice on the part of police and judge. Later in the same year, Alexander decided against persecution, but agreed to forbid any propaganda amongst the

Orthodox and any public manifestations of Raskol faith, such as processions with cross and banners, hymn singing outside a place of worship, solemn celebrations of baptism or marriage, funeral processions in which the clergy wore vestments and cowls, monastic habits, outward emblems of religion on churches, bells, etc. On the other hand Raskolniks were permitted to trade in November, 1863, and to earn medals and orders from the Government in 1864, unless indeed they belonged to the most noxious sects which eschewed marriage and prayers for the Tsar; they were allowed in 1861 with the consent of the Minister of the Interior to be admitted to public offices. In 1874 their marriages were legitimized, if duly registered in the records of the police and commune, and their licit character was made to depend not on the use of religious rites, but on the act of registration. The law obliging them to go through the mockery of baptizing their children in an orthodox church was now abrogated.

As early as 1864 the Tsar Alexander projected a revision of all the laws affecting the Raskol, and in 1867 charged his council to undertake new legislation. Committees of investigation were formed in consequence and men of special knowledge, like Melnikov, consulted. A new scheme of law was prepared and laid before the Holy Synod; but the political events of 1877, the war with Turkey, and the assassination of the Tsar in 1881 arrested the whole scheme, which was not resumed until 1883, when by Ukase of May 3 the new Tsar Alexander III gave sanction to the views of his council in favour of recognizing the civil rights of Dissenters and their liberty of worship. But the proscription of any outward signs or evidence of Raskol faith was kept up, and every measure taken to prevent propaganda and protect the Orthodox Church from being attacked. The general principle of religious liberty and toleration was admitted and even paraded in the new law, but in application sadly curtailed. The Orthodox Church was recognized as having a monopoly of religious truth and Government protection. No other religious body could make converts from other faiths, while no Orthodox person could leave the Church and enroll himself in the ranks of the Raskol. The statute forbidding any public manifestation of Raskol faith and opinion was to be vigorously enforced, and exile awaited any member of it who converted an Orthodox to his faith. Any who printed books with a view to Raskol propaganda, or gave lectures or distributed tracts for the purpose were liable to be imprisoned. Any who overtly spoke ill of the Orthodox clergy or vilified the Church were liable to the same penalty. The printing of the liturgical books of the Raskol was likewise forbidden, and any one selling them might be fined 300 rubles. No new churches, nor restoration of old ones, was to be attempted without the fiat of the provincial governor, and all Government officials and bureaucrats were pledged to assist the Orthodox bishops and clergy in the sacred duty of repressing the Raskol. The inferior clergy had to keep the bishop informed of any considerable defection on the part of the parishioners, in accordance with the principle that "the dominant Church, Orthodox, Catholic and Oriental, is invested with the right, as is no other, within the frontiers of the Empire to induce the heterodox by way of persuasion to embrace its doctrine." [1] The Government rewards those who assist in the work of converting Raskolnik by conferring the decoration of the third grade of the order of St. Anna on any missionary who is so fortunate as to make, with the aid of the police, one hundred converts among the Raskol or the infidels.

Mixed marriages between the Orthodox and members of the Raskol were only legal if celebrated in an Orthodox Church, with Orthodox rites, and if the Raskolnik party 'verted' to the Orthodox Church. Minors perverted to the Raskol or to any heresy were placed under the charge of the Minister of the Interior. All prosecutions directed against the Raskol had to be initiated by the ecclesiastical authorities, and the parish clergy could do no more than report cases to the bishop of the diocese. A request for a prosecution must be precise and clearly formulated.

Such in brief were the regulations in force before the year 1903. They purported to be inspired by goodwill and toleration, and the Imperial Senate in its commentaries on them mitigated them in a few particulars. For example, public vilification of an orthodox priest was to be condoned, if the latter by insolence or altercation had provoked it; and the mere performance of a rite by a Raskol priest for orthodox persons, especially if the latter were not of an age to appreciate dogmatic distinctions, was not to be classed as an attempt at religious perversion. Commenting on the clause forbidding Raskolniks to officiate for the Orthodox at baptisms, marriages or funerals, the Senate held that, in such cases, the ministrant alone be held responsible, and not the parents and other parties, even though they consented. In Russia it rests or rested with the bureaucracy, lay or spiritual, to enforce the laws of the Empire, very much as they please; and it can well be imagined, writes Palmieri (p. 411), that, under the superintendence of an intransigent Procurator of the Holy Synod like Pobedonostsev bureaucrats continued to use against the Raskol the weapons of an earlier legislation. To the protests of the Raskolniks no attention was paid; their chapels continued to receive the visits of the police who closed them when and as they chose; for it was this fanatical functionary's idea to beat down Catholicism, to suffocate the Raskol, and by such means bring about the religious unity of Russia.

[1] Skvortsov, *Zakony o raskolnikakh* (Laws concerning the Raskolniki), Moscow, 1903, p. 166, cited by Aurel. Palmieri, *La Chiesa Russa*, Firenze, 1908, to whom I am much indebted in this section.

Pobiedonostsev's Philosophy of Reaction

Konstantine Petrovich Pobiedonostsev, tutor and adviser to the last two Romanov tsars, affiliate of the Pan-Slavs and Procurator-General of the Holy Synod, possessed considerable power and great influence upon the Russian government of his day. The outstanding Russian protagonist of the theory and the practice of extreme conservatism, Pobiedonostsev was cordially detested by all Russian liberals as a black reactionary. Certainly his influence on both Alexander III and Nicholas II was staunchly anti-liberal and anti-democratic. An able scholar, he was the leading philosopher of reaction. The following passages are typical of his views and his teachings. The source is: K. P. Pobyedonostseff (R. C. Long, Tr.), *Reflections of a Russian Statesman.* London: Grant Richards, 1898. *Passim et seriatim.* (The original Russian edition was titled, *Moscow Conversations.*)

For, however powerful the State may be, its power is based alone upon identity of religious profession with the people; the faith of the people sustains it; when discord once appears to weaken this identity, its foundations are sapped, its power dissolves away. In spiritual sympathy with its rulers a people may bear many heavy burdens, may concede much, and surrender many of its privileges and rights. In one domain alone the State must not demand concession, or the people concede, and that is the domain where every believer, and all *together, sink the foundations* of their spiritual existence and bind themselves with eternity. There are depths in this domain to which the secular power dare not, and must not, descend, lest it strike at the roots of faith in each and all.

. . .

The oldest and most familiar system of relationship of Church to State is the system of Established or State Churches. Out of the multitude of religions, the State adopts and recognizes as the true faith one, which it maintains and protects exclusively, to the prejudice of all remaining Churches and religions. This prejudice in general means that the remaining Churches are not recognised as true, or entirely true, but practically it is expressed in many forms, with innumerable shadows, from non-recognition and alienation to persecution. In all cases where this system is in force the estranged faiths submit to more or less diminution in honour and prerogative as compared with the established faith. The State must not be the representative of the material interests of society alone; were it so, it would deprive itself of religious forces and would abandon its spiritual community with the people. The stronger will the State be, the more important in the eyes of the masses, the more firmly it stands as their spiritual representative.

Under these conditions alone will the sentiment of respect for the law, and of confidence in the power of the State, be maintained and strengthened among the people. No considerations for the safety of the State, for its prosperity and advantage, no moral principle even, is itself sufficient to strengthen the bonds between the people and its rulers; for the moral principle is never steadfast, and it loses its fundamental base when it is bereft of the sanction of religion. This force of cohesion will, without doubt, be lost to the State which, in the name of impartial relationship to every religious belief, cuts itself loose from all. The confidence of the people in its rulers is founded on faith—that is, not only on identity of religious profession, but on the simple conviction that its rulers have faith themselves and rule according to it. Even the heathen and Mahometan peoples have more confidence and respect for a Government which stands on the firm principles of faith—whatever that faith may be—than for a Government which acknowledges no faith, and is indifferent to all.

. . . The system of a "Free Church in a Free State" is founded on abstract principles and hypotheses. It embodies not the principle of belief, but the principle of religious indifferentism, and it is associated with doctrines which inculcate, not tolerance and respect, but a manifest or tacit contempt for religion, as an outworn factor of the psychical development of individual and national life. In the abstract conception of this system, which is the product of the latest rationalism, the Church appears as a political institution of abstract construction, with a definite aim; or as a private corporation established likewise with a definite aim, as other corporations recognised by the State. The conception of this aim is abstract also, for on it are reflected the diverse shades associated with one or the other conception of religion, from abstract respect for religion, as the highest element of psychical life, to fanatical contempt for it as the basest factor, and as an element of danger and disintegration. Thus, in the construction of this system we see at the first balance the ambiguity and indistinctness of its fundamental principles and propositions.

. . . Thus the free State may decree that the free Church concerns it not; but the free Church, if it be truly founded on faith, will not accept this proposition, and will not endure indifferent relations to the free State. The Church cannot abdicate its influence on civil and social life, and the greater its activity—the stronger its consciousness of internal working forces, the less is it possible for it to tolerate indifferent relations to the State; nor can such relations be tolerated if the Church is not to abjure its duties and abandon its divine mission. On the Church lies the duty of teaching and direction. To the Church pertains the administration of the sacraments, and the performance of ceremonies associated with the gravest acts of civil life. In this activity the Church of necessity is brought into constant contact with public and civil life: of this, marriage and education are sufficient instances. Thus, as the State, denying the Church, assumes control exclusively of the civil part of such affairs and renounces all authority in the spiritual-religious part, the Church assumes the functions surrendered by the State, and, in separation from it, takes possession, little by little but fully and exclusively, of those moral and religious influences which constitute for the State an indispensable element of strength. The State remains master alone of material and, it may be, of intellectual forces, but both one and the other are vain when unsupported by the forces of faith. Little by little, therefore, instead of the imagined equality of influence of the State and Church in a political alliance, inequality and antagonism appear. The position in any case is an abnormal one, which must lead either to the predominance of the Church over the apparently dominant State, or to revolution.

Such are the hidden dangers of the system, so lauded by Liberal theorists, of severance of Church and State. The system of State or Established Churches has many defects, many inconveniences, and many difficulties; it does not preclude the possibility of antagonism or conflict. But it is absurd to suppose that it has outlived its time, and that the formula of Cavour is the only key to the solution of all the difficulties of the most difficult of questions. The formula of Cavour is the fruit of that political doctrinarianism which regards all questions of faith merely as political questions of the equalisation of rights. It lacks spiritual insight, as lacked it another famous political formula, Liberty, Equality, and Fraternity, which to the present day weighs upon superficial minds with a fatal burden. In both cases the passionate apostles of freedom mistake in assuming freedom in equality. Bitter experience has proven a hundred times that freedom does not depend from equality, and that equality is in no wise freedom. It is equally absurd to believe that the equalisation of Churches and religions before the State must result in freedom of belief. The history of modern times demonstrates that freedom and equality are not identical, and that freedom in no way depends from equality.

What is this freedom by which so many minds are agitated, which inspires so many insensate actions, so many wild speeches, which leads the people so often to misfortune? In the democratic sense of the word, freedom is the right of political power, or, to express it otherwise, the right to participate in the government of the State. This universal aspiration for a share in government has no constant limitations, and seeks no definite issue, but incessantly extends, so that we might apply to it the words of the ancient poet about dropsy: *crescit indulgens sibi*. For ever extending its base, the new Democracy now aspires to universal suffrage—a fatal error, and one of the most remarkable in the history of mankind. By this means, the political power so passionately demanded by Democracy would be shattered into a number of infinitesimal bits, of which each citizen acquires a single one. What will he do with it, then? how will he employ it? In the result it has undoubtedly been shown that in the attainment of this aim Democracy violates its sacred formula of "Freedom indissolubly joined with Equality." It is shown that this apparently equal distribution of "freedom" among all involves the total destruction of equality. Each vote, representing an inconsiderable fragment of power, by itself signifies nothing; an aggregation of votes alone has a relative value. The result may be likened to the general meetings of shareholders in public companies. By themselves individuals are ineffective, but he who controls a number of these fragmentary forces is master of all power, and directs all decisions and dispositions. We may well ask in what consists the superiority of Democracy. Everywhere the strongest man becomes master of the State; sometimes a fortunate and resolute general, sometimes a monarch or administrator with knowledge, dexterity, a clear plan of action, and a determined will. In a Democracy, the real rulers are the dexterous manipulators of votes, with their placemen, the mechanics who so skilfully operate the hidden springs which move the puppets in the arena of democratic elections. Men of this kind are ever ready with loud speeches lauding equality; in reality, they rule the people as any despot or military dictator might rule it. The extension of the right to participate in elections is regarded as progress and as the conquest of freedom by democratic theorists, who hold that the more numerous the participants in political rights, the greater is the probability that all will employ this right in the interests of the public welfare, and for the increase of the freedom of the people. Experience proves a very different thing. The history of mankind bears witness that the most necessary and fruitful reforms—the most durable measures—emanated from the supreme will of statesmen, or from a minority enlightened by lofty ideas and deep knowledge, and that, on the contrary, the extension of the representative principle is accompanied by an abasement of political ideas and the vulgarisation of opinions in the mass of the electors. It shows also that this extension—in great States—was inspired by secret aims to the centralization of power, or led directly to dictatorship. In France, universal suffrage was suppressed with the end of the Terror, and was re-established twice merely to affim the autocracy of the two Napoleons. In Germany, the establishment of universal suffrage served merely to strengthen the high authority of a famous statesman who had acquired popularity by the success of his policy. What its ultimate consequences will be, Heaven only knows!

Among the falsest of political principles is the principle of the sovereignty of the people, the principle that all power issues from the people, and is based upon the national will—a principle which has unhappily become more firmly established since the time of the French Revolution. Thence proceeds the theory of Parliamentarism, which, up to the present day, has deluded much of the so-called "intelligence," and unhappily infatuated certain foolish Russians. It continues to maintain its hold on many minds with the obstinacy of a narrow fanaticism, although every day its falsehood is exposed more clearly to the world.

In what does the theory of Parliamentarism consist? It is supposed that the people in its assemblies makes its own laws, and elects responsible officers to execute its will. Such is the ideal conception. Its immediate realisation is impossible. The historical development of society necessitates that local communities increase in numbers and complexity; that separate races be assimilated, or, retaining their polities and languages, unite under a single flag, that territory extend indefinitely: under such conditions direct government by the people is impracticable. The people must, therefore, delegate its right of power to its representatives, and invest them with administrative autonomy. These representatives in turn cannot govern immediately, but are compelled to elect a still smaller number of trustworthy persons—ministers—to whom they entrust the preparation and execution of the laws, the apportionment and collection of taxes, the appointment of subordinate officials, and the disposition of the militant forces.

In the abstract this mechanism is quite symmetrical: for its proper operation many conditions are essential. The working of the political machine is based on impersonal forces constantly acting and completely balanced. It may act successfully only when the delegates of the people abdicate their personalities; when on the benches of Parliament sit mechanical fulfillers of the people's behests; when the ministers of State remain impersonal, absolute executors of the will of the majority; when the elected representatives of the people are capable of understanding precisely, and executing conscientiously, the programme of activity, mathematically expressed, which has been delivered to them. Given such conditions the machine would work exactly, and would accomplish its purpose. The law would actually embody the will of the people! administrative measures would actually emanate from Parliament; the pillars of the State would rest actually on the elective assemblies, and each citizen would directly and consciously participate in the management of public affairs.

Such is the theory. Let us look at the practice. Even in the classic countries of Parliamentarism it would satisfy not one of the conditions enumerated. The elections in no way express the will of the electors. The popular representatives are in no way restricted by the opinions of their constituents, but are guided by their own views and considerations, modified by the tactics of their opponents. In reality, ministers are autocratic, and they rule, rather than are ruled by, Parliament. They attain power, and lose power, not by virtue of the will of the people, but through immense personal influence, or the influence of a strong party which places them in power, or drives them from it. They dispose of the force and resources of the nation at will, they grant immunities and favours, they maintain a multitude of idlers at the expense of the people, and they fear no censure while they enjoy the support in Parliament of a majority which they maintain by the distribution of bounties from the rich tables which the State has put at their disposal. In reality, the ministers are as irresponsible as the representatives of the people. Mistakes, abuse of power, and arbitrary acts, are of daily occurrence, yet how often do we hear of the grave responsibility of a minister? It may be once in fifty years a minister is tried for his crimes, with a result contemptible when compared with the celebrity gained by the solemn procedure. . . .

Thus the representative principle works in practice. The ambitious man comes before his fellow-citizens, and strives by every means to convince them that he more than any other is worthy of their confidence. What motives impel him to this quest? It is hard to believe that he is impelled by disinterested zeal for the public good. . . .

On the day of polling few give their votes intelligently; these are the individuals, influential electors whom it has been worth while to convince in private. The mass of electors, after the practice of the herd, votes for one of the candidates nominated by the committees. Not one exactly knows the man, or considers his character, his capacity, his convictions; all vote merely because they have heard his name so often. It would be vain to struggle against this herd. If a level-headed elector wished to act intelligently in such a grave affair, and not to give way to the violence of the committee, he would have to abstain altogether, or to give his vote for his candidate according to his conviction. However he might act, he could not prevent the election of the candidate favoured by the mass of frivolous, indifferent, and prejudiced electors.

In theory, the elected candidate must be the favourite of the majority;

in fact, he is the favourite of a minority, sometimes very small, but representing an organised force, while the majority, like sand, has no coherence, and is therefore incapable of resisting the clique and the faction. In theory, the election favours the intelligent and capable; in reality, it favours the pushing and impudent. It might be thought that education, experience, conscientiousness in work, and wisdom in affairs, would be essential requirements in the candidate; in reality, whether these qualities exist or not, they are in no way needed in the struggle of the election, where the essential qualities are audacity, a combination of impudence and oratory, and even some vulgarity, which invariably acts on the masses; modesty, in union with delicacy of feeling and thought, is worth nothing. . . .

. . . What is a Parliamentary party? In theory, it is an alliance of men with common convictions, joining forces for the realisation of their views in legislation and administration. But this description applies only to small parties; the large party, which alone is an effective force in Parliament, is formed under the influence only of personal ambition, and centres itself around one commanding personality. By nature, men are divided into two classes—those who tolerate no power above them, and therefore of necessity strive to rule others; and those who by their nature dread the responsibility inseparable from independent action, and who shrink from any resolute exercise of will. These were born for submission, and together constitute a herd, which follows the men of will and resolution, who form the minority. Thus the most talented persons submit willingly, and gladly entrust to stronger hands the control of affairs and the moral responsibility for their direction. Instinctively they seek a leader, and become his obedient instruments, inspired by the conviction that he will lead them to victory —and, often, to spoil. Thus all the important actions of Parliament are controlled by the leaders of the party, who inspire all decision, who lead in combat, and profit by victory. The public sessions are no more than a spectacle for the mass. Speeches are delivered to sustain the fiction of Parliamentarism, but seldom a speech by itself affects the decision of Parliament in a grave affair. Speechmaking serves for the glory of orators, for the increase of their popularity, and the making of their careers; only on rare occasions does it affect the distribution of votes. Majorities and minorities are usually decided before the session begins. Such is the complicated mechanism of the Parliamentary farce; such is the great political lie which dominates our age. . . .

Such is the Parliamentary institution, exalted as the summit and crown of the edifice of State. It is sad to think that even in Russia there are men who aspire to the establishment of this falsehood among us; that out professors glorify to their young pupils representative government as the ideal of political science; that our newspapers pursue it in their articles and feuilletons, under the name of justice and order, without troubling to examine without prejudice the working of the parliamentary machine. Yet even where centuries have sanctified its existence, faith already decays; the Liberal intelligence exalts it, but the people groans under its despotism, and recognizes its falsehood. We may not see, but our children and grandchildren assuredly will see, the overthrow of this idol, which contemporary thought in its vanity continues still to worship. . . .

. . . In our age the judgment of others has assumed an organised form, and calls itself Public Opinion. Its organ and representative is the Press. In truth, the importance of the Press is immense, and may be regarded as the most characteristic fact of our time—more characteristic even than our remarkable discoveries and inventions in the realm of technical science. No government, no law, no custom can withstand its destructive activity when, from day to day, through the course of years, the Press repeats and disseminates among the people its condemnations of institutions or of men.

What is the secret of this strength? Certainly not the novelties and sensations with which the newspaper is filled, but its declared policy—the political and philosophical ideas propagated in its articles, selection and classification of its news and rumours, and the peculiar illumination which it casts upon them. The newspaper has usurped the position of judicial observer of the events of the day; it judges not only the actions and words of men, but affects a knowledge of their unexpressed opinions, their intentions, and their enterprises; it praises and condemns at discretion; it incites some, threatens others; drags to the pillory one, and others exalts as idols to be adored and examples worthy of the emulation of all. In the name of Public Opinion it bestows rewards on some, and punishes others with the severity of excommunication. The question naturally occurs: Who are these representatives of this terrible power, Public Opinion? Whence is derived their right and authority to rule in the name of the community, to demolish existing institutions, and to proclaim new ideals of ethics and legislation?

But no one attempts to answer this question; all talk loudly of the liberty of the Press as the first and essential element of social well-being. Even in Russia, so libelled by the lying Press of Europe, such words are heard. Our so-called Slavophiles, with amazing inconsistency, share the same delusion, although their avowed object is to reform and renovate the institutions of their country upon a historic basis. Having joined the chorus of Liberals, in alliance with the propagandists of revolution, they proclaim exactly in the manner of the West: "Public Opinion—that is, the collective thought, guided by the natural love of right in all—is the final judge in all matters of public interest; therefore no restriction upon freedom of speech can be allowed, for such restriction can only express the tyranny of the minority over the will of the mass."

Such is a current proposition of the newest Liberalism. It is accepted by many in good faith, and there are few who, having troubled to analyse it, have discerned how it is based upon falsehood and self-deception.

It conflicts with the first principles of logic, for it is based on the fallacious premise that the opinions of the public and of the Press are identical.

To test the validity of this claim, it is only needful to consider the origin of newspapers, and the characters of their makers.

Any vagabond babbler or unacknowledged genius, any enterprising tradesman, with his own money or with the money of others, may found a newspaper, even a great newspaper. He may attract a host of writers and feuilletonists, ready to deliver judgment on any subject at a moment's notice; he may hire illiterate reporters to keep him supplied with rumours and scandals. His staff is then complete. From that day he sits in judgment on all the world, on ministers and administrators, on literature and art, on finance and industry. . . .

This phenomenon is worthy of close inspection, for we find in it the most incongruous product of modern culture, the more incongruous where the principles of the new Liberalism have taken root, where the sanction of election, the authority of the popular will, is needed for every institution, where the ruling power is vested in the hands of individuals, and derived from the suffrages of the majority in the representative assemblies. For the journalist with a power comprehending all things, requires no sanction. He derives his authority from no election, he receives support from no one. His newspaper becomes an authority in the State, and for this authority no endorsement is required. The man in the street may establish such an organ and exercise the concomitant authority with an irresponsibility enjoyed by no other power in the world. That this is in no way exaggeration there are innumerable proofs. How often have superficial and unscrupulous journalists paved the way for revolution, fomented irritation into enmity, and brought about desolating wars! For conduct such as this a monarch would lose his throne, a minister would be disgraced, impeached, and punished; but the journalist stands dry above the waters he has disturbed, from the ruin he has caused he rises triumphant, and briskly continues his destructive work.

This is by no means the worst. When a judge has power to dishonour us, to deprive us of our property and of our freedom, he receives his power from the hands of the State only after such prolonged labour and experience as qualify him for his calling. His power is restricted by rigourous laws, his judgments are subject to revision by higher powers, and his sentence may be altered or commuted. The journalist has the fullest power to defame and dishonour me, to injure my material interests, even to restrict my liberty by attacks which force me to leave my place of abode. These judicial powers he has usurped; no higher authority has conferred them upon him; he has never proven by examination his fitness to exercise them; he has in no way shown his trustworthiness or his impartiality; his court is ruled by no formal procedure; and from his judgment there lies no appeal.

. . . In human souls there exists a force of moral gravity which draws them one to another; and which, made manifest in the spiritual interaction of souls, answers an organic need. Without this force mankind would be as a heap of sand, without any bond, dispersed by every wind on every side. By this inherent force, without preparatory accord, are men united in society. It impels them out of the crowd of men to seek for leaders with whom to commune, whom to obey, and whose direction to seek. Inspired by a moral principle, this instinct acquires the value of a creative force, uniting and elevating the people to worthy deeds and to great endurance.

But for the purposes of civil society this free and accidental interaction is not enough. The natural instinct of man seeks for power in unbroken activity, to which the mass, with its varied needs, aspirations, and passions may submit; through which it may acquire the impulse of activity, and the principles of order; in which it may find amid all the subversions of wilfulness a standard of truth. Thus, by its nature, power is founded on truth, and inasmuch as truth has as its source the All-High God and His commandments written indelibly in the consciences of all, we find a justification in their deeper meaning of the words, "there is no power but of God."

These words are addressed to subjects, but they apply with equal force to power itself, and O, that all power might recognise their import! Power is great and terrible, because it is a sacred thing. This word *sacred* (*svyastchennui*) in its primitive signification means *elect* (*otdyelennui*), dedicated to the service of God. Thus, power exists not for itself alone, but for the love of God; it is a service to which men are dedicated. Thence comes the limitless, terrible strength of power, and its limitless and terrible burden.

Its strength is unlimited, not in the material acceptation of the word, but in its spiritual meaning, because it is the strength of reason and of creation. The first act of creation was the appearance of the light and its separation from darkness. Thus, the first act of power must be the finding of truth and its discrimination from falsehood; on this is founded the faith of the people in power, and the gravitation towards it of all mankind. Many times and everywhere this faith has been deceived, but its fount remains intact, and cannot dry up, because without truth no man can live. From this also springs the creative force of power, the strength to attract just and rational men, to animate them and to inspire them to work and to great deeds. To power belongs the first and last word—it is the alpha and omega of human activity.

While humanity exists it will not cease to suffer, sometimes from power, sometimes from impotence. The violence, the abuse, the folly and selfishness of power raise rebellion. Deceived by their ideals of power, men seek to dispense with it, and to replace it by the authority of the law. This is a vain fancy. In the name of the law arise a multitude of unauthorised factions, which struggle for power, and the distribution of power leads to violence worse than that which went before. Thus poor humanity, searching for an ideal organisation, is borne on the waves of an infinite sea, without a guide, without a harbour in sight.

To live without power is impossible. After the need of communion the need of power is of all feelings most deeply rooted in the spiritual nature of man. Since the day duality entered into his soul, since the day the knowledge of good and evil was vouchsafed to him, and the love of good and justice rose in his soul in eternal conflict with evil and injustice, for him there has been no salvation save to seek sustenance and reconciliation in a high judge of this conflict; in a living incarnation of the principle of order and of truth. And, whatever may be the disenchantment, the betrayal, the afflictions which humanity has suffered from power, while men shall yearn for good and truth, and remember their helplessness and duality, they can never cease to believe in the ideal of power, and to repeat their efforts for its realisation. Today, as in ancient times, the foolish say in their hearts: There is no God, no truth, no good, no evil; and gather around them pupils equally foolish, proclaiming atheism and anarchy. But the great mass of mankind stands firm in its faith in the supreme principle of life, and, through tears and bloodshed, as the blind seeking a guide, seeks for power with imperishable hope, notwithstanding eternal betrayal and disillusion.

Thus the work of power is a work of uninterrupted usefulness, and in reality a work of renunciation. How strange these words must seem beside the current conception of power! It is natural, it would seem, for men to flee and to avoid renunciation. Yet all seek power, all aspire to it; for power men strive together, they resort to crime, they destroy one another, and when they attain power they rejoice and triumph. Power seeks to exalt itself, and words pass through our heads as something in no way concerning us, as yet the immutable, only true ideal of power is embodied in the words of Christ: "Whosoever of you will be the chiefest shall be servant of all." These words pass through our heads as something in no way concerning us, as especially addressed to a vanished community in Palestine. In reality, they apply to all power, however great, which, in the depth of conscience, does not recognise that the higher its throne, the wider the sphere of its activity, the heavier must become its fetters, the more widely must open before it the roll of social evils, stained by the weeping of pity and woe, and the louder must sound the crying and sobbing of injustice which demands redress. The first necessity of power is faith in itself and in its mission. Happy is power when this faith is combined with a recognition of duty and of moral responsibility! Unhappy is it when it lacks this consciousness and leans upon itself alone! Then begins the decay which leads to loss of faith, and in the end to disintegration and destruction.

Power is the depository of truth, and needs, above all things, men of truth, of clear intellects, of strong understandings, and of sincere speech, who know the limits of yes and no, and never transcend them, whose thoughts develop clearly in their minds, and are clearly expressed by their words. Men of this nature only are the firm support of power, and its faithful delegates. Happy is the power which can distinguish such men, appreciate their merit, and firmly sustain them! Unhappy is the power which wearies of such natures, promoting men of complaisant character, flexible opinions, and flattering tongues!

.   .   .

Men in authority must always remember the dignity of power. Dignity once forgotten, power decays, and relations to subordinates are falsified. With dignity is coincident, and should be inseparable, that simplicity which is necessary to impel subordinates to work, to inspire them with interest in their duties, and to maintain with them sincerity of relations. The consciousness of dignity engenders also freedom in relations to men. Power must be free within the limits of the law; being conscious of its worth, it need not consider the appearance it makes, the impressions it creates, or the conduct it should observe in its relations to men. But the consciousness of merit must be inseparable from the recognition of duty; as the recognition of duty is enfeebled, the consciousness of merit swells, till, swollen beyond measure, it degenerates to a disease which may be called the hypertrophy of power. As this disease advances on its course, power may fall into a moral obscurity, in which it considers itself as independent and as existing for itself alone. Then begins the disintegration of power.

While preserving the dignity of power, authority must not forget that it serves as a mirror and example for all its subordinates. As the man in authority conducts himself, so those who will succeed him are preparing to conduct themselves in their relations to others, in their methods of work, in their regard for their work, in their tastes, in their standards of propriety and impropriety. It would be wrong to imagine that power, when it takes off its robe of authority, may without danger mingle in the daily life of the crowd in the fair of human vanity.

Nevertheless, while cherishing his dignity, the leader must as steadfastly guard the dignity of his subordinates. His relations to them must be founded on trustfulness, for, in the absence of trustfulness, there can be no moral bond between him and them. He is a foolish man who fancies that he can know and judge all things without intermediaries and independently of the knowledge and experience of his subordinates; who wishes to decide all questions by his word and command, without recourse to the thoughts and opinions of those who stand directly beneath him. Such men, recognising their helplessness without the knowledge and experience of their subordinates, often end by becoming altogether dependent upon them. Still worse is the case of the leader who falls into the fatal habit of tolerating no objections or contradictions; and this is the attribute not only of narrow minds, but often of able and energetic, but vain and over-confident men. A conscientious worker must avoid everything absolute and arbitrary in his decision, the fruit of these is indifference—the poison of democracy. Power must never forget that papers and reports represent living men and living works, and that life itself demands and expects decisions and directions which conform with its nature. Truth must be in the leader himself, in his sincere, conscientious and practical views of work, and truth also corresponding to the social, moral, and economic conditions of the national life and the national history. Such truth is absent where the ruling principle of power is abstract theory, detached from life with its manifold conditions and needs.

The wider the field of the activity of the leader, the more complex the mechanism of government, the more he needs subordinates capable of work, and able to combine in single directions to a common end. Men are needed in all times and by all governments, but perhaps more than ever today. In our time governments must consider a multitude of forces now rising and affirming themselves—in science, in literature, in the criticism of public opinion, in social institutions with their independent interests. Ability to find and to choose men is the first essential attribute to power;

the second is ability to direct them and to establish due discipline upon their activity.

Alexander III as Seen by Witte

The outstanding Russian statesman of the late nineteenth and early twentieth centuries was Count Sergius Witte who served both Tsar Alexander III and Tsar Nicholas II. Nicholas did not like Witte whom he considered to be an unscrupulous and ambitious trouble-maker. Witte, on his part, held an exceedingly poor opinion of Nicholas and compared him most unfavorably with Alexander III whom he admired enormously. Here is Witte's description of his tsar-hero. The source is: Avrahm Yarmolinsky (Ed. and Tr.), *Memoirs of Count Witte*. Garden City: Doubleday, Page and Co., 1921. Pp. 37–41. (This is a one-volume abridgment of the original three-volume Russian version.)

The unfortunate brevity of Alexander III's reign, thirteen years in all, did not prevent the full growth and display of his noble, outstanding personality, to which the whole world paid homage on the day of his death. His Russian contemporaries and the succeeding generation did not highly esteem him, however, and many looked upon his reign with a scorn altogether unjustifiable, especially in view of the unhappy conditions of his youth and the deplorable circumstances under which he ascended the throne.

To begin with, his education and training were largely neglected, since the older brother, Nicholas, was the heir apparent during that period of Alexander's life. In addition, the family environment was unfavourable. The future emperor's sensitive moral feelings were grievously hurt by his father's late re-marriage at the age of sixty, when he already had numerous grown-up children and even grand-children. Then his uncompromising honesty was outraged by the prevalence in higher Government circles of a traffic in privileges and concessions to mercantile associations and particularly by the implication of Alexander II's morganatic wife, Princess Yuryevski, in this barter.

Consider, too, the unpropitious national situation. Having turned his back upon reform during the latter part of his reign, the Great Liberator (Alexander II) drove the liberals into the ranks of the revolutionists, so that when the heir apparent began to take an interest in politics, he was confronted with the existence of an extremely radical party and strongly impressed, therefore, with the necessity of stern measures to suppress subversive movements. The Heir was encouraged in this attitude by his preceptor, Pobiedonostzev.

Alexander III was undeniably a man of limited education. I cannot agree, however, with those who would class him as unintelligent. Though lacking perhaps in mental keenness, he was undoubtedly gifted with the broad sympathetic understanding which in a ruler is often far more important than rational brilliancy.

Neither in the Imperial family nor among the nobility was there anyone who better appreciated the value of a ruble or a kopeck than Emperor Alexander III. He made an ideal treasurer for the Russian people, and his economical temperament was of incalculable assistance in the solution of Russia's financial problems. Had not the Emperor doggedly warded off the incessant raids upon the Russian treasury and checked the ever-present impulse to squander the public funds accumulated by the sweat and blood of the people, Vyshnegradski and myself could never have succeeded in putting the nation back upon its feet financially.

Alexander III's prudence in government expenditures was matched by his personal thrift. Abhorring luxury and lavish spending, he led an extremely simple life. When he grew tired of his own table, he would ask for a common soldier's or a hunter's meal. This economy was sometimes carried too far. The Imperial table was always relatively poor, and the food served at the Court Marshal's board was sometimes such as to endanger the health. Alexander III was extremely economical with his wearing apparel. I had a curious proof of this when I accompanied the Emperor on one of his railway trips. Since I found it impossible, on account of my responsibility, to sleep of nights, I would often catch glimpses of His Majesty's valet mending the Emperor's trousers. On one occasion I asked him why he didn't give his master a new pair instead of mending the old so often. "Well, I would rather have it that way," he answered, "but His Majesty won't let me. He insists on wearing his garments until they are threadbare. It is the same with his boots. Not only does he wear them as long as possible, but he refuses to put on expensive ones. If I should bring him patent leather boots, he would angrily throw them out of the window." The Emperor's dislike of the expensive included gorgeous rooms. For this reason he never stayed at the Winter Palace, but always occupied the unpretentious quarters of Anichkov or Gatchina. There he took small rooms and lived frugally. He tolerated the Court's luxury as an unavoidable formality, but he always longed for a different mode of existence and created it for himself in his private life.

The entire Imperial family respected and feared Alexander III, who wielded the influence of a veritable patriarch. He believed that the royal family must set a moral example for the whole nation both in their private and social life. In his time dissolute conduct by Russian Grand Dukes in foreign countries, so common now, was very rare. Transgressing members of the Imperial family were sure to incur the Emperor's heavy displeasure. Remarriage was severely frowned upon in the case of anybody connected with the Government.

Alexander III himself led an unimpeachable life and his family was a splendid example of the old-fashioned, godfearing Russian type. He was a stern father and while the children did not fear him, they were uneasy and constrained in his presence with the single exception of Mikhail, the favourite son, who was not only unrestrained, but even inclined to take liberties, as the following amusing anecdote, related to me by his valet, will indicate. Becoming impatient at the boy's impertinence and inattention during a stroll in the gardens early one Summer morning, Alexander III snatched up a watering hose and gave Mikhail a good dousing. Without further ado they went in to breakfast, the youth changing his drenched clothing. After that the Emperor retired to work in his study and as usual indulged in his habit of occasionally leaning out of the window, but was met with an altogether unusual deluge from the upper window, where Misha had stationed himself with a pailful of water in anticipation of the Imperial appearance fenestral. There is very little doubt that none but Mikhail would have dared to think of such a stratagem, and there is no doubt whatsoever that nobody else could have executed it with impunity.

As a ruler, Alexander III made important contribution to the welfare and prosperity of his subjects and the international prestige of the empire. In the first place, he practically reconstructed the army, which had been thrown into a state of serious disorganization by the war with Turkey in the seventies. During the time that I was Director of Railways and later Minister of that department under Alexander III, railroad building, which had practically ceased some years before, was resumed with excellent results and plans were laid for future development. Alexander III also made possible the financial rehabilitation of Russia, in which I had the honor of participation as Minister of Finances. His salutary influence in this matter extended beyond his reign. In fact, it was only due to this that I was able to retain my position eight years after his death and thus complete the work, for Nicholas III was incapable of appreciating my endeavours and simply relied upon his deceased father's confidence in me.

The Trans-Siberian Railway

Witte's Account

> Sergius Witte served his country well. Among other things, he stabilized the currency, introduced the gold standard, induced foreign investors to lend huge sums of money to Russia, and was, in a manner of speaking, the father of the Russian Industrial Revolution. One of his most spectacular accomplishments was the Trans-Siberian Railroad. In the following excerpts from his *Memoirs* Witte tells of the beginnings of the undertaking and describes the moves which preceded the building of Chinese Eastern cut-off. It may be remarked that Witte was shrewd as well as able, scheming and tricky as well as vigorous, and, as these excerpts show, not at all lacking in vanity. The source is: Yarmolinsky (Ed.), *Memoirs*, pp. 52–54, 86–87, 89–90, 94–95.

It will not be an exaggeration to say that the vast enterprise of constructing the great Siberian Railway was carried out owing to my efforts, supported, of course first by Emperor Alexander III, and then by Emperor Nicholas II. The idea of connecting European Russia with Vladivostok by rail was one of the most cherished dreams of Alexander III. He spoke to me about it in the course of one of my first conferences with him following my appointment as Minister of Ways of Communication. As is known, Czarevitch Nicholas, the present Emperor, during his trip through the Far East, inaugurated, on May 19, 1891, the construction of the Ussurian Railroad, connecting Vladivostok with Khabarovsk. The Emperor complained that in spite of his efforts, which extended over ten years, his dream had failed to materialize owing to the opposition of the Committee of Ministers and the Imperial Council. He took my promise that I would bend my energies to the accomplishment of his desire.

In my capacity of Minister of Ways of Communication and later as Minister of Finances, both during the reign of Alexander III and afterwards, I persistently advocated the idea of the necessity of constructing the great Siberian Railway. As much as the former Ministers thwarted the plan, so I, remembering my promise to the Emperor, sought to advance it. As Minister of Finances, I was in a peculiarly favourable position with regard to furthering the project, for what was most needed for the construction of the railway was money. Had I remained Minister of Ways of Communication, I would have had to face the opposition of the Minister of Finances.

I devoted myself body and soul to the task, yet Emperor Alexander III did not live to see the realization of his dream, and it was only under Nicholas II that the immense railroad was completed. I was aided by the circumstance that the young Emperor took a personal interest in the matter. At my instance, while his father was still alive, he was appointed head of the Siberian Railroad Committee, which I had formed to promote the construction of the railroad. This committee was empowered to eliminate all manner of unnecessary delay and had the authority over both the administrative and the legislative matters involved in the construction. For the young heir-apparent this task was something in the nature of a preparatory school of statesmanship. He worked under the guidance of the vice president of the committee, Bunge, who was also his tutor. This was a very happy arrangement. The future ruler took his appointment in earnest and worked with enthusiasm. When he became Emperor, he retained the title of President of the Siberian Committee and did not lose his interest in the matter. This enabled me to complete the work within a few years.

. . .

In the meantime the great Trans-Siberian Railway, which was under construction, had reached Transbaikalia and the question arose as to the further direction which the railroad should follow. I conceived the idea of building the road straight across Chinese territory, principally Mongolia and northern Manchuria, on toward Vladivostok. This direction, I calculated, would considerably shorten the line and facilitate its construction. Considering the enormous mileage of the Trans-Siberian, it was natural to seek to shorten the route. Technically the Amur section presented great difficulties. Besides, the road would run along the Amur River and would thus compete with the Amur steamship companies. The Manchurian route would save 514 versts. In comparison to the Amur region this section also possessed the advantage of a more productive soil and a more favourable climate. The problem was how to get China's permission for this plan, by peaceful means based on mutual commercial interests. The idea appealed to me strongly and I found occasion to draw His Majesty's attention to it. The court physician, Badmayev, a Buriat by birth, who wielded a considerable influence over the Emperor, on the contrary, stood for the Kyakhta-Peking direction. I could not sympathize with his project, first, because I considered Vladivostok as the most desirable terminus for the Trans-Siberian, and, second, because I believed that a railroad to Peking would arouse the whole of Europe against us. It must be borne in mind that the great originator of the Trans-Siberian had no political or military designs in connection with the road. It was an enterprise of a purely economic nature. Alexander III wished to establish communication by the shortest possible route between the distant Maritime Province and Central Russia. Strategically, both Alexander III and his successor attributed a strictly defensive importance to the road. Under no circumstance was the Trans-Siberian to serve as a means for territorial expansion.

· · ·

In my conferences with Li Hung Chang I dwelt on the services which we had recently done to his country. I assured him that, having proclaimed the principle of China's territorial integrity, we intended to adhere to it in the future; but, to be able to uphold this principle, I argued, we must be in a position, in case of emergency, to render China armed assistance. Such aid we would not be able to render her until both European Russia and Vladivostok were connected with China by rail, our armed forces being concentrated in European Russia. I called to his attention the fact that although during China's war with Japan we did dispatch some detachments from Vladivostok, they moved so slowly, because of the absence of railroad communication, that when they reached Kirin the war was over. Thus I argued that to uphold the territorial integrity of the Chinese Empire, it was necessary for us to have a railroad running along the shortest possible route to Vladivostok, across the northern part of Mongolia and Manchuria. I also pointed out to Li Hung Chang that the projected railway would raise the productivity of our possessions and the Chinese territories it would cross. Finally I declared, Japan was likely to assume a favourable attitude toward the road, for it would link her with Western Europe, whose civilization she had lately adopted.

Naturally enough, Li Hung Chang raised objections. Nevertheless, I gathered from my talks with him that he would agree to my proposal if he were certain that our Emperor wished it. Therefore, I asked His Majesty to receive Li Hung Chang, which the Emperor did. I was practically a private audience and it passed unnoticed by the press. As a result of my negotiations with the Chinese statesman, we agreed on the following three provisions of a secret pact to be concluded between Russia and China:

(1) The Chinese Empire grants us permission to build a railroad within its territory along a straight line between Chita and Vladivostok, but the road must be in the hands of a private corporation. Li Hung Chang

absolutely refused to accept my proposal that the road should be either constructed or owned by the Treasury. For that reason we were forced to form a private corporation, the so-called Eastern Chinese Railroad Corporation. This body is, of course, completely in the hands of the Government, but since nominally it is a private corporation, it is within the jurisdiction of the Ministry of Finances.

(2) China agrees to cede us a strip of land sufficient for the construction and operation of the railway. Within that territory the corporation is permitted to have its own police and to exercise full and untrammelled authority. China takes upon herself no responsibilities with regard to the construction or operation of the road.

(3) The two countries obligate themselves to defend each other in case Japan attacks the territory of China or our Far-Eastern maritime possessions.

I reported the results of my negotiations to His Majesty and he instructed me to take up the matter with the Foreign Minister. I explained to Prince Lobanov-Rostovski that I had come to an oral agreement with Li Hung Chang regarding the provisions of a secret Russo-Chinese pact, and that the only thing left now was to embody the agreement in a formal written instrument. After listening to my statement of the terms of the agreement, the prince took a pen and wrote the text of the treaty. The document was drafted so skilfully that I approved it without the slightest reservation. The prince told me that the following day he would submit the document to His Majesty and return it to me if it was approved by the Emperor.

· · ·

Not the slightest information penetrated into the press regarding our secret agreement with China. The only thing Europe learned was the bare fact that China had agreed to grant the Russo-Chinese Bank a concession for the construction of the Eastern Chinese Railway, a continuation of the Trans-Siberian. The concession was drawn up under my instructions by the Assistant Minister of Finances, Piotr Mikhailovich Romanov, in consultation with the Chinese Minister in St. Petersburg, who was also China's envoy to Berlin. Winter and spring he usually spent in St. Petersburg, while the rest of the year he stayed in Berlin. Since it was then summer-time, Romanov went to Berlin and it was there that the terms of the concessions were drafted. The project was subsequently ratified by the two contracting Governments. At the time it was rumoured in Europe, I remember, that Li Hung Chang had been bribed by the Russian Government. I must say that there is not a particle of truth in this rumour.

The terms of the railroad concession granted by China were very favourable for Russia. The agreement provided for China's right to redeem the road at the expiration of 36 years, but the terms of the redemption were so burdensome that it was highly improbable that the Chinese Government would ever attempt to effect the redemption. It was calculated that should the Chinese Government wish to redeem the road at the beginning of the 37th year, it would have to pay the corporation, according to the terms of the concession, a sum not less than 700 million rubles.

An American's Description

> Mr. John W. Bookwalter, an American, traveled over the newly constructed Trans-Siberian from Moscow to Tomsk, which at that time (1898) was the eastern terminus although the railhead had already been pushed as far east as the Yenisei River. His report of this journey was privately published. The following excerpt is much condensed. The source is: J. W. Bookwalter, *Siberia and Central Asia.* Springfield, Ohio, 1899. Pp. 6–8, 43–46, 49–67, 87–94.

I set out to simply write you of my Siberian trip. The line of the Trans-Siberian railway runs in a general way through middle European Russia, the centre of the southern part of Western Siberia, and along the southern border of Eastern Siberia. Its western terminus is Moscow, and in the east, Vladivostok on the Pacific Ocean. It is difficult to determine its exact length, as the recent Russian-Chinese relations that have sprung up have caused Russia to change the original route down the Amur River in East Siberia. A commission has recently left here to make a new survey from a point about 1,200 miles west of Vladivostok, with the intention of radiating from that point several lines through Manchuria eastward, as China has recently given Russia extensive concessions in that province. One of these lines will run direct to Vladivostok through Manchuria, and, joining with the main line from Moscow, will thus make a much shorter route than the one originally designed to run down the Amur River, of which nearly 1,000 miles is now completed. Even under the new survey the line will not be less than 6,100 miles long.

.   .   .

There is now completed about 4,000 miles of road from Moscow east, on which trains are running. On the last 1,000 miles, however, only construction trains are running, with an occasional mixed passenger train at intervals of about a fortnight. In the last six weeks they have put on a through train that runs from Moscow to Tomsk, on the Tom River. This train leaves once in ten days and furnishes fairly comfortable facilities. Ordinary trains that break the journey at many points run also, at irregular intervals, as far as Omsk. The distance from Moscow to Tomsk is about 3,000 miles. It is the through train that I am taking. Whatever expeditions I make east of Tomsk will have to be done on construction trains, or over the old Siberian post-route by troikas or droshkies—curious vehicles drawn by three or five horses.

.   .   .

The Siberian railway, like all railways in Russia, is well constructed, the road-bed firm, track well ballasted, generally with stone, at least as far as Tscheljabinsk, and easy gradients. The road has a five-foot gauge, uniform with all the roads in European Russia. This gives an ample breadth to the cars, which, with their unusual height, imparts an air of comfort not possessed by roads of narrower gauge and less height of ceiling in the car. The stations, without exception, are clean and handsome, constructed often of wood, but frequently of brick or stone. It is a perfect delight to take a meal in the restaurants. They have a most agreeable custom of furnishing meals. On entering the dining-room, you will find at one end an immense sideboard literally groaning under a load of newly prepared Russian dishes, always piping hot, and of such a bewildering variety as to range through the whole gamut of human fancy and tastes.

You are given a plate, with a knife and fork. Making your own selection, you retire to any of the neatly-spread tables to enjoy your meal at your leisure, and, I might add, with infinite zest, for travel in this country, besides pleasing the eye, quickens the palate. The price, too, is a surprise to one accustomed to metropolitan charges. You can get soup, as fine a beefsteak as you ever ate, a splendid roast chicken, whole, done in Russian style, most toothsome and juicy; potatoes and other vegetables, a bottle of beer, splendid and brewed in this country, for one ruble—about fifty cents.

Safety seems to be the one idea uppermost in the minds of the railway ministry. Beside the electrical and other appliances used in the best railway practice they have an immense army of guards both for the train and the track. The road is divided into sections of one verst each—about two-thirds of a mile. For each section there is built a neat little cottage in which the guard and his family live. It is the duty of this guard or one of his family to patrol a section night and day. As soon as a train passes, the guard steps into the middle of the track, holds a flag, at night a lantern, aloft and watches the retreating train until it passes into the next verst or section. Where there is a heavy curve that prevents the view of the road for the distance of a verst, several guards are employed on a section. A train is, therefore, never out of sight of a guard.

I might add that women often perform this service, which is quite apart from that of the section gang, whose duty is to repair the road. On the Siberian railway, as far as Tomsk, there are to be nearly 4,000 of these cottages for the use of the guards; a very costly precaution, but one that gives a pleasing sense of security to the traveller. With the exception of the great post routes to Siberia, the Caucasus, and main highways in European Russia, which are first class and compare well with other countries, the common roads of Russia are indifferent, scarcely equal to those of our own country.

·

At Batraki, another important grain port, and celebrated for the fine quality of caviare, the railroad crosses the Volga. The bridge here, owing to its immense size and the difficulties encountered in its construction, deserves well to be classed among the world's great structures of this kind. It is only a little short of a mile in length, being built of fourteen sections, 360 feet span each. The bridge is 135 feet above the river at low water.

There were consumed nearly 7,000 tons of iron in its building, and it was designed and executed by a Russian engineer.

The Volga, where we crossed it, very much resembles the Mississippi River, as well in size as in other points. To form some notion of the size and volume of water in this mighty river, I would say, at the point where the railroad crosses the river it is just a mile wide at low water. At times of high water it is from four to eight miles wide. The channel near the bridge at low water has a depth of twenty feet, and a high water of 100 feet.

The velocity of the current when the river is at its flood is said to be thirty feet per second, and in its low stage, fifteen or twenty feet per second.

. . .

From Batraki to Wajsaowaja, a distance of 500 miles, there are the same fertile, treeless plains and prairies as from Moscow to the former place, a distance of 600 miles. At Wajsaowaja we encounter the foot-hills and get our first view of the Ural Mountains. We here also meet the Ufa River, whose sinuous course the road follows until the summit of the mountains is reached.

Those who from its great length—being over 1,700 miles from north to south—have been led to expect an imposing range of mountains, will be doomed to disappointment. The height is only moderate, being a little over 6,000 feet at the highest, in this respect scarcely equal to the Apennines. The summit is reached a little beyond Zlatoust, at an elevation of 3,000 feet. It is an easy grade and requires no special effort to surmount.

On reaching the summit, if one did not know it was the Ural Mountains, he might well believe he was on the railway summit of the Alleghanies near Altoona, so similar to it are the surroundings. Zlatoust, a large town, is most important in several particulars. It was until recently the "Botany Bay" of Russia. Here one occasionally sees prisoners chained in gangs destined to work in the mines or perhaps, doomed to the solitude of farther Siberia.

Zlatoust is in the centre of the iron regions of Russia. A very fine quality is produced here in great quantities, and being free from both sulphur and phosphorus, it is consumed principally in making sheets and bars for those purposes where the highest quality is required.

The region to the northward, extending to Perm and Ekaterinburg, abounds in gold, copper, malachite, lapis-lazuli, and other precious metals and minerals, all of which are being extensively mined and worked. At the former place, which is located on the Kama River, there are immense government works, employing over 2,000 men. It has one of the largest steam hammers in the world, and the foundry turns out steel cannon of unusual size and quality. They also manufacture firearms here, said to equal anything manufactured in Europe or America, and sidearms of unsurpassed excellence. It is from these localities in the Ural Mountains that what is known in America as "Russian iron" comes.

In Zlatoust, also, there are great government works for the manufacture of steel cannon and other arms. Cutlery of various kinds is made in large quantities, and it is said the swords are of exceptional quality. There are also produced marvellous castings from pig-iron. The statuettes cast out of this metal are marvels of artistic beauty and technical skill. Their quality, it is said, is due largely to the superior moulding sand produced in this region, but I am of the impression that it is more properly attributable to the rare qualities of the iron, which seems to flow with unusual fluidity, producing castings so delicate in detail as to be scarcely distinguishable from bronze. These art products are rapidly finding their way into European markets.

Shortly after leaving Zlatoust we pass a large stone monument erected at some distance from the railway. On one side is, in Russian, the word "Europe," and on the opposite side "Asia." It marks the boundary between Europe and Asia. One, however, does not need a monumental token to learn that he is passing from one great geographical division to another, for the sparce population, uncultivated lands, and general wild aspect only too clearly indicate that he has suddenly entered Siberia.

The eastern slope of the Ural Mountains is, for a space, more abrupt than the western, but it soon enters upon a gentle slope that continues until it touches the western edge of that great level plain which seems to stretch indefinitely to the east. On leaving the summit we joint the Isset, a small river, whose course we closely follow until it deflects to the northeast, becoming a tributary to the Irtish, itself one of the main branches of the great Obi River. Fifty miles farther on in the plains we come to Tscheljabinsk, where ends the first section of this great railway.

It may not be amiss to give the results of my observations respecting this year's crop conditions in the country through which I have passed, constituting as it does the finest cereal region in all European Russia. From a deficiency in rainfall, extending continuously over a period of almost four months, an alarming shortage of all crops, even grass, is certain to exist throughout an immense area, reaching through several hundred miles east and west, and perhaps five hundred miles north and south—an area about equally bisected by the Volga River and the railway line throughout this vast tract. This includes five of the largest and agriculturally the most important governments of Russia, containing from ten to twelve million people, and it is almost certain that enough cannot be raised this year to meet the wants of more than one-fourth of its population.

. . .

The government of Samara (said to be twice as large as Belgium) lies in the centre of the stricken region, and here already much distress had developed. I learn, on passing through, that the Czar has just given 500,-000 rubles for the relief of the sufferers. The region over which the drought extends is the finest wheat region in Eastern Russia, and in ordinary seasons supplies a large surplus for export to foreign countries. I was informed by a Russian officially connected with the ministry of railways, that they would probably have to bring into this region where the shortage has occurred, from other sections of Russia, from fifty to eighty million bushels of grain, to supply the necessary food to the inhabitants and seed to the farmers. The self-sustaining power of this great empire is fully made manifest by the fact that while so serious a shortage has occurred in one great section, in many others, such as the Crimea, the Caucasus, and the newly settled lands in Siberia, abundant and even excessive crops are reported, so that not only can the deficiency be fully supplied from her own home resources, but there will be left over a fair surplus for export.

. . .

The railway on leaving Tscheljabinsk takes an almost due easterly course, which it varies by a few points only until beyond the Yenisei River, a distance of about 2,000 miles, when it deflects to the southeast for nearly 800 miles, until it reaches Lake Baikal, only a short distance from the China border. It follows somewhat closely the old post route from Moscow to Irkutsk, running via Zlatoust, where at Tomsk it joins the more northern post route down the Tobol and Irtish rivers to Tiumen, and thence over the Ural Mountains to Perm and Nijni Novgorod to Moscow.

Curiously enough, the railway follows much the same course as that by which in ancient times the Huns, Tartars, and Moguls made through Southern Russia their numerous and dreaded incursions into Europe.

. . .

A sufficiently accurate general description of the Siberian railroad and its various appointments would, I think, be covered by the statement that it is fully equal to either the Union or Northern Pacific Railway, although the oldest portion east of Tscheljabinsk has been in operation scarcely two years, and the newer portions a few months only. The track is well laid, the grading firm and thorough, and the bridges almost wholly of iron, save a few of the original and temporary ones, which are rapidly being replaced by those of stone and iron. Those over the Irtish, Ishim, Obi, Tobol, Omsk, and Tom rivers I found to be well constructed, of the best materials and most approved modern pattern.

The stations, always artistic and picturesque, and never the same style, are neat, comfortable, of good size, and substantial, fully equal to the average depot on the New York Central or Pennsylvania. I noticed that recent surveys have been made along the line, and on inquiry was informed that they are preparing to build one or more additional tracks. This is a very timely provision as the road is already taxed far beyond its capacity.

A Russian Village in the 1890's

The following description of a peasant village in northern Russia was written after a residence of several years in Russia. Interesting rather than especially significant, it will help to build up a mental image of the Russian people as they were at the end of the nineteenth century. The source is: F. J. Wishaw, *Out of Doors in Tsarland. A Record of the Scenes and Doings of a Wanderer in Russia*. London: Longmans, Green and Co., 1893. Pp. 1–19.

Any one journeying through Russia must be struck by the exact similarity of each village to its fellows. He will see the same tumble-down wooden huts extending for a quarter of a mile on each side of the road, with the same solitary two-storied edifice in the centre of the village—the abode of the tradesman of the place, the same lean dogs will come out of the houses as he passes, to contest his right of way; the same herd of cows, at the same hour of the afternoon, will crowd down the street, monopolising every inch of the muddy road (there is no footpath), to this extreme discomfort and no slight alarm; and the same cowherd will wait until the stranger's ear is exactly opposite the end of his long pipe, and will then emit a nondescript sound which will make that stranger wish he had never been born, or at all events that he had been born deaf. It is this sound which brings the cows out of he wonders what hiding-places behind the huts. As the herd moves, wading slowly through the deep mud along the road, each house or yard seems to shoot out its contribution of one cow, or two cows, or six, according to the wealth of the owner, until the last hut is passed, when the whole herd turns abruptly to the side, gets over the ditch as best it can, and distributes itself over the communal pasture-land.

The casual passer-by will not see much of the inhabitants of the village unless he happens to wander through it late in the evening of a summer's day. Then indeed he will find it full of life and sound. A band of girls, all dressed in picturesque colours, are to be seen sitting upon a bench outside one of the houses, singing at the top of their voices, not in unison, but taking at least two and sometimes three parts, the first voice singing about an octave higher than ordinary sopranos can conveniently manage. Further on a band of men will be found standing or lounging about and enjoying similar vocal exercise, their higher tones being exceedingly nasal, but the basses excellent. All these good people are endowed by nature with the gift of harmony. A man with a bass voice can always improvise a bass or sing a second to a higher voice. As for the children of the village, they will have been hounded away to bed at this time of night; but earlier in the day they may be seen playing out in the road, generally with a species of knucklebones, or with a kind of ninepins or skittles played with clubs, which are thrown at the uprights, instead of a ball. The boys make marvellously good shots with these clubs, knocking over a small ninepin with certainty at a distance of twenty or thirty yards. The rival singing bands occasionally leave their seats and parade the village street, never mixing with one another, but occasionally indulging in loud personalities of a humorous but somewhat unrefined nature as they meet or pass.

Let us pay a visit, reader, you and I, to a typical village: let us choose Ruchee, which is not far from St. Petersburg. I shall prove an excellent guide here, for I have visited this hamlet many and many a time, and know it well. In one of yonder huts dwells a gamekeeper, one Ivan, who looks after the shooting interests of the district. Ivan is a great friend of mine, and is employed by an English gentleman, therefore you must not be surprised to find one *moujik* dressed differently from his fellows in this village of Ruchee. He will turn out when we reach his hut, for one of the children whose noses are for ever glued to the window-pane will cry out "Get up, father, here are the English *Barins!*" and when he appears you will see something like a costume!

But we have not reached the village yet. Yonder it lies; a long straight road, you see, as usual, with the houses built at uneven distances along each side. In the middle of the village the road takes a dip, down and up again, the lowest point being an extremely rickety bridge, consisting of wooden planks insecurely nailed to piles driven into the bed of the tiny stream which it spans. Beyond this village we can just see the first houses of another, Mourino. Mourino possesses a church, and is a *selo,* or chief of a group of villages. About Mourino I shall have more to say by-and-by.

Here is Ruchee. A few yards before we reach the first hut is a post with a notice-board upon it. Let us read the legend if we can; it is rather indistinct:

RUCHEE
46 souls

That is all. We knew it was Ruchee; but what does 46 *souls* mean? A soul is a man, not a woman. Women have no souls, according to the code of the Russian official district tax-collectors, for whose benefit the post and its information exist. I hope my reader, if I have one, is not a lady; for I feel that I shall incur her odium as the purveyor of this shocking evidence of the ungallant quality of the official Russian mind. But alas! it is too true. In Russia, so the proverb says, there is but one soul to seven women. The tax-gatherer, however, does not credit the ladies with even one seventh of a soul apiece, he ignores their claims altogether; in his eyes they do not exist, they are nonentities. The men have all the souls, for they pay all the taxes. Those who pay no taxes have no souls. But whether they have no souls because they pay no taxes, or whether they pay no taxes because they have no souls, I have not yet found a tax-gatherer sufficiently well-informed to tell me.

Well, then, Ruchee claims to contain 46 souls within its limits. A man-child, so soon as born, is a soul; so that some of these 46 souls may be infants. On the other hand, Ruchee may be teeming with a population of hundreds of girls and women, but it can only boast of 46 souls, for the poor girls do not count. I ought to explain, however, that the above estimate of the population of Ruchee dates from the last Government revision, perhaps ten years since. Therefore other souls may have been born to the village, which may of course contain more or less souls by this time, according to the balance of male births and deaths for the period. It is necessary to set up these official statistical posts because the total amount of tax imposed upon the village, as its payment for the use of the communal land, depends upon the number of "souls" alive in the village at the date of revision. The distribution of the land among the souls is looked after within the village itself, as I shall presently explain, without official interference from outside, and is guided by considerations of equity rather than by strict rule. For it is evident that to saddle a family of small male babies with the actual share of land and concomitant taxes for which as "souls" they are responsible, would be as unfair as to expect a widow with one son and five strapping daughters to live on the single share of land to which alone, as possessing but one soul among them, they are entitled.

But let us enter the village. What a barking of dogs greets us as we do so! Every hut seems to have contributed a cur, and every cur looks as if he would eat us up if he had time for anything besides barking. A stone deftly aimed produces a wonderful effect upon these Russian village dogs. They are not brave. Only one is struck, but his sorrow is pitiful to witness as he disappears full gallop down the street, going very much faster and farther than the occasion demands—the sight, and the pathetic sounds of his yelps, quickly discouraging the rest, who accept the inevitable and trot home again with a mourning aspect about the tail. Three small children rush shrieking and shouting from the first hut as we pass it, but stop dead on seeing us. They stare in silence until we have proceeded ten yards or so, when they set up a chorus of "Barin, dai kopaykoo" (Give us a kopeck, Mister).

Between the houses we can catch glimpses of the fields, which seem to be divided with mathematical accuracy into long strips. Upon these strips of land red-shirted peasants and women are hard at work, for, strange to say, it is not a holiday, and the villagers are actually up and about. At least half the week in Russia is "holiday" of so pronounced a kind that it is considered wicked to do work of any sort. As it generally takes a day or so to recover from a Russian holiday, which is spent brawling over vodka, in the village *traktir,* little time remains for work. The hay is just ready for cutting, and we may observe that out of yonder huge field of waving grasses an occasional strip is already cut, one patch here and another there. For this is one of the communal fields, and is divided in strips among the "souls" of the village, each soul possessing one, which he may generally cultivate how he pleases. The village owns three or four of these large fields, each subdivided as this one; but one is probably devoted to the growing of oats, another to a crop of rye, this one, as we have seen, is hay, and the fourth is probably lying fallow. The peasants will generally prefer to grow one crop over the entire field, each cutting his own portion when he thinks fit, or when he is not drunk, if he can find a day under the latter category. But if he prefers it he may grow a patch of oats in the middle of the hay-field, or a patch of potatoes amid the rye strips of his neighbours. Shall we enter one of these houses in order to see what ideas the moujiks and their families have as to making themselves comfortable at home? Very well, let us choose my friend Ivan's then. Here it is, no better than its neighbours, though Ivan receives his wages of ten roubles per month regularly, and is therefore richer than his fellows by about £12 a year. This consideration has not apparently induced him to mend his broken window, however, for the hole is stopped up with a piece of one of his wife's old dresses (I remember seeing her dressed in that very print a year or two ago). One of the children is of course staring out of the window—there! she has seen us. Now Ivan will appear. Here he is, rubbing his eyes with the back of his hand, and yawning cavernously. (Ivan! you have been drinking, little father! I shall think twice about presenting you with a rouble "for tea" next time you carry my game-bag after the ptarmigan.)

What an object the man is! On his shaggy head, which is covered with long yellow hair, he wears a soft English hat, the gift of his British employer. Over his broad shoulders is a Norfolk jacket, derived from the same source. So far he is an Englishman, though a disreputable one! From the coat downwards he is a moujik. His feet are encased in a pair of long boots, into which are tucked the ends of a pair of baggy cotton trousers. From beneath the Norfolk jacket protrude the tails of a red shirt, which tails are not tucked into the trousers, but are worn outside. There is a saying in Russia that so long as a Russian wears his shirt outside he remains honest; but when he begins to tuck it in, like a civilized Christian, he is no longer to be trusted. There may be some truth in this. The *chinovniks* and their tribe, being higher up the social ladder, have learned, among other arts, that of dressing themselves according to the usages of modern society. Whether the ancestors of these gentlemen ever were honest in their red-shirted days I am not in a position to state; but this I know, that their descendants are very far from it now. On the other hand, Ivan, who wears his red shirt in a manner which should have ensured his strict adherence to the paths of truth and righteousness, is a very considerable liar. I may say that I have known other moujiks not altogether immaculate. What then becomes of the proverb?

Ivan graciously permits us to enter and explore his domain. In the porch, reached by falling over three decayed steps into a pit, and then getting out of it and climbing, by a gymnastic effort, upon the platform which the steps originally led to—in this porch, hanging from a hook at the top, is a kind of earthen vessel something like a teapot, with two handles and a short spout. This is the family lavatory. When a member of the family desires to wash—which happens on very rare occasions—he stands underneath the water-vessel and tilts a very small quantity of the liquid into one hand. He then divides the water impartially between his two hands and applies both to his face. Part of his countenance thus receives a little attention from one or other of the damp hands, and lo! he is clean—a misleading expression signifying that his ablutions are over for several days. There is another method of washing, but my pen revolts from a description of it. Enough to mention that the mouth is applied to the spout of the teapot, and all further washing is done with the water thus procured. In a word, the Russian moujik considers his weekly or fort-nightly steam-bath quite as much in the way of personal cleansing as is good for him. I shall describe the village bath in its proper place, but meanwhile we are keeping Ivan standing outside his door, ready to show us in. As we enter the house three dogs rush out and nearly knock us over, whining and jumping on us with every demonstration of delight. You may see at once that these are English dogs. They belong to Ivan's employer, my old friend A., and are under the impression that we have come to take them out shooting. They know at a glance—perhaps I should say at a sniff—that we are Britons, and are looking about for our guns. Lie down, Bruce and York! we have come to see your house, there is no shooting to be done to-day. These dogs live with Ivan on terms of equality, and feed rather better than he does; but then Ivan gets plenty of vodka, and they do not. Ivan's is a one-roomed house—that is, there is but one room for general use. There is indeed a sort of black hole, opposite, quite dark and very small, where Ivan keeps his poultry, snowshoes, and other articles out of place in a drawing-room. The living room is a good size, perhaps fifteen feet by thirteen. It has two small windows, with four panes in each. Of these eight panes six are intact or nearly so, the seventh is half gone, the eighth entirely so—the latter being stopped up with a portion of Mrs. Ivan's old print skirt, as I have already mentioned. Round two sides of the rooms runs a narrow bench, about a foot in width. In front of this, at the corner, is the table. In another corner of the room is the stove, a huge brick structure reaching almost to the ceiling, five feet in breadth and four feet deep, and having a lower portion jutting out from the side to a length of six feet or so. This branch establishment is used by the family to sleep upon, and a nice warm bed it makes. As for the stove itself, a description of its working may be of interest to the reader. The door of the stove is a foot or so from the ground, and opens into a huge empty cavern formed by the whole of the inside of the stove. Into this logs of wood are thrust, in quantities, and ignited. This is only the beginning, and the heat of the wood while burning is a mere trifle. When the logs are reduced to red embers the door of the stove is shut up tight and the chimney securely closed. By this means all the heat is kept in the stove, which soon becomes a veritable "scorcher," and retains its heat for nearly twenty-four hours. But woe to the inhabitants of the house if the chimney be closed before the wood shall have been properly consumed, for speedy suffocation is their certain fate—death if they happen to be asleep, terrible nausea and sickness if awake and able to whisk off the iron covering which closes the chimney, in time to save their lives. I have spoken to an English gentleman who once nearly fell a victim to suffocation through the carelessness of a Russian servant. He was passing the night at a shooting-box near St. Petersburg, and, the cold being intense, had instructed the keeper, on retiring, to enter his room at six in the morning and relight the stove, in case it should have cooled down by that time. The keeper obeyed these instructions to the letter, but closed the chimney before the wood had been sufficiently reduced. At half-past seven my friend was awakened by the most violent headache he had ever experienced, accompanied by terrible sickness. He barely had strength to crawl out of bed and stagger into the fresh air—thus saving his life—when he fell insensible in the snow. There he was found shortly afterwards half-frozen and very ill, but alive enough to address remarks to that offending keeper which were almost sufficiently strong to thaw the snow in which he found himself outstretched.

Three small children climb down from the top of the stove as we enter Ivan's room, and stand staring up at us. On the table there is a *samovar* hissing comfortably, and Mrs. Ivan smiles and bows over it. She has been cutting hunks from a large round loaf of black bread, for this is dinner-time. There is also a smoked herring lying on the table, half wrapped in a truly horrible scrap of newspaper. Probably Ivan will get the whole of this dainty morsel, for he is a "soul" and must be fed up; black bread will do excellently well for the women, who have no souls to support. No, thank you, Mrs. Ivan, we won't take any tea, though it is very kind of you to offer it. As far as I can see, you only possess one tumbler, and that a remarkably unclean one. What would the Soul do, if we used his only tumbler? You suggest, reader, that Ivan would go to the *kabak* and drink vodka, and so he would; but he will do this anyhow, for we shall probably give him twenty kopecks for his services in showing us over his establishment, and Ivan's money all goes one way. There are small lumps of sugar lying promiscuously about the table. These are not placed in the tea, but are nibbled at before drinking in order to sweeten each mouthful as taken.

A few coppers will make those small children very happy; the money will be spent upon biscuits, and will go a long way.

Ivan's room is not too clean, and as for the scent thereof, well, if it were not for the half-broken pane of glass it would be still worse, and that is all we can say for it.

There is no second story, but there is a garret, under the roof. This is reached by a ladder from outside, and is used by Ivan for drying his clothes, on the rare occasion of a wash; for hiding away a store of grain, if he has managed to accumulate such; and for putting away sundry house-hold rubbish. Behind the house is a yard, knee-deep in mud, and at the end of the yard a shed. Half of this shed is used as a receptacle for Ivan's cart, plough, and sledge; the other half is the dwelling-place of the cows and horses, when these are at home; but the cows are out most of the day and night in the summer-time, on the pasture-lands, while the horses, at work during the day, herd with the cows at night.

So much for Ivan's establishment, which is the facsimile of every other moujik-home in the village, with the exception of that of the trader, whose house is much larger, and is built in two stories, towering thus over its poorer neighbours like a big policeman among a crowd of urchins. It will repay us to look in for a moment upon Abram Timofeyevitch Kapustyin, the powerful and wealthy individual who dispenses bread, vodka, herrings, calico prints, red shirts, and biscuits to the peasant folk of Ruchee. This gentleman is seated at a small table in his shop; he is drinking tea with lemon in it, and is engaged in conversation with a moujik, who turns out to be *Starost,* or elder, of the village. Of the latter, and of his office, I shall speak presently. As for the trader, he is a sleek, well-to-do, comfortable-looking personage. His power in the place is enormous, for every moujik owes him money, and depends upon him, not only for his daily supply of black bread (when the home-grown stock of rye comes to an end), but for his vodka, his clothes, everything he needs. This individual is often a large landholder, though a stranger to the place; for peasants who have fallen heavily into his debt, thanks, generally, to the national partiality for vodka, are glad to wipe off a portion of their indebtedness, and by so doing become qualified to consume further *vedra* of vodka on "tick," by letting their allotments of land.

We will take a cup of tea at Abram Timofeyevitch's invitation, and buy a red shirt and a startlingly coloured handkerchief or two to show our friends at home. The tea is good tea before it is drowned by Abram Timofeyevitch. How long he has been drinking from this one decoction in the small teapot I know not; but this I know, that his tea is the colour of the very palest sherry. We drink it out of tumblers and bite our sugar dry. The tea, or rather the very slightly bewitched water, is frightfully hot, and the bit of lemon floating in it gets terribly in the way as we try to dodge it in order to drink the scorching fluid. Abram will continue to replenish your tumbler until you sigh, turn the tumbler upside down, rise from your place, and shake hands with him as a sign that you have had enough. You must also shake hands with every other individual who has assisted in emptying Abram's huge *samovar,* thanking them "for their company."

There are several groups of peasants drinking tea at other tables; some are taking vodka and are rather noisy, but there is not much consumption of strong liquor at this time of day. At night the apartment will present a very different aspect. There will be such a babel of sound—singing and dancing and general uproar on the part of the Souls of the place—that were we to pass the house at a distance of half a mile we should conclude that this village must be the veritable home of Bacchus and his satellites. The shop itself is filthy, the counter being covered with a disorderly array of small bottles containing vodka, piles of black bread, many of the loaves being half cut, a keg of herrings whose odour is making a good fight for supremacy with that of the all-pervading vodka, some dishes of black-looking biscuits, which were once white but have lost their youth and good looks waiting for a purchaser among the children, who have evidently had no harvest of coppers lately, and a tub of Finnish butter. The handkerchiefs and calico prints are not displayed for sale in this room, but are sold in a similar shop adjoining; if you peep in, reader, you will see several women handling these articles and haggling over the price. Nothing, no article of commerce, ever changes hands in Russia without a bargain.

Russian Imperialism in Central Asia

The Russian counterpart of overseas expansion was overland expansion into adjacent territories. The second half of the nineteenth century saw a consistent and vigorous Russian drive in the general direction of Persia, India, and China. This expansion was of some concern to all

Europe but especially so to Great Britain. The constant hostility between Russia and Britain was in considerable measure due to the
Russian imperial advance which is summarized in the following selection. The source is: Norman D. Harris, *Europe and the East.* Boston: Houghton Mifflin Co., 1926. Pp. 129–131, 134–149.

One of the most remarkable movements of modern times has been the
expansion of Russia from the small duchy of Moscovy with an area of
748,000 square miles—approximately the size of Mexico—to a great
empire of over 8,300,000 square miles of territory and a population exceeding 170,000,000. After Peter the Great had wrested the supremacy of
the Baltic from Charles XII of Sweden, and secured an opening for Russia
on the seas of the north, and Catherine II had obtained a large portion of
Poland and a foothold upon the Black Sea, Russia found herself precluded
from further expansion on the west and southwest by reason of the established European states there and the jealous opposition of those same
states to her designs on Turkey and Constantinople.

Accordingly the Muscovite rulers early transferred their activities to
Asia. There they met with little opposition, for no established states of any
importance were encountered till the borders of the Chinese Empire were
reached. The Russian advance, however, was slow and not always the
product of deliberate design. Sometimes the gains were accidental or the
result of propitious circumstances; but ultimately some 6,000,000 square
miles of territory were acquired. This expansion took place in three regions: northern Asia—through Siberia to the Pacific Ocean; the "Heart of
Asia"—through Turkestan to China, Afghanistan, and India; and the
Caucasus—through Georgia and Daghestan to Persia. The chief motives
for increased territory were economic, commercial, political, and philanthropic. The economic were based upon the natural desire of a typically
agricultural nation for more territory and outlets for the development of its
economic life. The commercial centered in an ambition for increased trade
connections with the great trade centers of the East. The political was a
combination of a need for defensible frontiers on the east and southeast
(against the pillaging, wild, nomadic tribes of the Steppes and northern
Asia), of a national necessity for ice-free seaports and of a natural craving
for empire. And the philanthropic was a dual force composed of a desire
to bring order, good government, and civilization to Asia, and a racial
longing to give assistance and protection to all the brother Slavic nations
and followers of Greek Christianity, which should ultimately lead to a
triumph of Pan-Slavism, and which embraced other Christian and even
Mohammedan tribal states as well,—such as the native communities of
Khiva, Bokhara, and of the Caucasus.

The success of the Russian expansion was due primarily to four things:
a favorable geographical location, it being the only European state whose
borders touched the continent of Asia; an absolute monarchical form of
government which was especially adapted to continuous and effective
diplomacy, and which was understood by, and appealed to, Asiatics; the
absence of powerful and determined competitors, there being fifty-nine

different nationalities in Siberia, thirty-four in the Caucasus, and forty-two in Central Asia; and skillful method of dealing with Orientals. The Russians were adept in the use of bribery, of intrigue, and of force when necessary. As General Skobelev remarked, when referring to the Turkomans, "The harder you hit them, the longer they will be quiet afterwards." Moreover, the Russians were among the earliest Europeans to study the customs and languages of the East. And in asserting their supremacy they demanded of the subject peoples only recognition of the Czar, annual tribute, trade privileges, and cessation of pillagings, without insisting on any extreme or vexatious social or political changes. . . .

In 1554, Ivan the Terrible subdued Kazan and Astrakazan, extending the Russian territory to the Caspian Sea. The outpost of Orenburg on the Ural River was established; and a series of forts and trading posts created eastward, gradually, via Omsk to Semipalatinsk on the Irtish River. In 1732 and 1790, the Little and Middle Hordes of Kirghiz tribes submitted finally to Russia. And, by the beginning of the nineteenth century, the Russians had formed an irregular frontier—for approximately twelve hundred miles—across the Kirghiz Steppes, maintained by a series of fortified posts which were centers for military operations and commercial activities, and by a small force of twenty thousand Cossacks. This desert borderland remained, however, a constant source of trouble and annoyance to the Empire. The guard was never sufficient to prevent violations of the line; and marauding bands were frequently crossing into Russian territory to loot and destroy villages and property. Conditions of life and of trade were hard and uncertain. Communication with the outside world was difficult and infrequent. The attempts of the Russians to open trade routes to the chief marts of Central Asia were constantly thwarted, and their caravans pillaged by the roving, robber tribes of the steppes. Accordingly, the Russian statesmen determined to seek a defensible frontier and to take what steps they could to stabilize conditions in Turkestan. This movement, inaugurated in the early thirties and covering fifty years of activity, did not attain its full fruition till the Russians took Merv and reached the great Persian-Afghan-Hindu Kush mountain borderland in 1884.

Their progress for the first thirty years was very slow, for the difficulties of the undertaking were enormous, their officers and men inexperienced, and their resources limited. In the last twenty years, however, the Russian Government possessed much greater resources for its adventures in foreign expansion; and its forces were much better officered, manned, and equipped than in the earlier period. Consequently, their progress—directed by a superior group of able diplomats—was much more rapid. They had, fortunately, comparatively few setbacks; and their success was secured through a combination of exploration, intrigue, economic infiltration, and military force.

These Russian activities began at three points: Semipalatinsk on the Irtish River, Orenburg on the Ural River, and Krasnovodsk on the Caspian Sea—the movement from the last-named town did not take place, however, until nearly ten years after the Russians had occupied Krasnovodsk in 1869, and after the advance from the other points had been successfully accomplished. After Humboldt had explored successfully the region south of Semipalatinsk, the Russians established their first fort at Sergiopol—two hundred miles south of their outpost on the Irtish River just mentioned. Then followed another period of exploration to the south and southwest, in which Federov Karelin and Schrenk distinguished themselves. In 1884 the Great Horde of the South Steppes and Lake Balkash—the last of the Kirghiz national groups—submitted to Russia; and Prince Gortchakov advanced the Russian forces two hundred miles to Kopal at the foot of the Ala Tau Mountains, and built a fort there in 1846–47. By 1855, another two hundred miles had been traversed and Verni (Vernoe) and the valley of the Ili River occupied, where great numbers of peasants and settlers followed the military forces, seeking new homes. Once more the explorers pressed on: Semenov up the Ili River, Valekinov to Kashgar and south as far as the Pamirs, and Goluber and Matkov to Issik Kul Lake in 1858–59. Meanwhile, the Russian forces followed slowly. They seized and fortified Tokmak in 1860; and in the same year China transferred to them the Issik Kul region and the valley of the Naryn River to the south of this lake. Finally they pushed on some forty to fifty miles and in 1862 occupied Pishpek—two hundred and sixty miles from Kikand to which they were already advancing from another direction. And in 1867, the whole of this great region was organized into the Russian province of Semipalatinsk with Verni as a capital, which was later divided into the two provinces of Semipalatinsk and Semirechinsk having a combined area of over 322,000 square miles and a population of over 2,000,000.

Meanwhile, the second movement, inaugurated from Orenburg, had made equally good progress to the south and southeast via the Aral Sea. By 1834, the Russians, going via the Ural River, had reached Dead Bay—an arm of the Caspian Sea—and established a fort there. In 1847, we find them holding outposts on the Irgiz and Turgai Rivers, known as Forts Uralsk and Orenburg. The following year they reached Karabutak and set up another fortified post at Aralsk, near the northeastern extremity of the Aral Sea, called Fort Number One. From there the Russian outposts were gradually pushed southeastward along the Syr Daria (river) for one hundred and fifty miles to their next important station—Fort Perovsk—built in 1853. Their progress was expedited by a steamer brought from Sweden in parts and put together on the river. But, ere long, the Khivans and Tartars of Turkestan fortified the Syr Daria and effectively barred their advance for nine years.

Finally, General Chernaiev, with a large and well-equipped army and in accordance with a carefully planned program, forced his way rapidly one hundred and fifty miles to Djulek and the town of Turkestan, and then to Chimkent—a hundred miles farther—in 1864. When the news of this expedition reached Europe, it aroused considerable excitement in the capitals of the leading powers whose statesmen began at length to grasp the proportions of the Russian advance—although comparatively little was known of Turkestan in those days—and to begrudge her any considerable increase of territory or of trade. Great Britain, fearing chiefly for her Indian possessions, led the chorus of protests that ensued. But Prince Gortchakov —then Minister of Foreign Affairs—in a skillfully worded circular letter to the powers, dated November 21, 1864, succeeded in allaying all fears. He assured them that the chief motive of Russia in this advance was simply to secure an effective boundary in Central Asia—one that could be defended from border raids. It was highly desirable that the robberies and feuds of the Steppes should cease, but there was no chance of securing this while Russia merely bordered on the lands of a number of irresponsible tribes. It was therefore imperative: that the Russian Empire should advance her line till it touched the boundaries of the organized agricultural states of Khiva and Bokhara, and reached the mountains extending from Kikand to China; that a line of forts should be established to hold this line and to maintain peace; and that the "western civilization" should be given to the natives, who must be taught that trade is better than pillage. Accordingly, the Russians were permitted to pursue their advance unhampered; and General Chernaiev took Fort Niazbek and the populous and important city of Tashkent—sixteen miles northeast of it and commanding its water supply—in 1865, while General Romanovski occupied Khojent, a strong military town covering the roads to Kokand, Tashkent, Bokhara, and Balkh, in the following year.

By this time, the khanates and tribal chieftains of the interior of Turkestan had become suspicious of the motives of the Russians; and, in 1866, they all united, under the leadership of the Khan of Bokhara, in a "Holy League" against Russia. The Russian generals thereupon deliberately provoked a conflict with the ruler of the Khanate of Bokhara whose intentions were peaceful, by seizing the property of Bokharan merchants in Khojent and Tashkent, and by arresting some Bokharan envoys who had been sent on a mission of protest to St. Petersburg. The Amir retaliated indiscreetly by imprisoning the members of a Russian mission sent to his capital to reestablish friendly relations and to secure trade concessions; and General Chernaiev led an army across the Syr Daria at Chinaz against him—only to be defeated. The Russians succeeded, however, in capturing and holding the two forts of Jizak and Ura Tube within the Amir's domains before the year closed.

The next year the Russian Government organized the whole region already occupied southeast of the Aral Sea into the province of Turkestan, containing a population of about 1,500,000 people, with the town of Turkestan as its capital, and on November 17, 1867, appointed General Kaufmann commander-in-chief of its forces in Central Asia. Kaufmann proceeded promptly to organize an efficient expedition against Bokhara; and in 1868 he thoroughly defeated the Khan's forces on the Zerafshan River, took the important city of Samarkand—noted as the burial place of Tamerlane and as the religious capital of Turkestan with its marvelous Arab edifices—and compelled the Khan to sign a treaty of peace dated the 18th of June. By the terms of this agreement, the city of Bokhara was not to be molested; but the khanate was to be opened to the free trade and free passage of Russians. A small indemnity amounting to 125,000 gold tilla was to be paid Russia, to whom was to be transferred the valley of the Zerafshan and the cities of Smarkand and Katta Kurgan, which gave them control of the waters of the Zerafshan and the crops of the Khanate of Bokhara.

These successes again aroused Great Britain, whose statesmen viewed with apprehension every step taken by the Russians that brought their boundary nearer to the frontier of India. During the years 1869 and 1870, an attempt was made by the British Government to secure an agreement with Russia that should govern the future policy and protect the interests of both states in Central Asia. It resulted in what was afterwards known as the "St. Petersburg Correspondence" in the course of which the idea of a system of "buffer states" was evolved. Lord Mayo, who was Viceroy of India from 1869 to 1872, suggested that the British and Russian possessions should be kept safely aloof from one another by the maintenance of two series of independent buffer states. The three northern ones—Khiva, Bokhara, and Kokand—were to enjoy the protection of Russia, while the three southern—Kelat, Afghanistan, and Harkand—should have the support of Great Britain or India. In this way definite limits would be set to the territorial expansion of both powers, and each state would have its share in the trade and commercial development of Central Asia. Russia gave the scheme her tacit approval, but did not consent to any definite arrangement in the matter.

Meanwhile, difficulties were arising between Russians and Khivans. The latter resented the presence of the former in Central Asia and their interference in the affairs of Bokhara and neighboring states. Moreover, the Khivans were suspicious of the Russians and embittered because of the way the latter were obtaining the control of the trade of Central Asia. The presence of the Russians was as obnoxious to them as it was to the Bokharans and the other peoples of that region; while the intriguing, pushing manners of the western traders and settlers was equally irritating. There is little doubt that the Khivan chieftains were secretly taking what steps they could to retard the Russian advance and to keep them away from Khivan territory; for fear of annexation was ever hanging over their heads. In 1870, the Khan of Khiva forbade the exportation of grain or food into regions held by Russian forces; and an attempt was made to prevent all commerce between Russian forces and Khivans. And, in the next two years every effort was made diplomatically and commercially to hold up Russian progress; but all in vain.

The Russian Government, which considered a protectorate over the Khivans as an essential stepping-stone to the commercial and political domination of Central Asia, viewed these hasty, fruitless activities in defense of national independence as the unfriendly acts of a defiant competitor and enemy. And she began to look about for excuses to start a movement that not only would remove an irritating opponent, but also would furnish a pretext for the establishment of a protectorate over the khanates. It was not necessary to wait long. By the end of 1872, Russia was able to report to the powers that another military expedition into Central Asia would soon be necessary, owing to the unsettled conditions and raids upon trade along the Khivan border.

Khiva, to which Russia held a legitimate claim since certain Kirghiz chiefs had transferred to the Russian czars their family rights to Khiva, was reported as sheltering rebellious Kirghiz tribes, defying Russian power by the practice of brigandage, and conspiring with Bokhara, Kokand, and Kashgar to overthrow Russian control in Central Asia. In a well-authenticated interview in London in January, 1873, Count Schouvalov—then Russian Minister of Foreign Affairs—gave positive assurance to Lord Granville, at that time holding the portfolio of Foreign Affairs in the British Cabinet, that this would be merely a punitive expedition. Four and one half battalions only—about 4200 men—were to be sent. And there was no intention of taking possession since positive orders had been given that nothing should be done which would lead to a prolonged occupancy. What actually occurred was something quite different. General Kaufmann crossed the Khivan boundary with three columns composed of fifty-three companies of infantry and twenty-five Cossacks—about 14,000 men all told—and secured the submission of Khiva without difficulty, even though Bokhara, aroused at the invasion of territory belonging to her friend and ally, came rather tardily to the rescue. She, too, was forced to submit to the Russian army and to sign a treaty at General Kaufmann's dictation on September 28th, similar to that signed by Khiva on August 25th. These agreements provided for the opening of the Khanates and the Oxus River to the trade of Russia with but a two and one half per cent import duty on goods going into Bokhara or Russian territory. No person should be admitted into the khanates without a Russian passport; and the Russians admitted were to enjoy the right of holding property and carrying on business. And, while Bokhara the noble, with its four hundred mosques, its baths, its gardens, its great caravansaries, and its flourishing trade, was required only to receive a Russian agent and to send a representative to the Russian Government at Tashkent, its political status, as well as that of Khiva, became a dependent one. The direction of their foreign affairs passed into the hands of Russia, for they were forbidden to make any commercial or other treaty without the consent of the Russian Government; and they became subject protectorates of the Russian Empire, retaining, however, in other respects their local autonomy.

In this way were acquired two rich and fertile oasis communities, one (Khiva) having 24,000 square miles of territory and 800,000 population and the other (Bokhara) 83,000 square miles of territory and 1,250,000 population. And last, but not least, the slave-trade in Central Asia was abolished, commerce with the interior communities and peoples was unfettered, and protection afforded to life and property. For in the same year —1873—the Russian province of Samarkand, comprising some 26,000 square miles of territory and a population approximately 700,000, was established with the city of Samarkand as its capital; and three years later, General Kaufmann, taking advantage of an uprising started by the Khan of

Kokand—now a metropolis of Central Asia with 112,000 people—assisted by the leading chiefs of Khojent, divided and defeated these leaders, and added a large district to the east and southeast of Samarkand. The local chieftans all submitted and the whole region was organized the same year into the Russian province of Ferghana, which embraced 55,483 square miles of territory with a population of over 1,200,000.

Within a short time, a connection was established between the province of Ferghana and that of Semipalatinsk where we have seen the Russians advancing from Semipalatinsk to Pishpek. This completed the main Russian forward movement into Central Asia. Three things remained to be done, however, before the Russians could reap the full reward of their efforts and feel secure in their control of the region and its trade. The district between the Caspian Sea and the Khivan territory—known as Turkomania—had to be occupied; the Russian outposts had to be pushed forward till they controlled the northern outlets of the great passes through the mountain barriers of Persia, Afghanistan, and India; and all the centers of Turkestan had to be connected by rail with the Russian system.'

The Russians had early sought to obtain a foothold on the inhospitable eastern coast of the Caspian Sea. They made three attempts to establish a base of operations on its shore; one on the island of Ashoor-ada in the Bay of Astrabad in 1837–38 in the face of vain protests by Persia and England; a second at Krasnovodsk—south of Kara Bugaz Bay—in 1869; and a third at Chikishliar—above the Atrek River—in 1871. After the failure of General Lomakin's first attempt in 1877 to penetrate Transcaspia from Chikishliar, Kransnovodsk became the base of all the future Russian activities in that region as well as the starting-point of its Transcaspian railway in later years. It was a difficult region for military operations under the most favorable conditions, for it is a country of deserts and arid plateaus extending southward to the rugged, wild foothills of the Kopat Dagh (mountain range), then forming the northern border of Persia. And in these foothills dwelt the powerful Turkoman tribes—the most warlike people in all Turkestan.

The dangers and difficulties having been fully demonstrated by the crushing defeat of General Lomakin's second expedition at Geok Teppe on September 9, 1879, the St. Petersburg statesmen selected their ablest warrior—General Michael Dmitriavitch Skobelev—as the commander-in-chief of their next army of invasion. He was assisted by General Kuropatkin—then a young man—who, after a distinguished career, became commander-in-chief of the Russian armies in the Russo-Japanese War. After careful preparations, Skobelev's army left Krasnovodsk in July, 1880, 8,000 strong, and proceeded to occupy the inland territory by a series of marches toward the southeast. The brave Turkoman forces were defeated and driven back to their famous stronghold at Geok Teppe. Here the last remnant of their troops surrendered after a three weeks' siege on January 24, 1881, and 8000 of the garrison were deliberately slain as a warning to the other peoples of the region.

Thereafter, Skobelev's progress was steady and without serious opposition. On February 9, 1881, he took Ashkabad, and then moved his advance posts south-eastward toward the oases of Tejend and Merv, and the commercial centers of Kaaka-Kalch and Sarkhs. And the success of his operations enabled the Russians to conclude with Persia the Akhak-Khorassan Boundary Convention on December 21, 1881, which assigned to Russia all of the northeast rim of the plateau of Iran, north of the river Atrek, and confirmed her possession of the Merv and Sarakhs districts. This gave Russia access to the great mountain frontier of Persia and gave her a direct connection with the trade of Khorassan. Alexander III, who had no wish to draw the attention of Europe to these successes or arouse the suspicions of Great Britain, recalled Skobelev, after the receipt of a protest from the British Foreign Office, and appointed General Komarov in his place.

M. Alikhanov was sent on a special mission to Merv in 1882–83, where he secured a preferential commercial treaty by winning over the leading merchants to the Russian cause. And the Russian control became so extensive and effective throughout the whole region that, within a year, they were able to organize the vast area of 200,000 square miles lying between Persia, Afghanistan, the Khanates of Khiva and Bokhara and the Caspian and Aral Seas, into the Russian province of Transcaspia. General Komarov became its governor-general in the spring of 1883. On February 18, 1884, Komarov secured at Ashkabad the allegiance of four leading chiefs and twenty-four notables of the Merv Tekkes, and was then able to penetrate without serious resistance the remarkable Tejend Oasis in the Kara Kum Desert, where for centuries the famous town of Merv—the "Queen of the World"—had flourished amid cultivated fields and orchards. He occupied the place and its noted fortress—the Koushid—on March 16, 1884, and, pushing on steadily southward, took the fortress of Sarakhs in May of the same year. Thus the occupation of all the strategic centers of the region was completed and the Russian forces brought within striking distance of the Afghan frontier.

Meanwhile, in 1873, England and Russia had reached an agreement concerning frontiers in Central Asia. This Anglo-Russian understanding was the result of a correspondence between the Earl of Granville and Prince Gortchakov during the period from October 17, 1872, to January 31, 1873. At that time the Russian advance having reached the Khanate of Bokhara, the British were anxious to see limited the unmarked frontier between that state and Afghanistan. The agreement then reached provided that the boundary line of Afghanistan should run from Siri Kul, or Lake Victoria, to the junction of the Oxus and Kokcha Rivers, and follow the Oxus (Amu-Daria) and the district of Andkjui on the north and northwest to pillar number 79 on the Oxus, set at about the sixty-sixth degree of east longitude. In this way, Badakshan, Wakshan, Afghan Turkestan (including the districts of Kunduz, Khulm, Balkh, Andkhui), and Herat were retained by Afghanistan. The desert to the north and northwest of the Afghan boundary was referred to as "belonging to independent tribes of Turkoman" which included the Tekkes of Merv.

Therefore, when the Russian forces seized Ashkabad, Merv, Sarakhs, the British Government felt that this agreement of 1873 had been deliberately violated; and they entered a vigorous protest at St. Petersburg, which led to a spirited diplomatic controversy lasting nearly three years. The British statesmen were fully awake to the significance of the Russian advance in Turkestan, which now threatened to absorb Herat and push through Afghanistan to the border of India. But their hands had been tied by troubles in the Sudan where General Gordon was besieged in Khartoum, and by the reluctance of some of their leaders, such as Gladstone, to use force in the protection of the British interests abroad.

However, while the diplomats wrote dispatches, the soldiers of Komarov were gaining possession of the Zulfikar Pass on the road to Herat early in 1885; and in March they engaged with the Afghans in battle on the Kushk. The Government of India hastened to the aid of the Afghans; and there ensued the famous "race for Herat," as it was termed by the writers of that day. Before any serious conflict took place, however, the diplomats of the two empires had secured the appointment of a joint commission to settle this vexatious frontier question. It met in St. Petersburg, and its findings were embodied in the Russo-Afghan Boundary Convention in 1887, which determined the northwest frontier line of Afghanistan from the Persian border on the Hari-rud River to the Bokhara line on the Oxus (pillar number 79). Later this was surveyed and marked for one hundred and fifty miles with pillars. In the main, this was a favorable decision for Russia, since it gave her access to the chief passes and trade routes into northern Afghanistan. Yet it was a great advantage to Afghanistan and India to have this vexatious frontier problem settled, to have Herat retained by Afghanistan, and to have adequate protection provided for the caravans and trace of this region through the control exercised by Russia over the restless Turkomans and desert peoples to the north of the line.

This Russo-Afghan Agreement marks the third step in the final erection of the southern mountain frontier of Russia Turkestan (the first two being the Russo-Persian Convention in 1881 and the Russo-British understanding in 1873). The fourth and last step in this work was the determination of the boundaries of the Pamir plateau. This famous highland barrier is a tremendous plateau and mountain region with an altitude of from 14,000 to 25,000 feet, situated north of the Hindu Kush and opposite to Chitral in northern India. It is known locally as the "Roof of the World"; but little information existed in Europe concerning this region till the exploration of the eighties and nineties. Russian explorers appeared there from the north, while British travelers worked their way through from the south—notably the mission of Colonel Gromtchevski in 1889 and that of Colonel Younghusband and Davidson about a year later, both of which were forced to retire by the hostility of the Afghan natives. In 1891 Colonel Yonov attempted to occupy the plateau with a strong force. The Afghans resisted his advance stoutly, and England ordered several regiments of Goorkhas to their assistance. So Yonov was compelled to withdraw. But Russia apologized for the invasion of Afghan territory and agreed to a partition of the Pamir, after a long and heated correspondence. Finally, the matter was amicably adjusted in the Anglo-Russian Convention of March, 1895, and by the appointment of a commission in the following September to survey the region and mark the boundary line. By this convention it was agreed that this line should run from the eastern end of Lake Victoria (Siri Kul) to the Chinese frontier, and that it should mark, not only the boundary line between Afghan and Russian territory, but also the line of division between the Russian and British spheres of influence. The long strip of land, now stretching like a finger between Turkestan and India, was to be retained by Afghanistan, this preventing the possessions of the two empires from coming into direct contact. China was to be urged to mark her boundary, so that all cause for further disputes would be removed. And the whole region was carefully explored and studied by two Danish expeditions so that the world might have definite information concerning this heretofore inaccessible country.

Meanwhile, the work of railway construction had been begun, at the suggestion of General Annenkov, at Krasnovodsk, and a line built via Ashkabad and Merv to Bokhara and Samarkand, to which last-mentioned place the road was opened in 1888. Later, this was connected with a line from Orenburg coming by way of Kazalinsk, Turkestan, and Tashkent, and the railway extended to Khojent, Kokand, and Andiijan in Ferghanna, with a branch from Merv to Kushlk on the border of Afghanistan. In this way the Russian Government completed its expansion in Central Asia, rounded out its frontiers, and consolidated its possessions by railways and trade routes. And altogether the Russian acquisition in the Steppes, Turkestan, and Transcaspia amounted to 1,366,833 miles bearing a population of over 9,000,000 in 1910. Included in their new territory was a large district received from China when the Kuldkja affair was settled at the Treaty of Peking in 1881. This region, reaching from the Ala Tau range to the Tienshan Mountains, rounded out the Russian holdings along the great Chinese mountain barriers, including the Issik Kul district, and gave her an additional share of Turkestan which she added to the province of Semirechensk.

Where to Find More Information

BLACK, C. E. (Ed.) *The Transformation of Russian Society*. Cambridge: Harvard Univ. Press, 1960. Pp. 42–90.

CAREW HUNT, R. N. *The Theory and Practice of Communism*. 5th rev. ed. N.Y.: Macmillan, 1957. Chs. 1–7.

CHARQUES, *Short History*, chs. 14 & 15.

CLARKSON, *History*, chs. 17–19.

DOSTOEVSKY, F. *The House of the Dead*. (Many editions.)

————. *The Possessed*. Signet Classic.

FEUER, L. S. (Ed.) *Marx & Engels: Basic Writings on Politics and Philosophy*. A Doubleday Anchor Original.

FLORINSKY, *Russia*, vol. 2, chs. 33–38.

FOOTMAN, D. *Red Prelude*. New Haven: Yale Univ. Press, 1945.

GONCHAROV, I. A. *Oblomov*. Everyman's Library.

GORKY, M. *My University Days*. N.Y.: Boni & Liveright, 1923.

HAIMSON, L. H. *The Russian Marxists and the Origins of Bolshevism*. Cambridge: Harvard Univ. Press, 1955. Preface, pp. 1–117.

HARCAVE, *Readings*, vol. 2, sections 1–6.

HARE, R. *Pioneers of Russian Social Thought*. N.Y.: Oxford Univ. Press, 1951.

JELAVICH, C. *Tsarist Russia and Balkan Nationalism*. Berkeley: Univ. of Calif. Press, 1958.

KARPOVICH, *Imperial Russia*, pp. 35–55.

KOHN, H. *PanSlavism: Its History and Ideology*. South Bend: Univ. of Notre Dame Press, 1953. Pp. 103–179.

KORNILOV, *Modern*, vol. 2.

KROPOTKIN, P. A. *Memoirs of a Revolutionist*. Boston: Houghton Mifflin, 1899.

LANGER, W. L. *The Diplomacy of Imperialism*. 2 vols. N.Y.: Knopf, 1935. Vol. 1, pp. 3–60.

LOBANOV-ROSTOVSKY, *Russia and Asia*, chs. 7–9.

LYASHCHENKO, *National Economy*, chs. 15–21.

MARTIN, *Picture History*, pp. 144–160.

MAVOR, *Economic History*, vol. 1, pp. 375–418; vol. 2, pp. 103–135.

MAYO, H. B. *Introduction to Marxist Theory*. N.Y.: Oxford Univ. Press, 1960.

MAZOUR, *Russia*, chs. 17 & 18.

MENDEL, A. P. (Ed.) *Essential Works of Marxism*. Bantam Books.

MILIUKOV, *Outlines*, vol. 1, ch. 7; vol. 2, ch. 3; vol. 3, chs. 3 & 5.

PARES, *History*, chs. 19–21.

PETROVICH, M. B. *The Emergence of Russian Pan Slavism*. N.Y.: Columbia Univ. Press, 1955. Chs. 3, 5, 7–9.

ROBINSON, G. T. *Rural Russia under the Old Regime*. 2d ed. N.Y.: Macmillan, 1949.

SETON-WATSON, H. *Decline of Imperial Russia, 1855–1914*. N.Y.: Praeger, 1956. Pp. 1–184.

SHUB, D. *Lenin, A Biography*. Mentor Books.

TURGENEV, I. S. *Fathers and Sons*. Signet Classic.

WALSH, *Russia*, chs. 14–16.

WOLFE, B. D. *Three Who Made a Revolution*. Boston: Beacon Press, 1950.

WREN, *Course*, chs. 21–23.

Part VII

The Road to Revolution

Economic Developments, 1890–1914

The following description of some of the major economic developments in the late nineteenth and early twentieth centuries is intended only as a brief introduction. It begins with agrarian economy because, although by 1900 the total output of industry exceeded in value the aggregate output of agriculture, the great majority of the Russian people got their living directly from the land. The sketch, written by the editor, is based mostly upon Russian materials.

Between the Emancipation and the 1905 Revolution the peasants as a class acquired approximately fifty-two million acres of land, but the individual holding of the average peasant at the latter date was only about half what it had been in 1860. The figures for 1905 also show that the peasants, who made up at least 85 per cent of the total population, owned only 37 per cent of the land. Of the remaining land, the state owned 34 per cent; private landlords, 26 per cent; and the church, 3 per cent. Moreover, land prices had more than doubled during this generation and a half. This meant that the value of the peasant holding remained constant even though the amount of the holding was less. It also meant, of course, that it was twice as hard for the peasant to acquire additional lands. The peasant hunger for land might have been reduced and the situation might have been greatly eased had the production rates increased during these years. The average harvest returns of the Russian peasants, however, remained low as the following tables show.

AVERAGE HARVEST RETURNS (LBS. PER ACRE) BEFORE 1905

Nation	Wheat	Rye	Oats
Germany	1109	812	1064
United States	868	605	909
Russia	406	468	407

A somewhat different view of this same phenomenon at a later date may be gained from an international comparison of the figures for the per capita average production, export, and consumption of small grains.

SMALL GRAINS (STATED IN LBS. PER HEAD), 1909–1914.

Nation	Produced	Exported	Consumed
Canada	3730	811	2919
United States	2523	85	2438
Rumania	1925	1000	925
Russia	979	141	838

An arbitrary but typical account of the imaginary "average peasant" in 1905 shows an investment in land and buildings of 490 rubles upon which he paid 60 rubles a year in taxes and interest. Other annual money expense amounted to 160 rubles. He could expect an annual cash income from the sale of produce and livestock, supplemented by such extra work as he could get, of 134 rubles. His annual deficit would therefore be 86 rubles. Many peasants, as the official figures show, were on relief.

To put it in somewhat over-simplified form, there were too many peasants for the production per acre. As of the years 1903–1905, there were about 139 millions of persons in Russia. Approximately 111 Millions of these were classed as peasants; and 100 millions, more or less, were engaged in agriculture. It is a most significant commentary upon the situation that some 66 millions were unable to support themselves on the produce of their land and had to supplement their income by other work. The government relief figures show that many were not able to earn enough for subsistence. Government expenditures for the relief of poverty rose from approximately 12 million rubles for the period 1871–1890 to 268 million rubles for the period 1901–1906.

These mounting relief costs, as well as the rising expenses of a state which was slowly being modernized, had to be met either by some form of taxation or by borrowing. But taxation had its limits. The peasants paid —or at least were responsible for—90 per cent of the taxes, but tax collectors could not get blood from a turnip nor tax money from an impoverished peasant. The arrears of unpaid peasant taxes steadily increased. During the years 1871–1880, every peasant-owned acre owed tax arrears of eight cents to the state. By the period 1891–1900, every peasant-owned acre owed tax arrears of twenty cents.

The general agricultural situation, so gloomy in 1905, showed marked improvement in the years immediately before the first world war. The period from 1907 to 1914 was one of general prosperity, perhaps the most prosperous in Russian history. This happy condition was due to a combination of circumstances. First, there was a succession of good harvests, thanks to beneficent weather. Second, the breakdown of the commune as a result of the Stolypin Reforms resulted in an increase in the acreage occupied and cultivated by the more vigorous and progressive peasants. Third, the extension of credit by peasant banks and the steady growth of peasant co-operatives provided cheaper and better financing for peasant landowning and cultivation. The growth of the co-operative movement was especially striking. In 1901 there were roughly 2000 peasant co-operatives with a membership of 700,000. At the outbreak of war in 1914, there were 33,000 co-operatives with a total membership of 12 millions. Finally, prosperity fed upon itself to some extent. The improved economic well-being of certain peasant classes provided a better domestic market for manufactured goods. This, in turn, greatly aided by improvements in transportation, was reflected in the increase and improvement of markets for the peasants' products. Industry and commerce shared and participated in this prosperity.

In terms of self-comparisons—*i.e.,* of Russia with Russia—there were spectacular advances in both industry and commerce. The value of the aggregate industrial output of Russia rose from 541 millions of rubles in 1871 to nearly six billions of rubles in 1912. The production of pig iron increased from 1.3 millions of tons in 1894 to 5.1 millions of tons in 1913. Eighteen thousand tons of coal were mined in 1900; 40 million tons in 1913. Other figures bear out these samples as typical and the following table, showing the values of imports and exports in millions of rubles, rounds out the picture of the Russian commercial advance.

Yearly Average	Imports	Exports
1898–1902	617.4	739.6
1903–1907	723.3	1046.6
1908–1912	1047.4	1397.1
1912	1171.8	1518.8
1913	1374.0	1520.1

It is worth noting in passing that the bulk of the imports in 1913 came from Germany, which supplied 652.4 millions of rubles worth. Great Britain was a poor second with a figure of 207.6.

A somewhat false impression may be created, however, by these self-comparisons. A few international comparisons will balance the account. During the period 1912–1913, Russia mined 0.2 tons of coal per capita. This was much more than a decade before, but the United States in the same period was mining coal at the per capita rate of 5.12 tons. Similarly, in 1912–13, the United States, on a per capita basis, used 0.23 hp for manufacturing. Russia used 0.01 hp.

Finally, neither Russia nor the Russians owned all this new industrial and commercial wealth. The table below shows the amount of foreign capital entering Russia.

1851–1888	1,600,000 rubles
1889–1894	5,300,000 rubles
1895–1899	305,000,000 rubles
1905–1908	370,700,000 rubles

Between 1904 and 1913, more than three billions of rubles worth of Russian bonds were sold abroad. The foreign investment in Russian industries totaled two billion rubles by 1914. Of this, about 33 per cent was

French; 23 per cent, British; 20 per cent, German; and 14 per cent, Belgian. Approximately one-third of the capital in Russian stock companies was foreign owned. Nearly two-thirds of the pig iron and one-half of the coal produced were based on French capital. The government was also directly involved with foreign capital. The Russian state debt owed abroad increased from one billion, seven hundred and thirty-three million rubles in 1894 to four billion, two hundred and twenty-nine million rubles in 1914. France was the creditor for about 80 per cent of this debt, and Great Britain, for most of the remainder. Clearly there was some truth in the charge that imperial Russia was not far removed in some respects from semi-colonial status.

The Industrial Revolution

> The Industrial Revolution came to Russia much later than to Western Europe. The following selection gives a brief description and analysis of the movement in Russia. The source is: James Mavor, *An Economic History of Russia*. Second edition. Two volumes. New York: E. P. Dutton & Co., 1925. Vol. 2, pp. 363–367.

Apart from the question of the supply of labour, the general economical conditions in Russia prior to the Emancipation were not favourable to the growth of industry on any extensive scale. The economic life of the country was highly self-contained. Each estate, and sometimes each village, was a little world practically complete within itself. Even the noble landowners, who spent a portion of the year in the capitals, transported to their town houses from their estates almost the whole of the produce necessary for their support and for the support of their numerous retinue of servants. With the exception of iron, tea, cotton, and a few other staple commodities not at that time produced in Russia in sufficient quantities to satisfy the existing demand, only articles of luxury were imported, or even transferred from place to place. The great commerce which had been characteristic of early Russia, and which had been the basis of its economical and political strength, had disappeared. The "immobilization" of labour had as inevitable concomitant the "immobilization" of goods. There were, moreover, almost no railways. There was no banking system, and as yet there was but a trifling circulation of money in the country. Yet there are those who look back upon the age of bondage as an age of relative abundance—an age in which there was no freedom, but in which there was in general plenty to eat. All the conditions which have been described had to be greatly modified before extensive industry was possible. The changes began immediately after Emancipation. The creation of Land Redemption Banks and the negotiation of foreign loans provided a financial basis; railways were built rapidly in European Russia, and numbers of foreign capitalists—principally English, German, Belgian, and French—established factories for the manufacture of cottons, woolens, etc., in the late sixties and in the seventies. Some of the ancient towns developed into industrial centres. The regions specially affected by the industrial movement at this time were the Moskovskaya gub., St. Petersburg and its neighbourhood, the Baltic Provinces, and parts of Poland.

The growth of the railway system in the seventies and the protective tariff, which reached its fullest development in 1891, stimulated industry enormously. From this time onward the urban proletariat, which, owing to the various causes indicated above, had previously no considerable existence in Russia, began to become numerous and influential. Movement from the villages, ceased to be impeded by the Government, and artisans began to crowd into the towns. The excess of labour at once rendered labour cheap, and rendered the employers indifferent to the comfort of the labourers. The beginning of the process of industrial development on an extensive scale was not accompanied by the ameliorative legislation which, initiated in England, had been carried far in Germany and France—in all countries, in fact, in which the concentration of workmen in industrial towns had been taking place. Ere long the rigorous exploitation of labour brought the grievances of the workmen under the notice of the Government. Long hours, inadequate wages, and still more importantly, the knowledge that workmen in other countries were reputed to be better off than those in Russia, led to demands upon the Government to intervene. In countries where a measure of laisser faire existed, the natural and obvious method of labour association was productive, to a certain extent, of improved conditions. Even in such countries the power of the State was invoked in restricting the hours of labour, in regulating the system of "truck," and in providing for the protection of the working men against exposed machinery and in inevitably dangerous occupations. But in Russia such steps were taken slowly, and they were regarded by the workmen as inadequate, while labour association was practically prohibited.

Side by side with private enterprises, there were established Government factories for the manufacture of cloth, paper, tinned provisions, etc., together with metal refineries, foundries, porcelain works, etc., etc. These activities of the Government were supplemented by the factories belonging to the Udeli (The Imperial Appanage), in which large numbers of men were employed.

The circumstances that many of the private enterprises were brought into existence by the high protective duties, and that these enterprises were encouraged by the Government in its own factories, and in those of the Udeli, pursued methods similar to those of the private firms, made it inevitable that the responsibility for the situation should rest upon the shoulders of the Government. The labour question thus from the middle of the seventies assumed a definite political aspect.

In Russia, labour combination, in the West European sense, was prohibited. "Protection" appeared to exist solely for the manufacturer, whose enterprises received governmental assistance and encouragement. The Government not only facilitated the development of industries by high tariffs, but through the State Bank it financed industrial enterprises, and through the State domain it gave land, mining, and timber concessions to persons who were willing to undertake the task of industrial organization. Many of these persons were foreigners, or the agents of foreigners, who were specially protected by the Russian Government. In brief, the hand of the Government was everywhere.

The effect of this situation was to direct against the Government a large part of the irritation engendered in the minds of the working men against their employers. If, for example, a foreman in a factory lost his temper and beat a workman, the latter might complain to the Government factory inspector, but if the latter did not take the workman's view of the case, he came to be looked upon as a partner in the offence committed by the foreman. The chinovneke, or official class, came to bear the burden of the faults of its members, and the whole governmental system came to be called in question. Meanwhile the Government neglected to apply the ameliorating legislation which had been applied under similar conditions of protection and encouragement of industry by Germany, and the factory system, inspection notwithstanding, continued to be conducted in what the workmen now recognized fully to be an archaic manner.

The comparatively small number of working men in the cities, which before Emancipation were rather political and trading than manufacturing centres, accounts for the late appearance of labour organizations, excepting some of a rudimentary character.

·   ·   ·

While the development of industry on the large scale in Russia has lagged behind that of Western Europe in point of time, the late development, in the technical and commercial senses, has been accompanied by a late development in a social sense. The exploitation of the working men and women has been more severe than for many years it has been in any Western European country. The practice of "search," universal in Russia, the practice of beating workmen and other similar practices, are incidents in a system of oppression which survived the Emancipation, but which recent events have done much to mitigate. Low wages and unfavourable conditions of work have, as will be seen, played a conspicuous part in producing the "state of mind" which made the Revolution.

While the factory system has been developing in Russia with great rapidity, partly under the influence of a high protective tariff, there has been a spontaneous and very widespread development of the so-called kustarny or household industry in villages. In some gubernie, notably in Moskovskaya gub., the Zemstvos have encouraged the kustars or household artisans by organizing for them the direct supply of raw materials and by facilitating the formation of artels, or co-operative groups. It seems that in some industries, small iron ware, cardboard, leather, woodwork, etc., not only do the kustars compete with the large manufacturers, but they have in some cases succeeded in directing the trade wholly into their own hands.

The Growth of Russian Industry

The following excerpt from a recent study of Russian economic history by a scholar having full access to Russian materials will supplement the account given on pp. 535–538. Professor Lyaschenko was born and educated under the tsarist regime. He published three major studies before the 1917 Revolution and, despite the fact that he was a "legal Marxist," he held high academic rank at the University of Tomsk. After the revolution he served as a professor at the First Moscow State University and at the Institute of National Economy.

The first edition of his *History of the National Economy of Russia* was published in 1939 by the Soviet Academy of Sciences and was officially designated for use in "schools of economics." This edition is available in English translation. The 1947/48 edition from which the following excerpts were translated was approved by the Soviet Ministry of Education for use in "institutions of higher learning." There are major differences between the two editions.

The source is: P. I. Lyashchenko, *Istoriya narodnogo khoziaistva SSSR*. Two volumes. Moscow: State Publishing House, 1947/48. Vol. II (1948), pp. 148–160, 162, 170, 171, 214, 215. Abridged.

The 1890's

INDUSTRIAL PROGRESS IN THE 1890's

Year	No. of enterprises	No. of workers	Total value of production
1887	30,888	1,318,000	1,334.5 million Rs.
1890	32,254	1,424,700	1,502.7 million Rs.
1897	39,029	2,098,300	2,839.1 million Rs.
1900	38,141	2,373,400	3,005.9 million Rs.

During the decade 1887–1897, the number of enterprises increased 26.3 per cent; the number of workers, 59.2 per cent; and the total production, 112.8 per cent. But in the decade 1890–1900, the number of enterprises increased 18.3 per cent; the number of workers, 66.6 per cent; and the total production, 100 per cent. There took place not only an absolute increase in the number of enterprises, but also a concentration and rapid increase in productivity. . . . the rate of increase in the total industrial production during the 1890's, according to the official data was: 1878–1887, 26.1 million rubles a year; 1888–1892, 41.6 million rubles a year; 1892–1897, 161.2 million rubles a year.

. . . although the textile industry was foremost in absolute volume of production, the heavy industries (mining and metallurgy) were rapidly catching up with the light industries during these years. From 1887–1897, the total increase in production for industries was: mining, 11.2 per cent; chemical, 10.7 per cent; lumber, 9.3 per cent; metallurgical, 8.4 per cent; ceramics, 8 per cent; textiles, 7.8 per cent; and food, 1.7 per cent.

PRODUCTION IN MAJOR INDUSTRIES
(Stated in tons)

Year	Total coal mined	Total oil produced	Total iron mined	Pig iron smelted	Steel & iron produced
1860	329,400			352,800	223,200
1870	763,200	32,400	825,750	372,600	261,000
1880	3,610,800	612,200	1,083,600	469,800	635,400
1890	5,049,600	4,348,000	1,913,400	993,600	871,200
1895	9,999,000	6,948,000	3,024,000	1,561,900	1,121,400
1900	17,913,000	11,376,000	6,609,600	3,182,400	2,419,200

Iron and steel production for the whole country increased two times over during the five years, 1895–1900; iron and steel production in the south increased three to four times during the period. . . . The share of the Urals in the total production dropped from 67 per cent in the 1870's to 28 per cent in 1900, but that of the south increased from 0.1 per cent to 51 per cent.

The percentage increases in various phases of the cotton textile industry between 1890 and 1900 were as follows:

Number of spinning mills 65%
Number of weaving mills 42%
Number of spindles 76%
Number of looms 68%
Raw cotton used 94%
Unbleached cloth made 74%
Value of unbleached cloth 65%
Value of cotton 82%
Value of cotton yarn 107%

.   .   .

During the decade of the 1890's, therefore, Russian industry was rapidly being converted to large-scale capitalist techniques and to large-scale ways of production. . . . In 1879, factories employing less than 500 workers accounted for 79.7 per cent of all factories and 44.2 per cent of all workers. The respective figures for 1890 were almost the same, but by 1902, they stood at 73.8 per cent of all factories, and only 30.7 per cent of all workers. Factories employing more than 1,000 workers amounted to 7 per cent of the total in 1879; 7.6 per cent, in 1890; and 11 per cent in 1902. The percentages of workers employed in these large factories were, respectively: 32.8, 37.7 and 49.8. By the beginning of the twentieth century, large-scale enterprises accounted for half of all the workers; twenty years earlier, for only a third. . . .

TYPICAL FIGURES SHOWING INCREASES IN VOLUME AND IN CONCENTRATION
OF PRODUCTION IN THE METALLURGICAL INDUSTRY

	1880	1900	1909
Pig iron smelted per plant (tons)	4,559	12,888	36,900
Number of workers per plant	899	1,325	1,545
Horsepower per plant	255	1,286	1,805
Horsepower per worker	0.28	0.97	1.17
Pig iron smelted per blast furnace (tons) ...	9,296	22,644	40,968
Pig iron smelted per worker (lbs.)	10,152	18,676	
Open-hearth steel produced per furnace (tons)	7,164	15,804	
Bessemer steel produced per converter (tons)	25,992	41,148	

RAILROAD CONSTRUCTION. After the railway fever of 1870–1875—a five-year period during which railway trackage was increased by 7,500 versts, construction proceeded at a slower pace from 1876 to 1890. But from 1891 to 1895, new railway construction added 6,257 versts of new trackage, while the next five-year period (1896–1900) added 15,139 versts, and the total trackage was increased to 56,130 versts in 1901. During the single decade of the 1890's, in other words, 37 per cent of the total trackage (or half as much as had been built during the preceding half century) was laid down. . . . It should be noted that . . . the European part of Russia had 9.7 kilometers of railway trackage per thousand square kilometers of territory; england had 106 kilometers and Germany had 80 kilometers for the same unit. . . . At the beginning of the twentieth century, the total capital invested in railroads throughout the whole country amounted to 4.7 billion rubles, 3.5 billion rubles of which belonged to the government.

. . .

BASIC CAPITAL IN MAJOR INDUSTRIES
(in millions of rubles)

Industry	1890	1900	Percentage increase
Mining	85.7	392.2	358%
Metallurgical	27.8	257.3	826%
Chemical	15.6	93.8	501%
Ceramics	6.7	59.0	781%
Textile	197.5	373.7	89%
Food	87.6	153.1	75%
All industries	580.1	1,742.3	200%

ORIGIN OF EACH 100 WORKERS

Year	Peasants	Others
1884/5	91.5	8.5
1899	94.2	5.8

PERCENTAGE OF WORKERS WHOSE
FATHERS HAD BEEN FACTORY WORKERS

Year	Fathers Had	Fathers Had Not
1884/5	55.0	45.0
1899	55.6	44.4

. . .

AVERAGE WAGES IN LATE 1890's AND EARLY 1900's
(Stated in rubles per year for all workers in named industry)

Cotton manufacturing	171
Woolen manufacturing	170
Woodworking (mechanized)	215
Food products	182
Manufacture of mineral products	204
Chemicals	260
Metal works, machine work, etc.	341

. . .

Thus, in the course of the years 1890 to 1899, industrial capitalism overcoming low productivity, stereotyped techniques, and backward social conditions rapidly moved Russian industry far ahead. Russian industry, to be sure, still lagged far behind the advanced countries of the period in the volume of production in certain industries. But in those ten years, nonetheless, it had advanced very significantly, achieving a rate of concentration much higher than in the outstanding capitalist countries. Russian industry outstripped that of nearly all other countries in the speed of its development. For example, the smelting of pig iron during this decade increased in England, by 18 per cent; in Germany, by 72 per cent; in the U.S.A., by 50 per cent; and in Russia, by 190 per cent. . . . The production of iron during this time increased in England, by 8 per cent; in Germany, by 78 per cent; in the U.S.A., by 63 per cent; and in Russia, by 116 per cent. The English coal industry expanded by 22 per cent; the German, by 52 per cent; the American, by 61 per cent; and the Russian, by 131 per cent. Finally, in cotton manufacturing, the number of spindles in England increased 3.8 per cent; in the U.S.A., 25.6 per cent; in continental Europe, 33 per cent; and in Russia, 76 per cent.

. . .

1900–1909

The general European financial crisis which began in 1899 soon affected developments in Russia. There was a rapid fall in stocks, in bank capital, and in prices. Not all industries were hit equally hard, but there were many bankruptcies and rather widespread unemployment. The nadir of the crisis was 1902, but the Russo-Japanese War and the 1905 Revolution produced a slowdown if not a temporary recession which lasted until 1908/09. The following data, meant to illustrate the characteristics of the period from 1900 to 1909, have been adapted from the text and tables given by Professor Lyashchenko. The source is: Lyashchenko, *Istoriya,* vol. II, pp. 230–242 *passim,* 283, 284.

STOCK PRICES IN RUBLES

Company	1899	1900	1901
Petersburg Discount & Loan Bank	809	665	472
Briansk Factory	511.5	475	240
Donets-Urev	680	530	210
Baku Oil	950	830	695

* * *

DONBAS COAL MINES

	1900	1901	1902	1903
Mines operating ..	290	246	240	209
Production in tons	12,445,200	12,499,200	11,557,800	13,104,000

* * *

For example, at Moscow the price for iron girders fell from 2 rubles 30 kopecks in the middle of 1899 to 1 ruble 45 kopecks at the end of 1900, to 1 ruble 25 kopecks at the end of 1901, and to 1 ruble ten kopecks at the end of 1902. The price of structural iron fell from 1 ruble 68 kopecks in 1900 to 1 ruble 40 kopecks in 1901. The price of pig iron dropped from 70–80 kopecks at the middle of 1900 to 45–48 kopecks at the end of the year. The price of coal fell from 9–10 kopecks at the beginning of 1900 to 6–7 kopecks by the end of 1902. The price of crude oil went down from 17 or 18 kopecks in 1900 to 4 or 6 kopecks in 1902. The fall of prices began in the first half of 1900 and continued through most of 1902 when the crisis reached its lowest point.

* * *

PIG IRON SMELTED (IN TONS)

Year	Tons
1899	2,946,600
1900	3,195,000
1901	3,110,400
1902	2,817,000
1903	2,683,800
1904	3,250,800
1905	2,984,400
1906	2,952,000
1907	3,097,800
1908	3,079,800

* * *

INDUSTRIAL DEVELOPMENT, 1887–1908

Year	No. of Factories	Total production (in millions of rubles)	No. of workers
1887	30,888	1,334.5	1,318,000
1897	39,029	2,839.1	2,098,200
1908	39,866	4,908.7	2,679,700

RATE OF GROWTH IN PERCENTAGES

	1887–1897	1897–1908
No. of enterprises increased by	26.3%	2.1%
Total value of production increased by	112.7%	72.9%
No. of workers increased by	59.2%	27.7%

• • •

The General Situation

Lyashchenko, *Istoriya,* vol. II, pp. 287–289.

Despite the relative advances and the high degree of concentration in Russian industry, the general economic development undeniably lagged. A whole range of important and key branches were completely or almost completely lacking in Russia. Thus, the making of machine-tools was very backward. The greater part of the manufacturing equipment for factories and mills, especially of the more complicated types such as electrical equipment, turbines, machine-tools, etc. had to be obtained from abroad. There was absolutely no automobile industry. The basic chemical industry was very weak. . . .

How far Russia lagged behind the advanced countries of the West in industrial economics may be seen from the following figures. In 1913, the total volume of industrial production in Russia was 2.5 times less than that of France; 4.6 times less than that of England; 6 times less than the Germans; and 14.3 times smaller than that of the United States. This backwardness was most marked in certain industries, including some of the major ones. For example, in 1913, the Russian coal industry produced 36,000,000 tons; the German, 190,100,000 tons; the British, 292,000,-000 tons; and the American, 517,100,000 tons. Russian iron ore production was 9,500,000 tons; French, 43,000,000 tons; and the American, 63,000,000 tons. Russia produced 4,600,000 tons of pig iron; the United States, 31,500,000 tons; Germany, 16,800,000. American copper production was 557,200 tons; the Russian, 31,100. The backwardness of [Russian] industrial production is even more apparent when stated in terms of per capita production. Thus, in 1913, the production of electrical power in Russia was 14 kilowatt hours per capita against an American per capita output of 175.6 kilowatt hours; the smelting of pig iron was at the per capita rate of 30.3 kilograms in Russia compared to 326.5 in the U.S.A. . . . Per capita consumption of cotton was 19 kilograms in England, 14 kg. in the United States, and 3.1 kg. in Russia. An even more noteworthy fact is that Russia not only failed to overtake the more advanced capitalist countries but also continued to lag farther behind them. Thus, pig iron production on a per capita basis was eight times greater in the United States than in Russia in 1900; eleven times, in 1913.

• • •

A few scattered items computed from data given in the same source will round out this sketch. The production of farm machinery in 1912 was 570 per cent greater than it had been in 1897, 392 per cent greater than in 1900, and 136 per cent greater than in 1908. The number of cotton-spinning spindles was 137 per cent greater in 1913 than in 1900. Yarn production (cotton) increased by about 160 per cent in the same period. Pig iron production increased by 152 per cent between 1910 and 1913, steel production by about the same percentage, coal by 145 per cent, and the production of linen yarn by 149 per cent.

Labor, Wages, and Labor Legislation

The earliest attempt to ameliorate the lot of the Russian workers by fiat and law was made in 1741, eighty-one years before England's famous law limiting child labor in the textile mills. The Russian regulations covered wages, working hours, working conditions, medical assistance, and housing. A law of 1785 called for a sixty-hour work week. Both these eighteenth-century efforts were ineffective, but they at least established a precedent which the nineteenth century followed and expanded, first in the field of medical aid and later in workmen's insurance and regulatory legislation.

The first excerpt below sketches the history of medical aid to workers from 1866 to the end of the nineteenth century. The second selection deals with growth and changes in the industrial labor force and summarizes some of the measures taken for the protection of workers. The third recounts in greater detail the development of workmen's compensation insurance; the fourth shows, by means of a table, the actual operation of the disability insurance system from 1904 through 1908; the fifth summarizes the role of factory inspectors; and the final item gives the official figures on the average annual earnings of Russian workers in the early twentieth century. It should be noted for purposes of comparison with these figures that the average daily earning of women employees in Italy in 1902 was $0.23, and that the daily wages of Norwegian workers ranged (in 1907) from $0.268 to $1.25, or from about $80.00 to $375.00 annually.

The source for all these excerpts is: *Twenty-Fourth Annual Report of the Commissioner of Labor. 1909. Workmen's Insurance and Compensation Systems in Europe.* Two volumes. Washington: Government Printing Office, 1911. Vol. II, pp. 2087–2092, 2097–2103, 2117–2118, 2130, 2140–2141, 2207–2210.

History

To understand the development of Russian legislation in regard to medical assistance to workmen employed in factories it is necessary to point out that, in theory, medical aid is considered a proper governmental function, to be supplied in cities by the municipal government, and in the rural districts by the so-called "zemstvos"—organs of local self-government. In provinces where zemstvos have not been organized the duty of furnishing medical aid to the rural population devolves upon the governmental authorities. In practice only a very few municipalities have met this duty, and in those provinces which have as yet no zemstvos the organization of medical aid is purely formal and perfunctory. On the other hand, the zemstvos have, since their organization in the early sixties, always looked upon the organization of medical aid as one of their most important functions. The combined budgets of these zemstvos amount to many millions of dollars, and about one-fourth of the total expenditures is being devoted to medical aid in rural communities. There are many free hospitals and dispensaries in each county (*uyezd*) where a zemstvo exists, and the Russian peasant may be said to be fairly well provided with free medical assistance.

LAW OF 1866.—The law which imposed upon the factory owners the duty of furnishing medical aid to their factory employees dates from the year 1866. It owes its origin to the beginning of an epidemic of Asiatic cholera in Moscow. The governor of Moscow, considering the large factories with their insanitary conditions and large number of workers a possible means of spreading the cholera epidemic, in a report to the minister of interior suggested that the owners of large factories be required to establish hospitals and employ physicians in connection with their industrial establishments. As a result of this suggestion a decision of the committee of ministers was approved by the Emperor August 26 (Sept. 7), 1866, ordering as a temporary measure that "there be established in connection with each factory employing 1,000 workers a hospital with ten beds, and at each factory employing more than 1,000 workers 15 beds or more, and at each factory employing less than 1,000 workers 5 beds or more, at the rate of one for each 100 workers." Though the order was declared to be a temporary measure no time limit was mentioned, and the law is still in force.

The indefinite language of this law and the absence of any punitive measures for noncompliance with its demands or any organ of inspection and control, except the police authorities, left the entire problem in a very unsatisfactory condition. The language of the order showed that the intention existed at that time to follow it up with a systematic law regulating the question of medical aid to factory employees, for the minister of interior was ordered to present a plan for such legislation to the Imperial Council. In 1867, and again in 1874 in connection with a proposal of a law for regulation of conditions of employment, these legislative propositions were discussed, but without success, as the Imperial Council judged the law of 1866 to be sufficient and refused to go any further in this matter. The effect of this law was far from uniform; its execution depended mainly upon the zeal and energy of the provincial governors. In some factories good hospitals were established; in others the beds were left without medical attendance, and in a great many localities the law was entirely disregarded. In many factories the costs of these medical establishments were charged to the workmen.

LAW OF 1886.—This latter abuse was checked by the law of June 3 (15), 1886, regulating the conditions of employment and the relations between employers and employees, which among other things prohibited the deducting of the cost of medical aid from the wages of the workmen (Code, Vol. XI, 2, Industrial Code, sec. 102). On the other hand, it established serious limitations to the extent of medical aid to the workmen required of the employers, by laying down the rules that the employer could discharge any workman at two weeks' notice and immediately in case of a contagious disease. Evidently a dismissed employee had no claim to medical aid from the employer after the termination of the employment.

The law of June 3 (15), 1886, established municipal factory commissions for St. Petersburg, Moscow, Odessa, and Warsaw, and provincial commissions for the separate Provinces, and these commissions were intrusted among other things with the administrative regulations of the problem of medical aid to factory employees.

EXTENSION OF THE LAW TO MINING AND METALLURGY.—By a decree of March 9 (21), 1892, the provisions of the law of 1886 were extended to apply to the mining and metallurgical industries and were embodied in the Mining Code. Local mining commissions were established with functions parallel to those of the factory commissions, including the regulation of medical assistance to the employees. A law requiring proprietors of mining and metallurgical establishments to establish hospital facilities for treatment of sick employees had been on the Russian statute books for sixty years before similar provisions were made for factory industries, namely, in the general mining law of July 13 (25), 1806, for the mining industry was developed much earlier than manufactures. The greater danger to health and life from work in the mines was evident, and many of these establishments were owned from the beginning of Russian industry by the State or Crown, which was more inclined to take care of its employees.

According to this law, both the State and private mining and metallurgical establishments employing 200 persons or more were required to have a hospital and one or more resident physicians; but in the case of privately owned mines the law remained a dead letter until 1892. Finally both the local factory commissions and the local mining commissions were united into factory and mining commissions by the act of June 7 (19), 1899, which also established a central factory and mining commission and put it in control of the local commissions, for the purpose of unifying this work. The central commission is required to formulate general principles for the administration of the law of 1866, but the actual administration is still in the hands of the local commissions and exercised through the factory and mine inspectors. Provincial commissions were established in 64 provinces; in 35 of these such regulations were established, and in the remaining 29, mostly nonindustrial provinces, practically nothing was added to the ambiguous language of the law of 1866.

While the establishment of factory hospitals was mandatory according to the exact language of the law of 1866, it was nevertheless evident that for small industrial establishments with 100 or even less employees the organization of such a private hospital would either be a great hardship, possibly not demanded in view of the existence of good hospitals in the immediate vicinity, or would become a pure formality without any substantial benefit to the employees. Nor was it clear whether the law applied to factories with less than 100 workmen, whether 5 beds was the minimum number for a factory hospital, and what the requirements were in regard to medical attendance. In answer to inquiries from the Moscow provincial factory commission it was explained in 1887 that conditions had changed considerably during the preceding two decades, and that the growth of the activity of zemstvos and municipalities in supplying hospital facilities has made the organization of special factory hospitals unnecessary in many cases, and that as a substitute for the required hospitals factory owners may in certain cases be required to enter into agreements with zemstvos and other bodies for the supply of hospital and other medical facilities to their employees.

Regulations of Moscow

As an example of the regulations established by the provincial factory commissions, those in force since February 1 (13) 1897, in the province of Moscow, outside of the city of Moscow, may be briefly mentioned. Factories employing 500 or more workmen are required to have a factory hospital with one bed for each 100 workmen, a resident physician and a "feldsher" (a medical assistant of a somewhat higher grade than a trained nurse). When the number of workmen exceeds 3,000 two physicians must be employed, one of whom shall reside at the factory. Factories employing from 17 to 500 workmen may be freed from this obligation if they make arrangements with the zemstvo hospital or any other hospital, or several factories may combine for establishing a common hospital. In exceptional cases such arrangement may be permitted to factories having more than 500 workmen. When the factory hospital has less than 5 beds the physician need not reside at the factory, but must live not more than 7 versts (4.7 miles) from it, and must visit it at least three times a week, while the hospital must have a resident "feldsher." When the factory has no hospital of its own, and the distance to the hospital with which such arrangements have been made is more than 3 versts (2 miles), the factory must have an emergency room with all necessary appliances for first aid to sick or injured, and, if the number of workmen exceeds 200, also a "feldsher." Artisans' shops employing no more than 16 workmen are not subject to any of these requirements. In factories employing more than 500 workmen the hospital is required to consist of three divisions—a general ward, a contagious ward with facilities for isolation when necessary, and a dispensary for outside patients. Where both men and women are employed there must be separate rooms for each sex in both the general ward and the contagious ward. The rooms must contain a minimum air capacity of 3 cubic sazhens (1,029 cubic feet) per each bed; there must also be warm privies. In factories employing from 200 to 500 workmen the hospital must contain at least four rooms—two wards, an examination room, and a waiting room for outside patients. In factories employing less than 200 workmen at least two rooms are required, one for the beds and one for the outdoor patients. Where 200 or more women are employed, a special maternity room must be provided and also the services of a resident trained midwife; where less than 200 women are employed, such room and the services of a midwife must be furnished by the employer when necessary. Information must be furnished the factory commission in regard to the exact measures taken for compliance with these regulations.

. . .

The industrial development of the Russian Empire dates practically from the day of the emancipation of the serfs in 1861. Prior to that date manufacturing was conducted mainly in artisans' shops, and the few factories and mills then existing mostly employed serf labor. The problems of workmen's insurance could not have arisen in Russia until a comparatively recent date. Russia is primarily an agricultural country. The rural population, according to the census of 1897, constituted 108,811,626 out of a total of 125,640,021, or 86.6 per cent. Of the 33,201,495 persons gainfully employed, 18,245,287, or 55 per cent, were engaged in agriculture. Together with their dependents they constituted 93,701,564, or 74.6 per cent of the entire population.

But within the last thirty years the growth of Russian industry has been quite rapid. The urban population increased from 7,293,161, or 10 per cent of the total population, in 1858, to 16,828,395, or 13.4 per cent, in 1897.

According to the later census, the total number of persons employed in manufacturing and mechanical pursuits in 1897 was 5,169,919 and in transportation 714,745, making a total of 5,884,664 for the industrial army, or 17.7 per cent of those gainfully employed.

Table 1 shows the number and per cent of persons engaged in the various industries, according to the census of 1897 (*see next page*).

The industrial developement of Russia, as of any other country, manifested itself not only in the increase of the number of persons employed in industrial occupations, but also in the substitution of large manufacturing establishments for small, independent undertakings and the consequent growth of the wage-earning classes.

The problem of workmen's insurance concerns itself mainly with the wage-earner and not with the independent producer. For this reason the report published in 1906 by the Russian Government concerning the number of wage-earners in Russia, though based upon the data of the census of 1897, is of great importance. In Table II are shown the total number of persons employed as wage-earners in various branches of mining, manufacturing, transportation, commerce, agriculture, and unskilled labor and service.

According to these census figures the wage-earners in Russia numbered over 9,000,000, of whom about 2,400,000 were employed in manufacturing, 200,000 in mining, and 370,000 in transportation, giving a total of nearly 3,000,000 for wage-earners in industry, in the narrower sense of

TABLE 1

NUMBER AND PER CENT OF PERSONS ENGAGED IN THE VARIOUS INDUSTRIES OF THE RUSSIAN EMPIRE IN 1897

(Source: Premier Recensement General de la Population de l'Empire de Russie, 1897.)

Industry	Persons engaged in gainful occupations						Members of families of persons engaged in gainful occupations	Total	
	Male		Female		Total				
	Number	Per cent	Number	Per cent	Number	Per cent		Number	Per cent
Agricultural pursuits..........	16,159,118	60.0	2,086,169	33.3	18,245,287	55.0	75,456,277	93,701,564	74.6
Professional service..........	786,673	2.9	202,140	3.2	988,813	3.0	1,552,436	2,541,249	2.0
Personal service..........	2,958,070	11.0	1,817,283	29.0	4,775,353	14.3	2,748,943	7,524,296	6.0
Manufacturing and mechanical pursuits..........	4,187,826	15.5	982,093	15.7	5,169,919	15.6	7,115,643	12,285,562	9.8
Transportation..........	692,629	2.6	22,116	.4	714,745	2.1	1,236,265	1,951,010	1.5
Commercial pursuits..........	1,331,581	4.9	299,408	4.8	1,630,989	4.9	3,364,398	4,995,387	4.0
All other..........	824,631	3.1	851,758	13.6	1,676,389	5.1	964,564	2,640,953	2.1
Total..........	26,940,528	100.0	6,260,967	100.0	33,201,495	100.0	92,438,526	125,640,021	100.0

TABLE II

NUMBER AND PER CENT OF WAGE-EARNERS OF EACH SEX,
BY INDUSTRIES, 1897

(Source: Ministerstvo vnutrennykh diel. Chisiennost i Sostav rabochikh v
Rossii na osnovanii dannykh pervoi vseobshchei perepisi
naselenia Rossiiskoi Imperii 1897 goda. St. Petersburg, 1906.)

Industry	Total wage-earners	Males		Females	
		Number	Per cent	Number	Per cent
Mining:					
Miners	163,738	155,020	94.7	8,718	5.3
Smelters	42,638	40,940	96.0	1,698	4.0
Total	206,376	195,960	95.0	10,416	5.0
Manufacturing:					
Textiles	530,138	310,439	58.6	219,699	41.4
Animal products	74,270	71,246	95.9	3,024	4.1
Woodworking	173,043	166,295	96.1	6,748	3.9
Metal working	370,933	364,720	98.3	6,213	1.7
Minerals	83,138	74,469	89.6	8,669	10.4
Chemical products	61,094	45,247	74.1	15,847	25.9
Beverages—					
Alcoholic liquors	38,723	36,918	95.3	1,805	4.7
Other	4,220	4,035	95.6	185	4.4
Food products	194,703	183,941	94.5	10,762	5.5
Tobacco	27,994	10,620	37.9	17,374	62.1
Paper and printing	52,175	46,550	89.2	5,625	10.8
Instruments	8,030	7,722	96.2	308	3.8
Jewelry, etc.	25,767	25,213	97.8	554	2.2
Clothing	326,470	256,889	78.7	69,581	21.3
Building	345,724	345,724	100.0	......	...
Carriages and wooden boats	8,793	8,768	99.7	25	.3
Other	65,357	54,029	82.7	11,328	17.3
Total	2,390,572	2,012,825	84.2	377,747	15.8
Transportation:					
Post, telegraph, and telephone	5,463	5,439	99.6	24	.4
Water transportation	44,141	43,885	99.4	256	.6
Railroads	175,246	162,784	92.9	12,462	7.1
Carting	118,423	117,761	99.4	662	.6
Other	25,756	25,391	98.6	365	1.4
Total	369,029	355,260	96.3	13,769	3.7
Commercial pursuits:					
Commerce	118,787	113,171	95.3	5,616	4.7
Hotels, restaurants, etc.	76,970	72,266	93.9	4,704	6.1
Liquor trade	17,336	15,270	88.1	2,066	11.9
Cleaning, laundry work, etc.	42,495	11,751	27.7	30,744	72.3
Total	255,588	212,458	83.1	43,130	16.9
Agricultural pursuits, etc.:					
Agriculture	2,132,809	1,467,302	68.8	665,597	31.2
Cattle raising	411,817	341,596	82.9	70,221	17.1
Forestry	84,714	83,404	98.5	1,310	1.5
Other rural industries	57,990	44,820	77.3	13,170	22.7
Fishing and hunting	35,203	32,331	91.8	2,872	8.2
Total	2,722,623	1,969,453	72.3	753,170	27.7
Common (unskilled) laborers	1,094,848	809,426	73.9	285,422	26.1
Servants:					
In institutions	167,240	142,706	85.3	24,534	14.7
In factories, etc.	226,748	205,720	90.7	21,023	9.3
House servants (janitors, etc.)	162,053	160,089	98.8	1,964	1.2
Domestic servants	1,556,599	268,086	17.2	1,288,513	82.8
Total	2,112,635	776,601	36.7	1,336,034	63.3
Grand total	9,151,671	6,330,983	69.2	2,819,683	30.8

the word. Agricultural laborers numbered over 2,700,000, the servant class over 2,100,000, unskilled labor nearly 1,100,000, and wage-earners in commercial pursuits (not including salaried employees) over 250,000.

As a matter of fact this number is not as great as it would be but for the limitation put in Russia upon the designation "wage-earner" (*zabochi*). A great many persons who would be so designated in this country are classed with salaried employees in Russia, as, for instance, many railway employees.

On the other hand, a comparison between the number of wage-earners and the total number of persons employed in various occupations demonstrates the existence of a very large number of small independent producers in various branches of industry, as, for instance, in textile, woodworking, metal working, clothing, etc. This comparison, as made in Table III, shows that in manufactures in general only 48.3 per cent of the persons occupied were wage-earners, and more than one-half were independent producers.

Along with the industrial development the problems of protection of workmen against the results of accidents, sickness, and old age have been growing in importance and have commanded increasing attention.

The workmen's compensation act of June 2 (15), 1903, embracing all large industries, is perhaps the most important result in the domain of workmen's insurance. It has introduced a system of compensation of workmen against industrial accidents within a rather limited scope.

In the field of old-age insurance the existing provisions embrace almost exclusively the individual employees of the State. Of the private employees thus provided for the most important are the railroad employees, for whom old-age pension funds were established in 1888. In view of the extensive undertakings of the Russian Government, however, the existing old-age pension funds cover a very large body of industrial wage-earners. The pension fund for government railroad employees was organized in 1894, the fund for employees of the liquor monopoly in 1900, etc.

Very much less has been established in the domain of provision against sickness, though the earliest social labor legislation concerned itself with the care of the men in factories in case of sickness. Special laws concerning employees of certain state establishments were promulgated early in the nineteenth century, and general provisions in the form of temporary regulations were made in 1866, requiring the factory owners to furnish medical aid and if necessary hospital treatment to the sick employees. Thus from the very beginning the problem of medical treatment was separated from that of financial aid during sickness, and the burden of such medical treatment was placed upon the employer. Fairly satisfactory results were obtained in this branch of sickness insurance, but almost no progress was made in the other branch.

Thus, the entire situation in regard to workmen's insurance in Russia may be summarized as follows:

1. An accident compensation law of 1903, followed by a series of special laws for various groups of government employees.

2. The law of 1866 requiring the furnishing of medical treatment in factories (extended in 1886 to mines), and

3. A series of special institutions for old-age and invalidity insurance and relief mainly of government employees.

In addition to these provisions for the welfare of the wage-earners, as established by laws and governmental decrees, there is in Russia but little that can be traced to voluntary efforts, either of the employer or of the employees themselves.

TABLE III

PROPORTION OF WAGE-EARNERS TO TOTAL NUMBER OF PERSONS EMPLOYED,
BY INDUSTRIES, 1897

(Source: Premier Recensement General de la Population de l'Empire de
Russie, 1897. Relevé Génarel, St. Petersburg, 1905, Vol. II. Chisiennost i
Sostav Rabochikh v Rossii, St. Petersburg, 1906, Vol. 1.)

Industry	Number of persons employed	Wage-earners	
		Number	Per cent of persons employed
Mining:			
Miners	181,303	163,738	90.2
Smelters	47,560	42,638	89.7
Total	228,863	206,376	90.2
Manufacturing:			
Textiles	950,584	530,138	55.2
Animal products	154,221	74,270	48.2
Wood working	410,126	173,043	42.2
Metal working	624,954	370,933	50.4
Mineral products	125,781	83,138	66.1
Chemical products	76,800	61,094	79.5
Beverages—			
Alcoholic liquors	48,485	38,723	79.0
Other	3,740	4,220	48.2
Food products	343,794	194,703	56.6
Tobacco	31,485	27,994	88.9
Paper and printing	82,397	52,175	63.3
Instruments	23,391	8,030	34.3
Jewelry, etc.	54,570	25,767	47.2
Clothing	1,158,865	326,470	28.2
Building	726,926	345,724	47.6
Carriages and wooden boats	14,400	8,793	61.1
Other	106,468	65,357	61.4
Total	4,951,056	2,390,572	48.3
Transportation:			
Post, telegraph, and telephone	46,729	5,463	11.7
Water transportation	71,057	44,141	62.1
Railroads	262,180	175,246	66.8
Carting and drayage	302,956	118,423	39.1
Other	31,823	25,756	80.9
Total	714,745	369,029	51.6
Commercial pursuits:			
Commerce	1,256,330	118,787	9.5
Hotels, restaurants, etc.	154,470	76,970	49.8
Liquor trade	34,287	17,336	20.6
Cleaning, laundry work, etc.	135,902	42,495	31.3
Total	1,630,989	255,588	15.7
Agricultural pursuits, etc.:			
Agriculture	16,658.134	2,132,899	12.8
Cattle raising	1,121,828	411,817	36.7
Forestry	125,756	84,714	67.4
Other rural industries	199,807	57,990	29.0
Fishing and hunting	138,762	35,203	25.4
Total	18,244.287	2,722,623	14.9
Common (unskilled) laborers	1,120,156	1,094,848	97.7
Servants:			
In institutions	ᵃ167,240	167,240	100.0
In factories, etc.	242,011	236,743	93.7
House servants (janitors, etc.)	165,650	162,053	97.8
Domestic servants	1,578,412	1,556,599	98.6
Total	2,153,313	2,112,635	98.1
Grand total	29,043,409	9,151,671	31.5

ᵃBecause of differences in classification this item could not be obtained; it is therefore assumed to be the same as the number of wage-earners.

Within the last few years, and especially since the establishment of the National Legislature, considerable activity has manifested itself in the preparation of proposals for the comprehensive insurance systems, including all the three main branches of workmen's insurance, against accidents, sickness, and old age and invalidity. Such proposals were published in 1905, 1906, 1907, and 1908, and the last ones were formally introduced in the Duma and await the action of this body.

·   ·   ·

The problem of compensation of workmen for industrial accidents has been attracting the attention of Russian authorities as well as of Russian manufacturers since the beginning of the eighties, and the efforts for its solution may be divided into three classes: (1) The elaboration of plans for a general comprehensive law in legislative institutions; (2) organization by various departments of the Government of systems of compensation or insurance for special groups of workmen, mainly those engaged in state industries; and (3) voluntary efforts made by employers toward insurance of workmen, partly for humane and partly for business reasons.

The history of the legislative efforts will be discussed in the following section. The early special legislation concerning government employees will be discussed in connection with the chapter devoted to that topic, and the history of voluntary accident insurance will also be treated separately. [The two latter items are not reprinted here.]

Under the old regime of Russia prior to the granting of the constitution of 1905, legislative proposals were elaborated by the various administrative departments, and presented through the Imperial Council to the Emperor for his approval. As early as 1859, and several times since, commissions were created within the Ministry of Finance for revision of factory laws which, among other things, prepared drafts of a law defining employers' liability for industrial accidents, but the plans of these commissions never reached the stage of discussion in the Imperial Council.

In the development of the principle of compensation of workmen for results of industrial accidents, a considerable stimulus was given by the employers themselves.

As early as 1881, i. e., about three years before the German system of insurance against accidents was established, the influential Society for Encouragement of Russian Industry and Commerce elaborated a plan for obligatory state insurance of workmen against accidents, which guaranteed compensation for all injuries, unless incurred voluntarily, and placed the entire burden upon the employers, i. e., the industry. The plan was presented to the minister of finance, but did not proceed any further.

In the same year the congress of mining operators in Kharkov organized a miners' aid fund. In 1893 a petition was presented by the manufacturers of Moscow for a universal compulsory system of state insurance, to be realized by a tax upon the employers, and managed entirely by the governmental authorities. This feeling was not universal, for in the same year the publication of Von Witte's plan for employers' liability legislation called forth a formal protest from the "Congress of Mine Operators of Southern Russia and Poland," which was indorsed by the Council of Iron and Steel Manufacturers' Association. The whole subject of employers' liability, workmen's compensation, and compulsory insurance received a very prolonged and thorough discussion at the Pan-Russian Congress of Commerce and Industry, held at Nizhni Novgorod in August of 1896, in connection with the Pan-Russian Exposition. Two sessions of the congress and an entire volume of its reports were devoted to the consideration of the question of workmen's insurance. The board of the Moscow bourse forwarded a resolution favoring state compensation to the workmen for injuries caused by industrial accidents by a system of compulsory state insurance, the cost to be put upon all industrial establishments, by means of a tax upon the wage expense or the number of workmen, and proportionate to the degree of hazard presented by the various industries; two other chambers of commerce presented similar resolutions, proposing, however, an equal distribution of the burden between the employer and employee.

During the discussion of the problem at the session of the congress the strong preference of the manufacturers for a system of insurance as against employers' liability strongly asserted itself, and the congress resolved that "of the two methods of compensating workmen against accidents—workmen's insurance or a special employers' liability law—the system of insurance must be declared the more perfect one." Further, the congress resolved that "from the point of view of the interests of the employees as well as of the employers, the best method of providing for the worker disabled either through accident, sickness, or old age from earning a living would be such a system of compulsory insurance of the workers, which was not conducted for commercial profit and therefore should be placed under state supervision; it should not be limited to employees in factories and mills, but should include all workers employed in industrial activity. Should, however, the organization of a system of compulsory insurance under state supervision be found impossible in the immediate future, then it would be highly desirable that the employers make efforts to provide for insurance of their employees either in the existing private insurance companies or by organization of mutual insurance societies, the possibility of entry to which should be afforded to the proprietors of the small industrial establishments." Furthermore, the congress recognized that the existing legislation in regard to employers' liability was very deficient in that it did not conclusively establish the employers' liability for the trade risk of employment, and that for this reason private insurance must supplement existing legislation and specifically include the results of trade risk.

Thus the congress of commerce and industry recommended a material extension of the workman's rights for compensation. This recommendation may be explained by the statements made at the congress that a few heavy judgments of court in favor of the injured employees or the families of employees killed have demonstrated to the employers the preference of insurance over liability. The heavy cost of litigation was also felt by many manufacturers. Besides, with the introduction of insurance in one establishment the demand for it often spread rapidly through the whole industrial district, the workmen discriminating against employers who refused to provide for such insurance. The constant litigations were admitted to lead to strained relations between the employers and employees, which were destructive of factory discipline and efficiency. Besides, many representatives of large industrial establishments and almost all the representatives of the smaller establishments admitted that the danger of possible accidents, with the heavy burden of damages, was a disturbing factor in the calculation of cost of production, and that insurance was preferable, as it permitted an estimate of this element of cost.

Under the influence of the memorial of the Society for Encouragement of Russian Industry and Commerce, presented in 1881, the Council of Commerce and Manufactures, under the Ministry of Finance, was charged with the duty of preparing a draft of an employers' liability law. This draft was finally presented to the Imperial Council in 1889 by the minister of finance. This was the first important effort at a solution of the problem of industrial accidents.

The plan, while it proposed to establish a fairly liberal system of compensation, similar to that of the German law, up to a pension of 60 per cent of the earnings in cases of fatal accident, and even a pension equal to the full earnings in cases of total disability, on the other hand it strictly limited the liability of the employer to cases of his well-established negligence or that of a superintendent, thus virtually establishing a fellow-servant doctrine. Another provision of the bill placed upon the plaintiff the entire burden of proof of such negligence. Thus the plan decidedly limited the rights of the workman as they existed under the general law; far from relieving the injured workman from the expenses of a court trial, it would tend to create conditions under which the legal battles would have to be more persistent, and reduced the chances of the workman for a favorable private settlement.

The bill was therefore a step backward in the development of employers' liability and did not meet with the approval of the Imperial Council. The ministers of justice, of interior, of state domains, and of ways of communication raised objections.

This draft was referred back to the Ministry of Finance and in a few years a new draft was elaborated and introduced in the Imperial Council by the minister of finance, on March 15 (27), 1893.

This plan was in many respects much more thorough than that of 1889. It extended the liability of the employers to all accidents except those due to vis major, to actions of third parties, or to malicious intent or fault of the injured; in other words, the scope of liability was made practically equal to that of the railroad and steamship companies. The last limitation was undoubtedly an important one, but the burden of proof of the employee's fault or negligence was placed upon the employer, so that a considerable share of the trade risk was shifted, while in the plan of the bill of 1889 it rested upon the workman. Contributory negligence of the injured did not altogether relieve the employer of the responsibility, the draft providing that in such cases the courts could reduce the normal compensation by one-fourth to one-half. The plan of 1893 also applied to all employees, while the preceding project was limited to wage-workers only. Finally, it contained an important innovation in classifying trade diseases with injuries due to industrial accidents.

In the general scheme of pensions and allowances to the injured or his family the new plan followed quite closely after the old, with 60 per cent of the annual earnings of the injured as a maximum pension. It provided for peaceful agreements between both parties, from which there was no appeal, and for suits in common courts when no peaceful settlement was possible. Yet the large opportunity for litigation was evident, especially in view of the provisions in regard to contributory negligence. On the other hand, the liberal inclusion of the trade diseases called forth strong opposition among the manufacturers of St. Petersburg.

This plan did not meet with approval and was returned to the Ministry of Finance for further changes. The demand for legislation grew with the development of industry, and the discussion showed a considerable part of the manufacturers of Russia not unfavorably disposed to some regulation of this problem. In a few industrial centers the manufacturers organized mutual companies for insurance of their employees, and the liability assumed by these companies was much broader than that imposed by the laws. The activity of the manufacturers of Riga, which will be described in a later section, was very important in that connection.

In the spring of 1899 a new legislative scheme was announced by the Ministry of Finance. This plan bore evidence of the influence exerted by the Riga Mutual Insurance Company system. In fact, section 2 of the project of 1899, which contains an enumeration of exceptions to the liability of employers, repeated word for word the corresponding section 3 of the Riga society's by-laws. It excepted injuries due to accidents caused by (1) unpreventable and unexpected external forces (vis major), (2) acts of outsiders, who have no connection with the management of the industrial establishment, (3) such intentional acts of the fellow-servants as are not connected with the nature of the work, and (4) malicious intent of the injured. The by-laws of the Riga society stated "gross negligence of the injured," for which the legislative plan of 1899 substituted "malicious intent," thus limiting substantially the range of excepted cases.

The law was to apply to workmen and technical employees. Only factories were covered by the bill. Workshops employing less than 15 men and no mechanical power, mines, quarries, metallurgical establishments, agricultural, structural, and transportation employees were not included. Compensation offered included besides medical treatment an allowance of 50 per cent of the daily wages for temporary disability; a pension amounting to two-thirds of the annual earnings for complete permanent disability and a proportionate sum in cases of partial disability, while the Riga society offered 75 per cent to the married victims in similar cases; in cases of death the widow and children were to receive the same rate of compensation as under the Riga system, i. e., 30 per cent of the earnings to the former and 15 to 20 per cent to the latter. The new proposal extended the right to compensation not only to dependent parents, but also to dependent grandparents, brothers, and sisters, but the maximum was the same, and the claims of these relatives were recognized only in so far as the immediate family was not entitled to the 60 per cent maximum.

After four years consumed in the elaboration and adaptation of this plan, with vital changes, the final draft was approved June 2 (15), 1903, and went into effect on January 1 (14), 1904.

Workmen's Compensation—Present Status

The workmen's compensation act is entitled "Rules concerning the compensation of workmen and employees injured through accidents, as well as members of their families, in manufacturing, mining, and metallurgical establishments." It was accompanied by an extensive "Opinion of the Imperial Council" of the same date, containing amendments and modifications. Since that date many decrees and enactments in regard to this matter have been announced, and the entire law may be said to be still in the formative state.

Instructions to the factory and mine inspectors, referring to the details of the execution of the law, were approved by the ministers of finance and of agriculture and state domains on December 13 (26), 1903, and instructions to the police were issued by the central office of factory and mine inspection on March 5 (18), 1904. Instructions to physicians concerning the methods of determining the degree of disability were elaborated by the medical council of the Ministry of Interior, and approved by the latter on June 5 (18), 1904; new regulations regarding the collective insurance of workmen or the insurance of employers against their civil liability, harmonized with the new legislation, were approved by the minister of interior on December 22, 1903 (January 4, 1904).

By numerous acts the action of law was extended to various state establishments: To the workmen and civil employees of the artillery service, on June 9 (22), 1904, in effect January 1 (14), 1905; to the workmen and employees of manufacturing, mining, and metallurgical establishments of the Crown (i. e., the personal property of the Emperor and the imperial family), June 6 (19), 1905, in effect December 25, 1905 (January 7, 1906); to employees of the government printing office on December 19, 1905 (January 1, 1906), in effect July 1 (14), 1906; and of the senate printing office, March 6 (19), 1906, in effect July 1, 1906; of the navy yards, March 6 (19), 1906, in effect July 1 (14), 1906; and of the governmental industrial establishments connected with the department of ports and harbors, April 19 (May 2), 1906, in effect October 1 (14), 1906. Further extensions must follow to include all the industrial undertakings of the Government.

The application of the act is strictly limited to factories, mills, mines, and metallurgical establishments. Large sections of the working population are excluded, namely, the transportation employees (for whom special provisions exist, partly in section 683 of Volume X, part 1 of the code, as explained above, and partly in the pension and aid funds, which will be described elsewhere), the agricultural laborers, the building trades, and the commercial employees. Factories, mines, and metallurgical establishments owned by provincial governments and municipalities are included. Specifically excluded were industrial establishments of the Central Government, the workshops and other industrial establishments of private railroad and steamship companies, but the heads of the various ministries were instructed to present within one year after the law went into effect, i. e., after January 1, 1904, plans for extension of this law with necessary modifications, to the various state industrial establishments. Accordingly the main provisions of this law were extended to various governmental establishments, namely, all factories, mines, and metallurgical establishments which are personal property of the Emperor and the entire imperial family (so-called of his majesty's cabinet and the Crown), workmen and civil employees of the artillery, the government printing office, senate printing office, navy yards, and the industrial establishments of the department of ports and harbors, this latter group including also construction work. As yet the law was not extended to transportation companies. The extension of the law to the state and crown establishments is accompanied by modifications, more or less uniform, which makes it preferable to treat these establishments separately.

The essential limitation of the law is found in the term "factory." The Russian law recognizes two classes of manufacturing establishments, factories and "artisans' shops" (*remeslennya zavedenia*). The latter are not mentioned in the law and therefore are not subject to it. But the definition of a factory, contained in the Russian law, is not sufficiently specific; factories and mills are stated to differ from Artisans' shops in that they are large establishments using mechanical power, while artisans have none except hand machinery and tools. The decision in practice is left to administrative officers, and practically the law extends over all manufacturing establishments using machinery and mechanical power.

An exception is found in the exclusion of so-called rural industrial establishments. This includes a large class of certain small establishments located outside the city limits, namely, brick and tile yards, cement and starch factories, turpentine stills, wood distilleries, creameries, cheese factories, even if utilizing mechanical power, provided they do not employ more then 20 workmen, sawmills with only one mechanical saw, flour mills with four or less millstones, or only one rolling stone, wine presses, and a few other small rural industrial establishments.

The average sum of insurance against death varied from $336 to $381, and for total permanent disability from about $381 to $467. These rates of compensation do not appear to be high, but this may be partly explained by the general level of wages in Russia. For the last decade of the nineteenth century the average wages of an industrial worker (men, women and children) is stated in an official report to be equal to 187.60 rubles ($96.61); according to the factory inspectors' reports for 1900 to 1904 the annual earnings were as shown in Table V (*see next page*).

An average earning power of about $105 per annum gives an average daily wage of approximately 35 cents; the average compensation for death contracted for by the employers amounted to about $350, or 1,000 times

TABLE IV

NUMBER OF ACCIDENTS CERTIFIED, ANNUAL EARNINGS, AND COMPUTED
AMOUNT OF PENSIONS, IN CLAIMS CERTIFIED BY FACTORY INSPECTORS,
BY RESULT OF INJURY, 1904 TO 1908.

(Source: Ministerstvo Torgovli i Promyshlennosti. Statisticheskia Svedenia o
Resultatakh Primenenia Zakona 2 iunia 1903 goda. Svod otchotov fabrichnykh
inspectorov sa 1908 god.)

Result of injury	Number of cases certified	Annual earnings of injured		Computed amount of pensions		
		Total	Average	Total	Average	Per cent of earnings
1904.						
Death	105	$ 13,594.85	$129.47	$ 6,749.21	$ 64.28	49.6
Total permanent disability	17	2,720.68	160.04	1,815.00	106.76	66.7
Partial permanent disability	2,228	344,855.20	154.78	35,116.77	15.76	10.2
Total	2,350	361,170.73	153.69	43,680.98	18.59	12.1
1905.						
Death	197	26,151.00	132.24	12,093.08	61.38	46.2
Total permanent disability	45	6,151.29	136.70	4,107.66	91.28	66.8
Partial permanent disability	6,524	1,045,205.65	160.21	96,467.43	14.79	9.2
Total	6,766	1,077,507.94	159.25	112,668.17	16.65	10.4
1906.						
Death	228	30,279.40	127.80	14,248.74	62.50	47.1
Total permanent disability	46	7,767.35	168.86	5,043.40	109.66	64.9
Partial permanent disability	9,446	1,629,094.47	172.46	131,317.46	13.90	8.1
Total	9,720	1,667,141.22	171.51	150,609.60	15.49	9.0
1907.						
Death	213	30,680.56	144.04	14,422.48	67.71	47.0
Total permanent disability	43	7,844.53	182.43	5,219.28	121.37	66.5
Partial permanent disability	10,076	1,737,267.75	172.42	135,637.06	13.46	7.8
Total	10,332	1,775,792.84	171.87	155,278.82	15.03	8.4
1908.						
Death	199	35,526.42	178.46	15,765.82	79.23	44.4
Total permanent disability	42	8,349.65	198.80	5,448.42	129.72	65.3
Partial permanent disability	9,581	1,620,283.91	169.11	142,443.03	14.87	8.8
Total	9,822	1,662,159.98	169.23	163,657.27	16.66	9.8

TABLE V

AVERAGE ANNUAL EARNINGS OF WORKMEN IN RUSSIA, 1900 TO 1904

Year	Average annual earnings
1900	$ 99.95
1901	103.64
1902	104.27
1903	111.77
1904	109.03
Average	$105.73

the daily wages, and the average compensation for permanent disability was about $450 or about 1,200 to 1,300 times the daily wage. The pension for permanent disability varied from about 5 to 10 per cent of this sum, depending upon the age of the injured, and so may be estimated at from $22 to $45 a year. Small as these compensations were, the system of insurance on a whole was more liberal to the workman than the then existing legislation. An official report upon the activity of the insurance companies in this line stated that "industrial conditions have advanced ahead of existing legislation which does not any more meet the demand of actual life."

. . .

Complete lists of industrial and mining establishments in each district must be compiled by the factory or mine inspectors and kept on file by the provincial councils of manufactures and mining. All establishments subject to this law must be listed whether or not these institutions are otherwise subject to factory or mine inspection. Doubtful establishments must be entered in the lists, and the question of the application of the compensation act must be settled by the local council or referred to the central council in St. Petersburg, to which the proprietor of the establishment, who must be notified of its inclusion in the lists, has a right of appeal. Where there are no factory inspectors, other officers are instructed to collect the lists and furnish them to all officers who may be called upon in connection with accidents.

It is the inspector's duty to make a personal investigation of every industrial accident in his district, which takes place in an establishment subject to the compensation act, without waiting for the formal notice from the proprietor, and he must cooperate with the police to obtain all possible information. It is his duty to encourage amicable settlements between two parties; even if they had once failed to come to an agreement, as evidenced by a proper "act" of the factory inspector, and a lawsuit has been instituted, and even if the legal time limit had elapsed, nevertheless, if both parties enter a request for a voluntary agreement, such request must not be refused. If oral agreements are presented to him by both parties he can not decline to put them in writing as a preliminary to certification. In the case of a written agreement, acknowledged by a notary, appearance of the agreeing parties is not necessary and the request for certification may come in writing.

The inspector must decline to certify settlements by which the employer tries to avoid a direct obligation imposed by the law, or the employee signs away one of his undisputed rights, but before doing so the inspector on his initiative must suggest the changes necessary to obtain certification. With the written consent of both parties he may certify to some provision of the settlements and except others. When requests are made upon the inspector by one party for explanation as to his rights, the inspector may ask the other party to appear before him, and failure to appear must be considered as a refusal to enter into a voluntary agreement.

The factory inspectors may take the initiative to petition the court for appointment of the guardian for minor claimants. In case of pending voluntary liquidation, or transfer or public sale of an establishment, the inspector must remind the proprietors, orally or in writing, of their obligations under this act, and also inform all the beneficiaries, as far as possible, of the coming change in ownership. They must also inform the official conducting such liquidation or sale, of the obligations under this law. As defined by the regulations, the duties of the factory and mine inspectors are very broad and complex. Besides being charged with almost all the details of the execution of the law, they are practically made official mediators and conciliators, upon whose work the success of the law largely depends.

The Zubatov Plan

Sergei V. Zubatov, whose work as a police spy and agent provocateur won him appointment as Deputy Chief and, later, as Chief of the Moscow Political Police, developed a scheme for controlling the growing labor movement by means of "police socialism." The essence of the device was for the political police to sponsor and control labor unions, and to use the power thus obtained to steer the workers away from political action. The Zubatov Plan apparently was approved by Grand Duke Sergei, the reactionary governor general of Moscow, and by General Trepov, the head of the Moscow police. It was first put in effect in the spring of 1901, and had a considerable, though temporary, success.

Plehve, who became minister of the interior in 1902, opposed the Zubatov Plan but allowed it to continue in operation until Zubatov sought to extend his operations to Odessa. Plehve then used Zubatov's failures as ammunition against Witte whose policy of industrial expansion Plehve had long opposed. Zubatov was dismissed from office and exiled from the capital.

The following summation of the Zubatov Plan is from Mavor, *Economic History,* vol. 2, pp. 199–200. Professor Mavor suggests (p. 190) that Zubatov's primary motive was to use the scheme for his personal advancement.

The principal points in Zubatov's "programme" were as follows:

1. At present the law confides the safeguarding of the legal rights of employers and employees to the factory inspectorship; but this institution, in the opinion of the Political Police Department, has proved to be powerless to discharge this function, having forfeited the confidence of the workers owing to its partiality to the employers. Therefore the Political Police Department, from considerations of State importance, has not only decided to take upon itself that part of factory inspectorship duties which comprises the mutual relations of employers and employed, but even is almost inclined to put an end to the institution as an anachronism. . . .

2. The widening of the rights of factory workers (in spite of the statute law) shall consist in uniting the workers of each factory into separate

groups, each having its committee, voluntarily elected by workers of both sexes from among themselves. These committees must point out changes desirable for workers, in the scale of wages, distribution of working time, and general changes in the rule of internal order. The employer must communicate in future not immediately with his workers, but through the committee. The committees of separate factories of a given district are in communication with each other with a view to uniformity of action, the general supervision of the committees being centralized in the Political Police Department. For the purposes of this supervision the department appoints special agents from among the experienced and promising workers who are wise by long experience in the art of ruling the masses of the people.

3. In order to form this institution, mutually useful as it must be for employees and employers alike, the Political Police Department, in order that the coming occurrences should not take it unaware, took care not only to seek workers promising and experienced in strikes, even from among those who had been in administrative banishment, but also of establishing a school for training the future actors, under the management of people experienced in this branch. All these teachers receive decent remuneration.

4. The sums required for the support of this institution are afforded by the "Society of Mutual Assistance of the Workers in Mechanical Industries," the constitution of which was granted on 14th February 1902. In this society there are taking part as members thousands of workers of both sexes, and even those under age. Besides contributions from these, there are the subscriptions from high exalted personages, educated classes, clergy, and different persons, but as yet no merchants or manufacturers.

5. By the means described the Political Police Department succeeded in a short time in inspiring the most sincere confidence of the working men, because they became convinced that every humbled and insulted person finds in the Political Police Department paternal attention, advice, support, and assistance by word and deed; so that even the Museum of Labour, established by the Imperial Technical Society, began to lose ground.

The Kishinev Pogrom

The Russian word "pogrom" means literally "a little beating," and the usual pogrom lasted exactly three days. The most notorious of these violent anti-Semitic outbreaks in the early twentieth century occurred at Kishinev in 1903. A few months later, Plehve appointed as Governor of Bessarabia (of which province Kishinev was the capital) Prince Sergei Urussov. Urussov was an outstanding example of that apparent but not uncommon anomaly, a hereditary nobleman who was also a genuine liberal. After a very careful examination of the Jewish question in general and of the Kishinev pogrom in particular, Urussov wrote an account of the affair. As a measure of his views, it may be noted that Urussov served with distinction in the First Duma, and won merited renown there by a speech which castigated the government for its policies toward the Jews. The excerpts which follow are from: Prince S. D. Urussov (H. Rosenthal, Ed. and Tr.), *Memoirs of a Russian Governor*. New York: Harper and Bros., 1908. Pp. 77–82, *passim*.

First, I must say that in examining . . . the secret papers of the Kishinev case in the Central Police Bureau at St. Petersburg, I found not a thing to justify the assumption that the Ministry of the Interior thought it expedient to permit a Jewish massacre or even an anti-Jewish demonstration in Kishinev. Indeed, such a sinister policy on the part of that ministry is inconceivable; for A. A. Lopukhin . . . was at this time head of this department. . . . Whenever he was charged with being a reactionary, Plehve liked to point to . . . [Lopukhin] to show that he, Plehve, was seeking men with broad views and irreproachable names. . . . My intimacy with Lopukhin, based on our relationship and close friendship, enables me to assert that it is entirely inadmissible to suspect his department of engineering pogroms at that time.

I also entertain grave doubts of the authenticity of a letter alleged to have been addressed by the Minister of the Interior to the Governor of Bessarabia, and published in the English papers. [This is the *Times'* dispatch quoted by Mavor.] . . . Plehve was incapable of such an unguarded act . . . . . . Raaben [Urussov's predecessor at Kishinev] was not the proper agent to carry out any such projects. He was a very decent man . . . and, moreover, was quite tolerant towards the Jews. He himself, losing his official position, suffered from the pogrom. . . . Confidential agents carrying out delicate commissions do not get such treatment. . . .

A significant role in preparing for the pogrom was played by the press, this especially by Krushevan's local paper. . . . Krushevan's authority, in the eyes of his readers, was to a certain degree supported by the open patronage of the chief bureau of the press censorship. . . .

. . . The police, therefore, thought that a hostile attitude towards the Jews was a sort of government watchword; . . . . . . the conviction grew among the ignorant masses that hostile acts against the Jews could be undertaken with impunity. Things went so far that a legend appeared among the people that the Czar had ordered a three days' massacre of the Jews. . . . Thus, in my opinion, the central government cannot shake off its moral responsibility. . . .

But can one fully exonerate the government . . . [of taking] a direct part in the massacres? . . . I do not care to pass my suppositions for facts. I only pointed out the way in which the anti-Semitism of Plehve, possibly voiced by him as a mere matter of conviction . . . . . . rolling down the hierarchic incline of the gendarmerie corps, reached Lewandal head of the Kishinev secret police] in the guise of a *wish* on the part of the higher authorities, reached Pronin and Krushevan as a *call* for a patriotic exploit, and reached the Moldavian rioters as an *order* of the Czar.

This was undoubtedly the true explanation of the pogroms; and M. von Plehve must have known that in putting it in set terms, he was pronouncing his own sentence of death.

"The Liberation Movement"

Sir Bernard Pares, long regarded as the outstanding Western authority on Russia, was especially qualified to write of the development of political opposition which culminated in the establishment of the Duma. Not only was Sir Bernard intimately associated with the First Duma (he was a Gentleman Usher), but he also knew virtually all the political leaders of "The Liberation Movement." His studies on this subject have long been classics. The following excerpts are from his *Russia and Reform*. London: Constable and Co., Ltd., 1907. Pp. 87, 88, 487–490, 501–506.

The First Zemstvo Congress

The new Minister authorised the holding of a general Zemstvo Congress in St. Peterburg itself. At last the plan of Alexander II. was on the eve of realisation; but Mirsky had to fight with other influences far stronger than his own at the Court, and, if the people had issued from the atmosphere of suspicion which enveloped Russia, the Emperor had not. After some consultations it was decided that the Congress must be held in a private house, and its resolutions were communicated to Prince Mirsky, not officially, but as a piece of news to a personal friend; in this way they came to the ears of the Emperor.

This first Zemstvo Congress was held under the presidency of Mr. Shipoff. It was clear that the great majority of the deputies from the various Zemstva, who came rather by invitation than by any direct election, were ready to go farther than the minimum of Shipoff: in fact, but for his own great moral influence, the president might have found himself almost entirely isolated; but here, as so often afterwards, the difficulty of the whole task acted as a restraining influence, and the majority was wise enough to content itself with a unanimous vote in favour of the minimum. These so-called requests expressed before all things a desire for order, and for the corporate development of the whole country. The Congress states that Government has been separated from Society, and that this gap must be bridged at all costs. In the tenth out of the eleven articles it puts forward two resolutions, one representing the majority and the other the minority; both alike request that a national assembly should be summoned without delay, but the majority claim for the assembly definite legislative functions. Though the peasants were only indirectly represented on the Congress, a special article, which was accepted unanimously, emphasises the need of improving the conditions of peasant life. The eleven points may be summed up in the following requests:—No one without the sentence of an independent court of law ought to be subjected to punishment or limited in his rights. There must be means for bringing officials to account in the civil or criminal courts. There must be guarantees of freedom of conscience and religion, freedom of speech and press, and also freedom of meeting and association. The personal rights of citizens of the Russian Empire, both civil and political, ought to be equal. The peasants must be made equal in personal rights with the members of other classes. The country population must be freed from the wardenship of administrative authorities in all manifestations of its personal and social life. To peasants must be guaranteed a regular form of trial. Representation in the Zemstva must not be organised on class principles, and must include as far as possible all the actual forces of the local population. Small country units (Parish Councils) ought to be created. The sphere of local government should be extended to the whole province of local needs. Local self-government must be extended over all parts of the Russian Empire. The Conference expresses a hope "that the supreme power will summon freely elected representatives of the people in order, with their co-operation, to bring our country out on to a new path of Imperial development in the spirit of the principles of justice and of harmony between the Imperial power and the people." This great document, so vastly superior in spirit and substance to any proposals that had issued from the Government of the Reaction, marks the beginning of the reform movement. It bears at almost every point the personal impress of the mind of Shipoff. The nobility with which he pleads for reform, as essentially necessary to the cause of order and as the natural request of loyal subjects, continues to stamp the movement at many of its further crises. The minimum programme of Shipoff was accepted with enthusiasm by the whole country, and one public body after another ratified it; the volume of the national demand became so great that Russia could be said to possess a real public opinion which was practically unanimous.

· · ·

The Demand for "Freedoms" and a National Assembly

The Eleven Points adopted by the Zemstvo Congress of November 19 to 21, 1904, mark an epoch in Russian history. The document bore throughout the impress of Mr. Shipoff's loyalty to tradition and respect for the throne. Personal freedom from the arbitrary control of officials and the calling of some kind of national assembly were put forward, not as demands, but as requests, and the Government was left to settle all details. At the same time the principle that the Emperor must be brought into touch with his people was stated with a simple frankness, and it was clear that behind that modest petition stood practically the whole mass of the educated classes.

Soon after the Congress the Emperor called a meeting of his chief counsellors. Of this meeting we as yet have only one account. It represents that, when the question of reform was raised, Mr. Pobyedonostseff told the Emperor that he had not the right to infringe the principle of autocracy, that his position as Head of the Church would not allow it. Mr. Witte is said to have answered that an autocracy which had no power to make changes would not be an autocracy at all. In any case it is clear that the reactionaries won the day. Prince Mirsky asked leave to resign, and though his request was not at once granted, his power was already gone.

When, in the spring, the "Liberators" had attempted to organise a public banquet, they had found the war mood too strong for them. But on December 3 meetings were held in many towns to celebrate the fortieth anniversary of the reform of the Law-Courts. Many of these meetings took the form of public dinners. In St. Petersburg a dinner was arranged for December 2. It was postponed in consequence of a collision between the public and the police, but on the next day 600 guests met in the Pavloff Hall under the presidency of a well-known Liberator, Mr. Korolyenko; a resolution which followed closely on the lines of the Eleven Points was adopted and signed. In Moscow, on the same day, similar dinners ending with similar resolutions were held by the lawyers and by the Justices of the Peace; on December 4 lawyers, professors, and journalists met at a dinner in the Hermitage. On December 4 the lawyers of St. Petersburg organised a demonstration of protest against the postponement of a banquet arranged by them. Banquets were also held in the provinces; at Saratoff the guests numbered 1,500. In Russia members of the professions could under certain conditions meet to discuss professional subjects. The reformers had the tactical instinct to seize upon this means of making themselves heard. Doctors met presumably to discuss medical matters, and one of them would rise to say: "We cannot discharge our duty as doctors in Russia unless we have freedom of person, freedom of conscience, freedom of the Press, freedom of assembly, freedom of association, and a national assembly." In other words, the vast majority of intelligent opinion formed itself into line under the banner of the Eleven Points. The very fact that the professional unit could thus be used, that all doctors or all lawyers could be unanimous on a political question, made it all the more evident that the Government was quite out of touch with the nation. On December 18 there was a banquet of engineers in St. Petersburg, with a resolution on the needs of Russian industry; on December 27 there was a great dinner in honour of the Decembrists of 1825. The Government prevented some of the meetings; more frequently it punished the owners of the restaurants at which they had taken place. This led to important street demonstrations in St. Petersburg on December 11, and in Moscow on December 19. In the latter case the students came into conflict with the police.

On December 13 the Zemstva received the adhesion of another most important ally. The Town Councils, being elected largely from the merchant class, had so far been backward in the cause of reform; but in Moscow, at the last election, many Intelligents had been elected as representing important corporations, such as the University. The new Moscow Town Council, in the presence of a numerous audience, unanimously decided to telegraph to the Minister of the Interior that the "real obstacle to the further development of civic economy was to be found in those conditions which had been imposed by law upon the community"; the Council definitely adopted the principles of the Eleven Points; other Town Councils too followed the example of Moscow. Meanwhile the Zemstvo deputies had returned to their respective Zemstva, which proceeded in some cases to ratify what had been done at the Congress. Even the Marshals of the Gentry, elected as they were only by the large landowners, had met to make a moderate plea for reform, and one of them, Mr. Mukhanoff, who was also president of the local Zemstvo, carried through the Zemstvo Assembly a bold repetition of the Eleven Points. This address was telegraphed to the Emperor, and reached him in the midst of the congratulations on his name-day. Those who were present say that they never saw him so angry; on the margin of the telegram he wrote the words "Impudent and tactless." But the voice of public opinion was too powerful to be resisted, and on December 25, there was issued an Imperial Edict which spoke of reforms.

In this decree the Emperor desired to distinguish between "what really corresponded to the interests of the people" and the "faulty and temporary accident of a gust of aspirations." He was not unwilling to make material modifications in the laws if it were really necessary; peasant questions would be attended to. For the rest, the officials would be compelled to observe the law; the Local Councils would have their jurisdiction extended as far as possible; the Law-Courts would be unified and made more independent; workmen would be insured by the State; the administrative ordinances would be revised and their sphere of action limited as far as possible; the edict of toleration of March, 1903, would probably be extended; and the law of aliens would be modified. Superfluous restrictions on the Press would be abolished. The Committee of Ministers would be invited to suggest how these principles should be applied; that is to say, the bureaucracy was to undertake the reform of itself. The Official Communication which was issued two days later accused the popular leaders, such as Mr. Shipoff, "of trying to bring confusion into the life of society and of the State. . . . Their efforts had resulted in a series of noisy conventions which put forward various inadmissible demands, and in mob demonstrations on the streets, with open resistance to the appeals of the authorities." Such phenomena were declared to be "alien to the Russian people, which was true to the ancient principles of the existing Imperial order, though an attempt was being made to give to the above-named disturbances the unwarranted significance of a national movement." The leaders, "blinded by delusive fancies, did not realise that they were working not for their country, but for its enemies." Conventions of an anti-governmental character would be stopped by all means that legally pertained to the authorities. The Zemstva and Town Councils were ordered to return within the limits of their jurisdiction, and not to touch those questions which they had no legal right to discuss. Their presidents were threatened with punishment if they permitted such discussion, and the newspapers were ordered "to restore peace in the public mind, which had lately deviated from its proper direction." Clearly this pronouncement was hopelessly below the level of the situation. It is possible to explain the remarkable difference between the two twin documents, the Decree and the Communication; the second was to serve the purpose of a keeper ring; at the moment when the Government found it necessary to make concessions to a united public opinion, it reasserted its own supremacy. But this was not the way to secure the confidence of the people; on the contrary, the gap between it and the Government was now more visible than ever. At the beginning of January the Technical Congress in Moscow and the Natural Science Congress in Tiflis were closed, but these were trifling victories. At the other end of the Empire, General Stoessel surrendered Port Arthur to the Japanese, before the means of resistance were exhausted and against the advice of his council of war. Scarcely less significant of the demoralisation of the army was the shot fired against the Emperor on January 19 from the fortress of Peter and Paul. Nicholas left his capital, not to return for more than a year; and he was from this time onward more than ever cut off from all knowledge of his people.

The Zemstvo Constitutionalists were the natural link between the Zemstva and the professional classes. These last welcomed with special alacrity the invitation to send in their views to the Minister. From January to May they were rapidly organising themselves. Professional conferences of all kinds met in the capitals and in the chief towns, and each profession showed its unanimity on political questions by forming itself into a union. One of the first unions to form itself was that of the Engineers and Technicians. Its foundations were laid at the banquet of December 18, 1904. The Academic Union, consisting both of professors and students, was formed on the lines of a programme drafted by Professor Vernadsky, of Moscow, at the end of December. The Office Clerks and Book-keepers formed their union on March 12, the Teachers and Workers in Primary Education on March 25, the Medicals at the beginning of April, the Lawyers and the champions of Full Rights for Jews at the same time, the Pharmacists on April 15, the Writers on the 18th, the advocates of Full Rights for Women on May 9, and the Secondary School Teachers in the same month. One of the last and most important of the unions was that of the Railway Servants. From this list it will be clear that the unions embraced the mass of professional intelligence; to take an instance, nearly every doctor belonged to the Union of Medicals. Some amongst them, such as the Unions of Lawyers, Writers, and Advocates of Women's Rights, represented the more irresponsible section of the Intelligence, but others, such as the agricultural experts, the doctors, and the primary teachers, had a direct connection with the work of the Zemstva and Town Councils, which had done so much to put the educated classes in touch with the needs of the peasants and workmen. The engineers, who were always to the fore in the movement for reform, had secured in other ways a practical experience of the national needs. Many of the Russian Intelligents are not far removed by instincts and associations from the labouring classes, and in the Union of Railway Servants we see an instance of how it was possible for both Intelligents and working men to organise themselves on very similar lines. This union was a beginning of more definite organisation amongst the labouring classes. Later there were formed several other unions, including even a Union of Officials for the reform of official-dom and a Liberal Union of Policemen. The programmes of all the unions were practically identical, and were developed from the original minimum requests of the Zemstvo Congress of November: they claimed a National Assembly elected by universal, equal, direct, and secret suffrage, inviola-bility of person, and freedom of speech, of the Press, of association, and of meeting. The unions met in various buildings, as opportunity offered, and submitted suggestions to the public or to the Minister. Such were, for in-stance, the note of 198 engineers on the needs of Russian industry (De-cember 18), the note on the needs of education drawn up by the Academic Union, the resolution of the doctors (December 31st), the note on the necessity of abolishing the restrictions on the Jews (March 9), the note of the primary teachers (March 25), and the note on the needs of Secondary Schools. Many of these notes were the original programmes of the unions concerned.

Towards the beginning of this movement Professor Milyukoff, a "Lib-erator" in close touch with the Zemstva, and one of the most acute poli-ticians in Russia, had conceived the idea of massing all the unions into a Union of Unions. The meeting of protest on January 22 furthered the idea. A few persons constituted themselves as a central committee, and invited deputies from each union. So far they acted only as an intelligence depart-ment, and Professor Milyukoff never intended to swamp the individuality of each union in any central body. Many of the unions were themselves still in process of formation; but when the Congresses of the unions had en-abled men to acquaint themselves more nearly with political questions and with each other, Milyukoff's idea became capable of execution. On May 21, delegates from fourteen unions met in Moscow. Here was estab-lished a loose organisation, which left absolutely free the action of each union. All were, however, declared to be conducting a struggle for the po-litical liberation of Russia on the principles of democracy. A second Con-gress was held on June 4 in Moscow, after the battle of Tsushima. Without committing itself to any definite tactics, the Union of Unions made sugges-tions founded on the common experience of the several unions, and, by a vaguely worded resolution, recognised all means of combating the bu-reaucracy. Certainly one of the most effective of these means was sug-gested by the central committee itself. When, in June, some persons were prosecuted for belonging to the Union of Engineers, their fellowmembers filled up and forwarded to the police the following declaration: "In view of the prosecution of some members of the Union, in accordance with article 126 of the Criminal Code, for belonging to the Union, I declare that I belong to the Union, and if belonging to it is a crime within the meaning of article 126, then I am equally guilty with the persons who have been prosecuted, and am under the same responsibility." So many engineers signed this formula that the authorities, overcome by the hopelessness of the task, set free those who had been arrested. The policy of Milyukoff, then, was one of passive resistance; but the resolution which approved of all methods was easily interpreted to cover political assassination. Milyukoff himself was always opposed to such methods; but he had no business to tamper with the question. In presence of the overwhelming material resources of the bureaucracy, he was certainly bound to secure allies amongst the general public; but he ought never to have deferred to the views of the Terrorists. In so doing, he sought his allies in the wrong place; and thus put upon the beginnings of the new Liberal party a taint of opportunism and worse, which was later to weaken the claims of the first Imperial Duma.

The Union of Unions continued its activity throughout the summer; but obviously its value was only temporary. In the country, a doctor might find himself isolated from most other members of his union, and his natural affinity would be with the schoolmaster who was working in the same village. There was no reason why all the doctors in Russia should have one set of political views and all schoolmasters another. As a means of asserting the opinion of the professional classes, the unions had been of immense service; but their members now began to wish for more frankly political organisations. Milyukoff, who had foreseen this, tried to restrain the central committee from compromising itself by too many definitions; but after his imprisonment in the autumn the Union of Unions passed into the hands of irresponsible doctrinaires; and though it continued to exist, its pronouncements were no longer representative. The more moderate section of its members passed into the Cadet party; the more extreme section took some part in the abortive Moscow rising of December. The working men had by that time made themselves independent of the Union of Unions; and, as it now represented only a very small party, it failed to have any very sensible influence on the elections for the Imperial Duma. In the summer was founded the last of the unions and far the most important, that of the peasants. Though in loose connection with the main body, it had its own programme, and must be studied as a separate development.

The work of drawing up schemes of reform was not confined to the Zemstva and the unions. Obedient to the Imperial command, the Committee of Ministers, assisted by the officials of the different Ministries, plunged into the business of lawmaking; and in the course of five months, from January to June, there were published more new Acts than had before been produced in the course of years. The bureaucrats, who were themselves closely akin to the Russian Intelligents, had even more of a liking for report writing; but the very atmosphere of bureaucracy gave a nerveless character to much of this work. Much energy and time was spent on it, but there was a lack of humour which prevented the authors from seeing that their activity was belated, and a lack of seriousness which made the public think, in many cases very unjustly, that the whole work was insincere. Some measure of freedom of religion was given to the Old Believers on April 30, to alien confessions on May 14, and to the Jews on July 8; Edicts of April 13 and May 19 aimed at bettering the conditions of peasant life. The whole Ministry of Agriculture was hastily remodelled; certain vague and inadequate regulations dealt with the publishing of laws and with the modification of some of the Press laws. The one measure which could have quieted the country was the definite summons to a National Assembly. Over and over again the Government has offered concessions which might have given satisfaction three months before. The bureaucracy was now in that disordered state of mind which history has attributed to the Duke of Newcastle: it seemed to have lost half an hour in the morning, and to be hurrying all day in a vain attempt to catch it up. Its activity at least showed that it too was being driven by public opinion and was reluctantly submitting to the necessity of making concessions. But its conversion, if such it could be called, was only the result of the stress of events and lacked all conviction; the bureaucrats were therefore the last people who could be expected to make any practical settlement of the questions which were at issue.

The real leadership of the movement for reform was still in the hands of the Zemstvo men. The two parties which had formed themselves at the November Congress were now more precisely defined; but far the more numerous was that which followed the lead of the Zemstvo Constitutionalists. This party had very much the views of English Liberals, while the minority, under Shipoff, represented the best instincts of English Conservatism. The Liberal leaders, on the initiative of Mr. Golovin, president of the Moscow Zemstvo, had established an Organising Committee. At the beginning of May this committee summoned another Zemstvo Congress. This time some of the delegates sent by the local Zemstva were formally elected; but others still came by invitation of the committee, or represented no more than the progressive groups in their respective Zemstva. The Congress, by an overwhelming majority, decided that the National Assembly must be not merely consultative, but legislative. The formula of universal suffrage adopted by the Zemstvo Constitutionalists and their attitude towards the commission of Bulyghin were ratified by a large majority. The Zemstvo Conservatives held a separate Congress under the presidency of Shipoff; here a greater proportion of the members came simply by invitation. This too was the moment when the Town Councils also entered the political arena as a corporate unit. So far they had been disunited. Some of them had sent respectful addresses which vaguely reflected the general feeling of the people; some had addressed petitions to the Council of Ministers. Some Town Councils, like that of Saratoff, had put forward the most modest requests as to the constitution and functions of the National Assembly, but a large number had accepted the lead of the Town Council of Moscow. Moscow adopted the formula of universal suffrage; Stavropol spoke boldly of a Constituent Assembly; Erivan even raised the questions of Women's suffrage, land nationalisation, and the municipalisation of economic enterprises. Members of Town Councils began to get into touch with the Organising Committee of the Zemstvo Congresses.

Miliukov on the Zemstva Petition

Sir Bernard, in the preceding article, described the part played in the struggle for the Duma by the scholar-turned-politician, Paul Miliukov. Here is Professor Miliukov's own summary of the events of 1903–1904. The source is: P. Milyoukov, *Russia and Its Crisis*. Chicago: University of Chicago Press, 1905. Pp. 528–535.

The members of the Zemstvos, taken as a whole, are not at all identical with the "Emancipation Party." Yet so powerful is the present current of liberal public opinion that their program, recently formulated in the petition presented to the Tsar, is that of the "Emancipation." We have seen that as early as 1902 voices were heard in the local committees advocating the introduction of a constitution. But these voices were indistinct, and such as had a more positive ring were stifled, and their possessors sent into exile. The cry was, however, raised again—this time not by three or four isolated individuals, but by fully a hundred; and it was not in the local assemblies legally summoned in the districts, but in a semi-official meeting of the members of all the Zemstvos, first invited by the minister Svyato-polk-Mirskee, then forbidden, and finally tolerated to meet at St. Petersburg.

This was the first meeting in Russian history which represented the opinion of the Zemstvos, not about local and economic, but about general and political questions. This meeting formulated a demand which was much more positive than that of the few exiled members of 1902. In its petition it enumerated all the fundamental rights of the individual and the citizen: the inviolability of the person and of the private home; no sentence without trial, and no diminution of rights except by judgment of an independent court; liberty of conscience and of belief; liberty of the press and of speech; equal rights—civil and political—for all social orders, and as a consequence, enfranchisement of the peasants; a large measure of local and municipal self-government; and last, as a general condition and a guaranty for all the preceding rights, "a regular representation in a separate elective body, which must participate in legislation, in working out the budget, and in controlling the administration." Of the ninety-eight members present, seventy-one voted for this last clause as a whole, while the minority of twenty-seven was satisfied with its first half; *i.e.,* the most conservative asked for a "regular representation in a separate elective body, which must participate in legislation"; and they found this reform "absolutely necessary for the normal development of the state and of society." In the last paragraph of their petition the members of the Zemstvos requested that the anticipated reform be carried out with the assistance of the "freely elected representatives of the people"; *i.e.,* demanded the convocation of the "constitutional assembly."

This degree of unanimity in the St. Petersburg assembly has surpassed the boldest expectations even of those observers who have closely followed the latest events in the political life of Russia. "The Petition of Rights" of November 19–21, 1904, will remain a beautiful page in our annals; and whatever be its immediate practical consequences, its political importance cannot be overestimated. It was the first political program of the Russian Liberal party, openly proclaimed in an assembly which had full moral right to represent liberalism throughout the empire. Moreover, this petition of the Zemstvo men from all Russia was officially handed to the Tsar, and a deputation of the assembly was received by him. The pacification of Russia depended at that moment on the satisfactory answer of the Tsar to the petition. This answer seemed to have been more or less determined upon in advance; otherwise there would have been no political sense in permitting the assembly to gather in St. Petersburg, and in receiving the petitioners in a formal audience. All Russia was in a state of feverish expectation; and meanwhile all social groups—writers and journalists, professors and men of science, lawyers, engineers, individual Zemstvos, provincial circles of intellectuals, workingmen, students, learned societies, the general public in the street, each in his own way, in demonstrations, banquets, resolutions covered with thousands of signatures, etc., etc.—hastened to indorse the petition of the Zemstvos. No more united and "coordinated" political action has ever been witnessed in the history of the country. To be sure, socialistic publications drew a sharp line between their own demands and those of the liberals, and tried to introduce workingmen speakers into all the assemblies of the liberals, proposing to include in their resolutions a more positive demand for a "direct, equal, and secret" general vote, freedom of strikes and a constitutional convention, as well as for the immediate cessation of the war. In many cases these demands were agreed to, as practically they did not contradict—and often were even implied in—the demands of the liberals themselves. The freedom of discussion and the boldness of speech in these assemblies surpassed everything that Russia had ever seen before; and the same spirit pervaded the press. Conservative newspapers—as *Novoya Vraimya*—became liberal; liberal newspapers became radical; and two new daily papers were started in St. Petersburg to advocate the claims of the more advanced public opinion. Though severely censored, they used a bold, open language, which, with perhaps two exceptions—at the beginning of the era of the "Great Reforms" (1859–61), and in 1881—was unprecedented in the history of our press. Public manifestations in the streets, though peaceful, were treated with relentless cruelty. Policemen and "janitors" in groups of four or five fell upon single unarmed students and girls, beat them with their fists, and struck them with drawn swords, until the poor disabled victims lost consciousness. Some of them died; others were maimed for life. Evidently this was a deliberate and systematized attempt, intended to inspire horror. Instead, it only inspired hatred and a feeling of revenge.

At the same time the question of reform was under discussion in the Tsar's palace, Tsarskoya Selo; and in a cabinet session on December 15, under the presidency of the Tsar, it received a fatal solution which, instead of ending the conflict, hopelessly enlarged the gulf between the Tsar and his people. Mr. Mooravyov, the minister of justice, who was the first to speak, tried to prove that the Tsar had no right to change the existing political order. Mr. Pobedonostsev attempted to prove the same proposition by arguments from religion. He thought—in his own peculiar language —that Russia "would fall into sin and return to a state of barbarism," if the Tsar should renounce his power; religion and morality would suffer, and the law of God would be violated. It was such arguments as these which for a time decided the fate of Russia. Mr. Svyatopolk-Mirskee tried in vain to prove that the minister of justice talked nonsense; and Mr. Witte grimly concluded: "If it should become known that the emperor is forbidden by law and religion to introduce fundamental reforms of his own will—well, then a part of the population will come to the conclusion that these reforms must be achieved by way of violence. It would be equivalent to an actual appeal to revolution!" Mr. Witte played the prophet.

As a result of this discussion, the manifesto of December 26, 1904, was published. It began with the declaration that "when the need for this or that change shall have been proved ripe, then it will be considered necessary to meet it, even though the transformation to which this change may lead should involve the introduction of essentially new departures in legislation." The meaning of that solemn declaration was, however, ludicrously contradicted and narrowed by the opposite affirmation some few lines previously: "the undeviating maintenance of the immutability of the fundamental laws must be considered as an established principle of government." Such innovations as would interfere with that immutability of the fundamental laws were deliberately classified—and in advance—by the manifesto as "tendencies not seldom mistaken, and often influenced by transitory circumstances." These introductory principles were enough to annihilate any further concessions in the manifesto. All the demands of the Zemstvos, except political reform, were mentioned in the manifesto, but the promised changes were stated in such evasive and ambiguous terms and accompanied with so many "limitations," "possibilities," and other restrictions, that the impression produced was just opposite to what had been expected.

The immediate measures of the government still further increased the contrast between promises and good intentions, and the dire reality. While the manifesto promised to reconsider the "temporary" and exceptional regulations taken in its self-defense, as a matter of fact the government found itself obliged to resort to enforced measures of repression, domiciliary searches, arrests, imprisonments, etc. While it was promising to stop arbitrariness and to enforce a regime of "legality," in Nishnee Novgorod a crowd of policemen made a raid on a local club and treated the members of a party which they found in the clubroom just as they did the political demonstrators in the streets: they struck them with drawn swords—the feat remained unpunished. The manifesto promised to free the press from "excessive" repression; and there was a shower of repressive measures against the press: in three weeks of December there were doled out seven warnings, two prohibitions of retail sale, one "severe reproof," and two periodicals were stopped for three months. The manifesto answered, and tried to comply with, a political demand by the men of the Zemstvos; and at the same time an order was issued that no political demands should be permitted to be discussed in the Zemstvos. The Tsar promised to make more effective his promises of religious freedom given in an earlier manifesto of 1903; and at the same time the Holy Synod, led by Mr. Pobedonostsev, made public an address to the clergy which sounded very much like a disavowal of the Tsar and invited the priests to pray God to give the Tsar more power and wisdom.

In short, it was not pacification, but increasing irritation, that ensued from the publication of the manifesto.

• • •

The Raskol Reforms, 1903–1905

> The winds of change, described by Pares and Miliukov, affected religious matters as well as political affairs. The following brief summary is reprinted by permission of the publishers from F. C. Conybeare's previously quoted study, *The Russian Dissenters,* pp. 237–239.

A better epoch seemed about to dawn when on February 26, 1903, after the fall of Pobedonostsev, the young Tsar, Nicholas II proclaimed liberty of conscience; and in an Ukase promulgated by the Senate on December 12, 1904, a revision was promised of all the laws directed against the Raskol. Official persecutions, remarks Palmieri, far from having enfeebled the religious feelings and the spirit of abnegation of the Dissenters had only made them more tenacious of their beliefs, readier than ever to sacrifice everything rather than stoop to apostasy. Accordingly they formulated the following demands:—

1. That in official documents the offensive epithet *Raskolniki* or dissidents should be cancelled, and that of Old believers or Old Ritualists— the latter first used in Catharine II's rescript of August 13, 1775—should take its place. These substitutes the Orthodox objected to as implying that they themselves were the innovators in 1667.

2. They demanded juridical and religious autonomy for their parishes, and a corresponding right to possess what places of worship and charitable institutions they liked. Till now they had had mainly to meet for worship in private houses.

3. Liberty of cult, and a recognition of the legality of the so-called *metriki* or registers drawn up by Raskol ministers. They asked that there should be inscribed in these the names of those who, though they figured in the registers of the orthodox priests, had nevertheless declined their sacraments for a period of ten years. The law of 1883 only allowed Raskol chapels to be reopened which had been founded before 1826, when there were 1257 of them. Since 1883 and up to 1904 the number of their chapels had increased by 283.

4. The right of those, who in spite of their really being Raskolniks, figured as orthodox in civil documents, to inscribe their children in the Raskol registers. Members of the Raskol inscribed against their will in orthodox ledgers and lists generally refused on that account to report their births, marriages and deaths to the police. For example over fourteen years, 1889–1903, according to a fairly accurate estimate, out of 29,431 Raskolnik marriages only 1840 were reported to the police; out of 131,-730 births, only 552.[1]

5. Lastly the Raskolniks asked in 1904 for liberty to open elementary schools for their children in which their own catechisms should be taught; liberty for Raskol students, *not* to have to listen in secondary schools to a catechist's lectures *against* their religion; exemption of their priests from military service to which no orthodox priest is liable, and free access for their laity to all civil and military duties and offices.

Their demands, owing to Pobedonostsev's sudden fall from power and the disasters of the Japanese War, received some satisfaction, and an imperial Ukase of April 17, 1905, suppressed the offensive *Raskol,* and distinguished among Russian dissenters three categories: 1. of Old Ritualists who recognize the sacraments and dogmatic doctrines of the Orthodox Church, but differ therefrom on points of ritual; 2. of Sectaries, e.g. the Molokani, Stundists and Dukhobortsi; 3. the 'pernicious' sects, e.g. the Khlysty or Flagellants and the Skoptsy or Self-mutilators.

The first-named were henceforth to be allowed to organize themselves into a corporate Church and enjoy such rights as the Lutherans or Catholics already enjoyed; they were to divide themselves into parishes under rectors (*nastoyateli, nastavniki*), their clergy were exempted from military service, they might found schools of their own and move about without that machinery of passports which made them the special victims of police oppression and blackmail. The Council of Ministers, glossing the Ukase, furthermore gave them the right to *own* their churches, hospitals and cemeteries, the right of admission as students in military and naval academies, of receiving decorations and of printing their liturgies.

These concessions excited great hopes in the breast of the Raskolnik, while the orthodox journals also pretended to be overjoyed at so signal a proof that the Russian people is hostile to religious persecution. Skvortsov wrote as follows:—"We know by experience that police measures are repugnant to our aims. Religious errors are maladies of heart and soul, and it is best to use against them nothing but the gentle words of love and conviction. Government protection of a church by dint of law generates supineness in the pastors, somnolence and apathy; and it is all for the good if the Government, by withdrawing its aid from the Orthodox, constrains them to count on themselves and their own forces and to combat with their own weapons." [2] Yet Skvortsov had been, as Palmieri remarks, the ham-

---

[1] These figures from the *Pravoslavnyi Putevoditel* or "Orthodox Guide," an organ of the Russian Church, 1905, t. ii, p. 39.

[2] *Mission Review,* 1905, Tom. 1, p. 542.

mer of the Raskolniks, the loyal henchman of the arch-persecutor Pobedonostsev. "When the devil is sick, the devil a saint will be."

The real feeling of the Orthodox and of the Holy Synod was revealed
in the organ of the latter, the *Kolokol* or *Bell,* which objected particularly
to the liberty accorded to the Raskol to have its own parishes, and declared
that before long the best energies of the official Church would pass into the
ranks of the Raskol, seeing that the Orthodox Church in spite of the support, protection and tutelage of the State was unable to defend itself. The
young Tsar's Government impressed by these wailings of the Holy Synod
took a fresh tack, and a new Ukase of April 17, 1905, enacted a year's imprisonment for anyone who tries to seduce an orthodox person into any
of the rival confessions by means of sermons or dissemination of written
works or images.

Institutions of Imperial Government

The diagram below is a stylized "table of organization" of the imperial government as it existed just prior to the 1905 Revolution. It is included here as a convenient summary for reference purposes. The diagram was translated and slightly adapted from a chart prepared by N. P. Eroshkin and published in his book, *Ocherki istorii gosudarstvennyikh uchrezdenii dorevolyutsionnoi Rossii (An Outline History of State Institutions in Pre-revolutionary Russia).* Moscow, 1960. The translation was made by Miss Lucy Walsh.

THE HIGHEST INSTITUTIONS OF
THE RUSSIAN CENTRAL GOVERNMENT, 1905-1907

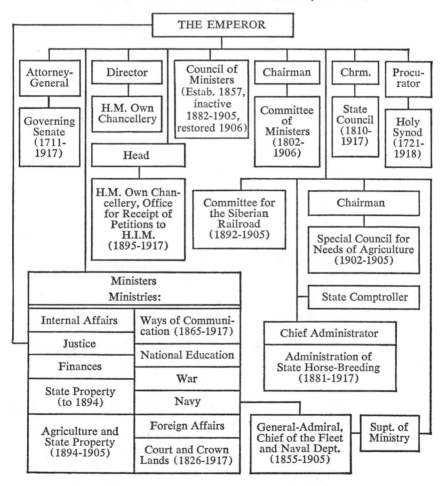

The Development of Lenin's Program

Official Soviet accounts often give the impression that Marxism was introduced into Russia by Lenin, which was not the case. The founder of Marxism in Russia was George Plekhanov who introduced the Russian intellectuals to Marx at a time when the future Lenin was only thirteen years old. Not until several years later (the dates are somewhat uncertain) did young Vladimir Ilyich Ulyanov (Lenin) become acquainted with the Marx-Engels doctrines, and he first learned of them through the writings of Plekhanov. For the next decade or so, Ulyanov regarded himself as the faithful disciple of Plekhanov.

The young convert threw himself into the work with enthusiastic vigor. His first Marxist writing intended for distribution appeared in 1893. It was the first of a long and voluminous series. Two years later, Ulyanov was arrested by the police, convicted of revolutionary activity and sent first to prison and later into exile. The authorities allowed him to have books and journals, to conduct an extensive correspondence, and to continue his writing. One of his articles served as the basis for discussion at the abortive 1898 Congress at Minsk.

Ulyanov himself was still in exile when nine delegates from various revolutionary groups met in three-day session at Minsk for the purpose of organizing a united party. They issued a manifesto calling for such an organization and elected a Central Committee of three to direct their work. Before anything could come of it, two of the committeemen and eight of the delegates were arrested. This failure made new tactics necessary, and Ulyanov took a leading part in the work, at first through correspondence and articles, later, in person.

Leaving Russia in 1900, Ulyanov sought out Plekhanov at Geneva. Already serious differences had begun to develop between the "old revolutionaries" (Plekhanov, Axelrod, and Zasulich) and the new generation which Ulyanov headed. After bitter quarrels among themselves it was finally agreed that they should seek to organize their movement by means of a revolutionary newspaper. This was Ulyanov's idea. He named the paper *Iskra* (*The Spark*) and chose as its masthead slogan Pushkin's line, "Out of the spark shall spring the flame." It was quite appropriate, therefore, that the leading editorial in the first issue should also be his work. Writing under the title, "The Urgent Tasks of our Movement," Ulyanov set forth the program of his party-to-be. A translation of this editorial, slightly abridged, follows. The source is: *Iskra. Central Organ of the Russian Social Democratic Workers Party.* Vol. I, no. 1 (December, 1900). P. 1.

The First Iskra Program

The Russian Social-Democrats have already declared more than once that the immediate political task of a Russian workers' party should be to overthrow the autocracy and secure political liberty. This was declared more than fifteen years ago by the representatives of Russian Social-Democracy, the members of the group known as "The Emancipation of

Labor." It was again stated two and one half years ago by the representatives of the Russian Social-Democratic organizations who formed the Russian Social Democratic Workers Party in the spring of 1898. But the question of what the political tasks of the Russian Social-Democrats should be is again coming to the front despite these repeated declarations. Many members of our movement are expressing doubts as to whether the answer given above is the right one. The economic struggle, it is claimed, is predominantly important; the political tasks of the proletariat are being narrowed, restricted, and pushed into the background. It is even declared that talk about forming an independent workers' party in Russia is merely an imitation of others, and that the workers ought to take part only in the economic struggle, leaving political matters to the alliance of intellectuals and liberals. This latest profession . . . (the notorious *Credo*) amounts . . . to a complete denial of the Social-Democratic program. . . . The Russian Social-Democratic movement is going through a time of vacillation and doubt. . . . The labor movement, on the one hand, is being cut off from Socialism: the workers are being helped to carry on the economic fight but nothing, or not enough, is being done to explain to them the Socialist aims and the political tasks of the movement as a whole. Socialism, on the other hand, is being cut off from the labor movement: Russian Socialists are once more asserting that the struggle against the government should be carried on by the intelligentsia alone and that the workers should confine themselves to the economic struggle.

. . . The "Economist" trend (if it can be called a trend) has given rise to attempts to raise this narrowness to a regular theory, and has tried to use for this purpose the currently fashionable Bernsteinism . . . which advocates the old bourgeois ideas under a new label. These efforts have resulted in the danger of a weakened connection between the Russian labor movement and Russian Social-Democracy, that foremost champion of political liberty. The most urgent task of our movement is to strengthen this link.

Social-Democracy is a union of the labor movement with Socialism. Its task is not passively to serve the labor movement in each of its separate stages, but to represent the interests of the whole movement, to point out to the movement its ultimate goal and its political tasks, and to protect its ideological and political independence. Cut off from Social-Democracy, the labor movement grows petty in character and tends, necessarily, to become bourgeoisie. By conducting only an economic fight, the working class loses its political independence, becomes a hanger-on to other parties, and betrays the great commandment: "The emancipation of the workers must be done by the workers themselves." There has been a period in every country when the workers' movement and the Socialist movement existed separately, each going its own way. And in every country this separation has resulted in the weakening of both movements. In every country only the union of Socialism and the workers' movement has given both a firm foundation. In Russia, the need for a union of Socialism and the labor movement was long ago set forth in theory, but it is only now being

achieved in practice. The process is very difficult and it is not at all surprising that it should be accompanied by doubts and vacillations. . . .

The whole history of Russian Socialism has brought it about that its
most urgent task is to fight the autocratic government and to win political
freedom. Our Socialist movement has become focussed, as it were, on the
struggle against the autocracy. History has shown, on the other hand,
that the gulf between Socialist thought and the advanced workers is much
wider in Russia than in other countries, and that as long as this persists the
revolutionary movement in Russia is doomed to impotence. It logically
follows that the task which is the mission of the Russian Social-Democrats
is to inculcate in the proletarian masses the idea of Socialism and of a
political awareness, and to organize a revolutionary party which will be in-
extricably linked with the spontaneous labor movement. The Russian
Social-Democrats have already done much along this line, but more remains to be done. As the movement grows, the field for Social-Democratic
action widens. As the work becomes more diversified, an increasing number of the members of the movement are concentrating their efforts on
doing various particular jobs. . . . This is unavoidable and quite legitimate, but we must be most careful lest these particular activities and special methods of fighting become ends in themselves. The preparatory work
should not be raised to the level of the main and only work.

Our principal and fundamental task is to assist the political organization and political development of the working class. Those who shove
this task into the background and do not subordinate all special jobs and
particular methods of fighting to it are straying along the wrong path and
are seriously hurting the movement. And it is being shoved into the background: first, by those who summon revolutionaries to fight the government with the help of isolated conspiratorial circles; and, secondly, by
those who reduce the scope of political propaganda, agitation, and organization—those who think it fitting and proper to treat the workers to
"politics" only on solemn occasions and at exceptional moments in their
lives—those who too zealously whittle down the fight against the autocracy
to demands for partial concessions from the autocracy, and who are not
sufficiently concerned with developing these partial demands into a systematic and implacable struggle by the revolutionary workers' party against
the autocracy.

. . . organize not only in mutual aid and strike benefit societies and in
workers' circles; organize also in a political party; organize for a determined struggle against the autocratic government and against the whole of
capitalist society. Unless the proletariat does organize in this way, it will
never rise to the level of a conscious class struggle. Unless the workers organize in this way, the labor movement is doomed to impotence. The
working class will never succeed in achieving its great mission, which is to
free itself and the whole Russian people from political and economic slavery, by strike funds, mutual-aid societies and circles alone. No class in
history has ever gotten power without producing as its foremost representatives political leaders capable of organizing and leading the movement.

The Russian working class has already shown that it can produce such men. The struggle of the Russian workers, so widely developed in the past five or six years, has shown how great the potential revolutionary energy of the working class is. It has shown that the most ruthless persecution by this government increases rather than decreases the number of workers who are eager for Socialism, political knowledge and the political struggle.

. . . we must set resolutely to work to do these tasks; we must undertake the questions of program, organization, and tactics for the Party. . . . We are way behind the old workers of the Russian revolutionary movement in this regard. We must admit this fault frankly, and devote our efforts to devising more secret methods, to carrying on systematic training in the rules of carrying on the work, in the ways of tricking the secret police and avoiding the traps of the police. We must train people who will devote not only their spare evenings but the whole of their lives to the revolution. We must build up an organization big enough to allow a precise division of labor. Finally, on the question of tactics, we shall speak here only of the following: Social-Democrats should not tie their hands, should not limit their activities to one preconceived plan or method of political struggle; they should accept all methods of fighting so long as these are commensurate with the forces under the Party's disposal and enable it to attain the maximum possible results under the given conditions. With a strongly organized party, one single strike may grow into a political demonstration, into a political victory over the government. With a strongly organized party, a local uprising may develop into a victorious revolution.

We must remember that the struggle with the government for partial demands, that the winning of partial concessions are only petty skirmishes against the enemy, minor engagements against the outposts—the decisive battle is still to come. The enemy's fortress, raining shot and shell upon us and mowing down our best fighters, stands before us in all its strength. We must capture that fortress . . . .

The 1902 Program

During the first eight years of writing and other revolutionary work Ulyanov used numerous pseudonyms, but in 1901 he first used the name which has become so much more famous than his real one. His choice, of course, was Lenin. In later years he customarily combined his own name and patronymic with the pseudonym, thus: Vladimir Ilyich Lenin. But in the earlier period he signed himself as N. Lenin. (He never used the name Nicolai or Nicholas. That was invented for him by others after 1917.)

N. Lenin, in March of 1902, published a book which not only was the point of departure for the debates at the 1903 Congress, but also remains to this day the basic strategical and tactical handbook of the Communist parties. The following excerpts show Lenin's pattern for the organization of a revolutionary party. He did not use the now familiar phrases "united front," "transmission belts," "fellow-travelers," etc., but the ideas are there.

The source is: V. I. Lenin, *What Is To Be Done? Burning Questions of Our Movement*. New York: International Publishers, 1929. Pp. 8, 28, 41, 56, 57, 65, 76, 77, 79, 82, 83, 84, 90, 105, 106, 107, 108, 109, 112, 116, 117, 118, 121, 123, 124. Greatly abridged.

Without a revolutionary theory there can be no revolutionary movement.

. . .

. . . the role of the vanguard can be filled only by a party that is guided by an advanced theory.

. . .

Hence, to belittle Socialist ideology in any way, to deviate from it in the slightest degree means strengthening bourgeois ideology. There is a lot of talk about spontaneity, but the spontaneous development of the labour movement leads to its becoming subordinated to bourgeois ideology. . . . Hence, our task, . . . is to combat spontaneity, to divert the labour movement, with its spontaneous trade-unionist striving, from under the wing of the bourgeoisie, and to bring it under the wing of revolutionary Social-Democracy.

. . .

Recently, the overwhelming majority of Russian Social-Democrats were almost wholly engaged in this work of exposing factory conditions. . . . So much so indeed, that they lost sight of the fact that this, taken by itself, was not substantially Social-Democratic work, but merely trade-union work. As a matter of fact, these exposures merely dealt with the relations between the workers in a given trade, with their immediate employers, and all that it achieved was that the vendors of labour power learned to sell their "commodity" on better terms, and to fight the purchasers of labour power over a purely commercial deal. . . . Social-Democrats lead the struggle of the working-class not only for better terms for the sale of labour power, but also for the abolition of the social system which compels the propertyless class to sell itself to the rich. Social-Democracy represents the working-class, not in its relation to any given group of employers, but in its relation to all classes in modern society, to the state as an organized political force.

. . .

The question now arises: What does political education mean? Is it sufficient to confine oneself to the propaganda of working-class hostility to autocracy? Of course not. It is not enough to explain to the workers that they are politically oppressed (any more than it was to explain to them that their interests were antagonistic to the interests of the employers.) Advantage must be taken of every concrete example of this oppression for the purpose of agitation (in the same way as we began to use concrete examples of economic oppression for the purpose of agitation.)

* * *

Up till now we thought . . . that a propagandist, dealing with say the question of unemployment, must explain the capitalistic nature of crises, the reasons why crises are inevitable in modern society, must describe how present society must inevitably become transformed into Socialist society, etc. In a word, he must present "many ideas," so many indeed that they will be understood as a whole only by a (comparatively) few persons. An agitator, however, speaking on the same subject will take as an illustration a fact that is most widely known and outstanding among his audience—say the death from starvation of the family of an unemployed worker . . . etc.—and utilising this illustration, will direct all his efforts to present a single idea to the "masses" . . . he will strive to rouse discontent and indignation among the masses against this crying injustice, and leave a more complete explanation . . . to the propagandist.

* * *

The workers can acquire class political consciousness only from without, that is, only outside of the economic struggle, outside of the sphere of relations between workers and employers. . . . To bring political knowledge to the workers, the Social-Democrats must go among all classes of the population, must despatch units of their army in all directions. . . . The Social-Democrats' ideal should not be a trade-union secretary, but a tribune of the people, able to react to every manifestation of tyranny and oppression, no matter where it takes place, no matter what stratum or class of people it affects; he must be able to group all these manifestations into a single picture of police violence and capitalist exploitation; he must be able to take advantage of every petty event in order to explain his Socialistic convictions and his Social-Democratic demands to all. . . .

* * *

. . . for he who forgets that "the Communists support every revolutionary movement," that we are obliged for that reason to emphasize general democratic tasks before the whole people, without for a moment concealing our Socialistic convictions, is not a Social-Democrat.

* * *

But if "we" desire to be advanced democrats, we must make it our business to stimulate in the minds of those who are dissatisfied only with the university or only with the Zemstvo, etc. conditions the idea that the whole political system is worthless. We must take upon ourselves the task of organizing a universal political struggle under the leadership of our party in such a manner as to obtain the support of all opposition strata for the struggle and for our party. We must train our Social-Democratic practical workers to become political leaders, able to guide all the manifestations of this universal struggle, able at the right time "to dictate a positive programme of action" for the discontented students, for the discontented

Zemstvo, for the discontented religious sects, for the offended elementary school teachers, etc., etc. . . . We would be . . . Social-Democrats only in name . . . if we failed to realize that our task is to utilise every manifestation of discontent, and to collect and utilise every grain of even rudimentary protest.

. . .

The spontaneous labour movement is able by itself to create (and inevitably will create) only trade-unionism, and working-class trade-union politics. The fact that the working-class participates in the political struggle and even in political revolution does not in itself make its politics Social-Democratic politics.

. . .

The workers' organisations must in the first place be trade organisations; secondly, they must be as wide as possible; and, thirdly, they must be as public as conditions will allow. . . . On the other hand, the organisations of revolutionists must be comprised first and foremost of people whose profession is that of revolutionists (that is why I speak of organisations of revolutionists, meaning revolutionary Social-Democrats.) . . . Such an organisation must of necessity be not too extensive and as secret as possible.

. . . every Social-Democratic worker should, as far as possible, support and actively work inside these [trade-union] organisations. . . . The wider these organisations are, the wider our influence over them will be. They will then be influenced not only by the "spontaneous" development of the economic struggle, but also by the direct and conscious action of the Socialists on their comrades in the unions.

. . .

We must also expose the conciliatory, "harmonious" undertones that will be heard in the speeches delivered by liberal politicians . . . irrespective of whether they proceed from an earnest conviction as to the desirability of peaceful cooperation of the classes, whether they proceed from a desire to curry favor with the employers, or are simply the result of not being able to do otherwise. . . . Trade-union organisations may not only be of tremendous value in developing and consolidating the economic struggle, but may also become a very useful auxiliary to the political, agitational, and revolutionary organisations.

. . .

A small, compact core, consisting of reliable, experienced and hardened workers, with responsible agents in the principal districts and connected by all the rules of strict secrecy with the organisations of revolutionists, can, with the wide support of the masses and without an elaborate set of rules, perform all the functions of a trade-union organisation, and perform them, moreover, in the manner Social-Democrats desire.

. . . I mean *professional revolutionists,* irrespective of whether they are students or working men. I assert: 1. That no movement can be durable without a stable organisation of leaders to maintain continuity; 2. that the more widely the masses are drawn into the struggle and form the basis of the movement, the more necessary is it to have such an organisation and the more stable must it be (for it is much easier then for demagogues to side-track the more backward sections of the masses); 3. that the organisation must consist chiefly of persons engaged in revolution as a profession; 4. that in a country with a despotic government, the more we *restrict* the membership of this organisation to persons who are engaged in revolution as a profession, and who have been professionally trained in the art of combating the political police, the more difficult will it be to catch the organisation; and 5. the wider will be the circle of men and women of the working class or of other classes of society able to join the movement and perform active work in it.

We can never give a mass organisation that degree of secrecy which is essential for the persistent and continuous struggle against the government. But to concentrate all secret functions in the hands of as small a number of professional revolutionists as possible, does not mean that the latter will "do the thinking for all" and that the crowd will not take an active part in the movement. . . . The centralisation of the secret functions of the organisation does not mean the concentration of all the functions of the movement. The active participation of the greatest masses in the dissemination of illegal literature will not diminish because a dozen professional revolutionists concentrate in their hands the secret part of the work; on the contrary, it will increase tenfold. Only in this way will the reading of illegal literature . . . and to some extent even the distribution of illegal literature almost cease to be secret work, for the police will soon come to realise the folly and futility of setting the whole judicial and administrative machine in motion to intercept every copy of a publication that is being broadcast in thousands. This applies not only to the press, but to every function of movement, even to demonstrations. . . . organisations intended for wide membership . . . can be as loose and public as possible, for example, trade unions, workers' circles for self-education . . . and Socialist, and also democratic circles for all other sections of the population, etc., etc. We must have as large a number as possible of such organisations having the widest possible variety of functions, but it is absurd and dangerous to confuse these with organisations of revolutionists. . . .

. . .

If we had such an organisation, the more secret it would be, the stronger and more widespread would be the confidence of the masses in the party, and, as we know, in time of war, it is not only of great importance to imbue one's own adherents with confidence in the strength of one's army, but also the enemy and all neutral elements; friendly neutrality may sometimes decide the outcome of the battle.

. . .

. . . our very first and most imperative duty is to help to train work-ing-class revolutionists who will be on the same level in regard to party ac-tivity as intellectual revolutionists (we emphasise the words "in regard to party activity," because although it is necessary, it is not so easy and not so imperative to bring the workers up to the level of the intellectuals in other respects.) . . . the working-class revolutionist must also become a professional revolutionist. . . . A workingman who is at all talented and "promising," must not be left to work . . . in a factory. We must ar-range that he be maintained by the party, that he may in due time go un-derground. . . . . . . When we shall have detachments of specially trained working-class revolutionists . . . no political police in the world will be able to contend against them, for these detachments will consist of men absolutely loyal and devoted to the revolution, and will themselves enjoy the absolute confidence and devotion of the broad masses of the workers.

. . .

The 1903 Congress

Friction increased among the members of the editorial board of *Iskra*, and it was decided to make another attempt to organize the party and to settle its program by means of another congress (or, as we would probably put it, conference). Because of the Russian police and because the most important leaders were in Western Europe, the meeting was convened in Brussels. Lenin took great pains (as far as he could) to arrange for the selection of delegates who would support him. He also carefully prepared detailed plans and arguments in support of them, and busily mended his political fences among the delegates as they ar-rived. The Belgian police soon ordered the delegates out of Brussels and the session was transferred to London. According to Lenin's count, forty-three delegates, representing fifty-one votes, attended the London meetings. Four of the delegates were or had been workers; the rest were intellectuals.

One of the most bitterly fought battles came on the nature of the party organization and, especially, on the qualifications to be demanded of members. Lenin demanded, as he had in his earlier writings, that membership be restricted to professional revolutionaries. He also wanted a strong centralization of authority and a most rigid discipline and obedience to the party's leaders. The veterans, Axelrod and Zasu-lich; Lenin's contemporary, Martov; and the neophyte revolutionary, Trotsky, all favored a party open to all who believed in its program and were willing to work under its leadership. This program (usually called Martov's) won on the first voting, 28 to 22. But Lenin was able to get the matter reconsidered after seven or eight delegates had with-drawn or been forced out. This time the victory went to Lenin by a slender majority.

The congress was, in fact, hopelessly split. Lenin, with great per-spicacity, arrogated to his faction the titles of *Bolshinstvo* (*Majority*) and *Bolsheviki* (*Members of the Majority*) thus forcing upon his opponents the titles of *Menshinstvo* (*Minority*) and *Mensheviki* (*Members of the Minority*). But the actual tabulation of the votes gives a more accurate picture. On the two very important matters of the election of the editorial board of *Iskra* and the election of the Central Committee the score was: delegates withdrawn or expelled—7; blank ballots —2; not voting—20; for Lenin's side—22. The London Congress actually created not one party but two, namely Lenin's Bolsheviks and Martov's Mensheviks.

Excerpts from Lenin's resolution which precipitated this split are given below. This is an official Soviet translation of a manuscript note in Lenin's handwriting. The original is in the Central Lenin Museum at Moscow.

1. A member of the Russian Social-Democratic Workers' Party is one who accepts its program, belongs to one of its organizations, and supports the Party both financially and by personal participation in its activities.

2. The supreme organ of the Party is the Party Congress. . . .

3. The following shall be entitled to representation at Congresses: (a) Central Committee; (b) Editorial Board of the Central Organ of the Party; (c) all local committees not belonging to special federations; (d) all federations of committees recognized by the Party. . . .

4. The Party Congress elects the Central Committee and the Editorial Board of the Central Organ of the Party. The Central Committee exercises direct leadership of the political struggle, co-ordinates and guides all practical activities of the Party, and administers the central Party funds. To serve the needs of the movement as a whole, the Central Committee may also appoint special agents or special groups under its direct control. The Central Committee shall settle all conflicts arising between various organizations and institutions of the Party, or within them.

5. The Editorial Board of the Central Organ leads the Party ideologically . . . and [makes] the decision of [on] tactical questions. The central Committee should be located in Russia and the Central Organ abroad. . . . In the event of the arrest of all the members and alternate members of the Central Committee, a new Central Committee shall be appointed by the Editorial Board of the Central Organ. . . .

The Lenin "Line" on the 1905 Revolution

As a result of the split which was so apparent at the London Congress, Lenin eventually lost control of *Iskra*. He then established a Bolshevik newspaper which he called *Vpered* (*Forward*) and used it as he had previously used *Iskra*, that is, to indoctrinate, organize, and direct his followers. The paper was published in Geneva. The issue for January 4 (N.S.), 1905, carried a lead editorial by Lenin in which he laid down the line for his followers in regard to events then taking place in Russia. The translation was made from a facsimile copy of the paper.

. . . For the proletariat, the fight for political freedom and a democratic republic in a bourgeois society is just one of the necessary steps in the fight for a social revolution which will overturn the bourgeois system. . . . The movement which is beginning in Russia is a bourgeois revolution. . . . No, the nearer the time of revolution approaches and the stronger the constitutional movement becomes, the more rigorously must the party of the proletariat uphold its class independence and not allow its class demands to be overwhelmed by the general talk of democracy. The more often and the more vigorously the representatives of so-called society bring forward what they claim to be the demands of the whole people, the more relentlessly must the Social-Democrats expose the real nature of this society. Take the notorious resolution of the "secret" Zemstva congress of November 6/8. You will find in it, shoved well to the background, deliberately vague and timid constitutional aspirations. You will find . . . exceedingly detailed suggestions for reforms in Zemstva and in municipal institutions—that is, in institutions which represent the interests of the landlords and capitalists. You will find mention of peasant reforms—freeing the peasants from guardianship and protecting proper court forms. It is wholly clear that here are representatives of the propertied classes who only desire to secure concessions from the autocracy and who have no desire to make changes in the foundations of the economic systems. . . .

Is there anyone who can't see that it is precisely the interests of all levels of landowners, merchant-industrialists, and middle class peasants which form the foundation and basis for the constitutional demands? Will we really be fooled because the democratic intelligentsia—which always and everywhere in all European middle class revolutions has taken on itself the role of publicist, speaker and political leader—represent these interests?

. . . The Proletariat must take advantage of the unusually favorable political position. The proletariat must support the middle-class constitutional movement, incite and rally the widest possible segments of the exploited masses of the people, muster all its forces, and start an uprising at the instant when the government's position is most desperate and the popular unrest is highest.

In what way should the proletariat immediately support the constitutionalists? The most important of all is to use the general unrest to agitate and organize among the least influenced and most backward sections of the peasants and workers. Of course, the Social-Democrats, the organized proletariat, ought to send its detachments among all classes, but . . . the more acute the struggle grows . . . the more should our work be concentrated in getting the proletarians and semi-proletarians ready for the direct struggle for freedom. . . . It is incomparably more important now to increase our ranks, organize our forces, and prepare for a more direct and open mass struggle. . . .

. . . A military disaster is inevitable, and it will inevitably be accompanied by the profound exacerbation of discontent, anger, and unrest. With the utmost energy, we must prepare for that moment.

. . .

Vpered (*Forward*) survived only until May (1905) when it was replaced by *Proletarii* (*The Proletarian*) with Lenin again as editor-in-chief. The first issue of this new "Central Organ of the Russian Social-Democratic Workers' Party" was published at Geneva on May 14/27. Its leading article was a brief report—written by Lenin, but signed by the Central Committee—of some of the decisions made at the Third Party Congress (held at London, April-May, 1905). The following excerpt is an official translation of a portion of that report.

. . . The Congress drew the attention of all Party members to the necessity of taking advantage of the waverings of the government, of every legal or practical extension of freedom for our activities, to strengthen the class organization of the proletariat and to prepare for open action by the proletariat. . . . The making of a victorious revolution and the defense of its conquests impose tremendous tasks on the proletariat. But the proletariat will not be dismayed by great tasks. . . . It will be able to take the lead of [sic] the armed uprising of the people. It will not shirk the difficult task of participating in a provisional revolutionary government, should such a task fall to its share. It will be able to repulse all counter-revolutionary attempts, ruthlessly crush all enemies of freedom, staunchly defend the democratic republic, and secure the fulfillment of our whole minimum program by revolutionary means. . . .

Father Gapon and Bloody Sunday

January 22, 1905 was a decisive date in Russian revolutionary history. On that day a peaceful procession of workers, led by the police-supported priest, Father Georg Gapon, advanced upon the Winter Palace to present a petition to the tsar. Nicholas was not in residence and the crowd was fired upon by troops. About one hundred and fifty were killed and another two hundred were wounded. The shock to public opinion was terrific and significant. The source for the following account of this incident is: Mavor, *Economic History*, vol. 2, pp. 456, 461–463, 467–468.

There thus came to be four elements in Gapon's movement: (1) the enthusiastic Gapon himself, apparently disinterested in the early stages, afterwards torn by conflicting interests and unable to pursue an independent course; (2) the police, participating partly overtly through the control provided by the constitution of Gapon's society, and partly covertly through spies, and probably, also, consciously or unconsciously on his part, through Gapon; (3) the small group of working men whose influence Gapon had found it necessary to enlist in order to secure adherents to his movement, and who afterwards forced Gapon into a position from which he would gladly have escaped; and (4) the mass of working men and working women members and strikers joining the society at the last moment, who, on the one hand, were depressed by low wages and by conditions of employment which they regarded as oppressive, and, on the other, were inflated with the promises of liberty and of improved conditions of life which were recklessly made to them by the progressive parties, and whose views about Gapon, as well as their adhesion to him, fluctuated from time to time.

. . .

On the 27th December (O.S.) the employees of all the St. Petersburg factories went on strike and decisive meetings were held on the following day, the 28th December, in Vasilyevsky Ostrov and other places.

On 2nd January 1905 (O.S.) there met in Gapon's house a hundred of the most influential of his adherents. Gapon again urgently pleaded for delay, but the working men "in the most categorical manner" insisted "that the fire of the excitement might die out," and that the strike at the Putilovsky Works presented an opportunity such as was not likely soon to occur again. They told Gapon also that if he did not lead them they would leave him. "We have been branded," some of them said, "as Zubatov's men, and as provocators, and here is the chance to wash out this detestable stain." This appeal was received sympathetically, and those present unanimously resolved upon going with the largest possible crowd to the Winter Palace with a petition on the following Sunday.

"So let it be!" Gapon said at last, worn out by the opposition to his appeals for delay.[1] From this time Gapon concealed himself from the police. They had been watching the proceedings at the branches, and it was evident that they had realized the change in the tendencies of the movement. . . .

Troops were hurried into the city on the night of the 8th [January, O.S.], and preparations were made to receive the petitioners. The mode of dealing with the crisis which was adopted is said to have been suggested by the late Grand Duke Vladimir [uncle of Nicholas II], while the military dispositions were placed in the hands of Prince Vasilchikov, Commander-in-Chief of the Corps of the Guard. The Tsar and the Imperial Family had gone to Tsarskow Selo some days earlier.

At the height of the movement of Gapon, the actual number of registered members of the branches did not exceed 9000, but the number of persons who attended the meetings of the branches was much greater— "some scores of thousands." The number of persons who took part in the procession of "Bloody Sunday" is difficult to estimate owing to the fact that many fractions of the procession were dispersed soon after they started. The usual estimate of the total number of those who set out upon the procession is 200,000.

Early in the morning of the 9th January [22 January, N.S.], red-cross arm-bands were distributed to the women and to some men. The object of

[1] The subsequent accusations of Petrov suggest that had Gapon not acquiesced in the demands of the majority at that time, he might then have been denounced as a police spy, or at least as a defender of the autocracy rather than of the liberties of the people.

this is rather difficult to explain, unless we realize that in so great a concourse, consisting of many widely separated groups, there were many different and even conflicting ideas. These red-cross bands may have been assumed to indicate that their wearers were not militant participants in the procession or they may have been assumed for the practical purpose of calling upon their wearers to act as nurses to the wounded in an anticipated sanguinary struggle. While it is not impossible that arms were carried by some, it is also true that in some of the groups, those who came to the rendezvous with arms were deprived of them by their fellow-workers before the procession started on its way. The more "class conscious" working men seem to have marched in front of the different processions with their arms linked, thus forming chains across the line of the processions.

The early morning of Sunday, 9th January was "bitterly cold, with a piercing wind and fine driving snow." People went to church as usual. There were no troops in the great square opposite the Winter Palace. Traffic across the Neva by the bridges was unimpeded. At ten o'clock in the forenoon the movements of troops began. It was the evident intention of the military authorities to deal with the crowd in detachments, and to hold the constituent elements of the procession at or near their respective starting-points. At the same time the bridges were strongly held, and the Palace square was occupied by troops, which early in the forenoon debouched from the courtyards of the Winter Palace.

The attacks by the troops upon the processions took place at many different points, and for that reason a connected statement of the occurrences is difficult. The procedure appears, however, to have been generally the same at all the points where the military came into collision with the crowd—a summons to disperse—followed speedily by a volley of blank cartridge and then a volley of bullets. The official account admits firing in the Schlusselburg Chaussee, at the Narva Gate, where the crowd was led by Gapon, in the Troitsky Square, in Vasilevsky Ostrov, in the Alexander Gardens, near the Winter Palace, and in the Nevsky Prospekt, especially at the Kazan Cathedral.

The Genesis of the Soviets

The soviets which played such an important part during and after 1917 were modeled on those first organized during the 1905 Revolution. The man chiefly responsible for the 1905 movement was George Khrustalyev-Nosar who escaped from his guards while being removed from the prison-fortress of SS. Peter and Paul in October, 1905. Mr. Khrustalyev-Nosar went first to Moscow where he organized a workingmen's association, and then to St. Petersburg where he established the first Soviet of Workers' Deputies. The following selections are excerpts from his own account of these events. The source is: G. Khrustalyev-Nosar, "The Council of Workmen Deputies" in *The Russian Review (A Quarterly Review of Russian History, Politics, Economics,*

and Literature). Published by The School of Russian Studies in the
University of Liverpool. Vol. II (1913), no. 1, pp. 89–100, *passim*.

Its story is a story of fifty days. It was constituted on October 26, 1905. Its
existence was interrupted by the recrudescence of reaction and by the
blind force of soldiers on December 16, 1905. In spite of its short existence,
the Council of Workmen Deputies played a decisive part. . . , giving to
the revolutionary movement an organised and regular character. . . .

Basing ourselves on this experiment [the organisation of the association
in Moscow], we began working to create another such autonomous organisation in St. Petersburg. Our appeal met with an enthusiastic reception
among the workmen. In spite of all the objectionable efforts of the Social
Democrats, the foundation-stone was laid, and in October took place the
first sitting of the new working men's organisation in the quarters of the
Technological Institute. At the start it did not possess either a precise title
or strictly defined functions. The workmen of the factories and works chose
one deputy for every 500 workmen. Small enterprises and the lesser workshops met together and sent a common delegate. Neither political nor religious nor national differences played any part in the matter. Thus the
whole mass of workmen scattered over St. Petersburg, who had no access to
professional unions or to political parties, was cemented and drawn into the
common work. Of course, the revolutionary fever and the general strike
which had just begun accelerated this process of organisation. All the workmen of St. Petersburg had every day at their meetings to discuss questions
raised by the Council of Workmen Deputies. The electorate of the Council
retained the right of referendum . . . [but the deputy could make decisions without consulting his electors]. In its external organisation, the
Council of Workmen Deputies was a most democratic "working men's parliament," and its discussions and resolutions were the equivalent of the
views and feelings of the agitated working classes in Russia during the
revolutionary epoch. They were obeyed *imperio rationis sed non ratione
imperii* [by order of reason, but not by reason of orders] as the Council
of Workmen Deputies had no means of compelling obedience. But at the
word of the Council the workmen struck work, and by resolution of the
Council they resumed it. . . .

But the work and the political significance of the Council reached far
beyond the limits of the working class. The whole democracy of St. Petersburg acknowledged the hegemony of the Council and its political authority. The Union of Unions . . . several times sought the honour of
sending its own delegates to the Council. Officials and the employees of
banks, offices, railways, post, telegraph, and telephone sent their representatives to the Council, and submitted to its decisions. The influence of
the Council extended over the Peasants' Union. In the country, there began to be formed Councils of Peasant Deputies. In the army and navy,
there were Councils of military deputies. In the Universities were organised
Councils of student deputies, in the secondary schools, Councils of deputies
from the secondary schools.

From St. Petersburg to Tiflis, and from Warsaw to Vladivostok, all Russia was covered with a network of various councils. Ordinary citizens came to the Council of Workmen Deputies for information, protection, and help. . . . . . . The peasants of an out-of-the-way village sent a complaint against Prince Repnin, and asked us to settle it. Lastly, Count Witte himself [then Prime Minister] being unable to send a Government telegram to . . . Kushka, was obliged to ask the help of the Council. . . .

In St. Petersburg there existed side by side, as the *Novoe Vremya* put it, "two Governments, the Government of Count Witte and the Government of Khrustalyev.". . . The former practically retired; the second took on itself the responsibility of securing the inviolability of citizens by forming a working men's militia; regulated railway, postal, and telegraphic communications and industrial life; realised in practice the freedoms promised by the manifesto of October 30; and appealed to the population to defend and maintain them. It goes without saying that the co-existence of these two governments could not long continue. . . .

The Russian Revolution [of 1905] was a *town* revolution. The overwhelming majority of the population . . . remained outside the movement. Certainly, later the town population found an echo in the "jacqueries" of the peasants. . . . [But] In a word, the town revolution did not find the necessary support among the country peasants. The town revolution made a mistake in counting on a country army of soldiers; the town revolution weakened itself by putting forward extreme social demands. The campaign of the Council of Workmen Deputies for an eight hours' day frightened away from the Council and armed against the Council the liberal elements of the industrial middle class. . . .

The October Manifesto

On 17/30 October, 1905, Tsar Nicholas II reluctantly issued a manifesto promising civil liberty and an extension of the right of suffrage and of the Duma's power over legislation. The chief architect of the manifesto was Witte who had bluntly told the tsar that he must either make concessions or establish a military dictatorship. As the reader can see from the full text of the manifesto, which follows, it was both brief and sweeping. The source is: Graf. S. Iu. Witte, *Vospominaniya* (*Reminiscences*). Two volumes. Berlin, 1922. Vol. 2, pp. 1–2.

On Improving the Form of Government

The troubles and disturbances in the capitals and in many parts of our empire fill Our heart to overflowing with great and heavy sorrow. The good of the Russian Sovereign cannot be separated from the good of the people, and the peoples' sadness is His sadness. From the disturbances now sprung up there may arise a profound popular discord and a threat to the unity and integrity of the All-Russian Power. The great of the Tsar's service enjoins us, with every power of our understanding and authority, to work for the speediest ending of troubles so dangerous to state. After ordering the proper authorities to take steps to eliminate direct displays of orderlessness, excesses, and violence and to secure the safety of peaceful persons who seek quietly to perform the duty which lies on everyone, We, for the more successful implementation of general measures designed by Us for the pacification of state life have found it necessary to unify the action of the supreme government.

We lay upon the government the responsibility for the execution of Our unchangeable will: 1) to give to the people immovable bases of civil liberty on the principles of true inviolability of person, freedom of conscience, speech, assembly and association. 2) Without halting the promised elections to the State Duma, to bring to participation in the Duma, so far as possible in the brief time remaining before its summons, those classes of the population which are presently deprived wholly of the rights of suffrage, leaving until later the further development of the principle of universal suffrage under the newly established legislative order (that is, according to the Law of 6 August [O.S.] 1905, the Duma and the Council of State.) 3) To establish as an immovable principle that no law can come into force without the consent of the State Duma, and that those elected by the people shall be guaranteed the opportunity for actual inspection of the legality of the actions of the authorities appointed by Us.

We call upon all the faithful sons of Russia to remember their duty to the country, to aid in ending the unprecedented disorder and, together with Us, to exert all efforts for the re-establishment of calm and peace in our native land.

The First Duma

The source is: Pares, *Russia and Reform,* pp. 546–560.

The Duma met on May 10, 1906. The Emperor, who had not visited his capital since the attempt made upon his life in January, 1905, in a firm and vigorous voice expressed his hope that the labours of the Assembly would be conducive to the welfare of Russia. The Duma, when it had met in the palace prepared for it, elected its President, Vice-Presidents, and Secretaries. There was no contest; nearly all were chosen from the ranks of the Cadets. All the prominent leaders of different parties had at one time or another been under the displeasure of the Government, and Professor Gredyeskul, a man of no particular eminence, was appointed Vice-President simply because he had been one of the last to suffer persecution. The Assembly made an admirable choice of a president: Professor Muromtseff is a trained lawyer of great distinction, whose nice legal sense and keen and conscientious discrimination would do credit to the English bench. His noble presence gave dignity to the Assembly; and his untiring concentration of mind, though it visibly aged him during the sittings, maintained throughout the debates the control of the spirit of law. In his absence, Prince Peter Dolgorukoff was an able and business-like chairman. Prince Shakhovskoy was a capable secretary.

The Emperor's Speech from the Throne had not contained any programme of legislation, nor did the Ministers suggest any. Of this great mistake the Duma took immediate advantage. We might say that the Emperor
wanted a German Parliament, and that the Duma intended to be an English one. It decided to take the initiative by putting forward a whole programme in its "Address to the Throne." This was a policy which would help
to keep the Assembly united; for the minimum demands of all sections
could be expressed together. The Address was very cleverly drafted. The
abruptness of some of the demands was masked by the loyal and moderate
tone adopted throughout. The needs of the peasants held a prominent
place; the more radical demands of the workmen received less recognition,
but then the workmen had by their boycott practically excluded themselves
from the Duma, and the object of the Cadets was to secure the unanimity
of those present. The debates were animated; a leading part was taken by
the Labour Group, which was still in process of formation. The Labour
leaders adopted the wise policy of leaving their more extreme claims unexpressed, supporting the Cadets in all their disputes with the Moderates, and
trying to secure the most decisive wording which could be passed unanimously. The Address was read three times; at the second reading it was
debated sentence by sentence. Discussion centered chiefly round the land
question, and the demands for an amnesty for political prisoners and for
the abolition of the death penalty. Count Heyden, standing for wise
moderation, used his excellent debating power to keep the demands within
reasonable bounds. On the land question the Moderates, who more than
anyone else represented the country gentry, showed their public spirit by
accepting the principle of expropriation of land; the measure of compensation was left to be decided later. Realising the numerical weakness of his
party, Mr. Stakhovich reserved his effort for the question of the amnesty.
In two great speeches, which came straight from his heart and would have
carried conviction to any who were not hopelessly prejudiced, he demanded
that the amnesty should be two-sided, and that the Duma, while condemn-
ing the death penalty as inhuman and demanding the immediate release of
political prisoners, should in the name of the country frankly express its
opinion that murders of officials should cease from that day. No more just
or more eloquent claim was heard during the sittings of the Duma. The
country gentry had not pleaded for themselves; they spoke in the cause of
the police, with whom they had nothing in common. Mr. Stakhovich had
seized the exact moment when, with only one dissentient, the Assembly had
decided on the abolition of the death penalty. But the Cadets, who always
kept their eyes fixed on the extremists to the left of them, and, in their
tactical manipulation of the votes, failed to appreciate the great mass of
opinion outside, now made their first crucial mistake; and Mr. Rodicheff
was put up to oppose the amendment of Stakhovich. Turning his back on
the Left, and adopting an almost threatening manner towards the Octobrists, he gradually worked himself up into a rhetorical piece of special
pleading, in which he maintained "that the time was not yet come for
moderation, that it would come only after the victory." The Labour Group

applauded, and on a division Mr. Stakhovich found himself in an insignificant minority. But the Duma had lost its best chance; Mr. Lvoff, one of the most able and honest of the Cadets, soon afterwards left the party.

The Address was piloted throughout the debate by Mr. Nabokoff. In a voice under whose soft inflection lay the suggestion of a great reserve of strength, he over and over again gave matter-of-fact and convincing answers to the objections of individual members. When he was not speaking, it was often more interesting to watch him than to follow the debates: he would rise in a casual way from his seat, move through the assembly much as an English gentleman might pass through the smoking room of his club, seat himself beside the terrible Aladin of the Labour Group, and work out with him some formula which could be accepted by that party. This, after very outspoken discussion, would at last be achieved, and Nabokoff, with his little slip of paper in his hands, would walk straight across to Count Heyden, the Conservative leader, with whom the same process would be repeated. It was to be noticed that almost anything proposed by Nabokoff was passed unanimously. The time came for the third reading. Heyden, Stakhovich, and a few others, being unable to accept certain phrases, retired to avoid breaking the unanimity of the House. At 3 A.M. the final draft was accepted in a full House by all present.

The Address expressed a number of general principles and suggested legislation on each. It was far more easy for the Government to break up the unity of the Duma than for Milyukoff to maintain it. Formally, the Address was simply an answer to the Emperor's speech; it remained that each demand contained in it should be turned into a separate Bill. If the Government were still so lacking in initiative as not to produce any Bills of its own, it might leave the Duma to go on with this work in the full assurance that there would sooner or later be divisions inside the Assembly. There was one way of keeping the Duma united against the Government, and that way was adopted by the Ministers. An unnecessary fuss was made as to the way in which the Address should be received by the Emperor. The Duma was ordered to send it to him, not directly, but through the Marshal of the Court. This made a very bad impression, as publishing to the nation the fact that the Emperor was isolated from the Duma. But the Ministers did not stop here: they solemnly came down to the Duma to pronounce a kind of judgment on the Address. The Premier, Mr. Goremykin, read out a long statement in which, while suggesting certain mild reforms, he characterised the chief demands of the Duma as "inadmissible." Above all, he strongly repudiated the policy of expropriation, which he declared to be anti-social. His manner was that of a schoolmaster reading a lesson, yet it was well known that he was not the real possessor of power. His remarks were listened to without the slightest interruption and in a painfully breathless silence. When he sat down, Mr. Nabokoff mounted the tribune. Speaking very simply and quietly, like a man who was thoroughly at his ease, he expressed the disappointment of the Assembly, and proceeded in a matter-of-fact way to move a vote of censure on the Government. Thus thrown upon their defence, the bureaucratic Ministers proved utterly incapable of meeting outspoken criticism. In their own Ministries they could order any critic out of the room; but here was a situation which they had never had to face before. They sat there bowing beneath the storm as one speaker after another drew instances from the vast store of official abuses, and catechised them point-blank on questions both of principle and of detail. Kovalyevsky asked whether the Emperor Alexander II. acted anti-socially, when he emancipated the serfs and endowed them with land. Kokoshkin, in defence of certain English principles to which the Duma had appealed, suggested that the maintenance of order was rather more successful in England than in Russia. One Minister, Mr. Shcheglovitoff, rose to almost apologise for the Government, very much to the chagrin of his colleagues. One can imagine how this scene would lower the prestige of the Government in the eyes of the average non-party peasant. After standing the racket for some time as best they might, the Ministers withdrew; and the vote of censure, which had the support of the Moderates, was carried without any opposition.

The Duma now settled down to its work of discussing separate Bills. The family atmosphere, which is so noticeable in Russia, was here peculiarly strong. The Assembly, having complete control of its own house, turned it into something like a vast caravanserai. The beautiful hall soon came to be regarded, even by the peasant members, as a kind of home. The long side lobbies were furnished with great tables covered with green baize, at which peasants and Intelligents sat down indiscriminately to write letters to their families. A constant stream of members was always passing through these rooms; and all congregated from time to time in the great noisy corridor. Here the chief leaders walked up and down arm in arm; and isolated peasants, Russian, Cossack, or Polish, sat about on the different benches and were quite ready to converse with any stranger. Members and correspondents gathered without distinction at the buffet and in the restaurant, and little groups of acquaintances wandered through the pleasant gardens outside. The building contained its own postal and telegraph office. If the Duma did nothing else, it brought together for the first time representatives of every class and of every interest in Russia. It was of course far more Imperial than any other European Parliament. It would be difficult to imagine a more picturesque gathering. Each man wore the costume of his class. The country gentry of the Intelligents dressed very simply, but there were Russian priests with long beards and hair, a Roman Catholic bishop in skull-cap lined with red, finely accoutred Cossacks from the Caucasus, Bashkirs and Buryats in strange and tinselled Asiatic dress, Polish peasants in the brilliant and martial costumes of their people, and a whole mass of staid, bearded, and top-booted Russian peasants. Strangers easily obtained admittance; and amongst the most picturesque visitors were the so-called "walking deputies" who were sent by peasant constituents to look after their members, and others who had tramped for hundreds of miles to ask the Duma to settle their private disputes. Groups of members and non-members formed in the corridor to discuss without reticence any question of the moment. Small party conferences, sitting in the committee-rooms, seemed in no way disturbed by passing strangers. Milyukoff, in the simple dress of an English country gentleman, walked up and down the corridor receiving the suggestions of various party leaders, which seldom induced him to deviate a yard from the tactics upon which he had determined. One noticed that the Cadets as a body quite failed to get hold of the non-party members. These peasants, who would not sink their individuality in any party formula, expressed the most fresh and interesting opinions of all. Count Heyden could often be seen discussing matters with them; he understood them, and they understood him; but Milyukoff was hardly ever to be seen talking to a non-party man. At one time it appeared that Kovalyevsky and Kuzmin-Karavayeff might capture a considerable section of the Cadets; but the Cadets arranged that every member should register his seat in the House, and this made it more difficult to pass from one party to another. The Labour Group, which continued its organisation throughout the sittings, tried in every way to absorb the Non-Party, but without success.

Bills were introduced into the Duma guaranteeing freedom of conscience and the inviolability of the person. The discussions were not very interesting; everyone was agreed as to these main principles, little more than the principles was expressed in the Bills, and almost as much had been said in the Emperor's manifestos. A month's delay had to pass after the notice of introduction, before the Assembly could deal effectively with any proposed measure. The Duma was allowed to discuss the franchise, and it of course declared in favour of the well-known formula "universal, direct, equal, and secret." The debate on woman's suffrage excited a lively interest. On this day the corridor was invaded by an active band of suffragettes, who evidently thought that they could give the necessary lessons to the non-party peasant. It was amusing to watch the peasants dealing with these young ladies. One very typical peasant admitted that it was most unfair that women should receive lower pay than men for similar work. "We will put that right for you," he said; "let us get on our legs first, then we will give you some rights." But the young ladies wanted not to receive, but to take, and claimed that women ought to be sitting in the Duma. "Look here," said he, "I will tell you what: you go and marry! You will have a husband and children, and your husband will look after you altogether." "Look after, indeed!" said the young ladies; but the peasant would not promise anything more. Equally interesting was the attitude of the Non-Party group towards the Jews: they spoke without any ill-will, but remarked: "Even without rights, the Jews are on the top of us." They were therefore almost the only dissentients on both these questions.

All these Bills were not really practical politics, for not a single measure of the Duma became law except a vote of credit to the Government to relieve peasant distress; they were rather appeals for popular support. Realising from the first that the bureaucracy was definitely hostile to it, and that no frank reform could successfully pass through the various stages ordained by the Government, the Duma naturally set itself to secure strength from elsewhere. With this object, it deliberately turned itself into a machine for propaganda. "The tribune," said one Labour member to me, "is the only part of this House that counts." Nearly every newspaper published the fullest reports of the sittings, and these were eagerly devoured in distant villages all over the country. Immobilised in its legislative work, the Duma put a number of carefully but firmly worded interpellations to the various Ministers. The abuses of the administration were thus brandished before the eyes of the country. This was already war, but it would be difficult to say which side had first declared it. Ministers, severally or together, continued to visit the Duma, to make explanations or to answer interpellations. Each such visit naturally led to a scene; when the Duma had, with one dissentient, abolished the death sentence, the Government sent down General Pavloff to explain that it refused this measure. Pavloff was generally believed to have hurried on the execution of certain death sentences contrary to law, and the Labour Group interrupted him with cries of "Murderer!" The President even had to adjourn the sitting. Aladin, who spoke with far more vehemence inside the Duma than amongst his own party, suggested that it was very amiable of the Ministers to continue to come down to the House after they had been told that the country did not want them. The situation was in fact an entirely false one for all concerned. The only Minister who knew how to face it was Mr. Stolypin. He answered interpellations with the utmost moderation, but with the utmost firmness; and once, when the Labour Group tried to shout him down, he turned on them and addressed the rest of his speech to them in a voice which rose loud and strong above all their clamour. He was the one Minister who was ever cheered by any member of the Duma. But Mr. Stolypin, though universally credited with honesty and courage, had to meet the strongest charges of all: he had to answer for the faults or omissions of his predecessors in office. On June 21 he had just replied to an interpellation on the "pogroms," when Prince Urusoff rose to make his memorable speech on the official circulation of appeals to murder, and the malignant activity of Komisaroff. The Prince spoke in so low a voice as to be almost inaudible; many of the peasant members in no way realised the importance of his speech; but it was published in full in most of the newspapers, and dealt to the Government by far the most crushing blow which it had yet received. The speech was exemplary in its moderation and loyalty; Prince Urusoff in no way inculpated the existing Ministry: the only inference which he drew from his disclosures was that the dualism within the Government itself must be abolished without delay, and that the Emperor must be put into real touch with his people. But to make his meaning clear, he had to attack "those obscure forces which," he said, "are arming against us." This was a more open declaration of war between the Duma and the unofficial advisers of the Crown.

Rumors of dissolution had been in the air ever since the passing of the Address. The Cadets desired to use every day to the full, in order to make the position of the Duma so strong in the country that dissolution would become practically impossible. This is why they gave such prominence to the land question, and why their Bill bore so pretentious a character. Mr. Milyukoff might almost be compared to the gambler in the famous opera of

Pushkin and Chaikovsky. Three cards will, he believes, give him fortune, and he dreams that the numbers have been revealed to him: he calls the three, (the three autonomies), and wins; he calls the seven, (the seven freedoms), and wins; he calls the ace, and the card produced is the Queen of Spades; pique—mort. The Queen of Spades was the land question.

The Land Bill of the Cadets was in many ways much less objectionable than it seemed. The principle of expropriation is in itself not revolutionary in Russia; it had been accepted by almost every section of public opinion, including the Conservative representatives of the country gentry; indeed, some reactionaries had blamed Mr. Goremykin for publicly opposing it. The Cadets were all in favour of compensation to the landowner, and were only divided on the question as to what would be a fair price; naturally, many objected to the artificial prices produced by the operations of the Peasants' Bank. Though the Cadets accepted the principle of the Labour Group that there should be a legal limit to the extent of estates, they fixed this limit so high as to rob the principle of all its force. The Cadets also agreed with the Labour party in declaring that land should be State property; but the long leases which they proposed knocked the life out of this declaration. Certainly Mr. Hertzenstein, the chief authority of the Cadets on this question, was not so much a land expert as an expert on land values, and his views were chiefly dictated by theories of almost a socialistic kind. Certainly nothing but theory could explain the assumption that Russia would prosper only on the basis of limited holdings. But leading Cadets themselves suggested in conversation that the Bill would come out of committee robbed of all its disagreeable characteristics. This is itself the sum of their condemnation. As it was they who had drafted the Bill, the pretence of Socialism in the original draft can only be looked upon as a hardly ingenuous piece of tactics, designed to preserve the unanimity of the Duma, and to capture the votes of the Labour Group. For all that, the Labour men introduced a separate Bill of their own. Their Bill was really that which the Cadet Bill only pretended to be, but the very similarity between the two justified the general opinion that the Cadets were almost Socialists. Beyond this, the Cadets had altogether misjudged their public. If I may trust the common conclusions of peasant members from almost every part of the Empire, only the least enterprising of the peasants were still in favour of the communal system of land tenure, though all wished to retain the Village Society. The most cherished dream of the intelligent peasant was that of personal property in land. The first land debates were ruled by the tactics of propagandism. Almost every peasant was encouraged to speak. Nearly all read their speeches; the speaker would afterwards proudly despatch the draft to his constituents. Thus the debate was rambling in the extreme. Next an enormous Commission was chosen to represent every section of the Duma; it was hoped that now the peasants would be willing to wait a little longer for the land; the Commission did not propose to hurry itself.

But the Government was getting ready to move. The recent pogrom in Byelostok, though presenting no signs of collusion with St. Petersburg, was undoubtedly in large part due to the neutrality or worse of local officials.

The Duma sent its own investigators to the spot, and they accepted without due examination any evidence offered to them so long as it was hostile to the police. It was now proposed, with the hearty concurrence of the Labour Group, to constitute in the country small committees to investigate the land question in each locality; in other words, the Duma was making a bid to gradually become the Government of the country. The tension between the representatives of the people and the Ministers was too severe to last.

More than once voices were raised even at the Court suggesting an accommodation. This could only be obtained by the resignation of the Ministers and the appointment of men who commanded the support of the Duma. Amongst those who were said to advocate this step the public were surprised to see the name of General Trepoff. The Ministers, it may be imagined, were not unwilling to retire from their exceedingly disagreeable position. From the appointment of a Cadet Ministry certain results were practically sure to follow. There would inevitably be an open conflict between the new Ministers and the so-called camarilla, or unofficial Court clique; but at the same time the Cadets would be forced by their new responsibilities to sever their connection with the Labour Group and to move more to the right; there would then be some kind of a split in the Cadet party itself, and thus there would be constituted inside the Duma a real Opposition. The governing Right Wing of the Cadets would be compelled to lean for support on the Moderates, and this new party of the Right would include nearly all those members of the Duma whom the Zemstva had trained in practical work. It could hardly have failed to take a tinge of class interests from the country gentry and the more responsible section of the middle class. The new Ministry, once in power, would be on its defence; every measure which it brought forward would be severely criticised, and men who had shown ability in opposition would now have to prove that they were more capable in administration than the bureaucracy. As the number of able Cadets was limited, and as they had been trained after all only in the sphere of local government, they could not have dispensed with the support of a certain number of the more Liberal bureaucrats. Such men would have to be retained both in the *personnel* of officialdom and in the Ministry itself. Any failure of the Cadets would help to develop in the public mind a natural movement of moral reaction which was already in process. For the Government, one of the strongest arguments in favour of a Cadet Ministry was that for once Russia possessed a Duma in which the strength lay near the centre. This phenomenon is comparatively rare even in constitutional assemblies of long standing; in Russia it was the artificial result of circumstances already explained; but it made for the formation of a great middle term between the sovereign and his people, and it was something to be seized upon and used to the utmost. Anyhow, the Court was half prepared to compromise; twice Mr. Shipoff was summoned to Peterhof, but as one who had failed to enter the Duma, and whose supporters in it were only a small and unorganised group, he once more refused office. There was much talk of a Ministry which should include both Mr. Muromtseff and Count Heyden. It was definitely resolved to invite Mr.

Muromtseff to Peterhof that he might suggest the names of possible colleagues; but a small disturbance in the Preobrazhensky regiment of the Guard led to a Court panic, and the step was deferred. Mr. Muromtseff, admirable as the President of the Assembly, would perhaps not have made a strong Prime Minister; and the Cadets seemed inclined to refuse to serve under any but their recognised party leaders. Certainly they represented the spirit of opposition in the country, and had given so many pledges to the public that they could hardly sink the individuality of their party in a coalition. But for these very reasons the personality of Mr. Milyukoff was highly distasteful to the Court. Not once during the session had the President been invited to Peterhof except as one of many guests at a Court banquet. If he had possessed a right of claiming interviews with the sovereign, or if there had been in the Assembly a responsible person in touch with the majority who reported the daily debates to the Emperor, the Court would have possessed more detailed knowledge of the actual political atmosphere. Anyhow all the chances of an accommodation came to nothing.

Meanwhile the Ministers could not but realise that the Duma was undermining their prestige amongst the people. The Land Bill was the most extreme bid of the Assembly for support against the Government; the Ministers drew up their own alternative measure, and, in a circular which they officially published all over the Empire, they condemned the principles of the Cadet Bill, thus making a direct appeal to the country against the Duma.

So far the propagandism of the Duma had been indirect; the Duma was precluded by law from issuing a direct address to the people; but such action had been equally illegal when these same Cadet leaders had carried their appeal through the Moscow Congress of July, 1905; and the fervour of the Labour Group and of the Cadets of the Left was not likely to be daunted by this formality. It was now that patience snapped on both sides. The Land Commission was the body specially attacked by the Government circular. All parties were represented on it; but its office-holders were not the chief leaders of the Cadets, and Milyukoff, as not being in the Duma, was of course excluded from it. At the Congress of July, 1905, a prominent part had been taken by Kuzmin-Karavayeff, who in the name of legality and order had begged the Congress to proceed with the greatest circumspection. This gentleman had played a prominent part in the Duma; he was supposed to be more Conservative than any of the Cadets; a speaker of remarkable grace and fluency, he always commanded attention. He now proposed to the Land Commission that it should send out to the country a weakly worded appeal asking the constituents not to believe in the Government circular, and to trust the Duma to make an effective Land Bill. The Commission, as representing all parties, adopted the address, and presented it for the acceptance of the whole Duma. The debate on this address was very remarkable. Late at night Mr. Lednitsky, sitting amongst the Cadets of the Right and also representing the Autonomist group, in vigorous language denounced the appeal as both feeble and irritating; he was loudly applauded both by the Moderates and by the Labour Group. But party discipline was strong amongst the Cadets; and the Labour Group preferred to compromise their rivals by a weak appeal rather than have no appeal at all. After pleading for the insertion of a stronger wording at certain points, they supported the address, and it was carried at the first reading by an immense majority.

On the next day there was no sitting, but in the evening there was a party meeting of the Cadets. Milyukoff and others of the leaders looked upon the address as a bad tactical mistake; they might be ready to appeal to the country, but this was neither the right time nor the right way. Many of their followers seemed inclined to break loose from them. However, the leaders in the end triumphed, and on the succeeding day Mr. Petrunkyevich rose at the second reading to suggest an entirely different wording of the whole address. This he moved by way of amendments to each paragraph. The Labour Group saw itself defeated on those points which it had most at heart, and the Cadets, in opposing the Labour amendments, had the support of the Moderates; finally the Labour Group left the hall *en masse,* and decided to draw up a more abrupt appeal of its own. After its departure, the Moderates contested the whole measure, and for the first time a proposal of the Cadets was passed only by a small majority. The suggestion that the address should be officially printed in the *Official Messenger* could not be discussed at all, because it was found that at this late hour the House did not possess the necessary quorum.

The wording of Petrunkyevich was far superior to the original draft. But the Duma had definitely decided to disregard the fundamental laws. Far more important was the obvious fact that the Duma and even the Cadet party were no longer unanimous. It seemed strange that a measure adopted almost unanimously by the Duma should be radically altered at the next sitting because a given party had decided to give it a different character; and an appeal to the people was precisely the measure which, of all others, most required firmness and solidarity. Naturally one asks why the Cadet members of the Land Commission originally adopted the first draft without ascertaining the will of their party. There had been similar mistakes before, as when Professor Petrazhitsky had risen apparently to introduce the Land Bill and had proceeded to condemn it. Tactical unity was hardly to be expected in the first Russian Parliament, and it is immensely to the credit of Milyukoff that he was ever able to keep the Duma united for so long. But now the Duma had published its dissensions before the world, and this was the moment which the Government might choose, if it desired a dissolution.

At Peterhof the counsels of General Trepoff were opposed by Mr. Stolypin, the only Minister who had followed the later debates in the Duma. Stolypin's view was clear and consistent; he recognised Russia as having passed into a constitutional régime: that is to say, there would always be a Duma to join in the work of legislation; but he refused to concede the principle that the Ministers should, as a matter of course, be selected from the party prevailing in the Assembly. He was against the formation of a Cadet Ministry, because it would be compelled by its pledges to surrender almost all the power of the administrative system in a single day. The Duma was at war with the Government; if the Government would not make way for a Cadet Ministry, the only step left for it was to dissolve the Duma. The discussion of the two views at Peterhof was long; but by the evening of Saturday, July 21, the view of Mr. Stolypin had prevailed, and the Emperor had signed the decree of dissolution. The decree expressed in no uncertain terms the Emperor's disappointment at what he regarded as the factious spirit of the Duma. It was read out in churches and posted up in public places all over the Empire; Stolypin himself accepted office as the new Prime Minister.

The dissolution of the Duma was the victory of a single strong-minded man. How he understood the difference between Constitutionalism and Parliamentarism was at once apparent; almost every newspaper in St. Petersburg was stopped except the *Official Messenger*. The public was stupefied and bowed beneath the yoke; it again felt the paralysing weight of an overwhelming governmental force hostile to the vast majority of expressed opinions. However, the Cadets and the Labour Group acted with a remarkable unanimity. They at once made their way to a common rendezvous at Vyborg, in Finland. Here a large majority of those members who had still remained in St. Petersburg discussed the drafting of a far more bold address to the people; Heyden, Stakhovich, and Lvoff, came out to confer with the majority, but were not able to join with it. Some forty of the Cadets, led by Hertzenstein, were against any strong expression of policy; but these were persuaded to make common cause with the rest, and a draft was discussed, accepted, and eventually signed by over two hundred members. In forcible language it invited the people to refuse recruits and the payment of taxes until there was a new Duma. The Cadets and the Labour Group could hardly have believed that isolated peasant communities would take the lead in resisting the Government with arms in their hands, and the Labour Group proposed the establishment of a central committee to represent the late Duma and to organise the resistance. This proposal, however, fell through in consequence of the attitude of the more moderate of the Cadets. A more effective article of the Vyborg manifesto was that which, in the name of the nation, refused responsibility for future foreign loans made to the Government; but the programme of a resistance to the Government all over Russia broke down when the Cadets, accepting the dissolution as final, practically retired into private life. Stolypin was expected to arrest all the members returning from Vyborg, but he was too clever to make this mistake. The Cadets continued to hold party meetings, but after making their great appeal for the support of the nation they themselves failed to take any action whatsoever. They were now looked upon as neither one thing nor the other; even the murder of Mr. Hertzenstein, which might have restored to them the sympathies of public opinion, resulted in nothing but a rather fussy expression of irritation. The artificial character of their tactical victory at the elections now became more and more apparent.

The Duma and the Budget

> The Duma's power over the budget was very severely limited. Its control covered only about half the budget at best and even this was somewhat uncertain since the upper house (the Imperial Council) also had some budgetary powers. If the two houses were unable to agree on a figure, the government could accept the figure it liked better. If no budget was passed, that of the preceding year remained in effect. The following excerpts are from an informal report given by the chairman of the Duma's Finance Committee. The reader may wish to compare these items with claims made by speakers in the Supreme Soviet (and elsewhere) on the nature of the tsarist budget. The source is: H. Lerche, "Five Years of Budget Work" in *The Russian Review*. Vol. 1 (1912), no. 3, pp. 14–48.

. . . The Imperial Duma is limited in the exercise of its legislative power, as to construction, technique, and economic administration of these Ministries [army and navy] and also their institutions and officials. Its part is restricted to the expression of wishes and the stating of views when the military and naval estimates and the various Bills are being debated, and to the granting or refusing of *new* credits for the requirements of the army and fleet.

Though it could only have a weak influence on the actual administration, the Imperial Duma was so possessed and penetrated with the dominant idea of the sacred duty of defending the country and restoring its military power, that it did not hesitate to raise the permanent expenditures for the army and voted large sums for special credits. By the estimates of expenditure of 1907, the ordinary expenditures of the Ministries for War were reckoned at 399.6 million roubles; by the Budget of 1912 which passed the Imperial Duma, the ordinary expenditures were estimated at 492.5 million roubles. . . . Besides this, in the course of the five sessions there were required for the payment of extra expenditures of the Ministry of War about 39 million roubles. For the extraordinary expenditures of the Ministry of War for the renewal of stores and material, the Imperial Duma granted . . . in the five years [1908–1912] 285. million roubles. The expenses of liquidating the war were estimated under a separate fund, and . . . amounted to 89.2 million roubles. The Imperial Duma considerably increased the ordinary permanent expenditure of the army . . . and granted 285.5 million roubles for restoring its military efficiency. . . .

In general, the ordinary expenses of the army and navy rose from 464.6 million roubles in 1907 to 651.6 million roubles in 1912, that is by . . . more than 40 per cent. . . .

Among cultural and productive expenditures we must dwell on public instruction, land settlement, agriculture, and public equipment. . . . the Duma aims at completing a system of universal free elementary instruction with a gradual increase in the number of local schools; it accepts, on behalf of the Treasury, the normal payment of teachers' salaries (which in 1912 demands 43 million roubles); it is helping in the construction of schools, and it is making a ten years' plan for financing schools in order to secure their further development. Unfortunately this plan meets with criticism in the Imperial Council.

The credits for schools are increasing. By estimates of 1907, the expenditures on elementary education amounted to 14.3 million roubles. For 1912, they have increased to 64.4 million roubles . . . or more than 4½ times. The total sum of expenditures on public instruction (including secondary and higher education and learned institutions) has risen from 45.9 million roubles in 1907 to 117.5 millions. . . . But these figures do not give all the expenditures of the State on public education, not to speak of the expenses of public bodies [the Zemstva], private persons, and societies. Besides the schools in the jurisdiction of the Ministry of Public Instruction, there are numerous schools of various classes in the jurisdiction of the Orthodox Church, and of the Ministries of Trade and Commerce, Ways of Communication, War, Justice, and others. The statistics of the expenditures of the State on instruction, science and art, enable us to make the following comparison: in 1907, the expenditures of the State under various jurisdictions amounted to 75.4 million roubles; in 1912, it is 156.7 million roubles. . . . . . .

The expenditures on land settlement rose from 11 million roubles in 1907, to 29 million roubles in 1912. Measures for developing agriculture . . . and improvements of the land (principally irrigation and draining works) called in 1907 for an expenditure of only 5.1 million roubles; for 1912, this expenditure amounts to as much as 31.5 million roubles. . . . . . .

Among public works, the first place belongs to railway construction. . . . Sixty million roubles were voted for the construction of State railways in . . . 1908; . . . and for 1912, 110.5 million roubles—a total, for the five years [1908–1912] of 338.2 million roubles. . . . ordinary expenditures have risen from 2173.4 million roubles in 1907 to 2668.9 million roubles in 1912, or a rise of . . . nearly 23 per cent. . . . The total of ordinary revenue of the State has risen from 2342.4 million roubles in 1907, to 2951 million roubles in 1911 . . . or a rise of . . . nearly 26 per cent.

Lenin and the Duma Elections

A part of Lenin's success was due to his shrewd and totally amoral opportunism. His program was absolutely fixed as to its ultimate goal, but it was extremely flexible as to tactics. He may have despised the day of small things, but he never made the mistake of being too proud to try to turn even small things to his advantage. He was always ready to adopt any means which seemed most promising in a given situation, and equally ready to abandon these for others when the situation changed. The following brief quotation from one of Lenin's editorials not only illustrates this characteristic, but also very concisely explains and justifies the tactic described. The source is: *Pravda,* 1/14 August, 1912. Only a portion of the editorial is reprinted.

. . . The workers realize fully that they need expect nothing from either the Third or the Fourth Duma. Nevertheless, we must take part in the elections, first, because the unification and political education of the toiling masses are characteristic of election times when party struggles and political life in general acquire a lively aspect and when the masses, in one way or another, learn about politics; second, for the purpose of getting our working class representatives into the Duma. The workers' deputies did a lot of good for the workers' cause even in the completely reactionary, landlord controlled [Third] Duma. They can continue to do so if they are genuine working class democrats, provided that they keep in touch with the masses, and if the masses learn how to supervise and direct them.

Political Parties in the Dumas

The following descriptive analysis of the first parliamentary political parties in Russia is based primarily upon data from the stenographic reports of the Duma. The source is: Warren B. Walsh, "Political Parties in the Russian Dumas," *The Journal of Modern History.* Vol. XXII, no. 2 (June 1950). Pp. 144–150.

"The supreme autocratic power belongs to the emperor of all the Russias. Acceptance of his authority is dictated not alone by fear and conscience but also by God Himself." [1] So ran the revised Fundamental Laws of the Russian Empire as promulgated on April 23/May 6, 1906 and great was the disappointment thereat. The preceding October, Tsar Nicholas II, albeit very much against his will, and promised to grant civil rights and liberties and to create an elected, national, legislative assembly. Nicholas himself shared the view that the implementation of these promises called for a constitution. This expectation was in no way dispelled when the government so extended the franchise as to put the elections almost on the basis of manhood suffrage. Then, just four days before the first meeting of the newly elected duma, there was issued not a constitution but only a revision of the existing Fundamental Laws.

There was created a legislative assembly, according to the letter of the promise, but the elected duma was yoked to a state council half of whose members were appointed directly by the tsar. Legislative authority was shared among the two houses and "the supreme autocratic power." The duma was to be summoned and could be adjourned or dissolved by the tsar, although the order of dissolution had to provide for a subsequent ses-

[1] "Svod osnovykh gosoudarstvennykh zakonov" [Code of laws on the foundations of the state], Sec. I, chap. i, art. 4, A. A. Dobrovolskii (ed.), *Svod zakonov Rossiiskoi Imperii* [Code of laws of the Russian Empire] (5 vols.; St. Petersburg, 1913), I, 1.

sion. The tsar was to make no changes in the Fundamental Laws without the concurrence of the duma and council, but the duma was forbidden to initiate such changes. It could interpellate ministers, but they remained responsible only to the tsar. Certain affairs, including such important items as military matters and control of about half the budget, were declared beyond the bounds of the duma's competence. The letter of the law was indeed restrictive, and Russia remained an autocracy. But it was no longer an unlimited autocracy. An assembly with an elected lower house had been created for the discussion of legislation properly proposed by itself, by the tsar, or by the council. Moreover, the tsar could no longer make laws by his authority alone. Legislation had to have the consent of the assembly.[2]

One of the concomitants of this change was the appearance and development of parliamentary political parties in Russia. The groupings were at first largely tentative and unstable, loosely organized and with little party discipline. The life-span of the first duma was too short to permit much stabilization. It held only forty sittings spread over seventy-three days.[3] There have been various estimates both as to the number and size of political parties in this session. The official records do not give any information on these matters although they do show the classes and/or occupations of the 497 members of this first duma.[4] In the absence of any official or uniformly accepted figures, Table 1 must be regarded as no more than guesswork, although it is based upon a careful comparison of many estimates.

TABLE 1

PARTY AFFILIATIONS, FIRST DUMA

Parties on the Right	45
National and Religious Groups	32
Kadets	184
Parties on the Left	124
No Party	112
Total	497

[2] "Svod uchrezhdenii gosudarstvennykh" [Code concerning state institutions], Sec. II, chap. i, art. 1, Dobrovolskii, I, 54; and "Svod osnovykh," Sec. I, chap. i, art. 7, *ibid.*, p. 1.

[3] The first duma was opened on April 27/May 10; held its last sitting on July 7/20; and was dissolved by the tsar's order on July 8/21, 1906. Data on the number of sittings and the dates are from Russia, *Gosudarstvennaya duma: stenograficheskiye otchety, 1906 god., sessiya pervaya* [State duma: stenographic reports, 1906, first session] (2 vols.; St. Petersburg, 1906–7), and from Russia, *Gosudarstvennaya duma: ukazatel k stenograficheskim otchetam 1906 god., sessiya pervaya* [State duma: index to stenographic report, 1906, first session] (St. Petersburg, 1907).

[4] "Spisok chlenov gosudarstvennoi dumy po izbiratelnym okrugam" [List of members of the state duma by electoral districts], *Ukazatel . . . 1906 god.*, pp. 3–17.

The "Parties on the Right" include seven men who have been customarily designated as "Rightists" and thirty-eight who had rallied together on the basis of accepting the October Manifesto as a sufficient concession from the autocracy. Though these "Octobrists" are listed as a party in the records of the second duma and will be discussed in connection with that session, they did not become an organized political party until the third duma when they were brought into line by Alexander Guchkov.

"National and Religious Groups" refers to the congeries of Poles, Mussulmen, and Kazaks. They usually voted with the Party of the Peoples' Liberty. This was the official title, rarely used, of what is more commonly known as the Constitutional Democratic party or Kadets. As the table shows, they formed the largest single group in the first duma. They were also the best organized and the most influential. Generally speaking they were more concerned with political than with social reforms, although they were not blind to the latter need. Their political aim was to build the duma into a strong, popular body similar to the British house of commons. The enthusiasm of their leaders, notably Paul Miliukov, was reflected in exaggerated reports of the party's size. Their voting strength fluctuated because they were often supported by other groups and by individuals who were not really affiliated with them except on specific issues.

The "Parties on the Left" included a loose coalition known as the Labor group (*Trudoviki*) and a variety of socialists ranging from Marxists to the breed which used to be known derisively as "parlor-pinks." [5] The Social Revolutionary party and the Social Democratic party had both boycotted the elections, but the Kadet newspaper claimed that there were two Social Democrats and seventeen Social Revolutionaries among the members on the Left.[6]

Over one hundred members of the first duma, mostly peasants, refused to affiliate with any party. They were much sought after by all groups and brief, personal alliances were frequently made.

There was an almost complete change in personnel between the first and second dumas. Only 31 persons were members of both.[7] This was due partly to the government's punitive measures against those who had signed the Viborg protest against the dissolution of the first duma, but mostly it reflected a change in the mood of the electorate. Sir Bernard Pares, for example, reported from firsthand study at the time that the peasants often deliberately chose professional revolutionaries to be their representatives in the second duma. This observation is supported not only by the spectacular increase in the parties on the Left from 124 to 216 members but also by the marked reduction in the No Party group which, as has been noted, was composed mostly of peasants in the first duma. It was still largely made up

[5] This coterie took the title of the Peoples' Socialists.

[6] Cited in A. Levin, *The second duma* (New Haven, 1940), p. 67.

[7] All data on the second duma, unless otherwise specifically indicated, have been calculated from Russia, *Gosudarstvennaya duma: ukazatel k stenograficheskim otchetam, vtoroi sozyv, 1907 god.* [State duma: index to stenographic report, second convocation, 1907] (St. Petersburg, 1907), pp. 3–26.

of peasants in the second duma but there were fifty to sixty fewer of them. The lifting of their boycotts by the Social Revolutionaries and Social Democrats was also a major factor. There were 20 more Social Revolutionaries and 64 more Social Democrats in the second duma than in the first.

The official records of the second duma are more elaborate and include information about party affiliations. The 520 members were divided among sixteen parties, five of which were "parties" only by courtesy. There was also a group of No Party persons. The tabular summary is given in Table 2.

TABLE 2

PARTY AFFILIATIONS, SECOND DUMA

Right	10
Moderate Right	23
Union of 17 October	19
Polish Kolo	46
Mussulman (Moslem)	30
Kazak Group	18
Party of the Peoples' Liberty (Kadets)	99
Labor Group	98
Peoples' Socialists	15
Social Revolutionaries *	37
Social Democrats	66
Miscellaneous (Party of Peaceful Restoration 2; Peasant Union 1; Christian-Socialist 1; Moderate 1; Party of Democratic Reform 1; Blank 1)	7
No Party	52
Total	520

* Includes three associates.

The Party of the Right was the most homogeneous. Every member but one was a landlord (*zemlevladelets*), and only two of the landlords owned less than two hundred dessiatins (540 acres) of land. It was the only party in which there were no farmers (*zemledelets*) and the only one in which the majority of the members were from the gentry/nobility (*dvoryanin*). Moreover, the party was unashamedly reactionary. It was opposed to the whole idea of a legislative assembly. It strove for the dissolution of the second duma, and it was intimately associated both with the notorious Black Hundreds and with the equally notorious Okhrana. Its goals, in short, were summed up in the famous slogan, "Orthodoxy, autocracy, and nationalism."

If the "haves" had been as class conscious as is sometimes alleged, the Party of the Right would presumably have been their home. But of the 116 landlords in the second duma only 9 were members of the Party of the Right, and only 37 were on the Right at all. Left, Right, and Center each had at least two landlords whose estates exceeded three thousand dessiatins. There was at least one landlord in every major party; even the Social Democratic and the Social Revolutionary parties each had one landlord of great wealth among their members. There were, however, only 11 landlords among the four parties on the Left as compared with 24 in the Center (Kadets), 34 among the national and religious groups, and, as noted, 37 among the three Rightist parties. Moreover, the Party of the Moderate Right, which was generally quite sympathetic with the aims and interests of the Party of the Right, was not exclusively a landlords' party. There were both farmers and professional men among its 23 members.

Although the 19 Octobrists were officially listed as a party, they were neither closely organized nor disciplined at this time. Thirteen of them were landowners, most of them wealthy. Ten were officials of one sort or another. They were not against reform, but they wanted no more revolution.

The Polish Kolo was the most heterogeneous of the three national and religious groups. Their members included a landlord with estates of over ten thousand dessiatins (the largest reported) and two landless workers. Most of the Poles were landlords but there were also a few farmers among them. The majority of the Mussulmen and Kazaks were not associated with the land either as owners or as farmers. They were mostly officials or professional men.

The Kadets were almost perfectly balanced between landlords and farmers with 24 of the former and 23 of the latter. The remaining 52 of their members, a slight majority, were not connected with the land. In the second duma, at least, the Kadets were not the party of professional people. Their frontal attempts to make the duma into a Russian house of commons having failed in the first duma, they sought, in the second, to use tactics which would win popular support for the institution and which would eventuate in the establishment of ministerial responsibility and a wider suffrage. Generally they had the support of the Poles, the Kazaks, and the Mussulmen.

The Labor Group continued to draw its strength mainly from among the small farmers. Seventy-one of its 98 members were farmers and most of them worked holdings of ten dessiatins or less.[8] A few Laborites reported connections with trade and/or industry, and three listed themselves as workers. There were also sizable groups of professional men and of officials among them.

The Social Revolutionary party is usually thought of as the great peasant party, but it was not so in the second duma. Less than half its members had any connection with the land. Most of them were professional men or holders of some official position.

The workers were strongest in the Social Democratic party, but even there they were in a minority—39 per cent of the party's total membership. The four landlords who were Social Democrats were among neither the

---

[8] Presumably most of the farmers, irrespective of party affiliations, had small farms. The data are not complete, however, since 73 farmers did not tell the size of their holdings. Of the 102 who did give the size, 73 reported less than ten dessiatins and an additional 20, less than twenty-five.

richest nor the poorest. One owned between eleven and twenty-five des-siatins; two between twenty-six and fifty; and one between one hundred and two hundred. Eighteen of the Social Democrats were professional men and two were of the gentry/nobility.

The No Party group was mostly made up of small farmers, but it in-cluded a few wealthy landowners and traders. The character of the Peoples' Socialist party is at least partly indicated by the fact that all but one of its 15 members were either officials or professional men.

Following the dissolution of the second duma and prior to the election of the third, the electoral law was drastically altered in violation of the Fundamental Laws of the Empire which provided that no such change should be made except with the concurrence of the duma itself.[9] The new law gave disproportional representation to the large landowners and to the

TABLE 3

PARTY AFFILIATIONS, THIRD AND FOURTH DUMAS

	DUMA AND SESSION							
	III, 1	III, 2	III, 3	III, 4	III, 5	IV, 1	IV, 2	IV, 3
Right.....................	49	49	51	53	51	64	60	61
National Group...........	26	20	...	...	...	...	...	...
Russian National..........	...	...	91	76	75	...	...	...
Moderate Right...........	69	75	...	...	...	...	...	...
Independent National......	...	...	...	16	16	...	...	...
Moderate Rt. & Rus. Nat'l.	...	...	...	...	...	88	88	86
Right of Octobrists Group..	...	...	11	11	10	...	...	...
Center...................	...	...	...	...	...	33	37	34
Union of 17 October.......	148	138	120	120	120	99	3	...
Zemstva-Octobrists........	...	...	...	...	...	...	66	65
Duma Group of Octobrists.	...	...	...	...	...	...	20	21
Polish-Lithuanian-Bielorus-sian Group.............	7	7	7	6	7	6	6	6
Polish Kolo..............	11	11	10	11	11	9	7	7
Progressive & Peaceful Restoration.............	25	36	...	...	...	...	...	...
Progressive...............	...	...	39	39	36	47	40	42
Mussulman Group.........	8	8	9	9	9	6	6	6
Peoples' Liberty (Kadets)...	53	51	52	52	53	57	55	55
Labor Group.............	14	15	14	14	11	10	10	10
Social Democratic.........	19	18	15	14	13	14	7	7
Rus. Soc. Dem. Worker's...	...	...	...	...	...	...	5	5
No Party.................	...	...	17	15	23	4	...	15
Independents.............	...	...	...	...	...	...	...	13
Miscellaneous............	...	...	...	...	...	...	13	...
Totals.................	429	428	436	436	435	437	423	433

[9] A detailed account of the dissolution is given by Levin, pp. 307–49. See also P. Harper (ed.), *The Russia I believe in* (Chicago, 1945), pp. 52–54; and Bernard Pares, *A wandering student* (Syracuse, N.Y., 1948), pp. 148–51. The best account in English of the electoral law is S. N. Harper, *The new electoral law for the Russian duma* (Chicago, 1908).

wealthy urban class. Most towns lost their right of direct representation and were submerged in the country districts surrounding them. Those which escaped this suffered a change in franchise which divided their voters into two classes, unequal in size but each electing the same number of deputies. The specific and detailed meaning of these changes is clearly revealed by the official personnel records of the third and fourth dumas.[10]

The members of the third and fourth dumas were, in general, men of substance. Ninety-eight per cent of the members of the third duma and 96 per cent of the members of the first session of the fourth duma reported themselves as owning some sort of property. This is in marked contrast to the second duma, only 51 per cent of whose members were property-owners. Furthermore, almost half the members in both the third and fourth dumas were landowners, as compared with less than a quarter of the members of the second duma. Half the landowners in the last two dumas held estates larger than seven hundred and fifty dessiatins.

The more extensive records which were kept for the third and fourth dumas make it possible to trace party changes throughout each of the sittings. These are summarized in Table 3, but certain aspects require some additional comments.[11]

[10] All the material on the third duma, except for the tabulation of party affiliations, has been calculated from "Lichnyi alfabitnyi ukazatel k stenograficheskim otchetam gosudarstvennoi dumy" [Alphabetical personal index to the stenographic reports of the state duma], in Russia, *Gosudarstvennaya duma: ukazatel k stenograficheskim otchetam (Chasti I–III), tretii sozyv, sessiya pervaya* [State duma: index to stenographic report (Parts I–III), third convocation, first session] (St. Petersburg, 1908), pp. 51–311. All the data on the first session of the fourth duma, except for the tabulation of party affiliations, are from "Lichnyi alfabitnyi ukazatel k stenograficheskim otchetam gosudarstvennoi dumy," in Russia, *Gosudarstvennaya duma: ukazatel k stenograficheskim otchetam (Chasti I–III), chetvertyii sozyv, sessiya pervaya* [. . . fourth convocation, first session] (St. Petersburg, 1913), pp. 55–224.

[11] The tabulation is based on "Spisoki chlenov gosudarstvennoi dumy po partiinym gruppirovkam" [List of members of the state duma by party groupings], in *Gosudarstvennaya duma . . . tretii sozyv, sessiya I* (St. Petersburg, 1908), pp. 13–18; *Sessiya II* (St. Petersburg, 1909), pp. 13–18; *Sessiya III* (St. Petersburg, 1910), pp. 13–18; *Sessiya IV* (St. Petersburg, 1911), pp. 13–18; and *Sessiya V* (St. Petersburg, 1912), pp. 19–24; and *Gosudarstvennaya duma . . . chetvertyii sozyv, sessiya I* (St. Petersburg, 1913), pp. 19–24; *Sessiya II* (Petrograd, 1914), pp. 19–24; and *Sessiya III* (Petrograd, 1915), pp. 291–334. Party "affiliates" have been tabulated as members. These figures do not agree with those compiled in a name-by-name count of the members listed in the "Lichnyi." For example, the "Lichnyi" for the third duma, first session, gives a total of 442 members for that session. The "Spisok" shows 429 members. Similar discrepancies also exist in the case of the fourth duma. The electoral law of June 1907 provided for 442 members (Dobrolovskii, I, 109–10). S. A. Piontkowskii, *Ocherki istorii SSSR* [Outline history of the U.S.S.R.] (Moscow, 1935), gives the following membership figures for the third duma: "Extreme Right," 144; Octobrists, 148; Polish-Lithuanian-Bielorussian Group, 7; Polish Kolo, 11; Progressives, 25; Mussulman, 8; Kadet, 53; Labor, 14; and Social Democrats, 19.

The Party of the Right, which had had only seven members in the first duma and ten in the second, shot up to fifty in the third and sixty in the fourth. It was, however, no longer exclusively a landlords' party. Among its members in the last two dumas were peasants, officials, and a sizable group of clergymen. It remained strongly reactionary, chauvinistic, and anti-Semitic. It also continued to be closely associated with the Black Hundreds and with the government's secret police. Its leaders in the third and fourth dumas were N. E. Markov, who was subsidized by the government, and V. M. Purishkevich, who was one of the murderers of Rasputin.

The labels "National Group," "Russian National," "Moderate Right," and "Independent National Group," which appear in the various sessions of the third duma, refer to the same people. These ninety-odd persons were all followers of P. A. Stolypin. After his murder they continued to form a loose alliance but took different party names. All of them are lumped together in the records of the fourth duma as the "Moderate Right and Russian National parties."

Certain splits and shifts also took place in the "Union of 17 October," which started out with 148 members in the first session of the third duma and dropped to 138 in the second session. A small segment split off to the right in the third session and took the title "Right of Octobrists Group." This group, with some additions, became the "Center" in the opening session of the fourth duma. During the next two sessions the Union disappeared. Most of its members moved slightly left to form the "Zemstva-Octobrists" and the "Duma Group of Octobrists."

The Octobrists were the wealthiest group in the last two dumas. Two-thirds of them in the third duma and 72 per cent of them in the fourth duma were of the gentry/nobility. In the third duma, the largest bloc of landlords was in this party, and the largest single holding reported (nine thousand, eight hundred dessiatins) belonged to an Octobrist. Of the 104 Octobrists who were landlords, 70 owned estates of over four hundred dessiatins, and 43 owned more than one thousand dessiatins apiece. The listing of earnings and/or property values was given for only 173 members of this duma, but on this incomplete basis the largest number of owners and the greatest concentration of wealth was among the Octobrists, twenty of whom had over 15,000 rubles a year. Two of them were millionnaires. The Union also had the largest number of officials among its membership. These facts did not change appreciably in the last duma.

The right Octobrists were quite thoroughly conservative, but the left Octobrists, led by A. Meyendorf, were quite liberal. This group sought to establish juridical and civil equality for the peasants and called for an equalization of tax burdens, for economic aid to the peasants, and for advanced labor legislation. Many of the most liberal among them were or had been high in the civil service.

The members of the Labor Group and of the Social Democratic party were at the opposite end of the social and economic scale from the Octobrists. There were no landlords in either party, although several members of each were of the gentry/nobility. All ten workers in the fourth duma were

Social Democrats. In the preceding duma eight of the ten workers had belonged to that party, one to the Labor Group, and one to the Party of the Right. For the third duma, seven Laborites listed their annual earnings and/or property value as follows: three under 2,000 rubles, three under 4,000 rubles, and one under 6,000. Thirteen Social Democrats listed their earnings or income. Eleven claimed less than 2,000 rubles and the other two, less than 4,000. Seven small farmers belonged to the Labor Group in the third duma, two in the fourth. The corresponding figures for the Social Democrats were four and six.

Until the second session of the fourth duma, "Social Democratic party" covered both Bolshevists and Menshevists. The Bolshevists split away at the opening of that session and entered the meeting as a separate group under the name of the Russian Social Democratic Workers' party. A. Badaev, who was one of them, says that of the fourteen Social Democrats listed for the first session, six were Bolshevists, seven were Menshevists, and one was a Menshevist follower. He also explains the emphasis upon workers in the new party name as a deliberate choice in order to distinguish the six Bolshevists from the Menshevists, none of whom, according to him, were workers. The chairman of the Russian Social Democratic Workers' party was the notorious criminal, revolutionary, and *agent provocateur,* Roman Malinovsky. Curiously enough, his name does not appear in the official reports.[12]

The Kadets, who were the main body of progressives in the third and fourth dumas, were, by that time, clearly the party of professional people. The largest single concentration of professional men was in that group, and they accounted for over half the party membership. The Kadets also included 20 landlords, most of them quite well off, 17 officials, and only 4 farmers. It was in general the party of the upper and middle classes.

A few other miscellaneous items may be noted in passing. There were 48 clergymen in the fourth duma and 40 of them belonged to the two parties farthest to the Right. Most of the wealthy were gathered on the Right and most of the poor on the Left, but there were a few strays like the Progressive who owned one hundred thousand dessiatins of land. Forty-five of the 65 peasant members in the first session were to the Right of the Kadets.

The duma had shifted toward the Right as the government had intended it should, but in the third session of the last duma there came to fruition a development which the government had not intended. This was the formation of the so-called Progressive Bloc, a coalition which included about three-quarters of the deputies. Included in it were the more liberal nationalists from the Moderate Right coalition, the Center, the Zemstva-Octobrists, the Duma Group of Octobrists, the Progressives, and the Kadets. Their slogan demanded the establishment of a "Ministry of Confidence," by which they meant a ministry in whose leader both the public and

[12] A. Badaev, *Bolsheviki v gosudarstvennoi dume* [Bolsheviks in the state duma] (Leningrad, 1939), pp. 67, 68, 200, 209, and 277. Two very interesting recent accounts of Malinovsky are given in David Shub, *Lenin, a biography* (New York, 1948), and Bertram D. Wolfe, *Three who made a revolution* (New York, 1948).

the tsar would have confidence and in whose members the public would have sufficient faith to enable the group to lead a united, co-operative effort. This was not a responsible ministry in the Western sense, but it was as far toward that as it seemed possible to go at the time. In August/September 1915, the Bloc presented its program to the government.[13] After some vacillation, the tsar's answer was the closing of the duma. The Bloc continued to exist, however, and its leaders continued to plan. By the end of 1916, their plans called for the establishment of a real constitutional monarchy. So far had the duma and its political parties moved before the revolution.

[13] The text of the program may be conveniently found in B. Pares, *The fall of the Russian monarchy* (New York, 1939), pp. 271–73.

The Tsaritsa and the Government

The personalities of the rulers are always a matter of tremendous importance in an autocracy because the wills and whims of autocrats affect the lives of millions of persons. There are few clearer illustrations of the soundness of this generalization than the story of the interrelationships of Nicholas II, Alexandra, and Rasputin. The source is: Sir Bernard Pares, (Ed.), *The Letters of the Tsaritsa to the Tsar, 1914–1916*. New York: Robert M. McBride and Co., 1924. Pp. ix–xii, xiv–xviii, xxviii–xxix, xxxi–xxxiii, xxxiv–xxxviii.

The future Empress of Russia, Princess Alix of Hesse-Darmstadt, was born on June 5, 1872, at Darmstadt. Her mother was the beloved Princess Alice of England, who died while nursing her children in 1878 at the age of thirty-five. Princess Alix was brought up largely in England at the court of her grandmother, Queen Victoria, whose ideas and discipline she fully assimilated. A large portrait of the Queen hung later in one of the chief living-rooms at Tsarskoe Selo; "She was very tiny," said the Empress, "but she was very forceful." The whole *morale* of Princess Alix was English. English was the language which she always spoke and wrote to the Emperor. The housekeeper of Tsarskoe Selo was an Englishwoman. In her family there was hereditary the hæmophilic ailment. One of her uncles had his life cut short by it, and her sister, Princess Irena of Prussia, married to Prince Henry, lost several of her children by it. This malady appears only in males and is transmitted only by females. The Empress herself was therefore immune from it, and though later she suffered very much from her heart, she had health to support a life full of trials and at times full of activities. Her eldest sister, Princess Victoria of Battenberg, was married in England. Another sister, Ella, married the Grand Duke Sergius, younger brother of Alexander III of Russia, and became on her conversion to the Orthodox Church (which was anything but nominal), the Grand Duchess Elizabeth. It was on a journey to this sister that Princess Alix was first contemplated as a possible bride for the heir to the throne. But nothing came of the idea this time. The whole nature of the Princess was deeply religious. Her strong Protestant honesty of conscience did not allow her to change her faith without conviction. An Orthodox Bishop was sent to Darmstadt to explain to her the Orthodox confession, and, as in her sister's case, it proved capable of satisfying the deepest instincts of her nature far more than was possible for Protestantism. There was in her father's family and also, perhaps, in her mother's a tendency towards mysticism. On the sudden illness of the Emperor Alexander III, in his anxiety for his son's marriage, Princess Alix was hastily summoned to Russia, and her first appearance to the Russian people as the future Empress was at Alexander's funeral.

She was, of course, a woman of wonderful beauty, fair and tall, with the dignity of an empress. But she was from the first painfully shy. Though this shyness gave way when she was with her very few intimate friends, it cannot be denied that she not only was thought, but actually was, very awkward, ill at ease, and unsympathetic in her appearances at the court. One does not need to take the description of one who hated her, Count Witte. M. Paléologue also finds that conversation is an effort to her, that she can hardly get out a word of welcome; and others too carried away the impression that her thought throughout court functions was, "When will this be over, and when will all these people be gone?" The life which she and her family led throughout, a life particularly of her choosing, was remote, not only from the culture and intellect of the country, but even from the other members of the Imperial family. The Grand Dukes themselves complained that they had the greatest difficulty in getting to the Emperor. The extraordinary limitedness and isolation of this life gave the whole atmosphere and background to the part which the Empress was to play in politics. And at the same time they solve the riddle of the extraordinary contrast between her private life and her public influence. It is this isolation which makes so intelligible the wonderful resignation and complete absorption in religion which marked the family life during imprisonment. Mr. Gibbs, colleague of M. Gilliard, and English tutor to the Tsarevich, said the Empress was never so worthy of herself as after the abdication. It was as if her nature could only expand in such a hermitage of remoteness and privation. From the outset, the "funeral bride" seemed marked for misfortune. The coronation festivities were completely marred by the terrible catastrophe on the Hodynsky Plain outside Moscow, where thousands were crushed through extraordinarily incapable arrangements for the distribution of presents to the people. The Emperor and Empress were not told of the extent of the disaster, and their decision to carry out their programme left with many the impression of heartlessness. The investigation which followed led to a conflict between the Court Ministry on the one side and the Moscow administration of the Grand Duke Sergius on the other, and this was a signal for one of those wars of court intrigue which were to disfigure the whole reign. The Empress's ardent wish to give an heir to the throne was disappointed time after time by the successive birth of four daughters, and when at last, in the midst of the disasters of the Japanese War, the little heir arrived in 1904, it was found that he was marked by the hereditary ailment of his mother's family. He was hæmophilic; the slightest scratch might lead to internal bleeding which there was no known means of stopping. Full of spirit, he had to be deterred as far as possible from any childish games and sports. The radiant health of his four sisters seemed a mockery of his ailment, and the Empress could not herself forget that the disease was transmitted through her.

In the most striking contrast with this succession of misfortunes stands out the picture of the home life of the Imperial family. While one is reading this story, one seems almost as much cut off from the outside world as were the actors in it; they had no ambitions, their requirements were healthy and of the most modest kind; there was nothing to make them wish to look outside their own life, everything to deter them from doing so. The Emperor, who as an emperor was so conspicuous a failure, was the most tender and devoted of husbands, and in the home circle that strong natural charm which impressed everyone who met him had full, free play. The Empress adored him, as is clear from these letters. There was no feeling of superiority, but a deep pity for the burden which he had to bear and the unsuitability of it to his yielding and lovable character.

•   •   •

The mystical tinge of the Empress's mind has already been mentioned. She had, we are told, "a very strong inner life" and could remain for hours absorbed in contemplation. She herself strongly disclaimed spiritualism. "It is a great sin," she said. But to everything mystic her miserable surroundings urged her strongly, and one cannot think that she saw any clear frontier between the two. A charlatan doctor of nervous diseases at Lyons, one Philippe, who worked in what he called "astral medicine" was introduced to the Grand Duchess Militsa, the Montenegrin Princess who had married the Grand Duke Peter Nikolayevich, and to her sister Anastasia, the Stana of these letters, married first to the Duke of Leuchtenberg and after her divorce in 1907 to the Grand Duke Nikolay Nikolayevich. Philippe, who was in person insignificant but had a remarkable attraction of manner, was through the Grand Duchesses presented to the imperial couple in 1901 at Compiègne during their visit to France and was later taken by them to Tsarskoe. We read of séances in which Philippe called up the spirit of Alexander III (whose wishes always possessed an immense authority for his son). We read even of a claim of Philippe that he could fix the sex of children, and from Witte's *Memoirs* and elsewhere we understand that the Empress was strongly persuaded that she was enceinte in the autumn of 1902. In 1904, however, Philippe definitely interfered in politics, and as his first steps in this field were very indiscreet—for instance, he promised quick success in the war against Japan—he left Russia in disgrace and died in France in August 1905. Philippe had told the Empress that she would have a second friend who would talk to her of God. He also, as we learn from the letters, gave her a bell as a symbol that she was to warn the Emperor against those who wished to influence him.

Philippe's successor was the famous Rasputin. The name itself is not a surname, but a nickname given him by his fellow-peasants and meaning "the dissolute." Gregory, who was born in 1871, was a simple peasant of the

village of Pokrovskoe, not far from Tobolsk in Siberia. After a most disorderly youth he retired to a neighbouring monastery, and on his return obtained among the peasants a reputation for wonderful spiritual powers. The
disorders of his life did not cease; they broke out from time to time with extraordinary violence. But this, it was claimed, only gave the more force to
his reiterated repentances. Rasputin was not a monk, but one of those
"holy" men who wandered about among the people claiming a direct commission from God, a type of extravagant and unlicensed individualism of
which there are many instances in the story of the Orthodox Church.
Throughout he claimed to be the typical man of the people, and it was as
such that he was welcomed in Petrograd by the Rector of the Theological
Academy, Bishop Feofan, who was confessor to the Empress. Certified by
Feofan, Rasputin entered the circle of the Montenegrin Grand Duchesses
and the Grand Duke Nicholas, and it was from them that he was passed on
to the Palace at Tsarkoe in the summer of 1907. Rasputin never sought to
flatter the sovereigns; he even spoke roughly to them from the first. He was
early associated with another charlatan, the Buryat doctor Badmayev, who
was guilty of money frauds. Rasputin's visits to the place have been greatly
exaggerated. M. Gilliard, who only once set eyes on him, says that Rasputin
did not see either of the sovereigns more than once a month and sometimes
much less frequently. According to Anna Vyrubova, it was only twice or
thrice a year before the war and from four to six times afterwards; she
maintains that Rasputin only saw the Emperor once throughout the critical
year, 1916. Most of the meetings took place not in the palace but in the little house outside the park tenanted by Vyrubova. Far more often the messages from Rasputin to the Emperor and Empress were, in the language of
these letters, "handed over" by Anna and often they were in the form of
telegrams to her. We must believe that the Empress never saw anything of
the man's vileness, though once she mentions in the letters that "he was not
tipsy." Both Madame Dehn and Anna Vyrubova strongly disclaim any
knowledge of this side of his character. Madame Dehn is convinced that
even for Anna Vyrubova Rasputin was nothing more than a holy man,
though her book, like the Empress's letters, represents Anna as a person
who would be in love with anyone. It is possible to believe this. But Petrograd itself could be in no doubt about the man's real character. He was a
standing outrage on decencies. Even Vyrubova admits that during the war
adventurers "took advantage of his simplicity," took him out to dinner and
gave him too much drink. As to the sexual exploits there can be no question. They were innumerable, and several of them were openly vaunted by
the women who fell victims to him. In March 1911, to counteract these public scandals, Rasputin made a visit to Jerusalem, but was back in Petrograd
by November. There followed further orgies, and Rasputin was now openly
condemned both by Bishop Feofan and by two others who had formerly
been his strong supporters—Bishop Hermogen of Saratov and the monk
Heliodore—who spat at him and struck him, and were very shortly afterwards relegated to monasteries. At this time the newspapers printed num-
berless instances of Rasputin's seductions. By the so-called press-reform

made during the Revolution of 1904–7, the preliminary censorship had been abolished, and papers could print what they pleased at the risk of being arbitrarily fined by the local governors after publication. This risk they were glad to take in the case of Rasputin, but the Empress secured from the Emperor an order that there should be nothing printed at all on the subject. Thereby the Emperor broke his own law and the leader of the Duma, Alexander Guchkov, seized the occasion for an interpellation and a public debate on Rasputin. In March 1912 the Prime Minister, Kokovtsev, a strong but enlightened Conservative, urged the Emperor to send Rasputin away from Petrograd. Rasputin departed of himself with an insolent threat to Kokovtsev, and when the Prime Minister visited the sovereigns in Livadia in May the Empress turned her back on him. At the beginning of 1914 Kokovtsev was summarily dismissed without explanation.

It may be true, as is urged, that in the main the Empress confined her interventions in politics up to the war to obtaining the dismissals of those Ministers who were hostile to Rasputin. As to Rasputin himself, the part which he took in politics was soon an active one. The pleas of Vyrubova on this point will not hold good for an instant. There is no need to regard him as a champion of any particular point of view except that of autocratic absolutism, which alone could enable him to penetrate an ignorant palace as the voice of the Russian peasants. But his good offices were constantly sought by political adventurers, and he himself was probably not conscious of the extent to which he was being used as a tool.

The foundation of Rasputin's influence with the Empress is quite clear. Before 1912 he had been called in to help with his counsel, and more than that, even with his prophecies, at moments critical to the health of the Tsarevich. In the summer of this year the Imperial family was at one of the Emperor's shooting-boxes in Poland, when Alexis fell while getting out of a boat so that he bruised his groin against the gunwale. This and a subsequent piece of negligence brought on a most serious crisis, and the parents were half beside themselves with anxiety. The doctors declared themselves helpless. Of course anything like an operation was at all times out of the question, and the internal bleeding could not be stopped. Recourse was made by telegraph to Rasputin, who replied at once: "This illness is not as dangerous as it looks. Let the doctors not torture him." It was from that moment that the danger rapidly passed away. In December 1915, while the Tsarevich was with his father at General Headquarters, there was another serious crisis, and the Emperor was bringing him back to Tsarskoe with little hope that the boy would arrive alive. Medical help was again impotent, and Rasputin intervened with a message which again coincided exactly with the passing of the crisis. Rasputin was certainly believed by most of his admirers to have the gift of prophecy. Anna Vyrubova says he was never wrong and gives several instances, some of them surprising. M. Gilliard thinks that Rasputin, who was certainly very astute, took care to be excellently posted as to all matters in which he ventured to intervene. As his influence increased, this certainly became much easier for him. Some of his messages almost amount to threats that the child is in danger if he, Rasputin, is not listened to. From this it was an easy step to demand, for instance, the dismissal of a minister or the promotion of a protégé. The Empress looked upon everything that he said as coming from a "Man of God."

. . .

Closer union with the Allies inevitably meant the progress of the constitutional cause in Russia. An appeal to the Duma and to the people had inevitably the same bearing. There was no question whatever as to the Empress's loyalty to Russia during the war, nor as to her devotion to the Russian Army; but constitutionalism was to her anathema. It meant the limitation of absolute power for her son. Since October 1905, no one could have stated exactly whether the Emperor had accepted that limitation of his authority which seemed the logical inference of the manifesto of October 30, 1905; nor could one say that the manifesto itself had ever been carried out with any sincerity. In any case this was the moment when the Empress abandoned all restraint and threw herself heart and soul into a battle with Russian constitutionalism. Rasputin had for some time been absent from Petrograd, but after the reverses of May his influence was stronger than ever. He was very fully informed and at first proceeded cautiously. The Empress herself at first, while urging his opinions on the Emperor, still offers excuses for her own interference. Rasputin on July 22 went to his Siberian home. He returned in the middle of August and threw himself more and more into the fight with the Duma. The Duma at this time with practical unanimity declared for a ministry which should have the full confidence of the people. This formula was a concession of the Liberal majority to those Conservatives who were not ready to demand that the Ministers should be chosen by the Duma. The great majority of the Duma, including nearly all the brains in it, formed into a single Progressive Bloc, for which the way had long been prepared, and was even able to propose a detailed unanimous programme of long-deferred reforms.

From July 11 the Emperor spent two months in Tsarskoe. This of course gave the Empress her opportunity, and the crisis of the struggle is not recorded in the letters. For her, even more odious and more dangerous than the Duma was the Grand Duke Nicholas. In her earlier letters we see that she is morbidly fearful that he would acquire a moral authority replacing that of the Emperor. Madame Vyrubova was always ready to repeat malicious gossip from officers at General Headquarters against the Grand Duke. She even at one time bunches together the names of all the foreign military attachés (including General Hanbury Williams, who was devoted to Nicholas II) as conspirators against the Emperor. The Grand Duke may have let fall the suggestion that the Empress should retire to a convent. This and more than this was current gossip at the time. Some even accused him of having allowed himself to be spoken of as Nicholas III. It can only be said that everything in the conduct of the Grand Duke (and there is plenty of light thrown on this question) is a flat contradiction to any possible doubt as to his loyalty. In any case, on August 24, the Ministers were summoned to Tsarskoe and there informed that the Emperor had decided to take over the

Command in Chief. They were astounded; and particularly Sazonov used every effort to dissuade him. Vyrubova relates how on his return to his family he says: "I was firm; see how I have been perspiring"; and tells how he held fast in his left hand throughout the interview the little ikon given him before it. The decision was received with consternation on all sides, but there was at least one point which it finally cleared up. By going permanently to the Army, and still more by the remarkably vigorous manifesto which he then issued, the Emperor showed friends and foes alike that he was absolutely committed to war to the end—a decision in which he never for a moment wavered.

With the Emperor at Headquarters, the Empress assumes an altogether new rôle in the Government. She describes herself later as "his wall in the rear." The Ministers, with a growing regularity, come to her with their reports. She herself remarks later that she is the first Russian Empress to have received them regularly since Catherine the Great—hardly a tactful thing to write to the new Catherine's husband. The change did not come all at once; but from the very outset she was in constant communication with Goremykin for the dismissal of the new more Liberal Ministers. The record of her letters here hardly needs any supplement or explanation. In letter after letter she urges the dismissal of Shcherbatov and of Samarin and more than suggests that of Polivanov and Sazonov.

·   ·   ·

Already in the autumn of 1915 it was clear that Rasputin was the most powerful man in Russia. For instance, General Mishchenko, with whom I was staying at that time, sent an A.D.C. to Petrograd to find out what was going wrong with army supplies, and the officer, who returned during my visit, explained that nothing at all could be done now without Rasputin's support. He did not assume the direction of affairs. He was still careful in his interventions, but that his approval was the first qualification for a ministerial post was already clear. The shame of this domination led to protests from two honest servants of the Emperor, already mentioned, General Dzhunkovsky and Prince Orlov. Rasputin had in the spring visited the tombs of the Metropolitans at Moscow and spent the evening at the most notorious place of entertainment in the town, a kind of Moulin Rouge, called by the name of Yar. Here he was both drunk and disorderly, and on being challenged used words which were deeply insulting to the Empress herself—"as to the old woman, I can do what I like." Dzhunkovsky, we are told, presented the police record of this scene to the Emperor, and he was dismissed from all Court appointments (September 8). Prince Orlov had more than once urged the dismissal of Rasputin. Now, we are told, he did so upon his knees, with the result that he was called upon to resign (September 5). Both these episodes have several echoes in the Empress's letters. One sees that the separation of the Sovereigns from the people is gradually becoming complete. Even the Moscow nobility, even the Imperial family, even the most loyal servants of the Palace are affronted, and from this time onwards we read in these letters, as a kind of running comment on every appointment or dismissal, "he venerates Our Friend" (that is, Rasputin), or, "he does not like Our Friend."

The prorogation of the Duma was from time to time prolonged. Old Goremykin, nearly ninety years of age, frankly feared to face it under the new conditions, and it was definitely his fear of the Duma and the Empress's own feeling of his weakness that led her in the end to recommend his resignation. The new appointment made on February 2, 1916, on the eve of the meeting of the Duma, was more astonishing than any that preceded it. The new Prime Minister, obviously the choice of the Empress, was Stürmer. He had been Governor in Yaroslavl and had conducted a savage repression of the Liberal County Council in Tver. He was also a Master of Ceremonies at the Court. He was simply known to the public for large defalcations, and typical enough was the report current at this time that at the outset of his premiership he informed his colleagues that a large sum was reserved to him for uncontrolled disposition, to which he asked their signatures. He was of course an obsequious follower of Rasputin. Stürmer himself was not really a man of any strength of character or of will. He was a puppet. With the most various of persons he left the impression of weakness and dishonesty. Stürmer was regularly received by the Empress for the conduct of affairs. The Duma was called for February 22, and on the suggestion of no other than Count Fredericks, who certainly wished the Emperor to stand well with his people, Nicholas took the occasion of the opening to pay his first visit to it. He was rapturously received. For the first time he addressed the Dumas as "representatives" of his people, and there was a great and unanimous outburst of patriotism. Rasputin, we are told, greatly deplored this incident. The Emperor the same day left for the front.

. . .

Rasputin's control of Russia was now complete. His reception-room was more than ever the rendezvous of all charlatans and adventurers. Rasputin would give them ill-written notes on slips of paper to the various authorities, who were simply requested to execute his wishes. Rasputin had all along predicted the greatest disasters from the war, so it was not surprising that he became the mouthpiece of a group of persons who wished to put an end to it. He even interfered in military operations, for instance discountenancing an offensive on the side of the Riga or dictating, or trying to dictate, arrangements as to transport of food or even of troops. He imposed on Bark, who had remained at his post, an enormous loan. The Synod, of course, was entirely in his hands, and so were all Church appointments. There were few sides of the administration of the Empire with which he did not deal. His instructions, handed over by "Ania," were sent on by the Empress to the Emperor. She sometimes even wrote them out for him or actually drafted a form of telegram for him to send to her with his signature. She herself complains more than once that her head goes round with the complications of the matters with which she deals. Yet she receives from the ante-room of Rasputin a man whom she had so far detested, Bonch Bruyevich, to hear his complaints against his chief, General Ruzsky, to which she begs the Emperor to listen. She is furious because Guchkov has written a letter to Alexeyev in which were the words "all depends on you," and she successfully urges that Alexeyev should be sent for a holiday.

At the beginning of July a party of members of the Duma, sent to England and France to promote closer contact with the Allies, returned to Russia. Its leader was Protopopov, Vice-President of the Duma, who had been picked by the President Rodzianko for this task. I had known him well in the summer of 1915 as right-hand man of Guchkov in the patriotic work for munitions. In England and France he had still maintained the same rôle, as he told me himself on the way back. Directly afterwards, while passing through Stockholm, he entered into long conversations on the subject of peace with a German diplomatist. In Petrograd he indeed maintained an appearance of loyalty to the Allies; but suddenly, through the agency of Rasputin, whom he had earlier met in connection with his taste for spiritualism, he was appointed Minister of the Interior (October 3). Of course after that, practically no one in the Duma would speak to him. Again the Empress imagined that a member of the Duma would be the best weapon for suppressing the Duma.

Protopopov himself was no strong man, though he posed to the Emperor as such. He was simply a mouthpiece of Rasputin. The direct slap in the face which had been given both to the Russian people and to the Allies was bitterly resented. Public affairs were now managed from some mysterious subterranean chamber and scandals of every kind flourished. There was the scandal of Manussein-Manuilov, a member of the secret police, journalist and speculator, who had actually been nominated by Stürmer as his principal private secretary. There were the financial scandals connected with the names of Manus and Rubenstein, big speculative financiers, unquestionably favourable to Germany. Rasputin in a visit to Moscow is reported to even have asked the Lefts why they too did not use his good offices. The case of Sukhomlinov was arbitrarily withdrawn on the repeated instances of the Empress contained in these letters. Sukhomlinov himself was removed from prison to a hospital on what seemed quite an insufficient plea of ill-health. She urges the same favour for Rubenstein. The Empress again demands that her husband shall contravene the ordinary course of law, and demand back all the papers on the case of Manuilov. Lines which were always ringing in one's head at this time of national abasement were those which immediately follow Shakespeare's magnificent description of England in *Richard II:* "Is now leased out Like to a tenement or pelting farm."

It is interesting that the Empress herself recognised the inevitableness of the Duma. She would advise the Emperor to "cleverly shut it"; but it was only tentatively that she hinted at its abolition. Stürmer, even more than Goremykin, was in mortal fear of the Duma. After all he, a weak and obsequious opportunist, would have to go there and answer for all the iniquities of Rasputin. After long delays the Duma met on November 14. Stürmer had arranged that immediately after the opening speech the Ministers followed by the Ambassadors would walk out. The crowded public remained, and the empty benches of the Ministers were assailed by a storm of national indignation. All along, it had been the policy of the Liberals to endeavour in every way to postpone revolution till after the war, and the Duma endeavoured by the vigour of its protests to represent, and thus to keep in hand, the wholesale indignation of the country. The Cadet leader, Milyukov, made use of a remark of the amiable and incompetent Shuvayev, who had said, "I am perhaps a fool, but traitor never." Turning this round, Milyukov exposed all the sins of the Government, concluding each item in his indictment with the question: "Is this folly or treason?" No less vigorous was Shulgin, the Nationalist; and in a later debate even the most brilliant of the Reactionaries, Purishkevich, came out with a terrible comparison between Rasputin and an earlier "Grishka," the monk Otrepyev, a pretender who in the seventeenth century actually ascended the throne of Moscow. Stürmer never dared to go to the Duma again; he asked of the Emperor and was refused leave to dissolve it and arrest Milyukov, and, with the agreement of the Empress and Rasputin, was dismissed.

Stürmer's successor was appointed by the Emperor at Headquarters without the Empress and against her wishes (November 23). He was an honest, capable, plain-spoken Conservative, Trepov, who had done good work in putting some degree of order into the chaotic administration of the railways. Trepov, who was a man, had demanded the dismissal of Protopopov as a condition to his own acceptance of the premiership. There follows the most feverish period in the Empress's correspondence. Letter after letter she writes to save Protopopov, and ultimately goes down with him to Headquarters herself. The Emperor kept Protopopov, and ordered Trepov to continue in office. On the other hand, Trepov, whose position was little understood by the public, had no success in the Duma, where three times he was shouted down. Trepov dragged on as best he could till January. Ultimately his resignation was accepted and with him went the last chance of saving the dynasty.

The administration was already really in the hands of Protopopov and his puppets. It is impossible that the Empress understood or approved of the outrageous swindles which her authority covered. Her letters show her to have been peculiarly ignorant of public affairs. She complained to a friend that honest Ministers could not be found—repeating a constant excuse put forward by the Russian Reactionaries for choosing the most dishonest. Clearly she had only one thing in mind: that no Minister must stand except by the approval of Rasputin. This comes out plainly in all the letters. Evidently she looked upon herself as saving Russia.

Gilliard Describes the Tsar

Pierre Gilliard had almost unparalleled opportunities to observe the Russian imperial family. Appointed Tutor in French to the Grand Duchesses Olga and Titiana in 1905, he became a member of the imperial household in 1911 and a tutor to the tsarevich in 1913. Gilliard's contacts with the family, to whom he was devoted, grew increasingly close. After the abdication in 1917, he chose to share the Romanov's imprisonment and exile. He lived with them at Tsarskoie-Selo and Tobolsk, and tried to accompany them to Ekaterinburg but this was not permitted. His account of the family and of his life with them is full of interest. Obviously it is not without bias. The source is: P. Gilliard, *Thirteen Years at the Russian Court.* (*A Personal Record of the Last Years and Death of Czar Nicholas II and His Family.*) New York: George H. Doran and Co., n.d. Pp. 205–206.

Why did Fate decree that Czar Nicholas II should reign at the beginning of the twentieth century and in one of the most troublous periods of history? Endowed with remarkable personal qualities, he was the incarnation of all that was noblest and most chivalrous in the Russian nature. But he was weak. The soul of loyalty, he was the slave of his pledged word. His fidelity to the Allies, which was probably the cause of his death, proves it beyond doubt. He despised the methods of diplomacy and he was not a fighter. He was crushed down by events.

Nicholas II was modest and timid; he had not enough self-confidence: hence all his misfortunes. His first impulse was usually right. The pity was that he seldom acted on it because he could not trust himself. He sought the counsel of those he thought more competent than himself; from that moment he could no longer master the problems that faced him. They escaped him. He hesitated between conflicting causes and often ended by following that to which he was personally least sympathetic.

The Czarina knew the Czar's irresolute character. As I have said, she considered she had a sacred duty to help him in his heavy task. Her influence on the Czar was very great and almost always unfortunate; she made politics a matter of sentiment and personalities, and too often allowed herself to be swayed by her sympathies or antipathies, or by those of her *entourage*. Impulsive by nature, the Czarina was liable to emotional outbursts which made her give her confidence unreservedly to those she believed sincerely devoted to the country and the dynasty. Protopopoff was a case in point.

The Czar was always anxious to be just and to do the right thing. If he sometimes failed, the fault lies at the door of those who did their utmost to hide the truth from him and isolate him from his people. All his generous impulses were broken against the passive resistance of an omnipotent bureaucracy or were wilfully frustrated by those to whom he entrusted their realisation in him which made him follow life rather than try to lead it. It is one of the characteristics of the Russian nature.

An essentially reflective man, he would have been perfectly happy to live as a private individual, but he was resigned to his lot, and humbly accepted the superhuman task which God had given him. He loved his people and his country with all the force of his nature; he had a personal affection for the least of his subjects, those *moujiks* whose lot he earnestly desired to better.

What a tragic fate was that of this sovereign whose only desire during his reign was to be close to his people and who never succeeded in realising his wish. The fact is that he was well guarded, and by those whose interest it was that he should not succeed.

Kerensky's Opinion of Nicholas II

Alexander Kerensky, a brilliant and courageous young lawyer under the old regime, was the only socialist member of the Provisional Government. It fell to him as minister of justice to place the imperial family under arrest, and so long as he was able, he protected them against the vengeance of the extremists. As minister and later as premier, Kerensky had several interviews with Nicholas and was therefore able to revise previous general impressions in the light of firsthand, specific experience. The source is: A. Kerensky, *The Crucifixion of Liberty*. New York: The John Day Co., 1934. Pp. 173–176. Slightly abridged.

There was always this mystery about Nicholas II: why, having been born to rule strictly as a constitutional monarch—to reign but not to rule—did he hate the very word "constitution" so much and refuse to let the burden of absolute rule slip out of his wavering hands, for which it was all too heavy? "Be as Peter the Great was" drummed the Empress into him. But to great Peter his autocratic powers were a mighty instrument of statesmanship: he ruled in order to build a great empire. Nicholas II made no attempt to build, he merely defended his powers, burdensome as they were to him, against internal foes. I do not think he knew the reason himself. He merely believed what his father and Pobiedonostsev had instilled into him: there could be no Russia without autocracy; Russia and the autocracy were one; he himself was the impersonation of the autocracy. So the magic circle closed. There was no way out, unless it was one into disaster and void. Perhaps the very reason why he took his enforced abdication so calmly was that he saw in it divine help, a relief from the burden of power which he could not throw off of his own accord because he was bound by his oath as "The Lord's anointed." Living in the twentieth century, he had the mentality of the Muscovite Kings, even though he had no blood connection with the Moscow dynasty. The daily work of a monarch he found intolerably boring. He could not stand listening long or seriously to ministers' reports, or reading them. He liked such ministers as could tell an amusing story and did not weary the monarch's attention with too much business. But I repeat that never—from the very beginning to the very end of his reign—did he willingly yield one inch of his autocracy. When it came to defending his divine right his usual indifference left him; he became cunning, obstinate and cruel, merciless at times.

·   ·   ·

Many is the time I have had cause to realize—both in my capacity of political lawyer and as a member of the Duma—that it was in the Czar's own study, and nowhere else, that the fiercest cruelty of the over-keen servants of the autocracy was invariably sponsored. When perusing a report concerning the suppression of revolutionary activities he would put a note of approbation opposite the place where a particularly harsh and lawless measure against the "seditionaries" was described. He stopped legal proceedings against officials accused of open, scandalous and quite unbearable abuses of power in the repression of revolutionary activities. He granted honors and official advancement to people known to the whole of Russia as the organizers of the Jewish pogroms. After 1905, when political parties were legalized in Russia, he took one of them openly under his patronage— that is, if one can call an organized bandit gang like the "Union of the Russian People" a party. From that moment he presented the country with the subversive spectacle of a monarch turned party member. . . . The headquarters of the "Union of the Russian People" were in secret communication with Tsarskoe Selo—through the medium of that evil genius of Russia, the Grand Duke Nicholas. Long before Rasputin came, there was already a second government—side by side with the official one—which engineered pogroms of the Jews and the intelligentsia and organized "political" assassinations (including an attempt against Witte himself). The official government—even Stolypin's government—was powerless to put an end to these outrages because at the decisive moment it was confronted by the Czar's personal, though camouflaged, interference. As I have already said, Nicholas II was in constant conspiracy against his own official decrees, laws and proclamations. He intrigued secretly against his own ministers, preferring the advice of the most manifest adventurers. Rasputin was merely the last of these, though admittedly the most powerful.

And another enigma: although he hated popular representation, although he fiercely fought each new Duma as it came, irrespective of whether it was radical or conservative, yet just as fervently did Nicholas II always seek some personal contact with the people, with the genuine, ordinary, uneducated, hard-working peasantry. He even had a kind of aversion for the courtiers and the aristocracy. He did not like people who were very well-born, rich or very cultured. Just as a surfeited epicure may sometimes be tempted away from champagne and oysters to beer and whelks, so the Czar was drawn towards the lowest of the low, towards the vagrant classes. The palace was never rid of a collection of monks, mad saints, pilgrims and holy beggars. Rasputin himself was a thorough muzhik with a peasant's sleeveless coat, a girdled shirt, greased boots, and an unkempt beard.

Gilliard Describes the Tsaritsa

Compare this description of Alexandra with that given above by Sir Bernard Pares. The source is : Gilliard, *Russian Court,* pp. 47–55.

The Czarina, Alexandra Feodorovna, formerly Alice of Hesse, and fourth child of the Grand Duke Ludwig of Hesse and Alice of England, youngest daughter of Queen Victoria, was born at Darmstadt on June 6th, 1872. She lost her mother early in life, and was largely brought up at the English Court, where she soon became the favourite granddaughter of Queen Victoria, who bestowed on the blonde "Alix" all the tender affection she had had for her mother.

At the age of seventeen the young princess paid a prolonged visit to Russia, staying with her elder sister Elisabeth, who had married the Grand-Duke Sergius Alexandrovitch, a brother of the Czar Alexander III. She took an active part in Court life, appeared at reviews, receptions, and balls, and being very pretty was made a great fuss of.

Everybody regarded her as the prospective mate of the Heir to the Throne, but, contrary to general expectation, Alice of Hesse returned to Darmstadt and nothing had been said. Did she not like the idea? It is certainly a fact that five years later, when the official proposal arrived, she showed signs of hesitation.

However, the betrothal took place at Darmstadt during the summer of 1894, and was followed by a visit to the Court of England. The Russian Heir at once returned to his country. A few months later she was obliged to leave suddenly for Livadia, where Alexander III was dying. She was present when his end came, and with the Imperial family accompanied the coffin in which the mortal remains of the dead Emperor were carried to St. Petersburg.

The body was taken from Nicholas station to the Cathedral of St. Peter and St. Paul on a dull November day. A huge crowd was assembled on the route of the funeral cortege as it moved through the melting snow and mud with which the streets were covered. In the crowd women crossed themselves piously and could be heard murmuring, in allusion to the young Czarina, "She has come to us behind a coffin. She brings misfortune with her."

It certainly seemed as if from the start sorrow was dogging the steps of her whose light heart and beauty had earned her the nickname of "Sunshine" in her girlhood.

On November 26th, thus within a month of Alexander's death, the marriage was celebrated amidst the general mourning. A year later the Czarina gave birth to her first child—a daughter who was named Olga.

The coronation of the young sovereigns took place in Moscow on May 14th, 1896. Fate seemed already to have marked them down. It will be remembered that the celebrations were the occasion of a terrible accident which cost the lives of a large number of people. The peasants, who had come from all parts, had assembled in masses during the night in Hodinskoie meadows, where gifts were to be distributed. As a result of bad organisation there was a panic, and more than two thousand people were trodden to death or suffocated in the mud by the terror-stricken crowd.

When the Czar and Czarina went to Hodinskoie meadows next morning they had heard nothing whatever of the terrible catastrophe. They were not told the truth until they returned to the city subsequently, and they never knew the whole truth. Did not those concerned realise that by acting thus they were depriving the Imperial couple of a chance to show their grief and sympathy and making their behaviour odious because it seemed sheer indifference to public misfortune?

Several years of domestic bliss followed, and Fate seemed to have loosened its grip.

Yet the task of the young Czarina was no easy one. She had to learn all that it meant to be an empress, and that at the most etiquette-ridden Court in Europe and the scene of the worst forms of intrigue and coterie. Accustomed to the simple life of Darmstad, and having experienced at the strict and formal English Court only such restraint as affected a young and popular princess who was there merely on a visit, she must have felt at sea with her new obligations and dazzled by an existence of which all the proportions had suddenly changed. Her sense of duty and her burning desire to devote herself to the welfare of the millions whose Czarina she had become fired her ambitions, but at the same time checked her natural impulses.

Yet her only thought was to win the hearts of her subjects. Unfortunately she did not know how to show it, and the innate timidity from which she suffered was wont to play the traitor to her kind attentions. She very soon realised how impotent she was to gain sympathy and understanding. Her frank and spontaneous nature was speedily repelled by the icy conventions of her environment. Her impulses came up against the prevalent inertia about her, and when in return for her confidence she asked for intelligent devotion and real good will, those with whom she dealt took refuge in the easy zeal of the polite formalities of Courts.

In spite of all her efforts, she never succeeded in being merely amiable and acquiring the art which consists of flitting gracefully but superficially over all manner of subjects. The fact is that the Czarina was nothing if not sincere. Every word from her lips was the true expression of her real feelings. Finding herself misunderstood, she quickly drew back into her shell. Her natural pride was wounded. She appeared less and less at the ceremonies and receptions she regarded as an intolerable nuisance. She adopted a habit of distant reserve which was taken for haughtiness and contempt. But those who came in contact with her in moments of distress knew what a sensitive spirit, what a longing for affection, was concealed behind that apparent coldness. She had accepted her new religion with entire sincerity, and found it a great source of comfort in hours of trouble and anguish; but above all, it was the affection of her family which nourished her love, and she was never really happy except when she was with them.

The birth of Olga Nicolaievna had been followed by that of three other fine and healthy daughters who were their parents' delight. It was not an unmixed delight, however, for the secret desire of their hearts—to have a son and heir—had not yet been fulfilled. The birth of Anastasie Nicolaievna, the last of the Grand-Duchesses, had at first been a terrible disappointment . . . and the years were slipping by. At last, on August 12th, 1904, when the Russo-Japanese War was at its height, the Czarina gave birth to the son they so ardently desired. Their joy knew no bounds. It seemed as if all the sorrows of the past were forgotten and that an era of happiness was about to open for them.

Alas! it was but a short respite, and was followed by worse misfortunes: first the January massacre in front of the Winter Palace—the memory of which was to haunt them like a horrible nightmare for the rest of their days —and then the lamentable conclusion of the Russo-Japanese War. In those dark days their only consolation was their beloved son, and it had not taken long, alas! to discover that the Czarevitch had hæmophilia. From that moment the mother's life was simply one dreadful agony. She had already made the acquaintance of that terrible disease; she knew that an uncle, one of her brothers, and two of her nephews had died of it. From her childhood she had heard it spoken of as a dreadful and mysterious thing against which men were powerless. And now her only son, the child she loved more than anything else on earth, was affected! Death would watch him, follow him at every step, and carry him off one day like so many boys in his family. She must fight! She must save him at any cost! It was impossible for science to be impotent. The means of saving must exist, and they must be found. Doctors, surgeons, specialists were consulted. But every kind of treatment was tried in vain.

When the mother realised that no human aid could save, her last hope was in God. He alone could perform a miracle. But she must be worthy of His intervention. She was naturally of a pious nature, and she devoted herself wholly to the Orthodox religion with the ardour and determination she brought to everything. Life at Court became strict, if not austere. Festivities were eschewed, and the number of occasions on which the sovereigns had to appear in public was reduced to a minimum. The family gradually became isolated from the Court and lived to itself, so to speak.

Between each of the attacks, however, the boy came back to life, recovered his health, forgot his sufferings, and resumed his fun and his games. At these times it was impossible to credit that he was the victim of an implacable disease which might carry him off at any moment. Every time the Czarina saw him with red cheeks, or heard his merry laugh, or watched his frolics, her heart would fill with an immense hope, and she would say: "God has heard me. He has pitied my sorrow at last." Then the disease would suddenly swoop down on the boy, stretch him once more on his bed of pain and take him to the gates of death.

The months passed, the expected miracle did not happen, and the ruthless attacks followed hard on each other's heels. The most fervent prayers had not brought the divine revelation so passionately implored. The last hope had failed. A sense of endless despair filled the Czarina's soul: it seemed as if the whole world were deserting her.

It was then that Rasputin, a simple Siberian peasant, was brought to her, and he said: "Believe in the power of my prayers; believe in my help and your son will live!"

The mother clung to the hope he gave her as a drowning man seizes an outstretched hand. She believed in him with all the strength that was in her. As a matter of fact, she had been convinced for a long time that the saviour of Russia and the dynasty would come from the people, and she thought that this humble *moujik* had been sent by God to save him who was the hope of the nation. The intensity of her faith did the rest, and by a simple process of auto-suggestion, which was helped by certain perfectly casual coincidences, she persuaded herself that her son's life was in this man's hands.

Rasputin had realised the state of mind of the despairing mother who was broken down by the strain of her struggle and seemed to have touched the limit of human suffering. He knew how to extract the fullest advantage from it, and with a diabolical cunning he succeeded in associating his own life, so to speak, with that of the child.

This moral hold of Rasputin on the Czarina cannot possibly be understood unless one is familiar with the part played in the religious life of the Orthodox world by those men who are neither priests nor monks—though people habitually, and quite inaccurately, speak of the "monk" Rasputin— and are called *stranniki* or *startsi*.

The *strannik* is a pilgrim who wanders from monastery to monastery and church to church, seeking the truth and living on the charity of the faithful. He may thus travel right across the Russian Empire, led by his fancy or attracted by the reputation for holiness enjoyed by particular places or persons.

The *staretz* is an ascetic who usually lives in a monastery, though sometimes in solitude—a kind of guide of souls to whom one has recourse in moments of trouble or suffering. Quite frequently a *staretz* is an ex-*strannik* who has given up his old wandering life and taken up an abode in which to end his days in prayer and meditation.

Dostoievsky gives the following description of him in *The Brothers Karamazof:*

"The *staretz* is he who takes your soul and will and makes them his. When you select your *staretz* you surrender your will, you give it him in utter submission, in full renunciation. He who takes this burden upon him, who accepts this terrible school of life, does so of his own free will in the hope that after a long trial he will be able to conquer himself and become his own master sufficiently to attain complete freedom by a life of obedience—that is to say, get rid of self and avoid the fate of those who have lived their lives without succeeding in sufficing unto themselves."

God gives the *staretz* the indications which are requisite for one's welfare and communicates the means by which one must be brought back to safety.

On earth the *staretz* is the guardian of truth and the ideal. He is also the repository of the sacred tradition which must be transmitted from *staretz* to *staretz* until the reign of justice and light shall come.

Several of these *startsi* have risen to remarkable heights of modern grandeur and become saints of the Orthodox Church.

The influence of these men, who live as a kind of unofficial clergy, is still very considerable in Russia. In the provinces and open country it is even greater than that of the priests and monks.

The conversion of the Czarina had been a genuine act of faith. The Orthodox religion had fully responded to her mystical aspirations, and her imagination must have been captured by its archaic and naive ritual. She had accepted it with all the ardour of the neophyte. In her eyes Rasputin had all the prestige and sanctity of a *staretz*.

Such was the nature of the feelings the Czarina entertained for Rasputin—feelings ignobly travestied by calumny. They had their source in maternal love, the noblest passion which can fill a mother's heart.

Fate willed that he who wore the halo of a saint should be nothing but a low and perverse creature, and that, as we shall soon see, this man's evil influence was one of the principal causes of which the effect was the death of those who thought they could regard him as their saviour.

The Tsaritsa and the Tsar

A vivid picture and a clear measure of the control which the dominant Alexandra exercised over the weaker Nicholas is given by her letters to him. A correlation of her letters with political events proves that she assumed the responsibility and the power of governing Russia. The letters also prove the influence upon her of Rasputin. The source of the following is: Pares (Ed.), *Letters,* pp. 113–116.

Tsarskoje Selo, Aug. 22-nd 1915

My very own beloved One,

I cannot find words to express all I want to—my heart is far too full. I only long to hold you tight in my arms & whisper words of intense love, courage, strength & endless blessings. More than hard to let you go alone, so completely alone—but God is very near to you, more than ever. You have fought this great fight for your country & throne—alone & with bravery & decision. Never have they seen such firmness in you before & it cannot remain without good fruit.

Do not fear for what remains behind—one must be severe & stop all at once. Lovy, I am here, dont laugh at silly old wify, but she has [trousers] on unseen, & I can get the old man to come & keep him up to be energetic—whenever I can be of the smallest use, tell me what to do—use me—at such a time God will give me the strength to help you—because our souls are fighting for the right against the evil. It is all much deeper than appears to the eye—we, who have been taught to look at all from another side, see what the struggle here really is & means—you showing your mastery, proving yourself the *Autocrat* without wh. Russia cannot exist. Had you given in now in these different questions, they would have dragged out yet more of you. Being firm is the only saving—I know what it costs you, & have & do suffer hideously for you, forgive me, I beseech you, my angel, for having left you no peace & worried you so much—but I too well know yr. marvelously gentle character—& you had to shake it off this time, had to win your fight alone against all. It will be a glorious page in yr. reign & Russian history the story of these weeks & days—& God, who is just & near you—will save your country & throne through your firmness.

A harder battle has rarely been faught, than yours & it will be crowned with success, only believe this.

Yr. faith has been tried—your trust—& you remained firm as a rock, for that you will be blessed. God anointed you at your coronation, He placed you where you stand & you have done your duty, be sure, quite sure of Him & He forsaketh not His anointed. Our Friend's prayers arise night & day for you to Heaven & God will hear them.

Those who fear & cannot understand your actions, will be brought by events to realise your great wisdom. It is the beginning of the glory of yr. reign, He said so & I absolutely believe it. Your Sun is rising—& to-day it shines so brightly. And so will you charm all those great blunderers, cowards, led astray, noisy, blind, narrowminded & (dishonest false) beings, this morning.

And your Sunbeam will appear to help you, your very own Child—won't that touch those hearts & make them realise what you are doing, & what they dared to wish to do, to shake your throne, to frighten you with internal black forebodings—only a bit of success out there & they will change. They will (?) disperse home into clean air & their minds will be purified & they carry the picture of you & yr. Son in their hearts with them.—

I do hope *Goremykin* will agree to yr. choice of *Khvostov*—you need an energetic minister of the interior—should he be the wrong man, he can later be changed—no harm in that, at such times—but if energetic he may help splendidly & then the old man does not matter.

If you take him, then only wire to me tail [*Khvostov*] alright & I shall understand.—

Let no talks worry you—am glad Dmitri wont be there now—snap up *Voyeikov* if he is stupid—am sure he is afraid meeting people there who may think he was against *Nikolasha* & *Orlov* & to smoothe things, he begs you for *Nikolasha*—that would be the greatest fault & undo all you have so courageously done & the great internal fight would have been for nothing. Too kind, don't be, I mean not specially, as otherwise it would be dishonest, as still there have been things you were discontented with him about. Remind others about Misha, the Emperor's brother & then there is war there too.—

All is for the good, as our Friend says, the worst is over.—Now you speak to the Minister of war & he will take energetic measures, as soon as needed—but *Khvostov,* will see to that too if you name him.—When you leave, shall wire to Friend to-night through Anai—& He will particularly think of you. Only get *Nikolasha's* nomination quicker done—no dawdling, its bad for the cause & for *Alexejev* too—& a settled thing quieten minds, even if against their wish, sooner than that waiting & uncertainty & trying to influence you—it tires out ones heart.

I feel completely done up & only keep myself going with force—they shall not think that I am downhearted or frightened—but confident & calm.—

Joy we went to those holy places to-gether—for sure yr. dear Father quite particularly prays for you.

Give me some news as soon as you can—now am afraid for the moment N. P. wiring to Ania until am sure nobody watches again.

Tell me the impression, if you can. Be firm to the end, let me be sure of that otherwise shall get quite ill from anxiety.

Bitter pain not to be with you—know what you feel, & the meeting with N. wont be agreeable—you did trust him & now you know, what months ago our Friend said, that he was acting wrongly towards you & your country & wife—its not the people who would do harm to your people, but *Nikolashna* & set *Gutchkov, Rodzianko Samarin* etc.—

Lovy, if you hear I am not so well, don't be anxious, I have suffered so terribly, & phisically overtired myself these 2 days, & morally worried (& worry still till all is done at the *Headquarters* & *Nikolasha* gone) only then shall I feel calm—near you all is well—when out of sight others at once profit—you see they are affraid of me & so come to you when alone—they know I have a will of my own when I feel I am in the right—& you are now —we know it, so you make them tremble before your courage & will. God is with you & our Friend for you—all is well—& later all will thank you for having saved your country. Don't doubt—believe, & all will be well & the army is everything—a few *strikes* nothing, in comparison, as can & shall be suppressed. The left are furious because all slips through their hands & their cards are clear to us & the game they wished to use *Nikolasha* for—even *Shvedov* knows it fr. there.

Now goodnight lovy, go straight to bed without tea with the rest & their long faces. Sleep long & well, you need rest after this strain & your heart needs calm hours.—God Almighty bless your undertaking, His holy Angels guard & guide you & bless the work of your hands.—Please give this little Image of St. *John the Warrior* to *Alexeiev* with my blessing & fervent wishes. You have my Image I blessed you with last year—I give no other as that carries my blessing & you have *Gregory's* St. Nicolas to guard & guide you. I always place a candle before St. Nicolas at *Znamenje* for you —& shall do, so to-morrow at 3 o'clock & before the Virgin. You will feel my soul near you.

I clasp you tenderly to my heart, kiss and caress you without end—want to show you all the intense love I have for you, warm, cheer, console, strengthen you, & make you sure of yourself. Sleep well my Sunshine, Russia's Saviour. Remember last night, how tenderly we clung to-gether. I shall yearn for yr. caresses—I never can have enough of them. And I still have the children, & you are all alone. Another time I must give you Baby for a bit to cheer you up.—

I kiss you without end & bless you. Holy Angels guard your slumber—I am near & with you for ever & none shall separate us.—

Yr. very own wife
Sunny.

Rasputin and the Imperial Family

> Gilliard's position at court enabled him to watch the rise and dominance of Rasputin from a rare vantage point. The following material deals with Rasputin, Anna Viroubouva, and the imperial family. The source is: Gilliard, *Russian Court*, pp. 59–65, 82–84.

About one hundred and fifty versts south of Tobolsk the little village of Pokrovskoie lies lost in the marshes on the banks of the Tobol. There Grigory Rasputin was born. His father's name was Efim. Like many other Russian peasants at that time, the latter had no family name. The inhabitants of the village, of which he was not a native, had given him on his arrival the name of Novy (the Newcomer).

His son Grigory had the same kind of youth as all the small peasantry of that part of Siberia, where the poor quality of the soil often compels them to live by expedients. Like them, he robbed and stole. . . . He soon made his mark, however, by the audacity he showed in his exploits, and it was not long before his misdoings earned him the reputation of an unbridled libertine. He was now known solely as Rasputin, a corruption of the word *rasputnik* (debauched), which was destined to become, as it were, his family name.

The villagers of Siberia were in the habit of hiring out horses to travellers passing through the country and offering their services as guides and coachmen. One day Rasputin happened to conduct a priest to the monastery of Verkhoturie. The priest entered into conversation with him, was struck by his quick natural gifts, led him by his questions to confess his riotous life, and exhorted him to consecrate to the service of God the vitality he was putting to such bad uses. The exhortation produced so great an impression on Grigory that he seemed willing to give up his life of robbery and license. He stayed for a considerable time at the monastery of Verkhoturie and began to frequent the holy places of the neighbourhood.

When he went back to his village he seemed a changed man, and the inhabitants could hardly recognise the reprobate hero of so many scandalous adventures in this man whose countenance was so grave and whose dress so austere. He was seen going from village to village, spreading the good word and reciting to all and sundry willing to listen long passages from the sacred books, which he knew by heart.

Public credulity, which he already exploited extremely skillfully, was not slow in regarding him as a prophet, a being endowed with supernatural powers, and in particular the power of performing miracles. To understand this rapid transformation one must realise both the strange power of fascination and suggestion which Rasputin possessed, and also the ease with which the popular imagination in Russia is captured by the attraction of the marvelous.

However, the virtue of the new saint does not seem to have been proof against the enticements of the flesh for long, and he relapsed into his debauchery. It is true that he showed the greatest contrition for his wrongdoings, but that did not prevent him from continuing them. Even at that time he displayed that blend of mysticism and erotomania which made him so dangerous a person.

Yet, notwithstanding all this, his reputation spread far and wide. His services were requisitioned, and he was sent for from distant places, not merely in Siberia, but even in Russia.

His wanderings at last brought him to St. Petersburg. There, in 1905, he made the acquaintance of the Archimandrite Theophanes, who thought he could discern in him signs of genuine piety and profound humility as well as the marks of divine inspiration. Rasputin was introduced by him to devout circles in the capital, whither his reputation had preceded him. He had no difficulty in trafficking in the credulity of these devotees, whose very refinement made them superstitious and susceptible to the magnetism of his rustic piety. In his fundamental coarseness they saw nothing but the entertaining candour of a man of the people. They were filled with the greatest admiration for the naivete of this simple soul. . . .

It was not long before Rasputin had immense authority with his new flock. He became a familiar figure in the *salons* of certain members of the high aristocracy of St. Petersburg, and was even received by members of the royal family, who sang his praises to the Czarina. Nothing more was requisite for the last and vital stage. Rasputin was taken to Court by intimate friends of her Majesty, and with a personal recommendation from the Archimandrite Theophanes. This last fact must always be borne in mind. It was to shelter him from the attacks of his enemies for many years.

We have seen how Rasputin traded on the despair which possessed the Czarina and had contrived to link his life with that of the Czarevitch and acquire a growing hold over his mother. Each of his appearances seemed to produce an improvement in the boy's malady, and thus increased his prestige and confirmed confidence in the power of intercession.

After a certain time, however, Rasputin's head was turned by this unexpected rise to fame; he thought his position was sufficiently secure, forgot the caution he had displayed when he first came to St. Petersburg, and returned to his scandalous mode of life. Yet he did so with a skill which for a long time kept his private life quite secret. It was only gradually that the reports of his excesses spread and were credited.

At first only a few voices were faintly raised against the *staretz,* but it was not long before they became loud and numerous. The first at Court to attempt to show up the imposter was Mademoiselle Tioutcheva, the governess of the Grand-Duchesses. Her efforts were broken against the blind faith of the Czarina. Among the charges she made against Rasputin were several which, in her indignation, she had not checked with sufficient care so that their falsity was absolutely patent to her sovereign. Realising her impotence, and with a view to discharging her responsibilities, she asked that in any case Rasputin should not be allowed on the floor occupied by the children.

The Czar then intervened, and Her Majesty yielded, not because her faith was shaken, but merely for the sake of peace and in the interests of a man whom she believed was blinded by his very zeal and devotion.

Although I was then no more than one of the Grand-Duchesses' professors—it was during the winter of 1910—Mademoiselle Tioutcheva herself told me all about this debate and its vicissitudes. But I confess that at that time I was still far from accepting all the extraordinary stories about Rasputin.

In March, 1911, the hostility to Rasputin became more and more formidable, and the *staretz* thought it wise to let the storm blow over and disappear for a time. He therefore started on a pilgrimage to Jerusalem.

On his return to St. Petersburg in the autumn of the same year the tumult had not subsided, and he had to face the attacks of one of his former protectors, Bishop Hermogenes, who employed terrible threats and eventually extracted a promise from Rasputin to keep away from the Court, where his presence compromised his sovereigns.

He had no sooner left the Bishop, who had actually gone so far as to strike him, than he rushed to his powerful protectress, Madame Wyroubova, the Czarina's all but inseparable companion. The Bishop was exiled to a monastery.

Just as futile were the efforts of the Archimandrite Theophanes, who could never forgive himself for having stood sponsor in some degree for the *staretz's* high moral character, and thus reassuring the Czar and Czarina by his personal recommendation. He did his best to show him up, but the only reward for his pains was to find himself transferred to the Government of Tauris.

The fact was that Rasputin managed to make the two Bishops seem low intriguers who had wanted to use him as an instrument, and then, becoming jealous of a favour they could no longer exploit for their own personal benefit, tried to bring about his downfall.

"The lowly Siberian peasant" had become a formidable adversary in whom an utter lack of moral scruple was associated with consummate skill. With a first-class intelligence service, and creatures of his own both at Court and among the men around the ministers, as soon as he saw a new enemy appear on the scene he was always careful to baulk him cleverly by getting in the first blow.

Under the form of prophecies he would announce that he was going to be the object of a new attack, taking good care not to indicate his adversaries too plainly. So when the bolt was shot, the hand that directed it held a crumbling missile. He often actually interceded in favour of those who had attacked him, affirming with mock humility that such trials were necessary for the good of his soul.

Another element which also contributed to keep alive the blind faith in him which lasted until the end was the fact that the Czar and Czarina were accustomed to see those to whom they paid particular attention become objects of intrigue and cabals. They knew that their esteem alone was sufficient to expose them to the attacks of the envious. The result was that they were convinced that the special favour they showed to an obscure *moujik* was bound in any case to raise a storm of hate and jealousy against him and make him the victim of the worst calumnies.

The scandal, however, gradually spread from the purely ecclesiastical world. It was mentioned in whispers in political and diplomatic circles, and was even referred to in speeches in the Duma.

In the spring of 1912, Count Kokovtzof, then President of the Council of Ministers, decided to take the matter up with the Czar. The step was a particularly delicate one, as hitherto Rasputin's influence had been confined to the Church and the Imperial family circle. Those were the very spheres in which the Czar was most intolerant of any interference by his ministers.

The Czar was not convinced by the Count's action, but he realised that some concession to public opinion was necessary. Shortly after Their Majesties went to the Crimea, Rasputin left St. Petersburg and vanished into Siberia.

Yet his influence was of the kind that distance does not diminish. On the contrary, it only idealised him and increased his prestige.

As in his previous absences, there was a lively exchange of telegrams—through the medium of Madame Wyroubova—between Pokrovskoie and the different residences occupied in turn by the Imperial family during the year 1912.

The absent Rasputin was more powerful than Rasputin in the flesh. His psychic empire was based on an act of faith, for there is no limit to the power of self-delusion possessed by those who mean to believe at all cost. The history of mankind is there to prove it!

But how much suffering and what terrible disasters were to result from the tragic aberration! . . .

The children saw Rasputin when he was with their parents, but even at that time his visits were infrequent. Weeks, and sometimes months, passed without his being summoned to Court. It became more and more usual to see him with Madame Wyroubova, who had a little house quite near to the Alexander Palace. The Czar and his heir hardly ever went there, and meetings were always very rare.

As I have already explained, Madame Wyroubova was the intermediary between the Czarina and Rasputin. It was she who sent on to the *staretz* letters addressed to him and brought his replies—usually verbal—to the palace.

Relations between Her Majesty and Madame Wyroubova were very intimate, and hardly a day passed without her visiting her Imperial mistress. The friendship had lasted many years. Madame Wyroubova had married very young. Her husband was a degenerate and an inveterate drunkard, and succeeded in inspiring his young wife with a deep hatred of him. They separated, and Madame Wyroubova endeavoured to find relief and consolation in religion. Her misfortunes were a link with the Czarina, who had suffered so much herself, and yearned to comfort her. The young woman who had to go through so much won her pity. She became the Czarina's confidante, and the kindness the Czarina showed her made her her lifelong slave.

Madame Wyroubova's temperament was sentimental and mystical, and her boundless affection for the Czarina was a positive danger, because it was uncritical and divorced from all sense of reality.

The Czarina could not resist so fiery and sincere a devotion. Imperious as she was, she wanted her friends to be hers, and hers alone. She only entertained friendships in which she was quite sure of being the dominating partner. Her confidence had to be rewarded by complete self-abandonment. She did not realise that it was rather unwise to encourage demonstrations of that fanatical loyalty.

Madame Wyroubova had the mind of a child, and her unhappy experiences had sharpened her sensibilities without maturing her judgment. Lacking in intellect and discrimination, she was the prey of her impulses. Her opinions on men and affairs were unconsidered but none the less sweeping. A single impression was enough to convince her limited and puerile understanding. She at once classified people, according to the impression they made upon her, as "good" or "bad,"—in other words, "friends" or "enemies."

It was with no eye to personal advantage, but out of a pure affection for the Imperial family and her desire to help them, that Madame Wyroubova tried to keep the Czarina posted as to what was going on, to make her share her likes and dislikes, and through her to influence the course of affairs at Court. But in reality she was the docile and unconscious, but none the less mischievous, tool of a group of unscrupulous individuals who used her in their intrigues. She was incapable either of a political policy or considered aims, and could not even guess what was the game of those who used her in their own interests. Without any strength of will, she was absolutely under the influence of Rasputin and had become his most fervent adherent at Court.

I had not seen the *staretz* since I had been at the palace, when one day I met him in the anteroom as I was preparing to go out. I had time to look well at him as he was taking off his cloak. He was very tall, his face was emaciated, and he had piercing grey-blue eyes under thick bushy eyebrows. His hair was long, and he had a long beard like a peasant. He was wearing a Russian smock of blue silk drawn in at the waist, baggy black trousers, and high boots.

This was our one and only meeting, but it left me with a very uncomfortable feeling. During the few moments in which our looks met I had a distinct impression that I was in the presence of a sinister and evil being.

Life in Political Exile

While Lenin was operating from exile abroad, other Russian revolutionaries, including those of an earlier generation as well as some of Lenin's contemporaries, were spending their lives in exile within Russia. One of the most famous of these earlier exiles was Mme. Breshko-Breshkovskaya, whose active political life spans the period from the *Narodniki* to the *Bolsheviks*. The following selection consists of an introduction, which identifies Mme. Breshkovskaya (as she was usually known), and several letters written by her from her Siberian exile in 1910 and 1911. The source is: Warren B. Walsh, "Some Breshkovskaya Letters," *The American Slavic and East European Review*. Vol. IV, nos. 10–11 (December, 1945). Pp. 128–140, *passim*.

Ekaterina Konstantinova Breshko-Breshkovskaya, née Verigo, was born in 1844 in the Vitebsk District and brought up on a large estate in the Chernigov District. Her father was the scion of an aristocratic Polish family and her mother was a member of the Russian aristocracy. Madame Breshkovskaya grew up in wealth and comfort with an assured social position. Her parents were liberally inclined, and she explained her own liberalism as being founded upon her father's teachings and influence. However, Madame Breshkovskaya went far to the left of her father's mild liberalism.

As a girl in her late teens, Madame Breshkovskaya went to St. Petersburg, where she at once became an active member of the liberal and revolutionary groups which centered around the University. Like others of her class among the intelligentsia, she was driven to the left by conviction and by a mysterious compulsion to expiate the sins of her peers. She became a follower of Mikhail Bakunin and an active member of the Narodniki.

Madame Breshkovskaya married in 1869. Her husband was of liberal persuasion, but, as had been the case with her father, Madame Breshkovskaya soon left him behind both literally and figuratively. Freed of family ties, Madame Breshkovskaya plunged wholeheartedly into her work among the peasants.

In 1874 she was arrested by the tsarist police and lodged in jail for some four years before being tried. At the trial she was not only found guilty, but also given an especially harsh sentence because she had had the temerity to deny the competence of the court. The sentence was for five years at hard labor in the mines at Kara. Madame Breshkovskaya served ten months at the mines and was then sent to Barguzin. An attempt at escape in 1881 resulted in recapture and the additional sentence of forty lashes and four years in the Kara mines. The flogging was not executed but she had to serve her term at Kara.

At the conclusion of this period, she was sent to Seleginsk where she remained for eight years. It was there that the American journalist, Mr. George Kennan, saw her and interviewed her. His account of that meeting, set as it was against the background of his exposé of the exile system, served to introduce Madame Breshkovskaya to American liberals.[1]

After her release from surveillance at Seleginsk, Madame Breshkovskaya was held in Siberia for four years longer but, as a "free exile," she was allowed to travel throughout the region. She returned to European Russia in 1896 after twenty-two years of imprisonment and exile. Promptly she set about her travels, organizing the Social Revolutionary Party of which she was one of the founders.[2] After many narrow escapes from the police she went into voluntary exile in 1903 for safety's sake. The next year she came to the United States, where she was enthusiastically received by liberal groups, especially by the "Society of American Friends of Russian Freedom."[3]

Following the 1905 Revolution, Madame Breshkovskaya continued her agitation against the tsarist government and was again arrested, along with her collaborator, Dr. Nicholas Chaikovski, in 1908. Dr. Chaikovski was released on bail and, at their trial, found not guilty. Madame Breshkovskaya, however, was kept in the prison fortress of Ss. Peter and

[1] George Kennan, *Siberia and the exile system,* two vols., The Century Co., N.Y., 1891. See II, 54, 119–122.

[2] There is a very brief statement concerning this activity of Madame Breshkovskaya in *Istoriya graždanskoi voiny v SSSR,* Moscow, 1938, I, 286.

[3] For information on this movement, see Alice Stone Blackwell (ed.), *The little grandmother of the Russian revolution; reminiscences and letters of Catherine Breshkovsky,* Little, Brown & Co., Boston, 1918, pp. 111–132, 332–333.

Paul until her trial and then was again sentenced to exile in Siberia. She arrived at Kirensk, her place of exile, in August, 1910. Later she seems to have been moved to Minussinsk, where news of the February (OS) Revolution reached her.

Returning immediately to western Russia, Madame Breshovskaya threw herself into the task of leading the Social Revolutionaries. The revolution had gone beyond her, as she had once outsped her contemporaries. In the Moscow State Conference, in the Pre-Parliament and in the Constituent Assembly she was the leader and spokesman of the right wing S.Rs.[4] Her cause lost after the October (OS) Revolution, Madame Breshkovskaya went again into exile abroad. After some wanderings, she settled in Prague. Her last years were largely spent in agitation against the Soviet regime, a fact which led Leon Trotsky to write of her: ". . . [Mme. Breshkovskaya] called 'the grandmother of the Russian Revolution,' but who zealously forced herself as godmother on the Russian counter-revolution."[5]

There was a spate of magazine articles about Madame Breshkovskaya in the years from 1917 to 1920. Thereafter she faded from notice, and in the last twenty-odd years there have been only about a half dozen short articles about her in the English language periodicals. Her death in 1934 brought only two short notices in American magazines. There are two books in English concerning Ekaterina Konstantinova Breshko-Breshkov-skaya: her letters which have already been cited; and *Hidden springs of the Russian Revolution; Personal memoirs of Katerina Breshkovskaya,* edited by Lincoln Hutchinson.[6]

The Kennan Collection of the New York Public Library contains a number of the Breshkovskaya letters.[7] All but two of these letters, which appear to be typescript copies of Madame Breshkovskaya's original letters to Miss Blackwell, were published in *The Little Grandmother,* etc. However, four of the published letters were presented *in extenso* but not *in toto,* and not always with accuracy. The omitted material gives a fuller and more vivid picture of Madame Breshkovskaya. I have retained Madame Breshkovskaya's original spelling and grammar except where correction was necessary to ensure understanding. Miss Blackwell, probably out of

[4] *Istoriya graždanskoi voiny,* pp. 240, 260; William H. Chamberlin, *The Russian Revolution,* two vols., The Macmillan Co., N.Y., 1935, II, 20, 451. See also Chernov, Mayor, *et al.*

[5] Leon Trotsky, *History of the Russian Revolution,* three vols., Simon & Shuster, N.Y., 1932, I, 230.

[6] Published in 1931 by the Stanford University Press.

[7] Avrahm Yarmolinsky, *The Kennan Collection,* N.Y. Public Library, N.Y., 1921. Dr. Yarmolinsky reported (p. 4) that about 40 of these letters had not been used in compiling the American edition of *The little grandmother,* etc. Upon later investigation, Dr. Yarmolinsky reported that "only about half a dozen of the letters have apparently remained unpublished" (letter to WBW, 2/Nov/44), and this was confirmed by Mr. Paul N. Rice of the Library staff (letter to WBW, 29/Dec/44).

pride for her friend, corrected both the English and the spellings of the letters. I have not made editorial comments, since these may be found in Miss Blackwell's work.

THE LETTERS

1.

Kirensk, Nov. 10, 1910[8]

I wanted to write you a cheerful and jolly letter as both these states of mind are not foreign to me,—on the contrary it is long a time since I have laughed as much as since my return to the world from the solitary confinement; and here I often laugh at every trifle and lovingly look at the few youngsters who like to take care of me and whom I like to see about me. But just on account of these youngsters I suffer a good deal of discomfort at present, not to say sorrow.

From the very beginning it was known that every one calling on me was entered on the "book of life." In the course of time it came to the notice of the police supervisor that some called on me seldom, others more frequently; that some did not stay long, others remained to chop wood, sweep out the rooms, go for provisions, or else to work at some foreign language or sit and wait until the time came to close the chimney with its heavy flue-plates; or else to take the old lady out for an airing or to the bathhouse and back, a trip of almost a half mile.# All these services were undertaken, mostly by those who had more time at their disposal, who had no necessary work the whole day.#

Particularly there was a young man living within a mile and half from the town, behind the Lena, supporting himself by odd jobs with little help from his relatives. He came every day after dinner for two or three hours; he was very kind to me and very attentive to all my household needs. He got into trouble once because he had given me a ride in his boat (it was only in the beginning of September) and now he is being constantly reminded that he has no right to remain in the city after eight o'clock in the evening. I have already told you that in Kirensk itself live only those who have obtained special permission (a few only) or those who are under special surveillance, like "poor" me; the rest have to live on the other side of the rivers and go a long way to their work. But as there is a dock on the other side as well, many work there in Glotov's steamboat shops, and in the city there are Gromov's work shops.

Well, about a month ago, another young man came, an assistant-surgeon# who does not want to practice in such places, where there are

[8] Miss Blackwell, *op. cit.*, pp. 197–202, dated this letter Nov. 10, 1911, and said that it was written to Dr. Chaikovski. Internal evidence suggests that it was written in 1910, not long after Madame Breshkovskaya's arrival in Kirensk. The last lines of the letter, which Miss Blackwell did not print, seem to indicate that it was not written to Dr. Nicholas Chaikovski. Passages which were not published by Miss Blackwell are indicated by the # sign at the beginning and end, but no attempt is made to indicate changes involving only a few words. The parentheses appear in the typescript copies.

neither medicines nor any other hygienic necessities.# He got employment as a carpenter at the city wharf, quickly made a success of this trade, and was already in hopes that by the end of the winter he would overcome all the difficulties and secrets of carpentry and house-painting, and in the spring would open somewhere a shop of his own. Being inclined to do favors for close friends, he called on me daily after his work and gave me massage treatment; in the afternoon he would call to take his scanty portion for dinner so as not to have to go one and a half miles to attend to me in whatever it might be necessary.

It appears that this sort of laborious life was considered a crime: ispravnik (district captain of police) has taken away from him his passport (a yearly one for travelling over the Kirensk district, which he had just obtained) then arrested him, imprisoned him, and on Saturday he is sending him away escorted by gendarmes to that volost (district) from which the assistant-surgeon had come to Kirensk. This was the Mukhtuiskaya volost, 700 versts down the Lena nearer to Iakutsk, a starving settlement where there is no work, deserted by its own population and filled with convict settlers who think it less dangerous to escape from there and be caught again than to remain there without work and without bread, #the price of which has reached four roubles a pood (36 lbs).#

Then again yesterday and today they are summoning other persons also to the police for examination, a short list of seven or eight names, alleged to be people particularly intimate with me. On another list all those who visit my hut are recorded and what will be done with them I cannot imagine, unless they station an armed guard to drive away all those who step upon my grass-plots. Aside from the fact that I like people generally, that a feeling of gratitude is deeply lodged in me, that distressed young lives are particularly affecting to me, so that I am simply ashamed to be the cause of anybody's misfortune or trouble,—I see that complete loneliness threatens me within a short time, either in the form of a hut prison here, in Kirensk, or somewhere in Bulum, on the Arctic Ocean, where they send exiles for complete isolation. What are they afraid of and what they imagine I cannot understand at all; I know only that I would rather stay in Bulum with white bears than to see how, on account of me, they are persecuting other people and depriving them of bread and of the most necessary freedom. They are even going to send away the sick so that they may not pass by me on their way to the hospital.

#I think, in fact I am sure, that all these precautions against some supposed great danger are being undertaken simply through the zeal of the whole hierarchical system (ladder) which creates fictitious causes not having any actual ones. Who could know, if not those who are persecuted, whether there is any ground for the persecution. And I know that there is absolutely no ground, and that all# their tricks, as the local police say, are the fruits of idle imagination and the attractive prospect of honors and promotion. But how can others be expected to endure all these pleasant jokes. In other words, one cannot be sure of a single day. I personally am used to these conditions of all my long life; nothing surprises me nor will surprise me in regard to that. But young hearts cannot feel hardened as well, and every unexpected unreasonable blow baffles them and leads to an enormous loss of energy. It is a good thing, however, that people are not angry at me and whence come these evil machinations, spreading out, net after net—plague take them!

#Today the books "Sovremenny Mir" (#10 arrived and I was very glad, because I shall be able to satisfy the demands of the poor volosts, which do not receive anything. Three magazines ("Viestnik Znania") and three papers (the promised "Retch," and "Russkoye Slovo" sent by some-one from Moscow), "Russkiya Vedomosti" will be good for sending about after they have been read at home; and you might send some illustrated magazines like "Nature and People," for which, by the way, Dr. N. N. [?] writes, as I have just noticed in an advertisement. Best of all let them send subscription "2," as it has a supplement with a good many pictures; you know pictures in prison and in exile give good food for the imagination, which is dulled by the eternal monotony. Another thing, the editor of the "Rusk [sic] Boz" has forwarded eight books, but no more, and "Viestn. Znania" none at all. In the meantime I ask not only for the magazines but for books of different kinds published by them.#

There is a common library here, but through the preponderance of foolish voters it has passed into the hands of careless people, so that now it will be either ruined entirely or reorganized in a more or less remote future. Since this mess was made before my time I do not intend to be responsible for it, the more so as I would be compelled to deal with various antagonistic interests. Therefore, I prefer to receive the books myself and to give them to whomever it seems best, keeping order and system. Do not think that I am greedy for myself personally; I do not read so very much, only what is necessary, but young brains need food.

Now the boasting begins: Today at last came the package with my prison belongings (coat, dresses, etc.). Taking into account things sent by you and donations received on the road and here, it appears that I have a half a dozen "costumes," one finer than the other. In other words, such a wealth as I have never before accumulated since I was born. I have hung them about the walls and I look at them and think: what shall I do with all these things even if I should order a wardrobe! And as to "handkerchiefs," gloves, little rags that have been sent—so many have accumulated that I can't imagine where to put it all. To my relief your gingham will go for shirts for the boys (I intend to cut as many as four out of 15 arshin) and for rags—

The new handkerchiefs I have given away to neighbors who have been kind to me and everything that is old I have left for myself except for the beautiful blanket which I hide under my pillow in the day time and at night spread over my ordinary every-day one which has seen many things in its days. It seems that even my old cloak is about ready to go into retirement. I have acquired two wadded coats and a few warm skirts—in a word—enough to get married on (such a bride) and the people are still dissatisfied and are always grumbling: a fur coat, grandma, a fur coat, by all means a fur coat. . . . I will show them a fur coat! Soon I shall have a bear skin for my feet and so far nothing but a "calf skin" from Iakutsk lies under my table as a beautiful rug and warms my feet which are clothed in felt shoes and rubbers. The hut would be good in every respect but there is a draft from the floor and the cold comes in. But we shall overcome that with the bear's help.

Heigh-ho! my life, nothing but a genuine carnival.

Abundant of earthly gifts and sincere love of the kind friends more than the wickedness of the enemies; so that the cup of joy outweighs that of bitterness. Just now, for instance, I have returned from my walk carrying in my hands a package of pies; one made of fish; another of carrots,—got them without paying a penny, and they took pleasure in wrapping them up in a newspaper. And if my clothes have to be washed, kind women are found (from our own circle) who will take them and wash them. But I myself like to freeze my washing out on the line in front of my window.

Oh what a great surprise for Boris and Marusia my hut would be, also to their friends. Only the heating of my little stove and baking potatoes in it would fill up many hours of the most pleasant occupation. The tin of which my samovar is made even reflects the moonlight during the night and its bright shining is the cause of no little admiration. And the small, queer cupboard, turned on one side,—that is my pantry—and my small windows consisting of a lot of little pieces of glass, and finally a hole in the wall opposite the stove, from which sometimes the bright sun beams full on the splinters of wood scattered upon the stove. This hole is open and many eyes have witnessed it, but how many that are not known nobody has any idea. But neither myself nor anybody else objects, since owing to these ventilators the air in the house is fine and no one ever has any headache #and it is easy to breathe. And only two roubles for thus hut, and one rouble for the water and but one and a half [?] of wood has been used for the months of September and October and there is enough yet for half of November; three roubles fifty copeins [sic] was paid for it. That's how we live—cheaply and well. Many kisses and thanks to you, my dear sister, for your care without which we could not live. Blessings to your children and embrace to your husband, remembrances and love to all the little ones.#

2.⁹

#Copy of post-card from Mrs. Breshkovsky to Alice Stone Blackwell.

Some days ago I sent a large envelope with letters addressed to many of my friends, praying you, dearest, to read them all and despatch them. There was written about my wanting of winter clothes: An overcoat, trousers, boots, and a cap. All these things shall be *warm* and *light*. Myself, I will never be able to get anything that is new and comfortable. You know why! Now it is the measure of these dresses:

⁹ Hitherto unpublished. No place or date is given, but the card was presumably written from Kirensk early in 1911.

The length:	132 centimetres
The breast:	112 centimetres
The arm:	63 centimetres
The foot:	31 centimetres
The head:	62 centimetres

So long and so large ought to be the clothes: The pelisse's length on its exterior side, and all other numbers for the interior side of the dresses. Kissing your hands, I pray pardon.#

. . .

5.[10]

#Copy of post-card from Mme. Breshkovsky to Alice Stone Blackwell. This card has the picture of a poor hut, roof and ground all covered with snow. Dated 8/21 September.

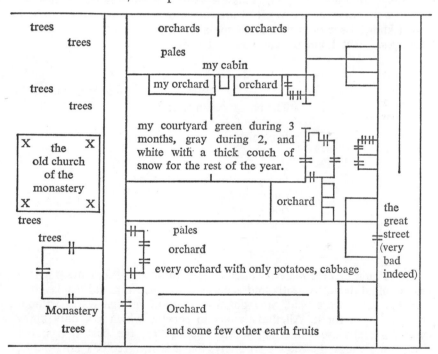

My cabin is much better as this one. Now I intend to inhabit a little mansion quite clean and bright. But there are new clouds about my existence of every days, and I will not be astonished when one of these days they come and take me away—don't know where. Searches and espionage do not cease. I never sure to awake in my own rooms. But all that does not matter. I am well and shall remain so. If removed to another place I will try to make you hear of your sister as well as till now. Never

[10] Hitherto unpublished.

afraid of the future for myself; for my heart and my mind will remain faithful to their creed. And my love and gratitude to you forever, for my sister.#

. . .

#My writings are till now in the hands of my foes and I am sure never to get them. I am sorry of it, but accustomed as I am to every sort of evils, I never mind, and hope only to realize my wishes to be understood by the youth of our country another time more propice to it.—Wishing to keep all your letters safe I do not keep them with me and often forget the quantity of those I received. Often do not answer the questions included there.— In my life, outside the change of dwelling for a better one,# there is a change concerning my custody: now there are four men spies going around my house and looking into my windows. They are two to accompany me when I am going out. This escort is so disgusting that I have no wish to walk out of doors. What of are they afraid to keep me imprisoned, I don't know! I see only they think me able to vanish like a cloud before their eyes.# But I am patient and will endure.

. . .

7.[11]

#The parcel contained:
    two night-gowns
    two shirts
    two pair drawers
    four pair stockings
    two pair gloves
    one overcoat
    one jacket
    one girdle
    one pair shoes
    one cap.   #

Everything of best material and made with accomplishment. #It is a pity to unfold them, so neatly and accurately they are put and displayed.# Even the duties were paid. So I got a quantity of foreign wares without paying a kopek for it. All that thanks to persons which not only know where the crabs are wintering, where one can get the best things, but which can arrange the matter so finely, that the receiver has no trouble, no outlay, all he shall do is to take and to use. #So it is with me. Till now I have not suffered from cold, for I never venture to go out. My dwelling is not so cold as to be frozen. But the highest degrees of cold are waiting on us yet.

[11] The first page of this letter is missing from the Kennan collection. Miss Blackwell, *op. cit.*, printed a few lines from this section as part of a letter to Mrs. Barrows, written Nov. 8/21, 1911. No place is given but it is obviously Kirensk.

	bath room	kitchen		cold closet
All is right in this house: water, wood, food, plenty, Platon [?] excellent.	bed	oven	cold antechamber	enough space, light and air
	my room Eng. book	dining room	little court yard	

TWO SPIES	THE STREET

I am so eagerly surveyed by the spies, that I cannot be sure you are getting all my letters, even as innocent as they are. Now I am sorry not to wire you some words of my hearty gratitude, dear friend, sister, and other friends. You can and must represent your selves what joy and what sympathy evoques in my soul your constant care and benevolence.

Yours forever,#

Russia Between Revolutions

Among the foreign observers and students of Russia in the early twentieth century, no one was more highly regarded by his peers than Harold Williams. A scholar, an accomplished linguist, and a penetrating observer, Mr. Williams wrote one of the best general descriptions of Russia as it was between the Revolution of 1905 and the fall of the monarchy in 1917. The following selections are from this book: *Russia of the Russians*. New York: Charles Scribner's Sons, 1915. Pp. 54–61, 333–350, 363–369.

The Civil Service

It would be quite wrong to say that the Russian Civil Service is wholly composed of bureaucrats pure and simple. There are bureaucrats, a great many of them, and there are also a number of Government employees who to-day are more or less tinged with the bureaucratic spirit, but to-morrow would do their duty just as well or even better if a Constitutional regime were in full swing. The Russian Government Service, taken as a whole, includes a large number of interesting types, from elegant men of the world to that pettifogging Dryzasdust familiarly known as a "Chancellory rat," from the rough red-faced police captain to the mild-mannered bespectacled excise clerk, from the dried-up martinet at the head of a St.

Petersburg department to the slow-moving, long-haired country postmaster. Governors, senators, clerks of court, tax collectors, school-inspectors, telegraph clerks, customs officials, wardens of the peasantry, heads of consistories, all are engaged in the business of the Empire, all are formally in the service of the Tsar. It is a State in uniform. The very schoolboys wear uniform, and even high-school girls have to wear brown dresses and brown aprons. Ministers wear uniforms, not in the routine of work in St. Petersburg, but on State occasions and when they travel about the country. Judges wear uniforms, and so do Government engineers and land-surveyors, and a host of other people whose salary filters down through many channels from the St. Petersburg Treasury. Brass buttons and peaked caps, peaked caps and brass buttons, uniforms with blue, red, or white facings meet the eye with wearisome monotony from end to end of the Empire, from the Pacific to the Danube. A Russian may wear uniform his whole life long. As a little boy of eight he goes proudly off to a preparatory school in a long grey overcoat, reaching almost to the ground, and in a broad-crowned cap with the peak tilted over his snub nose. When school days are over he dons the uniform of a student, and after a few years at University or Technical College, enters a Ministry and puts on one of the many official uniforms. The years pass, he is gradually promoted, and at fifty he is trudging in uniform with portfolio under his arm to his Ministry, just as with bag on shoulders he tramped to school when he was a little boy of eight.

All the Government officials are *Chinovniks,* that is to say, each of them stands in a definite *chin,* or rank. Peter the Great established an order of promotion called the *Table Rangov,* or Table of Ranks, and this order is in force to the present day. Once a man is drawn into the subtle mechanism of the Table of Ranks he may go on from grade to grade with hardly an effort on his part, by the mere fact of existing and growing wrinkled and grey-haired. When he enters the Government service he receives a paper called the *formulinary spisok* or Formular List, in which the events of his life are noted down from year to year—his appointment to a particular table in the Ministry of Justice, his marriage, the birth of his children, his leave, his illnesses, his appointment to a commission or committee, his despatch on special service, and then the long series of decorations and promotions, various degrees of the Order of St. Anne, St. Stanislav, St. Vladimir, and it may be high up on the last rungs of the bureaucratic ladder such coveted decorations as the Order of St. Andrew, or even the White Eagle. The orders are a reward for good service. But the *chins,* or grades, need not necessarily be so. A *chinovnik* may be promoted from grade simply for "having served the due term of years," as the phrase is, but his promotion may be hastened through favour in high places or in recognition of special diligence or ability. The names of grades have no meaning except as indicating the grade. They are the same throughout the civil service, and give no suggestion of the office held by the possessor. They were originally adapted from German titles, and look imposing when re-translated into German. Thus the grade of *nadvorny sovietnik* is not a particularly high one, but when it appears in German as Hofrat, or Court Councillor, the impression is given that the possessor is a personage of considerable importance. But the really important *chins* are that of *Staatsky Sovietnik,* which is perhaps not so important as it looks in its German guise of Staatsrath, or Councillor of State, but seems to secure a man against undue caprices on the part of Fortune, and to invest him with an air of respectability; and then the grades that make the man who attains to them a noble if he is not one by birth. There is a *chin* that conveys personal nobility, and the *chin* of *dieistvitelny staatsky sovietnik,* or Real State Councillor, conveys hereditary nobility. In this way the ranks of the gentry are constantly recruited from the bureaucracy, and the traditional connection between rank and Government service is maintained in actual practice. The grade of Real State Councillor also conveys the rank of a general in the Civil Service and the title of Excellency. The average *chinovnik* thinks himself happy if he reaches such as an exalted *chin* as this. Most professors become Real State Councillors by virtue of length of service, and it sounds odd to hear a stooping, frock-coated gentleman who is distinguished as an able lecturer on mediæval history, spoken of as a general. The grades of Secret Councillor and Real State Councillor are reserved for very old or for very distinguished members of the Civil Service, for ministers and ambassadors, and the like.

The system of grades is one of the forces that hold the bureaucracy together. It secures a certain uniformity of temper, tendency and aim. Russians are the most democratic people in the world, but this carefully adjusted system of grades, decorations, money premiums and, to close with, pensions, corresponding to the *chin* attained, appeals to an ineradicable human instinct for outward symbols of position, security and distinction, and makes of the bureaucracy a world apart, a world in which the interests of all the members are interwoven. It is curious how mortified even a Radical magistrate will be if his name fails to appear among the Real State Councillors in the annual promotion list, and, on the other hand, with what unalloyed pleasure he receives congratulations if he has been given the coveted grade after all. But there is another very characteristic feature of the bureaucracy, and that is its extraordinary centralisation. From the big dreary-looking yellow or brown buildings in St. Petersburg, in which the Ministries are housed, currents of authority, or directive energy go forth to all the ends of the great Empire in the form of telegrams or occasional oral messages by special couriers, but above all in the form of endless "papers." Pens scratch, typewriters click, clerks lay blue covers full of papers before the "head of the table"; the "head of the table" sends them to the "head of the department," to the Assistant Minister, if need be, and in the more important cases, the Assistant Minister to the Minister. Then back go the papers again with signatures appended, down through various grades for despatch to a judge, to another department, to a Governor, to a *chinovnik* on special service, or to some petitioner from the world without. Incoming and outgoing papers are the systole and diastole of the Chancelleries. All sorts of documents go under the general name of *bumaga* or "paper," from a warrant for arrest to a report on a projected railway, or a notification of taxes due. There are *doklady* or reports, and *otnoshenia* or communications between officials of equal rank, and *donesenia* or statements made to superiors, *predpisania* instructions or orders, and *proshenia,* applications or petitions. These and a hundred others besides, are all "Papers," and there is a special style for each of them, and a general dry and formal style for all of them known as the "Chancellery Style," which permeates Russian public life, and creeps into private letters and concert programmes, and newspaper articles, and into the very love-making of telegraph clerks waiting for trains on wayside stations. The "papers," their colour, the stamps upon them, their style, create an immense uniformity of mental content, and tend to level down the striking differences that exist between say, the Tartar policemaster in a town on the Caspian Sea, and the son of a Russian priest who serves as a clerk in the financial department in Tver. It is extraordinary discipline. The lack of variety in the system increases its hold on all its members. There are hardly any of the curious divergencies and inconsistencies of which the English administrative system is so full, hardly any quaint anachronisms left to linger on because of some wise use they have for the affections. There are certain inevitable modifications in the Caucasus, in Central Asia, in Bessarabia and in Siberia, Poland and the Baltic Provinces. But, generally speaking, the system as outlined in mathematical order on smooth white paper, is embodied with surprising accuracy in the network of institutions that cover the great plain from limit to limit. Authority is delegated from the big yellow Ministers in St. Petersburg to the dreary white buildings in the head towns of the governments or territories into which the whole Empire is mapped out, and from the government towns to the head towns of the districts into which each government is divided, and then down to the smallest towns and to the Wardens of the Peasantry. The uniformity of it all is both imposing and depressing, and as wearing as the inevitable redcapped stationmaster and brown-coated gendarme on every one of the scores of railway stations between Wirballen and Harbin.

The integrity and uniformity of the bureaucratic system is maintained, the system is held in its framework, so to speak, by means of the army. The army, in its turn, by means of the conscript system, subjects almost the whole male population to a uniform discipline, levels down, for a time at any rate, the distinctions between various regions and various nationalities, and serves as a most potent means of Russification. Russification, indeed, is not the word, though it is the Russian language that is used in the process, for it is not the interests of the Russian people that are primarily in question but the interests of the State. It is a moulding of all the human material of the Empire upon one State pattern, a persistent elimination of divergencies, a grandiose attempt to subordinate all the wayward impulses of 160 millions of human beings to one common aim unintelligible to the mass. The army supplies the clamps by which the vast mechanism of the bureaucracy is held in position.

But it is through the police that the bureaucracy carries out its function of maintaining order. And the police have of late years assumed an over-weening importance in the State because the bureaucracy has constantly tended more and more to limit its functions to the maintenance of order. It has subordinated everything to this end. It has become immensely suspicious. The very success, the very efficiency of the bureaucracy has been its ruin. In so far as it governed well, administered justice, prevented crime, promoted education, built roads and railways, and furthered trade, it encouraged individual initiative, fostered the desire for liberty. And at the same time it opened the eyes of many to its own corruption, to the depredations on the national wealth and welfare carried on under the veil of order, strict uniformity and long-armed discipline. On both occasions when the clamps were loosened, when the army was defeated in the Crimea in 1854-5, and in Manchuria fifty years afterwards, the evils of the bureaucracy were vividly revealed, the system almost fell asunder. Almost, but not quite. For after the Crimean War reforms were effected and the system was modernised, and again after the Japanese war reforms were granted and a further attempt was made at modernisation. But on each occasion concessions were followed by a reassertion of bureaucratic authority by means of the police. The nineteenth century was a century of movement, even in Russia. The emancipation of the serfs meant the freeing of an enormous amount of pent-up energy of economic development, it aroused a hum of fresh and vigorous movement all over the Empire. But for that strange complexity of widely extended, exclusive interests for which the bureaucracy stands, and for that rigid external uniformity which is the aim of its efforts, movement was dangerous. The bureaucracy took fright at the new, high-spirited movement of the sixties and, instead of steadily promoting economic and educational development, set to work to devise a system of checks. It tried to render its own reforms innocuous, set bureaucratic safeguards on its own judicial system, and bound and weakened those Zemstvos, or elective County Councils, which impaired the integrity of the bureaucratic system by exerting the functions of local government in thirty-four governments of European Russia. And the maintenance of order interpreted as the prevention of movement became the bureaucracy's prime care.

The Peasantry

It is the peasant who embodies most distinctly the connection with the soil, and the peasant is the most interesting person in Russia. But there are so many types of peasant, there is such a variety of character and custom that it is difficult to make general statements that will be absolutely true of all. "Not a village but has ways of its own," is a Russian saying. A Siberian peasant on the Yenisei is a very different kind of man from the Tula peasants on Leo Tolstoy's estate of Yasnaia Poliana, and the Cossack of the Don is at once distinguishable from the peasants of the northern governments of Olonets and Archangel. Within the limits of a single government very different types may be met with. In the northern districts of the Chernigov government the peasants have thin, sharp features and speak a dialect of Great Russian. In the southern districts of the same government a dark, broad-faced, broad-shouldered type prevails and the language is Little Russian. Even a single district may display considerable variations. In the Nizhnedievitsky district of the Voronezh government there are three distinct groups, known as Shchekuny, Tsukany, and Galmany, and representing clearly-defined varieties of custom, costume, dialect, and character. The Shchekuny are extremely conservative, ignorant, poor, dirty, and have the reputation of being great thieves. Their neighbours, the Tsukany, pronounce many words differently, are a trading folk, busy, open, communicative, eager for novelties; their women often wear silk and satin, whereas those of the Shchekuny wear only picturesque, old-fashioned, homespun costumes. The third group again, the Galmany, speak a slightly different dialect, are not averse from innovations, but are laughed at by their neighbours for their big, many-coloured, baggy trousers. In fact, the variety of types even within the limits of the Russian nationality is inexhaustible. There are many degrees of prosperity. Side by side with well-to-do peasants there are whole villages that live in wretched poverty. Judging by the dull-eyed, bent-shouldered White Russian peasants one sees amongst the Jews on the railway stations in the governments of Vilna and Minsk, one might easily jump to the conclusion that the White Russian peasants generally were a dead and alive, down-trodden people. Their life is certainly not a cheerful one, but that even the White Russians are not the dumb, driven cattle that many of them seem is shown by a little peasant's paper published in Vilna which prints numbers of stories and a good deal of pretty verse written by peasants, as well as reports of co-operative and educational work undertaken in various villages in the Western Governments. There are three main groups of Russians—White Russians, Little Russians, and Great Russians—and the differences between them are frequently greater than those between an educated Russian and an educated Englishman.

It would be absurd, then, to attempt to describe in a chapter the life of the Russian peasantry as a whole. In the present chapter some account may be given of certain villages on the river Volhov in the Novgorod government, not far from St. Petersburg, it being premised only that a great many of the features noted here are characteristic of all the central and northern governments of European Russia.

The village of Vladimirovo stands on the river bank about ten miles from the St. Petersburg-Moscow railway line, and about half a mile away from a large country house to which the inhabitants of the village were a little over half a century ago attached as serfs. The village consists of one street, containing about thirty-five cottages and lined with birch trees. Behind the village stretch open fields with a long line of forest in the background. The broad, swiftly-flowing river is a highway in the summer. Steamers maintain communication between the railway station and Novgorod. Great rafts of timber with red-shirted raftsmen drift from the rivers beyond Lake Ilmen down the Volhov to Lake Ladoga and so out to the Neva and St. Petersburg. Barges are towed up early in the season and come down later with timber cut small or with immense stacks of hay. Sometimes the long, yellow barges spread magnificent sails and fly many-coloured flags, and with a fair wind go floating past bright green fields triumphantly up the stream, the steersman dexterously managing the heavy rudder. Then there are curious bulging craft, painted in stripes, with covered decks and sharp stern, big rudder and coarse sails. Such vessels as these come down by various rivers from the distant Borovichi district bringing crude pottery which the boatmen sell in the villages by the way. There are plenty of fish in the river and the peasants cast their nets and catch enough for food and for sale. All through the summer the river is alive with unceasing traffic, though nowadays the trade is nothing like what it was in the Middle Ages when Novgorod was a great commercial republic, and German and Italian merchants were constantly bringing their ware up the Volkov and carrying away rich stores of furs and skins.

But in November the Volhov freezes hard and remains frozen till April. Then all the steamers and boats and barges lie still, and the river becomes simply a smooth, white road over which sleighs go gliding in a long and silent procession. But the peasants of Vladimirovo are not greatly affected by the change. Unlike the peasants of the opposite bank they do not trade and they fish very little. Considering that they live on a great river and so near the railway they are surprisingly unenterprising.

Their cottages are built of wood and are unpainted, yellow when new and grey within a year or two; with sloping shingle or thatched roofs and with the gable-end and glazed windows facing the street. The entrance is from the side. You mount a wooden staircase or ladder, push open a door, and find yourself in the upper or main floor of the cottage, the ground floor being mostly used for storage purposes. On the upper floor there may be one, too or three rooms, according to the wealth of the owner and the size of his family. A big, white-washed, brick stove occupies a promi-nent position in the main room, and on this stove the older people and the children sleep in winter. There is a rough table and a few chairs, a bed, and square, wooden trunks adorned with gaudy pictures; on the walls, cuttings from illustrated papers, in the corners ikons or sacred pictures, and in the middle of the room a child's cot suspended from the ceiling. Pots and pans on the shelves; on the landing at the head of the staircase a barrel of water and a dipper for washing—which is effected not by plung-ing and rinsing, but by getting another person to pour on the head and hands; then behind the landing lies the hay-loft where half the family sleeps in summer, and under the hay-loft is the stable. Living-rooms and stable are practically under one roof, but men and animals are far apart, and they do not herd together as is the case in Western Ireland, and the cottages are, as a rule, remarkably clean. Some of the women pile upon shelves and walls an incongruous variety of ornaments such as may often be seen in English farm-houses. Often there are pot-flowers in the win-dows. On the floor are mats of rough canvas, and occasionally there are family photographs on the walls. There is only one flower garden in the village and that exists because, in the first place, the owner's wife is cook at the manorhouse where there is a pretty garden, and in the second place the owner himself is the strong man of the village, and the boy who pulled up his narcissi would know what to expect. Behind some of the cottages are vegetable gardens with a fruit tree or two.

At the end of the village and behind many of the cottages are *banias* or Russian bath-houses, which are a necessity of life to the Northern Russians. The *bania* is a low, wooden building, containing a large brick stove on which when it is heated cold water is poured so that the room is filled with steam. There are boilers for hot water. On one side of the room there is a tier of benches, and to lie on the highest bench where the air is hottest is the most effective way of taking the bath. The bath is a combination of perspiring and washing in hot and cold water, and the peasants aid the process by beating themselves with birch twigs. In winter the youths sometimes rush out of the *bania* and roll naked in the snow. Every Saturday the villagers take their bath, and this right through the year, so that it is altogether unfair to describe the peasants of Northern and Central Russia as being indifferent to cleanliness. On the contrary, they are exceptionally scrupulous in this respect.

In the centre of the village is a shop kept by a widow-woman, where sugar, tea, sweetmeats, cotton-fabrics, and a score of odds and ends are sold at a high price, often on credit. There is a tiny chapel or rather a shrine in which services are rarely held. The parish church is several miles away, but the church in the neighbouring parish is just across the river and the Vladimirovo peasants as a rule go there when they go to church at all.

Outside the village is a big, two-storied school building where about sixty children from all the villages in the neighbourhood are taught the elements. The girls are taught sewing, and there is a carpentry class for the boys, with a special teacher and a well-furnished shop. This school, which owes its existence to the neighbouring landowner, is unusually large and well equipped. Very often in the villages the school is held in an ordinary peasant's cottage, roughly adapted for the purpose. The Vladimirovo school is now maintained by the Ministry of Education. There are two teachers, a man and a woman, and the priest from over the river gives religious instruction. The only children's festival in the year is the Christmas tree which is usually provided by the landowner's family. Then the little boys and girls march round the fir-tree in a stumbling, hot, disorderly procession and gaze in wonder at all the marvels agleam in the candlelight amongst the dark branches. They sing lustily the songs they have been taught for the occasion and are full of struggling, despairing eagerness when the time for the distribution of presents comes. On the whole, the children live a jolly life. There are so many of them and they are always trooping about the village street together, the little girls arm-in-arm and sometimes singing in imitation of their big sisters, and the little boys striding about barefoot contemptuous of mere girls with hands deep in the pockets of long, baggy, patched trousers, or else racing off at full speed when big people find them robbing birds'-nests or getting within dangerous reach of forbidden fruit trees. In winter the most absorbing care of the mothers is to see that the children are warmly clad, but in the summer the boys go mostly bareheaded and their hair is bleached to a uniform white. There is no end to the children, six, seven, or eight being quite a normal number in a family, and it is a relief to the mother if a girl of eleven or twelve can go out as nurse to a neighbour for keep, or if one of the small boys is made a shepherd lad. The bigger boys help their fathers, and the bigger girls may go out to service or else find work in the factory down the river. But in any case it is not easy to make ends meet, and the peasants frankly admit that it is not an unmixed evil if one of the children dies.

The problem of "What shall we eat, and what shall we drink, and wherewithal shall we be clothed?" is for the peasants a tolerably simple one, especially as far as eating is concerned. The staple food is home-made rye bread, which is called black, but it is not coal-black, as most of us imagined when we read German stories in our childhood, but dark brown. This bread is pleasant to the taste and very nourishing, but to assimilate it a long training is necessary. It seems ill adapted to English digestions, and the older peasants often suffer violent aches and pains as a result of its use. Black bread is the staple, and the peasant can do an enormous amount of field-work on black bread alone. But this fact is not an absolute argument in favour of vegetarianism, for as soon as a peasant goes to work in a factory he finds that his strength fails him unless he eats meat; and even the workmen in a brickkiln near the village declare they cannot do without flesh food. The peasant cats meat rarely, as a rule only on festival days. But every day there is a meatless soup of some kind, most frequently *shchi,* in which preserved cabbage or sauerkraut is the chief ingredient. Potatoes are eaten as a kind of sauce or condiment to bread; altogether the chief art in eating is to find ways of consuming the largest possible quantity of bread. Barley and buckwheat porridge is frequently eaten. For special occasions the women bake *pirogi* or pasties filled with cabbage, more rarely with rice, and still more rarely with meat. On their simple but monotonous diet the peasants seem to thrive fairly well, although digestive complaints are not infrequent.

To drink there is plain water and tea. Every peasant cottage has its *samovar* or tea-urn, and tea is drunk regularly, very weak and very pale, without milk. In drinking tea a small lump of sugar is made to go a long way; a tiny morsel is bitten off and held between the teeth and gradually melts as the tea is sipped. Peasants eat slowly and with great decorum, crossing themselves before and after meals.

But there is another beverage to which the Russian peasant is greatly addicted, and that is *vodka,* a spirituous liquor as innocent-looking as water, but a most potent kind of brandy. On the whole, the peasant does not drink such an enormous amount of *vodka* as is supposed. The average consumption of alcohol per head is less in Russia than in Great Britain. But the peasant drinks at intervals. He remains sober all the week and celebrates Sundays and festival days by consuming enough *vodka* to raise his spirits; a very small quantity of *vodka* suffices to intoxicate him. On special holidays as the festival of the patron saint of the village, there is heavy drinking, often leading to fierce quarrels in which knives are used; and sometimes murders are committed. Vodka-selling is the monopoly of the State. All over the country there are Government brandy-shops, in which the salesman or saleswoman hands out through a hole in a netting like that of a telegraph office bottles from long rows of shelves like those in a dispensary, for consumption off the premises. There is no State brandy-shop in Vladimirovo, but during one year there was a great deal of illicit grog-selling, and that was a bad time for the village, for the men were always drinking and their earnings melted away. Then the women revolted and took matters into their own hands. They went about the village and broke the windows in the cottages of the sly grog-sellers and made them give up the trade. Only one they left in peace. She was a widow, and they gave her permission to sell *vodka* until she could save enough to buy a cow. After this revolt the peasants were compelled to make journeys to other villages when they needed brandy. The women in this district do not drink, but that is not the case everywhere. In some of the districts around Moscow the women drink at least as much as the men and make a boast of doing so. And the nearer peasants are to the cities or to manufacturing districts the more they drink and the more demoralised they become. Sometimes a revulsion of feeling occurs, and in Vladimirovo several of the hardest drinkers occasionally go to the priest and take a vow not to drink, or in other words sign the pledge for six months or more. And although they are by no means pious men they keep their vow.

. . . The question of dress in the country is at once simpler and more difficult than it used to be. In former days all garments were home-made, the fashions remained unchanged for generations and valuable costumes were handed down from mother to daughter and long kept in the family as heirlooms. In the remoter districts, where the influence of the cities is not strongly felt, the older costumes are still worn, and often the women's costumes are complicated and beautiful, with gorgeous headgear and veils and rich adornment or silver coins of various times and peoples. Occasionally, as in some villages on the Gulf of Finland near St. Petersburg, the old costumes are retained in defiance of the factories and proudly worn on Sundays. But in Vladimirovo the modern spirit rules. Of the typical, red, close-fitting woman's dresses known as the *sarafan,* which is eagerly sought after as a curiosity, not a specimen is now to be found in the village; probably all have been cut up or worn to shreds. There are a few spinning-wheels and rough hand-looms, and the women weave a kind of coarse canvas and linen table-cloths and towels from the flax which is one of the staple crops in the district. Some of the women embroider for sale. But most of the clothing material comes from the factories. About once a month a Tartar comes round with a waggon full of cotton fabrics, and of these the peasants buy what they need for their garments. The women make their own and the children's clothing and also the men's shirts or blouses. In the autumn a tailor goes from cottage to cottage and makes rough suits and overcoats for the men. There is a feltmaker, too, who makes the round of the villages and beats out felt for winter boots. Very often nowadays the men buy their clothing ready-made, and the boys have to be content with more or less clumsy adaptations of their father's or elder brother's garments.

In the district here described, and this is true of most districts near the main highways, the women dress in cotton skirts and blouses, and on their heads wear coloured cotton kerchiefs. The men wear a kind of rough European dress—German dress they call it here—with high boots and cotton blouses, known as Russian shirts, and in colder weather double-breasted coats buttoned up to the neck. Their head-gear is usually a soft peaked cap. On Sundays the younger men flaunt shining top-boots and gaudily embroidered shirts. The younger women are quickly adapting town fashions which they probably bring home from the factory down the river where so many of them are employed. The daughter of a compara-tively poor peasant will walk on Sundays in elaborate dresses of a town pattern; none of them dare yet do such an unheard-of thing as wear a hat in the village, though probably they have hats stored away. But it is to be feared that some of them have already gone so far as to complete their transformation by wearing false hair. *O tempora, O mores!*

The inhabitants of Vladimirovo are neither well-to-do nor very poor. They are not geniuses and are not enterprising, but they are no fools, and they are not stubbornly conservative. They have no pronounced political opinions of any kind, take things very much as they come, rarely read newspapers, although during the war and the revolutionary years some of them went so far as to subscribe to the cheaper journals. Few of the men read books, but sometimes the younger women and girls read the story-books to be found in the school library. Nearly all the men have served in the army, but it is difficult to see what trace army life has left on them. Several served in the Japanese War and took part in some of the fiercest engagements, but they tell of their experiences in a humdrum way without the slightest display of emotion. One snub-nosed, broad-cheeked peasant, Alexei, received for his services in the war a premium of £50, which he spent on building a new cottage. He was also appointed military instructor in the school under the new boy-scout system, and aroused the merriment of the whole countryside by his attempts to drill rebellious schoolboys into the proper use of wooden guns. There are hardly any among the villagers who remember the days of serfdom. An old forester and his wife can sometimes be induced to recall the time when they were serfs. But they will not admit that there was any profound and essential difference be-tween then and now, except that in the old days a peasant was bound to be more industrious, which they are inclined to consider was rather a good thing. A former blacksmith, Gerasim, now dead, used to tell with pride that he was rarely flogged and enjoyed the favour of his master, who got him a very pretty bride, naturally also a serf, from another estate of his about twenty miles away. Gerasim fell in love with her at first sight, but he seems to have been a dull fellow and by no means handsome, and the girl cried her eyes out at being compelled to marry him. There was no help for it. It was the master's will, and they were the master's property. But for months after the marriage the bride would not look at Gerasim and turned her back on him every time he approached her. Of the stern master who effected this marriage and who lived in the early part of the last century it is related, amongst other things, that during haymaking and harvest he used to stand on a hill and watch the work through a telescope; any peasant who showed sign of slackness he immediately had flogged. But the pre-emancipation period with its three days a week of compulsory labour on the big estate, the constant floggings, the purchase and sale of men and women, is a fading memory now. The younger generation has hardly an idea of what serfdom meant.

The effects of serfdom linger on, however, in Vladimirovo in a very curious way. Most of the peasants are very good fellows, not idle, and some of them witty and original. But, on the whole, they are strangely flaccid and lacking in initiative, and this is characteristic of most of the villages for a considerable distance along the left bank of the river. On the right bank a very different spirit is manifested. Just opposite Vladimirovo is a large village called Vysoko, which the German traveller, Olearius, notes having visited during his journeys up to Novgorod in the seventeenth century. Here the peasants are much more prosperous, are more industrious, better dressed, have better houses, are more wide-awake and alert, more receptive of new ideas, more enterprising in every way. The chief explanation of the difference is a very simple one. Along the left bank the peasants were the serfs of private landowners. On the right bank they were the serfs of the State, which meant that after the payment of a heavy tax a great deal of room was left for individual initiative. Then there is one other important fact that accounts for the difference in character. The villages on the right bank are the remains of the military settlements founded by Count Arakcheiev early in the nineteenth century. Arakcheiev was a fierce disciplinarian, and applied martial law to field-work and to every detail of life in the settlements. With the help of the cat-o'-nine-tails he got a fine highroad lined with birch trees built from Gruzino some distance down the river to Saraia Rusa beyond Lake Ilmen. The discipline was intolerable, and led to a terrible revolt which was ferociously quelled. But the sense of order and duty inculcated in the settlements in Arak-cheiev's stern days has left its impress on the character of the inhabitants of the right bank until now. At the present time the difference between the two banks makes itself continually felt, and while the left bank on the whole remains passive and is sunk in routine, the right bank is undergoing some very remarkable changes. But before describing these changes it is necessary to give some account of the prevailing system of peasant land tenure and of the *mir* or village commune.

In Vladimirovo, which is a small village, the commune exists in a simple form. All the peasants of the village hold their land in common, and there is no rented or bought land to complicate ownership rights. Fifty years ago at the time of the emancipation the Vladimirovo peasants received a portion of the land of the estate to which they had been attached. This land was in effect purchased by them, but the purchase was made through the State, the peasants gradually extinguishing their debt in the form of annual redemption payments which constituted an extra tax. The State in its turn compensated the landlord by means of a complex financial operation. The result, as far as the Vladimirovo peasants were concerned, was that they secured in all about 630 acres of land. The way they put it is that they received 5½ desiatins per soul, a "soul" then being a male householder. At the time of the emancipation there were forty-six souls, so that the total amount was 253 desiatins. This land was divided up amongst the members of the community in such a way that each received his share of forest, meadow, and field. But the system of allotment is a very curious one. If each peasant had his lot in one compact area he could deal with it fairly easily. This is not the case. Justice requires that good and bad soil, forest and bog, the far lands and the near lands should be as nearly as possible equally apportioned. So the land is cut up into narrow strips, and these strips cause considerable confusion, especially if they happen to become entangled with Crown lands or with landlords' land or land that has been bought or rented by individual peasants. This overlapping of strips is one of the most perpetually irritating of land problems in Russia.

In Vladimirovo, however, this particular difficulty is felt less acutely than in other villages, because the peasants' land is fairly clearly marked off from that of the estate on one side, and from that of the neighbouring village community on the other. And, indeed, the Vladimirovo peasants got such a small share of land that they have little difficulty in managing it. Every peasant knows his lot though it is not divided from others by fences or ditches, and disputes are rare. The land is owned legally by the whole community, and each member holds his land only in virtue of his membership. This does not mean, however, that all members of the community are equalised in the matter of wealth. Even if they were equalised at the beginning the lapse of years makes them unequal. The growth of population causes changes. Some families increase, others diminish and disappear. One family has many sons, each of whom has a right to land. Another family has many daughters who are married off and lost to their father's house. Sometimes if there are several males in the family, some go to work in the towns or on distant estates and leave their father or brothers to work the land which in time practically passes into the hands of the workers. Some families are industrious and enterprising, others indolent and ready to forego their rights. In fact, there is no end to the possibilities of inequality. There exists a legal corrective to the growth of irregularities in the form of a repartition which may be undertaken by the community at certain intervals. But the peasants of Vladimirovo have not once effected a repartition since the emancipation. They seem to have thought it hardly worth while. Part of the surplus of population brought by the years has gradually drifted away and left the community very little larger than it was at the time of the emancipation. And there is a natural disinclination to upset established relationships. But a considerable disproportion now exists. Some families are richer and some are poorer.

Some hold the share of two souls or more, others have only half a soul, and some have practically nothing more than the tiny plot of land on which their cottage stands.

The communal land was, until a few years ago, inalienable. It could not be sold or leased, and every peasant, so long as he was a member of the commune and had not forfeited his rights, had a certain safe and sure anchorage to which he might return when life in the world outside buffeted him too severely. The commune is a kind of mutual aid society, and the habit of united action ingrained as a result of centuries of communal life is one of the most marked features of the Russian peasants' character. Living together in a village, not scattered about on separate lots of land, possessing strongly developed social instincts, they are communicative, gossipy, given to lending and borrowing, observant of custom, retentive of tradition. And the communal system largely explains the extreme con-servatism of the Russian peasant in methods of cultivation. It is not easy to effect innovations when, after all, your land is not your own and the other members of the community resent the implied aspersion on the traditional methods. The peasants of Vergezha and all the other peasants in the neighbourhood, might get very much more out of their land than they do. With intensive culture a good deal might be done even with thirteen acres. There are, in fact, German and Lettish colonists in the district who prosper greatly on land of the same quality, but the Russian peasants have not shown the slightest disposition to adopt their methods.

The affairs of the community are managed by a *skhod,* or mote of which all the adult males are members. The *skhod* annually selects a *starosta* or elder, who on occasion summons the men for the transaction of necessary business by walking through the village, striking each cottage with a rod and crying, *"Na skhod!"* (To the mote!). In the exercise of his duties the elder is assisted by another peasant who acts as policeman, or *desiatnik.* The chief business of the starosta is to collect the taxes, to note their payment in a register and to convey them to the centre of the canton, or volost, a few miles away. The village mote discusses all matters that concern the whole village; the hire of a shepherd for the cattle during the summer months, the amount to be paid to the neighbouring landlord for the right of pasturing the herd on his estate, and many other such details of the communal life. Sometimes bigger questions are discussed. The peasants of the village of Kurino, up the river, decided some years ago after long discussion to acquire, through the Peasant's Bank, a Govern-ment institution which facilitates the purchase of land by the peasantry, a considerable portion of a neighbouring estate. The question of the interest to be paid to the Bank is now one of the many questions discussed by their mote. More general questions are occasionally touched upon. The mote may pass a resolution (called a *prigovor,* or sentence) urging the removal of an unpopular school teacher or priest, or the retention of one whose dismissal is threatened. During 1905 and 1906 many communes discussed political questions, and a large number of peasants' resolutions were sent to the First Duma demanding a great variety of reforms, chiefly concerning land-tenure. Discussions of this kind have, however, now been pretty thoroughly checked by police measures.

For the peasants are not allowed to act independently. They are under constant tutelage. All the villages in a given area called a canton or volost converge on an administrative centre in the chief village of the canton which has a cantonal mote and a cantonal court under the presidency of a *starshina,* or elder. The books of the canton are kept by a *pisar,* or secretary, who is also the mainspring of the activity of the court. In the cantonal court cases are tried by customary law, but these courts are notorious for their corruption, and it is a common saying among the peasantry that a gift of a bottle of beer to the *starshina* and a rouble to the *pisar* is sufficient to secure judgment in the desired direction. The *uriadnik,* the lowest representative of the Government rural police, lives in the cantonal centre.

The canton contains another personage of great importance to the peasantry. It will be noted that the whole organisation of the canton is concerned only with the peasants. The gentry and other inhabitants of the area are not included in the administrative arrangements. The peasants are, indeed, regarded as being, as a class, in the position of minors, and this fact is emphasised by the appointment of special officials, known as *Zemskie Nachalniki,* Rural Overseers or Wardens of the Peasantry, whose duty it is to exercise a general oversight over the peasants in their respective districts each of which may include two or three cantons. Usually a prominent landowner of the neighbourhood is appointed Warden, and care is taken that his views shall be agreeable to the Government. The Warden has judicial rights with power to fine and imprison, and minor criminal cases are tried before him. If he is politically active and heavy-handed he may make things very unpleasant for the peasants, and as an institution the wardenship is unpopular. But the peasants regard the Warden as the chief authority in the district, and their favourite threat is to appeal to the Zemsky. Thus Anna, the wife of Nikolai the forester's son in Vladimirovo, had endless trouble with her husband who had not only beat her, which would be considered a normal and a natural thing and a sign of affection, but openly insulted her, and although he earned a great deal of money practically starved her and the children. Several times she retired to her father's house to parley from there, but Nikolai never kept his promises, and finally she went off to lay all her troubles before the Warden. Kusha, a widow in a village down the river, had an incorrigible son of sixteen who beat her, turned her out of her own house, and threatened to kill her. She, too, applied to the Warden and had the boy put in prison.

The Landowners

But if the peasant is changing so is his neighbour the landed proprietor, or *pomieshchik.* The estates of the country gentry are a characteristic feature of the landscape in Central and Northern Russia. The house stands perferably on a river-bank or on a hill-side. It is half-hidden amidst a grove of trees. Frequently, especially if the house was built, as a great many of the houses of the country gentry were, at the beginning of the nineteenth century, it has a veranda and a balcony supported by massive white columns. Near the house there is almost sure to be a lime-tree avenue, leading to an orchard of apple, pear, and cherry trees. A flower garden, sometimes with artificial ponds, and a variety of outbuildings complete the number of immediate appurtenances to the manor-house. Indoors a wide entrance-hall, a big dining-room, a drawing-room, a kitchen full of busy, chattering life, stairs leading to all sorts of quaint nooks and corners, well-stocked storerooms, libraries often containing old and valuable books, pretty, old-fashioned mahogany furniture, family portraits on the walls and generally a snug and soothing sense of leisure, security, and remoteness from the bustle of the world. Such is the home of the average *pomieshchik*. The government of Orel, of which Turgeniev was a native, was studded with such homes as these, and no one has described them more vividly than he. "Gentlefolks' Nests," he calls them, and this name with its lulling note of defence and security is still largely applicable, although the gentry no longer wield, as formerly, exclusive authority in the country side, and the distributing forces of a new time are beating up against the white-columned mansions.

In some of the great estates stand splendid palaces with magnificent grounds as in Arkhangelskaia and Marfino in the Moscow government. And, on the other hand, there are landowners who by rank belong to the gentry, but who possess little land and live in a condition hardly differing from that of the peasantry. The steppe *pomieshchik,* again, is a type apart and so are pomieshchiks from beyond the Volga. In the south-eastern region and Siberia the conception of a *pomieshchik* as understood in the centre and the north of European Russia is simply lost amidst various categories of Cossacks, peasants, colonists, and big and small farmers of a more or less American type.

The typical *pomieshchik* has no exact counterpart in England. He is neither a country squire nor a yeoman farmer, though he may have features characteristic of both. Very often he is in the government service and devotes his chief energies to administrative work, regarding his estate merely as a place of repose and, under favourable conditions, as a source of income. During the winter months he and his family live in the city, and the estate is left in charge of a steward who may possibly be a German or a Lett, but is, as often as not, a shrewd peasant from a neighbouring village. There are honest stewards, but the average steward has an elastic conception of his rights and privileges, and the absenteeism of many proprietors, and the light-hearted indifference they often display to the business of the estate when they do come down to it during the summer months almost irresistibly tempt to speculation. Even if the proprietor is not in the Government service he probably prefers to live in the city or in the government town, and then it may easily happen that the owner of a considerable estate can barely scrape together enough money to pay the rent of his flat, while his steward on the distant estate builds himself a roomy and comfortable mansion. A landowner in the Novgorod government built on his estate a house of stone. One day his steward came to St. Petersburg with a melancholy story of a storm having risen and the house having been swept away by the river Volhov. The landowner shook his head sadly, but it was long before he learned that the steward had simply pulled the house down and sold the materials. This experience must have disheartened the landowner for he sold his estate through the Peasants' Bank, then made unfortunate investments and was finally ruined.

Indeed the habits acquired by the gentry during centuries of serfdom are not to be thrown off in a day. When a man inherited an estate which, having serfs upon it, produced wealth almost mechanically, fed and clothed its proprietor and provided him almost without any exertion on his part with the money he needed for living in the cities and for travelling, he would naturally pay close attention to working of the estate only if he were personally interested in agriculture or were resolutely bent on adding to his wealth. There were, under the old system, many *pomieshchiks* who scraped and saved and sat year in, year out on their estates without ever visiting the city, who flogged the maximum of work out of their peasantry, outwitted their weaker neighbours, and by dint of economy, careful calculation, and endless litigation succeeded in greatly increasing the extent of their property. These were the methods that secured for the Grand Princess of Moscow their supremacy over their neighbours. But the Grand Princess of Moscow also brushed aside the laws which led to an incessant disintegration of big estates by providing that all the sons should inherit equally. The ordinary *pomieshchik* could in no way evade this law, and the consequence was that after a father had spent a lifetime in extending the frontiers of his property farther than the eye could reach, his death would mean the splitting up of the estate into five or six fragments, and it was not to be expected that all the sons would inherit the acquisitive instincts of their parent. Moreover, the habit of recruiting the ranks of the administration and of the army officers from among the country gentry encouraged the growth of the type of *pomieshchik* who drew his income from his estate without ever troubling as to how it was raised.

This passive and receptive attitude to the soil lingers on to a great extent among the country gentry, and its traces are constantly met with even on estates the proprietors of which are enlightened and progressive Zemstvo-workers, are eagerly interested in agriculture, and personally superintend the cultivation of the soil. A subtle fatalism seems to be latent in the homes of the gentry. There are endless difficulties, but it seems to the proprietors incredible that they should be insurmountable. A way out is sure to be found, things cannot be as bad as they appear. Some one is sure to help, either the Government or the elements or some vague, friendly Providence. Indeed, the gentry are just as responsible as the peasantry for the prevalence in Russian conversation of such comfortable optimistic phrases as *Obrazuietsia* ("It wil come out all right"), or the expressive interjections, *Avos* and *Kak-nibud* ("May hap!" and "Somehow or other").

The Government does a great deal to justify the confidence of the gentry. There is an institution called the State Land Bank which was formed twenty-four years after the emancipation when it had become clear that the gentry for all their wealth in land could not cope with the difficulties of this new situation without direct financial aid. The Government needed a class of landed gentry, and since the gentry showed a tendency to let their land slip out of their hands, to turn it into money as soon as possible and then to squander the proceeds, it was the policy of the Government to find means for maintaining the connection between the gentry and the land. The Gentry's Bank accordingly advances sums on mortgage at a low rate of interest, and on such easy conditions that the advance practically amounts to a donation which enables the Government to hold the land in trust for the mortgagee and to prevent its passing too rapidly into the hands of private money-lenders, or members of other classes. Even such paternal action often fails of its effect, however, and a quarter of the estates now mortgaged are registered as having passed from the possession of gentlemen into that of representatives of other classes. The total number of estates mortgaged in the Bank is over 26,000, the amount advanced on which is nearly 660 million roubles, or about 67 million pounds sterling. The greater number of estates mortgaged are in such central governments as Tula, Orel, Kursk, and Riazan. The Bank is a kindly institution, and until recently it was very tolerant of the weaknesses of the gentry, though it is growing stricter now. There is a pleasant ritual when the *pomieshchik* comes to pay interest on the mortgage; complaints on the part of the pomieshchik of hard times and inability to pay the full sum, commiseration on the part of the Bank officials, but insistence on the absolute necessity of paying the entire amount, expostulation from the pomieshchik, further demurring from the official, a little gentle bargaining, the retirement of the official to inner rooms where consultations are held, after which the official with a sigh accepts the smaller amount and remits the remainder until the following term when the scene is re-enacted.

All the benevolence of the Government does not avail, however, to establish any great fixity of tenure for the families of gentry. The inheritance law is responsible for constant perturbations. The right of primogeniture does not exist in respect of purely Russian estates—the eldest son has an advantage only if the family possesses an entailed estate in Polish districts where the right of Primogeniture does prevail—and all the sons inherit equal portions, while a daughter's interest is one-fourteenth. Then the growing economic strength of other classes menaces the gentry. An emancipated serf makes money as a contractor and advances cash to his former master on the security of considerable areas of meadow or forest land; the security is not redeemed, the land falls into the peasant's hands. He becomes a timber merchant, buys or mortgages forests from the neighbouring gentry who are usually glad enough to sacrifice timber to save their estates, to pay for the education of their children or for travelling, or to cover a variety of debts that have been contracted in the cities. The estates of the gentry grow smaller, those of the timber merchant grow larger. The merchant's sons inherit a large property and develop it. The surrounding peasants earn good money in timber-felling and rafting, for the merchant and the gentry find the wages for agricultural labourers rising and the difficulty of securing labour increasing. Some of the gentry shrink back in alarm before the growing difficulties, and after exhausting all possible methods of raising money on their land abandon the task in despair, finally dispose of their estates and become townsmen pure and simple. Others devise new methods of production and cultivation, build a starch factory and grow acres of potatoes to keep it going, start a brick-kiln if the soil is suitable, or a flour-mill, a distillery or some similar enter-prise, or, if there is access to a good market engage in dairy-farming, or else try to improve the quality of their land by scientific manuring or by draining swamps. Those landowners who take their estates seriously and exploit their resources according to modern methods as a rule succeed in keeping their heads above water, but that section of the gentry which is unable to take a keen interest in agriculture and resigns itself to the will of kindly fates is being gradually elbowed off the land by pushing merchants and well-to-do commission agents and shrewd peasants and various keen-eyed financiers. Often the landowner sells his estate for a song, and has the bitterness of seeing the purchaser make a fortune out of land that he him-self had considered valueless.

This flux in land tenure is inevitable under the modernising process through which Russia is now passing. The break-up of the peasant com-mune and the creation of a class of peasant farmers with private property means that these farmers, in so far as they are successful, will add to their property by purchasing land from the gentry. And so there will be from all sides a steady encroachment which only economically strong proprietors will be able to resist. The result will undoubtedly be immensely to increase the productiveness of the soil in European Russia—for it is in European Russia that the change is chiefly felt. It is obvious, even to the inexperi-enced eye, that far less is made of Russian estates than might be made, not to speak of the land of the peasants. The traveller who makes the railway journey via Berlin to Moscow or St. Petersburg is inevitably struck by the contrast between the level of cultivation in the estates and farms of East Prussia and those in Russia, and the difference between the agriculture of Central Russia and that of the Baltic Provinces is also very marked. A Western farmer habituated to the microscopic niceties of intensive cul-ture on small patches of land is astonished at the waste, at the indifference to rich opportunities so often met with on Russian estates. The final break with the traditions of serfdom, the development of individual initiative and of a determination to exploit the resources of the soil to the utmost, to make money by farming instead of depending on barely aided nature, should mean a startling increase of national wealth.

The Bolsheviks and the First World War

The First World War divided the socialist groups, both in Russia and elsewhere, even more than they had been before. Generally the socialists rallied to the support of their respective countries, but Lenin's position permitted no such action. Under his leadership, the Bolshevik Central Committee uncompromisingly stated its position in a manifesto which was issued in the fall of 1914. The manifesto was signed by the Central Committee. It had been drafted by Lenin, and was published, among other places, in his newspaper, *The Social Democrat*. (This paper had replaced *Forward* as the "Central Organ of the Russian Social Democratic Workers' Party.") The following excerpts from the manifesto are reprinted from an official Soviet translation of it.

The European war, for which the governments and the bourgeois parties of all countries have been preparing for decades, has broken out. . . . The seizure of territory and the conquest of foreign nations; the ruination of a competing nation and the plundering of its wealth; the diversion of the attention of the working classes of Russia, England, Germany, and the other countries from internal political crises; the division of the workers, fooling them by nationalism, and the wiping out of their advance guard with the object of weakening the revolutionary movement of the proletariat —such is the only real meaning, substance and importance of the present war.

The first duty of the Social-Democrats is to reveal the true meaning of the war and ruthlessly to expose the falsehood, sham, and "patriotic" phrase-making spread by the ruling classes . . . in defence of the war.

The German bourgeoisie heads one group of belligerent nations. It is fooling the working class and the laboring masses. . . . . . .

The other group . . . is headed by the French and British bourgeoisie, which is fooling the working class and the toiling masses. . . . . . .

But the more zealously the governments and the bourgeoisie of all countries strive to divide the workers and to set them against each other . . . the more urgent is the duty of the class-conscious proletariat to preserve its class solidarity, its internationalism, its Socialist convictions . . . .

It is with a feeling of deepest chagrin that we have to record that the Socialist parties of the leading European countries have not discharged this duty. . . .

. . . The Russian proletariat has not shrunk from making any sacrifice to rid humanity of the disgrace of the tsarist monarchy. But we must say that if anything can . . . delay the fall of tsardom, if anything can help the tsardom in its struggle against the whole democracy of Russia, it is the present war which has put the wealth of the British, French, and Russian bourgeoisie at the disposal of the tsardom for its reactionary aims. . . .

It is impossible to decide, under present conditions from the standpoint of the international proletariat, the defeat of which of the two groups of belligerent nations would be the lesser evil for socialism. But for us, the Russian Social-Democrats, there cannot be the slightest doubt that from the standpoint of the working class and toiling masses of all the nations of Russia, the lesser evil would be the defeat of the tsarist monarchy, the most reactionary and barbarous of governments . . . .

The only correct proletarian slogan is the transformation of the present imperialist war into a civil war . . . .

Lenin's Orders on Tactics

The Bolsheviks in Russia attempted to carry out Lenin's instructions concerning the war. The Russian government, quite naturally, regarded such actions as treasonable. Eleven Bolsheviks were arrested and sentenced to exile in November, 1914. Lenin's editorial comment on the trial contained the following orders as to the proper behavior of Bolsheviks who found themselves in like circumstances. The source is: *The Social Democrat*. Geneva. No. 40 (29 March, 1915). Abridged.

The aim pursued by the defendants was to obstruct the efforts of the prosecutor to discover the identity of the members of the Central Committee in Russia and of the Party agents in its varied relations with workers' organizations. This goal was attained. And for its future attainment, the method long officially recommended by the Party should be adopted, namely: refusal to give evidence. . . . Our comrades should have refused to testify about the illegal organization [the Party underground]; they should [also] . . . have taken advantage of the fact that this was a public trial to make a direct statement of the views of the Social Democrats. . . .

The February/March Revolution in Petrograd

Approximately nine months before the events described in the following letter, Mr. Edward T. Heald arrived in Petrograd to begin his service as a Y.M.C.A. secretary there. It is apparent from the letter that he was neither a trained observer nor politically acclimated to Russia. The letter makes no pretense to analysis or profundity. It is, however, an honest, informal record of what Mr. Heald saw, heard, and thought during the first week of the February/March Revolution, and it captures some of the excitement and uncertainty of those stirring days.

Mr. Heald's letters, written to Mrs. Heald, remained unpublished for a quarter of a century until Mr. Heald gave the editor permission to publish them. The letter which follows is one of a series which was originally published in the *American Slavic and East European Review*. It is reprinted here with the generous permission of Mr. Heald and of the journal.

The source is: Warren B. Walsh (Ed.), "Petrograd, March-July, 1917. The Letters of Edward T. Heald." *American Slavic and East*

European Review. Vol. VI, nos. 16–17, pp. 118–133. The footnotes, which relate Mr. Heald's particulars to the general scene, retain their original numbering.

Vosnesensky Prospect [2]
Petrograd
March 16, 1917
[Friday]
Dear Emily:

I am not sure whether the new regime and the new freedom which have so suddenly come to this land will give the censor the liberty to allow an American citizen to write to his wife in detail about the thrilling experiences of the past few days, but by avoiding military matters that have a bearing upon the Great War, I will take the chance on getting this detailed account through to you.[3]

I realize that we are living too near the events to grasp their real significance, but I feel that they transcend in greatness any revolution in the world's history, affecting as they do the lives of 170 million people. And from all that we can now see, the entire change from one end of the Empire to the other has been completely made in a week's time and with an order and absence of violence that is a wonderful revelation of the natural self-restraint and good-nature of the Russian people.

Little did we realize a week ago today that the strike which had started in the shops here had such a tremendous significance.[4]

The government and military officials seemed to have little more realization of it than we, for the Committee of the Empress met on Thursday

[2] My apartment address (ETH).

[3] "Dear Emily" is Mrs. Heald. This letter went through without censorship as did most of those written after the Revolution. (ETH.)

[4] Strikes which had already been numerous from January on, now increased rapidly both in seriousness and numbers involved. Chamberlain retails an estimate of 197,000 strikers on March 9th. *Vide,* W. H. Chamberlin, *The Russian Revolution,* 2 vols., N.Y., Macmillan, 1935, I, 75.

Government leaders and government critics both realized the increasing gravity of the whole situation and sought to bring an understanding of it to the tsar. Chiefly under the direction of Protopopov, Minister of the Interior, plans were made to quell the uprising expected in the capital. Heavy batteries were emplaced, machine guns were brought in, and Gurko, Chief of Staff, sent three crews of sailors to maintain order. Despite the urgings of Alexandra and of his advisors and ministers, Nicholas left for Headquarters on March 8th. That same day, the Duma castigated the government's policy on food, and street disorders broke out in Petrograd. For a detailed account, *vide* B. Pares, *Fall of the Russian Monarchy,* Knopf, N.Y. 1939. 412 *et sqq.,* esp. 436–471; Chamberlin, *op. cit.* I; 70–98. For the official Bolshevik interpretation, *vide,* M. Gorki *et al.* (eds), *Istoriya grazhdanskoi voinyi v SSSR,* Moscow, 1938, I: 55–75. This source places the number of strikers on that day (March 9th NS) at "about 200,000."

night with Mr. Harte [5] and laid plans for the war prisoners' work as if nothing unusual was in progress. That the strike was far-reaching, however, speedily became apparent. Street car traffic became irregular Friday [the 9th] and practically ceased during the afternoon. The sleighs with their drivers likewise disappeared from the streets, so that when Day and I had to deliver a letter to Premier Golitsyn, on the other side of the city, we had to walk. We were informed at the palace of the Premier that he was not at home, but had gone to the Tsarskoe Selo that day.[6]

Crowds of unarmed strikers and [their] families gathered on the Nevsky Prospect during the day, and order was preserved by the Cossacks. We anticipated a repetition of former times of disturbances when women and children were ridden down by the Cossacks. This time, however, they used no violence, but merely rode through the open lanes of the people, while the latter shouted at them "You're ours!" and the Cossacks smiled back.[7]

That Friday night, six of us attended the performance of Gogol's *Revisor,* greatest of Russian comedies, at the Alexandrinsky Theatre. The house was filled and everybody [was] in a lively humor at this satire on the political weaknesses of the mid-nineteenth century. Few of them realized that a greater drama was at that moment unfolding in real life throughout the capital. The Tsar's empty box was guarded by two sentries who maintained their inflexible poise and stare during . . . [the performance].

B. . . . did not go to the show with us, but continued his walk up the Nevsky. He says that while we were at the play there were volleyings up and down the Nevsky several times; the soldiers [were] firing upon the people.

That day, Friday [the 9th], a notice was posted by the Chief of Police [8] warning people to stay indoors for the next three days, as order would be preserved even if it required the use of arms. The order further stated that those who were promoting the trouble were playing the enemy's game.

[5] Dr. A. C. Harte was one of two representatives sent to Europe by the Y.M.C.A. to arrange for service to war prisoners. After consultations with the Central Powers, he reached Moscow in May 1915. Partly because the Y was suspected as pro-German, the Russians were not inclined to cooperate and it was only after considerable difficulties that Dr. Harte won the support of the Empress. Dr. Harte continued to serve as the general European agent of the Y's International Committee, with special responsibility for Russia. *Vide* W. H. Taft, *et. al., Service with fighting men,* 2 vols., Association Press, N.Y., 1922, II: 231 *et sqq.*

[6] George M. Day was a Y.M.C.A. secretary with long experience in Russia. Prince N. D. Golitsyn was President of the Council of Ministers from January to March, 1917.

[7] This is confirmed by many sources both Bolshevik and Tsarist.

[8] Presumably, the City Prefect, Balk. Actually he was subordinate to General Habalov, Commander of the Petrograd Military Area. Habalov's own testimony concerning the events of these days is to be found in *Padenie tsarskogo rezhima,* 7 vols., Moscow, 1924–27. I: 182–219.

Saturday [March 10th] things became noticeably more unsettled. Streetcar traffic entirely ceased. We learned that the motormen had taken off the grips so that the cars could not be started. We were told that the cordial feeling existing the previous day between the soldiers and the strikers had changed owing to the fact that one of the officers had been killed while protesting the taking of the grips. . . .

. . . One of the office girls was called up at noon by her mother and notified that the police had instructed that she should come home at once as it was getting unsafe to go through the streets in that part of the city (near the American Embassy). [She left and] the other girls were not long in following suit, all except Miss Golubeva who stayed to get out the mail and telegrams. Nevsky Prospect was closed to traffic except two blocks at the end of our street. When we had to cross the Nevsky on our way to lunch at the Malo Yaroslavets, Saturday noon, the bridges were heavily guarded by soldiers. We could see a dense crowd of the strikers a couple of blocks further up the Prospect, in front of Kazan Cathedral, waving a big red flag at their head.

Saturday evening three of us walked down to the Mayak, but the attendance at the gym class was small.[9] Mr. Gaylord was there and I asked him how this compared with the Revolution of 1905 through which he had passed. He said that there had been more excitement on the Nevsky this time, but less in the rest of the city.

But on Saturday the real movement had not yet gotten underway. The police still had control of the situation, at least in the center of the city. There were reports, however, that there were three hundred thousand armed strikers on the outskirts, in the factory districts, and that when they should break through into the center of the city, nothing could stop them. We also heard that the Government had brought in quantities of ammunition, machine guns, armored automobiles and tanks, as well as large numbers of Cossacks.[10]

Sunday was a beautiful sunshiny day. I attended church in the morning and the English pastor was very much perturbed over the conditions in the city. Then I visited the art gallery and the attendance was not a quarter of what it had been the preceding Sunday. Many people were obeying the warnings to stay off the streets. Then George Day and I set out from our apartments for dinner at the Malo Yaroslavets about three o'clock. We started in the direction of the Admiralty Building, but were stopped, along with many others, at the end of our block by mounted police who ordered us back. We went to the Morskaya and succeeded in crossing the Nevsky

[9] The Mayak (Lighthouse) was founded in Petrograd in 1900 by Franklin A. Gaylord. Although engaged in work very similar to that of the Y, it did not officially affiliate with the Y until 1917. Taft, *op. cit.* II: 421.

[10] On this evening, Nicholas wired Habalov: "I command that the disorders in the capital shall be stopped tomorrow, as they are inadmissible in this serious time of war with Germany and Austria." *Padenie*, I: 190; *cf. Istoriya*, 56; and Pares, *op. cit.*, 442. Pares comments, "By this message he signed his own dethronement."

on that street. I shall never forget the sight looking up the Nevsky that beautiful afternoon. For the whole length of the Prospect not a person was going along the street, either in the roadway or on the sidewalks, but persons were crossing at each cross street.

After dinner we tried to return by the way we came, but the approach to the Nevsky was blocked by a dense crowd of people and by mounted police, who waved us back. So we had to go back through the Arch of the Winter Square and try to reach our apartment by the route that was closed when we started out. As we crossed . . . the Nevsky at the Admiralty corner there rounded the Square more than five hundred Cossacks, armed with lances, who started up the Nevsky. You could not imagine a more brilliant and martial sight than the Cossack cavalrymen glittering in the sunlight.

. . . There had been volleys up the Nevsky as well as on the other two Prospects frequently that day . . . . towards the Siberian Railroad Station . . . [B] had seen the soldiers form lines across the street and fire upon the unarmed crowd. He saw two dead and a number injured. . . . He said that the crowd kept crying "Bread! Bread!" as they came with outstretched arms towards the soldiers.[11]

B. . . . and his wife had been on the Nevsky later in the afternoon and had seen one of the workingmen step from the crowd and go up to a policeman and say something that seemed to be insulting. At any rate, the policeman hauled back and struck the man down with the flat of his sword. The workingman jumped up again and began spitting in the face of the policeman. . . .

Monday, March 12th, was the great day that suddenly sounded the knell of the old regime, though we were slow to realize what was taking place.[12] It was quieter on the Nevsky than the day before. I walked up the Prospect to the Sadovaya at noon, and saw nothing exciting though the banks and most of the business places were closed. The center of action Monday was on the other side of the city. . . .

Mr. Harte, who always treated our predictions of a revolution with a smile saying that nothing of the sort would happen, was still planning to go

---

[11] During the day, the Pavlovsky regiment mutinied and there was much disorder with many casualties. The primary question was still one of food. Pares, *op. cit.*, 442; *cf.* also, Chamberlin, *op. cit.*, I: 77. For a "White" view *vide* A. I. Denikin. *The Russian Turmoil,* E. P. Dutton & Co., N.Y., n. d., 40–46: and *The Memoirs of Baron N. Wrangel,* J. B. Lippincott Co., Philadelphia, 1927, 254–275. So many memoirs covering these events have appeared that it would extend this beyond all reason to list even part of them. Very useful bibliographies may be found in works of Pares and Chamberlin, already cited, and elsewhere. F. A. Golder, *Documents of Russian History,* The Century Co., N.Y., 1927, contains translations of various important primary materials.

[12] On this day the Duma heard the Tsar's order for its dissolution; the Volynsky regiment mutinied and was followed by many others; the Cabinet, after many sessions, dispersed; and, in the words of Chamberlin (*op. cit.,* I: 80) "So the city passed completely into the hands of the revolutionaries."

to Sweden the next morning. His secretary, Penn Davis, had to go through the trouble zone this Monday morning to complete passport arrangements and secure documents for Mr. Harte and himself. When he arrived at the Liteiny Prospect he found barricades, and was stopped by the strikers who had some student soldiers with them. After showing his American passport and explaining his business he was allowed to go on, and got back alright.

During the day the sound of firing became louder in our part of the city. Neither Baker nor I understood what was taking place when we started over to the Narodni Dom after tea that evening to hear Shaliapin in *The Roussalkas*. There was an atomsphere everywhere of excitement, uncertainty, and danger. Volleys and shots started at every crossing and corner. Around the Winter Palace Square people clung to sides of buildings, and if they came to street intersections where they had to cross they darted across. The gloomy sombre red buildings seemed to be sitting in judgment on the country's doom.

When we reached the middle of the New Nicholaievsky Bridge over the Neva we stopped on the high middle and looked back over the city. We saw flames rising over the Liteiny region, which we afterwards learned were burning law courts. Machine guns were keeping up an incessant rat-atat-tat in a dozen different quarters of the city, and particularly loud in the direction of the Narodni Dom. At the further end of the bridge was a squad of soldiers forming a line across. I went up to the officer and asked if there was any objection to our proceeding on to the Narodni Dom. He asked for passports and when I showed them he said "Alright." As we neared the bridge over the Little Neva a little further on, another squad of soldiers stood facing us. When we were about fifty paces off the crowd of women and working people in front of us broke and ran, and looking ahead we saw the guns raised in our direction. We immediately reversed our direction, and while we didn't run, we never walked faster until we put a building between us and the raised guns. We decided to hear Shaliapin some other evening. Later we learned that no performance was held at the Narodni Dom that night.

We saw no policemen during this walk. It was the first time that they had not been on the streets in the center of the city. We haven't seen any since. They disappeared from the streets late that afternoon.

The real surprise awaited Baker and me when we got back to Mr. Harte's room at the Grand Hotel. He had given up his trip to Sweden the next morning. But not until he and Day had taken a trip to the station that had been full of thrillers. They had loaded the trunks and baggage on one of the high Russian sleds known as lamovois, to take to the station for checking purposes the night before the train leaves according to the Russian custom. As their lamovois passed the big square in front of the Winter Palace they were fired upon. As they continued down the narrow Millinaya Ulitza they were fired upon again. They ducked their heads and Mr. Harte prayed while George used his Russian on the driver to speed him up. The driver didn't need any coaxing. They arrived at the Liteiny Bridge only to be surrounded and held up by a crowd of about a hundred and fifty strikers, students and soldiers. The leader was a student. The strikers thought that Harte and Day were trying to take ammunition over the river to the enemy, and demanded that the trunks be opened for search. There were these two Americans standing up on the high sled, with the crowd of revolutionists thronging around them from every side. What Mr. Harte feared most was that some of the Tsar's cavalry or police would suddenly appear on the scene and proceed to fire upon them, in which case Mr. Harte and George, standing high above the crowd, would be the best targets.

Another thing was troubling Mr. Harte. He had forgotten to bring one of the trunk keys which he had left with Penn Davis at the Hotel. What would the strikers think when he told them that he did not have the key? But he had one of the keys and opened the trunk it fitted. After carefully searching it, the mob was satisfied and did not ask to look in the other trunk. They provided an escort of soldiers to conduct him to the station. As soon as they got their trunks off the lamovois at the station, the driver disappeared with his horses and sled. Then Mr. Harte could find no one to take charge of their baggage. The customary crowd of porters was nowhere in sight. No officials were to be seen. The platform was almost deserted. Finally a lone official appeared who looked at the Americans in wonderment, and told them that there would be no train in the morning; that the officials had been unarmed by the strikers; that no one was in authority; and that there was no one to look after their trunks.

It was in vain that Mr. Harte and Day searched for another vehicle of any kind to take them and their baggage back to the Hotel. They were almost giving up hope of finding a place to store their baggage when a man appeared who showed them a closet where they could lock their things up. It was characteristic of Mr. Harte that the excitement did not keep him from seeing to it carefully that his wardrobe trunk was set up in the right position, doubtful though it was that he would ever see it again. Then he and Day walked the four miles back to the Hotel, arriving there shortly before we returned. Mr. Harte was ready to acknowledge that the situation was serious. Half of the city that he had been through was in the hands of the strikers.

The next big surprise awaited us at ten o'clock when Day and I returned to our apartments. A Russian sailor was there, who was a friend of Madame Stepan. He gave us the astounding news that the old government was overthrown, that a new government had been established with a committee of twelve at its head responsible to the Duma, and that the entire city was in the hands of the revolutionists, excepting the Police Districts which were all under the fire of the revolutionists. He lived in the Morskaya Police District. Most of the soldiers had already gone over to the strikers and the people and the others were rapidly following suit. Not until then did we realize that we were in the midst of a great revolution that so many of our friends had talked about and dreaded.

One of the pieces of information which our marine friend gave us, which was later verified, was that the same Monday morning the Tsar had appointed Minister Protopopov dictator, ordering the dissolution of the

Duma. But the Duma ignored the orders of the Tsar and immediately went into executive session thus defying the Tsar and his government. That was the point where the real revolution began.[13]

Our marine friend said that he could not get home on account of the siege against the Police District near his home. He said that most of the firing then going on in the city was at the Police Districts, and also by boys who had secured fire-arms and were shooting them off in the air for sport. Crowds of soldiers and strikers were holding jubilee meetings over the city, as comrades in a common cause, adopting the red flag of the revolution. Officers who stood by their oath of loyalty to the Tsar were being arrested.

One of the first efforts of the revolutionists was to clean out the Police Department, and the lives of the police were unsafe if seen on the streets. The wrath of the movement seemed directed chiefly towards this institution, the records of which were dumped out of the windows on to the streets and sidewalks below and burned. Russians with whom we talked called the police system a treacherous German institution that had been foisted upon the people back in the time of Peter the Great, and that it had been used as an instrument to keep the masses in ignorance and bondage ever since.

The next piece of news came when B. . . . arrived home at midnight. He and G. . . . met an officer in the same block that our apartments are located. Across the street is the building of the War Ministry. This officer asked B. . . . and G. . . . if they were English. They replied that they were Americans. The officer replied "Good, I also foreigner. I Finnlandsky. To-morrow that building is ours," pointing to the war ministry. He spoke in Russian and B. . . . and G. . . . knew just enough of the language to guess that he said that they were going to blow up the building. We accordingly wondered as we turned in that night whether we would be awakened by an explosion. The Finn was as happy as a boy. Immediately after talking with B. . . . and G. . . . he went over to the building and passed into the court between lines of soldiers who evidently held the building for the revolutionists.

A half hour after midnight Eric Christensen, our big Dane secretary, came home. Ordinarily he is very calm, but this time he was dancing and shouting with excitement. He had just shaken hands with a couple of men who had been released from the famous Peter and Paul Fortress. Both the prisoners were Finns, and had a thousand rubles each furnished by some

---

[13] The order proroguing the Duma was signed by Nicholas on the 10th and countersigned by Golitsyn on the 12th. The leaders of the political parties in the Duma resolved that the members should not disperse. *Cf.* Golder, *Documents,* 277–278. According to Chamberlin (*op. cit.,* 80–81) and *Istoriya,* 63, the Duma accepted the order of dissolution but removed as "private citizens" to another room in the Tauride Palace and held an extralegal conference. At any event, the Duma organized an Executive Committee and, a few hours later, a Provisional Committee. The latter undertook the tasks of government. Golder, *Documents,* 280–281. Protopopov, on the demand of the ministers expressed by Golitsyn, resigned and went into hiding on the evening of the 12th. *Cf.* Pares, *op. cit.,* 451–452.

Finnish revolutionary committee, to pay their expenses home. The Fortress had been taken by the soldiers that evening, and all the prisoners, who were there for political and religious reasons, were released, including nineteen soldiers who had been imprisoned during the last few days.

It was hard to shake off enough of the excitement that night to get to sleep.

Tuesday March 13th dawned a beautiful clear day. We were awakened by volleys and artillery fire at an early hour, which increased in intensity. People hugged the courtways in the street below us, and if they crossed the streets they did so with a dash. If they began to take to the sidewalks a sudden volley would send them scattering for shelter. Our soldat told us that the Dvornik (house-porter) gave orders to stay in that day.

At nine o'clock, however, I started out as usual for the office planning to stop at Mr. Harte's room in the Grand Hotel on the way. As I reached the end of the block, at the corner of Gogol Street and Vosnesensky Prospect, an imposing sight was before me. Directly ahead, a block away, the square opposite the Astoria Hotel (headquarters for the officers) was full of soldiers. Down the Morskaya came column after column of soldiers, in martial order, greeted with the rousing shouts of the people assembled in the square in front of St. Isaac's Cathedral. The sun shining on the masses of soldiers made a brilliant spectacle. The soldiers stopped short when they came even with the statue of Nicholas, where they faced the Astoria Hotel.

Suddenly there was a tremendous volley and the sidewalks and squares were emptied of people in the twinkling of an eye. I was half way across Gogol Street when the volleys came, and I had that naked feeling the soldiers are said to have when they go over the top. I wasted no time covering the remaining half of the street and was soon in Mr. Harte's room. While we stood at his window looking out on the street, soldiers began to come along the middle of the street leading officers to the Duma to swear allegiance to the new government. These were the officers who surrendered and said they were willing to swear allegiance to the new order. Some of them looked downcast and others happy.

During a lull in the fighting I crossed the street to our office building, and with some of the other secretaries looked down from our sixth floor directly on top of the Astoria Hotel roof at the end of the block on the opposite side of the street, and on the fighting in the street and square in front of the hotel. We could see the marines lying on Gogol Street in front of St. Isaac's shooting at the hotel. We saw several men fall, and some of them afterwards crawled off dragging a wounded arm or leg. The Red Cross automobiles came and went rapidly. The famous storming of the officer's headquarters was in full swing. More and more detachments of soldiers came along leading officers to the Duma. Some of the officers offered resistance and were killed on the spot. Others shouted "We're for you" and were allowed to keep their swords and arms and often given commands. At the height of the fighting we noticed a commotion on top of the Astoria Hotel roof. A machine gun had been placed there and the officers had begun firing down on the sidewalk below. It did not take long for the soldiers to spot the mischief and put an end to it with short shrift for the unfortunate officers.

While we were watching this affair from our windows B. . . . and G. . . . had an exciting time down on the street. They were on the Morskaya under the Astoria Hotel when the machine gun began its work from the roof. In the rush for shelter, B. . . . fell and had many a kick and cuff before he regained his feet. He said he got all the excitement he wanted that time.

We saw the soldiers smashing bottles of liquor on the sidewalks, and we saw the contents running down the street. We saw only a few soldiers carrying off or drinking the liquor.

The battle lasted about a half hour, and by that time the soldiers had everything in their own hands, and the officer had flung out the white flag. This was the day of the private soldier. They told their officers to go home and stay out of sight until things were quiet again. The officers, having taken their individual oath of allegiance to the Tsar, considered themselves more bound to it than the soldiers who took allegiance in groups. For the officers it was a great moral struggle, many [?] of them being in sympathy with the revolution. Caught as they were in a situation where they had to make instant decision, there was a variety of reactions on their part, many paying with their lives for their hesitation.

The way the soldiers took things in their own hands was a revelation. They showed perfect confidence, tackled most difficult tasks with a practical efficiency and did all with a buoyant, smiling assurance and mastery that gave everyone confidence that they knew what they were doing. The "children of the Tsar" this day stepped forth as their own men and masters.

Probably the predominant impression that an American received from the events of the day was the self-restraint and order of the soldiers, as well as of the workingmen. There were cases of killing and bloodshed, and during the day many were taken to the hospitals, but considering the size of the revolution, the number of men and soldiers engaged in the struggle, the amount of bloodshed was small. Outside of the destruction of property in the police districts, the officers' quarters, and the homes of the suspected aristocracy, there was little looting. And this order was maintained despite the fact that there was an indiscriminate distributing of firearms to workingmen and boys. This was one time when prohibition was a blessing to Russia. If vodka could have been found in plenty, the revolution could easily have had a terrible ending.

One of the problems of this day was the snipers. The soldiers quickly handled such cases by bringing up an armored car or tank against the building from which the shots came, and playing the machine gun upon it. Many of the police were in hiding, concealed often through the connivance of dvorniks, who formed a part of the old police system. The H. . . .'s had an exciting experience in their apartments. Shots were fired into the court from some upper floors. A group of fifty or sixty soldiers immediately came in and made a thorough search of every room at the point of a gun.

The starshy (head) dvornik was almost shot, but was saved at the last moment by one of the captors who had an argument that had an effect upon the other soldiers.

The center of action was transferred from the Liteiny District to the Gogol and Morskaya District. We had the full benefit of it. In the afternoon the magnificent palace of Baron Friederichs, the German sympathizer, who was the Tsar's personal advisor and Chamberlin, was in flames. It was in plain view up the Gogol from our office and was completely burned out.

Towards evening of this day I picked up on the streets a news-sheet entitled *"Izvestiya Petrogradskago Soveta Rabochikh deputatov"* [14] dated 28 February [O.S.] 1917, and calling upon the workingmen of all lands to unite. It announced that the bourgeois system had been overthrown, the capitalistic class destroyed, and urged the workingmen and soldiers to elect deputies for a central labor council or soviet. This was the first printed matter that had appeared in the capital for several days. It was also the first announcement of or by the Soviet. The newspapers had all been closed since Friday. We didn't know what was going on in the rest of the world or Empire. The wildest rumors were afloat.

One rumor had the Kaiser overthrown and a revolution successful in Germany. Another had the Tsar's army on the way from the front to put down the revolution. The discovery of five hundred machine guns on the roofs of the buildings in Petrograd, carrying an apparent threat of a St. Bartholomew's Eve massacre to put down the revolution if necessary, did not dispel our nervousness. The minister Protopopov, had ordered one thousand machine guns placed, according to report, but had only succeeded in getting five hundred up when the plan was discovered. The plan was for all the machine guns to begin playing upon the multitudes at the same instant, signal for which was to be an airplane that would come over the city from Tsarskoe Selo. Rumor had it that the Tsarina was to give the fatal order that would start the airplane, but that she lost her nerve at the last moment. Well, to pick up this red revolutionary bulletin on top of these rumors did not quiet our nerves. All restaurants and stores were closed, at night the streets were pitch dark, the street lamps not being lighted. It was a disquieting evening.

Wednesday [the 14th] conditions became more normal. At ten-thirty I started afoot for the American Embassy. Cheering on the Morskaya attracted my attention, and when I arrived on the street I found a great parade in progress, all revolutionists carrying the red flag and the bands playing the Marseillaise. I followed the parade along the Nevsky and shall never forget the wonderful sight. From the Morskaya to the Liteiny, over a mile and a half, the great Nevsky Prospect was packed with people from the buildings on one side to the buildings on the other side.

---

[14] There were no regular newspapers during the first week of the Revolution. The news-sheet to which Mr. Heald refers was the first number of the Soviet *Izvestiya*. Its name was changed several times during the first year of its existence. Golder (*op. cit.*, 277) lists the changes.

The parade itself consisted of soldiers, officers, marines, workingmen all marching in order, and every division hoisting the big red banners. The marching columns stretched from the curb-stone to the middle of the broad Prospect. The spectators packed the rest of the street, a continuous deafening cheer greeting the marching columns along the whole route. Now and then armored cars darted along with soldiers armed to the teeth. I never expect to see a more thrilling sight in my life.

During the whole time I saw only one drunken man, and heard only two shots fired. The order was wonderful. The people were not so much wild with enthusiasm as they were joyously, freely, intensely, spiritually happy. There was an exhilaration to it that was thrilling and indescribable. One felt that it must be a dream; that it was impossible that such things were happening in Russia. Well dressed people were in evidence and apparently as happy as the bent gray-haired working men who looked about with a dazed sort of happiness, while their faces shone with a rapturous glow. There seemed to be the best of feeling between the officers and soldiers.

When I reached the Embassy I learned that the Tsar was expected to be at the Duma that afternoon to proclaim a new constitution. The people at the Embassy thought he could still save his dynasty if he would grant the constitution and appoint new ministers who would represent the people. But the Tsar never appeared. He let this last chance slip by. Sixty thousand soldiers at Peterhof this day gave their allegiance to the Duma. This same day Grand Duke Cyril went out to the Duma and tendered his allegiance and the service of the marines under his command to the new government. We also got our first outside telegraph news this day, to the effect that Moscow was also in the hands of the revolutionists. The struggle there had been brief and an easy victory for the revolutionists. The Mayor of the city was a liberal. The police took refuge in the Kremlin but had to surrender speedily.

While I was at the Embassy word came that Protopopov, the former Minister of the Interior, had surrendered. He had been in hiding with the other ministers of the old regime at the Admiralty since Monday. At eleven-fifteen Wednesday he appeared at the Tauride Palace, where the Duma meets. A student was at the entrance. Protopopov went up to the student and said, "You are a student?" "I am," was the reply. "I have always been interested in the welfare of our country," said Protopopov, "and therefore I come and give myself voluntarily. I am former Minister of the Interior Protopopov. Lead me to whatever person is necessary." The student led him to the Temporary Executive Committee. On the way the soldiers, recognizing him, gave vent to their indignation, and threatened him, and when he arrived at the committee, he was pale and tottering. Kerensky, the new Minister of Justice, pacified the crowd and prevented violence.[15]

At noon this day the Admiralty passed into the hands of the revolution-

[15] *Cf.* the stirring account of this in Shulgin's memoirs, quoted in Pares, *op. cit.*, 454–455.

ary soldiers, and the ministers who had been in hiding either fled or gave themselves up.

On my way home from the Embassy I saw armored cars racing through the streets filled with armed soldiers who were scattering bulletins. I picked one up. It was called *Prikaz No. 1,* was dated March 1, and was signed by the Soviet of the Workers' and Soldiers' Deputies, the uniting of these two groups apparently having taken place during the preceding twenty-four hours. This order called upon the soldiers not to salute their officers except when on duty. All titles were to be dropped. Soldiers could no longer be addressed by their officers with the familiar "Thou" but only by "Sir" and the polite "You." The day before (Tuesday) there had been no saluting, but during the big parade Wednesday morning saluting was general. With the appearance of Prikaz No. 1 however, saluting stopped. Trouble brewed in the atmosphere.

Thursday noon Zemmer [16] showed up at the office. All his enthusiasm for the new regime was gone. "Everybody is out for what he can get for his own profit," said Zemmer. "There is no patriotism. Everything was beautiful the first two days, then differences arose and harmony disappeared." Zemmer had been at the Duma the preceding day to swear allegiance to the new government, along with two thousand other officers. He was worried as to the outcome, as out of eight thousand officers in the city only two thousand had shown up at the Duma. It was reported that a large number had gone out to Tsarskoe Selo to the Tsar. Others were in hiding. Moreover there was a serious struggle going on between the radical revolutionists who wanted a social revolution, and the conservative liberals, who wanted a constitutional monarchy. Zemmer was afraid that they might split and give the old regime its opportunity to regain control. It was reported that a large army loyal to the Tsar was on the way from the front to put down the revolution. Regarding Prikaz No. 1, Zemmer said that it had been dispatched with haste by the truck-load to the front, and that it would ruin the discipline of the whole army.

Banks opened up until one o'clock Thursday. Many stores of provisions were brought to light. Butter, which had been selling at three rubles and twenty kopeks (about $1.00) per pound, dropped to eighty kopeks by revolutionary order. Soldiers were on hand to see that no more than that was charged. Sugar, which had been issued only on tickets, could now be secured without tickets. Great stores of meat were brought forth from cold storage and placed on the market. Out at Nevsky Monastery a couple of thousand tons of sugar were seized by the revolutionists and placed at the disposal of the government. There was a rush for provisions from every hand all day.

In the evening we heard that the Tsar's army had arrived from the front and was engaging the revolutionists in a great battle at the edge of the city near the Baltsky Station. We walked over that way, but heard and saw nothing out of the ordinary and concluded that the rumor was false.

[16] A Russian officer, transferred from the Russian Red Cross to assist the Y.M.C.A. (ETH.)

Friday morning [the 16th] we were thrilled to see in the windows of the *Novoye Vremya* newspaper a bulletin reading that Nicholai Romanov (all titles removed) had abdicated at three o'clock that morning [17] for himself and his heir, Alexei, in favor of Michael Alexandrovitch, the next in line. Alongside it another bulletin read that Michael Alexandrovitch declined to accept the throne, stating that the people wanted a Republic, and that he wanted to get back to the front where he belonged. The abdication of the Tsar had been written on his special train near Pskov, after it had been shunted back and forth in vain efforts to elude the revolutionists.

The story of the worries and remarks of the Tsar during those last hours, as reported in the newspapers, reads like a chapter from the Middle Ages. When it was all over and he had signed the abdication he sighed, "How I long to be with my roses in the Crimea." Baron Friederichs, whose palace was burned, was with him to the last.

With the appearance of the morning bulletins the new Cabinet was announced. The new Minister of Justice is Kerensky, a Socialist, and his first order was that any important papers or documents which were found in the Police Headquarters and were worthy of saving were to be transferred to the Academy of Science. He seems to know how to attract the attention and seize the imagination of the people. There was also appointed a new Minister, one for Finnish Affairs, to take the place of the old Governor General of Finland, who has been arrested. Also the man who was responsible for the new restrictive and repressive measures in Finland in 1905 is in custody.

In the same bulletins the Cabinet announces that it will be guided by the following principles: (1) Full and immediate amnesty in all political and religious affairs; (2) Liberty of word, press, assembly, unions and strikes with extension of political liberty to those in military service within the confines permissible by military technical conditions; (3) Abolition of all class, religious and national limitations; (4) Immediate preparations to convoke on the basis of universal, equal, direct, and secret suffrage, a Constitutional Assembly, which will establish the form of administration and constitution; (5) Substitution of national militia in the place of police, with elected leaders and subject to local administration; (6) Elections to local administration on the basis of universal suffrage. On the following day a proclamation was issued removing all restrictions from the Jews.

On Friday [the 16th] the old flag of Russia was replaced by the red flag in all quarters of the city. Soldiers were busy all day pulling down the coats of arms of the old regime, including those on the Winter Palace. The Singer Sewing Machine Building protected the American Eagle on its top by having it wrapped in the American flag, but all other eagles in the city came down.

Little Alexander, our office boy, when asked what he thought of the revolution, said "Tsar ne nado." (No need of a Tsar.)

---

[17] Actually the document was dated Pskov, 3 P.M., March 15th. The abdication of the Grand Duke Michael was dated the 16th.

One of Mr. Harte's friends, Count Stackelburg, was killed Monday. Revolutionists came to his palace on the Millionaya, and when he refused to open the doors, he was shot down. Sturmer is reported dead in prison. Count Pallen has not been heard of since Monday. He went down to one of his estates in the country near Moscow just before the revolution, and his life is feared for. The girls in our office are back at work, and all seem happy at the new day.

We now feel that we can draw a full breath; that what we see is no longer a dream but a reality; that a new era has opened with consequences beyond imagination. We are thrilled with the new energy, purpose, and enthusiasm that has taken hold everywhere. It has been good to be alive these marvelous days. We can take our hats off to the Russian people; they know how to put great things across. Their good-nature is impressive; even in the course of the fighting they seemed to retain their good-nature. They don't seem to have the natures that would lead to the excesses of the French Revolution. They handle the most exciting emergencies in a cool matter-of-fact way. And I am struck with their continued loyalty to the Allies. I talked with a number of the soldiers during the week. "Give us a week to clean this up," they said, "and then we'll go back and clean up the Germans so quick no one can stop us."

Lenin Comes Home

The Bolsheviks were as surprised and as unprepared for the first (February/March) 1917 Revolution as was the rest of the world. Lenin was in Switzerland and the lesser leaders were either also in exile or were operating clandestinely and rather ineffectively on a very small scale. The party membership had dropped to under 24,000. Lenin at first tried to continue his leadership by remote control through his "Letters From Afar," but this proved inadequate and very unsatisfactory from his point of view. The amnesty granted by the Provisional Government permitted the Bolsheviks to return to Russia from abroad or from Siberia. Lenin determined to take advantage of the amnesty if a way could be found by which he could return to Russia. The Western Allies correctly regarded him as their enemy and refused to permit him passage across their territories.

According to the official Communist history, Martov, the Menshevik leader, first suggested that Lenin seek permission to travel across Germany. The German High Command, who evidently agreed with their opponents' belief that Lenin would make trouble for Russia, gave the necessary permission. Lenin and his party crossed Germany by train, went then to Sweden, and finally entered Russia through the frontier station at Tornio, Finland. There is a certain irony in the fact that the Russian officials at Tornio treated Lenin just as they did any other Russian who returned from abroad. He had to fill out a standard "Inquiry Form" and to get a standard entry permit. The permit was signed by the head of the Tornio station. A translation of one side of the Inquiry Form is given below. The reverse side bore the notation that "Vlad. Ulyanov" had been given a travel permit by the Russian consul-general in Sweden on March 31st (O.S.). The original is in the Central Lenin Museum.

Inquiry Form

For Russian subjects arriving from abroad through the frontier station of Tornio.

2 April [O.S.], 1917.

Name, Patronymic, surname, rank: Vladimir Ilyich Ulyanov

Last residence: Stockholm (Sweden) (Hotel Regina, Stockholm)

Age, nationality, religion: Born 10 April [O.S.], 1870 at Simbirsk; Russian; Orthodox

For what purpose did you go abroad?: Political refugee. Left Russia illegally.

Give address and purpose of visit if stopping in Finland: No intention of stopping.

To what city are you going? Give address: Petrograd. Sister's address: Mariya Ilyichna Ulyanova, Shirokaya St. 48/9, Apt. 24.

Profession: Journalist

Signature: [s] Vladimir Ulyanov

Kerensky's Speeches and Pronouncements

Alexander Fedorovich Kerensky was a member of the Third and Fourth Dumas, and was the registered head of the "Labor Group." (Some forty years after the February/March Revolution, Kerensky told the editor that his true affiliation had been with the Social Revolutionary party.) Kerensky had been a member of the Executive Committee of the Duma and of the Provisional Committee which was created on February 27/March 12, 1917. He also became a vice-president of the Petrograd Soviet and minister of justice in the Provisional Government. He later became minister of war and navy and, finally, head of the Provisional Government. The documents below consist of excerpts from a few of Kerensky's many speechs and proclamations during the first three months after the February/March Revolution. The material was translated by the *National Geographic Magazine* from documents furnished it by the Imperial Russian Embassy in Washington. The source is: *The National Geographic Magazine.* Vol. XXXII, No. 1 (July, 1917), pp. 24–45, *passim.* Interpolations omitted. Slightly abridged.

Speech to the Petrograd Soviet

Comrades, do you believe me? Do you have faith in me?

I speak, comrades, from the very depths of my heart. I am ready to die should it become necessary.

Comrades, in view of the organization of the new government [*i.e.,* the

Provisional Government], I felt it my duty immediately, without awaiting your formal sanction, to reply to the invitation extended me to assume
the responsibilities as Minister of Justice. . . . I received the invitation
and became a member of the Provisional Government as Minister of
Justice.

My first step was the issuing of an order calling for the immediate liberation of all political prisoners, without any exception; also that our comrades, the deputies of the social democratic faction [sic. The reference is
to the Bolsheviks.] now in Siberia, be escorted here with honors.

In view of the fact that I have assumed the responsibilities of the
Minister of Justice prior to receiving your formal sanction, I now resign as
vice-chairman of the Council of Soldiers and Workmen [the Petrograd
Soviet of Workers' and Soldiers' Deputies]; but I stand ready to again
assume that title should you find it necessary. . . . Every minute is dear.
I call you to organization, discipline; I ask you to extend help to us, your
representatives who are ready to die for the people.

Public Speech

Comrades, soldiers and citizens, I am the member of the Duma, Alexander Kerensky, Minister of Justice. I declare in the presence of all of you
here that the new Provisional Government has assumed its responsibilities
and duties in agreement with the Council of Soldiers and Deputies [the
Petrograd Soviet]. The agreement between the Executive Committee of
the Duma and the Executive Committee of the organization of Soldier
Deputies has been approved by the Council of Workmen and Soldier
Deputies with a majority of several hundred against fifteen.

The first step of the new government is the immediate publication of
the act of full amnesty. Our comrades of the second and fourth Duma,
who were illegally sent to the wilderness of Siberia, will be immediately
liberated and brought here with honors.

Comrades, in my power are now all the representatives of the ex-
Council of Ministers and all the ministers of the old order. They will
answer, comrades, for all crimes committed by them, before the people, in
accordance with the law.

Comrades, free Russia will not stoop to those humiliating means of
struggle which characterized the acts of the old regime. No one will be
punished without trial; all will be judged in an open peoples' court.

Comrades, soldiers and citizens, every step taken by the new government will be public. Soldiers, I beg of you to cooperate. Free Russia has
become one, and no one will succeed in tearing freedom from the peoples'
grasp. Do not mind the exhortations coming from the agents of the old
order. Pay attention to your officers. Long live free Russia!!

First Proclamation

Citizens! So far every order coming from the Provisional Government,
and having in view the complete defeat of the old regime and the establishment of the new order, has been executed by the people without bloodshed.

The honor of the nation demands that the first radiant days of liberty be not befogged by thoughtless and intolerable acts of violence; such acts must be avoided in spite of the natural unrest of citizens.

Conscious of the greatness of the moment, all citizens must voluntarily take all the necessary steps tending to preserve the liberty of every individual without the slightest exception. Be it known to all that the guilty will be put to just trial, which will result in punishing all according to their deserts.

Citizen A. Kerensky, Member of
the Duma, Minister of Justice

Public Speech

Nicholas II is resigned to his fate and has asked the help of the Provisional Government. I, as Minister of Justice, am holding his fate, as well as that of his dynasty, in my hands; but our marvelous revolution was almost bloodless, and I do not want to be the Marat of the Russian revolution. There should be no place for vengeance.

Speech to the Council of Deputies

I have heard there are rumors afloat among you to the effect that my attitude toward the old authorities and the Imperial family is gradually weakening. I have heard that there appear among you people who dare to express a lack of confidence in me. I warn all who speak thus that I will not permit a disbelief in me, and through me insult Russian democracy [sic].

I ask of you to either exclude me from your midst or to give me your full confidence. You accuse the Provisional Government and myself of being too indulgent with members of the Imperial family; you say that we leave them free and treat them with consideration.

I was at Tsarskoye Selo, where I met the officer in command there and spoke with the soldiers. The commandant of the Tsarskoye Selo Palace is a good friend of mine, in whom I have absolute confidence. The garrison promised me to obey all my commands.

You doubt because there are several members of the Tsar [sic] family who are still at liberty, but at liberty are those only who in common with you have protested against the old regime and the rascalities of Tsarism. Dmitry Pavlovich is free because he, too, struggled with the old order up to the very last. He worked out a plan to kill Rasputin, and therefore he has a full right to remain an officer of the Russian army in Persia.

Comrades, soldiers and officers, remember that the work of the Provisional Government is one of enormous responsibilities. The Provisional Government stands for liberty, right, and Russian independence, and it will stand there up to the very last. The equal responsibility for the fate of our country rests on us, on your Provisional Government. In the name of your debt to the country, we must all work together in full unity. I became a member of the Provisional Government as your representative and I endeavored to the utmost of my power to champion your interests and opinions.

I worked for your good, and I will continue doing so as long as you believe in me and as long as you are frank with me; but there appear people who want to create enmity between us. Remember that it is the duty of all of you to continue your good work, and if you will I shall work with you; if this be not your wish, I shall step aside. I want to know, Do you believe me or do you not?

First Order

Having assumed the military powers of the country, I declare:

First. The country is in danger, and a duty devolves upon every one to extricate her from it, regardless of difficulties. I will therefore refuse to accept resignations prompted by a desire to avoid responsibilities in this grave hour.

Second. Those who have voluntarily left their military and fleet units (deserters) must return at the appointed time (the 28th of May).

Third. Those guilty of violation of this order will be punished under the full severity of the law.

To read this order to all companies, squads, batteries, and crews on the battleships.

A. Kerensky
Minister of War and Navy

Order of 25 May

Warriors, officers, soldiers and sailors!

In this great and sad hour in the life of our country, I am commanded by the will of the people to take my place at the head of the Russian armed forces. Infinitely heavy is my new burden; but as an old soldier of the revolution, submitting to the severe discipline of duty, I have assumed before the people and the revolution the responsibility of the army and fleet.

All of you warriors of free Russia, from soldier to general, are fulfilling a glorious debt [? obligation], the debt of defending revolutionary Russia. By defending Russia you are at the same time battling for the triumph of the great ideals of revolution—for liberty, equality, and fraternity. Not a drop of our blood will be spilled in the name of untruth.

You will march forward where your leaders and the government will direct you, not for the purpose of conquest and violence, but in order to save free Russia. It is impossible to drive away the enemy while standing in one place.

On the tips of your bayonets you will bear peace, right, justice, and fair play. In straight ranks, strengthened by discipline of duty and undying love to the revolution and country, we will go forward, free sons of Russia. Without discipline there is no unity of action; without discipline there can be no salvation. The fate of our liberty depends on whether the army and fleet will fulfill their duty to their country up to the very last. By vanquishing Tsarism the army has performed a great deal, having shown how one must love and battle for liberty. But I believe that the army will perform still greater deeds; they will show how to understand liberty, cherish her, and die for her.

Let the freest army and fleet in the world prove that in liberty there is strength and not weakness; let them forge a new and iron discipline of duty, and let them raise the battle strength of the land; let them add to the will of the people that grandeur of might which will hasten the hour of the realization of the people's hopes.

Forward to liberty, land, and freedom!! . . .

Brothers, I greet you in the name of the Russian revolution; I bow before you in the name of the great Russian people!

To read the order to all companies, squads, batteries, and to all the crews on all men-of-war.

A. Kerensky,
Minister of War and Navy

Order for the Brusilov Offensive

Russia, liberated from the chains of slavery, is firmly resolved to protect, at all cost, the rights of honor and liberty. Having had faith in the fraternal feelings of nations, the Russian democracy has called the warring countries with an ardent appeal to cease the carnage and to conclude an honorable peace, securing tranquillity for all nations; but, in response to this fraternal appeal, the enemy has proposed to us treason.

The Austro-Germans have offered to Russia a separate peace and tried to blind our vigilance by fraternization, hurling themselves at the same time against our allies with the hope of crushing us after their defeat. Being now convinced that Russia will not allow herself to be tricked, the enemy is threatening us and concentrating troops on our front.

Warriors, our motherland is in danger. Freedom and revolution are in peril. The time has come when our army must accomplish its duty. Your commanding general, beloved through victory, proclaims that each day lost adds new strength to our enemy, and that only an immediate decisive blow can disrupt the plans of the foe.

Therefore, being fully conscious of the great responsibility of the country, in the name of the free Russian people and its Provisional Government, I call upon the armies, strengthened with vigor by the revolutionary genius, to start the offensive. The enemy must wait before celebrating victory. All nations must know that it was not through weakness that we talked peace. Let them know that liberty augments our forces. Officers and soldiers, you must realize that all Russia is blessing your acts on the field of honor. In the name of liberty, future prosperity, and in the name of a lasting and honorable peace, I command you, Forward!

A. Kerensky,
Minister of War and Navy

The April Theses

> Until Lenin's arrival in Petrograd in April, the lesser leaders of the Bolsheviks (including Stalin) had produced no clear-cut program and had not progressed beyond the stage of general obstructionism and trouble-making. Lenin at once set to work to change that situation. The day after his arrival, he presented a specific program of revolution. His proposals evoked a stormy dissent even among the other Bolshevik leaders, but within a month he had won the majority of the party's Central Executive Committee to his side. It is not too much to say that Lenin here changed the course of history. The Bolshevik leaders (for example, Stalin, Kamenev, and Molotov) who had returned to Petrograd before Lenin had no such plan as his even if they had had the force to carry it through. It was Lenin who took over full control of the party; trained, disciplined, and prepared it; set the goals; determined the strategy and picked the tactics; and, finally, chose the time for action.
>
> The statement of the program which he presented on April 17th (N.S.) has been widely reprinted. The version given here is translated from the program as it was published in *Pravda* on April 20, 1917.

1. In our attitude toward the war, which on the part of Russia still remains, under the new government of Lvov and Co., unquestionably a predatory, imperialist war because of the capitalist nature of that government, not the slightest concession ought to be made to "a revolutionary movement in favor of defending a capitalist fatherland."

The class-conscious proletariat might give their consent to a revolutionary war, truly justifying a revolutionary movement in favor of defense of a capitalist fatherland, only on condition: (a) that power be transferred to the proletariat and to the poor peasantry which is close to the proletariat, (b) that all annexations be renounced in fact and not just in words, (c) that a genuine break be made with all capitalist interests.

In view of the indubitable good faith with which large sections of the masses accept the war as necessary for the defense of the country . . . , in view of the fact that they are being fooled by the bourgeoisie, it is necessary to explain their mistake to them . . . , to explain the indissoluble tie between capitalism and the imperialist war, to prove to them that it is impossible to end the war by a really democratic, free peace without the overthrow of capitalism. Organize the most widespread propaganda for this view among the troops on active duty. [Preach] fraternization.

2. The uniqueness of the current moment in Russia lies in the transition from the first stage of revolution in which, because of the lack of class-consciousness and organization among the proletariat, power fell to the bourgeoisie to the second stage in which power ought to be put in the hands of the proletariat and the poor peasants.

This transition stage is characterized, in the first place by a maximum of legality (Russia is now the freest of all the warring countries in the world); in the second place, by an absence of violence against the masses; and, finally, by a totally unwarranted confidence in the capitalist government which is really the worst enemy of peace and of socialism.

This situation demands of us flexibility in adapting ourselves to the unique requirements for Party work among unprecedently large masses of the proletariat who have been aroused to political awareness.

3. There must be no support given to the Provisional Government. The complete falseness of its promises, particularly those relating to annexations, must be explained. [There must be] an exposure of the unpardonable, illusion-breeding "demand" that this government, a government of capitalists, cease to be imperialistic.

4. We must recognize the fact that in most of the Soviets of Workers' Deputies our Party is a minority and so far a small minority compared to the bloc of all the petty-bourgeois, opportunist elements who have surrendered to bourgeois influences and who transmit those influences to the masses.

It must be explained to the masses that the Soviets are the only possible form for a revolutionary government; and our task, therefore, as long as this government surrenders to bourgeois influences, is patiently, systematically and persistently to expose—in a way especially adapted to the practical needs of the masses—the errors of their tactics.

So long as we remain a minority, we must carry on the work of criticizing and explaining errors so that the masses may overcome their mistakes through experience; and, simultaneously, we must advocate the transfer of the entire power of the state to the Soviets of Workers' Deputies.

5. [There must be] No parliamentary republic—to return to a parliamentary republic from Soviets of Workers' Deputies would be retrogression —but a republic of Soviets of Workers', Farm-hands', and Peasants' Deputies throughout the land, "from top to bottom."

Abolition of the police, the army, and the bureaucracy. (i.e., the standing army to be replaced by the universally armed people [peoples' militia]).

All officials to be elected and subject to recall at any time, and their salaries shall not be greater than those of good workers.

6. In the agrarian program, the emphasis must be on the Soviets of Farm-hands' Deputies. All landowners' estates to be confiscated. All land in the country to be nationalized; the distribution of the land to be in the hands of the Soviets of Farm-hands' and Peasants' Deputies. Separate Soviets of Poor-Peasants' Deputies to be organized. Model farms to be set up on each large estate (from 270 to 810 acres, depending on local conditions and at the discretion of the local bodies) under the direction of the Soviets of Farm-hands' Deputies and for the common good.

7. All banks in the country to be merged at once into a single national bank which shall be controlled by the Soviet of Workers' Deputies.

8. Our immediate job is not to "introduce" Socialism but only to bring the production and distribution of goods under the control of the Soviet of Workers' Deputies at once.

9. Party tasks:
a) To summon a Party congress at once;
b) To change the Party program, mainly: 1) on the question of im-
    perialism and the imperialist war; 2) on the question of our attitude
    toward the state, and our demand for a "Commune state" (i.e., a
    state of which the prototype was the Paris Commune.); 3) amend-
    ment of our antiquated minimum program.
c) A new name for the Party (instead of "Social Democrats," whose
    official leaders . . . have betrayed socialism . . . , we must call
    ourselves a Communist Party.)

10. A new International. We must take the lead in creating a revolutionary International, an International directed against the social-chau-
vinists and against the "Center" (. . . i.e. [against] Kautsky & Co. in
Germany, Longuet & Co. in France, Chkeidze & Co. in Russia, Turati &
Co. in Italy, MacDonald & Co. in England, etc.)

The Land Question, 1917

Throughout Russian and Soviet history, no problem has been more
persistent and more resistant to solution than the agrarian problem. It
is, in fact, not one problem, but a complex of many problems involving
climate and soil fertility, agricultural practices and tools, as well as
problems of landownership and control. Members of the Provisional
Government recognized the seriousness of the problem but were unable
to compose their deep differences about solutions to be attempted. The
results of their temporizing, as well as some measure of the difficulty
of their position, are set forth below in a series of excerpts from the
official archives.

The source is: M. Martynov (Ed.), "Agrarnoe dvizhenie v 1917 g.,"
Krasnyi Arkhiv ("Agrarian Movements in 1917," *Red Archives*). Vol.
XIV, pp. 185–226, *passim*. The documents were translated and the
translations made available to me by Professor Kenneth I. Dailey.

Telegraphic report (No. 1) from V. Samoulenko, Commissar of the
Minsk Gubernia to Prince Urusov, Deputy Minister of the Interior;
dated 12 May, 1917.

The agrarian movement has not yet reached a particularly hot stage here.
There have been no great events. Mass phenomena—prohibition against
cutting the forests, preparation of timber, and illegal pasturing of cattle.
The movement grows since the Peasants' Convention because they consider the resolutions of their Convention as law. The Commissariat issued
and published a memorandum that such actions are illegal. The results of
this memorandum are not yet clear. . . .

Increasing disorders are observed among the military at the front. . . .
in the Novogrudsk District, two battalions attached to the estate of Prince
Svyatopolk-Mirsky looted the wine cellars, got drunk, burned down the
palace, and looted his property. The looting continues. Warnings do not
help. They do not obey their superiors. . . . . . Fires assume an epidemic character; the woods of the Krukovsk State Forest are burning; 25

houses (farm units) burned down at the village of Zagorye; 186 buildings, in the little town of Sverzhene; 18, in the village of Pishkovtsy; 16 houses, in the village of Savichky.

> Telegraphic report (No. 2) from Kliott, Deputy Commissar of the Vilno Gubernia, to Prince Urusov, Deputy Minister of the Interior; dated 16 May, 1917.

The agrarian movement in Vilno Gubernia took the form of the transfer to the volost committees of privately owned and some state owned forests. Forest guards are dismissed. These committees permitted the peasants to graze their cattle in forests and pastures everywhere. Private ponds have been declared community property. In the District of Desna, Boginnsk volost, Count Plyater's steam mill was seized by the peasants.

> Report by the Commissar of the Novoalexan-
> drovsk District, Kovno Gubernia; dated 14 June, 1917 (No. 207).

On the 4th of June, at the town of Desna, Vitebsk Gubernia, the Commissar convoked a Peasants' Convention of the Vitebsk Gubernia and of that part of the District of Novoalexandrovsk which has been attached for administrative matters to the Government of Vilno. About 400 representatives, peacefully minded peasants, appeared. Speakers from the extreme left wing parties (the Socialist Revolutionaries) appeared and excited the whole assembly. [They declared:] "All the land is ours, and you may now take all you need in accordance with the resolutions of the volost committees—fields, forests, meadows, ponds, etc.—and in order to legalize this, so that it will not be considered as a seizure, you have to pay, not to the owners but to the volost committees—the very lowest rent per dessyatin."

It was suggested that they replace all foresters on privately owned and state owned lands with persons of their own choice. The charge for grinding grain was set at the lowest figure imaginable, and the millers, unwilling to work for such pay, refused to work. In such cases, the volost committees seize the mills. All waters, ponds and rivers are taken over by the volost committees . . . and former tenants are sent away. Private owners are permitted to harvest hay for their own use, but only up to 10 July and on condition that they do it by their own efforts without hired help. So, according to this convention, private owners and their tenants are completely excluded from managing their land, and everything goes over to the hands of the volost or village committees. Persons unqualified for the duties are elected to the volost committees. Those who promise to take all private land from the owners and give it to the peasants are elected. Private owners are entitled only to that which they can cultivate by their own strength. Until this resolution was adopted, I managed, although with great difficulty, to restrain the peasants of the Novoalexandrovsk District from more seizures, illegal grazing, forest cutting, etc. But I am no longer able to do this. When the peasant delegates return from the convention, they recount all the speeches they heard, and they take no notice of my protests, saying that they heard differently at the convention. . . .

The duties of the elected District Commissars are very difficult. When trying to stop seizures, and when remonstrating with the peasants at volost meetings, they cry: "We elected you and if you won't stick with us, we will fire you." Besides, when the volost committee makes decisions, it does not present these to the District Commissar for approval, and the decisions go into effect at once. I request the Department to send out, as quickly as possible, instructions as to the rights and duties of the volost committees, and to emphasize that not a single decision of a volost committee can be put into effect without the approval of the District Commissar or district committee. . . .

> From a note to the Central Land Committee, written by a convention of landowners of Kirsanovsk, Tambov Gubernia; dated 12 June, 1917.

Old people, rich people, and women who were still left in the country accepted the *coup d'etat* quietly, and explained it as a consequence of the Tsar's irrational management of the country. It could be expected that the demand for a socialist revolution would not quickly penetrate into the countryside so that the movement, in the beginning, would remain simply a demand by soldiers and workers. But the change of the whole local government, the liquidation of the police force and of every former authority in the village, and the amnesty of criminals speeded the revolutionary process. The revolution, moving into the village, found no governmental institutions there. . . .

At Kirsanovsk, there was a self-constituted committee for public safety —not picked on the basis of general elections, but consisting of people chosen by chance because general elections were impossible. This committee initiated the formation of committees in the volosts. Part of the people protested the illegality of these actions, but their protests received no support. Because of this, people came to the conclusion that—according to the new order, as the peasants called it—the desires of the people as expressed by the committees were the highest law of the country, and that there were no limits whatever on popular rights. The peasants came to this conclusion because none of the decisions made by the committee, despite their illegality, has ever been revoked by the Government. . . . The village was left to itself. Here are some of the excesses of the peasants and of the committees.

[The peasants fired the managers of the estates of Count Perevsk and Senator Martinov, and arrested the manager of Mr. Nosov's estate.] The volost committee of Kurdyukovsk has taken all oat seed from the landowners, and has sold it to the peasants at prices below the fixed prices. In many volosts, peasants searched the landowners' houses, seized their documents, took their weapons, prohibited the sale of their agricultural products and their transportation from the estate. All sales and deals were superintended by the volost committee, and prices and agreements were changed. . . . . . . It became impossible to manage the farms, and many landowners left their estates and went into town. . . . For a time, the committee assumed the right to collect all duties, payments and arrears; assumed the right to hold auctions and . . . [forbid] residents of other volosts to take part in these auctions. . . . The District Committee decided to reduce land rents by 25% compared to last year. The volost committee went still further and decided to lower the rents by 60%, and in some places the peasants took possession of lands entirely without compensation to the owners.

[After noting that low rents encouraged peasants to grab more land than they could till, and that the peasants of a village or an estate refused to share the lands with "strange peasants," the statement continues:] . . . they were convinced that the right to own lands taken from the landlords could be granted only to those peasants who had previously belonged to that same landlord. In this way, former serfs were again overloaded with land while the smaller (i.e., state) peasants got nothing. And the first attempt of socialism . . . did not end the anarchy in Russian life. . . .

In vain did the landlords apply to the volost and district commissars. The commissars agreed as to the complete illegality of the [committees'] regulations, but said they were not allowed to cancel them. They merely suggested that the landlords liquidate their estates.

> From the notes of the Manager of the State Banking Department in Chistopolsk (No. 1); dated 2 July, 1917.

The fatal consequences of the slackening of power are already at hand. All the arable land, the woods, and the meadows have passed from their owners into the hands of the peasants and, therefore, we can expect for next year neither the quantity (many lands will be empty) nor the quality of grain (the ploughing is done negligently, even worse than the previous ploughing done by the peasants.) The thoroughbred cattle have been seized; part of them butchered on the spot, and part of them sold and driven away. Horse-breeding farms were destroyed, and race horses hitched to ploughs, harrows, seeding machines, and harvesters; and because of the lack of experienced hands all this inventory is already out of order. Well-kept gardens were destroyed, young trees were uprooted and the bark was torn from old trees. . . . The proprietors . . . were told: "You have lived long enough by our labor, and you have drunk our blood long enough. Now it is our turn.". . .

> A report from the District Commissar of Ranenburg, Ryazan Gubernia, dated 28 July, 1917, struck an entirely different note. Although admitting that the harvest would be very poor (three to five times less than in the preceding year), the commissar reported that matters were going well with a maximum of cooperation and a minimum of disorder. But even this optimistic report concluded that there was " . . . an existing tendency to undermine the authority of the committee and to create distrust among the population. . . ." Commissar's reports from the Gubernias of Kazan and Simbirsk stressed the growth of disorder and violence in these areas during July and August. "The peasants of the village of Yashkino, supported by the volost and village committees, seized horses, harnesses and tools. . . . The enforcement of the law on grain monopoly meets strong resistance from the peasants. . . . The food question does not show any im-

provement, and the shortage of food is great. . . . a member of the Chertanovsk Food Committee was seized by the people while carrying out his official duties. . . . the soldiers Frolkin and Rezkin are making propaganda against the grain monopoly. . . . Steps are being taken to stop the activities of agitators." But soldiers sent out to help the committee collect grain ". . . went over to the side of the peasants instead of helping the authorities induce the peasants to deliver their grain. . . . They crossed their rifles before the doors of the barns and declared that they would not allow the grain to be taken."

From a report to the Minister of Agriculture by A. V. Granov, representative of the Ministry in Kherson Gubernia (no. 3); dated 29 August, 1917.

. . . I had to speak at a meeting of the District Land Committee at Odessa, and I met very serious opposition. There was a dull discontent among the peasants. Everyone apparently wanted to say: "We are tired of waiting. In Petrograd, they talk and busy themselves, but we have to plough.". . .

Resuming, I have to repeat what I already said . . . [to] the Central Land Committee and personally to A. F. Kerensky: that it is impossible to procrastinate any more in the matter of an agrarian law. . . . the present moment seems a great deal less favorable for carrying out any measures of the Provisional Government than it was three or four weeks ago. The prestige and the authority of the Government have fallen from the high point they held after the happenings of 3–5 June and after the formation of the present coalition cabinet.

Lenin Calls the Revolution

The complete breakdown of the July offensive, the breaking away of Ukraine and the consequent resignation of the Kadet ministers from the coalition government brought new turmoil to Petrograd. A group of irresponsible enthusiasts, including some Bolsheviks, promoted an uprising against the government. Lenin, whose preparations were not completed, correctly judged the movement to be premature and sought to restrain it. When he found that he could not stop it, Lenin made a quick tactical change and ordered his followers to join the movement in the hope of thus being able to control it. After three days of disorder, the rising gradually petered out. Lenin and some of his colleagues were forced to go into hiding in nearby Finland in order to escape arrest. However, he continued to keep in constant contact with his group and was able to maintain his control over it.

By October, Lenin judged that the situation had changed completely. His own preparations were completed, and the government was much weaker, largely as a result of the Kornilov affair. On October 7/20, Lenin returned secretly to Petrograd, and at the meeting of the Central Executive Committee of the Bolsheviks on October 10/23, he proposed the resolution which is the first of two following documents. The resolution was vigorously opposed by some of the committee, but Lenin finally succeeded in getting it adopted.

The second document is Lenin's "Letter to the Members of the Central Committee," written on the literal eve of the Petrograd coup. The originals of both documents are in the Central Lenin Museum. They are here translated in full.

The C[entral] C[ommittee] recognizes that both the international position of the Russian Revolution (revolution in the German Navy which is an extreme manifestation of the world Socialist Revolution, and the threat by the imperialists to make a peace in order to stifle the revolution in Russia)—and the military situation (certain decision of the Russian bourgeoisie and Kerensky and Co. to surrender Petrograd to the Germans)—and also the securing of a majority in the Soviets by the party of the proletariat—all this in conjunction with the peasant uprisings and the increase of public confidence in our Party (Moscow elections), and lastly the obvious preparations for a second Kornilov affair (removal of the soldiers from Petrograd, sending of Cossacks to Petrograd, encirclement of Minsk by Cossacks, etc.)—all this places armed insurrection on the order of the day.

Therefore, recognizing that armed insurrection is inevitable and that the time is completely ripe for it, the C[entral] C[ommittee] calls upon all Party organizations to govern themselves accordingly, and to discuss and settle all practical questions from this standpoint (Congress of Soviets of the Northern Region, troop withdrawal from Petrograd, action in Moscow and Minsk, etc.)

• • •

I am writing these lines on the evening of the 24th [Oct. 24/November 6, 1917]. The situation is critical in the extreme. It is absolutely clear that to delay the insurrection now would be truly fatal.

I exhort my comrades with all my strength to realize that everything now hangs by a thread; that we are being confronted by problems which cannot be solved by conferences or congresses (even Congresses of Soviets) but exclusively by peoples, by the masses, by the struggle of the armed masses.

The bourgeois onslaught of the Kornilovites and the removal of Vekhovsky show that we must not wait. We must at all costs, this very evening, this very night, arrest the government, first disarming the Junkers (defeating them if they resist) and so forth.

We must not wait! We may lose everything!

The value of the immediate seizure of power will be the defense of the people (not of the congress, but of the people, the army and the peasants in the first place) from the Kornilovite government, which has driven out Verkhovsky and has hatched a second Kornilov plot.

Who must take power?

That is not important at the moment. Let the Revolutionary Military Committee take it, or "some other institution" which will declare that it will relinquish the power only to the true representatives of the interests of the people, the interests of the army (immediate proposal of peace) the interests of the peasants (land to be taken immediately and private property abolished) the interests of the starving.

All districts, regiments, forces must be mobilized at once and must immediately send their delegations to the Revolutionary Military Committee and to the Central Committee of the Bolsheviks with the insistent demand that under no circumstances must the power be left in the hands of Kerensky and Co. until the 25th—not under any circumstances; the matter must be decided without fail this very evening, or this very night.

History will not forgive revolutionaries for procrastinating when they could be victorious today (will certainly be victorious today) while they risk losing much, in fact, everything, tomorrow.

If we seize power today, we seize it not in opposition to the Soviets, but on their behalf.

The seizure of power is a matter of insurrection; its political purpose will become clear after the seizure.

It would be a disaster, or a sheer formality, to await the wavering vote of October 25. The people have the right and the duty to decide such questions not by a vote, but by force; in critical moments of revolution, the people have the right and the duty to direct their representatives, even their best representatives, and not to wait for them.

This is proved by the history of all revolutions; and it would be an infinite crime on the part of the revolutionaries were they to let the moment slip, knowing that upon them depends the salvation of the revolution, the proposal of peace, the salvation of Petrograd, salvation from famine, the transfer of the land to the peasants.

The government is wavering. It must be given the finishing blow at all costs.

To delay actions will be fatal.

[s] V. I. Lenin

A Revolutionary Proclamation

This is a translation of the proclamation which announced the Bolshevik *coup* in Petrograd. It was printed as a poster. The original is in the Central Lenin Museum.

FROM THE REVOLUTIONARY MILITARY COMMITTEE OF THE PETROGRAD SOVIET OF WORKERS' AND SOLDIERS' DEPUTIES

TO THE CITIZENS OF RUSSIA

The Provisional Government has been overthrown. Governing power has passed into the hands of the agent of the Petrograd Soviet of Workers' and Soldiers' Deputies, the Revolutionary Military Committee, which stands at the head of the proletariat and garrison of Petrograd.

The cause for which the people fought: the immediate proposal for a democratic peace, the abolition of landlordism, control of production by the workers, the creation of a Soviet government—is secure.

Long live the revolution of the workers, the soldiers, and the peasants!

The Revolutionary Military Committee for the Petrograd Soviet of Workers' and Soldiers' Deputies.

25 October, [O.S.] 1917
10 A.M.

His Opponents Talk

The reader may wish to compare Lenin's dramatic call to planned action with the following account of the activities of the Council of the Republic on October 25/November 7. The description was written by Professor Pitirim Sorokin, then a leading member of the Right-Wing Social Revolutionaries and secretary to Kerensky. The dialogue is meant to convey the sense of what was said; it is not a literal record of the remarks. The source is: Pitirim A. Sorokin, *Leaves from a Russian Diary—and Thirty Years After*. Enlarged edition. Boston: Beacon Press, 1950. Pp. 98–100.

On October 25, in spite of illness, I set out for the Winter Palace to get news. In the streets I saw the familiar spectacle of speeding automobiles full of sailors and Latvian soldiers, firing recklessly as they passed; no trams, no droshkies. But so accustomed had all of us grown to this condition of things that I went on quite indifferently. Approaching the Winter Palace, I found it surrounded by Bolshevist troops. It would have been sheer folly to walk into their arms, so I turned around and sought, in the Mariinsky Palace, the Council of the Republic. There I learned that while Kerensky had fled to the front to seek military assistance, Konovaloff and the other Ministers, with the Governor of Petrograd, Rutenberg and Palchinsky, were barricaded in the Winter Palace defended only by a regiment of women soldiers and three hundred military cadets.

"This is outrageous!" stormed a Social Democrat deputy. "We shall certainly protest against such violence."

"What! Are we going to pass another resolution?" I asked.

"In the name of the Soviet, the Council of the Republic and the Government we shall appeal to the country and to the world democracy," he replied, offended at my levity.

"And what is that but another resolution?" I asked banteringly.

"We shall appeal to the military forces."

"What military forces?"

"Officers and Cossacks are still faithful."

"The same men whom the revolutionary democracy treated as counter-revolutionaries and reactionaries," I persisted. "Have you forgotten how you insulted them, especially after Korniloff's failure? After that do you imagine they will be willing to defend us? I think, on the contrary, that they will be rather gratified at what has happened."

The Council of the Republic convened, and a proposal to protest against the criminal attack on the rights of the people and of the Government was made and debated. But the discussion did not last very long, for suddenly the Hall was invaded by a troop of soldiers who announced: "According to a decree of the new Government the Council of the Republic is dispersed. Leave here immediately or submit to arrest."

The chairman of the council said: "The resolution of protest has been heard. All in favor raise their hands." The resolution was carried. Then the chairman said: "Under pressure of violence the Council of the Republic is temporarily interrupted." Such was the end of the first Republic, an end scarcely more heroic than that of the Duma.

The Revolution in the Provinces

The five selections which conclude this section are excerpts from the unpublished diary and letters of Mr. Graham R. Taylor who was an eyewitness of the events described. Mr. Taylor, who had been on the staff of *The Survey Magazine* since 1910, was specially recruited by the Department of State and sent to Russia in 1916 as one of a staff of special assistants requested by Ambassador David R. Francis to assist him in administering funds sent by the German and Austrian governments for the relief of their civilian nationals interned in Russia. There were roughly 200,000 such persons, and most of them were interned in remote villages. Mr. Taylor was assigned to improve the distribution of these funds and to improve the lot of the internees in Orenburg Province. He was in the provincial capital (Orenburg) when the February/March Revolution took place. His description of events there supplies a useful complement to Mr. Heald's account of events in Petrograd. The confusion and uncertainties, the improvisations, and the optimism which Mr. Taylor noted were characteristic of the early weeks of the revolution.

Responsibility for German and Austrian interests was turned over to the Swedish and Danish embassies after the United States entered the war, and Mr. Taylor was assigned to other special duties by the embassy. He was in Moscow, except for one brief absence, from April, 1917 until January, 1918 when he was sent to Petrograd to head the office of the American Committee on Public Information there. Along with other members of the "Compub" staff, Mr. Taylor was removed from Russia by the State Department in May, 1919. He was subsequently sent to Siberia to carry on the "Compub" work and remained there until April, 1919. From 1922 until his death in 1942, Mr. Taylor was Director of the Division of Publications of the Commonwealth Fund.

Neither the diary nor the letters were written for publication, and I am indebted to Mrs. Graham R. Taylor for permission to use excerpts from them. I have omitted all purely personal matters, but have not otherwise altered the material.

1. DIARY

March 15, 1917

. . .

No especial turbulence in Orenburg. Crowds around Orenburg Slovo office. The telegrams—short handbills issued by the papers—and the papers themselves appear with no reference to the Censor in them. The customary line "Passed by the Censor" does not appear.

Everyone is wondering what the Governor will do—he is associated with extreme reactionaries—is a member of the famous "Black 100"— Union of the Russian People. But the great question is what will the Tsar do.

. . .

Citizens Committee put up a statement on Kiosks and had boys distribute calling on people to support new Govt. Gov. issued proclamation to be careful about paying any attention to this Committee.—Patrols of Cossacks in the streets. Bare report that the Tsar has abdicated his throne.

March 16, 1917

Publication of Tsar's Manifesto resigning the throne and designating Michael, his brother, as successor.

March 17, 1917

Everybody relieved to know that the Gov. has sent a telegram accepting the new Govt. List of ministers printed: . . .

Everybody here is incensed at finding out that the censor in the P.O. held up a telegram two days while another wire was sent to Petrograd to find out if the news was true. This delayed the news of the Revolution two days in Orenburg. . . .

March 18, 1917

The Orenburg news is interesting. A meeting of 5,000 soldiers and officers of the town garrison was held in the circus last evening and a telegram was sent to Petrograd demanding the dismissal of Gen'l. Sandetsky in Kazan and Gen'l. Pogoretsky. The latter was arrested last night. So also was Col. Kashinseff, head of the gendarmerie on whom I have frequently called—a very decent chap. He is held in the house of the Police Master who announced that he w'd [would] follow the orders of the Citizens' Committee. There seem to be new police officers in town—the old uniforms, but a white band tied around the arm to indicate the new citizen police.

With the acceptance of the *new* Govt. by the Govt. and the coming into line of the Police Master and of the soldiers of the garrison, all danger of disturbances here seems over. But in Tver, the Gov[ernor] was killed and the Gov[ernor] of Kursk has fled no one knows where. . . .

March 20, 1917

Went to call on former Gov[ernor] Tulin. A changed atmosphere at the very doorstep of the palace—for a "citizens' militia"—man stood at the door—that sign on the white band around his arm. He said when I explained I only wanted to see "His Excellency" on a personal matter— that Tulin was inside. And so he was, just inside the door. He said he would be very glad to see me presently. So I went upstairs. The place seemed deserted. No haughtiness of doorkeepers and servants—very different demeanor. Not a soul in the ante room, where formerly a group of officials was always waiting to see the chief. After a moment—during which I overheard Tulin phoning to someone: "Think of me no more as the Governor; I am going to the front where I was." The door of his chamber opened and out came an orderly who bid me come in. Another change—his desk had not a paper on it. The place was like a room to which a family returns in its town house from summer vacation.

He looked as if he had gone through worries. There was none of the grave "important" and preoccupied air as formerly—but geniality as usual, but of a somewhat more leisurely and more human sort. I think he felt his changed position, for he opened the conversation by saying: "Of course I am no longer Governor, but only Ataman of the Cossacks."

March 22, 1917

Manch read in the paper about special message sent by Kerensky to have Madame Breshkovsky released. Thanks be to God.

March 25, 1917

A day which has thrilled me in every fibre. A demonstration for the new government and in honor of those who died two weeks ago today in the streets of Petrograd. With McConnaughey and Manch, I started out to the great open Ploshaty between the Forstadt and the Main city. The place was a mass of soldiers and citizens. The latter mainly on the west side, covering hillside and roofs; the soldiers drawn up in long ranks facing the west. Their heads were bare and in front of them were gorgeously arrayed priests performing an out of doors Mass. The soldiers' backs were toward the Monument erected in honor of the 300th year of the Romanoff dynasty. Over the inscription on the building cloths were stretched, while in front of it were two red flags.

Soon the droning of the priests ended and as with one hand the hats of the soldiers went on. Then they marched so as to form the eastern and northern side of a great square. Across the square were masses of citizens. Both citizens and soldiers had scores of red flags and banners with all sorts of inscriptions. Then the military band played a funeral march in memory of the Petrograd martyrs. Also a good old Congregational hymn tune. I walked along behind the rows of soldiers, to see the banners. They read, "Cheers for the Freedom of Russia."—this on a red flag held aloft by Cossacks! "Hurrah for the Constitutional Assembly." "Freedom, Equality,

Fraternity" was on many banners. One red banner held between two sticks showed on one side two figures of bureaucrats in court regalia. One was holding a chain which extended to the shackled wrist of a soldier. The other's chain went to a student. The words were, "The old Regime: men rot in its chains." The other side showed the two officials toppling on the ground, the chains broken—the soldier and the student looked happy— beaming. The inscription read "The New Order," "Freedom breaks the chains." My eyes could hardly believe the sight of that held aloft by the Cossacks.

The bands played the Marseillaise and the vast assemblage sang a labor hymn to its strains. Then the citizens' committee of 27 headed by Mayor Clientov and the new commander of [the] garrison here walked all around the inside of the great square—the crowds hurrahing and the committee bowing.

This ended, the soldiers began to march past the east side of the square, their faces showing their great pleasure at the shouts of the citizens for "our soldiers." Always previously when soldiers were marching in the streets the people seemed utterly indifferent.

As the citizen leaders tried to keep the crowd from pressing in on the line of march, I heard one of them rather impatiently say, "You have no organization; be organized." I could not help thinking of the enormous problem ahead and how slow and difficult it would be as compared with that simple yet earnest command or exhortation.

Many banners reminded one of socialist demonstrations in New York: "Proletariat of all nations: Unite." "The Eight Hour Work Day." etc. I could not help thinking of the great crowd of peasants on the steppe last September accompanying the sacred image and contrasting that mediae- valism with this radical modernism and wondering how it will all work out. But as I saw the banner "Advance: Free Russia." I could not help think- ing of Breshovsky and the other exiles in Siberia and with what joy they would get the news that Russia is at last Free.

2. LETTER OF APRIL 3, 1917

. . . I left Moscow on Thursday, March 8, the very day when all un- known to us the bread rioting began in Petrograd—which was to lead, in five days to the new Government. On the way I made the acquaintance of a prominent Petrograd business man who was in the next compartment to mine. He was most interesting and well informed and we had one of those talks of which I have so longed to write you, about politics here. We dis- cussed the impending revolution—everyone I have talked with ever since I came here has talked of nothing else. The war has been decidedly second- ary in the people's thought, as compared to the internal situation. The great question all along has been whether the revolution would come be- fore or after the end of the war, and whether it would be a quick overturn at the top—especially after the assassination of that most extraordinary and revolting character Rasputin. All the stories about him—and indeed a lot of the events during these few months in Russia have made me feel as if I were in an Arabian Nights sort of existence. But my companion on the train told me that he gave the Tsar only a few more weeks of power and perhaps of life. How little did we know that the period would not be weeks, but just 4 days from that very conversation.

I started to work to finish up in Orenburg and clear out for good. They gave me a banquet on Tuesday night—the very night when the crisis was reached in Petrograd and the new Government was sure, the soldiers rallying that day to the support of the revolution. Yet not a word of all the great events reached us until Thursday. We found out afterward that the news actually arrived in Orenburg by telegraph on Tuesday—as to the events up to that time in Petrograd—but the head of the telegraph in Orenburg pocketed the news and kept the entire city in ignorance for two days.

At once all sorts of rumors went around. The crowds gathered in front of the local newspaper office—the very newspaper of which an edition had been confiscated a few weeks before, because of anti-government expressions, my best friend among the officials in Orenburg personally directing the confiscation. The Governor, a man of high standards and intelligence, but very conservative, posted his proclamation alongside of one which had been posted by an anonymous citizens committee, telling the people to pay no attention to the citizens committee announcement bespeaking support for the new government. For a time we were afraid there would be violence, which there certainly would have been, if the Governor had persisted in that policy. For of course he could call upon the 50,000 troops in the town.

But in two days he announced that he recognized the new government, and all was peaceful. He was one of a very few governors not arrested by the citizens. My old friend, the Col. of the Gendarmerie was at once clapped into jail. The Gendarmerie was abolished all over Russia as you know—and what that means you can imagine, for they were the special police whose sole duty was to uphold the dynasty—they are the ones who sent people to Siberia.

The "Persuader-in-Chief"

The somewhat derisive nickname of "persuader-in-chief," which was given to Kerensky, was more accurate than its sponsors may have realized. The Provisional Government lacked coercive authority. It could only request, suggest, and seek to persuade—and Kerensky's voice was the most persuasive it possessed. The following passages from Mr. Taylor's diary describe Kerensky's appearance at two meetings in Petrograd.

June 8, 1917

Spent much time trying to get a box for Mr. Crane at the Kerensky meeting this afternoon. Finally got some seats in the Tsar's box at Bolshoi Theatre. Also a box for tomorrow's meeting in the Zemena Theatre. But we didn't care to go to this P.M.'s meeting. So Bakeman, Lewis and I went, a great demonstration. Difficult to squeeze into the theatre. Felt embarrassed when we were ushered in alone into the Tsar's box. Later [Bruce] Lockhart, [the] French Consul and [the] Jap Consul came.

Big orchestra, about 200—70 violins and 12 bass viols. Played Marseillaise. With chorus rendered new Russian hymns. Speeches by Chernov. And then Kerensky appeared. Dramatic—simple uniform of a private— not even shoulder straps—nothing glittering—only a red rose on his blouse. He jumped on a table, disregarding speakers' pulpit and with one gloved hand (on acct. of a recent injury) he [spoke] with hoarse, jerky voice and jerky fore arm gestures, he bit off his speech—a phrase or a word at a time—impression of great intensity—pauses between. Rasping voice but crisp and incisive; every word to count. He said, "In Riga a man said the people have been so long oppressed that they don't know how to use freedom now that they have it. All is disorder and the people show no initiative to construct the new order. I say that it is an insult. But we must work to show that we do know what to do with freedom. I tell you, from my observation at the front that the army is heroically doing its part— and they suffer hunger and cold. I wonder how many of you ought to be 'out there.' "But the only way for the army to do its best effectively is for you to do your part here. You must work to supply the army."

He used simple words and he threw in "tovareesh" occasionally and looked at the galleries most effectively. When he concluded people rushed down the aisles, and threw roses at him and all sort of flowers. Soldiers on the stage kissed him. Fortunately I got down by the door just as he passed out to his auto—so jammed in the crowd it could not move for some time. Face brown and he looked full of vigor, though tired. Fine build and looks as young as his 36 years. Hard to believe that with tb of the kidneys he is not likely to last long.

June 9, 1917

We all went down to the Zemena Theatre—meeting of the Social-Revolutionary Party—Kerensky's own party. Great crowd. He said: "No one has the right to be pessimistic. The Revolution was not a holiday, but the start of a great era of self-sacrifice. As Minister of War, I find it hard to send men to the trenches to die—instead of myself. But I do it because there is no other way of keeping up our revolution. I expect all of the mass of the people—all of us—to throw away the little trivial interests and look on the whole movement for the new life as if we—each one of us—had full responsibility. Each one in practising self-denial will bring that spirit into the whole crowd."

Collection was taken to send literature to men in the trenches—who say they are willing to undergo all physical hardships but don't want to starve their brains.

Speech by Aksenticff—a political exile in Paris for 10 years—who came back after the Rev. Said he loves Moscow—wants to seek out the spot where the greatest crowds tramp the soil of Moscow and there kiss the earth of free Russia.

Referred to the comments on the impracticability of the New Russia, but said that the work of destruction was over and the work of construction beginning and that the socialists would not be in it if they did not know it to be not merely destructive but constructive. "It is all very well to sing about Free Russia and the Revolution, but we must also work."

Election of the Metropolitan

Mr. Taylor was one of the fortunate few who witnessed the ceremonious election of the Metropolitan of Moscow—an event, as he remarks, which had not taken place since the time of Peter the Great. The Mr. Crane who is mentioned was the Honorable Charles R. Crane, an American long interested in Russia. "Sam Harper" was Professor Samuel G. Harper of the University of Chicago, one of the first American professors to specialize on Russian affairs. The description represents a brief segment of a long letter from Mr. Taylor to his father. It was written on July 4, 1917.

I would give anything if you could have been in my place to-day. You would have been so much interested in the rare occasion I was permitted to see. It was the election of the Metropolitan of Moscow. There are three Metropolitans in the Russian Church—Moscow, Petrograd and Kiev, but the Moscow one is the most important. The election to-day was a new thing, so far as its being a result of the revolution is concerned. But it is a very old thing judged by the standard of centuries. It was the first such election held in 200 years, but the Church is just going back to its methods as they were prior to the time of Peter the Great. The Church has always been restive under the regulations—"reforms"—of Peter the Great, and so far as the Church is concerned the revolution is mainly an effort to revert to its old time ways.

Mr. Crane, Mr. Mott and Mr. Hart of the Y.M.C.A. and Sam Harper came down from Petrograd in charge of High Procurator Lvov, of the Holy Synod—the cabinet minister who is the head of the Church so far as the government is concerned. So we were some of the very few outsiders who got right in on the floor of the big Cathedral for the occasion. Such of the Moscow public as even got inside the church were standing in far off galleries.

The ballot box from the Duma in Petrograd was brought down for the occasion and stood in the middle of the Cathedral. There had been a preliminary congregational election—everyone being allowed to vote—women as well as men—for delegates to the final election to-day. So to-day these delegates, mostly priests, but some laymen, and even some women among them, cast their ballots for the two candidates, Tikhon and Samarin. Tikhon was at one time the head of the Russian Church in America. He is a very good man and only a little more conservative than Samarin on the question of the freedom of the Church from the government. In fact, as Mr. Crane said, it was most fortunate that there were two such good men as candidates. Tikhon was elected by 418 to 303. After the count of the ballots, the result was given to the bishops who retired behind the high altar to go through the purely formal deliberation and approval of the election.

The final part of the election was a procession of the bishops out from behind the high altar to stand in a row in front of it while a priest with a marvelous deep voice announced that Tikhon was elected. Then the whole crowd of 700 and more sang a Te Deum. It was most impressive.

The Galician Campaign Recoils

> The Galician campaign of which Mr. Taylor speaks is more often written of now as the second Brusilov offensive. After a brilliant start, the whole effort collapsed, thus further discrediting the Provisional Government. The "trouble in Petrograd" was the July Rising which Lenin first opposed but finally permitted his Bolsheviks to join in the hope of controlling the affair. After its failure, Lenin fled to Finland— not to Germany. It was quite generally believed at the time that Lenin was a German agent. Technically he was not, but he did not hesitate to use German support (including funds) to advance his own purposes. "The right-hand lieutenant of Lenin" was Trotsky. This selection is an excerpt from a letter of July 26, 1917 to Mr. Taylor's family.

The Russians advance in Galicia was encouraging, but none of us really thought it would be much more than a flash in the pan, and now the army seems to be bent on running away about as fast as it can. My Russian friends are so ashamed that they hardly can talk with me.

The operations at the front come closest home to us in our apartment by the arrival of the wounded. I told you, I think, that this big apartment house is mainly a great hospital for the wounded. Every day during the Galician advance there were more frequent arrivals of ambulances at the door, the wounded being carried out of them on stretchers and up into the wards by the convalescent soldiers.

The psychology of the situation in the army is clear, however. You suddenly take away from the Cossacks the figure of the Tsar, the symbol at least of something for which they fought, also the flag they were accustomed to rally around, also the great swinging national anthem, also the dream of putting the Cross in place of the Crescent on St. Sophia—the main things that they have for generations been trained to regard as the sacred things of their country. Then you start a discussion of the dividing up of the land around their home villages. The whole thing means that there is a new balance of interest—and with death in front of them, and the chance to get the land they have longed for at home, small wonder that they simply leave the front and go home.

I understand that the commanders are at their wits' end as to how to maintain discipline. There have been instances of regiments cut to pieces because other regiments did not come up as expected—they were holding a meeting to decide whether to fulfil the orders that were given them. That is the naive way in which a lot of the ignorant interpret "liberty."

But it is tragic for those who have the cause of the war at heart. In the Galician advance the proportion of officers killed was simply overwhelming, I am told. They went to their death by hundreds in vain effort to stir the soldiers to follow their example. One of the tragic figures of the situation is that of Guckhoff, the former minister of war—first minister of war after the revolution. Mr. C. told me that he feels the situation so keenly that he has gone to the front as an officer, asking to be put in the front firing line in the hope that he may die in battle.

Meanwhile the Leninites are causing all sorts of trouble in Petrograd. Mr. C. told me they actually had the city in their grasp after the street fighting of last week, only they simply failed to close their hands on it until the troops loyal to the government came up from the front. It is absolutely sure that Lenin is in the pay of the Germans, and I have it on good authority that he has now escaped over the frontier into Germany. If he had stayed a few more days I am told he certainly would have been killed in Petrograd.

One of the ignominious things is that a right hand lieutenant of Lenin was in America last winter and sailed on the same boat that brought Mr. C. and Lincoln Steffens. The British took this man off the boat at Halifax, but . . . [he was later allowed to resume his journey to Russia].

The November Revolution in Moscow

The Bolshevik Revolution began in Petrograd and spread almost immediately to Moscow where it met a brief but stiff resistance. This time, as the following excerpts from his diary show, Mr. Taylor found himself very close to the center of events.

November 10, 1917

While we were at breakfast Nikolai Alexandrovitch telephoned to us that there was much trouble—street fighting between the Bolsheviki and the Gov't troops in the vicinity of the Kremlin and the Theatre Square, that no trains were running and that before going out we should phone our consulate to find out if it was safe for us to come to it. Our maid, Olga, also told us there was shooting all around.

We started out, however, for the 2d Division. All seemed quiet and we saw only an occasional small group of people talking. As we crossed the Pokrovka, we met young S. of the 2nd Div. who said he had been there but that the door was locked . . . Randolph evidently not having come—having been from 8:15 to 9:45 coming over from his lodgings. Was stopped on the Tverskaya where much shooting was to be heard and people were peeking around the corner from the side streets. He got across at last and then made his way over to Lubyanka Ploshatz where many soldiers were on guard.

One block up the Miasuitzkaya, he found a barricade consisting of two automobiles turned sideways across the street. He had then come on to the office.

When we came in the building, all the householders from the upper apartments were down by the front door. They eagerly questioned us as to whether we had seen any trouble. Forgot to say that when we arrived at the 2d Div. in the morning, we telephoned to A. M. in her apt. at the Kremlin. She said the fighting had been pretty strenuous early in the morning and that about 15 soldiers had been killed and many wounded on both sides— fighting especially at three of the Kremlin gates. She and the rest of the family were safe.

After sitting around the office for an hour, we went out to buy some provisons at a market out from the center of town and then came around by the 2d Div. and back home for lunch. About 3 we started out to go to the Consulate.

We had no trouble in reaching the Lubyanka Ploshatz, where report had it that there had been much shooting earlier in the morning. There was a crowd looking down toward the Theatre Ploshatz where the firing seemed to be heavy, some rifle fire but also some from heavier pieces. As we stood watching also a motor with a Red Cross flag on it came whizzing up and through the crowd with a wounded man in it.

We went around by the Kuznetski Most to the Petrovka—all the time hearing incessant firing from the direction of the Theatre Sq; the Duma and the Kremlin. We then went up the Petrovka to the Statechinkov and across on that to the Dmitrovka where a soldier stopped us. It was quite evident that there would be much difficulty in crossing the Tverskaya. We went up the Dmitrovka to the Boulevard and then over to the Tverskaya, but again a soldier stopped us. A group of people seemed to be looking up at the belfry of the church at the corner as if there were snipers hidden up there.

We then went around and out beyond the Boulevard to cross the Tverskaya. As we walked out the Malaya Dmitrovka, we saw a motor truck filled with armed soldiers, one of them with a drawn revolver standing on the step by the driver. A few minutes afterward we heard heavy firing in the Strasnaya Ploshatz and imagined that the truck load of soldiers— probably of the govt. had run into a crowd of Bolshevikis at the Ploshatz —perhaps encountering snipers in the church tower.

It appears as if the Tverskaya is the main street of the Bolshevikis— perhaps especially because the Soviet of Workman's deputies has the old palace of the Gov. General. When we had tried to cross over to the Tverskaya a block beyond the Gov. General's palace, a soldier had stopped us. When we told him we were from the American Consulate, he told us to go on—toward the Tverskaya. But just as we started to we saw a lot of soldiers and civilians—all armed—come down from the Tverskaya to a gate of a big apt. house. They acted as if watching out for the enemy. Just after they got in the gate, a truckload of armed soldiers came from the other direction up toward the apt. As we were in between, it wasn't very pleasant and would be dangerous if the two groups began firing at each other.

By going a couple of blocks beyond the Boulevard, we were able to swing over through side streets to the Nikitskaya Vorota and then down toward the Consulate. As we came near the Cherneshevsky Per. we met T., who said that everyone had left the Consulate but that they had had an exciting day, for there had been shooting up and down the street all day— the Governor General's house. Also it seems that there was shooting back and forth between one crowd who used the English Church as their fort (next door to the Consulate) and the Russki Viedomosti office across the street.

As T. was showing us the places in the walls of the building near the Consulate, some soldiers up the street called to us to "go on," which we did without delay—back to the Nikitskaya and up it beyond the Boulevard— and so on home to Lubyanka Ploshatz.

The bullet marks on the walls by the Consulate (where the American Flag was up at the gate) seemed as if they might have been made with something larger than a rifle.

I judge from the heavy noises that small field pieces must be used.

Bought a paper on the way home and found it told of the capture of the Kremlin by the Govt. troops. Proclamation of the Military Commander stating that the city is under martial law, prohibiting gatherings and also people from going out on the streets unless they have permission of the Household Committee.

Also dug out a handbill printed by the Soviet of Workman's Deputies which had been handed to me near the Tverskaya. It said that the Provisional Govt. is arrested in Petrograd and that the outcome of the Revolution is now in the hands of the workmen and soldiers and peasants. It calls on railway men to send Kerensky to Petrograd.

All streets are dark. Miss M. called to say that they were all safe at the Kremlin and that the government troops have the place. She said that there was still much shooting, and that during the day dead bodies lay on the pavement, some time before removed. It seems queer to talk with her when you can't get within five blocks of the Kremlin without running the risk of getting shot in the street battles. . . .

November 11, 1917

We started out for a walk to see how things seemed in the streets. Walked up to Lubyanka Ploshatz and joined the small crowd there looking down toward the Metropole. The sound of shooting was incessant including field pieces as well as rifle fire. Occasionally three or four struggling figures, heads bent down, would scurry across the street in front of the Metropole—looking as if they were hurrying in out of a pelting sudden thundershower. But the bright still day made it seem unnatural. We heard that the Bolsheviki were holding the Malo Theatre against the efforts of the Junkers to dislodge them.

We stopped to look at bullet holes through store windows in Lubyanka Ploshatz. Some looked as if they might have been merely wilful and wanton as we did not remember having seen them yesterday morning and had heard of no fighting in the Lubyanka Ploshatz since yesterday morning. And they did not seem to have come from the direction of any nearby fighting area.

We then walked down the Kuznetski Most to the Dmitrovka where we saw a Bolshevik crowd and a Bolshevik soldier arrest a cadet in uniform.

Where to Find More Information

CARR, E. H. *The Bolshevik Revolution, 1917–1923.* 3 vols. N.Y.: Macmillan, 1951–1953. Vol. 1.

CHAMBERLIN, W. H. *The Russian Revolution.* New ed. 2 vols. N.Y.: Macmillan, 1952. Vol. 1, pp. 1–117.

CHARQUES, *Short History,* ch. 16.

CLARKSON, *History,* chs. 20–25.

FISHER, G. *Russian Liberalism.* Cambridge: Harvard Univ. Press, 1958.

FLORINSKY, *Russia,* vol. 2, chs. 39–48.

———. *The End of the Russian Empire.* New Haven: Yale Univ. Press, 1931.

GANKIN, O. H. and FISHER, H. H. (Eds.) *The Bolsheviks and the World War.* Stanford: Stanford Univ. Press, 1940.

GOLDER, F. A. *Documents of Russian History, 1914–1917.* N.Y.: Century, 1927.

HARCAVE, *Readings,* vol. 2, sections 7–11.

KARPOVICH, *Imperial Russia,* pp. 55–96.

LOBANOV-ROSTOVSKY, *Russia and Asia,* chs. 10 & 11.

MARTIN, *Picture History,* pp. 161–202.

MAZOUR, *Russia,* chs. 19–28.

MEISAL, J. & KOZERA, E. *The Soviet System.* Ann Arbor: Wahr, 1953. Pp. 1–56.

PARES, B. *The Fall of the Russian Monarchy.* Vintage Russian Library.

———. *History,* chs. 22–24.

SETON-WATSON, *Decline,* pp. 185–381.

TREADGOLD, D. W. *Lenin and His Rivals.* N.Y.: Praeger, 1955.

———. *Twentieth Century Russia.* Chicago: Rand McNally, 1959. Pp. 3–145.

WALSH, *Russia,* chs. 17–20.

WREN, *Course,* chs. 24–27.

Part VIII

The Soviet Period

Trotsky's Analysis of the Bolshevik Revolution

Trotsky did not fully identify himself with Lenin and the Bolshevik movement until July, 1917, but thereafter he quickly became Lenin's closest associate and one of the chief leaders. He was, for example, instrumental in establishing Bolshevik control over the Petrograd Soviet. His accounts of the events are important because he was a leading participant. There is an additional significance to the material below. In Trotsky's own words, "[it was] . . . written in snatches . . . between the sittings of the [Brest-Litovsk] Peace Conference . . . [and was] designed to acquaint the workers of the world with the causes, progress and meaning of the Russian November Revolution." It thus is the picture of their work which the Bolshevik leaders wished the world to see in 1918, and its simple eloquence shows why Trotsky had earned the nickname of "The Pen." The source is: L. Trotsky, *The October Revolution*. First Indian edition. Bombay: Modern India Publications, 1952. Pp. 1–4, 7–8, 11–12, 13, 14, 24, 25–28, 30–31.

What distinguished our party almost from the very first stage of the Revolution was the firm conviction that the logic of events would eventually place it in power. I am not speaking here of the theoreticians of our party, who, many years before the Revolution, even before the Revolution of 1905, had come to the conclusion, from a close analysis of the class relations in Russia, that the victorious course of a revolution would inevitably place the power of the State in the hands of the proletariat, supported by the wide masses of the poorest peasantry. The main foundation for this belief was the insignificance of the Russian middle-class democracy and the concentrated character of Russian industry, and, therefore, the immense social importance of the Russian working class. The insignificance of the Russian middle-class democracy is but the obverse side of the power and importance of the proletariat. True, the war temporarily deceived many people on this point, and, above all, it deceived the leading sections of middle-class democracy itself. The war assigned the decisive role in the Revolution to the army, and the old army was the peasantry.

Had the Revolution developed more normally, that is, in conditions of

717

peace-time, such as prevailed in 1912, when it really began, the proletariat would inevitably have taken the leading role throughout, whilst the peasant masses would have been gradually towed along by the proletariat into the revolutionary whirlpool. But the war imparted an entirely different logic to the course of events. The army had organized the peasantry, not on a political, but on a military basis. Before the peasant masses found themselves united on a common platform of definite revolutionary demands and ideas, they had already become united in regiments, divisions, corps, and armies. The lower middle-class democrats, scattered throughout this army, and playing a leading part in it both in a military and intellectual sense, were almost entirely imbued with middle-class revolutionary sentiments. The deep social discontent of the masses grew ever deeper and strove for expression, particularly owing to the military debacle of Tsardom. Immediately the Revolution broke out, the advanced sections of the proletariat revived the traditions of 1905 by calling upon the popular masses to organize in representative bodies, *viz*. the "Councils" of delegates (Soviets).

The army thus had to send representatives to revolutionary bodies before its political consciousness in any way corresponded to the level of the rapidly developing revolutionary events. Whom could the soldiers send as their representatives? Naturally, only those intellectuals and semi-intellectuals who were to be found in their midst and who possessed at least a minimum amount of political knowledge, and were capable of giving utterance to it. In this way, by the will of the awakening army, the lower middle-class intellectuals found themselves suddenly raised to a position of enormous influence. Doctors, engineers, lawyers, journalists, who in pre-war days had led a humdrum private life and laid no claim of any sort to political influence, became, overnight, representatives of whole corps and armies, and discovered that they were the "leaders" of the Revolution. The haziness of their political ideas fully corresponded to the formless state of the revolutionary consciousness of the masses themselves. They contemptuously looked upon us as mere sectarians because we were urging the social demands of the working class and the peasants in a most resolute and uncompromising fashion. At the same time these lower middle-class democrats, in spite of their proud demeanour or revolutionary upstarts, felt a profound diffidence both in their own capacities and in the masses who had raised them to such an unexpectedly high place. Calling themselves Socialists and really regarding themselves as such, these intellectuals looked up to the political authority of the Liberal bourgeoisie, to its knowledge and its methods, with all ill-concealed respect. Hence the endeavour of the lower middle-class leaders to obtain, at all costs, the cooperation of the Liberal middle-class by way of an alliance or coalition. The programme of the party of Socialist Revolutionaries, based as it all is on vague humanitarian formulae, and employing general sentiments and moral constructions in the place of class-war methods, was the most suitable spiritual dress that could have been found for these improvised leaders. Their political helplessness in the impressive political and scientific knowledge of the bourgeoisie found a theoretical sanction in the teaching of the Mensheviks, who argued that the present Revolution was a bourgeois revolution, and could not, therefore, be carried through without the participation of the bourgeoisie in the Government. A natural *bloc* was thus formed between the Socialist Revolutionaries and Mensheviks, expressing both the timid and hesitating political mind of the middle-class intellectuals and its vassal attitude towards Imperialist Liberalism.

To us, it was perfectly clear that the logic of the class struggle would sooner or later destroy this temporary combination and fling aside the leaders of this period of transition. The hegemony of the lower middle-class intellectuals was at bottom the expression of the fact that the peasantry, suddenly called to take part in organized political life through the machinery of the army, had by sheer weight of numbers pushed aside and overwhelmed the proletariat for the time being. Even more, in so far as the middle-class leaders had been raised to a dizzy height by the powerful mass of the army, the working class itself, with the exception of its advanced sections, could not but become imbued with a certain political respect for them and try to maintain political contact with them for fear of finding themselves divorced from the peasantry. And this was a very serious matter, for the older generation still remembered the lesson of 1905, when the proletariat was crushed, just because the massive peasant reserves had not come up in time for the decisive battles. That is why in the first phase of the new Revolution also the proletarian masses showed themselves highly accessible to the political ideology of the Socialist Revolutionaries and the Mensheviks—especially as the Revolution had aroused the hitherto slumbering backward masses of workers, and thus made the hazy radicalism of the intellectuals a sort of preparatory school for them. The Council of Workers', Soldiers', and Peasants' Delegates meant in these conditions the predominance of peasant amorphousness over proletarian Socialism, and predominance of intellectual Radicalism over the Peasant amorphousness.

The structure of Soviets rose so rapidly to a gigantic height mainly because of the leading part played in their labours by the intellectuals, with their technical knowledge and middle-class connections. But to us it was perfectly clear that this grand structure was built on deep internal contradictions and would inevitably collapse at the next stage of the Revolution.

· · ·

It was during the first All-Russian Congress of the Soviets that the first alarming crash of thunder occurred, which warned of the coming storm. Our party had projected an armed demonstration at Petrograd for June 23rd. Its proximate object was to bring pressure to bear upon the Congress. "Take over the power in the State"—this it was that the Petrograd workers wanted to tell the Socialist Revolutionaries and Mensheviks who had come from all parts of the country. "Spurn the bourgeoisie! Have done with the idea of coalition, and take the reins of power into your own hands!" We were quite certain that if the Socialist Revolutionaries and Mensheviks broke with the Liberal bourgeoisie, they would be compelled to seek support from the most energetic and most advanced elements of the proletariat, which would thus obtain the leading role in the Revolution. But that was just what frightened the lower middle-class leaders. In conjunction with the Government, in which they had their own representatives, and shoulder to shoulder with the Liberal and counter-revolutionary bourgeoisie they opened a truly savage campaign against the projected demonstration so soon as they got wind of it. Everything possible was set in motion against us. We were at that time a small minority at the Congress, and we gave way; the demonstration did not take place. But all the same it left a very deep mark in the minds of the two contending parties, and made the gulf between them deeper and their mutual antagonism more acute. At the closed sitting of the Presidential Bureau of the Congress, in which also representatives of the various parties took part, Tsereteli, then a member of the Coalition Government, speaking with all the resoluteness of a narrow-minded lower middle-class doctrinaire, declared that the only danger threatening the Revolution was the Bolsheviks and the Petrograd workers who had been armed by them. He therefore argued that the people "who did not know how to use arms" must be disarmed. Of course he had in mind the Petrograd workers and that portion of the Petrograd garrison which supported our party. However, no disarming took place, as the political and psychological conditions were not yet ripe enough for such an extreme measure.

To compensate the masses for the loss of their demonstration, the Congress of the Soviets itself organized an unarmed demonstration, on July 1st. And that day became the day of our political triumph. The masses turned out in overwhelming numbers, but although they came out in answer to the call of the official Soviet authority—a sort of counterblast to the miscarried demonstration of June 23rd—the workers and soldiers had inscribed on their banners and placards the demands and battle-cries of *our* party: "Down with the secret treaties!" "Down with the policy of strategical offensives!" "Long live an honourable peace!" "Down with the ten capitalist Ministers!" "All power for the Soviets!" There were only three placards with expressions of confidence in the Coalition Government: one from a Cossack regiment, another from the Plekhanoff group, and a third from the Petrograd "Bund," an organization consisting largely of non-proletarian elements. This demonstration proved not only to our opponents, but also to ourselves, that we were far stronger in Petrograd than had been imagined.

· · ·

The correlation of forces inside the Soviets at the time was such that a Soviet Government would have meant, from a party point of view, the concentration of power in the hands of the Socialist Revolutionaries and Mensheviks. We were deliberately aiming at such a result, since the constant re-elections to the Soviets provided the necessary machinery for securing a sufficiently faithful reflection of the growing radicalization of the masses of the workers and soldiers. We foresaw that after the break of the Coalition with the bourgeoisie the radical tendencies would necessarily gain the upper hand in the Soviets. In such conditions the struggle of the proletariat for power would naturally shift to the floor of the Soviet organizations, and would proceed in a painless fashion. On their part, having broken with the bourgeoisie, the lower middle-class democrats would themselves become the target for its attacks, and would, therefore, be compelled to seek a closer alliance with the Socialist working class, and sooner or later their political amorphousness and irresolution would be overcome by the labouring masses under the influence of our criticism. This is why we urged the two leading Soviet parties to take the reins of power into their own hands, although we ourselves had no confidence in them, and frankly said so.

But even after the Ministerial crisis of July 15th, Tsereteli and those who thought with him did not give up their pet idea of a coalition. They explained to the Executive Committee that the chief Cadet leaders were, it was true, demoralized by doctrinairism and even by counter-revolutionary sympathies, but that in the provinces there were many bourgeois elements who would march side by side with the revolutionary democracy and whose cooperation would be secured by the co-option of some representatives of the upper middle-class in the new Ministry. Dan was already placing high hopes on a new Radical-Democratic party which had been concocted about that time by a few doubtful politicians. The news that the Coalition had broken to pieces only to give rise to a new Coalition spread rapidly throughout Petrograd, and created a wave of dismay and indignation in the workers' and soldiers' quarters. This was the origin of the events of July 16th–18th.

. . .

There was still some hope that a demonstration of the revolutionary masses might break down the obstinate doctrinairism of the Coalitionists and compel them to realize at last that they could only maintain themselves in power if they completely broke with the bourgeoisie. Contrary to what was said and written at the time in the bourgeois Press, there was no intention whatever in our party of seizing the reins of power by means of an armed rising. It was only a revolutionary demonstration which broke out spontaneously, though guided by us politically.

. . .

The movement of July 16th–18th showed with perfect clearness that the leading parties of the Soviet lived in Petrograd in a complete political vacuum. It is true that the garrison was by no means entirely with us at that time. There were among it units which still hesitated, were still undecided and passive. But apart from the ensigns, there was not a single unit among the garrison, which was willing to fight against us in defence of the Government or the leading parties in the Soviet. It was from the front that troops had to be fetched. The entire strategy of Tsereteli, Tchernoff, and others, during those July days was to gain time so as to enable Kerensky to draw "reliable" troops into Petrograd. Delegation after delegation entered the Tauride Palace, which was surrounded by a huge crowd, and demanded a complete break with the bourgeoisie, energetic measures of social reform, and the commencement of peace negotiations. We, Bolsheviks, met every new detachment of demonstrators, either in the street or in the Palace, with harangues, calling on them to be calm, and assuring them that with the masses in their present mood the compromise-mongers would be unable to form a new Coalition Ministry. The men of Kronstadt were particularly determined, and it was only with difficulty that we could keep them within the bounds of a bare demonstration. On July 17th the demonstration assumed a still more formidable character—this time under the direct leadership of our party.

.   .   .

Meanwhile the internal situation was deteriorating and becoming more and more complicated. The war was dragging along without aim, without sense, without any perspective. The Government was taking no steps to extricate itself from the vicious circle.

.   .   .

At the front the state of affairs was going from bad to worse. A cold autumn, wet and muddy, was drawing near. There was the prospect of a fourth winter campaign. The food supply was becoming worse every day. In the rear they had forgotten about the front. There were no reliefs, no reinforcements, and no warm clothing. The number of deserters was increasing daily. The old army committees, elected at the beginning of the Revolution, still remained in their places and supported Kerensky's policy. Re-elections were prohibited. An abyss was formed between the army committees and the masses of the army, and finally the soldiers began to detest the committees. Again and again delegates from the trenches would arrive at Petrograd and ask point-blank, at the sittings of the Soviet: "What are we to do now? Who will end the war, and how shall it be done? Why is the Petrograd Soviet silent?"

The Petrograd Soviet was not silent. It demanded the immediate assumption of authority by the central and local Soviets, the immediate transference of the land to the peasants, the establishment of control by the workers over industry, and the immediate initiation of peace negotiations. So long as we had been in opposition, the cry "All power to the Soviets!" was a battle-cry of propaganda, but since we became a majority on all the chief Soviets it imposed upon us the duty of taking up an immediate and direct struggle for power.

In the villages the situation had become complicated and confused to the last degree. The Revolution had promised the land to the peasants, but had forbidden the latter to touch the land till the meeting of the Constituent Assembly. The peasants at first waited patiently, but when they began to lose patience the Coalition Government resorted to measures of repression. In the meantime the prospect of the meeting of the Constituent Assembly was becoming dimmer and dimmer. The bourgeoisie was insisting that the Constituent Assembly should not be summoned until after the conclusion of peace. The peasant masses, on the other hand, were becoming more and more impatient, and what we had predicted at the beginning of the Revolution was now coming true. The peasant masses began to grab the land on their own authority. Reprisals became more frequent and severe, and the revolutionary land committees began to be arrested—here and there. In some districts Kerensky even proclaimed martial law. Delegates from the villages began to stream to Petrograd, and complained to the Soviet that they were being arrested while trying to carry out the programme of the Soviets and handing over the estates of the private landowners to the peasants' committees. The peasants demanded our protection. We replied that we could only help them if the government power were in our hands. Hence it followed that if the Soviets did not want to become mere talking-shops they were bound to make an effort to get the power into their own hands.

· · ·

All power to the Soviets: such was the demand of our party. In the preceding period this meant, in terms of party divisions, complete authority for the Socialist Revolutionaries and Mensheviks as against the coalition with the Liberal bourgeoisie. Now, however, in November 1917, this demand meant the complete supremacy of the revolutionary proletariat, headed now by the Bolshevik party. The question at issue was the dictatorship of the working class, which was leading, or, to be more correct, was capable of leading, the millions of the poorest peasantry. This was the historical meaning of the November rising.

Everything conspired to lead the party along this path. From the very first days of the Revolution we had insisted on the need and the inevitability of the assumption of the entire government authority by the Soviets. The majority of the Soviets, after an intense internal struggle, adopted our standpoint and took up this demand. We were getting ready for the second All-Russian Congress of the Soviets, at which we expected a complete victory for our party. The Central Executive Committee, on the other hand, under the direction of Dan (the cautious Tshkheidze left for the Caucasus in good time) did everything possible to hinder the meeting of the Soviet Congress. After great efforts, supported by the Soviet group at the Democratic Conference, we at last obtained the fixing of a definite date for the Congress: November 7th. This date has now become the greatest date in Russian history. As a preliminary, we called together in Petrograd a conference of the Soviets of the Northern Provinces, including also the Baltic Fleet and the Moscow Soviet. We had a definite majority at this conference. We also obtained some protection on the right flank from the left wing of the Socialist Revolutionaries, and laid the foundation for the business-like organization of the November rising.

. . .

And so the whole conflict in Petrograd was coming to an issue over the question of the fate of its garrison. In the first place, of course, it affected the soldiers, but the workers, too, evinced the liveliest interest in it, as they feared that on the removal of the troops they might be crushed by the military cadets and Cossacks. The conflict was thus assuming a very acute character, and the question over which it was tending to an issue was very unfavourable to the Kerensky Government.

Parallel with this struggle over the garrison was also going on the previously mentioned struggle for the summoning of the Soviet Congress, in connection with which we were proclaiming openly, in the name of the Petrograd Soviet and the conference of the Soviets of the Northern District, that the second Soviet Congress must dismiss the Kerensky Government and become the real master of Russia. Practically the rising was already proceeding, and was developing in the face of the whole country.

During October the question of the rising played also an important part in the internal life of our party. Lenin, who was in hiding in Finland, wrote numerous letters insisting on more energetic tactics. Amongst the rank and file there was great fermentation and growing discontent, because the Bolshevik Party, now in a majority in the Soviets, was not putting its own battle-cries into practice. On October 28th a secret meeting of the Central Committee of our party took place, at which Lenin was present. On the order of the day was the question of the rising. With only two dissentients it was unanimously decided that the only means of saving the Revolution and the country from complete destruction was an armed rising, which must have for its object the conquest of supreme government authority by the Soviets.

The Interventions: a Soviet View

Soviet historians for quite obvious reasons, and other historians for reasons which are less clear, have fallen into the habit of treating the Bolshevik Revolution as if it were completed in October/November, 1917. It was not; its violent and uneven course required several years to complete. Part of this course was a bitter struggle of Russian against Russian (as well as of other national groups against the Russians) which makes it easy to label the events as a civil war. In one sense, it certainly was a fratricidal struggle; but in a broader sense, it was a continuation of the revolution which began in Petrograd in October/November.

Another aspect of the years immediately after 1917 was the "interventions" of foreign powers. French and British agents and missions, both military and civilian, had actually intervened directly in Russian

affairs from the beginning of the war, and there were American interventions as well after the February/March Revolution. These actions
were motivated primarily by a desire to maintain Russia as an effective, fighting ally. Two other factors came into play after November,
1917: a feeling that the Bolsheviks were wittingly or unheedingly helping Germany, and a fear—pointed out in the second selection below—
of world revolution. Soviet spokesmen do not mention either of these
factors in their discussions of "interventions." An excerpt from a typical Soviet interpretation, designed for "popular reading," is printed below. The source is: M. Mitin, *Twenty-Five Years of Soviet Power,
1917–1942*. Moscow: Foreign Languages Publishing House, n.d. Pp.
11–14.

The respite gained by the Soviet State proved to be shortlived. The peaceful labours of the peoples of the Soviet Republic were soon interrupted by
foreign invaders and by the Russian counter-revolutionaries who in the
early part of 1918 united for the purpose of overthrowing the Soviet
regime and of transforming Russia into a colony of the foreign imperialists.

Without declaring war, the Entente imperialists landed their troops
in Russia and commenced hostilities. The German imperialists also did
their best to subjugate the country, in spite of the fact that they had concluded peace with the Soviet Government. The foreign troops helped to
organize the anti-Soviet forces in the country, and kulak revolts broke out
in a number of places.

The foreign invaders and the Russian Whiteguards captured Archangel
and Murmansk, the Far Eastern Provinces and Siberia, the Ukraine and
the Caucasus, the Urals and part of the Volga region. Three-fourths of
the country was thus occupied, Soviet Russia was cut off from her main
sources of food, raw materials and fuel. The foreign invaders instituted a
blockade and the country was cut off from the outside world. The Soviet
Republic was like a besieged island in a raging sea of counter-revolution.

The sitiation was critical. The food shortage was extremely acute.
The workers' bread ration in Moscow and Petrograd was as low as two
ounces per two days. There was a shortage of arms, ammunition, clothing,
raw materials and fuel. Factories were closed down one after another. The
very existence of the country was imperilled. But the Soviet people led
by the heroic Russian working class did not despair. They found means of
surmounting these gigantic difficulties and saved their revolution and their
country's independence.

The Bolshevik Party roused the people for a *patriotic* war against the
foreign invaders and internal counter-revolutionaries. Lenin said: "The
issue is as follows: we are at war, and the fate of the revolution will be
determined by the outcome of this war." He issued the slogan: "Everything for the front!" This helped the Bolshevik Party and the Soviet Government to mobilize all the forces and resources of the Republic to defeat
the foreign and internal enemies. The issue was: "Victory or Death!"
And this was the battlecry of the sons of the people as they joined the Red
Army and went off to the front. The Bolsheviks set an example to all.

Nearly half the membership of the Communist Party and of the Young Communist League joined the army to fight for the cause of the people and to protect the gains of the October Revolution.

With a firm and sure hand Lenin and Stalin led the Soviet people to victory. They created and reared the army and personally directed the work of defence. Lenin's political and military genius, his iron will, his immense political experience, and all his titanic energy, were concentrated on the organization of victory over the enemy. He drew up the main strategical plans, daily watched the situation at the various fronts, issued instructions to the military commanders and verified their execution. All the threads of military leadership were concentrated in Lenin's hands.

Stalin was Lenin's true and worthy associate in this work. The Central Committee of the Communist party always commissioned Stalin to direct operations on the crucial sector where the fate of the Republic was being decided. With the foresight and skill of a great military leader, Stalin was able quickly to appraise the situation and to work out the strategy and plan of operations in conformity with it. With a firm hand he swept away all disruptive elements at the front and in the rear, introduced iron discipline in the Red Army, inspired the commanders and men to display the utmost heroism in the fight and thus ensured victory. *The most brilliant victories achieved during the Civil War are associated with Stalin's name* [sic].

During the Civil War the Soviet Republic often found itself in a critical situation. On more than one occasion the enemy succeeded in achieving important military successes. A critical situation arose in 1918, when the Whiteguards directed their blow at Tsaritsyn (now called Stalingrad), and also on the two occasions when Yudenich was approaching Petrograd. In the spring of 1919, Kolchak seized the whole of the Urals and was marching towards the Volga. Particularly grave danger menaced the country in the autumn of 1919, when Denikin captured Orel, marched on Tula, and threatened Moscow, the heart of Soviet Russia.

The Bolshevik Party made no attempt to conceal from the people the gravity of the situation, but appealed to them to strain their efforts to the utmost to repel the enemy. The people eagerly responded to the Party's appeal and each time succeeded in averting the danger. As Lenin said subsequently: "The distinguishing feature about Russia is that in the most critical situations she had at her command masses who could be put toward as reserves, as a reservoir of fresh forces, when the old forces became exhausted."

The heroic defence of Tsaritsyn and Petrograd, and the defeat of Denikin when he was pressing towards Moscow, have gone into history as unforgettable examples of the staunchness, pluck and heroism of the Soviet people. The memory of the defenders of the Land of Soviets of that period is covered with unfading glory.

The Soviet Republic and its Red Army defeated all the Entente's military campaigns against Russia, drove their troops from Soviet territory, defeated the German invaders and one after another defeated the numerous tools of the foreign imperialists, such as Kolchak, Yjdenich, Denikin, Krasnow, Wrangel, and the Polish Whiteguards.

Why was the Soviet State able to vanquish all its enemies in the period of the Civil War? Because it waged *a just war of liberation* [*sic*], a war in defence of the freedom and independence of the country and for the protection of the Soviet regime. The Red Army fought to preserve the gains of the October Socialist Revolution which had placed the entire wealth of the country and all the achievements of science, engineering and culture at the service of the people.

A World to Win

Lenin and his colleagues believed that the revolution in Russia was only the first stage of a world-wide revolution. In fact, Lenin concluded his first speech after his return to Russia by hailing the world socialist revolution. He and his associates continued for some years to think that world revolution was impending and that a European socialist revolution was imminent. And they spent much thought, effort, and money to accelerate its coming. This was partly a reflection of their confidence in the Marxian "revelations," but it was also, in part, a reflection of general European developments immediately after the First World War. Discontent and unrest were almost everywhere apparent; riots and other disorders were common; mutinies and rebellions occurred in some countries; and there were full-scale revolutions which won temporary successes in Hungary and in Germany.

As a result of events in Germany in the fall of 1918, the German Spartacist (Communist) leader, Karl Liebknecht, was released from jail. Lenin and his associates immediately ordered their ambassador in Berlin to present their congratulations to Liebknecht. The second sentence documents the statement that they believed the day of world revolution to be at hand. The message to the ambassador was handwritten on a sheet of notepaper. The original is in the Central Lenin Museum.

To the Russian Ambassador in Berlin

Convey our most ardent greetings to Karl Liebknecht. The release from prison of the representative of the revolutionary workers of Germany is a sign of a new epoch, the epoch of victorious socialism which is now beginning for Germany and for the whole world.

On behalf of the Central Committee
of the Russian Communist Party (Bolsheviks)
Lenin, Sverdlov, Stalin

Lenin and the Kulaks

The food shortages which had plagued the Provisional Government grew worse after the October/November Revolution. The Provisional Government had had too many scruples and too little power successfully to carry out their attempted levies of grain. The Bolsheviks had more power and no scruples. To supply the city proletariat, chief supporter of the Bolsheviks, with food was an absolute necessity if the party was to retain power. Food levies were extended and enforced by armed gangs from the cities, operating under Bolshevik leadership and sanction. "Committees of the Poor" were organized among the peasants to cooperate with these "food-requisitioning squads" in a deliberate class war against the middle class and richer peasants (*kulaks*).

The following telegram, sent by Lenin to the Zadonsk Soviet, is typical of his ruthlessness and of the methods employed. The original copy is in the Central Lenin Museum.

Take most vigorous action against kulaks and their allies, the Left Socialist-Revolutionary swine. Issue an appeal to the poor peasants. Organize them. Request help from Elets. The Kulak bloodsuckers must be unmercifully suppressed. Wire reply.

Lenin

Lenin's Report for 1921

Lenin, as Chairman of the Council of People's Commissars, delivered a report on "the state of the nation" to the Ninth Congress of Soviets which met in December, 1921. The major points of his report were printed in poster form for wide distribution. An official Soviet translation of this poster is given below. The original poster is in the Central Lenin Museum.

1. THE INTERNATIONAL SITUATION

A certain equilibrium has been achieved, but it is rather unstable.

The first commandment in our policy, the first lesson to be drawn from this year of the work of our government, a lesson which must be mastered by all workers and peasants, is: be vigilant, remember that we are surrounded by people, classes, governments, which openly proclaim their deepest hatred for us. Therefore we shall always be but a hair's breadth from new invasion.

2. ECONOMIC RELATIONS WITH EUROPE

In 1921 (the first year of trade with foreign countries) we made great progress. If we take the three years, 1918, 1919, and 1920, we shall find that our total imports for this period were a little over 17 million poods [612,000,000 tons]; in 1921 we imported 50 million poods [1,800,000,-000 tons] or three times as much as in all three preceding years together.

3. Our Internal Situation and the New Economic Policy

The most fundamental and basic question is [*sic*] the relations between the working class and the peasantry, the alliance between the working class and peasantry.

No other economic bond is possible between the peasantry and the workers, that is, between agriculture and industry, than exchange, trade. The substitution of the food tax for the surplus-appropriation [food-levies] system is the essence of our economic policy, and that essence is a very simple one. In the absence of a flourishing large-scale industry capable of immediately satisfying the peasants with its products, there is no other way for the alliance of workers and peasants, for the gradual development of a powerful alliance, than the way of trade.

4. The Famine and Agriculture

About 75% of the winter crop area in the famine-stricken provinces, 102% in the provinces partially affected by the crop failure, 123% in the producing provinces and 126% in the consuming provinces were sown in the autumn. This at any rate shows that, devilishly hard as the conditions were, we did give some assistance to the peasantry in extending the crop area and combating famine. With conditions as they are now, we are entitled to believe, without the least exaggeration and without fear of error, that in the matter of supplying seed for spring sowing, we shall also render appreciable assistance to the peasantry. I repeat, this assistance will by no means be complete. We shall by no means be able to meet all requirements. That must be made clear. All the more, therefore, must we exert every effort to extend this assistance.

5. The Food Tax

Tortured as we were by imperialist war and by civil war, and hounded by the ruling classes of every country, there is and can be no way out of our situation without the greatest hardships. And therefore we must say quite distinctly, without evading the bitter truth, and affirm it in the name of the congress to all our people in the localities, although they realize the hardships: "Comrades, the very existence of the Soviet Republic, our very modest plan of restoring transport and industry, will wholly depend on our fulfilling the general program of food supply. Therefore one hundred percent collection of the food tax is absolutely essential."

6. Fuel is the Foundation of Industry

As regards the supply of wood fuel, I must again say: "comrades, the utmost exertion of effort in your localities in this field must be the slogan!"

The total output of the Donets Basin in 1920 was 272 million poods [9,792,000,000 tons]; in 1921 it was 350 million poods [12,600,000,000 tons].

7. IRON AND STEEL

Difficult as our position is, we can here observe great progress. In the first half of 1921 we produced 70,000 poods [2,520,000 tons] of pig iron, in October 130,000 poods [4,680,000 tons], and in November 270,000 poods [8,720,000 tons], or nearly four times as much.

8. ELECTRIFICATION

In 1918 and 1919 together, the number of power stations started was 51 with an aggregate capacity of 3,500 kilowatts. In 1920 and 1921, the number of stations started was 221, with an aggregate capacity of 12,000 kilowatts. Our output of peat in 1920 reached 93 million poods [3,348,-000,000 tons], in 1921 it reached 139 million [5,004,000,000]—the only sphere, I should say, in which we have left pre-war figures far behind.

9. TRADE IS THE TOUCHSTONE OF THE NEW ECONOMIC LIFE

Productive forces have already begun to develop, thanks to the New Economic Policy. There is one other aspect of the matter—we must learn. And therein lies the significance of the New Economic Policy. Learn! This learning is a very hard matter. It is not at all like hearing lectures at school and passing examinations. Every attempt to evade this task, every attempt to close our eyes, and to pretend that this is not our affair, would be most criminal and most dangerous conceit—Communist and trade union conceit.

10. THE REFORM OF THE VECHEKA [Cheka]

This institution was our avenging sword against the innumerable plots, the innumerable attempts on the existence of Soviet government made by people who are infinitely stronger than we are. That is the merit of the Vecheka. But at the same time we definitely declare that we must reform the Vecheka, define its functions and jurisdiction and limit it to political tasks. The problem which we are tackling this year, and which up to now we have been tackling with such difficulty and so inadequately—the union of the workers and the peasants in a durable economic alliance—even amidst the utmost ruin and want, that problem we have solved correctly, the line we have adopted is correct—about that there can be no doubt.

Lenin's Electrification Scheme

The development and wide distribution of electric power was one of Lenin's pet dreams. Speaking of it at the Eighth Party Congress in 1920 he said: "Communism is the Soviet government plus the electrification of the whole country."—a statement which clearly indicates the importance Lenin attached to this matter. In 1921, Lenin wrote the following letter to G. M. Krzhizhanovsky, an old Bolshevik who was then Chairman of the State Planning Commission and a member of the party's Central Committee. This is an official Soviet translation of the original letter which is in the Central Lenin Museum.

Gleb Maximilianovich,

The following idea has occurred to me.

We must make propaganda for electricity. How?

Not only by word, but by example.

What does this mean? It means, above all, popularizing it. For this purpose a plan must be worked out at once for the installation of electric light in every house in the RSFSR.

That will be a long business, for it will be a long time before we have enough wire and the rest for 20,000,000 (—40,000,000) lamps.

Nevertheless, we need a plan at once, if only for a few years ahead.

That is the first thing.

The second thing is that an abridged plan must be worked out at once, and then—this is the third thing, and the most important—we must promptly kindle both emulation and initiative among the masses, so that they tackle the matter immediately.

Could not a plan (approximate) be worked out for this purpose at once on the following lines?

1) Electric light to be installed in all rural district centers (10,000–15,000) within one year.

2) In all villages (500,000–1,000,000, probably not more than 750,-000) within two years.

3) In the first place—village libraries and Soviets (two lamps each).

4) Secure the poles immediately in such and such a fashion [sic].

5) Secure the insulators immediately yourselves (the porcelain factories, if I am not mistaken, are local ones and small?) in such and such a fashion [sic].

6) Copper for the wire? Collect it yourselves in each county and rural district (a subtle hint at church bells and so on).

7) Organize the teaching of electricity on such and such lines [sic].

Cannot something along these lines be devised, elaborated and decreed?

Yours, Lenin

Lenin's Description of Himself

All the delegates to the Tenth All-Russian Congress of the Russian Communist party had to fill out a four-page party questionnaire. Lenin answered his questionnaire as follows. Lack of space makes it impossible to reproduce the form of the questionnaire in facsimile, but his answers are reproduced exactly except that where he used abbreviations which might not be familiar the entire words are given. The document is preserved in the Central Lenin Museum.

Name: Ulyanov (Lenin), Vladimir Ilyich

Party organization: Central Committee, Russian Communist Party, Moscow

Number of delegate mandate (voting/advisory): No. 21 advisory

By whom elected: Central Committee

*No. of Party members represented at
    meeting at which elected:* Central Committee—19 members

*Which All-Russian Party Congresses
    have you attended:* All except July (August?) 1917

Date of birth—age: 1870—51 years

State of health: Good

Family—no. of members of dependents: Wife and sister

Nationality: Russian

Native tongue: Russian

Knowledge of other languages: English, German, French—poor, Italian—
    very poor

*What parts of Russia do you know well,
    and how long have you lived there:* Know Volga country where I was
    born best; lived there until age 17

*Have you been abroad (when, where,
    how long):* In a number of West European countries—1895, 1900–
    1905, 1908–1917

Military training: None

Education: Graduated (passed examination as externe) Petrograd University, Law Faculty, in 1891

Basic occupation before 1917: Writer

Special training: None

*Occupation since 1917 besides Party, Soviet,
    trade union, and similar work:* Besides those enumerated, only writing

What trade union do you belong to: Union of Journalists

Positions held since 1917: October 1917 to March 1921; Moscow; Council
    of People's Commissars and Council of Labor and Defense; Chairman

Present position: Since October 1917; Moscow; Chairman, Council of
    People's Commissars and Council of Labor and Defense.

How long have you been a member of the R.C.P. (Bolsheviks): Since
    1894

Have you ever belonged to any other parties: No

Participation in the Revolutionary movement before 1917: Illegal Social-
    Democratic circles; member of the Russian Social-Democratic
    Workers' Party since its foundation. 1892–3, Samara; 1894–5. St.
    Petersburg; 1895–7, prison; 1898–1900, Siberia; 1900–05,
    abroad; 1905–07, St. Petersburg; 1908–1917, abroad.

Penalties incurred for revolutionary....
    Activities: 1887 prison; 1895–7 prison; 1898–1900 Siberia; 1900
    prison

How long in prison: Several days and 14 months

How long at hard labor: None
How long in exile: Three years
How long a political refugee: 9–10 years
Party functions since 1917: October 1917 to March 1921, Moscow, Member of the Central Committee
Present Party function: as above
Have you ever been tried by the courts of the RSFSR or of the Party: No
Date: 7 March, 1921
Signature of delegate: V. Ulyanov (Lenin)

Among Lenin's Legacies

During periods of partial recovery from the illness which finally proved fatal, Lenin sought to give continuing leadership to his associates by means of written communications. Among these were notes which Lenin wished to have placed before the first party congress which should follow his death. Many of these documents were not published until 1956. It is believed that they were distributed among the delegates to the Twentieth Party Congress in connection with Khrushchev's speech on Stalin. The versions which are printed below were released to the press on 30 June, 1956 by the U.S. Department of State which had received them "through a confidential source." Five of the eighteen documents released by the State Department are included here.

[1]

FOR THE EXCLUSIVE USE OF PARTY ORGANIZATIONS

I transmitted the notes which V. I. Ilyich [*sic*] dictated to me during his illness from 23 December to 23 January—13 separate notes. This total number does not yet include the note concerning the national question (Mariya Ilyishna has it). Some of these notes have already been published (on the Workers-Peasants Inspection, and on Sukhanov). Among the unpublished notes are those of 24–25 December '22 and those of 4 January '23 which contain personal characterizations of some CC [Central Committee] members. Vladimir Ilyich expressed the definite wish that this note of his be submitted after his death to the next Party Congress for its information.

N. Krupskaya [Mme. Lenin]

The documents mentioned in the declaration of Com[rade] N. K. Krupskaya, which are to be transmitted to the CC Plenum commission, were received by me on 18 May '24.

L. Kamenev

Vladimir Ilyich's notes mentioned above and transmitted to Com. Kamenev—are all known to me and were earmarked by Vladimir Ilyich for transmittal to the Party.
18. V. 24.

N. Krupskaya

[2]

Having familiarized itself with the documents which were transmitted to Com. Kamenev by N. K. Krupskaya on 18. V. 24, the CC Plenum Commission decided: To submit them to the nearest Party Congress for its information.

19. V. 24. [S.] G. Zinoviev, A. Smirnov, M. Kalinin, N. Bukharin, J. Stalin, L. Kamenev.

> Lenin died on 21 January, 1924. The Thirteenth Party Congress was held from the 23d to the 31st of May, 1924.

[3]

Letter to the Congress

I should very much like to advise that a series of changes in our political organization be undertaken at this Congress.

I should like to share with you those thoughts which I consider to be most essential.

I submit, as of primary importance, that the size of the CC membership be enlarged to several dozen, possibly even to one hundred members. It seems to me that our Central Committee would be exposed to great danger in case future developments would not be favorable to us (and we cannot rely on it)—if we had not undertaken such a reform.

. . .

Referring to the first point, i.e. enlargement of CC membership, I am of the opinion that it is necessary for the raising of CC authority and for the serious work aimed at raising the efficiency of our apparatus, as also for the prevention of conflicts between small CC groupings which would gravely affect the fate of the Party as a whole.

I think that our Party has the right to demand 50–100 CC members from the working class whom it can give up without taxing its strength too highly.

This reform would lay the foundation for a greater stability of our Party and would help it in its struggle in the encirclement of hostile nations, a struggle which in my opinion can and must greatly sharpen in the next few years. I think that thanks to such a move the stability of our Party would increase a thousandfold.

23. XII. '22.   Lenin
Written by M. V.

Continuation of the notes

24 December '22

By the stability of the Central Committee, of which I spoke above, I mean measures to prevent a split—if such measures can at all be found. Because the White Guardist from *Russkaya Mysl* (I think it was S. F. Oldenburg) was of course right when, in the first place, in their action aganst Soviet Russia, he banked on the hope of a split in our Party and also when, in the second place, in speaking of this split, he banked on very serious differences of opinion in the Party.

Our Party rests upon two classes and this may possibly result in the violation of its stability; and its fall could not be prevented if these two classes did not reach an agreement. Under such conditions to apply this or that solution, and even to discuss the stability of our CC, is useless. No preventive measures would in such an event avert a split. I hope, however, that this [the possibility of a split in the Party] would threaten only in the remote future, that it is so improbable that we need not even talk about it.

I have in mind stability which would make a split impossible in the near future and I intend to examine here a series of a purely personal nature [sic].

In my opinion, and from this viewpoint, such CC members as Stalin and Trotsky present the most important factor pertaining to stability. The character of relationship between them contains, to my mind, the greater part of the danger of that split, which could be avoided; this preventive aim can, I think, best be served along with other purposes by raising the number of CC members to 50, to 100 persons.

Com. Stalin has, having become Secretary General, concentrated enormous power in his hands and I am not at all certain that he is capable of utilizing this power with sufficient caution. Com. Trotsky, on the other hand, as was already demonstrated in his fight against the CC in connection with the question of the People's Commissariat of Communications, distinguishes himself not only as possessing great abilities. He is probably the most able man in the present CC but at the same time he possesses an exaggerated self-confidence and an exaggerated attraction to the purely administrative side of affairs.

These two traits of the able leaders of the present CC might quite innocently lead to a split; if our Party does not take steps to prevent this, the split can occur unexpectedly.

I will not further attempt to characterize other CC members as to their personal qualities. I will recall only that the October episode of Zinoviev and Kamenev was, of course, not an accident, but we should use it against them even less than non-Bolshevism against Trotsky. [The "October episode" refers to the opposition of Kamenev and Zinoviev to Lenin's plan to start the Bolshevik revolution in October (O.S.) 1917.]

Speaking about the younger CC members, I want to say a few words about Bukharin and Pyatakov. In my opinion they are the most able forces (of the younger men); but in regard to them we should be aware of the following: Bukharin is not only a very valuable and very prominent Party theoretician, but is properly regarded as the favorite of the whole Party; his theoretical views, however, can be accepted as fully Marxist views but only with a very large grain of salt, because there is something of the scholastic in him (he never studied and, I think, has never completely understood, the dialectic).

25. XII. Now for Pyatakov; he is a man of unquestionably strong will and of great ability; he is, however, too much tempted by administrativeness, and by the purely administrative side of things, to be relied on in an important political question.

It is clear that the first as well as the second observation refers only to the present, but both are made just in case these two able and loyal workers are not able to find an occasion to round out their knowledge and get rid of their onesidedness.

25. XII. 22.   Lenin
Written by M. V.

[4]

Supplement to the Letter of 24 December, 1922

Stalin is too rude and this defect, which can be freely tolerated in our midst and in contacts among us Communists, can become an intolerable defect in one holding the position of the Secretary General. Because of this, I propose that the comrades consider ways and means by which Stalin can be removed from this position and another man selected, a man who, above all, would differ from Com. Stalin in only one quality, namely, greater tolerance, greater loyalty, greater kindness and more considerate attitude toward his comrades, less capricious temper, etc. This circumstance could appear to be a meaningless trifle. I think, however, that from the viewpoint of preventing a split and from the viewpoint of what I have written above concerning the relationship between Stalin and Trotsky, this is not a trifle, or if it is one, then it is a trifle which can acquire a decisive significance.

Written by L. F.   Lenin
4 January 1923

Continuation of notes
26 December 1922

The enlargement of the CC membership to 50 or even 100 persons should serve, as I see it, a two- or three-fold purpose; the more CC members there are, the more persons will get to know the CC work and the smaller will be the danger of a split as a result of taking some careless step. Enlistment of many workers into the CC will help our workers improve the efficiency of our apparatus, which is very bad. Actually we have inherited it from the old regime, because it was entirely impossible for us to reorganize it completely in such a short time, especially during the period of war, of famine, etc. For that reason the "critics," who, in a derogatory or sarcastic manner, point out the defects of our apparatus, can be boldly answered that they have no concept whatever of the conditions of our present revolution. Effective reorganization of the apparatus within five years was entirely impossible—especially during the period of the revolution. It is enough that during five years we managed to create a government of a new type in which workers at the head of peasants stand against the bourgeoisie, and this at a time when we are encircled by a hostile world; this was a tremendous accomplishment. This knowledge should not, however, blind us to the fact that it is actually the old apparatus which we have taken over, the apparatus of the Czar and the bourgeoisie, and that now, when we have attained peace and have satisfied our minimal needs, we should devote all our effort toward improving the efficiency of the apparatus. I picture this to myself in this manner; several dozen workers taken into the CC machinery will be more able than anyone else to occupy themselves with the control, efficiency and transformation of our apparatus. It became evident that the Workers-Peasants Inspection which initially possessed this function, is incapable of performing it and can be used only as an "auxiliary," or, under some conditions, as an assistant of these CC members. Workers drawn into the CC should, in my opinion, not be recruited from among those who have behind them a long period of service in the Soviet apparatus (in this part of my letter I count the peasants as workers in every case) because these workers have acquired certain habits and certain prejudices, which we specifically consider it necessary to combat.

The CC staff should be enlisted largely from among the workers who are below the level of the group which were promoted during the last five years to positions in the Soviet apparatus, and from among those who are close to the common workers and peasants, who are not directly or indirectly in the category of exploiters. I think that such workers, now attending all CC meetings, and all Politbureau meetings, and having the opportunity to read all CC documents—are capable of creating the cadre of loyal supporters of the Soviet system; they will be able also, firstly, to add to the stability of the CC itself, and secondly to work actually on rebuilding the apparatus and making it efficient.

Written by L. F.

26. XII. 22.

Continuation of the notes
29 December 1922

When raising the number of CC members, it is necessary, in my opinion, to solve—probably first of all—the problem of control and efficiency of our apparatus, which is good for nothing. For this purpose we should utilize the services of highly qualified specialists; the task of making these specialists available belongs to the Workers-Peasants Inspection.

How the work of these control specialists, who also have sufficient knowledge is to be coordinated with the work of these new CC members—practice should decide. It appears to me that the Workers-Peasants Inspection (as the result of its development and also as the result of doubts in regard to this development) has reached a stage, which we now observe, namely, a stage of transition from a separate People's Commissariat to the assignment of special functions to CC members. This transition is away from an institution which inspects absolutely everything—away from a group consisting only of a few members who are, however, first-class inspectors who have to be well-paid (this is particularly indispensable in our era when everything has to be paid for and in the situation when the inspectors are employed only in those institutions which offer better pay).

If the number of CC members is adequately raised and if they attend each year a course on administration of governmental affairs, benefiting from the help of the highly qualified specialists and of the members of the Workers-Peasants Inspection who are highly authoritative in every sphere of activity—then, I think we will successfully solve this problem which has so long evaded solution.

Therefore, totally: about 100 CC members and no more than 400–500 assistants, who, in their capacity as members of the Workers-Peasants Inspection, control in accordance with their directives.

29 December 1922   Lenin
Written by M. V.

"The Carrot and the Stick"

> The rulers of the USSR have skillfully and successfully combined coercions and rewards to increase industrial and labor productivity. The 1918 Russian Constitution made all citizens between the ages of fifteen and fifty-one years liable to compulsory labor. This legal compulsion was abolished after 1922 (except in cases of emergency), but it was decreed that a worker who had taken a job thereby became subject to the Labor Code which prohibited his leaving that employment without the specific consent of the head of the enterprise. This proved very difficult to enforce.
>
> Absenteeism remained a grave problem despite the decree against it issued in 1932 by the party's Central Executive Committee and the Council of Peoples' Commissars of the USSR. Excerpts from this decree are given below. The decree was published in *Izvestia* on November 16, 1932. It was signed by Kalinin, Molotov, and Yenukidze, and was dated November 15, 1932.
>
> There have been several modifications of this law both by new decrees and by court interpretations. According to an interpretation made in 1939, a single tardiness of over twenty minutes was equivalent to a day's absence and was therefore punishable by dismissal. This ruling was reversed after Stalin's death. A decree of June 26, 1940 provided that absenteeism should be punished by compulsory labor at reduced wages but without confinement, the sentence (which might be as long as six months) to be served at the offender's regular place of employment. This was obviously an effort to maintain disciplinary controls without disrupting production.

Decree on Absenteeism

. . . the Central Executive Committee [of the Communist Party] and the Council of Peoples' Commissars resolve: . . .

2. To order that even in the case of one day's absence from work without sufficient reasons the worker shall be dismissed from the services of the

factory or enterprise, and shall be deprived of the ration cards issued to him as a member of the staff of the factory or enterprise, and shall also be deprived of the use of lodgings which were given him in houses belonging to the factory or enterprise.

3. To instruct the governments of the federated republics to amend their Labor Codes to correspond with this.

*   *   *   *   *

Decree on Labor Passports

In an effort to reduce the distressingly high labor turnover, the Presidium of the Supreme Soviet of the USSR ordered the introduction of Labor Passports (or Labor Workbooks) in 1938. The system was largely in abeyance immediately after the 1941–1945 War, but it was subsequently restored and expanded. The decree, which is self-explanatory, was issued on December 20, 1938, and was signed by Molotov and Bolshakov. It was published in *Izvestia* on December 21, 1938.

. . . the Council of Peoples' Commissars decrees:

1. The introduction, effective January 15, 1939, of Labor Workbooks for workers and employees in all state and cooperative institutions and enterprises, [the Workbooks] to be issued by the administrative boards of the institutions (enterprises).

2. Labor books are to contain the following information about the owner of the book: surname, name, and patronymic; age; education; profession; information about his work and about his movement from one institution (enterprise) to another, the causes of such shifts, and also [a record] of encouragements and rewards received.

.   .   .

6. Workers and employees must produce their Labor books for inspection by the managing board of the institution (enterprise) when signing on [for a job]. Managing boards have the right to employ workers and employees only if the latter present their Labor books. . . .

7. Managing boards . . . must complete the issuance of Labor books to their workers and employees by January 15, 1939. Persons signing on for work for the first time after that date must get a Labor book not later than five days thereafter.

8. Labor books must be kept for all workers and employees, including seasonal and temporary workers, who work . . . for more than five days.

9. The Labor book is to be kept by the management . . . and returned to the worker or employee on his dismissal.

. . . [The decree also gave detailed instruction to management as to the information required to be shown on the Labor book, the time and manner of recording the data ("All entries in Labor books are to be made in ink."), manner of issuance, manner of replacement if lost, etc.]

Decree Establishing the "Hero of Socialist Labor"

> Inducements designed to increase industrial and other production have included: differential wages, bonuses, larger rations, better housing, and the award of special honors and recognitions. The decree of the Presidium of the Supreme Soviet of the USSR establishing one of the honors is printed below. The decree was signed by Kalinin and Gorkin on December 27, 1938 and was published in *Izvestia* on the following day.

1. To establish the supreme grade of distinction in the sphere of economic and cultural construction: the rank of Hero of Socialist Labor.
2. Persons promoted to the rank of Hero of Socialist Labor are simultaneously awarded the Order of Lenin.

Soviet Labor Law

> The following historical description and analysis of Soviet labor law was written by the late Vladimir Gsovski, a leading specialist on Soviet law. It was published originally in the *Monthly Labor Review* (March–April, 1951), and was later reprinted as "Bulletin No. 1026" of the U.S. Department of Labor. The reprint below is from the latter source, pp. 1–6, 12. Dr. Gsovski's article is an excellent introduction, written for laymen, to an important technical subject.

> *"Soviet Russia does not know of any 'free' contract of employment, nor of any legal relations usually connected with the concept of the employment contract. . . . In Soviet Russia labor duty is the basis of labor relations."* [1]

Thus did a contemporary Soviet authority on labor law characterize the situation in 1920. He was not referring to forced labor, so widely used in Soviet Russia, especially after 1930, but to the Soviet equivalent of "free" labor, the subject of the present article.

Generally speaking the concept put forward in the quotation is largely held today by the Soviet State; it governs to a great extent the functions of the trade-unions and reflects the attitude of the Communist Party. Over the years it resulted in separate labor laws which are punitive rather than protective.

True, in 1920, private enterprise had been effectively barred under the policy known as Militant Communism. This was superseded in 1922 by the so-called New Economic Policy (N.E.P.),[2] under which private enterprise, within certain limits, was readmitted and freedom of the employment contract was accorded some recognition. But this policy came to an end about 1929 with the inauguration of the first Five Year Plan, which,

---

[1] Z. Tettenborn, Soviet Legislation on Labor (in Russian, 1920) p. 16.

[2] For description and analysis of major stages of the Soviet policies and their expression in law, see Gsovski, Soviet Civil Law, University of Michigan Press, Ann Arbor, Vol. 1 (1948) pp. 10 *et seq.*, 791, *et seq.*, Vol. 2 (1949) p. 537 *et seq.*

according to Stalin, had been framed and executed to eliminate capitalist elements and to create an economic basis for a socialist society.[3] Since then private enterprise has been banned.

When private enterprise finally disappeared in Russia the great majority of persons engaged in industry and commerce—from top executives to manual laborers—became employees of a single owner—the government.[4] In that sense there is no contrast between capital and labor in the Soviet Union. The Soviet Government claims that there is a "unity between the interests of the toilers of the Soviet Union and those of the Soviet Socialist State," as an official textbook on labor law stated in 1946.[5] However, such unity can hardly be demonstrated in reality. Soviet industrial organization shows that the fixed relationship between labor and State management took the place of the free relationships between labor and capital in capitalist countries.

Government-owned industry and commerce now operate on a different basis from that of the first years of the Soviet regime (1918–21). At that time, private enterprise and profit-making were outlawed without offering a substitute for satisfaction of personal ambition or an opportunity for extra earning.

In contrast, the policy adopted after the drive began for total socialization was popularly called "whips and cookies." On the one hand, concessions are made to the ever emerging personal ambition; but on the other, criminal law is put into operation in an effort to check the inefficiency of the entire economic system.

Government agencies engaged in business operate on a "commercial" basis (*Khoziaistvenny raschet*) and enjoy a degree of formal independence and enter into contracts with each other and with private persons. Although they are government agencies they are supposed to act with the competitive vigor of a private enterprise (the principle of "socialist competition"). This "independence" should not be overrated. As a Soviet text puts it: "The commercial basis is merely a special method of management of the national economy." [6] Planned assignments of higher bureaus set definite limits to their independence, to say nothing of continuous supervisory control by various government agencies and political control by the secret police and Communist Party.

Nevertheless, the management of a Soviet quasi corporation is as interested in obtaining the lowest unit labor cost as its capitalist prototype. A single executive is appointed by the head of the bureau under whose authority the enterprise (called "trust" in industry and *torg* in commerce) operates. He hires and fires, allocates wages, imposes penalties, and

[3] Stalin, Problems of Leninism, English Edition, Moscow (1940) p. 409.
[4] Members of the so-called productive cooperatives are in fact paid for their work and not according to their shares. See Gsovski *op. cit.* Vol. 1, p. 411, *et seq.*
[5] Aleksandrov and Genkin, Soviet Labor Law (in Russian, 1946) p. 312.
[6] Evtikhiev and Vlasov, Administrative Law (in Russian, 1946) p. 36. *See also* Gsovski *op. cit. supra* note 2, Vol. I at 382 *et seq.*

grants bonuses. Bonuses are paid from a special director's fund based on a percentage of the profits or savings. His own bonus also depends upon the efficiency of the enterprise. In case the output falls below standard quantity or quality, he is liable to imprisonment up to 8 years.

Private profit-making is barred and the earnings of the bulk of the population are practically limited to wages and salaries. But the governmental scale of compensation for work, whether in money or comfort, aims to offer a substitute for profit-making to stimulate efficiency. A system of wages and salaries is designed to allow wide latitude for differentials in wage, salary, and bonus payments. To this end, the principles of piecework and bonuses for efficiency, without any guaranteed minimum wage, constitute the basis of compensation for work in government industry, in collective farming, and in cooperatives.

Regardless of whether the employee is paid by time or by piece, he must attain a standard of output established by the management. If he fails to do so through his fault he is paid according to the quality and quantity of his output.[7] Progressive scales of piecework and bonuses for extra efficiency are issued by the government for individual industries and industry groups.

Numerous honorary titles—"Hero of Labor" and others—and medals carry with them distinct material benefit, such as tax exemption, right to extra housing space, etc. There are also "personal salaries" and "personal pensions" awarded without reference to any scale, and Stalin prizes amounting to as much as 300,000 rubles in a lump sum.

All this affords professional, managerial, and skilled labor remuneration in money and comfort greatly exceeding that given to the ordinary laborer. For example, a scale of salaries and wages for electrical power plants, established in 1942 and still in force as late as 1946, ranged from 115 to 175 rubles monthly for janitorial services to 1,000 to 3,000 rubles for a director.[8]

In 1934, Stalin frankly declared the underlying philosophy of his policy as follows: "Equalization in the sphere of demands and personal life is reactionary, petty bourgeois nonsense, worthy of a primitive ascetic sect and not of a socialist society organized in a Marxian way."[9]

However, material benefits thus promised evidently proved to be insufficient stimuli for good work.

[7] Soviet Labor Code, Sec. 57 as amended in 1934. "If an employee at a governmental, public, or cooperative enterprise, institution, or business fails through his own fault to attain the standard of output prescribed for him, he shall be paid according to the quantity and quality of his output but shall not be guaranteed any minimum wage. In other enterprises and businesses (private enterprises including those under a concession) such an employee shall be paid not less than two-thirds of his scheduled rate."

[8] Handbook of Wages in Electrical Power Plants (in Russian, 1946) pp. 8–12, 25.

[9] Stalin, "Speech at the 17th Congress of the Communist Party (1934)" quoted from his *Problems of Leninism* (10th Russian edition, 1938) p. 583.

Heavy responsibility is imposed upon both workers and management. Inefficiency involves not only loss of material benefits and possible loss of job, but prosecution in court as well. Workers are subject to penalties imposed by managers for "loafing on the job" and to court action for absenteeism and unauthorized quitting of the job. From 10 to 25 years in a forced labor camp,[10] with or without confiscation of property, can be imposed for "misappropriation, embezzlement, or any kind of theft" of the property of the principal employers, the government, or public bodies. Prior to 1946, the death penalty could be invoked.[11] In case of damage to or loss of property of the employer—tools, raw materials, fuel, even work clothes—if due to employee negligence can result in deductions from wages, in some instances in an amount 10 times the value of the property.[12]

A series of laws penalize inefficient management for such things as poor quality or small volume of output, failure to penalize workers for absenteeism and other violations of labor discipline.[13]

A potent incentive to the efficiency of the individual establishment is the principle that earnings depend in part upon the efficiency of the whole enterprise (principle of "check by ruble"). Business success brings definite individual profit; business failure incurs heavy punishment for those holding administrative posts. Although the total amount of regular wages to be paid in an individual enterprise is established by central government bureaus ("wages fund"), bonuses are dependent upon the profits or savings of an individual enterprise.

Under such an arrangement there is no less reason for the rise of labor conflicts than under capitalism. But under the Soviet system labor is deprived of the main effective devices by which it may protect itself in a labor dispute in the capitalist world. Neither the constitution nor any law or decree mentions the right to strike and the strike is tacitly outlawed.

In general, all the channels through which labor can pursue its objectives in the capitalist world—legislation, courts, administrative agencies, the press, and trade-unions—are in Soviet Russia agencies of the principal employer of industrial labor—the State.

For a time when private enterprise was tolerated under N. E. P. (1922–28) the Soviet leaders visualized the protection of the interests of labor in this conflict through trade-unions. But the unions were regarded as an arm of government and of the Communist Party rather than as an independent force. Still they were to be an arm specialized in protection of labor. As the drive for socialization progressed, this special protective quality of the unions was pushed to the background. Instead, the notion of

[10] Statute of June 4, 1947 concerning the crimes against government and public property, *Vedomosti* 1947, No. 19.

[11] Law of August 7, 1932. For its translation and discussion see Gsovski *op. cit. supra* note 2, Vol. I pp. 562, 728.

[12] Soviet Labor Code Secs. 83–83 [4] (as amended), Act of June 20, 1942, Sec. 12; Instruction of the People's Commissar for Labor of June 1, 1932, Secs. 1–3. For further citations, see Gsovski *op. cit.* Vol. I pp. 823–825.

[13] Act of Dec. 28, 1938; Edict of July 10, 1940, *id.* p. 821.

the identity of interests of the workers and the Soviet State was put forward, and the primary function of Soviet labor unions is to serve the interests of the State.

The eleventh congress of the Communist Party in 1922, when the N. E. P. was inaugurated, recognized that if government enterprise operates on a commercial basis "inevitably certain conflicts of interests on the issue of labor conditions in the enterprises are created between the working masses and the directors, managers of the government enterprises, or the government bureaus to which the enterprises are subordinated." Consequently the resolution "imposed upon the trade-unions the duty to protect the interests of the working people." [14]

Thus, the Labor Code of 1922, then enacted, relegated to the collective agreements between management and trade-unions the settlement of all the basic working conditions, including wage rates, standard of output, shop rules, etc.

Nevertheless, even then, both before and after this period, the trade-unions were not considered as a force independent from the Communist Party or the Soviet Government. The ninth congress of the Party (1920) had stated that "the tasks of trade-unions lie primarily in the province of economic organization and education. The trade-unions must perform these tasks not in the capacity of an independent, separately organized force but in the capacity of one of the principal branches of the government machinery guided by the Communist Party." [15] The tenth congress went further and in 1921 passed the resolution, drafted by Lenin, and stressing the role of the trade-unions in Soviet Russia as a "school of communism." [16] The fifteenth congress in 1925 stressed that "trade-unions were created and built up by our [Communist] Party." [17]

"The most important task of the trade-unions," says the official textbook on Civil Law of 1944, "is the political education of the toiling masses, their mobilization for building up socialism, and the defense of their economic interests and cultural needs . . ." [18]

"Formally," says the official textbook on Administrative Law of 1940, "the trade-unions are not a party organization but, in fact, they are carrying out the directives of the Party. All leading organs of the trade-unions consist primarily of Communists who execute the Party line in the entire work of the trade-unions." [19]

Thus the trade-unions were transformed from a labor protecting arm into an arm for execution of government policy, and achievement of production goals. According to Soviet jurists, "the socialist industrialization of

[14] All-Union Communist Party on Trade Unions, Collection of Resolutions (In Russian, 1930) p. 55. See also Deutsch, Soviet Trade Unions, London, 1950.

[15] Ibid. p. 35.

[16] Ibid. p. 36.

[17] Ibid. p. 87.

[18] Agarkov and others, Civil Law (in Russian, 1944) Vol. I, p. 190; Civil Law Textbook (in Russian 1938) Vol. 1, pp. 108–109.

[19] Denisov, Soviet Administrative Law (in Russian, 1940) p. 60.

the country required that labor law . . . serve the successful struggle for productivity of labor and strengthening of labor discipline." [20]

Such transformation of the trade-unions into a government arm, enforcing official economic policy, began soon after the onset of the first Five Year Plan. Accordingly, the sixteenth congress of the Communist Party directed in 1930 that the trade-unions, striving in collective agreements for improvement of the standard of living of the workers, must take into account the financial status of the enterprise with which the agreement was made and the interests of the national economy. In making the agreement, the resolution insisted, each party must undertake definite obligations in carrying out the financial and production plan of the enterprise. The unions in particular were obligated to guarantee, on behalf of the workers, the productivity of labor contemplated by the plan.[21]

The central agency of all the Soviet trade-unions—their Central Council—was granted the status of a government department in 1933. It officially took the place of the People's Commissariat for Labor, which was then abolished, and the Council was also charged with administration of social insurance. But then the Central Council of Trade-Unions lost the character of a representative body of trade-unions even in terms of the Soviet "democracy." Under law this Council must be elected by the Congress of Trade-Unions which is designated as "the supreme authority of the trade-unions of the Soviet Union." Nevertheless, since the Ninth Congress in 1932 no such Congresses were convoked for 17 years, during which the whole Soviet social order and the position of labor were radically changed.

When the Tenth Congress convened in 1949, no explanation was asked or offered for the delay. The Congress adopted a new statute which reaffirmed the total control of the Communist Party over the trade-unions:

"The Soviet trade-unions conduct their entire work under the direction of the Communist Party—the organizing and directing force of the Soviet Society. The trade-unions of the U.S.S.R. rally the working masses behind the Party of Lenin-Stalin." [22]

Among numerous tasks assigned by the new statute to the trade-unions the generalized political objectives are described in the first place at great length. For example, the trade-unions "strive to enhance in every way the socialist order in society and State, the moral-political unity of the Soviet people, the brotherly cooperation and friendship between the peoples of the Soviet Union; they actively participate in the election of the agencies of governmental power; they organize workers and clerical employees for the struggle for the steady development of the national economy."

In contrast, "the duty to protect the interests of the working people" which had been emphasized by the Party Congress in 1922 is not expressly stated. It may have been considered unnecessary because the stat-

[20] *Op. cit. supra* note 5, p. 90.
[21] Ibid. p. 98.
[22] Trud (in Russian) May 11, 1949. See Bureau of Labor Statistics, Notes on Labor Abroad No. 11, May 1949, pp. 39–40.

ute assumes that "in the conditions of the Soviet socialist order the State protects the rights of the working people." But in any event the labor-protection tasks of the unions are couched in cautious language.

At the very end of the above quoted passage it is mentioned that the unions "look after (*zabotiatsia*) the further rise of the material well being and the full satisfaction of the cultural needs of the toilers." At another place the unions' monopoly to represent the workers is stated with a hardly accidental lack of specificity: "[unions should] act on behalf of workers and clerical employees before the governmental and social bodies in matters concerning labor, culture, and workers' everyday life."

Collective bargaining, provided for in the Labor Code of 1922, was discontinued in 1933. As the official Soviet text on labor law explained in 1946: *"The collective agreements as a special form of legal regulation of labor relations of manual and clerical employees has outlived itself.* Detailed regulation of all sides of these relations by mandatory acts of governmental power does not leave any room for any contractual agreement concerning one labor condition or another." [23]

In plain English, this means that the Soviet leaders chose to abandon the last vestige of contract in relations between labor, even as represented by party-controlled trade-unions on the one hand and State management on the other, for the sake of outright government regimentation. Capitalist free collective bargaining was frankly declared unfit in the socialist surroundings of the Soviet Union.

However, in 1947 a campaign for making new collective agreements was suddenly ordered after a lapse of 14 years.

Collective agreements were declared the most important measure "to achieve and exceed the production plan, to secure further growth of the productivity of labor, improvement of the organization of labor, and the increase of responsibility of management and trade organizations for the material condition of living of the employees and cultural services rendered to them." [24] Nevertheless, the new policy is far from introducing free collective bargaining. Certain matters are definitely excluded from any negotiation and agreement and are reserved for government regulation.

The new rules positively require that "the rates of wages, of piecework, progressive piecework, and bonuses as approved by the government must be indicated" in the agreement. It is expressly forbidden to include any rates not approved by the government. In other words, wage rates are excluded from bargaining, but if included in the agreement are no more than applications of the governmental schedule to the establishment for which the collective agreement is drawn. This is true, to a large measure, of other points covered, particularly standards of output. The official act and the jurisprudential writings insist that the primary purpose of

[23] *Op. cit., supra* note 5, p. 106. Italics in the original.

[24] Resolution of the Presidium of the Central Council of the Trade Union approved by the Council of Ministers, Preamble, *Trud* (in Russian) Apr. 18, 1947. See Bureau of Labor Statistics, Notes on Labor Abroad No. 2, June 1947, p. 28, and No. 13, December 1949, p. 36.

such agreements is to translate the abstract terms of the general plan for economic development into specific assignments and obligations within each particular establishment. They appear to be merely a form in which the orders of the government are made more precise.

A Soviet writer of authority comments:

> It is understood that the present day collective agreements could not but be different by content from collective agreements which were made at the time when the rates of wages and some other conditions of labor were not established by the law and government decrees.
>
> The purpose of the present day collective agreement is to make concrete the duties of the management, shop committees, workers, technical, engineering, and clerical personnel toward the fulfillment of the production plans and production over and above the plan as well as to raise the responsibility of business agencies and trade-unions for improvement of material living conditions of workers and cultural services rendered to them.[25]

As before, the new regulations are based on the assumption that "the interests of the workers are the same as the interests of production in a socialist state" and that the collective agreements are designed to be the "juridical form of expression of this unity." [26] Accordingly, a model agreement is drafted by each ministry upon consultation with the central offices of the appropriate trade-unions. Then the model agreement is sent as a fait accompli to the establishments concerned.

While such collective agreements are not the result of collective bargaining, it may be observed that when the Soviet Government faced the task of postwar rehabilitation of its economy, it preferred to give decreed labor conditions the appearance of an agreement.

Negotiation and mutual agreement are in fact proscribed in the Soviet Union in many important respects. Government regulation of wages and other basic conditions of labor took their place. However, it does not mean that labor is thus protected by law as we understand it. True, a Code of Labor Laws still exists on the statute books of the republics of the Soviet Union. But it was enacted in 1922 when private enterprise was within some limits tolerated and the government was not the sole employer in industry and commerce. At that time the code sought to regulate labor relations on the basis of free contract and to protect labor by methods resembling advanced democratic labor legislation.

However, these provisions of the code were either repealed or for the most part became inoperative being superseded, without a formal repeal, by various laws and decrees.

Under the totalitarian concept of government power, the accepted rela-

---

[25] Aleksandrov and other compilers, Goliakov, editor, Legislation concerning Labor (in Russian 1947) p. 15.

[26] Moskalenko, "Legal Problems Involved in Collective Agreements" in *Trade Unions* (in Russian 1947) No. 8, p. 16 *et seq.; Trud* (in Russian) Apr. 18, 1947, Editorial.

tionships of the administrative and legislative branches of the government do not apply. Although the terms "constitution," "legislative act," and "administrative decree" are used in Soviet law, the authority attached to each of these sources of law in the Soviet Union is different from that associated with these terms in the democratic countries. A constitutional provision may be set aside by an administrative decree and the newly enacted rule is incorporated into the constitution only at a later date. For example, the 7-hour working day was provided for in the 1936 constitution (section 119).

However, on June 26, 1940, the Presidium of the Supreme Soviet, an executive body in terms of the constitution, decreed the 8-hour normal working day. This edict became operative immediately. It was ratified by the Supreme Soviet in August 1940, but without following the procedure prescribed for constitutional amendment. Not until 7 years later was section 119 constitutionally amended.

The Soviet jurists are fully aware of such practices. In discussing the sources of Soviet labor law in the treatises on this subject, they seek to blur the distinction between the authority of a constitutional provision, a legislative enactment, and an administrative decree or directive. In a recent (1949) standard treatise,[27] designed for use in university law schools, a doctrine of "normative acts" (rule making) as the source of Soviet labor law is promulgated. Normative acts are in general terms defined as "acts by which the will of the ruling class is 'elevated to law.' " This not too clear definition is fortunately followed by an enumeration of the specific acts issued by Soviet authorities which, according to the author, fall under the defintion. These are "laws" enacted by the Supreme Soviet (Soviet equivalent to legislature), "edicts" by its presidium (a body of 47 members constituting the Soviet collective President), "normative resolutions" (i. e., rule-making resolutions) of the Council of Ministers (cabinet), joint resolutions of the Council of Ministers and the Central Committee of the Communist Party, regulations issued by individual ministers and by the Central Council of the Trade-Unions.

In other words, any decree or order by any of the central governmental authorities is law. No matter what it is called and by what body it is issued, it prevails until the action of another authority supersedes it.

The survey of recent trends in the Soviet legislation thus far made suggests the conclusion that the disappearance of private enterprise from the Soviet economy has not been followed by the increase of rights of labor in labor law. If compared with the time when private enterprise was tolerated, the legal status of labor has worsened. Another striking feature of the Soviet regulations on labor are the numerous penal provisions.

·   ·   ·

These elements of conscript and forced "free" labor exist in the Soviet Union in addition to the outright convict labor in labor camps operated by the Ministry of Interior (M. V. D.). Discussion of them is outside the

[27] Aleksandrov, editor, Soviet Labor Law (in Russian, 1949) p. 53.

scope of this article, which is devoted exclusively to the Soviet group which is the nearest counterpart of our free labor.

In discussing the general situation of postwar free employment, Soviet writers themselves plainly indicate that "voluntary" employment under Soviet conditions is not much different from conscript labor. A treatise by Dogadov on the development of the Soviet labor law, which appeared in 1949, states:

> In the socialist society there is no difference in principle and quality between drafted labor and labor performed by voluntary entering into labor relations by taking of employment. When we are saying that in the socialist society the principle of voluntary labor is recognized we are not speaking of recognition of some kind of abstract principle of free labor and trade in a liberal and bourgeois sense, a principle which would be treated as a value per se.

> Under the conditions of socialist society . . . it is impossible to secure the principle "from each according to his ability" without a pressure by the state and law regarding the universal duty to work.[47]

It is clear that the "voluntary employment" still to be found in some branches of Soviet industry is far from our concept of free labor.

Jobs are frozen. Worker and manager are under equally heavy penalties, both criminal and civil. Millions of future Soviet citizens, while still only 12 to 14 years old, are assigned for training at jobs selected for them by the authorities, without necessary regard for personal preferences or those of their parents or guardians. Professionals, for considerable time after graduation, are denied the right to go into a job of their own choosing. This is the general picture of "free" labor in the Soviet State.

The Labor Decree of 1956

> Several major changes were made and earlier decrees were annulled by a new labor law which was issued in April, 1956. Portions of the new law were quoted verbatim, and other sections were summarized by Mr. Yu. P. Mironenko in the *Bulletin* of the Institute for the Study of the USSR (Munich). Vol. III, no. 9 (September, 1956). Pp. 20–23. The verbatim quotations and parts of the summaries given by Mr. Mironenko are printed below.

The reasons for the decree's publication were given in the following words:

As a result of the growth of the workers' consciousness, the increase in their material well-being and cultural standards, discipline at enterprises and institutions has strengthened. Under these conditions the existing legal responsibility of workers and salaried employees for unwarranted departure from enterprises and institutions and for repeated or prolonged absence without due cause is not a necessity and can be replaced by measures of a disciplinary and social nature.

[47] Dogodov, "History of Development of the Soviet Labor Law" in *Ucheniye Zapiski* of Leningrad University, Series of Legal Sciences, No. 2 (in Russian 1949), p. 163, 166.

On the basis of this, the Presidium of the Supreme Soviet made the following decisions:

1. To abolish workers' and salaried employees' legal responsibility for unwarranted departure from enterprises and institutions and for repeated or prolonged absence without due cause.

2. To set aside sentences of persons convicted of unwarranted departure from enterprises and institutions and for absence without due cause.

3. To dismiss all cases of unwarranted departure from enterprises and institutions and of absenteeism not examined by the court up to the time of publication of this decree.

4. To rescind the conviction of citizens previously convicted and who have carried out their sentences for unwarranted departure from enterprises and institutions and for absenteeism and also of persons who under the provisions of the present decree are no longer subject to sentence.

. . .

Article 5 of the new decree under discussion establishes that now workers and salaried employees, when leaving of their own volition, are obliged to give two weeks' notice to the administration of the enterprise or institution. This article also reestablished the norms . . . under which a labor agreement may be dissolved at the request of the employee, with the difference that notice was increased from one to two weeks. This reestablishes the situation existing prior to June 26, 1940.

Article 6 of the decree establishes that workers and salaried employees leaving of their own accord lose their seniority and are granted the right to receive benefits for temporary disability only after working at least six months at the new place of employment. This article reestablishes the provisions . . . which were in effect until June 26, 1940.

. . .

Article 7 of the decree lists the penalties imposed by the director of the enterprise or the head of the institution concerned on workers and employees absenting themselves without due cause. They are as follows:

1. Disciplinary action in accordance with the internal labor regulations, or, at enterprises and institutions where there are special statutes on discipline, in accordance with these statutes.

2. The deprivation for three months of the right to a percentage increase for service or a decrease up to 25% of a one-time bonus for length of service.

3. Dismissal with a corresponding entry in the labor book to the effect that the employee had been dismissed for being absent without due cause. The person dismissed loses his seniority and regains the right to temporary disability benefits only after working six months or more at the new place of employment.

Forced Labor

The penultimate application of "the stick" has been forced or slave labor, more euphemistically known in Soviet terminology as "corrective labor." Although the West did not become generally aware of the existence of forced labor in the Soviet Union until after World War II when the testimony of many escapees and defectors became available, forced labor had been an integral part of the Soviet economic system at least since 1930. The system of forced labor was originally controlled by the OGPU. When this organization was abolished, control passed to the NKVD and, subsequently, to the MVD. Both these organizations had a special department, called GULAG (Chief Administration of Collective Labor Camps and Colonies) to handle the work.

No exact or unchallenged figures are available, but it appears that GULAG was the largest single employer of labor through the 1930's and 1940's. One carefully compiled listing of labor camps and colonies contains 485 entries. Their inmates worked at the following occupations, among others: lumbering, railway construction, mining, farming, port construction, quarrying, canal construction, fisheries, textile manufacturing, petroleum industry, and all kinds of maintenance jobs.

Forced labor, in addition to its economic aspect, was also an instrument of political control. Since Stalin's death, it has apparently been used less for this purpose. There have been some amnesties and a number of forced labor camps and colonies are reported to have been closed. The system does not, however, appear to have been abandoned.

The documents which follow are of two types. The first, which reports the completion of a canal and the preparations for turning the canal over to the government, gives conclusive proof of the use of forced labor on that project. Yagoda, who signed the report, was tried and convicted in the treason trials of 1938 (a portion of his testimony at that trial is reprinted in this book), but at the time of the report, as his signature indicates, he was second in command of the secret police. The translation was made from a photograph of Yagoda's typescript letter which was published in the Soviet magazine, *The USSR in Construction*. Moscow: State Publishing House of Graphic Arts, 1933. No. 12.

The other two documents deal with NKVD arrests and deportations in the Baltic countries after these were occupied by the Soviets. Both of them are translations of photostatic copies of Soviet documents.

[1]

To the SECRETARY of the C[entral] C[ommittee] of the C[ommunist] P[arty] (B)[olshevik], Comrade Stalin:
To the SECRETARY of the C. C. of the C. P. (B), Comrade Kaganovich:
To the CHAIRMAN OF THE COUNCIL OF COMMISSARS OF THE USSR, Comrade Molotov:

By a government decree of November, 1931, the OGPU was charged with the construction of the White Sea—Baltic Canal, connecting the White

Sea with the Baltic, from Provonets on Lake Onega to Soroka on the White Sea, a total distance of 227 kilometers [141.05 miles].

I now report that the work of construction, begun at the end of November, 1931, was completed on June 20, 1933, i.e., in one year and nine months.

The entire canal and all its equipment appeared, in preliminary tests and observations, to be in good working order.

A total of 118 structures were built on the White Sea—Baltic Canal, as follows: 19 locks, 15 dams, 12 spillways, 40 embankments, 32 canals—length 40 klm.

For these the following amounts of work were required: [There follow seven items concerning the amount of dirt moved, of concrete poured, etc.]

[?] A technical commission is examining the canal in preparation for its acceptance by the government.

Asst. Head of the OGPU,

[s] Yagoda

26 June, 1933.

[2]

Destinations and Routings for Deportees from Latvia, Lithuania, and Estonia on 13/14 June, 1941.

(Extract from NKVD telephonogram, abridged.)

Riga.   Comrade Serov: Comrade Avakumov:
Echelons from Latvia to proceed as follows: . . .
From the Lithuanian SSR to the Altain Region: . . .
From Estonian SSR: . . .

37. Station	Kotielnicki,	Gorki Railway		1,600	persons
38. "	Shakjunya,	"	"	300	"
39. "	Kirov,	"	"	500	"
40. "	Slobodskoye,	"	"	400	"
41. "	Filenki,	"	"	300	"
42. "	Vekanskaya,	"	"	300	"
43. "	Muraski,	"	"	100	"
44. "	Orichi,	"	"	100	"
45. "	Yurya,	"	"	100	"
46. "	Pinyur,	"	"	100	"
47. "	Koparino,	"	"	100	"
48. "	Lusa,	"	"	100	"
49. "	Novosibirskr, Tomsk	"	700		"
50. "	Chany,	"	"	1,000	"
51. "	Kargat,	"	"	1,000	"
52. "	Promysklennaya,	"	"	1,000	"
53. "	Starobielsk, Moscow-Donbas Railway				
	Men only without their families			1,930	persons

54. Station Babynino, Moscow-Kiev Railway
Men only without their families   1,000 persons
55.   "   Solikamsk, Perm Railway
Criminal offenders   472   "

Bills of lading to be prepared in accordance with above destinations.
Heads of echelons to report progress once daily to Transport Department of the NKVD of the USSR.

Chernyshev

No. 30/5698/016   Delivered: Kotliarev
June 13, 1941   Received: Vorobiev—June 13

[3]

Strictly Secret

Instructions Regarding the Manner of Conducting the Deportation of the Anti-Soviet Elements from Lithuania, Latvia and Estonia.

1. General Situation

The deportation of anti-Soviet elements from the Baltic States is a task of great political importance. Its successful execution depends upon the extent to which the county operative triumvirates and operative headquarters are capable of carefully working out a plan for executing the plans and foreseeing in advance all indispensable factors. Moreover, the basic premise is that the operations should be conducted without noise and panic, so as not to permit any demonstrations and other excesses not only by the deportees, but also by a certain part of the surrounding population inimically inclined toward the Soviet administration.

. . .

2. Manner of Issuing Instructions

The instructing of operative groups should be done by the county triumvirates within as short a time as possible on the day before the beginning of the operations, taking into consideration the time necessary for traveling to the place of operations.

3. Manner of Obtaining Documents

After the issuance of general instructions to the operative groups, they should definitely be issued documents regarding the deportees. Personal files of the deportees must be previously discussed and settled by the operative groups of townships and villages, so that there are no obstacles in issuing them.

After receiving the personal files, the senior member of the operative group acquaints himself with the personal files of the family which he will have to deport. He must check the number of persons in the family, the supply of necessary forms to be filled out by the deportee, and transportation for moving the deportee, and he should receive exhaustive answers to questions not clear to him.

At the time when the files are issued, the county triumvirate must explain to each senior member of the operative group where the deported family is to be settled and describe the route to be taken to the place of deportation. Routes to be taken by the administrative personnel with the deported families to the railway station for embarkation must also be fixed. It is also necessary to point out places where reserve military groups are placed in case it should become necessary to call them out during possible excesses.

Possession and state of arms and ammunition must be checked throughout the whole operative personnel. Weapons must be completely ready for battle, loaded, but with the cartridge not kept in the chamber. Weapons should be used only as a last resort, when the operative group is attacked or threatened with an attack, or when resistance is shown.

4. Manner of Executing Deportation

. . .

Having arrived in the village, the operative groups must get in touch (observing the necessary secrecy) with the local authorities: chairman, secretary or members of the village soviets, and should ascertain from them the exact dwelling of the families to be deported. After that the operative groups together with the local authorities go to the families to be banished.

The operation should be commenced at daybreak. Upon entering the home of the person to be banished, the senior member of the operative group should gather the entire family of the deportee into one room, taking all necessary precautionary measures against any possible excesses.

After having checked the members of the family against the list, the location of those absent and the number of persons sick should be ascertained, after which they should be called upon to give up their weapons. Regardless of whether weapons are surrendered or not, the deportee should be personally searched and then the entire premises should be searched in order to uncover weapons.

. . .

Should weapons, counter-revolutionary pamphlets, literature, foreign currency, large quantities of valuables, etc., be disclosed, a short search act should be drawn up on the spot, which should describe the hidden weapons or counter-revolutionary literature. Should there be an armed resistance, the question of arresting the persons showing armed resistance and of sending them to the county branch of the People's Commissariat of Public Security should be decided by the county triumvirate.

. . .

After the search the deportees should be notified that upon the decision of the Government they are being banished to other regions of the Union.

The deportees are permitted to take with them household necessities of not more than 100 kilograms [220.46 lbs.] in weight:

1. Suit
2. Shoes
3. Underwear
4. Bed linen
5. Dishes
6. Glasses
7. Kitchen utensils
8. Food—an estimated month's supply to a family
9. The money at their disposal
10. Haversack or box in which to pack the articles.

It is not recommended that large articles be taken.

Should the contingent be deported to rural districts, they are permitted to take with them a small agricultural inventory: axes, saws, and other articles which should be tied together and packed separately from the other articles so that when embarking on the deportion train they are loaded into special freight cars.

. . .

5. Manner of Separating Deportee from His Family

In view of the fact that a large number of the deportees must be arrested and placed in special camps and their families settled at special points in distant regions, it is necessary to execute the operation of deporting both the members of his family as well as the deportee simultaneously, without informing them of the separation confronting them. After having made the search and drawn up the necessary documents for identification in the home of the deportee, the administrative worker shall draw up documents for the head of the family and place them in his personal file, but the documents drawn up for the members of his family should be placed in the personal file of the deportee's family.

The moving of the entire family to the station, however, should be done in one vehicle, and only at the station should the head of the family be placed separately from his family in a railway car specially intended for heads of families.

. . .

6. Manner of Convoying the Deportees

. . .

7. Manner of Embarking

. . .

The deportees should be loaded into railway cars by families; it is not permitted to break up a family (with the exception of heads of families subject to arrest). An estimate of 25 persons to a car should be observed.

After the railway car is filled with the necessary number of families, it should be locked.

After the people have been taken over and loaded in the echelon train, the commander of the train shall bear responsibility for all the persons turned over to him reaching their destination.

After turning over the deportees, the senior member of the operative group shall draw up a report to the effect that he has performed the functions entrusted to him and address the report to the chief of the county operative triumvirate. The report should briefly contain the name of the deportee, whether any weapons and counter-revolutionary literature were discovered, and how the operation went.

Having placed the deportees on the echelon of deportees and submitted reports of the results of the operations performed, members of the operative group shall be considered free and shall act in accordance with the instructions of the chief of the county branch of the People's Commissariat of Public Security.

DEPUTY PEOPLE'S COMMISSAR OF STATE SECURITY OF THE USSR

Commissar of State Security of the Third Rank
Correct: (signed) MASHKIN   (signed) SEROV

> Another secret Soviet document listed thirty-eight categories of "persons to be registered by the NKVD for later arrest or deportation." The list included the following: Trotskyites, anarchists, terrorists, Social Revolutionaries, Social Democrats, Liberals, Small Farmers, Agrarians, members of the Bund and of Zionist organizations, "counter-revolutionary Fascist elements," members of anti-Soviet organizations, "mystics such as Free Masons and theosophists," policemen, "persons who occupied prominent positions in the Estonian civil or public service," opponents of collectivization, industrialists, wholesale merchants, great landowners, shipowners, owners of hotels and restaurants, persons who have been in the diplomatic service, relatives of persons who have escaped abroad, spies, prostitutes, owners of brothels, persons of aristocratic descent.

The Death Penalty

> The ultimate "stick" is execution of an individual by the state. The following summary of the use of the death penalty in the Soviet Union is reprinted by permission from the *Bulletin of the International Commission of Jurists.* Geneva. No. 12 (November, 1961). Pp. 55–58. The footnotes have been omitted.

On July 21, 1961, *Pravda,* the official Communist Party newspaper in the USSR, published the following article:

> The USSR Prosecutor General (*sic*) appealed to the Russian Republic Supreme Court concerning the lightness of the sentence passed

by the Moscow City Court in the case of Ya. T. Rokotov and V. P. Faibishenko, sentenced on July 15 to 15 years' deprivation of freedom each for large scale speculation in currency.

The judicial collegium for criminal cases of the Russian Republic Supreme Court upheld the appeal and the case was returned for a new court hearing.

On July 18 and 19 the Russian Republic Supreme Court, consisting of Comrade A. T. Rubichev, Chairman of the Supreme Court, and two people's assessors—Comrade A. N. Vasilyev, electric locomotive engineer of the Moscow Railroad, and Comrade A. I. Maurin, tool mechanic at Plant No. 569—held an open court session to hear the criminal case against Ya. T. Rokotov and V. P. Faibishenko for speculation in especially large sums of currency.

Comrade G. A. Terekhov, senior assistant to the USSR Prosecutor General (*sic*) and legal counsellor second class, represented the state prosecution.

Comrades N. I. Rogov and V. Ya. Shveisky, defense lawyers, represented the defendants.

The Court recognized that Rokotov and Faibishenko were guilty of regularly and for purposes of profit buying large amounts of foreign currency and gold coins from foreigners and some Soviet citizens, and of selling them at speculative prices.

The Court established that Rokotov bought a total of 12,000,000 rubles' worth of currency and gold coins and had resold them and that Faibishenko had bought and resold currency in the total amount of 1,000,000 rubles (in old currency).

Rokotov and Faibishenko led a parasitic type of life and enriched themselves through the benefits created by the working people.

Considering that Rokotov and Faibishenko had committed a grave state crime, the Russian Republic Supreme Court, on the basis of Art. 25 of the Law on State Crimes, sentenced Rokotov and Faibishenko to death by shooting with confiscation of all their valuables and property.

The sentence is final and there can be no appeal.

The sentence was heard with approval by those present in the court room.

The death sentence was passed, with retroactive effect, by invoking Decree No. 291 of July 1, 1961, which amended Article 25 of Law of State Crimes. This decree is the latest step in Soviet legislation concerning the death penalty, which has had in the USSR a varied history.

Following the overthrow of the Czarist regime, the Provisional Government, which had been established before the Bolsheviks took over in November 1917, abolished the death penalty on March 25, 1917, but later restored it for the armed forces. It was totally abolished—much against the wishes of Lenin—on November 10, 1917, immediately after the seizure of power by the Communists, but re-introduced on January 21, 1918. On January 17, 1920, the death penalty was abolished again to be restored in May of the same year.

On May 26, 1947, a decree was issued abolishing the death penalty in peacetime. The foreword to the decree of the Presidium of the Supreme Soviet stated:

> ". . . meeting the wishes of the trade unions of workers and employees and of other authoritative organizations which express the opinion of broad public circles, the Presidium . . . believes that the application of the death penalty is no longer necessary in peacetime conditions."

Within a matter of three years, however, on January 12, 1950, the same body restored the death penalty "for traitors, spies, and those seeking to undermine the State."

The decree was promulgated

> "in view of declarations received from the national republics, from labour unions, peasants' organizations, and also from those working in the arts, to the effect that a change in the decree abolishing the death penalty is necessary . . ."

There was no exact definition of the crimes, since the decree did not indicate precisely the sections of the Criminal Code under which the crimes were punishable. On April 30, 1954, this decree was extended to persons committing murder under aggravating circumstances.

When in 1958 the new "Principles of Criminal Legislation for the USSR and the Union Republics" were drafted, former decrees on the death penalty were incorporated in the newly drafted rules, as well as later in the new Criminal Code of the Russian Federated Socialist Republic, which came into force on January 1, 1961. Accordingly the death penalty was to be imposed on crimes of banditry and terrorism, treason, espionage, sabotage and murder.

More recently, soon after the enactment of these basic criminal codes, referred to above, the scope of capital punishment has been broadened twice.

The official Gazette of the Supreme Soviet of the USSR (Vedomosti Verkhovnovo Soveta SSSR) No. 19, 1961, contained Decree 207 of May 5, 1961 on "intensifying the struggle against especially dangerous crimes" which extended the application of capital punishment for the pilfering of State or public property in especially large amounts and for counterfeiting money on a business scale. No. 27 of the same official Gazette published Decree No. 291 of July 1, 1961, extending the application of capital punishment once more, this time for speculation with foreign currency. The decrees amended Articles 22 and 25 of the "Principles of Criminal Legislation" to include the above provisions as follows:

> Capital punishment, by shooting, may be applied as an extraordinary penalty, pending its complete abolition, in cases of high treason,

espionage, sabotage, terrorist acts, banditry, making for the purpose of uttering, or uttering counterfeit money or securities, conducted as a business; speculation with foreign currency or securities conducted as a business or on a large scale; violation of rules concerning foreign currency by a person who was formerly sentenced for violation of rules concerning foreign currency or for speculation with foreign currency or securities; premeditated murder under aggravating circumstances stipulated in the articles of the criminal codes of the USSR and the Union Republics establishing liability for premeditated murder; and the pilfering of state of public property in especially large amounts; and also, in wartime or under combat conditions, for other serious crimes in cases specially stipulated in the legislation of the USSR.

Capital punishment by shooting may also be applied in the cases of especially dangerous habitual offenders and persons convicted for serious crimes who, at places of detention, terrorize prisoners who have taken the path of reform, who commit attacks on the administration or organize criminal groupings for this purpose and also actively participate in such groupings.

This long, impressive list of crimes punishable by death includes murder and special crimes committed in wartime. These two categories are the standard cases for the application of capital punishment in Criminal Codes, including military codes. Next on the list are the political crimes, such as treason, espionage, etc. In these cases the justification for the death penalty has been debated for two hundred years. In practice, however, capital punishment for political crimes is imposed by several States.

Much more striking, however, are categories recently included on the list: crimes committed at places of detention and the series of economic crimes. The commission of a crime at a place of detention is generally an aggravating circumstance in criminal law, without, however, meriting capital punishment. Such a severe measure might be reasonably explained only by a serious deterioration of the discipline at those places of detention. In the case of pilfering of State and public property and other economic crimes violating the State-run Soviet economy, one must bear in mind that State ownership of the means of production is the very basis of the Soviet social and economic system, the protection of which is considered vital. One wonders, however, if, as was declared "the growing might of the new (Socialist) world system guarantees the permanence of the political and the social and economic gains of the Socialist (Communist) countries," why does internal protection need the deterrent of the death penalty? A fortiori, if we recall the statement of last May of Procurator-General Rudenko:

"As Socialist Statehood gradually develops into Communist selfgovernment, persuasion and education of the masses is gradually becoming the principal method of protecting public order and fighting its violators."

Capital punishment by shooting is by any standards not a progressive method for persuasion and education of the masses.

The latest contribution to this problem from Soviet authorities are the resolutions of the recent plenum of the USSR Supreme Court. The plenum dealt with the application of the Decrees of May 5 and July 1 1961 on "Intensifying the struggle against especially dangerous crimes." It was stated that the supervisory examination of the cases of the lower courts showed serious errors in the application of the above mentioned decrees. The tribunals, the Supreme Court noted, did not realize the social danger of the economic crimes involved and meted out light sentences, something which could not be tolerated. These faults had to be remedied, the Supreme Court said, and the struggle against this type of crime was to be led with efficiency and vigour.

All Hail Stalin

The virtual deification of Stalin as the charismatic leader (*vozhd*) is exemplified by the following samples chosen at random from many thousands. The first, titled "Joseph Stalin," is from F. Gordon, *First Grade Reader.* (Approved by the Peoples' Commissariat of Education of the RSFSR.) Moscow: State Textbook Publishing House, 1935. The second selection is a portion of a "Hymn to Stalin," published in *Pravda* on 28 August, 1938. The third is from the Moscow *Daily News* and is a part of the "Song of Stalin." The fourth example is from the *Information Bulletin* of the Embassy of the Union of Soviet Socialist Republics (Washington, D.C.). It was published on 20 December, 1945. Only excerpts are reprinted here. The final item is from a speech by Beria on the "Thirty-fourth Anniversary of the Great October Socialist Revolution," published by the *USSR Information Bulletin* in November, 1951. Another example of sycophantic adulation will be found under the heading, "The Truth Is—." (p. 838)

Joseph Stalin

Conrad Stalin is known all over the world. Stalin is the son of a Georgian worker. Stalin was a very young boy when he began to work for the workers' cause. Stalin worked with Lenin. Stalin was sent to prison many times under the tsar. The last time he spent four years in exile. In the October revolution, he helped the workers to drive out the landlords and the capitalists. They did not give up at once. They tried to make things as they had been in the past. They began a war against the Soviets. In this war Stalin was the leader of the workers. Under his leadership the Red Army was successful. It defeated the enemy. At the same time, Stalin together with Lenin and other comrades began to build a new life. Lenin died, but the party which he helped to build, the Bolshevik Party, remained. It worked to help the workers create a new life. Stalin is its best leader and worker. We now have hundreds of new factories. There we make new machines, tractors, and airplanes. More peasants now live on the Kolkhozes. They work together. In the Kolkhozes, there are machines, schools, also nurseries for the little children. Now we have very few people who cannot read. The children and the grown-ups are studying. All the children must go to school. The workers and peasants stand for the land of the Soviets. The Red Army protects the land of the Soviets from its enemies. Its enemies are the landlords and capitalists of all countries. The friends of our Soviet country are the workers and peasants and the oppressed of all countries. From everywhere they send greetings to Stalin. We school children also send him our children's greetings.

* * * * *

Hymn to Stalin

O Great Stalin, O leader of the peoples,
Thou who brought man to birth,
Thou who fructifies the earth,
Thou who restores the centuries,
Thou who makes the spring to bloom,
Thou who makes vibrate the chords of music.

* * * * *

The Song of Stalin

Who broke the chains that bound our feet, now dancing,
Who opened lips that sing a joyous song,
Who made the mourners change their tears for laughter,
Brought back the dead to life's rejoicing throng.
Who is in heart, in every thought and action,
Most loving, true and wise of Lenin's sons—
Such is the great Stalin.

* * * * *

"Stalin's Birthday—December 21"

Joseph Vissarionovich Stalin (Djugashvili), the great continuator of the cause of Lenin and leader of the peoples of the USSR was born on December 21, 1879, in the town of Gori, Georgia. . . . He founded the revolutionary organs in Transcaucasia which supported the policy of Lenin. . . . During the Revolution of 1905–07, Stalin, at the head of the Transcaucasian Bolsheviks, directed the revolutionary struggle of the Transcaucasian workers and peasants. He upheld and brilliantly developed Lenin's principles of organization and tactics and the theoretical principles of the Bolshevik Party. . . .

After the February Revolution of 1917 he was released from his last exile and went to Petrograd where he directed the activities of the Central Committee and the Petrograd Committee of the Bolshevik Party and edited the Party newspaper, *Pravda*. . . . During the October days of 1917 he was at the head of the Party Center to direct the uprising. Together with Lenin, Stalin was the inspirer and leader of the Great October

Socialist Revolution. . . . Since Lenin's death Stalin has been leading the peoples of the USSR along the road mapped out by Lenin. Stalin is Lenin's devoted disciple, his closest associate and friend. Jointly with Lenin he founded and built up . . . the Bolshevik Party. He upheld the principles of Leninism in the struggle against the treacherous Trotskyites, Bukharinites and other enemies of the people.

A profound theoretician who defended and further developed the theories of Marx, Engels and Lenin, Stalin further elaborated Lenin's teachings regarding the victory of socialism in one country, socialist industrialization, collectivization of agriculture, the Socialist State, and the building of socialism and communism in one country. . . . Stalin is the author of the new Constitution of the USSR. . . .

Under the leadership of the great Stalin the peoples of the Soviet Union, in the days of the Patriotic War, united to fight and defeat the German-fascist invaders. Stalin is the organizer, great strategist and leader of the armed forces of the Soviet Union. Stalin is today's Lenin. With the name of Stalin, the Soviet people associate their present and future, all their achievements and victories.

* * * * *

Beria's Eulogy

Comrades: The peoples of the Soviet Union are today celebrating the 34th anniversary of the Great October Socialist Revolution, which was illuminated by the genius of Lenin and which set mankind on the road to a new, socialist world. Every new year of advance along this road is productive of fresh achievements for our country.

All the activities of the Bolshevik Party and the Soviet Government in the period between the 33rd and 34th anniversaries of the October Revolution proceeded, as they have in all the years since the death of the great Lenin, under the wise direction of our leader, Comrade Stalin. (*Prolonged applause.*) [sic] The perspicacity of Comrade Stalin's genius orients our Party and our people in the complexities of internal and foreign affairs and outlines the perspective of our further development. Comrade Stalin's inexhaustible energy in the day-to-day direction of affairs, large and small, and his faculty for determining the chief tasks of the Soviet State and directing all our energies toward their accomplishment ensure the great victories of the peoples of the Soviet Union in the building of communism. (*Applause.*) [sic]

. . .

These projects were undertaken on the initiative of Comrade Stalin, who displays constant solicitude for the welfare and prosperity of our country and for lightening the labor and improving the living conditions of the Soviet people. Comrade Stalin's initiative has met with the ardent support of all our people, who rightly call these projects the Stalin Great Construction Works of Communism. (*Prolonged applause.*) [sic]

. . .

In the effort to accomplish the great program of communist construction, the Soviet people have rallied still more closely around their own Communist Party, around the inspirer and organizer of our victories, the great Stalin. (*Stormy applause.*) [*sic*]

The Treason Trials

There was a very extensive party purge in 1933 which resulted in the expulsion of about a third of total party membership. Purgings—equally drastic or more so but not as extensive numerically—went on continuously through 1938. After the murder in December of 1934 of Stalin's close associate, Sergius Kirov, there was a virtual reign of terror highlighted for the world by several spectacular treason trials. Zinoviev, Kamenev, and several of their colleagues were tried for treason, convicted, and sentenced to imprisonment in January, 1935. In August of the next year, Zinoviev, Kamenev, and some of their followers were again brought to trial on charges of conspiring under the leadership of Trotsky for the overthrow of the regime with the help of foreign powers. The accused confessed to the charges and sixteen of them were convicted and executed.

Radek, Pyatakov, and various other "old Bolsheviks" were tried for treason and convicted in January of 1937. Thirteen of them were executed. Eight of the top-ranking army officers, including Marshal Tukhachevski, were executed as traitors after a secret court-martial in the following June. The sensational climax came with the trials of Bukharin, Rykov, Yagoda, and eighteen others in March of 1938. The accused were charged "of having on the instructions of the intelligence services of foreign states hostile to the Soviet Union formed a conspiratorial group named the 'bloc of Rights and Trotskyites' with the object of espionage . . . wrecking, diversionist and terrorist activities, undermining the military power of the USSR . . . dismembering the USSR . . . for the benefit of the aforementioned foreign states, and, lastly, with the object of overthrowing the Socialist social and state system existing in the USSR and of restoring capitalism, of restoring the power of the bourgeoisie." The accused confessed their guilt in open court and, since several of them had been among the most prominent leaders of the party, the event can only be described as sensationally spectacular.

No attempt is made here, explicitly or implicitly, to explain, interpret, or evaluate the purges and the trials. The excerpts by no means give anything like the whole story or even one side of it. They do, however, give some idea of the nature of the trials and of the confessions. The "last plea" of Bukharin is especially revealing. The court was composed of four "Military Jurists" and the prosecuting attorney was Andrei Vishinsky, then Procurator-General of the USSR. The excerpts are from the authorized English version of the verbatim report of the trial which was published by the People's Commissariat of Justice of the USSR. The title is: *Report of the Court Proceedings in the case of the Anti-Soviet "Bloc of Rights and Trotskyites" heard before the Military Collegium of the Supreme Court of the USSR, Moscow, March 2–13, 1938, etc.* Moscow: 1938. Pp. 401–405, 465–466, 476, 575–578, 777–778, 785–787. The testimony of Bukharin follows.

BUKHARIN: I cannot say "No" and I cannot deny that it did take place.

VYSHINSKY: So the answer is neither "Yes" nor "No"?

B——: Nothing of the kind because facts exist regardless of whether they are in anybody's mind. This is a problem of the reality of the outer world. I am no solipsist.

V——: So that regardless of whether this fact entered your mind or not, you as a plotter and a leader were aware of it?

B——: I was not aware of it.

V——: You were not?

B——: But I can say the following in reply to your question: since this thing was included in the general plan, I consider it likely, and since Rykov speaks of it in a positive fashion, I have no grounds for denying it.

V——: Consequently, it is a fact?

B——: From the point of view of mathematical probability it can be said, with very great probability, that it is a fact.

V——: So that you are unable to give a plain answer?

B——: Not "unable," but there are some questions that cannot be answered outright "Yes" or "No" as you are perfectly well aware from elementary logic.

V——: Allow me to ask Rykov again: was Bukharin aware of this fact?

RYKOV: I did not speak to him about it.

V——: Now, did Bukharin know about it or not?

R——: I personally think with mathematical probability that he should have known of it.

V——: That's clear. Accused Bukharin, were you aware that Karakhan was a participant in the conspiratorial group of Rights and Trotskyites?

BUKHARIN: I was.

V——: Were you aware that Karakhan was a German spy?

B——: No, I was not aware of that.

V——: (to Rykov) Were you aware, accused Rykov, that Karakhan was a German Spy?

RYKOV: No, I was not.

V——: Were you aware that Karakhan was engaged in negotiations with certain German circles?

R——: Negotiations regarding the centre of the Rights?

V——: Yes, of course, regarding the centre of the Rights.

R——: Yes, yes.

V——: Treasonable negotiations?

R——: Treasonable.

V———: With whom did he conduct these negotiations, and with what institution?

R———: (No reply.)

V———: Well?

R———: I don't know that.

V———: In that case, tell the Court: what was the line of negotiations?

R———: The line was. . . . At that time negotiations were conducted with German government circles.

V———: With which circles?

. . .

V———: . . . Can the conclusion be drawn from this that Karakhan, with your knowledge, engaged in negotiations with fascist circles regarding support for your treasonable activity on definite conditions? Was that the case?

R———: Yes.

V———: And what were the conditions?

R———: Firstly, a number of economic concessions, and secondly the so-called dismemberment of the USSR.

V———: What does that mean?

R———: That means the separation of the national republics and placing them under a protectorate, or making them dependent, formally not dependent, but actually dependent on . . .

V———: That is to say, territorial concessions?

R———: Of course.

V———: Did Karakhan propose in the name of your bloc to cede to the Germans some part of the territory of the Soviet Union?

R———: The matter was somewhat different.

V———: I speak of the meaning of these concessions.

R———: I myself did not meet Karakhan. I know this from Tomsky who explained it in my presence and in that of Bukharin.

V———: So that means Burkharin also knew? Allow me to ask Bukharin. Did you know?

BUKHARIN: I did.

RYKOV: He explained it this way: the German fascists accept these conditions, i.e., privileges as regards concessions, trade agreements, etc., but on their part they demand that the national republics be given the right to free separation.

V———: Well, and what does this mean?

R———: It was not what we had proposed. This was a new demand on the part of the Germans. In plain language, this means, of course, the dismemberment of the USSR.

V———: That is to say, handing over part of the USSR to the Germans?

R———: Of course.

V———: That is to say, you were aware that Karakhan, with your knowledge, engaged in negotiations with German circles to hand over part of the USSR. Precisely what part?

R——: There was no talk about that.

V——: Did your plan include a point about severing the Ukraine for the Germans, or did it not?

R——: I personally cannot say about the Ukraine, I repeat, not because we were against the Ukraine being severed.

V——: But were you against or for its being severed?

R——: There was simply no talk among us about the Ukraine being severed, and the question was not decided then.

V——: Did you have in view severing the Ukraine in favour of German fascism?

R——: Such was the formula.

V——: Not a formula—but in practice?

R——: In practice the question at issue could be that of Byelorussia.

V——: And of the Ukraine?

R——: No. We could not decide this question without the consent of the Ukrainian counter-revolutionary organizations.

V——: Then I address myself to the accused Bukharin. Did you in 1934 engage in negotiations with Radek on this subject?

BUKHARIN: Not negotiations, but conversations.

V——: All right, conversations. Did they take place or not?

B——: They did, only not about that.

V——: Then about what?

B——: Radek told me of his negotiations with Trotsky, that Trotsky had engaged in negotiations with the German fascists regarding territorial concessions in return for help to the counter-revolutionary organizations.

V——: That's it, that's it.

B——: I then objected to Radek.

V——: Did Radek tell you that on Trotsky's instructions the Ukraine was to be ceded, yielded to the Germans?

B——: I definitely remember about the Ukraine.

V——: Were there such conversations or not?

B——: Yes.

V——: And about the Far East?

B——: About the Ukraine I definitely remember; there was talk of other regions, but I do not remember which.

V——: You testified as follows: "Trotsky, while urging the intensification of terrorism, yet considers the main chance for the advent of the bloc to power to be the defeat of the USSR in a war against Germany and Japan at the cost of territorial concessions (the Ukraine to the Germans, and the Far East to the Japanese.)" Was that so?

B——: Yes it was.

V——: That is to say, these are the concessions?

B——: I was not in agreement.

V——: Further it states: "I did not object to the idea of an understanding with Germany and Japan, but did not agree with Trotsky on the extent."

B——: Read the next phrase as well, where the extent and character are explained.

V——: I have read and want to speak about this. [*sic*]

B——: I said I was against territorial concessions.

V——: No. I want to speak about this. And so Radek told you that Trotsky gave instructions to cede the Ukraine to the Germans. Did he say this?

B——: He did, but I did not consider Trotsky's instructions as binding on me.

V——: Was Rykov aware of this conversation with Radek or not?

RYKOV: Whom are you asking?

V——: Bukharin.

BUKHARIN: I don't remember whether I told Rykov.

V——: And Rykov?

RYKOV: He did not tell me.

V——: Consequently you were unaware of Bukharin's conversation with Radek?

RYKOV: (No reply.)

V——: But did he talk privately to Bukharin?

RYKOV: Who?

V——: Radek. Accused Bukharin, how did Radek talk to you? What post did you occupy at that time?

BUKHARIN: It is not a matter of the post.

V——: What post did you occupy?

B——: I was the editor of "Izvestia."

＊ ＊ ＊ ＊ ＊

[Examination of Ossinsky.]

THE PRESIDENT: Accused Bukharin, have you any questions to put to witness Ossinsky?

BUKHARIN: I have. In the first place, I should like to ask Ossinsky whether he could tell us something about the central group of "Left Communists" in Petersburg. Whom did it consist of?

THE PRESIDENT: This question has no bearing on the conspiracy.

B——: It has because inasmuch as negotiations were carried on . . .

THE PRESIDENT: We are now concerned with the accused Bukharin.

B——: Why I am appearing here as a representative of the group of "Left Communists" and its centre. When we are asked about the Right and Leftist centre, that concerns us, but if it relates to the centre of the group of "Left Communists," we cannot talk. . . .

THE PRESIDENT: In any event the case concerns Nikolai Ivanovich Bukharin.

B——: Citizen the Procurator stated that this was not the case because, owing to the lapse of the time limit prescribed by law, there is no case.

THE PRESIDENT: Accused Bukharin, do you want to put questions to witness Ossinsky?

B——: Yes, I do. I want to ask witness Ossinsky whether Ossinsky was a member of the central group of "Left Communists."

OSSINSKY: Of course I was.

B——: I want to find out from witness Ossinsky whether he wrote the general theses which served as the main platform of the "Left Communists" in that period.

O——: Quite right.

B——: Together with whom did you write those theses?

O——: Together with Bukharin, Radek and Preobrazhensky.

B——: And who was the author of the basic text of these theses?

O——: The author of the basic text was Ossinsky.

VYSHINSKY: And who edited it?

O——: It was edited by all those participating, including Nikolai Ivanovich Bukharin.

B——: Then I should like to ask witness Ossinsky whether he was in Moscow on the eve of the October uprising.

O——: Yes, on the eve of the October uprising I was in Moscow.

B——: I should also like to know if witness Ossinsky was in Moscow during the October uprising.

THE PRESIDENT: What need is there for these questions?

B——: I need them for my defence, because later on I will have no opportunity to get answers to these questions.

VYSHINSKY: If the accused Bukharin states that he needs these questions for his defence and since, according to our laws, each accused has the right to defence in its full scope, I plead that this question be not ruled out.

B——: In this case I plead for putting again all the questions which the Court has ruled out before.

THE PRESIDENT: Accused Bukharin, do not engage in obstructing the work of the Court.

V——: If the accused Bukharin has need of putting all these questions for his defence, I, as Prosecutor, do not object to these questions being put here.

THE PRESIDENT: But the Court objects to these questions being put here, because they have no bearing on the case.

V——: I submit to the decision of the Court.

B——: I submit, too.

* * * * *

[Examination of Mantsev.]

MANTSEV: The attempt [an explosion on the premises of the Moscow Committee of the Communist Party] was directed against the Moscow Committee of the Communist Party.

VYSHINSKY: And was Bukharin the secretary of the Moscow Committee at that time?

M——: He was not the secretary.

V——: Was he present at this meeting of the Moscow Committee?

M——: In my opinion, he was not.

BUKHARIN: What do you mean, I was not present? I was contused during the explosion.

M——: It is possible he was there, I do not remember it.

* * * * *

[Examination of Yagoda.]

THE PRESIDENT: Have you any questions, Comrade Procurator?

VYSHINSKY: Of course. Hence, if we sum up your explanations, we may say the following: First—that you plead guilty to the fact that your participation in the underground work of the Rights was of long standing.

YAGODA: Yes.

V——: Second—that you plead guilty to having been one of the leaders of the underground "bloc of Rights and Trotskyites."

Y——: Yes, I do.

V——: Third—that, together with this bloc, you pursued the aim of overthrowing the Soviet government and restoring capitalism in the USSR.

Y——: Yes, I do. We set ourselves the task of seizing the Kremlin.

V——: That for the purpose of overthrowing the government you chose the method of an insurrection timed primarily for the outbreak of war. Is that so?

Y——: No, it is not so. An armed insurrection—that was nonsense. Only these babblers here could think of that.

V——: Well, what were you thinking of?

Y——: Of a "palace coup."

V——: That is to say, of a violent coup, carried through by a small group of plotters?

Y——: Yes, the same as they did.

V——: Timing it preferably for a military onslaught on the USSR by foreign powers, or did you have various plans?

Y——: There was one plan, namely, to seize the Kremlin. The time was of no importance.

V——: Was it your point of view that it was expedient in case of war to prepare and secure the defeat of the USSR?

Y——: That was the point of view of the bloc, and therefore it was mine too.

V——: Do you also admit being guilty of espionage work?

Y——: No, I do not admit being guilty of this activity.

V——: But you yourself have said that several spies were at work under your direct leadership.

Y——: Yes, I admit that.

V——: Did you know they were spies?

Y——: Yes, I did.

.   .   .

V——: And do you admit being guilty of organizing and effecting terrorists acts: first—the murder of Comrade Kirov on the orders and instructions of the bloc?

Y——: I admit being guilty of complicity in the murder.

V——: Do you admit being guilty of complicity in the murder or in causing the death of Menzhinsky?

Y——: I do.

V——: Do you admit of being guilty of organizing the murder of Kuibyshev?

Y——: I do.

V——: Do you admit being guilty of the murder of Alexei Maximovich Gorky?

Y——: I do.

V——: I have no more questions.

THE PRESIDENT: Have Counsel for Defence any questions?

COUNSEL FOR DEFENCE KOMMODOV: Does the accused Yagoda confirm the testimony he gave at the preliminary investigation with reference to his meetings with Pletnev?

Y——: I said that.

K——: Is the same true as regards meetings with Kazakov?

Y——: I confirmed that.

K——: I have no more questions.

COUNSEL FOR DEFENCE BRAUDE: Who conceived the idea of death from disease?

Y——: I have said—Yenukidze.

BRAUDE: Allow me to ask you, what methods did you employ to secure Levin's consent to commit these terrorist acts?

Y——: In any case not such as he described here.

BRAUDE: You yourself went into detail about this at the preliminary investigation. Do you confirm this part of your testimony?

Y——: It is exaggerated, but that doesn't matter.

BRAUDE: I have no more questions.

* * * * *

[A portion of Bukharin's "last plea."]

I shall now speak of myself, of the reasons for my repentance. Of course, it must be admitted that incriminating evidence plays a very important part. For three months I refused to say anything. Then I began to testify. Why? Because while in prison I made a reevaluation of my entire past. For when you ask yourself: "If you must die, what are you dying for?"—an absolutely black vacuity suddenly arises before you with startling vividness. There was nothing to die for, if one wanted to die unrepented. And, on the contrary, everything positive that glistens in the Soviet Union acquires new dimensions in a man's mind. This in the end disarmed me completely and led me to bend my knees before the Party and the country. And when you ask yourself: "Very well, suppose you do not die; suppose by some miracle you remain alive, again what for? Isolated from everybody, an enemy of the people, in an inhuman position, completely isolated from everything that constitutes the essence of life. . . . [*sic*]" And at once the same reply arises. And at such moments, Citizens Judges, everything personal, all the personal incrustation, all the rancour, pride, and a number of other things, fall away, disappear. And, in addition, when the reverberations of the broad international struggle reach your ear, all this in its entirety does its work, and the result is the complete internal moral victory of the USSR over its kneeling opponents. . . .

The point, of course, is not this repentance, or my personal repentance in particular. The Court can pass its verdict without it. The confession of the accused is not essential. The confession of the accused is a medieval principal of jurisprudence. But here we also have the internal demolition of the forces of counter-revolution. And one must be a Trotsky not to lay down one's arms.

* * * * *

[A portion of Yagoda's "last plea."]

I want to correct the Procurator and make an objection on a part of the charges which he has made. . . . the Procurator is not right in considering me a member of the centre of the bloc. . . . I did not take part in the decisions of the bloc. . . . I was informed *post factum*. . . . . . . Rykov . . . made the decisions.

. . . the Procurator announced it proved beyond doubt that I was a spy. This is not true. I am not a spy and have never been one. . . .

It is not only untrue to say that I was an organizer but it is untrue to say that I was an accomplice in the murder of Kirov. I committed an exceedingly grave violation of duty . . . , but I was not an accomplice. . . .

My objections on these points are not an attempt to belittle the significance of my crimes. My defence would have no practical meaning here, because for each millionth part of my crimes, as the Procurator says, he wants my head. I staked my head and I surrender it, but I want to reduce my enormous debt to the Procurator. I know what my sentence will be, I have been awaiting it for a whole year. In the last hours or days of my life I do not want to play the hypocrite and say that I want to die. This is not true. I have committed heinous crimes. I realize this. It is hard to live after such crimes, it is hard to sit in prisons for tens of years. But it is terrible to die with such a stigma. Even from behind the bars I would like to see the further flourishing of the country which I betrayed.

Citizens Judges! I directed vast construction jobs—the canals. [See the document quoted on pp. 751–752.] Now these canals are the adornments of our era. I do not dare ask to be sent there even for the most arduous work. Citizens Judges! Our laws and our Court differ greatly from the laws and the courts of all bourgeois countries. . . . Our laws are based on a different principle, our Court is a different court. The Soviet Court differs from bourgeois courts in the fact that this Court, when trying a criminal case, does not base itself on laws as on a dogma, but is guided by revolutionary expediency. Our country is mighty, strong as never before, purged of spies, diversionists, terrorists and other scum, and I ask you, Citizens Judges, in passing your sentence on me, to consider whether there is revolutionary expediency in my execution now? . . . I address myself to the Court with the plea: forgive me if you can.

The Supreme Soviet of the USSR

According to the *Fundamental Law of the Union of Soviet Socialist Republics,* more popularly known as the 1936, or Stalin, Constitution, the Supreme Soviet of the USSR is "the highest organ of state power," and is invested with exclusive legislative power. It is a bicameral body in which the Union Soviet is charged with representing national interests while the Soviet of Nationalities is concerned with the interests of the various national groups. Either chamber may initiate legislation, but both must consent to it. The two chambers have parallel committees and commissions (e.g., Credentials and Budget); exercise some powers separately, others jointly; and have both separate and joint sessions as business requires.

The next nine selections, grouped together for the reader's convenience, deal with various aspects of the election and operation of the Supreme Soviet from 1937 to 1962. Among the subjects emphasized are the elections, including the speeches of certain prominent candidates whose words give the official interpretation of the meaning of the elections, and illustrative legislative actions. There have, of course, been changes in personnel, in particular business brought before the Supreme Soviet, and in other matters. The budget figures, for example, represent not only growth, but also inflation and currency reforms. Some matters which were of prime concern in 1938—Japanese aggression being one case in point—were no longer of moment in 1962. But, as these selections show, there have been relatively few over-all changes and the Supreme Soviet of the USSR remains primarily a consent-building body.

The constitutional provisions about elections, which form the first selection, and the excerpts from the election speeches will be more meaningful if the following information is kept in mind. The first Supreme Soviet of the USSR, elected in 1937, was prolonged until 1946 despite the statutory four-year term. The official explanation was that the Second World War made the holding of elections unfeasible. The second Supreme Soviet was elected in 1946; the third, in 1950; the fourth, in 1954; the fifth, in 1958; and the sixth, in 1962. The number of deputies varied over the years. There were 1,143 in 1938; 1,339 in 1948; over 1,600 in 1958; and 1,443 in 1962. There were also some slight variations in the voting records as well as changes in the numbers of eligible voters. The 1962 record was, however, typical. According to the official reports of the 1962 election, 139,957,809 (99.95

per cent) of the 140,002,771 eligible voters voted. (The comparable figure for 1946 was 99.7 per cent.) Of those who voted, 139,210,431 (99.47 per cent) voted for the candidates for deputy to the Union Soviet; 746,563 (0.53 per cent) voted against the candidates, and there were 815 spoiled ballots. 139,931,455 (99.6 per cent) voted for the candidates for deputy to the Soviet of Nationalities; 564,155 (0.4 per cent) voted against them, and there were 706 invalid ballots. (*Pravda* 25 April, 1962.)

The selection below is an abridgment of Chapter XI, Articles 134–142, of the *Fundamental Law of the Union of Soviet Socialist Republics,* adopted 5 December, 1936.

The Electoral System

Article 134

Members of all Soviets of Working People's Deputies—[federal, republican, regional, district, city, and rural] . . . are chosen by the electors on the basis of universal, equal and direct suffrage by secret ballot.

Article 135

. . . all citizens of the USSR who have reached the age of eighteen, irrespective of race or nationality, sex, religion, education, domicile, social origin, property status or past activities, have the right to vote in the election of deputies, with the exception of insane persons and persons who have been convicted by a court of law and whose sentences include deprivation of electoral rights.

Every citizen of the USSR who has reached the age of twenty-three is eligible for election to the Supreme Soviet of the USSR, irrespective of race or nationality, sex, religion, education, domicile, social origin, property status or past activities.

Article 136

. . . each citizen has one vote; all citizens participate in elections on an equal footing.

Article 137

Women have the right to elect and be elected on equal terms with men.

Article 138

Citizens serving in the armed forces of the USSR have the right to elect and be elected on equal terms with all other citizens.

Article 139

. . . all Soviets . . . are elected by the citizens by direct votes.

Article 140

Voting at elections of deputies is secret.

Article 141

Candidates are nominated by election district. The right to nominate candidates is secured to public organizations and societies of the working people; Communist Party organizations, trade unions, cooperatives, youth organizations and cultural societies.

Article 142

It is the duty of every deputy to report to his electors on his work and the work of his Soviet of Working People's Deputies, and he may be recalled at any time upon decision of a majority of the electors in the manner established by law.

"The Higher Organs of State Power"

The form, functions, and powers of the Supreme Soviet of the USSR are formally stated in Chapter III, Articles 30–56, of the 1936 Constitution. Samples, taken from the *Fundamental Law, etc.,* adopted 5 December, 1936, are printed below. These form one measure of the place of the Supreme Soviet in the Soviet political system, but a much more accurate determination of political reality can be made by measuring the complexity of agendas of the Supreme Soviet against the brevity of its sessions and the size of the body. There are two regular sessions each year, but the two together last only a week or or two. During the interims, the Presidium has full power. The Presidium's actions are subject to review and confirmation by the Supreme Soviet which, during its first twenty-five years, unanimously ratified all actions taken by the Presidium.

There were eight items on the agenda of the second session (1938) of the first Supreme Soviet. These included the adoption of the federal budget, a complicated act establishing the judicial system, the election of the Supreme Court of the USSR, and approval of interim actions and appointments. The session listened to many long reports and acted on all eight agenda items in eight working days. The first session of the second Supreme Soviet lasted six days and dealt with the budget and all interim decrees, appointments, and dismissals.

According to Soviet press reports of the first 1948-sitting of the Supreme Soviet, three days were devoted to a "debate" on the budget, and 47 of the 1,339 deputies spoke to the question. The Soviet press reported only 19 of these speeches, 5 of which were made by federal officials. Six of the 19 made specific criticisms of the work of certain ministries, 4 asked larger appropriations for the speaker's home area, and 9 endorsed the budget as presented. The finance minister of the USSR promised to consider all suggestions and criticisms, and the budget as originally presented was adopted unanimously by both chambers.

A special session of the third Supreme Soviet was held following Stalin's death in 1953. It required just sixty-seven minutes to ratify the most sweeping changes to be made in Soviet government and administration since Lenin's death in 1924. The pattern continued, as shown by one of the selections below which deals with the fourth Supreme

Soviet, and by the following data. The sixth session of the Supreme Soviet required four days to deal with four major agenda items—the reorganization and development of the national economy, the national budget, international affairs and foreign policy, and all interim actions. The seventh session of the fifth Supreme Soviet lasted six days; its final session, three days; and at its final sitting (8 December, 1961) this Supreme Soviet adopted a new civil code, approved the economic plan for 1962, and passed the budget by a show of hands with no "nays" and no abstentions.

Article 30

The highest organ of state power in the USSR is the Supreme Soviet of the USSR.

Article 32

The legislative power of the USSR is exercised exclusively by the Supreme Soviet of the USSR.

Article 36

The Supreme Soviet of the USSR is elected for a term of four years.

Article 37

The two chambers of the Supreme Soviet of the USSR, the Soviet of the Union and the Soviet of Naitonalities, have equal rights.

Article 38

The Soviet of the Union and the Soviet of Nationalities have equal powers to initiate legislation.

Article 39

A law is considered adopted if passed by both chambers of the Supreme Soviet of the USSR by a simple majority vote in each.

Article 46

Sessions of the Supreme Soviet of the USSR are convened by the Presidium of the Supreme Soviet of the USSR twice a year. Extraordinary sessions are convened by the Presidium . . . at its discretion or on the demand of one of the Union Republics.

Article 48

The Supreme Soviet of the USSR at a joint sitting of the two chambers elects the Presidium of the Supreme Soviet of the USSR. . . . The Presidium . . . is accountable to the Supreme Soviet of the USSR for all its activities.

Article 49

The Presidium of the Supreme Soviet of the USSR:
a) Convenes the sessions of the Supreme Soviet . . . ;

b) Issues decrees;
c) Give interpretations of the laws . . . ;
d) Dissolves the Supreme Soviet . . . and orders new elections;
e) Conducts nation-wide referendums . . . ;
f) Annuls decisions and orders of the Council of Ministers of the USSR and of the Councils of Ministers of the Union Republics if they do not conform to law;
g) In the intervals between sessions of the Supreme Soviet . . . releases and appoints Ministers . . . subject to subsequent confirmation by the Supreme Soviet . . . ;
j) Exercises the right of pardon;
l) Appoints and removes the high command of the Armed Forces of the USSR;
m) In the intervals between the sessions of the Supreme Soviet . . . proclaims a state of war . . . when necessary . . . ;
n) Orders general or partial mobilization;
o) Ratifies and denounces international treaties of the USSR;
r) Proclaims martial law in separate localities or throughout the USSR in the interests of the defense of the USSR or of the maintenance of public order and the security of the state.

Article 53

On the expiration of the term of office of the Supreme Soviet . . . , or on its dissolution prior to the expiration of its term of office, the Presidium of the Supreme Soviet of the USSR retains its powers until the newly elected Supreme Soviet . . . shall have formed a new Presidium. . . .

Article 54

On the expiration of the term of office of the Supreme Soviet . . . , or in the event of its dissolution . . . the Presidium . . . orders new elections to be held within a period not exceeding two months. . . .

Article 55

The newly elected Supreme Soviet . . . is convened by the outgoing Presidium . . . not later than three months after the elections.

Article 56

The Supreme Soviet of the USSR, at a joint sitting of the two chambers, appoints the Government of the USSR, namely, the Council of Ministers of the USSR.

Adopting the Federal Budget

At the first joint sitting of the two houses in the second (1938) session (10 August, 1938), "Comrade Zverev, People's Commissar of Finance of the USSR" presented a fourteen thousand to fifteen thousand word report on the "Unified State Budget." The joint session then adjourned and the two houses considered the budget in their separate sessions. The matter was introduced in each chamber by a further report of some seven thousand words delivered by the chairmen of the respective budget commissions. Each Soviet then devoted three sittings (11, 13, and 14 August) to "debates" on the budget. Fifteen deputies (out of 569) and two administrators spoke in the Union Soviet; fifteen deputies (out of 574) and one administrator spoke in the Soviet of Nationalities. Zverev and the respective chairmen of the budget commissions then "replied to the debate." The speeches, all but one of which are quoted in full, are not quite typical because they contain certain criticisms. In fact, they were selected to illustrate the nature of the criticisms as well as the general character of the "debates."

Speech of A. F. Nikanorov of the Archangel Area and Region in the Union Soviet.

Comrades, members of the Supreme Soviet. The unified State Budget of the USSR for the year 1938, presented by the Government to the Second Session of the Supreme Soviet for consideration and approval, will unquestionably be approved and ratified by the Session of the Supreme Soviet. It will unquestionably be fully approved by the millions of the people of our great country. This Budget, both in its total, aggregating 125,184,200,000 rubles, and in its structure, is a truly popular Budget of the country of victorious socialism.

Our Budget is a striking manifestation of how, under the leadership of the Communist Party, under the leadership of our great Stalin, the Soviet people are firmly and confidently marching towards communism.

The People's Commissar of Finance, in his report, and the deputies who spoke here were right in stressing the sharp distinction between the Budget of the Land of the Soviets, where the people are free, and the Budgets of the capitalist countries, where the working people are kept under the yoke of exploitation and oppression.

It is necessary, comrades, that we ourselves, the whole people and our class brothers abroad should remember that quite recently our country was under the yoke of an autocracy of landlords and capitalists. This found its reflection also in the Budget of tsarist Russia. In an article entitled, "Apropos of the State Revenue Roll," written in 1902, Validimir Ilyich Lenin analysed the Budget of the tsarist government drawn up by Witte and exposed the entire system of robbing the people. In discussing the fact that one of the items of revenue was foreign loans, Lenin showed that the tsarist Budget reflected the policy of enslaving a great country to foreign capital.

As to our Budget, not a single kopeck of its huge total goes into the pocket of any sort of capitalists, not a single kopeck goes to pay any loans advanced by foreign capitalists, as was the case in tsarist Russia.

In the same article Lenin showed what huge funds were assigned in the Budget for the maintenance of "personages of the imperial family."

At the same time all that the Budget of the Tsarist government provided for in expenditures through the Ministry of Public Education, which

Lenin dubbed the "Ministry of Obscuration," amounted to 36,000,000 rubles. If the expenditures made through the various departments are included, the allocations for education comprised a little over 4 per cent of the entire Budget of tsarist Russia. At present we are expending 20,000,-000,000 rubles, or 17 per cent of the Budget, on public education.

In those years in tsarist Russia all the schools, from lowest to highest, were attended by a little over 6,000,000 people, i.e., less than 50 for ever 1,000 population. In 1938, however, in the USSR the elementary and intermediate schools are attended by 33,300,000 children, and approximately 2,000,000 students receive instruction in the higher educational establishments, training colleges, and schools for adults. And think, comrades, of all the people taking various kinds of courses! Here, for example, is our Archangel Region, which formerly was a place of exile for revolutionaries. In the city of Archangel alone there are 50,000 people, and in the region as a whole approximately 200,000 people who are studying.

I am deliberately comparing today's data with those referring to the years of the Russo-Japanese War. Today, when the Japanese military, not without the knowledge and approval of other imperialists, are trying to invade the Land of the Soviets, we may point to the vast distance which we have travelled under the leadership of the Party of Lenin and Stalin.

27,000,000,000 rubles for the People's Commissariat of Defence and the People's Commissariat of the Navy! A Budget aggregating 125,000,-000,000 rubles! The moral and political unity of the 170,000,000 people of the Soviet Union.

These are our arguments, which shall serve as a stern warning to the aggressors.

It was with pride and joy that Lenin, after the revolution, announced to the delegates who attended the Congress of the Comintern that the Soviet state had accumulated 20,000,000 rubles in gold for the realization of an advance in industry. And in 1933 Comrade Stalin announced in his report to the January Plenum of the Central Committee of the CPSU that the Party had brought about not only the restoration of our industry, but also its rapid development, by using our internal resources, without usurious loans and credits from abroad.

Since then 350,000,000,000 rubles have been expended on strengthening the might of our country, on the development of industry, the collectivization of agriculture, the advancement of culture. We see the great victories of Socialist industrialization and of Socialist agriculture throughout our vast country, from end to end, from sea to sea.

In our Archangel Region, on the shores of the White, Barents and Kara Seas, in the regions of the Far North, Socialist life is seething like a hot spring, just as in every other part of our great country. This is attested to by our mechanized sawmills—as, for instance, the V. M. Molotov Mill —the Sulphate Works now under construction in Archangel, the paper mills, the 2,165 collective farms, representing 96.3 per cent of all peasant households in the region, the hundreds of mechanized timbering stations, the thousands of tractors, harvester combines and other agricultural machinery cultivating our fields.

We, the deputies to the Supreme Soviet from the Archangel Region, are of the opinion that the economic development of the North can and should be further advanced, and that it can and should be done more vigorously.

Timber is the principal resource of the Archangel Region. But the timber industry includes not only timber cutting and floating, but also the wood-chemical industry; however, the wood-chemical industry is still very little developed in our region. This is the result of the activity of the wreckers who for a long time had a hand in the administration of the region.

Valuable timber waste, which furnishes the raw material for chemical products and the production of furniture, remained unutilized in our region. Moreover, this waste represents a constant danger of causing fires. It is necessary to build not only large factories and enterprises, but also small factories and special shops for the utilization of this waste.

Timber is not the only item of wealth of the Archangel Region. We are also very rich in water. We have the greatest possibilities for the development of fisheries and of the canning industry. But these are very little developed. In some districts of the region, particularly in the extreme north, in Pechora, Bolshaya Zemlaya and Kanin-Timan districts, there are rich deposits of coal and other minerals. The Soviet tundra is not only a pasture for deer; it can become a base for the development of powerful industries. The working people of the Archangel Region—Russians, Nentsy and Komi—will do everything the Party and the Government demand in order to get the lights of Socialist industry to outshine the lights of the aurora borealis.

Under the conditions prevailing in the Archangel Region, agriculture occupies a comparatively small place in the economic life. But there are great possibilities for its development, since the harvest yields are fairly stable and high. The Archangel Region is the home of the fine Kholmogory breed of cattle, and we can achieve the introduction of this breed on a larger scale in other parts of the Soviet Union.

We are rich not only in an economic respect, but also in that we have remarkable people. There is not a single branch of economy in which we could not find people who are known not only in the Region, but throughout the country.

The enemies of the people tried to retard the development of our Region. They have been exposed by the organs of the People's Commissariat of Internal Affairs, directed by Nicolai Ivanovich Yezhov, and, on the whole, have been weeded out.

The capitalists are preparing to attack the Soviet Union. The working people of Archangel will never forget the hard labour prisons which the interventionists instituted on the islands of Mudyug and Yokanga in 1918–19, and in which many Soviet people perished. Like the whole Soviet people, the working people of our region—Russians, Nentsy, and Komi—will rise at a moment's notice to the defence of our sacred Soviet borders!

It will be absolutely necessary in the Budgets of the coming years to provide for an even more rapid development of the country of the North, for an even more rapid development of mechanization in timber cutting and floating. But in the current year some funds could also be provided for improvements in Archangel. The question of the utilization of timber waste should be tackled at once.

A few critical remarks concerning some People's Commissariats. These remarks are based on the experience of the work of the Budget Commission of which I am a member.

First, with regard to the work of the People's Commissariat of Finance. When we discussed questions of estimates and plans, when we discussed special financial assessments, the officials of the finance organs showed that they knew their business. But when it came to the question of control, of checking up on how the finance organs are directing the carrying out of the Budget provisions, we established the fact that this work was unsatisfactory. The finance organs must draw from this very serious conclusions for themselves. We have impermissably big arrears in the collection of taxes from the rural population, particularly from the individual peasants. As for the collection of taxes from persons of the so-called liberal professions, it is particularly badly organized. In July 1938 the Budget Commission could not even get an answer to the question as to the sum of the arrears on this item in 1937.

The People's Commissariat of Finance has given an unsatisfactory account of itself in the work of developing the savings bank system. Most of the savings banks and the greatest part of the depositors are in the cities, while in the rural districts the savings bank system is very little developed.

The People's Commissariat of Finance has not been paying proper attention to the question of state insurance. With good work we should be able in the immediate future to double and treble the number of citizens insuring their lives and property.

The Government must demand that the People's Commissariat of Finance and other People's Commissariats should definitely improve their work in drawing up their Budgets. We cannot tolerate a situation when plans of financing are drawn up before the plans dealing with production, labour productivity, utilization of equipment, etc.

When the Budget Commission examined the Budget of the People's Commissariat of Agricultural Stocks, this Commissariat appeared in a very unfavorable light. We know that our country is very rich in grain, that in the rural districts there is plenty of grain and flour. We know that the population now wants to get a higher grade flour, that the population demands better work on the part of the trading organizations and the Commissariat of Agricultural Stocks. Instead of improving the work, the People's Commissariat of Agricultural Stocks proposed to the Budget Commission to curtail the plan of realization of flour, which also meant curtailment of receipts from the turnover tax. This was wrong, for the Budget Commission had information from a number of towns about difficulties in satisfying the demand for higher grade flour.

The shortcomings in the work of other People's Commissariats have already been mentioned. But it would be wrong, while criticizing the People's Commissariats, to pass by those shortcomings in the work of securing 100 per cent fulfillment of the Budget provisions for which we, the members of the Supreme Soviet, and the local Party and Soviet organizations are responsible. For instance, in our region the fulfillment of the Budget provisions in the first half of the current year was as follows: revenues 52.3 per cent, expenditures 49.3 per cent. At first glance, this seems not bad; but a closer scrutiny of the various items reveals that the revenue from local industry amounted to only 29 per cent of the estimate for the year. This is intolerable, and we, the leading workers of the region, are no less to blame for it than the workers of the People's Commissariats, for the Archangel Region has very extensive possibilities for the development of local industry.

A few words about the People's Commissariat of the Timber Industry. Its share in the Budget revenues is not a large one, but, as has been currently pointed out both in speeches and in the press, its work is unsatisfactory. We, the leading workers of the Archangel Region, cannot disclaim responsibility for the state of the timber industry. We are now bending our efforts to ensure the carrying out of the Government order about discarding log-floating on the Northern Dvina. Perhaps some of the comrades do not know what this log-floating represents. It means that the timber is floated not in rafts, but in single logs. On such a fine river as the Northern Dvina, these logs have caused great damage to our economy: steam boats have been smashed up through collisions with them, and an enormous amount of timber has been carried out into the White Sea. In 1932 approximately 2,000,000 cubic metres of timber drifted away into the sea. This year we shall make sure that our timber does not drift away into the White Sea.

Comrades, under the leadership of our Government, under the leadership of the Communist Party, the people of our country distribute the wealth they create along such channels as are necessary in the interests of Socialism. Consequently, the fulfillment of each item in the Budget depends upon all of us, upon every Soviet citizen. We members of the Supreme Soviet must remember Comrade Stalin's words about the duties of deputies and we shall have to improve our work for fulfillment of the provisions of the Budget.

Comrades, the approval of the unified state Budget for 1938 by the Supreme Soviet of the USSR will signify our full endorsement of the foreign and internal policy of the Soviet Government and the Communist Party. The approval of the state Budget by the Supreme Soviet will again demonstrate the unity and solidarity of the millions of the multi-national Soviet people, confidently marching towards communism under the leadership of our Party, under the leadership of the greatest man of our epoch— Comrade Stalin. (Applause.)

* * * * *

Speech of A. G. Smagina (Stalinabad City Area, Tadzhik SSR) in the Soviet of Nationalities.

Comrades, members of the Supreme Soviet. The state Budget of the USSR for 1938 submitted to the Session displays in bold relief the growing might of our Socialist country. Our Budget is evidence of tremendous victories in all spheres of Socialist construction. The Soviet people have won these victories under the leadership of the Bolshevik Party and our beloved leader, Comrade Stalin. (Applause.)

We are discussing the state Budget at a tense moment in the international situation. The fascists are becoming more brazen every day. The Japanese militarists are striving with might and main to involve Japan in a war with the Soviet Union. But the Japanese *samurai* have made a big mistake. Our heroic Workers' and Peasants' Red Army has taught them a good lesson. Our mighty Red Army is battle-tried, it defends the vital interests of the working people. It is invincible because it was formed and reared by the great leaders, Lenin and Stalin. (Loud and prolonged applause.)

Let the fascists and their hirelings be advised that our Red Army, led by one of Comrade Stalin's closest comrades, by the First Marshal of the Soviet Union, Klim Voroshilov (loud applause) will make havoc of the enemy on his own territory. Comrades, I am working as an aviatrix in the civil air service. At the first summons of the Party and the Government I am ready together with the whole Soviet people to go to the defence of our country, and am prepared at any moment to change over to a war plane for the defence of the Soviet Union. (Prolonged applause.)

The moral and political unity of the Soviet people was made particularly evident to the world during the elections to the Supreme Soviet of the USSR and the Supreme Soviets of the Union and autonomous republics. Let the fascists and their hirelings be advised that all the Soviet people are united as never before around the Bolshevik Party and are infinitely devoted to Comrade Stalin, their leader and teacher. (Loud and prolonged applause.)

In the Budget, as is quite right, great attention is given to questions of defence of our country. There is no doubt that the Soviet of Nationalities will unanimously approve and sanction the 27,000,000,000 rubles which the Budget provides for the defence of the Land of Socialism.

Comrades, before the Great Socialist Revolution, the working people of Tadzhikistan were ruthlessly oppressed by the tsarist government and the Emir of Bokhara. The people of Tadzhikistan lived under a double yoke, in bondage and poverty. The working population of Tadzhikistan were prey to extortion and tyranny. Only one half of one per cent of the population could read and write. Tadzhikistan has been completely transformed in the two Stalin Five Year Plans. Scores of universities and intermediate schools have been opened. The republic has a total of 4,000 schools, attended by over 200,000 children. Over 250,000 adults are studying too, in the republic. Now 70 per cent of the population of Tadzhikistan have become literate. Expenditure on public education has increased from 34,000,000 rubles in 1932 to 219,000,000 rubles, the 1938 assignment. There was only one hospital in Tadzhikistan before the revolution, and even that was accessible only to *bais,* landowners, and mullahs. Now the republic has over 100 hospitals, and over 400 dispensaries for out-patients.

In the past Tadzhikistan had no industries or railways at all. Under the two Stalin Five Year Plans industrial development has made great headway in Soviet Tadzhikistan. I need only mention enterprises such as the "KIM" and "Nefteabad" oil fields, the Shurab collieries, the silkreeling mills, a giant cannery and many other industrial enterprises. Stalinabad, the capital of the republic, is being built up on a wide scale. The population of our towns is growing continually. For instance, since 1929 the population of Stalinabad has increased from 5,000 to 70,000.

I should like to call attention to the great victories Socialist agriculture has won in our republic. The peasantry of the Tadzhik SSR has taken the path of collective farming once and for all. 92 per cent of all peasant holdings in the republic have been collectivized. Agricultural machines have superseded the antediluvian *omach* and *ketman* on the fields of Tadzhikistan. The collective farmers of Tadzhikistan have made great progress in cotton cultivation. In 1937 the collective farmers picked 16 centners of cotton per hectare, whereas in 1934 the yield was 6.2 centners per hectare. On the basis of these economic achievements, the collective farmers have attained a cultured, prosperous life.

The friendship of the peoples of the whole Soviet Union is unbreakable. All our victories are due to a resolute application of the national policies of Lenin and Stalin; we have won them in a ruthless struggle against the Trotskyite, Bukharinite and bourgeois-nationalist fascist spies, diversionists and wreckers, who tried to thwart our victorious advance. The splendid men of the People's Commissariat of Internal Affairs, led by the Stalin People's Commissar, N. I. Yezhov (applause) discovered the enemies' dastardly plans in time and destroyed them.

Under the leadership of the Party of Lenin and Stalin, under the leadership of the Soviet Government and Vyacheslav Mikhailovich Molotov (applause) and Mikhail Ivanovich Kalinin personally (applause), with the help of the Great Russian people, Tadzhikistan has become a prosperous Soviet republic. The working people of Tadzhikistan have attained this happy and prosperous life as a result of the masterly leadership and constant care of Joseph Vissarionovich Stalin, the leader of peoples. (Loud applause. All rise.)

Comrades, conditions in Tadzhikistan are such that arterial roads are of great importance to the republic's economic life. In this year's Budget, the People's Commissariat of Finance of the USSR has made no provision even for repairs to existing roads. Therefore I ask that in the operation of the Budget, the People's Commissariat of Finance should find the necessary funds for repairs to arterial roads and for the construction of new roads, especially in the mountainous and frontier districts of our republic.

Comrades, the Budget of the Soviet Union, the Budget of all her republics, speak eloquently for the soundness of the national policy of the Party of Lenin and Stalin, and for the further economic and cultural progress of the peoples of the Soviet Union.

Under the leadership of Comrade Stalin (applause) the great strategist and tactician of the proletarian revolution, the leader of the working people, we shall go on boldly and confidently to new victories for Communism. (Applause.)

* * * * *

Speech of S. M. Ivanov (Ulan-Ude Rural Area, Buryat-Mongolian ASSR) in the Union Soviet. Abridged.

. . . I fully second the motion made by a number of deputies to approve the Budget of the USSR. A great part in all the successes which we have achieved in the past years was played by our finance system; for, unlike the Budgets of capitalist countries, the primary purpose of our Soviet Budget is to advance the national economy of our country, to improve the material well being of the masses of the working people. It reflects the constant concern of the Bolshevik Party, the Soviet Government and Comrade Stalin personally for the flourishing of the former backward and downtrodden peoples, for raising their economy and culture to the level of the advanced peoples of the Soviet Union. Our Buryat-Mongolian ASSR furnishes a striking example of this. . . . [There follows a review, partially statistical, of developments in this republic.]

Soviet-Buryat Mongolia is a flourishing Socialist republic—a strong outpost of Socialism in the East. Under the leadership of the Bolshevik Party, and with the help of the Great Russian people, the peoples of Buryat-Mongolia, formerly doomed to extinction, have now obtained a happy and joyous life. . . . All our successes have been achieved under the leadership of the Party of Lenin and Stalin and the Soviet Government, with the daily help and attention of our great leader and teacher, the inspirer of our victories, Comrade Stalin (loud and prolonged applause) and his faithful associate, Comrade Molotov. (Loud and prolonged applause.) . . . [After a brief reference to spies, wreckers, etc. who were caught "with the help of the glorious Soviet intelligence service," the speaker continued.]

Comrades, I shall draw your attention to a number of defects and errors made by the People's Commissariat of Finance of the USSR, and the People's Commissariat of Finance of the RSFSR in drawing up the local Budgets. These Commissariats sometimes pay little attention to the distinguishing features of the remote republics, as in the case of Buryat-Mongolia. . . . First, I wish to point to the insufficient appropriations for the repair of school buildings and the purchase of school supplies. That is why many of our schools are badly repaired and ill-equipped. Secondly, I must draw the attention of the deputies to the fact that the People's Commissariat of Finance of the RSFSR and the Art Department do not provide sufficient funds for the development of our national art. . . . The most backward section of our work is in housing and municipal services. . . . the State Planning Commission and the People's Commissariat of Finance of the RSFSR are holding back the development of the municipal services, and our housing accommodations are hardly growing at all. This situation has obtained for a number of years. . . .

> [The speaker complained briefly that the RSFSR Commissariat of Finance "did not take into consideration the special features of each republic," and did not give the governments of the autonomous republics any chance to amend or correct the proposed budgets in view of local knowledge and needs. He spoke specifically of the need for more attention to irrigation and transportation.]

A few words about the establishment of a fixed percentage of allocations from the Budget revenues, particularly the turnover tax. This year the People's Commissariat of Finance has changed the percentage of allocations from the revenue items of the Budget twice, and as a result placed us twice in financial difficulties.

I am confident that the Government of the USSR and the People's Commissariat of Finance will take these remarks into account. . . .

> [The speaker endorsed the appropriation for defence ("We live in a capitalist encirclement.") and referred briefly to the international situation, especially to the Japanese threat. He pledged the support of the Buryat-Mongolians and asked Molotov to continue his policy of "Resolution and firmness." The speech closed with the usual tributes to the CPSU (B).]

Long live the organizer and inspirer of the gigantic victories of Socialism—our great and wise, our own Comrade Stalin! (Loud and prolonged applause. All rise.)

* * * * *

I. I. Sidorov, Chairman of the Budget Commission of the Union Soviet, replied to the "debate" as follows.

Comrades, members of the Supreme Soviet. Inasmuch as all the deputies who spoke in the debate on the Budget expressed their agreement with the findings of the Budget Commission, and inasmuch as Comrade Zverev, People's Commissar of Finance of the USSR, in announcing the opinion of the Government, did not object to the majority of the amendments proposed and the criticisms made, the Budget Commission considers that its recommendations to increase the revenue side of the Budget by 1,553,775,000 rubles as against the draft submitted was fully and entirely justified.

The debate on the Unified State Budget was maintained on a high political level. Every deputy spoke in a statesmanlike way. The Unified State Budget of the USSR is a splendid Budget. It must be carried out both as regards revenue and expenditure in a Bolshevik way. A determined fight must be waged against violations of Budget discipline, and we must demand that all People's Commissariats, departments, organizations, all citizens of our country fulfill their duties to the state Budget. And we, too, the members of the Supreme Soviet, must work hard to ensure that the provisions of the state Budget are carried out.

Comrades, the debate on the Unified State Budget has shown that all the items of revenue and expenditure meet with the unanimous approval of the deputies who have spoken and of the whole Soviet of the Union. Great enthusiasm and satisfaction are occasioned by the appropriation of 27,000,000,000 rubles for defence purposes, for the purpose of strengthening the military might of our Socialist country. This testifies to the ardent love of the working people for their native land, it testifies to the unanimous desire to strengthen the might of our Red Army, Navy and Air Force still further, it testifies to the moral and political unity of our people, and to the fact that the Soviet people in their millions are prepared to thoroughly smash any enemy on his own territory. (Prolonged applause.)

The fascists of Germany and Italy and the imperialists of Japan are trying to provoke us to war. The fascist agents within our country—Trotskyites, Bukharinites and bourgeois nationalists—have been smashed. The Soviet people are united more solidly than ever around the Bolshevik Party, around our leader and teacher, our great Stalin. (Loud applause.)

But, comrades, the fight is not over, it is still going on. We must therefore show even greater determination in rooting out and destroying the enemies of our people, no matter what mask they may hide behind. We declare to the fascists and the Japanese imperialists, and let them bear it well in mind, that we fully and entirely approve of the firm policy and practical acts of our Soviet Government, and that if we are subjected to military attack, our valorous Workers' and Peasants' Red Army will destroy the enemy on his own territory. Let the fascists know that war on us will end in the destruction of fascism. Communism will triumph all over the world! (Loud applause.)

Comrades, where, in what other country, does a Budget submitted by the government meet with such unanimous approval? There is no such country, nor can there be, under capitalist rule. It is possible only in our country, the country where Socialism is victorious, and where the Budget is like a mirror reflecting the vital interests of our population.

I call upon you to vote for and adopt such a Budget unanimously. (Prolonged applause.)

The work of the Session testifies to the unity of the Soviet people, to their love and devotion to the Soviet government and its leader, Vyacheslav Mikhailovich Molotov (loud and prolonged applause. All rise. Cries: "Long live Comrade Molotov!" "Hurrah for Comrade Molotov!") their love and devotion to our Bolshevik Party and its Leninist-Stalinist Central Committee, their love and devotion to the leader and teacher of all working people, the man who is leading us from victory to victory, our dear and great Stalin! (Loud applause and cheers. All rise. Cries: "Hurrah for

Comrade Stalin!" "Hurrah for our leader and great teacher, Comrade Stalin!" "Long live our great Stalin!" Cheers.)

* * * * *

Zverev's "reply to the debate" in the Soviet of Nationalities.

Comrades, members of the Supreme Soviet. At the sittings of the Soviet of Nationalities and the Soviet of the Union we have had a comprehensive discussion of the draft Unified State Budget for 1938. The unanimous approval of the Budget bears witness to the fact that the proposed Budget reflects, both in the revenue and in the expenditure side, the great tasks that confront our country in the year 1938.

In discussing the Budget, the Chairman of the Budget Commission of the Soviet of Nationalities, Comrade Khokhlov, proposed some amendments to the draft submitted. One of the motions made by the Budget Commission of the Soviet of Nationalities is to increase the total revenues in the Budget by over 1,500,000,000 rubles, including an increase of 591,500,000 rubles from the turnover tax. An analogous motion . . . has been made by the Budget Commission of the Soviet of the Union. The Budget Commission of the Soviet of Nationalities has moved that the revenues in the Budget be increased by 208,310,000 rubles from the profits tax on our economic organizations and industrial People's Commissariats. The Budget Commission has also moved to increase the revenues by 300,000,000 rubles through an increase in the receipts from state loan bonds purchased by the savings banks with the funds attracted in deposits from the population. The Budget Commission also proposes to increase the expenditures in the Budget by more than 1,500,000,000 rubles.

The Council of People's Commissars of the USSR has instructed me to state before the Session of the Supreme Soviet that it recognizes the expediency of the motions of the Budget Commissions for an increase in expenditures and revenues in the draft Budget submitted. With regard to the turnover tax, the Council of People's Commissars considers it possible to accept an increase in receipts not in the amount of 591,500,000 rubles, as proposed by the Budget Commission of the Soviet of Nationalities, but by 627,500,000 rubles as recommended by the Budget Commission of the Soviet of the Union.

The Budget Commission of the Soviet of Nationalities has raised the question of increasing the profits tax by 208,000,000 rubles. The Council of People's Commissars of the USSR is of the opinion that it is expedient and necessary to increase Budget revenue from the profits tax by 132,610,000 rubles.

The Council of People's Commissars of the USSR has no objections to the motion of the Budget Commission to increase the taxes and levies on the population by 30,000,000 rubles, and to increase the Budget revenues by attracting deposits to the savings banks. The improvement in the material well being of the working people, and the prosperity of the population both in the cities and in the countryside, create favourable conditions for the participation of the workers and all the working people in the work of the savings banks. The revenues that accrued from this source in the first half of the year amounted to 1,200,000,000 rubles. If the savings banks and finance organs work energetically, the 300,000,000 rubles which the Budget Commission refers to in its motion will undoubtedly accrue to the Budget revenue of the state. That is why the Council of People's Commissars considers it expedient to raise the Budget estimate of receipts from this source as well.

Nor has the Council of People's Commissars of the USSR any objection to increasing the estimates of receipts from the state social insurance fund by 75,000,000 rubles and from customs revenues by 250,000,000 rubles. Decisions adopted by the Council of People's Commissars of the USSR after the draft had been submitted to the Budget Commission fully ensure the receipts accruing to the Budget from customs revenues. As regards other revenues, the Council of People's Commissars considers it expedient to include in the Budget the sum of 122,094,000 rubles as additional revenue.

Beside the amendments to the draft Unified State Budget, remarks have been made by the Budget Commissions . . . , as well as by individual members of the Supreme Soviet, in criticism of the work of various economic People's Commissariats. Members of the Supreme Soviet have pointed out that some People's Commissariats, . . . have not been discharging their financial obligations to the state Budget, and have not been fulfilling their plans for the output of industry and the lowering of the cost of production. The Council of People's Commissars of the USSR has instructed me to inform the members of the Supreme Soviet that in the near future the Council of People's Commissars will take additional concrete measures to improve the financial and production activity of these People's Commissariats.

Members of the Supreme Soviet and the Chairman of the Budget Commission of the Soviet of Nationalities, Deputy Khokhlov, have also criticized the work of the People's Commissariat of Finance of the USSR. I fully agree with these critical remarks. Unquestionably there are still many deficiencies in the People's Commissariat of Finance.

Some members of the Supreme Soviet of the USSR have pointed out that the People's Commissariat of Finance is not sufficiently acquainted with the financial affairs of the Union republics, and has therefore committed mistakes in drawing up the Unified State Budget. I must state that when the People's Commissariat of Finance submitted the draft Unified State Budget to the Council of People's Commissars, the latter pointed out the mistakes and corrected the draft. However, the criticism to the effect that the People's Commissariat of Finance is not acquainted with the specific features of economy in the . . . various republics is justified. At the same time we must demand of the Councils of People's Commissars of the republics, and of the executive committees of the territories and regions, that in estimating their expenditures and filing their claims to the Union Budget they should approach the matter from the viewpoint of the interests of the state.

The work of drawing up the Budget for 1938 has shown that in some instances the statements and claims presented to the Union and republican organizations had been accepted without a critical analysis. It is this that explains the fact that at first the demands upon the Budget totaled 45,136,000,000 rubles, while now, after the Budgets of the various republics have been examined into by the Council of People's Commissars of the USSR, this part of the Budget, as you see, represents a sum of 34,747,000,000 rubles. Thus the claims of the Union republics had been exaggerated to the amount of 10,389,000,000 rubles. It is quite obvious that a situation like this cannot be tolerated in the future. It is necessary to conform to strict state discipline in putting claims to the Union Budget. Only that should be demanded which is actually needed. An impermissible attitude with regard to drawing up claims was displayed by the organizations of the Kirghiz SSR.

The state Budget of the Kirghiz SSR for 1937 totaled 235,000,000 rubles, and for 1938 this republic drew up a Budget in the amount of 617,000,000 rubles. The Council of People's Commissars of the USSR could not agree to this sum and, after an examination into the Budget, decided to allow Kirghizia the sum of only 312,844,000 rubles. The unfounded claims put in by the Kirghiz comrades show how in some instances the attitude to the Union Budget betrays a lack of consideration of the interests of the state.

Exaggerated claims had also been filed by the Tadzhik, Turkmen, Kazakh and Armenian SSRs and by a number of autonomous republics and regional executive committees. At the same time the exaggerated claims to expenditures were usually accompanied by a demand for an increase of revenues from Union sources, while the possibilities of the local sources were clearly underrated. Instead of mobilizing all forces to increase the sources of revenue, instead of bringing to light new possibilities and disclosing concealed resources, the People's Commissariats of Finance of the Union Republics followed the line of least resistance. They demanded an increase in the percentage of the allocations from the turnover tax in order thus to obtain the sums that would enable them to draw up the republican and local Budgets without a deficit.

The governments of the various Republics do not always show a critical attitude to the claims of the People's Commissariats and other institutions. In 1937 the expenditures on village reading rooms in the Kazakh SSR, as shown by the summary of the local Budgets, totaled 4,000,000 rubles, yet for 1938 the Republic filed a claim for 21,602,000 rubles. It acted in exactly the same way in regard to the expenditure on physical culture and on sports, which it raised to 890 per cent of the expenditure of the preceding year.

The People's Commissariat of Finance of the USSR is unquestionably in duty bound to improve its work and draw up its financial plans in conformity with the specific features of the various republics. But it is also necessary to enhance the sense of responsibility in dealing with Soviet state funds in the republics and regions. The workers in charge must demand only what is needed for the realization of the various measures, without putting in any extra claims.

The prompt collection of state taxes is the most important task of the finance bodies. However, there are many who fail to realize this. I have already pointed out that in some regions and republics the finance bodies have failed to organize the timely collection of taxes and levies on the population.

The situation as regards the utilization of the resources allotted for housing and municipal development is very bad. A checkup on the work of housing, municipal and public service development has shown that most of the republics are not fulfilling their plans. In the first half of the year the Tadzhik Republic completed only 17.3 per cent of the year's plan for housing, municipal and public service development, the Byelo-russian Republic 22 per cent, the Kirghiz Republic 24.4 per cent, the Turkmen Republic 25.7 per cent, and the Kazakh Republic 26.5 per cent. The failure to fulfill the plans is explained by the fact that the local Soviets have not made the proper preparations for the construction work. Plans and estimates have not been drawn up on time, and in many cases the construction jobs have not been supplied with labour power.

The Central Municipal Bank and the Municipal Banks in the localities are not exercising proper control over housing, municipal and public serv-icc dcvclopment. At best the managers of these banks read the state-ments of the amount of money drawn. But they do not fight to reduce the cost of construction and to make the builders keep within the estimates in their expenditures.

A serious deficiency in the Budget work is the poor state of account-ing. The existing system of accounting with regard to the realization of the state and local Budgets does not provide an opportunity for a day-to-day control of the financial transactions of the Budget institutions and eco-nomic organizations. This system prevents the timely disclosure of viola-tions of financial and Budget discipline. It will be necessary for the Peo-ple's Commissariat of Finance of the USSR, together with the Central Administration of National Economic Accounting, to revise the forms of bookkeeping and statistical accountancy on the state Budgets and local Budgets. It is necessary to submit definite terms for and the order of sub-mitting accounts.

The remarks of the Chairman of the Budget Commission and of mem-bers of the Supreme Soviet impose upon the People's Commissariat of Finance of the USSR the obligation of drawing the necessary conclusions and setting itself the immediate task of effecting a radical improvement in all spheres of finance work.

With the help which the People's Commissariat of Finance of the USSR receives from the Government and from Comrade Stalin, we will by all means accomplish the tasks set us in the Budget for 1938. (Ap-plause.)

Voting on the Budget

The voting procedure was the same in both chambers. First, the budget was voted on section by section. Then the budget as a whole was voted on. Next the Budget Act was voted on article by article (there were ten articles in the Budget Act of 1938) and, finally, the vote was taken on the Budget Act as a whole. Here are typical motions and votes.

(Voting on sections of the Budget in the Union Soviet.)

ZVEREV: Expenditures on the People's Commissariat of Defence and the People's Commissariat of the Navy—27,044,020,000 rubles.

CHAIRMAN: I shall take a vote on expenditures on the People's Commissariats of Defence and Navy in the amount of 27,044,020,000 rubles. Those in favor of the adoption of this sum, please raise their hands. Please lower your hands. Anybody against? No. Any abstentions? No. Adopted unanimously.

(Voting on articles—Soviet of Nationalities.)

ZVEREV: In Article 7 some editorial changes were made after the draft had been distributed. I shall read it in its final form. "Article 7. To note the unsatisfactory organization of the collection by the People's Commissariat of Finance of the USSR, and its local organs in 1937 of the legally established rural taxes and levies. To make it the duty of the People's Commissariat of Finance of the USSR and the local Soviet organs to adopt measures to improve the work of the finance bodies."

CHAIRMAN: Are there any remarks on Article 7?

VOICES: Adopt.

CHAIRMAN: Those in favor of adopting Article 7, please raise their hands. Please lower your hands. Anybody against? No. Any abstentions? No. Article 7 is adopted unanimously.

(Voting on the whole budget—Union Soviet.)

Chairman: . . . We have concluded voting on the Union Budget section by section. I shall now take the vote of the Soviet of the Union on the Union Budget for 1938 as a whole. Those in favor of the adoption of the Union Budget as a whole, please raise their hands. Anybody against? No. Any abstentions? No. Adopted unanimously.

(Voting on the Budget Act—Soviet of Nationalities.)

Chairman: . . . I shall take a vote on the unified State Budget of the USSR (1938) Act as a whole. Those in favor of adopting this Act as a whole, please raise their hands. Please lower your hands. Anybody against? No. Any abstentions? No. The Unified State Budget of the USSR (1938) Act is adopted unanimously.

* * * * *

The 1946 Elections

> The second Supreme Soviet of the USSR was elected in 1946. The following Soviet account of this event exemplifies the image which the Soviet rulers wished the world to have. Note the references to and quotations from Stalin, the understandable feeling of triumph, and the claims of what the election returns "prove." The source is: *New Times.* Moscow. No. 4 (February 15, 1946), pp. 1–3.

On February 10, 1946, 99.7 per cent of the voters went to the polls to elect a new Supreme Soviet of the Union of Soviet Socialist Republics. All the candidates of the Communist and Non-Party Bloc were elected to the supreme organ of the Soviet State. These candidates—workers, farmers and intellectuals—are genuine representatives of the Soviet people. Among them are experienced statesmen, prominent public leaders and rank-and-file collective farmers, outstanding scientists and humble young workers.

The election was a great triumph for socialist democracy: it revealed the complete moral and political unity of the Soviet people, whose numbers run into many millions, and the strength and monolithic structure of our multi-national state. It was a demonstration of the profound confidence the people place in the Soviet Government and in the Communist Party, and of the love and devotion of the vast masses of the people to the great leader of the Soviet State, J. Stalin.

The Supreme Soviet elections were also of great international importance.

An interval of eight years separates us from the first election of a Supreme Soviet. This period was replete with events of the greatest magnitude, the like of which had not been witnessed before in the history of mankind. During this period the Soviet Socialist State passed through grave dangers and severe trials and its Red Army, under the leadership of Generalissimo J. Stalin, achieved gigantic victories in the war against Hitler Germany and her allies. These victories over a dangerous and powerful enemy, who threatened to enslave all the freedom-loving nations, were possible thanks to the strength, unity and stability of the Soviet State. The social and political system of the Great Soviet Power gave practical proof, by the success with which it passed the great tests of the past few years, of its viability and superiority over every other form of social and political organization.

> "The war was something like an examination for our Soviet system, for our state, for our Government, for our Communist Party, and it summed up the results of their work. . . ." said J. Stalin in the speech he delivered to the voters.

The brief report made by the leader of the Soviet State on the work of the Communist Party in having prepared our country for active defence was striking and convincing. The leadership of the Communist Party ensured the triumph of the policy of socialist industrialization and collectivization of agriculture in the Soviet Union; and it ensured the progressive development of Soviet society on the basis of scientific socialist planning. Thanks to this leadership, the Soviet Union was transformed into a mighty and progressive industrial power and played a decisive part in the war waged in common by all the freedom-loving nations against the German and Japanese imperialists, in the war which "actuality became a war of the nations for their existence" (Stalin).

No less convincing were the plans of work of the Communist Party for the future as outlined by Stalin, plans providing for the rehabilitation and development of the country's economy, the consolidation of the Soviet State in every aspect—plans which, when carried out, will enable us to say that our Motherland is ensured against all contingencies. With the experience of previous years behind them, the vast masses of the working people of the U.S.S.R. do not for a moment doubt that these plans will be realized in their entirety. This explains why the Communist Party, which came out in the elections not alone but in a bloc with the non-party people, enjoys the boundless confidence of the whole of Soviet society; it explains why the workers, farmers and intellectuals unhesitatingly cast their votes for the candidates of the Communist and Non-Party Bloc.

The results of the elections for the Supreme Soviet of the U.S.S.R. are the natural continuation and fixation of the victorious results of the great war of liberation against fascism, in which the Soviet State and the Soviet people honourably performed their duty to mankind.

These results show that the Soviet Union has emerged from the stern trials of the war politically, economically and militarily stronger and more consolidated than ever it was before. The Soviet State has come still further to the front as a major factor in international life. No serious problem in international relations can now be solved without the participation of the Soviet Union. This situation accords with the interests of all other peace-loving nations and countries pursuing the path of democratic development and of the consolidation of their independence. The foreign policy of the Soviet Union unswervingly follows the course of strengthening peace and hence enjoys the full support of the masses of the people, whose needs and interests it fully protects.

Those foreign politicians who, blinded by their reactionary prejudices, refuse to reckon with this indisputable fact run the risk of making themselves ridiculous. They should take warning from the ignominious failure and gross miscalculation of those irresponsible critics of the Soviet social system who repeatedly foretold its inevitable collapse as the result of "a slight push from outside."

Arguments have appeared in the foreign press to the effect that the Soviet State was unstable because it was a multinational state. Those who advanced these arguments could not, or would not, understand the essence of the multinational Soviet State, grown up not on a bourgeois basis which stimulates sentiments of national distrust and national dissension, but on a Soviet basis, which, on the contrary, cultivates sentiments of friendship and fraternal co-operation among the nations and knows neither racial, colonial nor national oppression.

In certain countries abroad reactionary elements still endeavour to poison the international atmosphere. Significant, for instance, is the manner in which some reactionary newspapers and periodicals abroad commented on the election campaign in the Soviet Union. Some decided to gloss over the fact, rather unpleasant for them to swallow, of the unity and solidarity of the one hundred million Soviet voters, a unity become possible and realized on the basis of socialist democracy. Others resorted to falsification in their descriptions and appraisals of the Supreme Soviet elections, by deliberately distorting the election speeches of Soviet leaders, and by trying to conceal from public opinion the genuinely democratic election platform upon which the splendid victory of the Communist and Non-Party Bloc was achieved.

The impressive unity of the Soviet people demonstrated by the election returns enhances still more the international influence and authority of the Soviet State. The election has shown that the Soviet Union contains no social groups or strata that question the necessity of ensuring stable peace and security for all peace-loving nations, big and small, for those free and for those still fighting for their liberation. No people can be found in the Soviet Union to preach or justify aggressive war against any peace-loving country whatsoever, to sap the foundations of the edifice of international security.

Everybody knows that there are some democratic countries in which the course to be followed by their foreign policy is often the subject of acrimonious controversy, in which the reactionary forces anxious to sow discord and animosity among nations sometimes gain the upper hand. Here lies the source of vacillation, inconsistency and deviation from a peace policy in countries the peoples of which view with understandable alarm the dangerous talk of a "third world war."

The Soviet Union pursues a thoroughly consistent policy designed to ensure peace all over the world. This policy of the Soviet Government, which persistently exposes the machinations of reaction in the world arena and facilitates the triumph of the principles of democracy in the relations between peoples, has the unanimous, undivided support of the whole of the Soviet people. This is confirmed by the election of the Supreme Soviet of the U.S.S.R.—eloquent testimony of the unqualified support on the part of the electorate of both the domestic and foreign policy of the Soviet Government and of their full approval of the post-war plans for the economic and cultural development of the country.

The execution of these plans will make the Soviet Union a still mightier state, an impregnable bastion of peace and the security of nations.

It was for this that over a hundred million voters in the Soviet Union cast their votes on February 10, 1946.

* * * * *

The 1950 Elections

> Excerpt from an election speech by Georgii M. Malenkov, 9 March, 1950.

Comrades:

On March 12 elections to the Supreme Soviet of the USSR will be held. We are all certain that the citizens of the Union of Soviet Socialist Republics will unanimously cast their ballots for the candidates of the bloc of the Communists and non-Party masses.

The Soviet people will go to the polls convinced that the policy of the Communist Party and the Soviet Government is right—a policy directed toward the further advancement of all branches of our country's national economy, the steady improvement of the material welfare of the working people and the preservation of peace throughout the world.

Beyond a doubt our people on that day will demonstrate once again their solidarity with their beloved Communist Party and the Soviet Government.

The State Budget and Consumer Goods, 1953

> Georgii M. Malenkov, then Chairman of the Council of Ministers of the USSR, addressed the Supreme Soviet on 8 August, 1953. He addressed himself first to the budget, and then introduced his famous proposal to increase consumer goods. This was later used by Khrushchev and others in their attacks upon Malenkov. The source is: *G. M. Malenkov's Speech*. London: Soviet News, 1953. Pp. 3-5, 8-9.

Comrades deputies! The draft State Budget submitted by the government to the present session of the U.S.S.R. Supreme Soviet completely ensures the financing of tasks connected with the development of the national economy in 1953, the third year of the Fifth Five-Year Plan, the implementation of which will be an important step forward on the path of building a communist society in our country.

The State Budget reflects the policy of the Soviet government and of our Party, which aims at the development and the steady progress of the socialist national economy.

Of the budget revenue, totalling 543,357 million roubles, the overwhelming part, amounting to 86 per cent, comes from industry, agriculture, and other branches of the national economy. Among the items of budget expenditure, in its turn, the greatest is the financing of the national economy.

For the further development of the national economy, the 1953 Budget provides 192,500 million roubles, or over 36 per cent of all budget expenditure, as compared with 178,800 million roubles last year. Apart from budget allocations, in accordance with the national economic plan, for these same purposes almost 98,000 million roubles are being allocated from enterprises' and economic organisations' own funds made up from their profits and other sources. Thus altogether, for the financing of the national economy this year, there will be allocated more than 290,000 million roubles as compared with 265,000 million roubles in 1952. With all this one must bear in mind that, as a result of the price reduction which has been carried out, the purchasing power of the rouble has increased, and consequently the amount for the financing of the national economy is *de facto* being increased even more.

Funds allocated for the development of the national economy ensure the uninterrupted growth of social production as the basis for the further advance of the people's wellbeing and a still further strengthening of the defensive capacity of our country.

The State Budget reflects the concern of the Soviet state for the steady raising of the material and cultural standard of life of the working people.

Expenditure on education, the health services, social and cultural measures, on pensions, as well as payments to the population on loans, will amount this year to 139,500 million roubles, as compared with 129,600 million roubles in 1952. In addition to this, expenditure is being incurred out of the Budget on the reduction of state retail prices, which ensures for the population a gain of over 46,000 million roubles, calculated on the basis of one year, and on a number of other measures directly aimed at raising the people's wellbeing.

Altogether, the population will receive from this year's Budget 192,000 million roubles, or over 36 per cent. of the entire budget expenditure, as against 147,000 million roubles last year. At the same time from their personal incomes the working people will contribute to the Budget in the form of taxation and duties, and also by subscribing to the loan, 65,000 million roubles i.e., 21,000 million roubles less than last year. Thus, during the current year factory and office workers and collective farmers will receive from the Budget 127,000 million roubles more than they will contribute to it out of their personal incomes. In 1952 the population received 61,000 million roubles more than it contributed to the Budget.

The State Budget provides for expenditure on defence to the amount of 110,200 million roubles. This sum represents 20.8 per cent. of the entire budget expenditure, as against 23.6 per cent. in 1952.

In proposing the allocations for defence, the government has proceeded from the premise that we are obliged untiringly to perfect and strengthen the Soviet armed forces in order to ensure the safety of our motherland and be ready to give a crushing rebuff to any aggressor who might seek to violate the peaceful life of the peoples of the Union of Soviet Socialist Republics (*stormy and prolonged applause*). [*sic*]

·   ·   ·

We must always remember that heavy industry is the very foundation of our socialist economy, because without the development of heavy industry it is impossible to ensure the further development of light industry, the growth of the productive forces of agriculture, and the strengthening of the defensive power of our country.

Now, on the basis of the successes achieved in the development of heavy industry, we have all the conditions for organising a sharp rise in the production of consumer goods.

We have every possibility and we must do so. During the past 28 years the output of means of production as a whole has grown in our country about 55 times over, while the production of consumer goods during the same period has increased only 12 times over. A comparison of the 1953 production level with the prewar year of 1940 shows that during this period also the output of means of production increased over three times, while the production of consumer goods increased by 72 per cent.

The volume of production of consumer goods which we have reached cannot satisfy us.

Hitherto we have had no possibility of developing light industry and the food industry at the same rate as heavy industry. At the present time we can—and therefore we must—in the interests of ensuring a more rapid increase in the material and cultural standards of life of the people, promote by every means the development of light industry.

Over a long period of time, we directed our capital investment mainly towards the development of our heavy industry and transport. During the years of the Five-Year Plans, i.e., since 1929 and up to 1952, the amount of state funds invested in capital construction and equipment, calculated in accordance with current prices, was: Heavy industry, 638,000 million roubles; transport, 193,000 million roubles; light industry, 72,000 million roubles; agriculture, 94,000 million roubles.

The government and the central committee of the Party consider it essential to increase considerably the investment of funds for the development of light industry, the food industry, and, in particular, the fishing industry, and for the development of agriculture, and consider it essential to correct the output targets for goods consumed by the people by considerably increasing those targets, to draw the engineering and other enterprises of heavy industry on a wider scale into the production of consumer goods.

The urgent task lies in raising sharply in two or three years the provision for the population of foodstuffs and manufactures, meat and meat produce, fish and fish products, butter, sugar, confectionery, textiles, clothing, footwear, crockery, furniture, stationery and other household goods; in raising considerably the provision of all kinds of consumer goods to the population (*stormy applause*). [*sic*]

As we know, the Fifth Five-Year Plan provides for an increase in consumer goods by 1955 by approximately 65 per cent. as against 1950. We have every possibility of developing the production of consumer goods on a scale to fulfil this task much sooner.

One must not, however, be satisfied with a quantitative growth alone in the production of consumer goods. The question of the quality of all manufactured goods for general consumption is of no less importance.

It must be admitted that we lag behind in the quality of consumer goods, and that we must introduce considerable improvements in this matter. Many enterprises are still producing articles of an unsatisfactory quality, not meeting the requirements and tastes of the Soviet consumer.

General consumer goods produced by our industry, though as a rule of solid quality, leave a great deal to be desired in finish and external appearance. To the shame of workers in the industry, the customer frequently prefers to acquire goods of foreign production, only because they have a better finish. Meanwhile we have every possibility of producing good quality and attractive textiles; good quality and smart clothes; and durable and elegant footwear. We have every possibility of providing a good finish to all the goods which serve to satisfy the people's requirements.

The Soviet people are right to demand from us, and primarily from the workers in the industries producing consumer goods, goods which are lasting, well finished, and of high quality. We must respond to this demand by action. It is the duty of every enterprise to produce high-quality goods, and to care constantly for the durability and good finish of production.

The task is to make a drastic change in the output of consumer goods and to ensure a speedier development of the light and food industries.

But, in order to ensure a sharp development in the output of consumer goods, we must first of all take care of the further growth and development of agriculture, which supplies the population with food, and light industry with raw materials.

Our socialist agriculture has attained great successes in its development. Year after year the commonly owned economy of the collective farms is growing and becoming stronger, the output of agricultural products is increasing.

Our country is assured of bread. As compared with pre-war times, deliveries to the state of cotton, sugar beet, and livestock products have considerably increased. In 1952 the deliveries were: Raw cotton, 3,770,-000 tons, 70 per cent. more than in 1940; sugar beet, 22 million tons, nearly 30 per cent. more than in 1940. Last year deliveries to the state of meat amounted to three million tons, which is 50 per cent. more than deliveries in 1940. Deliveries of milk were 10 million tons, or nearly 60 per cent. more than in 1940. In addition to state procurements, our agriculture supplies a large quantity of meat, milk, and other foodstuffs through the co-operative and collective farm trade.

The deliveries of bread grain and other agricultural produce are being carried out this year successfully and in an organised manner.

Great progress has been made in equipping agriculture with new and up to date machinery, which has made it possible completely to mechanise many types of operations so as to lighten the work of the collective farm peasantry and make that work more productive.

The successes of agriculture are considerable. They are an undoubted achievement of our collective farms, of our machine and tractor stations, our state farms, our socialist system.

However, it would have been a serious mistake not to see the lag in many important branches of agriculture, not to notice that the present-day level of agricultural production does not correspond to the increased technical equipment in agriculture, to the potentialities inherent in the collective farm system.

We have still quite a number of collective farms, and even of entire areas, where agriculture is in a neglected state. In many areas of the country collective and state farms gather in low harvests of grain and other agricultural crops and allow big losses in harvesting. As a consequence of the underdevelopment of agriculture, some of the collective farms still have insufficient revenue in money and kind and yield little to the collective farmers in money, grain, and other produce for every workday unit.

Elections to the Fourth Supreme Soviet (1954)

> This selection consists of short excerpts from three election speeches. All were delivered in March, 1954. The first speaker was G. M. Malenkov; the second, V. M. Molotov; and the third, N. S. Khrushchev. It is ironic in view of what later happened that the publishers accorded the speakers this priority. The source is: *"Elections to the Supreme Soviet of the USSR. Speeches by G. M. Malenkov, V. M. Molotov, N. S. Khrushchev."* A "Soviet News" Booklet. London, 1954. Pp. 5, 15–16, 25–26, 30, 36.

Comrades, allow me to express to you and, in your persons, to all the voters of the Leningrad constituency, my heartfelt gratitude for the great honour and trust you have shown me by nominating me as your candidate for the Supreme Soviet of the USSR (prolonged applause.) I assure you that I will continue, honestly and devotedly, to serve the cause of our glorious Communist Party, our great people, to give all my energy to our socialist motherland (prolonged applause.)

The election of the highest organ of power is an event of paramount importance in our democratic state. The Soviet people, masters of their country, in preparing for the forthcoming elections, are reviewing the path traveled during the four years that have passed since the previous elections to the Supreme Soviet of the USSR. . . .

The Soviet man looks toward his future confidently, cheerfully and boldly. He knows that the Communist Party devotes all its energies to his happiness, to the peaceful prosperity and development of our glorious motherland (prolonged applause.)

* * * * *

Comrades, allow me, first of all, to express to you and to all the electors of the Molotov constituency who have nominated me as candidate for the Supreme Soviet of the USSR, my heartfelt gratitude for this high honour and for the confidence placed in me. (Applause.) I shall consider it my first duty, my duty as a communist, to justify your trust, Comrade Electors! (Applause.)

The foundation of our Party's successes is that steadfast confidence which it enjoys among the working people. All of us must value that confidence. It is the sacred duty of every communist to make it his concern to strengthen that confidence and to continue honestly to serve his people, and to rally the working people around our Party, its central committee and the Soviet government (prolonged applause.) . . .

The elections to the Supreme Soviet of the USSR serve as a general testing of the home and foreign policy of the Communist Party and the Soviet government. These elections at the same time bring the Soviet people still closer to the Party and the government.

The bloc of communists and non-party people, in which the growing ties of our Party with the broad masses of the working people and the rallying of our people around the Party have found expression, is growing and becoming stronger! (Tumultuous and prolonged applause.)

* * * * *

Comrades! The working people in the Kalinin constituency of our glorious capital, Moscow, have shown great confidence in me in nominating me as their candidate for the post of Deputy of the supreme organ of state power—the Supreme Soviet of the USSR. Allow me, in the first place, to thank you sincerely for this high honour and to assure you that I shall do my utmost to justify your trust (applause.) Every one of us communists who have [sic] been nominated for the important state post of Deputy of the USSR Supreme Soviet, realizes that we owe the confidence of the people to the Communist Party that has reared us, to its central committee (applause.)

Created by our brilliant leader and teacher, the great Lenin, the Communist Party is confidently leading the people along the road to communism. By its heroic struggle for the cause of socialism and by its selfless service to the people, the Communist Party has won the unbounded love and confidence of all working people. The glorious 50th anniversary of the Communist Party of the Soviet Union provided a striking demonstration of the all-conquering strength of the teachings of Marx, Engels, Lenin and Stalin. From their long years of experience, the working people have proved to their satisfaction that the Communist Party has no interests higher than the interests of the people, that it is truly the party of the people. The Communist Party is strong in its unbreakable ties with the people, through the steel-like unity of its ranks and its loyalty to Marxism-Leninism. Our party today is solid and united as never before (prolonged applause.)

The peoples of our country come to the elections to the Supreme Soviet of the USSR firmly united around their beloved Communist Party, its central committee and the Soviet government. The Soviet people give their warm approval and unanimous support to the policy mapped out by the Communist Party. . . . The Communist Party's policy is directed towards the strengthening of the might of the Soviet motherland, towards a further powerful development of economy and culture, towards ensuring the security of the USSR and strengthening the cause of world peace.

The Soviet people are enthusiastically striving to carry out this policy. . . .

Vladimir Ilyich Lenin, the founder of the Communist Party and the Soviet state, taught us that the people test political parties and persons in public life, not by their declarations and promises, but by their deeds. The Soviet people have learned this wise teaching of Ilyich's by heart and they demand from their elected representatives devoted service to the people and constant implementation of the policy drawn up by the Party. It is, therefore, quite natural that every election to the Supreme Soviet is for us a countrywide testing of how the policy of our Party is actually being carried out.

Four years separate us from the last elections. At the present time, at the many election meetings, millions of Soviet people are discussing the manifesto of the central committee of the Party to the electors [sic], the results of our work, and the main aims of our home and foreign policy. . . .

In the period immediately ahead, we must do everything possible to ensure that we have plenty of fine fabrics, and see to it that the colours are better, to ensure that the footwear is of good quality and in attractive styles, and to ensure that better quality articles are produced in sufficient quantities to improve the life of Soviet men and women. The Party is tackling this job in the proper way, and there need be no doubt that it will be carried out successfully (applause.)

At the time of the last elections, the Communist Party set the aim of developing socialist agriculture. . . . But we can by no means be content with these successes.

In the course of the past six months the central committee of the CPSU, at its plenary meetings, has twice discussed the urgent tasks for further developing agricultural production in the country, and has outlined a program for a big advance in agriculture. This is an indication of the great attention the Party is paying to the development of agriculture. And the Party is basing itself on the need to secure, within the coming two or three years, a level of agricultural production that will abundantly satisfy the requirements of the population as regards foodstuffs and of light industry as regards raw material. . . .

For the victory of the bloc of communists and non-party people in the forthcoming elections to the Supreme Soviet of the USSR! (Tumultuous applause.)

Speedy Legislation

The fourth Supreme Soviet, having been duly elected and called into session, proved itself no less able than its predecessors to handle complex legislation with a speed which can hardly fail to cast doubt on the thoroughness of its deliberations and the genuineness of its political stature. The source is: *Intelligence Report No. 7307. (Unclassified.) July 27, 1956.* Washington: Office of Intelligence Research, Department of State. Abridged.

. . . On the morning of July 11, the Councils of Elders of the two houses met jointly, ostensibly to give "fullest consideration" to the formulation of an agenda. One hour later the Council of the Union convened and without delay unanimously adopted the five-point agenda proposed by the Councils of Elders. In the afternoon, the Council of Nationalities followed suit.

The first agenda item involved a new state pension law, and occupied nearly four of the five days of the session. The other major agenda items—a disarmament appeal to other parliaments, a declaration on a Japanese parliamentary proposal to ban nuclear weapons tests, the transformation of the Karelo-Finnish constituent republic into the Karelian autonomous republic within the USSR—were all discussed and disposed of on the final day. Except for the first and last day, each house met for only half days.

The state pension bill had been published in draft form on May 9. During the succeeding two months an alleged 12,000 letters had been received "from the working people" containing comments and suggestions on the bill. These letters were averredly considered by the Legislative Proposals Commissions of each house, which began "hearings" on the bill on June 25. When the bill came up for "debate," each house heard a report from its Legislative Proposals Commission. These reports were substantially alike, containing a total of 15 proposed changes, many of which Premier Bulganin had referred to in his speech at the opening session. The amendments, all of which were adopted, were generally in the direction of more liberal benefits for pensioners and will cost the state approximately 500 million rubles annually.

Apart from the two major reports, a total of 33 brief speeches were made on the draft legislation, many containing additional proposed amendments. After the "debate" was closed, Bulganin again appeared, this time before each house separately, and stated categorically which amendments were acceptable (all those made by the Legislative Proposals Commissions) and which had to be rejected (all amendments initiated by individual deputies on the floor). After the Premier spoke, the bill was voted upon, first in sections and then as a whole, each vote winning unanimous endorsement. No amendment which bore the official seal evoked objection, and no proposal which failed to gain the government's support was accorded the privilege of a floor vote. This procedure was essentially the same as that followed by past sessions of the Supreme Soviet in considering the state budget.

The "Reality-World" of a Soviet Citizen

There is no more difficult task for a student of another time or of another culture than that of trying to grasp what constitutes the reality-world of other people. Though every individual's reality-world is his alone, he is likely to share it in some degree with others who have had the same training and background. Also, to some degree, what a person perceives as reality—that is, what seems real to him—is determined by assumptions which he has learned. Again, a common training is likely to produce similar assumptions in those who share it. The three short paragraphs below illustrate one aspect of an assumption commonly and repeatedly taught to Soviet citizens. The source is: M. B. Mitin, *Soviet Democracy and Bourgeois Democracy*. Moscow: Foreign Languages Publishing House, 1950. Pp. 49–51.

One of the striking indexes of the majesty of Soviet democracy is the complete equality of rights exercised by women in the Soviet State. Lenin said that woman's position in society shows particularly clearly the difference between bourgeois and socialist democracy.

There is not a single bourgeois-democratic country in the world where women enjoy full equality of rights. In bourgeois countries women either play no part at all, or participate to a limited degree, in public and political life; female labour there is exploited and counted as the very cheapest. The proportion of female labour employed in the more important branches of industry, in the leading professions and in the different branches of culture, is negligible. Not a single bourgeois republic has given women equality with men, either formally or in fact.

The picture is absolutely different in the U.S.S.R. In the Soviet State women enjoy all rights to the full, on a par with men. They take a most active part in the economic, political and cultural life of the country, and fully and comprehensively display their creative abilities in the most diverse spheres of socialist construction. The history of the development of the Soviet State has shown what an enormous number of talented people, and of individuals with a capacity for organization are to be found among the masses of working women. Women occupy a place of honour in our country—in the kolkhozes and in industry, in all spheres of culture and science, in political and public organizations—and side by side with the menfolk are fulfilling the tasks facing the Soviet Land.

How the Party Operates (I)

There is usually a distinct difference between the official, formal descriptions of an institution and the way in which it is actually organized and operated. The ideals of organization and operation are usually only approximated at best, and often appear ignored or forgotten in practice. The description which follows emphasizes the facts as opposed to the theory, and shows how the rank and file party organizations really function. The material is from one of a series of analyses of the Soviet social system made for the United States Air Force by the Russian Research Center of Harvard University. The studies made use of published documentary materials, complemented by interviews with former Soviet citizens and by questionnaires. The research was conducted in 1950 and 1951. No similar material of more recent date is available for publication.

The selection consists of two unbroken excerpts from: Sidney Harcave, *Structure and Functioning of the Lower Party Organizations in the Soviet Union. Technical Research Report No. 23.* Maxwell AFB, Alabama: Air Research and Development Command, Human Resources Research Institute, January, 1954. Pp. iv, v, 47–49.

I

This report examines the *base of the party pyramid* in the Soviet Union along both its territorial and functional divisions. The research tools are the available written sources supplemented by oral interviews with DP's who had personal experience in party activities. Though dealing mainly with the late 1930's and early 1940's, these eyewitness accounts describe a party structure that has remained essentially unchanged today.

The aims of lower party organs are concentrated on the politicization of all activity, primarily production in factories, farms, and mines. Because of their share in responsibility for output according to plan, primary party organizations often find themselves pushed from their ideal vantage point as management's assistant and critic to the extremes of either usurping directorial functions or covering up management's shortcomings to avoid censures. Because of a smaller membership density and dispersal of the population in the countryside, rural party organizations have greater powers and responsibilities than their urban counterparts. The functions of party units in schools consist in the narrow interpretation of the party line and the execution of directives from higher party organs. Since the party membership of primary and secondary school teachers is low, directors who belong to the party, Young Communist students, and the district department of education serve as additional control mechanisms.

Controls on science exist on the higher, creative, as well as the lower, execution levels through respective party organs. Except for offices of the security police and the prosecutor, local government branches submit to local party control, too; higher government organs submit only their administrative practices to the scrutiny of their primary party organizations. There is also evidence of informal meetings and lines of communication between party officials in ministries. The territorial-functional principle of party organization is varied in the armed forces and transport where combined governmental-party organs take direct charge of political work.

The structure and rights of a primary party organization, which must consist of at least three party members, depend on its size. Primary organizations unite to form a district organization, consisting of a conference, the district committee, the bureau and the apparatus, in turn equipped with at least four departments: cadres, propaganda and agitation, organization and instruction, and military. Since the purges of the late 1930's district officers have been invariably hand-picked from above, receiving "confirmation" by a sham election of conference members. The bureaus seem to have embodied, in their weekly meetings, the major decision-making power for the district, and include the half-dozen or so key persons in the area.

The first secretary is in charge of the apparatus, responsible for the district committee, and ranks first socially as well as politically on the district scene. The instructor serves as a direct link with primary party organizations, while party organizers of the Central Committee act as roving agents of the center. The selection of key party and non-party personnel in its domain forms one of the few remaining sectors of autonomy for the primary organization.

Although the dissemination of full and timely information from the center to local party organizations is still the letter of party directives, the spirit gives members only as much as is considered necessary for them to know in order to fulfill their assigned tasks. The upward flow of information, however, has been emphasized, so that a variety of open and secret means is used to collect statistical, disciplinary, operational, and morale data. Besides several official channels used to cross-check each other, networks of informers and letters of complaint to the party or to newspapers afford ways of siphoning material to the leadership. While never complete, the downward flow of information was rather diversified and detailed until the end of the 1920's, but has become ever slighter since. Only a small inner circle has access to classified material; the mass of the party is fed on the same line available for the population at large.

The center's inspection services weaken the formal chain of command within the party; though keeping the leaders abreast of what is happening in the lower ranks, they make life for both rank-and-file party members and officials highly unstructured and uncertain. Complexity is introduced into the formal hierarchy by Party Control Commissions and "Party Life" departments of newspapers, not to mention the power of higher organs over primary unit personnel and decisions.

In addition to the formal requirements, unpublished rules operate to bar politically unreliable persons from party membership: those with records of arrest for political reasons, workers for the Germans under the occupation, and applicants with relatives abroad. The prime quality sought in party workers is loyalty, with formal education and specialized training increasingly important in recent years. Competence in primary organization work is frequently a means of attaining full-time party positions, though positions so gained seldom entail much responsibility. The full-time workers enjoy exemption from outside work and greater authority, prestige, and chances for advancement than the part-time workers who constitute the bulk of the officials on the lower levels.

In conclusion, (1) cycles of apathy and crisis are detected in the pace of party work at the primary level; (2) the myth that theory and practice are one is found necessary for the continued existence of the party; and (3) the primary party organizations are divided into officials serving as the regime's political superintendents and the rank and file exercising little power but gaining greater career chances and a feeling of importance and identification with the regime.

· · ·

II

The history of the Communist Party of the Soviet Union has been one of recurrent crises, of frequent purges, and numerous alterations in organizational forms. These periodic convulsions have been and apparently will continue to be part of a normal rather than an abnormal condition in the party. They are in part the result of the continuing effort of the leadership to force the development of the country at a pace too rapid to enlist the support of an overburdened populace; as a consequence frequent whipping-up drives are necessary. And in part they are—to make a simple statement about a far from simple situation—the product of the Soviet system of dictatorship.

Rulers in authoritarian systems like the Soviet one are constantly faced with the possibility of losing contact with the realities of life among their subjects, and the accompanying possibility of the development of weakening and destructive forces among them. To avoid this danger, each ruler tries to create an organ which will keep him accurately informed of real conditions without weakening, by its very existence, his powers. In Imperial China, the censorate was such an organ; in Nazi Germany, the *Sicherheitsdienst* was the chief one; in Russia, under Nicholas I, the Third Section. In the early days of the Soviet regime, the party was expected to serve the dictatorship as a self-adjusting mechanism incapable of weakening the dictatorial power, yet allowing it sufficient flexibility to preserve and perpetuate itself. Since then the political police has become another important means of maintaining contact with the real situation, but the party still provides significant service in that respect.

That the Soviet leaders have attempted to maintain the party as an instrument to provide flexibility to the regime is attested by the unrelenting stress on criticism and self-criticism. They want the lower party organs to uncover errors and shortcomings, to keep the center properly informed, and to show initiative. But the leaders' own policies make it difficult for the lower party organs to perform those tasks honestly. Centralization of power has steadily narrowed the area in which initiative can be applied; and unwarrantedly excessive punishment, meted out whenever the exercise of initiative has indicated any independence in policy-making, has turned the lower party functionaries and the rank-and-file members toward caution rather than initiative.

Another policy conflict arises from the effort to maintain incompatibles: one-man management and collective party control. The result of these conflicts is that the party recurrently shows a tendency to slow down: recruitment of members falls off, p.p.o. meetings are held infrequently, faults and shortcomings are concealed rather than revealed, and a spirit of apathetic bureaucratism overspreads the party. Then the old story begins to repeat itself: apathy is treated by shock therapy, and crises again become commonplace. Shake-ups in personnel and wholesale disciplinary actions follow; new leaders replace old ones, and older leaders are relieved of their positions or are demoted to lower ones where they can reflect on their follies and try to redeem themselves. In consequence, a new surge of energy sweeps through party work, but it can be expected to signify nothing more than the beginning of another cycle.

Many myths publicized by the Communist Party are dispelled by the simple expedient of comparing the party's theories with its practices. A study of lower party organizations brings into prominent focus a particular one: the myth of the single standard within the party. Accounts of party activity are filled with evidence that the theoretical single standard is wholly disregarded in practice and that actually a rigid double standard is applied. The highest party leaders may ignore basic party rules whenever it is convenient for them to do so; yet they condemn and punish lower party leaders who ignore the letter of the Party Charter. Lower party leaders are not only prohibited from treating these high-level derelictions as derelictions, but are also required to act as if the highest party leaders are shining examples of correct party behavior. The sins of the leaders may even become virtues. Thus the tenth anniversary of the opening of the Eighteenth Congress was treated as an occasion for rejoicing despite the fact that the Nineteenth Congress was *seven years overdue*. Stalin's practice of summoning government and party leaders personally to his office was treated as an example of proper collective leadership and not as an evidence of one-man rule. Directives which have been ignored for as many as twenty years are cited as if they were still operative and binding. In short, the lower party leaders and the rank and file are prohibited not only from saying that the emperor is naked but also from averting their eyes from his nakedness; like true gentlemen, they must look and act as if he were clothed.

Reason prompts one to believe that there must be some rationale for these conditions. Certainly the situations have not been deliberately manufactured, for the existence of a double standard and contrasts between theory and practice can at best only tax the credulity of the older party members. But the retention of rules and beliefs which have no basis in present-day reality is, apparently, deliberate. Belief in the myth that practice and theory are one is necessary for continued existence of the party. Its basic dogma is that it and it alone is the custodian of Marxist-Leninist orthodoxy, and to admit departure from orthodoxy would be to destroy that dogma.

Older party members, being aware of the disparity between theory and practice, either rationalize or anesthetize themselves to it. But the younger party members who do not remember the pre-Stalinist days of the party and who learn about them only from expurgated history may believe that myth is reality, that every act consummated in the Soviet Union is proof of the eternal truths of Marxism-Leninism as interpreted by Stalin. Knowing only Soviet "reality," they may believe that what they experience is in fact inner-party democracy.

If such beliefs can be engendered in the party member, his behavior can be directed into ways of usefulness to the regime without the danger that he will interpret the myths in ways adverse to it. He may, for example, be encouraged to exercise the right of "criticism and self-criticism" in such a way as to help the party center discover weaknesses in the work of the lower organizations without creating either the possibility of the undermining of the authority or that of organization of opposition. In his hands, party elections can serve as instruments with which the party center can restrain the lower leaders from abuse of their delegated authority. Although it is true that party elections are generally "means of registering assent rather than forums of free choice," party members have on occasion withheld their assent to the election of persons recommended from above; and, on such occasions, punishment went not to those casting the rejecting votes but to the persons rejected, for by Soviet logic the loss of a prearranged election could only prove that those rejected are unworthy.

In considering the place of lower party personnel in the general Soviet scheme, it is necessary to separate—roughly, at least—the party functionaries in the lower party organizations from the rank-and-file members. The functionaries are, broadly speaking, the directing and supervising agents of the regime. Together they make up a body of faithful, able, and experienced men in whom the regime places great (though far from complete) confidence as executors of its will. Or, to put it in a somewhat more realistic way, they make up the regime's corps of political superintendents and foremen.

One of their chief duties is to serve as propagators and guardians of the Communist gospel, the keepers and expounders of the sacred texts. If they were placed in Monnerot's picture of Communism as an atheistic form of Islam, they would be the *ulema,* the body of the learned.

The power exercised by these officials is determined by their position in the party hierarchy. It narrows down rapidly between the provincial and the district level and even more rapidly between the district and the p.p.o. levels. The power of district committees, as has been noted, varies in different parts of the country and in different branches of district life. Even within the committee, power is unevenly distributed; the first and occasionally the second and third secretaries outrank their colleagues by far, while many of the other functionaries are distinguished from the rank and file only by their responsibilities, not their privileges. The same diversity of power and position is also found among p.p.o. officials.

In considering the position of the rank-and-file members, it is well to distinguish between the subjective and objective meaning of being a rank-and-filer. The subjective meaning, of course, is elusive and not demonstrable by limited evidence; state of mind defies documentation. Former party members among the respondents could speak with authority only about themselves and a few intimate friends, and they were inclined, because of the nature of their positions as displaced persons, to color their recollections. Those who were never in the party could speak more authoritatively about the bearing of party members than about their state of mind; and, even on the subject of bearing, they were likely to over-generalize and to ignore historical changes in the position of the party rank and file. However, the statements of respondents showed enough agreement to give at least an impression of the subjective meaning of being a rank-and-file party member. Most non-party persons, when asked how one could distinguish between a party and a non-party person, replied that party members appeared to have confidence and a feeling of importance, and could be distinguished at a glance from the non-party persons, who seemed insecure and uncertain. A few respondents, some of them former party members, felt that only party functionaries felt self-confident and important while rank-and-filers felt themselves part of the gray masses.

On the matter of whether or not any of the original mood of the party is still left among its members, whether or not they still have any feeling of belonging to a body with a historical mission, a body set apart either because it is dedicated or because it is privileged, the same difficulties present themselves. One respondent told an illustrative story, probably fictitious, of a scene which he claimed to have witnessed in the 'twenties. A drunken worker was sitting on a dock in Saratov and cursing the Soviet regime with great abandon, while a man who appeared to be an ex-Menshevik (he was dressed like an intellectual, had a well-trimmed goatee and wore a pince-nez) sat nearby listening to him. Finally, the seeming ex-Menshevik offered his agreement with the worker—and received a sound rebuff for his interest. The worker jumped up, ready to fight, and shouted angrily, "I can curse the Soviets because they belong to us. But they don't belong to you; so keep quiet!"

Fictitious or not, the story illustrates a sense of identification with the regime which rank-and-file members, by all accounts, felt in the earlier years. Events since then have undoubtedly robbed party members of much if not all of that feeling of identification. But the distinction between party and non-party rank and file, small as it is now, may still give the party member a sense of belonging. There are some who at least feel privileged by 1) the right to attend closed party meetings at which discussion, limited though it is, is freer than at other meetings; 2) the right to transmit derogatory information through party channels; and 3) the right to be a propagandist, to harangue one's colleagues, to play roles allotted by the party, and to have access through the functionaries of the p.p.o. and the district committee to influence—even though its attainment is uncertain —which is denied to non-party persons.

The objective meaning of being a rank-and-filer is more easily determined. In recent years, he has had little real power and few privileges beyond those of the non-party rank-and-filer. He has no preferential position with respect to housing, food, or clothing, and he appears to have little with respect to type of employment. However, it is said that, all other conditions being equal, he will be chosen for a position in preference to a non-party person. Perhaps his most important advantage comes from the fact that entry into the party opens paths of advancement closed to others. Though not attained by many, responsible positions in the government bureaucracy, press, industry, agriculture, transportation, armed forces, police, foreign service, and the bureaucracy of the party come within the realm of the attainable upon his entry into the party.

The "Agitprop"

One of the very important agents of party control is the "agitprop," or agitator-propagandist, who interprets the party line and explains the party's will to the masses. The place and function of an agitprop are clearly set forth in the following article which also provides an excellent example of the famous "Bolshevik criticism and self-criticism." Note how the anonymous author first praises effective agitprops and then scolds those who fail to come up to the ideal. The source is: *Bloknot Agitatora* (*The Agitators' Notebook*), a biweekly publication of the Agitation and Propaganda Section of the Moscow Committee and the Moscow City Committee of the Communist Party of the Soviet Union. No. 13 (May, 1950). Pp. 20–27. The translation was made by Messrs. Richard Newell and James Richmond. Slightly abridged.

CONDUCT DAILY AGITATION WORK AMONG THE POPULATION

Bolshevik agitator! They meet him everywhere with love and esteem. He carries the ardent Bolshevik word; explains the policy of the party and government, [answers] questions of the international situation and foreign policy of the Soviet state; educates all his listeners in the spirit of Soviet patriotism.

The Soviet people warmly thank the agitators for their great work. How many letters are received by party organizations with the expression of sincere gratitude! Here, for example, the residents of house #3 on Staropanskaya Lane sent to the Party organization of the factory "Red Seamstress" such a letter:

"We, constituents, transmit our thanks to the agitators for the attention they have paid to us. Their talks, lively and absorbing, and also the clear answer to all inquiries, helped us to understand still more deeply the electoral system of the USSR and the entire situation in which the country of Soviets lives. We sincerely liked the considerate relation of the agitators to the residents of our house."

At the time of the elections to the Supreme Soviet of the USSR hundreds of thousands of agitators and propagandists of the capital and *oblasts* carried out mass-political work. Party organizations further strengthened their connections with the masses, accumulating the rich and varied experience of agitation-mass work among the population. Diversified forms of political agitation were employed widely: gatherings and meetings of constituents, meetings with candidates for the Supreme Soviet of the USSR, lectures and reports, group and individual talks, evenings of questions and answers, etc.

Wide circles of the party and komsomol actives, and non-party comrades carried on mass-political work. Up to one-third of the agitators led mass-political work for the first time.

In the period of the preparation for the elections to the Supreme Soviet of the USSR in Moscow and the *oblasts,* more than 4,500 agitation points stood as real centers of mass-political work among the population.

The most widespread forms of political agitation were the talks of agitators in apartments, dormitories and Red Corners. Here proceeded group and individual conversations with the constituents. Many agitators did not cease their work with the population for a number of years. An agitator of one of the party organizations of the Stalin *raion,* engineer Maria Sergeevna Khayurova, has carried on mass-political work among the residents of her home since 1945, conducting talks regularly.

In the city of Lyublino, lecturing bureaus were arranged for the constituents at the time of the election. Reports and lectures on political and scientific-instructive themes, etc., were conducted for the population.

At the time of the electoral campaign, the agitators carried on work differently with consideration [given] the inquiries and interests of the constituents. They arranged meetings separately for the youth and housewives. The political agitation also included invalids, pensioners, etc.

In Perov, for example, soirees of young constituents and organized cycles of lectures for youths were conducted. The lectures attracted 200–300 people to the auditorium.

Various forms of mass-cultural work had wide circulation in the pre-election campaign among the population: excursions to museums and exhibitions, collective visits to theatres and movies, television broadcasts, concerts with the forces of artistic self-improvement, literary evenings, organization of portable libraries in the homes, etc.

In the Krasnopolyanskii *raion* at the time of the elections to the Supreme Soviet of the USSR several agitation brigades worked. The brigades had automobiles at their disposal and served distant collective farms. Agitators presented reports and talks on political and scientific-instructive themes. With the help of the editorial staff of the collective, the agitation brigade gathered local material and issued a well-formulated wall newspaper.

The success of the work among the masses at the time of the electoral campaign was guaranteed by the increased quality of agitation. Party organizations systematically gathered agitators, gave them directions about the forms and methods of work, conducted an interchange of the experience of the agitators.

The agitators showed much attention and care about the satisfaction of the desires of the constituents. With the help of social actives and of Soviet organizations they assisted in deciding a number of questions concerning the improvement of the living conditions of the workers. Thus the agitators of the Central Statistical Administration under the Council of Ministers of the USSR achieved the speeding of major repairs on a house [and] the installation of gas in the apartments.

Rich experience of agitation work was accumulated from the time of the electoral campaign. Political work among the masses was raised to a new height. These achieved successes must be fortified. In many party organizations mass-political work at the time of the electoral campaign was summed up, having in view work among the population in the near future.

Agitators of the factory "Sickle and Hammer" continue the work in the former electoral district in the same form as at the time of the elections. Agitation points are preserved here. More than 500 agitators conduct talks among the population regularly. In the former electoral district No. 47, after March 12th, agitators conducted 200 talks. At all agitation points agitators are on duty.

Agitators of the "Stalinogorskugol" trust and of Mine No. 26 continue mass-political work among the population. In Lyublino a lecturing bureau works as before.

The experience of the organization of agitation brigades in the Krasnopolyanskii *raion* and Moscow *oblast* is utilized even after the elections. An agitation brigade is formed for the accommodation of the workers of the MTS [Machine Tractor Station] in the period of the sowing. The agitation points continue their work in a number of collectives of the *raion*. Here talks and reports are conducted about the spring sowing, about the three-year plan for the development of animal husbandry, on international themes, etc.

The agitation collective of the Central Statistical Administration under the Council of Ministers of the USSR does not break off close communication with the population in their homes. Here a list of desires is compiled, showing the agitators the nature of the requests of the workers and their families, which they [the agitators] answer in order that concrete measures be taken.

However, many agitators, after the elections to the Supreme Soviet of the USSR, ceased mass-political work among the population. There are agitation collectives where, after March 12th, not one agitator went to a home where he had carried on work at the time of the elections. This is incorrect. Our party demands that the connection of the agitators with the workers at their homes not be cut off, that the agitators systematically conduct work with the population. The agitation points must be preserved. They must be used for reports and mass-cultural measures. As before, libraries, clubs and Red Corners of enterprises and institutions can prove a great help in the work.

The task of the leaders of the agitation collectives is not only not to decrease the number of agitators, who worked among the population, but to attract new agitators to the work, to correct their work, to systematically train, to furnish necessary materials, newspapers and literature. Special attention must be paid to the raising of the quality of mass-agitation work. In order to explain clearly and well the movement of events, the policy of our party, the international and domestic situation, to broaden the political scope of the workers, the agitator himself must increase his knowledge, work by himself, study deeply the works of Marx, Engels, Lenin and Stalin, read newspapers, magazines, and political literature.

The sacred responsibility of the agitator is to educate the workers in the Communist spirit, to lift them to the struggle for new successes in the building of Communism.

It is necessary even now, after the elections, to carry on work selectively, considering the needs of various groups of the population— housewives, youths, etc.

Individual and group talks, lectures and reports, meetings with scholars, writers, poets, artists, collective visits, to theatres and moving pictures, evenings of questions and answers, literary evenings, organization of agitation brigades and other forms and methods of political agitation, which were applied at the time of the elections, must be even further practiced in the work in former electoral districts.

In all mass-political work with the population, the social active, who must be widely utilized even in the future, proves a great help to the agitators.

The duty of all agitation collectives is to carry on mass-political work daily among the population, to strengthen the positive experience of the work, accumulated from the time of the elections to the Supreme Soviet of the USSR.

The Agricultural Problem

No problem faced by the Soviet regime from Lenin to Khrushchev was so persistent, more stubborn, and less susceptible of solution than the agricultural problem. Actually, it was not one problem, but an agglomerate of interrelated problems involving climate, soil fertility and arability; farming methods and equipment; peasant aspirations, apprehensions, and needs; planning and administration. Significant information on various aspects sometimes can be found in unlikely places. The selection below consists of excerpts from speeches before the second session (1938) of the first Supreme Soviet on "The State Horse Tax on Individual Peasant Farms." The speakers touched on the following points, among others: the policy of collectivization, its successes and failures to date; private property; the techniques of administration and the use of coercion; and the reality of power. The speeches are quoted from the official, verbatim report of the session. The bill which the speakers were discussing was adopted unanimously by both chambers of the Supreme Soviet, and went into immediate effect.

By way of a very brief background it may be pointed out that the forcible collectivization of agriculture during the Second Five Year Plan represented one of Stalin's greatest successes, his most dangerous gamble, and his most ruthless action. Lenin had tried but failed to accomplish the socialization, so-called, of agriculture. It had been one of the objectives of the First Five Year Plan, but it was not achieved then. Stalin recognized that he could not build "a socialized state" unless he could get the peasants—the majority of the Soviet people—into "socialized organizations." The continuance of his regime depended upon his doing so, but peasant opposition, though disorganized, was extremely strong. He spared no pains and no persons to win his gamble. Literally millions of peasants were deprived of their homes, their possessions, their families, their freedom, and their lives. By brutality combined with later concessions, Stalin won his gamble, collectivized agriculture, and saved his regime.

The material below indicates that the peasants were still fighting rear-guard actions in 1938 though the main struggle was then over. Statements in the Soviet press as late as 1962 indicated that peasant opposition to collectivization and "socialist discipline" still remained a problem.

Speech of R. E. Melnikov (Smolensk Rural Area, Smolensk Region) in the Union Soviet.

Comrades, members of the Supreme Soviet. I move that the Bill on the State Horse Tax on Individual Farms introduced by the Legislative Bills Commission of the Soviet of the Union be passed *in toto*.

This Bill is an expression of the Stalin policy of our Bolshevik Party and Government in the countryside, which is directed towards strengthening the collective farms in all ways, towards their further development and the transformation of all collective farms into Bolshevik collective farms and all collective farmers into prosperous farmers.

The Bolshevik Party, under the leadership of Comrade Stalin, has achieved historic victories in the bitter struggle against the most malicious enemies of the people. Agriculture has been reconstructed along Socialist lines on the basis of collective and state farms, on the basis of the introduction of modern machine technique into the process of agricultural production. Our Party, under the leadership of the great genius of toiling humanity, Joseph Vissarionovich Stalin, has solved the most difficult and complex problem of the Socialist revolution in our country.

The collective farm system in the countryside has conquered finally and irrevocably. The collective farm peasantry is a loyal, steadfast support of the Soviet power. The collective farms have inexhaustible opportunities for further increasing the harvest yields and carrying out Stalin's slogan of producing 7,000,000,000–8,000,000,000 poods of grain annually.

In his report at the Extraordinary Eighth All-Union Congress of Soviets, Comrade Stalin characterized our Soviet peasantry with exceptional vividness. He said: "Our Soviet peasantry is an entirely new peasantry. In our country there are no longer any landlords and kulaks, merchants and usurers to exploit the peasants. Consequently, our peasantry is a peasantry emancipated from exploitation. Further, our Soviet peasantry, the overwhelming majority, is a collective farm peasantry, i.e., it bases its work and wealth, not on individual labour and on backward technical equipment but on collective labour and up-to-date technical equipment. Finally, the farming of our peasantry is based, not on private property, but on collective property, which has grown up on the basis of collective labour.

"As you see, the Soviet peasantry is an entirely new peasantry, the like of which the history of mankind has never known before."

Comrades, the broad masses of the collective farm peasantry fully understand that their prosperous, cultured and happy life is inseparably linked up with the growth and consolidation of the national economy and the defensive power of the great Union of Soviet Socialist Republics. Therefore the peasant collective farmers manifest a high political level in their comprehension of state tasks. Therefore the collective farm peasantry considers honest Bolshevik fulfillment of all its obligations to the Soviet state its prime duty.

I should like to dwell on a few facts characterizing the tremendous changes which have taken place in agriculture in the Smolensk Region during the years of the Stalin Five-Year Plan periods. Before the revolution the overwhelming majority of the peasants in the old Smolensk Province owned but insignificantly small plots of land and eked out a miserable existence. Under pressure of landlord and kulak bondage the peasants abandoned the villages in search of remunerative work. Now 94.5 per cent of the peasant households in our region have united in collective farms and are therein building a happy, joyous and prosperous life. Thanks to the solicitude of the Bolshevik Party, the Soviet Government and our great Stalin personally, the collective farm peasantry of our Region has at its disposal modern agricultural technique. A total of 85 machine and tractor stations, 4,500 tractors, over 600 harvester combines, 1,750 flax pullers, complex threshing machines, tractor sowers and other agricultural machines are operating on the collective farm fields of the Smolensk Region. Modern agricultural technique has brought about fundamental changes in peasant labour, made it lighter and ensured a rapid expansion of the sown area, primarily of the area sown to the most important industrial crop in our region—flax. These successes forcefully demonstrate the brilliant results of the Stalin policy of collectivization of agriculture, achieved on the basis of the development and consolidation of the collective farm system.

The enemies of the people—the Right and Trotskyite traitors to their fatherland—having wormed their way into the leadership of what was formerly the Western Region, tried with all their might to retard the growth of the collective farms, used wrecking methods to disrupt collective farm economy, created conditions that were more favourable for the individual peasants than for the collective farmers. As a result of this hostile work the percentage of collectivization of peasant households in the region remained on one and the same level for a long time.

On January 1, 1938, there were 29,000 individual farms in the region, or 6.4 per cent of the total number of farms. Of these individual farms, 11,394 owned horses, and many of the individual peasants used these horses not for agricultural work on their farms but for purposes of speculation and profiteering.

There were many cases in our region where as a result of the subversive activities of wreckers, as a result of the fact that local Soviet government organs in the region violated the decisions of the Party and the Government concerning non-collective farm peasants, the individual peasants were either not taxed at all or were taxed less than was due, not all the sources of income being estimated. For instance, in the Andreyevsky district of the Smolensk Region, the individual peasant Peter Belmachev owned two draught horses, large cattle [*sic*] and a large number of small livestock. All this property was incorrectly taxed. The amount of the tax was obviously underestimated, and even this reduced tax was systematically left unpaid.

For a number of years the local finance organs did not apply the measures required by law to compel this individual farm to carry out its obligations. In the village of Vertensk in the Duminich district, an individual peasant woman by the name of Senyushkina, who owned two horses, regularly used them not for her own agricultural work but for purposes of profiteering, engaging in carting and stacking bark. It is characteristic that in estimating the tax on Senyushkina's farm, the local organs took no account of this main source of income. The wrecking practice whereby the local Soviet organs tolerated cases of under-taxation with regard to individual farms had a harmful effect on the economic growth and consolidation of the collective farms and gave rise to unhealthy sentiments among some collective farmers.

Thanks to the exceptional sagacity of our great leader, Comrade Stalin, the glorious Soviet Intelligence service, headed by the Stalinite Commissar N. I. Yezhov, exposed and destroyed the hornets' nest of the Right and Trotskyite hirelings of fascism.

The Central Committee of the CPSU(B) and the Government rendered the Smolensk Region tremendous assistance, ensuring the successful elimination of the consequences of wrecking activities in agriculture.

The decisions of the Council of People's Commissars of the USSR and the Central Committee of the CPSU(B) adopted on April 19, 1938—"On the Prohibition of the Expulsion of Collective Farmers from Collective Farms," "On the Incorrect Distribution of Income in Collective Farms" and "On Taxes and Other Duties on Individual Peasant Farms"—played a big role in strengthening the collective farms and in rapidly eliminating the consequences of wrecking activities in agriculture.

These decisions vividly reflect the Stalinite solicitude for the collective farms and collective farmers.

In our Smolensk Region, 7,446 peasant farms entered collective farms during the first half of 1938.

It is our most important task to liquidate in a Bolshevik manner the consequences of wrecking activities in the agriculture of the region.

The Bill on the State Horse Tax on Individual Peasant Farms, which is up for adoption by the Session of the Supreme Soviet, meets the desires of the broad masses of collective farmers. This law will be a powerful weapon with which to suppress the profiteering carried on by the non-collective farm peasants. It will facilitate the still greater consolidation and development of Socialist agriculture, the further growth of a prosperous, cultured and happy life for the collective farm peasantry.

Comrades, we are all certain that our great Socialist fatherland will achieve wonderful new successes in all fields of Socialist construction in town and country. A guarantee of this is the fact that we are guided by the glorious Bolshevik Party, that we are being led from victory to victory by the great leader of toiling humanity, a man of the most profound wisdom and steel will—our own great Stalin. (Applause.)

* * * * *

Speech of A. S. Yezhov (Budyonny Area, Ordjonikidze Territory) in the Union Soviet. Somewhat abridged.

Comrades . . . I fully support the motion to pass the Bill. . . .

The collective farm system has been finally and irrevocably victorious. . . . As Deputy Ugarov said here, 93 per cent of the peasant households are united in collective farms. A total of 99 per cent of the sown area of the farms in our country belongs to the collective farms. . . .

Comrades, the Bill . . . is a document of great political importance. In our country only 7 per cent of the peasantry are on individual farms. But even this insignificant proportion of individual peasants demands serious attention. We cannot allow part of the working people—the individual peasants—to disregard Soviet laws. . . . We cannot permit individual farms to find themselves in more favourable conditions than the collective farmers.

At the plenum of the Leningrad Regional and City Committees of the CPSU(B) on October 10, 1934, the unforgettable Sergei Mironovich Kirov said: "If we want to complete the collectivization of our region, we must, first, actually ensure the advantage of the collective farmers over the individual peasants, and, second, compel the individual peasants to fulfill their state and social obligations as they should be fulfilled."

The facts are that some individual farms which own horses do not fulfill their state and social obligations from year to year. Thus . . . [in the district where I work as Party secretary] there are 625 individual farms. The majority of them own horses but from year to year fulfill neither their plans of agricultural work nor all their obligations to the state.

The enemies of the people who operated in the territory encouraged and cultivated this anti-state practice. Individual farms took absolutely no part in the repair work of our hospitals, schools, reading rooms and clubs, or in road construction, but they enjoyed the results of the work of the collective farmers. I am not opposed to the individual peasants using the schools, hospitals and roads built with the help of the collective farmers. They should enjoy all the benefits created in our country. But I am opposed to the practice of rotten liberalism on the part of some local officials in respect to those individual peasants who do not fulfill their social and state obligations. . . .

* * * * *

Excerpts from the speech of A. I. Ugarov (Smolny Area, City of Leningrad) before a joint sitting of the two chambers of the Supreme Soviet, party and government leaders being present.

. . . The Legislative Bills Commission . . . has charged me to report to you on the . . . Bill. Day by day the collective farm system in our country is gaining in strength. . . . The toiling peasants all over the world, languishing under the yoke of bourgeois, landlord and kulak exploitation, and burdened by imposts and taxes of all kinds, can see in the collective farm system in our country a great example of how life can be made new, free and bright. . . .

Our Constitution, as you know, permits the existence and operation of the small private economy of individual peasants and handicraftsmen, based on their personal labour and precluding the exploitation of the labour of others. We cannot, however, overlook the fact that the individual peasants indulge in economic practices which actually represent a circumvention of the Soviet laws and an infringement of the interests of the collective farmers and of the Soviet state. The economic activities of the individual peasants are sometimes of a nature that places the individual peasant farm in an advantageous position as compared with the collective farm—a state of affairs which is fundamentally at variance with the policy of our Communist Party and of our Soviet State. . . .

As far back as February 1933 . . . Comrade Stalin said that "one section of the individual peasants has become utterly corrupt and gone in for profiteering." The use of horses for profiteering purposes has become quite widespread. The individual peasants are sometimes known to purchase additional horses for the same profiteering purposes. In the Chernigov region . . . between August 1, 1937, and August 1, 1938, 938 horses were purchased by individual peasants. Of these, 718 horses are being used for carting and 167 in logging and peat extraction. . . . The incomes derived . . . amount to quite big sums . . . as much as 4,000–6,000 rubles a year, and sometimes even more, per farm. . . .

The widespread use of horses for profiteering undermines the discipline of the individual peasants as regards discharging all their duties to the state, furnishes them with an opportunity to evade the Soviet law, and has a decidedly bad influence on the less stable elements among the collective farmers. This state of affairs, comrades, cannot but have an undesirable effect on the remaining individual peasants as regards their joining collective farms.

It is in order to put a stop to the practice of individual peasants using their horses for profiteering, in order to improve the discipline of individual peasants as regards carrying out all their duties to the state, and in order to do away with the harmful influence which the individual peasants who have gone in for profiteering exert on the less stable elements among the collective farmers, that the Legislative Bills Commission has submitted to the Session the Bill on a State Horse Tax on Individual Peasant Farms.

* * * * *

Farms and Farming

Under the Exchange Agreement signed in 1958 there were inter-
changes of visits between Soviet and American specialists, students,
and others. One group of American specialists on the mechanization of
agriculture made a thirty-day visit to the Soviet Union in the late summer of 1958. Much of the group's report was highly technical, but the
three excerpts below are of wider interest. The original order of the
the material has been changed. The source is: *Farm Mechanization in
the Soviet Union. Report of a Technical Study Group.* Washington:
Government Printing Office, November, 1959. Pp. 8–10, 6–8, 30.

A collective farm is called a "voluntary association of peasant farmers."
The collective farm members "elect" or sustain a chairman, who may be
selected from outside the membership. They also endorse a board selected
from the membership. The number of board members varies among farms.

One collective farm we visited has a board of 11 and a revision committee of 7. Another has a board of 9 and a revision committee of 5. The
chairman and the board members are elected for a term of 1 or 2 years,
but any of them can be ousted by decision of a general meeting at any
time.

Each collective farm holds monthly management conferences, division
meetings, and an annual meeting (which sometimes lasts all day).

The chairman, along with the collective farm board, draws up the program for the year. He must report at the annual meeting.

Each collective farm has a District Executive Committee made up of
specialists who are employees of the Republic. This committee inspects and
supervises the collective farm operations, sets quotas, approves programs,
and sees that plans are carried out on the farms. The Communist Party
organization also supervises.

It is part of the function of the Ministry of Agriculture of the Republic
(within the framework laid down by the U.S.S.R. Ministry of Agriculture) to oversee the work of its regional and district committees. The
budget is approved by the Ministry of Agriculture of the Republic.

Detailed records are kept of work performed, and each worker shares
in the income of the common enterprise.

We were told that each month the collective farmers get an advance
on future income. At the end of the year, when all information is in and
recorded, a final distribution of income is made to each member on the
basis of workday units and work performance norms.

Each collective farm family is allowed to use a small plot of land (usually not exceeding 1 acre) for a garden, fruit trees, raising chickens, a
cow, a few pigs, and similar enterprises.

We learned of various schemes and efforts to get the farmers to spend
less time on their own plots and more effort on the large collective enterprises. For example, the collective farm sometimes sells the farmer milk

for one-half or one-third the price received for milk delivered to the combine.

Outstanding workers who have filled many times their quotas or their daily norms are rewarded for their efforts, and they are held up as ideals to work toward. People are paid incentives for production over quotas or for their efforts to reach the records set by the people who have received awards.

Officials claim that what is inspiring to the people is that these innovators or front-rank workers enjoy fame and honor and become distinguished people regardless of their origin—whether they have been peasants, executives, or government workers, or leaders in the Communist Party.

Here in essence is what we were told at the Lenin Collective Farm near Zaporozhe:

At the annual meeting, a board of nine people is elected, also a separate revision board of five people. They determine the amount of work that is to be considered a workday and the days on which workers are paid.

For technical advice, a Regional Agricultural Executive Committee of 18 is elected. Each oblast nominates one candidate for the executive committee. When we inquired further, we were told that there are really two elections. One is the election of the electoral committee by open ballot. Most of these people are from trade unions. Then there is the final vote on the candidate by secret ballot.

This committee meets at least once a year. If a worker is dissatisfied with his pay for workday units, he sees this committee, which sets quotas and workday units.

The committee elects its own chairman, and its decisions must be approved by a general meeting of the able-bodied people who have a right to vote. At the annual meeting, the general body can disapprove and change the workday units. Work units may be changed from year to year as output varies. Differences in work units between collective farms are not great.

The committee has a number of divisions such as education, public health, and agriculture (Regional Agricultural Board).

When some emergency arises that is not covered by the program for the year (such as costs or revision of the building program), a meeting is called.

We were told that if a state official finds something he thinks is not right on the farm, he can make recommendations for consideration by the chairman and the board, but the final decision rests with the farmers at their general assembly.

At the Telman Collective Farm, Minsk Region, the chairman's salary is based on 120 workdays per month. This is fixed at a general meeting and amounts to 2,500 rubles per month, plus 1 per cent of the farm's gross income. The salaries of the agronomist and the agricultural engineer are 80 per cent of that of the chairman (or 96 workdays), plus ½ of 1 per cent of the gross income.

A norm is set on this farm, but a good worker can fill two or three norms in 1 day. The norms, as recommended by a committee, must be approved at a general meeting on the farm. A quorum consists of three-quarters of the able-bodied workers.

Rather than altering the base pay of tractor drivers and other skilled workers the number of workday credits per actual day worked is increased, possibly up to 3 workday units per day.

This farm has a Regional Executive Committee supervised by employees of the Republic's Ministry of Agriculture. This committee has several divisions, including education and agriculture. Probably some committee members are elected, but most are staff people; and they supervise the details of operation of the collective farm.

As the name indicates, state farms are outright state enterprises. All farmworkers, from the directors to the field workers, are employees of the state.

State farms often operate alongside collective farms. Virtually all "new lands" agricultural developments are state farms, and more and more farmland is coming under state farm operation. There are indications that government leaders would like all farms eventually to be state farms.

State farms are favored for electrification, mechanization, and other modernization. For example, we were told that 40 per cent of the collective farms have electricity, whereas all state farms are electrified.

State farms are larger than collective farms. As stated earlier, the MTS's did not serve state farms, as each farm owned its own equipment, but now the RTS's serve state farms just as they do collective farms.

A state farm is responsible to the Regional Executive Committee of the Republic's Ministry of Agriculture, which is under the supervision of the U.S.S.R. Ministry of Agriculture.

Each employee is paid wages and each family has the use of a small plot, somewhat similar to the system on collective farms.

Some state farms are general farms, but most are specialized, such as grain, dairy, and sugar beet farms.

There are trade unions for state farms for all the U.S.S.R. We asked whether it was necessary for a worker to belong and were told, "It is not compulsory but very convenient, and all do." There are no strikes.

· · ·

As mechanization of agriculture increased in importance in Soviet planning, it was necessary to devise a way to apply this technology. Who would own the equipment? Who would operate it? How would it be maintained and kept in repair?

Since no land was privately owned and it was impossible for individual farmers to own and maintain tractors and other equipment, a system within the framework of a universally socialized agriculture had to be devised. Farms were being collectivized throughout the U.S.S.R.

So, in 1928, the first so-called Machine Tractor Station was set up. The MTS owned the equipment in the name of the state; and each strategically located station allocated the equipment to the various collective farms in its immediate vicinity.

Repair facilities were installed. A program to train maintenance personnel was established at institutes set up for this specific purpose. The idea and organization spread, until by 1957 more than 8,000 Machine Tractor Stations were in operation.

The system multiplied many problems. Management of the collective farms was separate from the centrally-owned tractors and equipment. We were told, however, that the equipment was usually field-operated by residents and employees of the farms. There was contradiction on this point.

The MTS built up great power, kept detailed records, and virtually spelled life or death to a farm enterprise because the farm was subservient to the allocation of equipment.

The MTS not only furnished the equipment, but was responsible for technical personnel, major repairs, supply of lubricants and fuel, and supervision of work accomplished with equipment. By 1957, we were told, these stations employed more than 2 million tractor drivers, mechanics, and other semitechnical people. By 1957, it was estimated that more than 277,000 specialists in all phases of agriculture, including tractor and equipment operators, were functioning.

By officials' own admissions, the divided responsibility between the MTS's and the managers of collective farms often caused delays, duplication, misunderstanding, and general inefficiency.

In 1958, following a lengthy speech by Khrushchev, it was decreed that the MTS's would be replaced by Repair Technical Stations. Ownership of tractors and equipment was to be taken over by the farms, and necessary services would be handled by the RTS's.

We were told that impartial committees were set up to appraise the equipment and to help determine the prices that should be paid by the farms for the used equipment being transferred from the state-owned MTS's to the state-controlled collective farms.

At the time of our visit, much of this transfer of ownership had been carried out.

State farms have always had jurisdiction over the equipment they use. Therefore, with the abolition of the MTS's, collective farms may gradually approach a par with state farms, so far as equipment is concerned.

Whereas the MTS serviced about 10 or more collective farms, one RTS now services the farms previously covered by 3, 4, or more MTS's.

The RTS assembles orders for tractors and equipment from the farms and then forwards requests to the planning agencies so that production schedules can be worked out for delivery of equipment on a quarterly basis.

Collective and state farms place their requests with the Repair Technical Station for equipment they want to purchase during the year and take
delivery each quarter. These requests are submitted to the Ministry of
Agriculture. The Ministry assembles them, and they are discussed by the
Scientific Council of Agriculture.

The Scientific Council of Agriculture then takes its recommendations
of GOSPLAN, the overall planning and control group.

GOSPLAN fits the recommendations into the general overall economy and designates which factories will produce what and how many.

The RTS not only distributes the manufactured equipment to the farms,
but also does the major repair work on all equipment, especially tractors,
and in most cases supplies fuel, oil, grease, fertilizers, pesticides and other
supplies, and important technical and supervisory services attendant to the
farm equipment industry. It also displays equipment and holds demonstrations, distributes literature, and performs other general services and
educational functions relating to the mechanization of agriculture.

The RTS has its own staff of workers, technicians, engineers, and
other necessary help. Each year it makes agreements with the farms it
serves and by which it is paid for services performed.

The RTS still has rather rigid control over operation of tractors. For
example, daily reports on amount of work done and fuel consumed are
mandatory.

No equipment can be traded in, although a farm can sell used equipment to another farm if a buyer can be found.

Nearly every collective and state farm had fairly good machine shop
and repair facilities; but for major repair jobs, tractors and equipment are
taken to the RTS's.

It is a rather determined practice to have every tractor brought to the
RTS for a complete overhaul once every 2 years, but apparently the farms
have some choice as to when they bring them in and what repairs are
made. The facilities we saw at the RTS's were good.

When the RTS repairs an engine or replaces one in a tractor, the farm
is charged the cost of the repairs plus rental of equipment used while repairs are in progress. We were told that the average cost of rebuilding a
tractor is about 29 per cent of the original cost.

During the peak season the RTS, tractor operators, and combine
operators work "around the clock." The operators work in two shifts,
10 hours each.

Drivers and operators are trained in trade schools. A "Review Commission" considers both practical tests and written tests prior to issuing
operators' licenses. Licenses are issued in two grades, 1st and 2d, and
operators are relicensed each year.

Our group visited several RTS's including one at Kharkov and another near Krasnodar.

The Kharkov RTS provides service to 19 farms and 50 other enterprises, in an area approximately 50 kilometers in radius. It has about 40
personnel, including 20 engineers and other technical men, and provides

service for more than 200 tractors and 100 combines. In addition, about 60 machine operators work on the farms and cooperate in repair programs with the RTS. Two-way radios connecting the RTS and the tractor and combine brigade camps, together with mobile repair shops, help to keep the machines operating during rush times.

A schedule of repair and maintenance of tractors and machines is set up by agreement with the collective and state farms, the major overhauls taking place during the autumn and winter. The machine operators help the repair staff. Complete disassembly and repair is given a tractor at about 4,500 hectares ([or] approximately 10,000 hours).

The Kharkov RTS adds about 12.8 per cent to the "factory" price of the machines as a handling charge. It accepts no trade-ins. The RTS sends out forms on which orders are placed for machines and tractors. Orders for 1959 tractors and combines had been placed prior to our visit on September 5, 1958. This RTS does not conduct an educational program. Repair kits and subunit parts (such as fuel pumps, transmissions, and starting engines) are available for sale or temporary replacement while damaged units are being repaired. The RTS has special machines for rent to prevent crop disasters.

This RTS is self supporting, with the exception of three state-paid specialists—the chief inspector, inspector, and agronomist. The agronomist is concerned with diseases, pest control, and the like, whereas the inspectors are concerned with the proper use and maintenance of all tractors and machines. They give advice and recommendations regarding care and maintenance. If no attention is given to "advice" the inspector has the authority to suspend the operator's license. He has authority to collect damage costs from the salary of the operator if the damage is due to negligence or misuse. Collection is arranged through the bookkeeper for the farm. The judgment of the inspector is based on "well-known" rules of operation. An example is the rule for "thorough inspection" after 1,500 hours of operation. If the rule is not complied with, there is first a warning and then some action by the inspector. The record keeper for the brigade makes daily reports on the kinds of operation and the machines used with each tractor.

The new parts building of the Kharkov RTS was relatively small. They had a nice machine shop, a short assembly line for the repaired tractors, engine dynamometers, fuel injection unit repair and test section, sheds for new machines, fuel delivery trucks, repair trucks, and a large area surrounding the buildings.

The Krasnodar RTS is similar to but larger than the Kharkov RTS. It has responsibility for 450 tractors, 400 trucks, and 150 grain combines. There are 180 workers plus 31 engineers and other technicians.

Machine Test Stations (MTS's), as their name implies, were organized to evaluate the prototype machines developed by the various research and machine building institutes and construction bureaus. Our group visited several MTS's and found the time both interesting and profitable. We were told that 23 MTS's are now functioning and 3 more are being organized.

The testing season is from April to December. The usual practice is to test two machines of each model. The factory representative may be present and, if he disagrees with the findings, he may write a report which is considered by the Scientific Council of the Agricultural Ministry. Results of the tests are published in the Agricultural Ministry magazine, "Tractors and Agricultural Machines." We were told that in the near future bulletins will be published showing specifications, identification of the manufacturing plant, and test results.

The "state" standards for testing machines and tractors are prepared by many scientists from the different educational and research institutes and approved by the Scientific Council. Reports on tests, covering quality of work, labor required, reliability, ease of handling, safety, amount of metal used in construction and the like, are made to the Council.

·   ·   ·

(Summary) The manufacture and distribution of farm machinery in the U.S.S.R. is controlled by GOSPLAN, the overall state planning commission. GOSPLAN is divided into about 25 sections; one section is concerned with automobiles, tractors and farm equipment. Although many older machines show evidence of being patterned after U.S. models, new machines are largely of Soviet design. The machinery manufactured in the U.S.S.R. is on display in the impressive All-Union Agricultural and Industrial Exhibit in Moscow.

Machine Tractor Stations, the first of which was established in 1928, formerly owned and managed the equipment used on collective farms. However, state farms owned and operated their own machinery. The divided responsibility between the machine tractor stations and the collective farms apparently resulted in general inefficiency and, in 1958, ownership of the machines was taken over by the collective farms. At this time Repair Technical Stations (RTS's) were set up for central control of major repairs and other services.

Machine Test Stations, not to be confused with Machine Tractor Stations, have been organized to evaluate prototype machines developed by the various research and machine building institutes and bureaus. Twenty-three test stations were operating at the time of our visit.

Farm machines are produced in subassembly and assembly lines, similar to those in the U.S.A., but with less output per worker. The work week in the factories, at the time of our visit, was 43½ hours. Production incentives are highly regarded as a way of increasing production per worker. Goals are established for each plant and awards made to those who meet and exceed the quota. Premiums are also paid to designers for developing machines that gain acceptance.

Farm building development in the U.S.S.R. has lagged behind farm machinery development. Electricity is used for many tasks around the farmstead, such as grain cleaning and operation of milking machines. It is also available in many of the homes but is used principally for lighting and not for appliances.

As in the U.S.A., institutions for educating the Soviet "agricultural engineer" carry on programs of research as well as teaching. In addition, other research institutes and construction bureaus are charged specifically with the development of new machines. The institutes appear to be staffed by competent engineers who were well equipped with research tools and instruments.

The U.S.S.R. has seven institutes for the mechanization and electrification of agriculture where agricultural engineers are trained. The typical engineering diploma graduate (approximately equal to a B.S. degree in the U.S.A.) will have completed 10 years in grade and high school plus 5 years of institute study or he will have completed 7 years of grade school plus 4 years of technical high school plus 5 years of institute study. Graduate work is offered in some institutes.

Birobidzhan: Two Views

Few aspects of Soviet life have been more boastfully reported or more vigorously contested than those dealing with the question of nationalities. The first statement below is typical of official Soviet reporting on this subject, with special attention to anti-Semitism and to the so-called Jewish homeland, The Jewish Autonomous Province of Birobidzhan. The source is: M. Chekalin, *The National Question in the Soviet Union.* New York: Workers Library Publishers, 1941. Pp. 3, 24–25. The second, contrasting statement is from a pamphlet published by "Jews in Eastern Europe" (London, no date but probably 1961.) The author was Moshe Abramovich, and the title is *Jews in the 1959 Soviet Population Census: An Analysis.* Pp. 7, 15–16.

Numerous nationalities inhabit the Soviet Union. Like an older brother, the great [*sic*] Russian people have helped the formerly exploited peoples rise from poverty and disfranchisement to economic prosperity and cultural progress, to political equality and independent state life. All the peoples of the land of socialism live in peace and friendship with one another. This peaceful collaboration of the various nationalities, inconceivable under capitalist conditions, has been fully successful on the basis of socialism. . . .

The position of the Jews in the U.S.S.R. is a particularly striking example of the triumph of Soviet nationality policy. In July, 1918, by a Soviet Government decree signed by V. I. Lenin, anti-Semitism was proclaimed a criminal offense. In the very first days of its existence, the Soviet power created a number of Jewish national districts in the Ukraine and in Byelorussia, where there is a concentrated Jewish population, and in 1934 a Jewish Autonomous Region—Birobidjan—was formed in the Far East.

For the first time in the history of the Jewish people its ardent desire to create its own homeland, to create its own national state system has materialized. Under the leadership of the great Bolshevik Party and actively supported by all sections of Soviet society, the Jewish toiling masses are developing and consolidating a Soviet state system in Birobidjan, whose forms correspond to the customs and modes of life of their people. The Jewish Autonomous Region consists of five districts and occupies a territory of 80,000 square kilometers. It is being settled by Jewish working people who are voluntarily migrating there from all the republics of the Soviet Union as well as from abroad.

Now that they have their own state and their own land, the Jewish collective farmers are successfully engaging in socialist agriculture and achieving splendid results, refuting indeed the age-old bourgeois-philestine falsehood that the Jewish people is unable to master agricultural labor. A number of factories and mills have been erected in the city of Birobidjan. A new, socialist culture is developing in the native language of the Jewish people.

The formation of the first and only Jewish autonomous region in the world is the most striking proof to the working people of the world that only under the conditions of a Soviet system is the complete social and national emancipation of the oppressed nationalities possible, that only in the land of socialism does the economic and cultural life of the national minorities truly flourish.

* * * * *

On May 10th, 1959, the Soviet press carried general figures on the "preliminary results" of the census, and comparisons with previous censuses indicating a population increase in the Soviet Union. These numbers contain no reference to Jews, but the following figures on the population of Birobidzhan, the Jewish Autonomous Region, are instructive.

Birobidzhan population in January 1959   163,000
    of which
Urban population   118,000
Rural population   45,000

In 1939, Birobidzhan had a total population of 108,419 which subsequently increased by about 50 per cent during the next twenty years. But neither the 1939 nor the 1959 figures mention the percentage of Jews in the population of their "own" region.

The above figures, however, give indirect information on the Jews in Birobidzhan. A Soviet source had estimated, shortly before the 1939 census, that Jews in Birobidzhan represented 20 per cent of the region's total population, *i.e.*, 21,000 individuals. It should be assumed that in 1959 Jews represented no more than 20 per cent of Birobidzhan's population and possibly even less. In 1959, the average of rural population in the Soviet Union was 42 per cent, whereas in Birobidzhan it was only 28 per cent. It is furthermore doubtful whether the majority of the rural population consists of Jews. That means that after the total extinction of Jewish agriculture in Belorussia and the Ukraine during the war, and the 1947 migration of the Crimean settlers' survivors to Birobidzhan, hardly any Jewish agriculturalists actually remained.

Only a small part of the data collected and compiled in the census, has, as yet, been published. This survey, which is based on these fragmentary details, must therefore be incomplete. However, after decades of assumptions and estimates on Soviet Jewry, we have now been given some information to work on.

In spite of the extinction of all Jewish cultural and social activity in the Soviet Union, the terrifying period of the "Doctors' Plot," and present-day discrimination and persecution, 2,268,000 Jews have affirmed their membership of the Jewish nation. Though these very circumstances prompted some Jews to declare their nationality as Jewish they induced others to disavow or conceal their origin. The number of declared Soviet Jews is therefore considerably smaller than their real numbers. According to available data, it may be assumed that Soviet Jews constitute 25 per cent of World Jewry.

The second and only other means of identification in the Soviet census conditions is the declaration of native language. It cannot be doubted that some Soviet Jews have assimilated Russian culture and become estranged from Yiddish, though the census results gave a distorted picture of this. We do not know how many of those Jews who regard Russian as their mother tongue still read or understand Yiddish. Neither do we know how many of them would have declared Yiddish as their mother tongue had it not been for the prohibition and repression suffered. Under these conditions the half-million Jews who declared Yiddish as their mother tongue represent only part of those whom this language serves as a living link with their brethren.

Ever since the establishment of the Soviet regime, there have been two basic methods used for "solving the Jewish problem": the open door to assimilation, and the step by step extinction of Jewish religious, cultural and social life. The census results prove that in spite of these policies and their effects, the Jews of the Soviet Union constitute a defined and recognised national body within the Soviet national framework, even from the quantative point of view.

The "solution of the Jewish problem" by these methods is still a long way from success after 43 years of Soviet rule.

Nationalism as an Instrument of Control

Since General Suvorov lived in the eighteenth century, this article is chronologically out of place. But it is published here less as an account of General Suvorov than as an illustration of the Communists' use of Russian nationalism. The theme of nationalism first appeared in Soviet literature in the late 1920's, and was used increasingly during the 1930's. World War II, called by the Soviets "The Second Great Fatherland War" (or "The Great Patriotic War"), brought a crescendo of nationalism as might have been expected. It was not generally anticipated that emphasis on this theme would continue after the war, but it did.

The source is: V. Markov, "A Great Russian General," *Bloknot Agitatora*. No. 13, May, 1950. Pp. 28–33. The translation was made by Messrs. Richard Newell and James Richmond.

A GREAT RUSSIAN GENERAL

(On the 150th anniversary of the death of A. V. Suvorov)

The 18th of May of this year marks the 150th year since the death of the great Russian general Alexander Vasilyevich Suvorov. Very long ago the famous Suvorov battles and campaigns resounded. Since that time our Fatherland and our people have been transformed beyond recognition. But the glory of this great Russian general has not dimmed; his noble image lives and will live eternally in the memory of the people.

Suvorov is near and dear to the Soviet peoples for his outstanding war deeds, in which the military endowments, bravery and heroism of the great Russian people found striking embodiment.

Suvorov imortalized his name by his ardent love for the Fatherland, for the people.

Suvorov spent forty years of his life in combat. And from his first baptism of fire in 1760, on the battlefields of the Seven Years' War, to the last, the Swiss campaign, at the end of 1799, he never experienced defeat, raising to unprecedented heights the glory of Russian arms by his great numbers of splendid victories.

To Suvorov belonged the honor of victory at Fokshany in 1789, where a Turkish army of 30,000 was destroyed. Suvorov was the author of the victory of Russian arms at Rymnik, where, with one-quarter less forces, he defeated a Turkish army of 100,000. With the name Suvorov is connected one of the most famous pages of military history, the capture of the powerful Turkish fortress of Ismail in 1790. The storming of Ismail, prepared and brilliantly achieved under the leadership of Suvorov, has not to this time lost its meaning as a most instructive model of exalted military art.

Everywhere Suvorov and his valiant armies battled, fortresses considered invincible collapsed, and the most famous generals and most select troops suffered terrible and inglorious defeat. He undertook such courageous and original maneuvers as to upset all plans and jumble all maps of the enemy. He inflicted such powerful and violent blows on the enemy that none could recover. At the time of the Italian campaign Suvorov defeated the three best generals of France—representatives of the Napoleon school of military art.

Enviers of Suvorov tried to explain his numerous victories as a simple game of chance, as blind luck. But Suvorov simply answered: "One time luck, another time luck. God forgive! There must be skill sometime or other."

The "luck" of Suvorov was in his military genius, his indomitable will and his supreme devotion to his Fatherland and to his people.

"A good name is the property of every honest man," wrote Suvorov in one of his private letters, "but I wagered my good name on the glory of my

Fatherland, and attributed all successes to its prosperity." Suvorov lit the sacred flame of love for the Fatherland, for the people, in the heart of every soldier. "You are Russians," he said to his soldiers in minutes of danger, "Act like Russians!"

The "archrussian general," by Engels' definition, he embodied in himself such precious qualities of his great nation as a clear mind, brave creative daring, inflexible courage and unyielding firmness, simplicity, and a cordial attitude toward the people. In this fertile soil blossomed the military genius of Suvorov, creating a system of military art most advanced for his time, [a system] triumphantly tested in battles.

The instruction and training of the soldiers constituted the basis of the Suvorov "science of conquest." While for Western European generals, contemporaries of Suvorov, the soldier was only a mechanism, a sightless weapon, the great Russian general saw in the soldier his fighting comrade in arms, a defender of the Fatherland. He had paternal concern for his subordinates, persistently developing in them combat enterprise and intelligence, hardening their courage and daring. The soldiers of Suvorov repaid the beloved general a hundredfold for his care.

History preserves the memory of the innumerable exploits of the Suvorov soldiers. Not without reason were they called the wonder knights [bogatyri, from a hero of Russian folklore]. The most outstanding of these exploits was the Swiss campaign of 1799. At the time of this campaign, with the general, already burdened by his years, at their head, Russian troops crossed the Alps from northern Italy to Switzerland, overcoming incredible difficulties and destroying the enemy. This campaign along mountain slopes, between cliffs and ice, was a heroic epic poem, sung afterwards by many artists with words and brushes.

Suvorov is great not only because he, as no one else in his time, knew how to instruct and train victorious troops. Suvorov is also great because he knew no equal in the ability to lead troops, to achieve victory on the field of battle in any, even the most difficult conditions, in any situation.

In 1773, at the time of the war with Turkey, the enemy troops to the number of about 12,000 stormed the populated point of Hirsovo, defended by the troops of Suvorov, numbering in all 3,000. Suvorov ordered that the enemy be allowed to approach as close as possible, and then threw his soldiers in a bayonet attack from the flanks. The Turks did not stand but turned in flight. The Suvorov forces followed the panicky retreating enemy for 30 kilometers.

Repeatedly, superiority in numbers of troops was on the side of the Turks, even in the battle at the fortress of Kinburn in 1787. Suvorov was wounded twice, but did not relinquish the leadership of the troops from his hands. Notwithstanding the extremely grave situation, he withheld his reserves to the last possible moment, and they decided the outcome of the conflict. The select Turkish troops were utterly put to rout.

"Judgment of eye, speed and attack are the basis of victory," said Suvorov, and in every conflict he showed in fact the classic models of this sharp judgment of eye, amazing speed and all-destructive attack.

As distinct from the western European military school, Suvorov never aimed for a pattern, for a prepared scheme, but always acted flexibly, originally, proceeding from concrete conditions. He created a system of Russian offensive tactics to which his enemies could not contrast anything [even] nearly equal.

The name Suvorov brought fear and panic to the enemies. This name called forth love and pride from all the Russian people. Victories, achieved by the Russian troops under the leadership of Suvorov, live for centuries as the embodiment of the invincible power and valor of Russian arms.

The Soviet Army is the worthy successor of all the best that military art has given from the past. Soviet soldiers preserve with care the precious Suvorov legacy. The principles of the Suvorov military art have not lost their vital strength even to the present day. It is not accidental that, in the formation of our army, in the first model of the Red Army text, approved by V. I. Lenin, were written as a combat manual the ten basic rules of Suvorov tactics.

In the years of the difficult ordeal for our Fatherland—in the years of the Great Patriotic War [World War II], Comrade Stalin, addressing the Soviet troops, said: "Let the courageous image of our great forefathers— Alexander Nevsky, Dmitri Donskoi, Kuzmin Minin, Dmitri Pozharsky, Alexander Suvorov, Mikhail Kutuzov—inspire you in this war."

The courageous images of our great forefathers inspired the Soviet troops to immortal military deeds in the conflict with the German usurpers.

Many precepts of Suvorov—as, for example, how to beat the enemy "not by numbers, but by skill"—have become military law in our units. The unbroken connection of Soviet military art with the Suvorov science of conquest has found reflection in the institution of the Order of Suvorov —the high award for mastery of generalship.

With the name Suvorov is also connected our future army—the education of her young cadres. The military academies, established by the resolution of the Council of Peoples' Commissars and the Central Committee of the All-Union Communist Party of Bolsheviks on August 21, 1943, for the training of youths for military service in the officer ranks, carry the name of Suvorov.

Soviet soldiers, progeny of Suvorov, live in a different age, in different conditions, than their great forefather. Autocracy shackled the creative forces of our people. Suvorov, persecuted by the envious and ungifted tsarist clique, stood his entire life, by his own expression, "between two batteries," and concluded his life in disgrace.

With the establishment of Soviet power, with the triumph of Socialism in our country, all forces of the people blossomed unprecedentedly. Under the leadership of the Party of Lenin-Stalin, the free Soviet people attained unsurpassed achievements in all fields, among them the military. Our patriotic military science, developed and enriched by Comrade Stalin, was raised to a rare height. The war convincingly demonstrated that Stalinist military science is the most advanced science in the world.

The outstanding victories of Soviet arms in the battles of the Second

World War eloquently attest that the progeny of Suvorov preserve with dignity the glorious traditions of their great forefather. Marking the 150th year since the death of the genial Russian general and paying tribute to his bright memory with love, all Soviet peoples are aware with pride, that guarding the peace and security of our Fatherland stands the mighty Soviet Army, an army trained and [battle-]hardened by the great Stalin.

Strategy and Tactics, 1955

There was published in Moscow in September, 1955 a small booklet setting forth the official interpretation of strategy and tactics. Like all such publications, its real function was less the presentation of an abstract or theoretical discussion than the dissemination of a new directive. Because of its subject matter and because it was published in relatively small quantities, several Western specialists on Soviet affairs believe that the pamphlet was intended for the guidance of party officials. It was not given mass circulation. Care has been exercised in making the excerpts not to alter the meaning by removal from context. The source is: N. V. Tropkin, *Ob Osnovakh Strategii i Taktiki Leninizma* (*Concerning the Strategy and Tactics of Leninism*). Moscow, 1955. *Passim.* The translation was originally made by Miss Erika Orle.

The strategy and tactics of Leninism are one of the most important parts of the great Marxist-Leninist doctrine about the reorganization of the world on a new, Communistic basis. This is the science of leadership in the class struggle of the proletariat and of all oppressed and exploited for their social and national liberation; a science about the struggle of millions of workers who, in a gigantic social battle, destroy the world of oppression and slavery, and build a world of Socialism.

By generalizing the experiences of the Workers' and Communists' movements of the whole world, and particularly by considering the great victorious experience of the Communist Party of the Soviet Union, the strategy and tactics of Leninism determine the trends and methods of the struggle, contribute to the unification into one channel of the different streams of the liberation movement, plan the concrete means for overthrowing the domination of landowners and capitalists, for the establishment of the dictatorship of the working classes, and for the abolition of all forms of oppression and exploitation. The strategy and tactics of Leninism show Communist and Workers' parties how to form political armies for the liberation struggle and how to lead the revolutionary actions of these armies.

The aim of the strategy and tactics is to secure, with a minimum of losses, a maximum of revolutionary movements, to direct the liberation movement of the working class and all toiling masses by the shortest route to the end in view. The Marxist-Leninist doctrine teaches that the working class and the toiling masses would not profit from favorable conditions for the development of a victorious struggle for liberation if the Communist Parties did not know how to decide on a general strategic line and how to select and use tactical methods and forms of revolutionary activities corresponding to the local historical conditions.

Each truly Marxist Party, leading the revolutionary struggle of the proletariat and all toiling masses, bases its activities on the strategy and tactics of Leninism.

• • •

The strategy and tactics of Leninism are passing a great historical test and are achieving a brilliant affirmation in the successful movements of democratic countries toward Socialism, in the revolutionary struggle of the working class in capitalist countries, in the growth of a movement for national liberation in colonial or subordinated countries. It teaches the World Communist Movement the complicated art of leadership in the great revolutionary struggle for common democratic, socialist aims.

• • •

The Marxist-Leninist theory, scientifically disclosing the objective laws of social development, permits the working class and its party to take advantage of these laws in the interests of all workers, to manage the liberation struggle successfully, to foresee its course and, sometimes, without giving up the final great goal of the revolutionary movement, to lead the masses of the people to it competently. Without knowing these objective laws, it is impossible to set the strategic aim correctly and to determine the tactical form of the struggle. Refusal to reckon with the objective laws of social development damages the revolutionary movement, leads to hazardous activity, and to the separation of the Party from the masses.

• • •

The most important starting point for the strategy and tactics of Leninism is the undeniable Marxist statement about the masses of people being the creators of history. The strategy and tactics of Leninism are filled with a deep faith in the gigantic revolutionary strength of the working class, in the great revolutionary capacities of the peasants and of all other toiling people, and it most emphatically denies any show of the cult of personality. The strategy and tactics of Leninism have as their main aim the awakening of the creative energy of the working classes, the support of the most complete and effective manifestation of the revolutionary energy of the people, the furtherance of the widest possible raising of the masses for the liberation struggle, the organization of this struggle, the emphasis of its aim, the transformation of the masses into a victorious revolutionary army, and the direction of them by the shortest way to their great goal—the destruction of all forms of exploitation of man by man—to the realization of Scientific Communism.

The immovable foundation of the strategy and tactics of Leninism is the basic thesis of Marxism on the unavoidability of the downfall of capitalism, this being the most important point in the Marxist doctrine about the dictatorship of the proletariat as the most radical means for reconstructing society according to the spirit of Socialism. Lenin's theory of the Socialist Revolution is most important in planning the strategy and tactics of the revolutionary poletariat. It gives a scientific basis for their strategy and tactics. Many of the most important statements and rules of Leninist strategy and tactics flow directly and immediately from his theory of the Socialist Revolution—Lenin's theory of the hegemony of the proletariat, the theory of the transformation of bourgeois-democratic revolutions into Socialist Revolutions, the doctrine about the probability of a Socialist victory in some countries.

. . .

Leninism teaches that the proletariat has to attain the leadership of the liberation movement in order to destroy the bourgeoisie, and it is therefore necessary to develop within the proletariat an ability for political leadership of the masses, to learn how to vanquish the bourgeoisie in the struggle for influence over the vast masses of workers, to learn how to achieve the complicated task of uniting others around oneself, and how to weld into one complete revolutionary front all those classes and groups of the population who can participate in all or in some stages of the struggle.

. . .

Proletarian leadership in the struggle for liberation does not establish itself by itself, but is gained in a hard struggle with the bourgeoisie which through its many agencies tries to seize the leadership of the revolutionary movement in order to weaken and betray it. There can be no thought of a victorious end to the struggle unless the bourgeoisie are removed from the leadership of the liberation movement.

. . .

The highest expression of the proletarian leadership in the struggle for liberation is the leadership of the Communists and Fraternal Parties in the struggling, revolutionary actions of the workers. Only by creating its own political Marxist party is the proletariat able to participate consciously in the struggle for liberation, to give the basic liberating movement a conscious, purposeful character, and rise to the position of the leader in the struggle for democracy and Socialism.

. . .

By a deep analysis of imperialism, Lenin discovered the law of irregularity in the political and economic growth of capitalism. By showing the main point of this law, Lenin demonstrated that, in capitalistic surroundings, separate enterprises, branches, even countries develop irregularly; some advance, some lag behind in their development. During the epoch of imperialism, this irregularity increases greatly, achieves a decisive importance, becomes a competition of one country against another, alters the balance of forces, destroys the equilibrium of the world arena. The struggle between the imperialistic vultures for markets for their goods and capital; the struggle for colonies, for sources of raw materials increases. All this sharpens the collisions between imperialistic countries, leads to predatory wars, and to a new redistribution of the world. Wars diminish the strength of imperialism and make it possible for the proletariat to pierce the front of imperialism at its weaker points. . . . Therefore, under the conditions of imperialism, it is not advisable to cling to the old, out-of-date marxist formula about the possibility of attaining a Socialist victory only as a result of the simultaneous triumphs of the proletariat in all the capitalist countries.

. . .

. . . Leninism teaches that the proletariat is first victorious in countries which are the weak links in the chain of imperialism. Weak links in the chain of imperialism are not always the countries with the highest industrial level. According to the law of the irregular development of capitalism, such countries might be politically unripe for a Socialist Revolution. At the very beginning, according to the Leninist theory, a victorious Socialist Revolution was possible only in a country having at least a medium level of capitalist development; but subsequently, thanks to the support of the country which had had a victorious Socialist Revolution, Socialist changes are possible even in backward countries. . . . Lenin's theory of a Socialist Revolution opened wide possibilities for the struggle for democracy and Socialism in colonial and dependent countries and, at the same time, it confronted the proletariat in imperialistic countries with the importance of the fight to end the yoke of imperialism not only in the colonies but in the mother countries as well.

. . .

One of the main foundations of the strategy and tactics of Leninism is the principle of proletarian internationalism. . . . The world front of imperialistic reactionism is opposed by a united front of the revolutionary movements of all countries, and the revolutionary forces of each country consider themselves as one unit of this front. The liberation movement in each country becomes a substantial part of the world liberation movement, and a revolution on a national scale becomes part of the World Revolutionary Movement. . . . No proletariat of any country can seize political power unless it has the support of the workers of other countries. . . . Only the close cooperation and mutual support by the workers of different countries can assure success to the struggle for liberation. Therefore, the strategy and tactics of any Workers' Party . . . must put the interests of the international proletariat at the top.

. . .

At the present time, there are no countries in the world where a bourgeois-democratic revolution would have only an anti-feudal character or where it would not be connected with a national liberation struggle. All the countries of the world which have been slow in destroying feudalism and which, therefore, are backward in their economic development have already been transformed into colonies or dependent countries by the big imperialist states. The presence in these countries of considerable remains of feudalism is combined with a foreign, imperialist yoke so that the People's Democratic Revolution is not only an anti-feudal movement but also an anti-imperialist, national liberation movement. This widens the social base for revolution in colonial and dependent countries. The proletariat can count on attracting into the liberation movement not only the peasants, but also the small bourgeoisie, the intellectuals, the nationally-minded middle class who are interested in the liberation of markets and of the national economy from foreign competition and in the destruction of the remains of feudalism.

· · ·

The Communist Parties of the imperialist countries base their activities on another strategic plan for the liberation struggle. In these countries the dictatorship of the bourgeoisie, consolidated as a result of previous bourgeois revolutions, has existed for many decades. During that time the bourgeoisie created an enormous state machinery, gained great experience in the sphere of political cheating of the working people, set up colonial domination over many backward countries and, by means of colonial exploitation, bribed and corrupted the leaders of the working class—"the working aristocracy," and placed its agents in the workers' movement. All this complicates the attainment of the strategical aims of the Workers' Parties in those countries.

The strategy of this stage of the liberation struggle has found a clear expression in the program of the British Communist Party's "Britain's Way to Socialism," which orients the British working class toward a revolutionary reformation of the bourgeois democracy into a People's Democracy. The program says that "the people cannot progress toward Socialism without using the present political power which must be taken away from the capitalist minority and given into the hands of the majority of the people, with the working class at the top."

· · ·

China and the European People's Democracies, as well as the Soviet Union, have reached the third strategic stage which begins with the establishment of the political power of the proletariat. The times when the USSR was the only country building Communism have gone forever. Today the Socialist System is represented not by one country but by a whole Socialist Camp covering over 900 million people. The removal from the imperialist system of China and of the European People's Democracies began a new stage in the development of International Socialism. The beginning of this stage created new and incomparably more favorable conditions than ever before for the liberation movement in the capitalist world.

· · ·

If strategy plans the general direction of the proletariat's struggle throughout a whole stage of the revolution and aims at winning the war over the full run of that stage, then tactics involve other tasks. The function of tactics is not to win the war as a whole, but to win separate battles, to carry out single attacks successfully. Tactics are a part of strategy. . . . The tactics may change many times during every strategic stage of the revolutionary struggle. The liberation movement cannot develop in the form of a continuously swelling wave. It develops by tides and ebbs, by attacks and retreats.

* * *

One of the most important tactical forms of the struggle is the work done by Communists in unions and other mass organizations of the working class. The relationship of the Communist Party to the unions is a concrete example of the relations between the vanguard of the proletariat and the vast masses of workers. Leninism teaches that the Communist Parties have to lean on the unions in order to become a strong power. . . . Without the unions, it is impossible to conquer or to retain the proletarian dictatorship. The unions are a mighty weapon in the revolutionary struggle. They are the schools for the Communist education of the workers.

* * *

Communists also believe in the use of parliamentary forms of struggle by the revolutionary proletariat. . . . Revolutionary Communism, as far as relations to bourgeois parliaments are concerned, does not consist in cowardly refusals to participate, but in the creation of a truly revolutionary group within the parliament.

* * *

While recognizing the admissibility of compromise as a principle, Communist Parties cannot accept ideological compromises. There can be no compromises which do not reserve a freedom of action to the Party; a freedom for Communist propaganda and agitation, a right of criticism, and a right to fight temporary allies who are basically loyal to other ideas.

* * *

Marxism-Leninism is for compromises and understandings which assure the winning over to the cause of Communism of the majority of the proletariat; which further the growth of Communist influence among non-proletarian groups of the working class and strengthen the position of the Party; which provide a chance for a breathing space in order to mobilize forces, and rebuild the lines in order to get ready for the final attack against the enemy; which permit taking advantage of contradictions among the enemies in the interest of a victorious revolution; and which avoid unprofitable battles in order to conserve strength and to win under new and more favorable conditions.

There is now no country in the world where there is not a revolutionary Marxist-Leninist Party. Communist and Workers' Parties have grown into a great army of men fighting for Socialism. This army covers the whole globe, and is the brains, bones, and conscience of all progressive humanity. They number their forces at over 250 million, and are a power which can lead humanity to a complete rebuilding of the world on the basis of true democracy and Socialism. Borrowing an unshakable conviction as to the inevitable victory of Socialism from the treasury of Marxism-Leninism and from the experiences of our great Communist Party, the Communist Parties abroad are successfully leading the struggle of nations for liberation from capitalist slavery. As the fighting vanguard of the Camp of World Peace and Democracy, they attract ever wider masses. The unceasing growth of their influence on the wide masses of people is an indisputable law of historical development. But the successes of the World Communist Movement do not relieve the Communist Parties in capitalist countries of their obligation further to increase their influence and to attract still greater masses of the people.

* * *

The experience of the Communist Party of the Soviet Union in forming victorious, mass-political armies for the fight for democracy and Socialism is of great importance to all Communist Parties. Lenin's instructions about the necessity of combating all forms of sectarianism are of greatest significance. The most dangerous forms of sectarianism under present circumstances are the underestimation of the task of widening the base of mass movements for peace, the underestimation of the struggle for democratic freedoms and national sovereignty, the underestimation of work in the unions and other mass organizations among the workers, and the treatment of members of Catholic and Right-Socialist organizations as identical with the reactionary leaders of those groups. . . . Fraternal Communist and Workers' Parties should intensify their ideological work, educate their members in the spirit of proletarian internationalism and in a spirit of irreconcilability to all kinds of deviations from the principles of Marxism-Leninism, teach the proletarian vanguard to understand correctly and to use knowledgeably the basic principles of the strategy and tactics of Leninism. Communism is the most powerful and unconquerable social movement of our time. . . . And hopeless are the mad efforts of the bourgeoisie, condemned by history to inevitable destruction, to stop the growth of Communist forces.

"The Truth Is ———"

The first of the two selections below consists of a few excerpts from a pamphlet written by Georgii Malenkov in honor of Stalin's seventieth birthday. The source is: G. Malenkov, *Comrade Stalin—Leader of Progressive Mankind*. Moscow: Foreign Languages Publishing House,

1950. The second selection contains excerpts from the famous speech by Nikita S. Khrushchev before the Twentieth Congress of the Communist Party of the Soviet Union (1956).

[1]

A quarter of a century ago Comrade Stalin vowed in the name of the Party to fulfill the behests of Lenin with credit. This vow . . . was the guiding star in the historic struggle . . . for the building of socialist society.

Comrade Stalin led our Party and the Soviet people along Lenin's path. He upheld and developed Lenin's theory of the possibility of building Socialism in one country. Carrying out Lenin's behests, our Party, led by Comrade Stalin, effected the socialist industrialization of our country and the collectivization of our agriculture, and converted the Soviet Union into a great industrialist and collective-farm socialist power.

Comrade Stalin understood Lenin's inspired ideas regarding a Marxist party of a new type with a profundity equalled by none; he protected the purity of the teaching of Marx-Engels-Lenin, developed the Marxist-Leninist theory, and steeled the Party in battle against numerous enemies; he has trained, and continues to train, cadres capable of advancing the causes of our Party.

Together with the great Lenin, Comrade Stalin founded the first Socialist State in the world. Under the banner of Lenin, under the leadership of Comrade Stalin, our mighty Motherland, the Soviet Land, whose peoples are bound by amity and friendship, is alive, growing, and gaining strength.

·   ·   ·

In the second world war . . . Comrade Stalin, heading the Soviet Union, personally directed the defeat of Hitler's hordes, secured the victory of the peace-loving nations, was the recognized leader in the grim struggle for the liberation of mankind from the fascist yoke.

·   ·   ·

That is why the peoples of the Soviet Union, and all progressive humanity, look upon Comrade Stalin as their recognized leader and teacher. That is why today they so express their warm love and devotion to Comrade Stalin and acknowledge his great services in the struggle for a happy life and for peace among nations.

·   ·   ·

Under the leadership of Comrade Stalin, our people are confidently marching to Communism.

The eyes of the people of the Soviet Union and of hundreds of millions in all countries turn with deep gratitude to Comrade Stalin. Progressive mankind looks upon Comrade Stalin as its beloved leader and teacher, and believes and knows that the cause of Lenin and Stalin is invincible.

[2]

Lenin's wisdom in dealing with people was evidenced by his work with cadres.

Stalin was characterized by an entirely different relation to people. Lenin's traits—patience in working with people, persistently and painstakingly educating them . . . were entirely alien to Stalin. He discarded Lenin's methods . . . for administrative violence, mass repressions and terror.

. . .

Stalin . . . used extreme methods and mass repressions when the revolution was already victorious, when the Soviet state had already been strengthened, when the exploiting classes had already been liquidated. . . .

It is clear that Stalin showed his intolerance, his brutality and his abuse of power in a whole series of cases. Instead of mobilizing the masses by proving his political correctness, he often chose to use repression and physical annihilation, not only against genuine enemies, but also against persons who had committed no crime against the Party or the Soviet government. Here we see no wisdom, but only a demonstration of that brutality which had once so alarmed V. I. Lenin.

. . .

Facts prove that many abuses were committed on Stalin's orders. . . . Stalin was a very distrustful man, sick with suspiciousness; we know this from our work with him.

. . .

During and after the war, Stalin advanced the thesis that the disasters which our nation experienced in the first part of the war were due to the "unexpected" attack of the Germans against the Soviet Union. But, comrades, this is completely untrue. [Khrushchev then cited warnings from Great Britain and the United States as well as from Soviet sources.]

. . .

Despite these particularly grave warnings, the steps necessary to prepare the country properly for defense and to prevent it from being taken unawares were not taken. Did we have time and capabilities for such preparations? Yes, we had the time and the capabilities.

. . .

Therefore, the menace which hung over our Fatherland at the beginning of the war was largely due to Stalin's erroneous methods of directing the nation and the Party.

However . . . even after the first stage of the war Stalin demonstrated nervousness and hysteria which interfered with actual military operations and caused serious damage to our army. Stalin was a long way from understanding the real situation which developed at the front. [Khrushchev then recounted an incident in which Stalin, against the advice of Khrushchev and others, ordered, "Let everything remain as it is."]

And what was the result of this? The worst that we had expected. Our army concentrations were surrounded by the Germans and in consequence we lost hundreds of thousands of our soldiers. This was Stalin's military "genius"; this is what it cost us.

Stalin on History and the Future

> The following excerpts are part of the authoritative Stalinist version of dialectical and historical materialism. During his lifetime, Stalin was usually credited with the authorship of this discussion which was printed in the 1939 edition of the *History of the Communist Party of the Soviet Union (Bolshevik)* and in many other forms.

Dialectical materialism is the world outlook of the Marxist-Leninist Party. It is called dialectical materialism because its approach to the phenomena of nature, its method of studying and apprehending them, is *dialectical,* while its interpretation of the phenomena of nature, its conception of these phenomena, its theory, is *materialistic.*

Historical materialism is the extension of the principles of dialectical materialism to the study of social life, an application of the principles of dialectical materialism to the phenomena of the life of society, to the study of society and its history. . . .

The dialectical method regards as important primarily not that which at the given moment seems to be durable and yet is already beginning to die away, but that which is arising and developing, even though at the given moment it may appear to be not durable, for the dialectical method considers invincible only that which is arising and developing. . . .

The demand for a bourgeois-democratic republic when tsardom and bourgeois society existed, as, let us say, in Russia in 1905, was a quite understandable, proper and revolutionary demand, for at that time a bourgeois republic would have meant a step forward. But now, under the conditions of the USSR, the demand for a bourgeois-democratic republic would be a meaningless and counter-revolutionary demand, for a bourgeois republic would be a retrograde step compared with the Soviet republic.

Everything depends on the conditions, time and place.

It is clear that without such a *historical* approach to social phenomena, the existence and development of the science of history is impossible, for only such an approach saves the science of history from becoming a jumble of accidents and an agglomeration of most absurd mistakes.

Further, if the world is in a state of constant movement and development, if the dying away of the old and the upgrowth of the new is a law of development, then it is clear that there can be no "immutable" social systems, no "eternal principles" of private property and exploitation, no "eternal ideas" of the subjugation of the peasant to the landlord, of the worker to the capitalist.

Hence the capitalist system can be replaced by the socialist system, just as at one time the feudal system was replaced by the capitalist system. Hence we must not base our orientation on the strata of society which are no longer developing, even though they at present constitute the predominant force, but on those strata which are developing and have a future before them, even though they at present do not constitute the predominant force. . . .

Hence, in order not to err in policy, one must look forward, not backward.

Further, if the passing of slow quantitative changes into rapid and abrupt qualitative changes is a law of development, then it is clear that revolutions made by oppressed classes are a quite natural and inevitable phenomenon. Hence the transition from capitalism to socialism and the liberation of the working class from the yoke of capitalism cannot be effected by slow changes, by reforms, but only by a qualitative change of the capitalist system, by revolution. Hence, in order not to err in policy, one must be a revolutionary, not a reformer.

Further, if development proceeds by way of the disclosure of internal contradictions, by way of collisions between opposite forces on the basis of these contradictions and so as to overcome these contradictions, then it is clear that the class struggle of the proletariat is a quite natural and inevitable phenomenon. Hence we must not cover up the contradictions of the capitalist system, but disclose and unravel them; we must not try to check the class struggle but carry it to its conclusion.

Hence, in order not to err in policy, one must pursue an uncompromising proletarian class policy, not a reformist policy of harmony of the interests of the proletariat and the bourgeoisie, not a compromiser's policy of "the growing of capitalism into socialism." Such is the Marxist dialectical method when applied to social life, to the history of society . . .

Hence the science of the history of society, despite all the complexity of the phenomena of social life, can become as precise a science as, let us say, biology, and capable of making use of the laws of development of society for practical purposes. Hence the party of the proletariat should not guide itself in its practical activity by casual motives, but by the laws of development of society, and by practical deductions from these laws. . . .

This means that the history of the development of society is above all the history of the development of production, the history of the modes of production which succeed each other in the course of centuries, the history of the development of productive forces and people's relations to production.

Hence the history of social development is at the same time the history of the producers of material values themselves, the history of the laboring masses who are the chief force in the process of production and who carry on the production of material values necessary for the existence of society.

Hence, if historical science is to be a real science, it can no longer reduce the history of social development to the actions of kings and generals, to the actions of "conquerors" and "subjugators" of states, but must above all devote itself to the history of the producers of material values, the history of the laboring masses, the history of peoples.

Hence the clue to the study of the laws of history of society must not be sought in men's minds, in the views and ideas of society, but in the mode of production practised by society in any given historical period; it must be sought in the economic life of society. Hence the prime task of historical science is to study and disclose the laws of production, the laws of development of productive forces and of the relations of production, the laws of economic development of society.

Hence, if the party of the proletariat is to be a real party, it must above all acquire a knowledge of the laws of development of production, of the laws of economic development of society. Hence, if it is not to err in policy, the party of the proletariat must both in drafting its program and in its practical activities proceed primarily from the laws of development of production, from the laws of economic development of society. . . .

. . . the capitalist relations of production have ceased to correspond to the state of productive forces of society and have come into irreconcilable contradiction with them. This means that capitalism is pregnant with revolution, whose mission it is to replace the existing capitalist ownership of the means of production with socialist ownership. This means that the main feature of the capitalist system is a most acute class struggle between the exploiters and the exploited. . . .

Here there stands out in bold relief the *tremendous* role of new social ideas, of new political institutions, of a new political power, whose mission it is to abolish by force the old relations of production. Out of the conflict between the new productive forces and the old relations of production, out of the new economic demands of society there arise new social ideas; the new ideas organize and mobilize the masses; the masses become welded into a new political army, create a new revolutionary power, and make use of it to abolish by force the old system of relations of production, and firmly to establish the new system. The spontaneous process of development yields place to conscious actions of men, peaceful development to violent upheaval, evolution to revolution. . . .

Stalin on Capitalist Encirclement

Stalin wrote this statement in 1937. Like most of his pronouncements, this was reprinted in many media. This version is from Joseph Stalin, *Mastering Bolshevism.* New York: New Century Publishers, 1945. Pp. 7–9.

What are these facts which our Party comrades forgot, or which they simply did not notice? They forgot that Soviet power has conquered only one-sixth of the world, that five-sixth [*sic*] of the world is in possession of capitalist powers. They forgot that the Soviet Union is in the conditions of capitalist encirclement. It is an accepted thing to talk loosely about capitalist encirclement, but people do not want to ponder upon what sort of thing this capitalist encirclement is.

Capitalist encirclement—that is no empty phrase; that is a very real and unpleasant feature. Capitalist encirclement means that here is one country, the Soviet Union, which has established the socialist order on its own territory and besides this there are many countries, bourgeois countries, which continue to carry on a capitalist mode of life and which surround the Soviet Union, waiting for an opportunity to attack it, break it, or at any rate to undermine its power and weaken it. Our comrades forgot this fundamental fact. But it is that precisely which determines the basis of relations between capitalist encirclement and the Soviet Union.

Take for example the bourgeois states. Simple-minded people may think that extremely good relations reign between them, as between states of the same type. But only simple-minded people can think so. In reality the relations between them are far from being those of good neighbors. It has been proved as plainly as two and two make four that the bourgeois states shower their spies, wreckers, diversionists and sometimes murderers on each other, behind their frontiers; give them instructions to worm themselves into the factories and institutions of these states, to create their own network there and "in case of necessity" to smash them from the rear so as to weaken them and undermine their power. Such is the case at the present time. . . .

The question must be put: why should the bourgeois countries be gentler and more neighborly to the Soviet socialist government than they are to bourgeois states of their own type? Why should they send fewer spies, wreckers, diversionists and murderers behind the frontiers of the Soviet Union than they send behind the frontiers of bourgeois countries which are akin to them? Where did you get this from? Will it not be truer, from the point of view of Marxism, to suppose that the bourgeois states must be sending twice to three times as many wreckers, spies, diversionists and murderers behind the lines of the Soviet Union than behind those of any bourgeois state?

Is it not clear that as long as capitalist encirclement exists, there will be wreckers, spies, diversionists and murderers in our country, sent behind our lines by the agents of foreign states?

Our Party comrades forgot about all this, and having forgotten were caught unawares.

This is why the spying and diversive work of the Trotskyite agents of the Japanese and German secret police was completely unexpected by some of our comrades.

Khrushchev on Capitalist Encirclement

By way of illustrating the twin aspects of history, change and continuity, as well as by way of contrast to Stalin's theorizing, here is a brief excerpt from Khrushchev's report to the Twenty-first Extraordinary Congress of the Communist Party of the Soviet Union (January, 1959.) The source is: N. S. Khrushchev, *Control Figures for the Economic Development of the USSR for 1959–1965.* Moscow: Foreign Languages Publishing House, 1959. P. 132. Italics in the original.

. . . Marxists understand the final victory of socialism to mean its triumph on an international scale. Having built socialism, our country remained for a long time the world's only socialist state, living in a hostile capitalist encirclement. It could not consider itself fully guaranteed against armed intervention, against the danger of a forcible restoration of capitalism by international reaction, for the capitalist states then surrounding the land of socialism were much stronger economically and militarily.

The world situation has changed radically [*sic*] since then. The Soviet Union is no longer in a capitalist encirclement. There are two world social systems: capitalism, which is living out its day, and socialism, a full-blooded and growing system that has the support of the workers of all lands. (*Applause.*)

The Soviet Union, as every other socialist country, is not guaranteed against the possibility of imperialist aggression. But the relation of real forces in the world today is such that we shall be able to repel any attack by any enemy. (*Stormy applause.*)

There is no power in the world that can re-establish capitalism in this country or crush the socialist camp. The danger of capitalist restoration in the Soviet Union is ruled out. And this means that *the triumph of socialism is not only complete but final.* (*Stormy, prolonged applause.*)

It can therefore be said that the question of building socialism in one single country and its complete and final victory has been decided by the course of the historical development of society.

Stalin on War

The first of the two following selections is Stalin's analysis of the causes of war in general and of World War II in particular, plus some of his comments on what victory meant to the Soviet Union. The occasion was his famous election speech of February, 1946. The source is an official Soviet translation of "Speech by J. V. Stalin at an Election Rally in Stalin Electoral Area, Moscow February 9, 1946," published by the Soviet Embassy in Washington, March, 1946.

The second excerpt deals with the question of the inevitability of war. It is from Stalin's essay, "Economic Problems of Socialism in the

USSR." The essay was translated into many languages and widely distributed in October, 1952. These two pronouncements constituted the core of the official "line" until after Stalin's death.

It would be wrong to think that the Second World War was a casual occurrence or the result of mistakes of any particular statesmen, though mistakes undoubtedly were made. Actually, the war was the inevitable result of the development of world economic and political forces on the basis of modern monopoly capitalism. Marxists have declared more than once that the capitalist system of world economy harbors elements of general crises and armed conflicts and that, hence, the development of world capitalism in our time proceeds not in the form of smooth and even progress but through crises and military catastrophes.

The fact is, that the unevenness of development of the capitalist countries usually leads in time to violent disturbance of equilibrium in the world system of capitalism, that group of capitalist countries which considers itself worse provided than others with raw materials and markets usually making attempts to alter the situation and repartition the "spheres of influence" in its favor by armed force. The result is a splitting of the capitalist world into two hostile camps and war between them.

Perhaps military catastrophes might be avoided if it were possible for raw materials and markets to be periodically redistributed among the various countries in accordance with their economic importance, by agreement and peaceable settlement. But that is impossible to do under present capitalist conditions of the development of world economy.

Thus the First World War was the result of the first crisis of the capitalist system of world economy, and the Second World War was the result of a second crisis.

That does not mean of course that the Second World War is a copy of the first. On the contrary, the Second World War differs materially from the first in its nature. It must be borne in mind that before attacking the Allied countries the principal fascist states—Germany, Japan and Italy—destroyed the last vestiges of bourgeois democratic liberties at home, established a brutal terrorist regime in their own countries, rode roughshod over the principles of sovereignty and free development of small countries, proclaimed a policy of seizure of alien territories as their own policy and declared for all to hear that they were out for world domination and the establishment of a fascist regime throughout the world.

Moreover, by the seizure of Czechoslovakia and the central areas of China, the Axis states showed that they were prepared to carry out their threat of enslaving all freedom-loving nations. In view of this, unlike the First World War, the Second World War against the Axis states from the very outset assumed the character of an anti-fascist war, a war of liberation, one of the aims of which was also the restoration of democratic liberties. The entry of the Soviet Union into the war against the Axis states could only enhance, and indeed did enhance, the anti-fascist and liberation character of the Second World War. . . . That is how matters stand as regards the origin and character of the Second World War.

By now I should think that everyone admits that the war really was not and could not have been an accident in the life of nations, that actually this war became the war of nations for their existence, and that for this reason it could not be a lightening quick affair. As regards our country, for it this war was the most bitter and arduous of all wars in the history of our Motherland. . . .

The war was something like an examination for our Soviet system, for our State, for our Government, for our Communist Party, and it summed up the results of our work. . . . This was one of the positive aspects of the war. . . .

And so, what are the results of the war? . . . We concluded the war with complete victory over the enemies. That is the chief result of the war. But that result is too general and we cannot stop at that. . . . how is our victory over our enemies to be understood? What is the significance of this victory as regards the State and the development of the internal forces of our country?

Our victory means, first of all, that our Soviet social order has triumphed. That the Soviet social order has successfully passed the ordeal in the fire of war and has proved its unquestionable vitality.

As you know, it was claimed more than once in the foreign press that the Soviet social order was a "risky experiment" doomed to failure, that the Soviet order was a "house of cards" which had no roots in real life and had been imposed upon the people by the Cheka, and that a slight push from without was enough for this "house of cards" to collapse.

Now we can say that the war refuted all these claims of the foreign press as groundless. The war showed that the Soviet social order is a truly popular order springing from the depths of the people and enjoying their mighty support, that the Soviet social order is a form of organization of society which is perfectly stable and capable of enduring.

More than that, there is no longer any question today whether the Soviet social order is or is not capable of enduring, for after the object lessons of war none of the skeptics ventures any longer to voice doubts as to the vitality of the Soviet social order. The point now is that the Soviet social order has shown itself more stable and capable of enduring than a non-Soviet social order, that the Soviet social order is a form of organization, a society superior to any non-Soviet social order.

* * *

The principal aims of the new Five-Year Plan are to rehabilitate the ravaged areas of the country, to restore the prewar level in industry and agriculture, and then to surpass this level in more or less substantial measure. To say nothing of the fact that the rationing system will shortly be abolished (*stormy, prolonged applause*), special attention will be devoted to extending the production of consumer goods, to raising the living standard of the working people by steadily lowering the prices of all goods (*stormy, prolonged applause*), and to the widespread construction of all manner of scientific research institutions (*applause*) that can give science the opportunity to develop its potentialites. (*Stormy applause.*)

I have no doubt that if we give our scientists proper assistance they will be able in the near future not only to overtake but to surpass the achievements of science beyond the boundaries of our country. (*Prolonged applause.*)

. . .

(*All rise. Prolonged, unabating applause turning into an ovation. From all parts of the hall comes cheers: "Long live our great Stalin! Hurrah!" "Hurrah for the great leader of the peoples!" "Glory to the great Stalin!" "Long live Comrade Stalin, the candidate of the entire nation!" "Glory to Comrade Stalin, the creator of all our victories!"*) [Italics in original.]

* * * * *

Some comrades hold that wars between capitalist countries have ceased being inevitable because of the development of new international conditions since World War II. They consider the contradictions between the socialist and the capitalist camps to be more acute than contradictions among the capitalist countries; they believe that the U.S.A. has brought other capitalist countries sufficiently under its influence to be able to prevent them from going to war among themselves and thus weakening each other; they think that the leading capitalist intellects have learned enough from two world wars and the damage which these caused the whole capitalist world not to again run the risk of involving capitalist countries in war with each other; and, because of this, they believe that wars between capitalist countries are no longer inevitable.

These comrades are mistaken. They observe the outward, surface phenomena, but they do not understand those deeper forces which, although so far operating imperceptibly, will, nevertheless, determine the course of developments. Outwardly, everything would seem to be going well. The United States of America has put Western Europe, Japan and other capitalist countries on rations. Western Germany, Britain, France, Italy and Japan have fallen into the clutches of the United States, and are meekly obeying its orders. But it would be a mistake to suppose that things can continue to "go well" for ever, that these countries will always tolerate the domination and the oppression of the United States, that they will not try to break loose from bondage to America and seek a path of independent development.

Take Britain and France first of all. They are undoubtedly imperialist countries. Cheap raw materials and secure markets are doubtlessly of paramount importance to them. Can it be assumed that they will forever tolerate the present situation in which, under the cloak of the Marshall plan aid, Americans are penetrating the economies of Britain and France and are trying to convert them into adjuncts of the economy of the United States, and American capital is seizing raw materials and markets in the British and French colonies and so plotting disasters for the high profits of British and French capitalists? Would it not be more accurate to say that capitalist Britain and, after her, capitalist France, will eventually be compelled to break away from the embrace of the United States, and to enter into conflict with the U.S.A. in order to secure a position of independence and, of course, profits?

Let us turn to the major, conquered countries, West Germany and Japan. These countries are now languishing in misery under the jackboot of American imperialism. Their industry and their agriculture, their trade, their foreign and their domestic policies, and their whole life are enchained by the American occupation regime. Yet, only yesterday, these countries were great imperialist powers and were shaking the foundations of British, American and French domination in Europe and in Asia. To think that these countries will not try to rise again, will not try to smash American domination and force their way to independent development, is to believe in miracles.

It is said that contradictions between capitalism and socialism are stronger than contradictions among capitalist countries. That is theoretically true, of course. Not only is it true today; it was true before the Second World War, and it was realized, more or less, by the leaders of the capitalist nations. Yet World War II began as a war between capitalist countries and not as a war between them and the USSR. Why? First, because war with the socialist land, the USSR, is more dangerous to capitalism than wars between capitalist countries. War between capitalist countries brings into question only the supremacy of certain capitalist countries over others; war with the USSR certainly raises a question of the existence of capitalism itself. Second, the capitalists do not believe that the USSR is aggressive despite their clamor, for propaganda purposes, about Soviet aggressiveness. They are aware of the peaceful policy of the Soviet Union, and they know it will not attack capitalist countries.

Just as certain comrades now believe that Japan and Germany have been definitely put out of action, so was it similarly believed after the First World War that Germany had been definitely put out of action. It was also then said and proclaimed in the press that the United States had put Europe on rations; that Germany would never again rise, and that there would be no more wars between capitalist countries. In spite of this, Germany rose again as a great power within the space of some fifteen or twenty years after her defeat, having broken out of bondage and taken the path of independent development. And it is significant that it was none other than Britain and the United States which helped Germany to recover economically and to enhance her war potential. Of course, when the United States and Britain assisted Germany to economic recovery, they did so with a view to setting a recovered Germany against the Soviet Union, to utilizing her against the land of socialism. But Germany directed her forces, in the first instance, against the Anglo-French-American bloc. When Hitler Germany declared war on the Soviet Union, the Anglo-French-American bloc, far from joining with Hitler Germany, were compelled to enter into a coalition with the USSR against Hitler Germany. The struggle of the capitalist countries for markets and their desire to crush their competitors proved in practice, therefore, to be stronger than the contradictions between the socialist and the capitalist camps.

What guarantee is there that Germany and Japan will not rise again, will not attempt to break free from American thralldom and live their own independent lives? I think there is no such guarantee.

It follows from this that the inevitability of wars between capitalist countries remains in force.

It is said that Lenin's thesis that imperialism inevitably produces war must now be regarded as obsolete because powerful, popular forces have now come forward against another world war and in defense of peace. This is not true.

The object of the present day peace movement is to rouse the masses of the people to fight for the preservation of peace and for the prevention of another world war. Consequently, the aim of this movement is not to overthrow capitalism and establish socialism—it confines itself to the democratic aim of preserving peace. The present peace movement differs in this respect from the movement at the time of World War I for the conversion of the imperialist war into a civil war. The earlier movement went further and pursued socialist aims.

It is possible that, here or there, in a particular combination of circumstances, the fight for peace will develop into a fight for socialism. But then it will no longer be the present day peace movement; it will be a movement for the overthrow of capitalism.

What is most likely is that the present day peace movement will, if it succeeds as a movement for the preservation of peace, result in preventing a particular war, in its temporary postponement, in the temporary preservation of a particular peace, in the resignation of a war-like government and its replacement by another which is prepared to keep the peace temporarily. That will be good, of course; even very good. It will not be enough, all the same, to eliminate the inevitability of wars between capitalist countries generally. It will not be enough because, despite all the successes of the peace movement, imperialism will remain, will continue in force, and, consequently, the inevitability of wars will also continue in force. To eliminate the incvitability of war, it is necessary to abolish imperialism.

Khrushchev on War

The Twentieth Congress of the Communist Party of the Soviet Union, held in February, 1956, will perhaps be best remembered for Khrushchev's speech "down-grading" Stalin. However, the "First Party Secretary" also gained headlines throughout the world by his remarks at that congress on "the inevitability of war." It appeared to some observers that Khrushchev had discarded a major Communist doctrine. More careful analysis indicated that this hasty interpretation required modification. The first of the two following selections consists of the full published text of Khrushchev's declaration on the subject. The second selection is composed of excerpts from an analysis of the Communist position. The source for both selections is: "The 20th CPSU Congress and the Doctrine of the 'Inevitability of War,' " *Intelligence Report No. 7284. (Unclassified.)* Washington: Office of Intelligence Research, Department of State, June 22, 1956.

[1]

The possibility of preventing war in the present era:

Millions of people all over the world are asking whether another war is really inevitable, whether mankind, which has already experienced two devastating world wars, must still go through a third one. Marxists must answer this question, taking into consideration the epoch-making changes of the last decades.

There is, of course, a Marxist-Leninist precept that wars are inevitable as long as imperialism exists. This precept was evolved at a time when, first, imperialism was an all-embracing world system and, second, the social and political forces which did not want war were weak, poorly organized, and hence unable to compel the imperialists to renounce war.

People usually take only one aspect of the question and examine only the economic basis of wars under imperialism. This is not enough. War is not only an economic phenomenon. Whether there is to be a war or not depends in large measure on the correlation of class, political forces, the degree of organization, and the awareness and resolve of the people.

Moreover, in certain conditions, the struggle waged by progressive social and political forces may play a decisive role. Hitherto the state of affairs was such that the forces that did not want war and opposed it were poorly organized and lacked the means to check the schemes of the war-makers.

Thus it was before World War I, when the main force opposed to the threat of war—the world proletariat—was disorganized by the treachery of the leaders of the Second International. Thus it was on the eve of World War II when the other Great Powers, to all intents and purposes, encouraged the aggressors, and the right wing social democratic leaders had split the labor movement in the capitalist countries.

In that period, this precept was absolutely correct. At the present time, however, the situation has changed radically. Now there is a world camp of socialism which has become a mighty force. In this camp, the peace forces find not only the moral but also the material means to prevent aggression.

Moreover, there is a large group of other countries, with a population running into many hundreds of millions, which are actively working to avert war. The labor movement in the capitalist countries has today become a tremendous force. The movement of peace supporters has sprung up and developed into a powerful factor.

In these circumstances, certainly, the Leninist precept that so long as imperialism exists the economic basis giving rise to wars will also be preserved, remains in force. That is why we must display the greatest vigilance. As long as capitalism survives in the world, the reactionary forces representing the interests of the capitalist monopolies will continue their drive toward military gambles and aggression and may try to unleash war.

But war is not fatalistically inevitable. Today there are mighty social and political forces possessing formidable means to prevent the imperialists from unleashing war, and, if they actually try to start it, to give a smashing rebuff to the aggressors and frustrate their adventuristic plans.

To be able to do this, all anti-war forces must be vigilant and prepared; they must act as a united front and never relax their efforts in the battle for peace. The more actively the peoples defend peace, the greater the guarantees that there will be no new war.

[2]

Analysis of Communist statements on the "inevitability of war" is complicated by the ambiguity inherent in the Communists' use of the word, "inevitability." Engels said that what Darwin did for biology, Marx did for sociology, and the boast that the "science of Marxism" permits the formulation of "laws" and predictions regarding social phenomena equal in accuracy to those of modern natural science has been a prime article in the stock-in-trade of Communism. Nevertheless, when Marxists say a future social happening is "inevitable," the sense in which the term is used differs from its conventional meaning, as when we speak of death as inevitable. For all its emphasis on historical processes and "objective" social forces, Marxian causality is not deterministic in the "mechanistic" sense of Newtonian physics; rather it is "dialectical," which is to say it takes into the equation the element of human volition or "free will." The "proletarian revolution" depends as much on the "subjective factor," on conscious and purposeful human action, as it does on the "historical situation," the "objective factor" which makes revolution possible. Hence, the "inevitability" of the social revolution is always subject to the proviso that human beings (in this case the proletariat) play their assigned role.

It is the essence of the Marxist faith that human action is itself historically conditioned, that men will, in fact, act as historic necessity bids them to act. Nonetheless, Marxists would concede that if for any reason they do not, the whole scheme falls apart: if men do *not* act, if the proletariat does *not* fulfill its historic mission, then the revolution is *not* inevitable. Therefore, when Marxists use the word "inevitable," it must be interpreted in the context of the Marxian fusion of determinism and free will. When Marxists say that war is inevitable, they express their belief not that men *cannot* prevent it but that men *will not* prevent it.

In the Communist view, then, war becomes inevitable or avoidable depending upon what the Communists, at any given moment, think the likelihood is that men will prevent war, or depending on what impression they wish to create regarding their belief as to the likelihood that men will prevent war. In the light of these observations it becomes easy to understand the facility with which the Communist leadership can switch from pronouncements that war is inevitable to pronouncements that war is avoidable. It is not an objective matter at all, as the word "inevitable" might suggest, not even in the sense of belief in the objective validity of a theory. . . .

. . .

In assessing Communist doctrinal pronouncements on war, it is essential to distinguish between inter-capitalist wars and "imperialist" wars against the USSR. The Communist theory of the "inevitability of war" dates back to Lenin's tract on *Imperialism* (1916), in which he purports to deduce the inevitability of war *between capitalist states* from a Marxian analysis of the international economics of capitalism in its "imperialist" stage. On the other hand, if the statements about the inevitability of "imperialist" wars against the USSR are analyzed with due allowance for the qualifications inherent in the dialectical use of words, it becomes clear that Communist doctrine has never regarded such wars as inevitable.

Khrushchev, who appears concerned to deny that war between the Communist and capitalist camps is inevitable, confuses the issue by failing to mention that the "Marxist-Leninist precept" on inevitability of war relates to inter-capitalist wars only. This raises the possibility that there may be no inconsistency between the 20th Congress thesis that war is avoidable and earlier Communist doctrine on war, which would mean that Khrushchev's claim that he is revising Lenin's theory is, in fact, false.

The answer is that while Khrushchev has not altered the Communist doctrine on war between Communist and capitalist states, he has nonetheless introduced a considerable innovation into Communist dogma on the subject of war: the 20th CPSU Congress has, by implication, scrapped Lenin's (and Stalin's) doctrine that war *between the "imperialist powers"* remains inevitable until capitalism has vanished from the earth. . . .

How the Party Operates (II)

Professor Harcave's earlier analysis may now be compared with the image which the party leaders wished to project concerning some of their operations in 1962. The material has been translated and abridged from *Pravda*, 27 January, 1962.

. . . Very important questions of the work of local party committees in carrying out the decisions of the 22d Party Congress and improving party organizational leadership were broadly discussed at the recent Central Committee CPSU conference of heads of party organs sections of oblast and kray party committees and union republic central committees and of organizational instructors of sections of a number of city and rayon party committees. . . .

Many rayons, enterprises, Kolkhozes, and sovkhozes are lagging and poorly utilizing their rich reserves and possibilities. Major shortcomings and mistakes have been disclosed recently in the work of party organs of Turkmenistan and Tadzhikistan and Kirovskaya, Vologodskaya, and several other oblast party committees. Kolkhoz and sovkhoz leaders are often changed. All this testifies to an inattentive approach by party committees to the study of people in practical work and to the selection and indoctrination of cadres.

Modern conditions demand of all cadres, and primarily of leaders, a high theoretical knowledge, selfless devotion to the ideas of Communism, high skill, and great energy and persistence in the fulfillment of party and government decisions. All party organs must firmly and consistently carry out the Leninist principles of the selection and indoctrination of cadres, select people according to their political and business-like qualities, and achieve a correct combination of old experienced officials and young energetic organizers who know their work well. There is no place in leading work for backward, ideologically barren, unprincipled people who have lost their ties with reality.

Systematic rejuvenation of elected organs is an inviolable norm of party, state, and public life. Elected organs should be rejuvenated so that the most capable people who are devoted to the cause of the party are drawn into leadership. Without a doubt, succession of leadership should be secured in the rejuvenation.

Speakers at the conference cited cases whereby the practical carrying out of the theses of the Party Program and Party Statutes concerning systematic rejuvenation of elected organs has elicited a pained reaction from several officials. Once having penetrated the sphere of leadership, some officials decided that this was awarded them almost for life; they became convinced of their "irreplaceability." Therefore, a transfer to other work, less important yet within their capability, has been taken as a personal insult.

Party committees, and primarily party organs sections of oblast and kray party committees and of union republic central committees, must strictly fulfill the demands of the 22d Party Congress on rejuvenating elected organs and observing the principle of removability and succession. . . .

Many examples of serious shortcomings in work with cadres were cited at the conference. Some secretaries of rural rayon party committees do not possess the necessary organizational capabilities and have a poor understanding of agricultural production. For example, among the first secretaries of rural rayon party committees in Ivanovskaya, Kalinisnskaya, Orlovskaya, and Chitinskaya oblasts, there are no agricultural specialists with a higher education.

There are no agronomists or zootechnicians on 137 kolkhozes in Pskovskaya Oblast. At the same time, more than 1,000 agricultural specialists work in industrial enterprises and in institutions. Sixty agricultural specialists have "settled down" in the Pskov Telephone Plant alone. Recently, 12 graduates of an agricultural tekhnikum arrived in Pskov and were registered as apprentices of metalworkers and lathe operators. . . .

Outmoded forms of work and an unsuitable style of leadership must be resolutely discarded. The features of a party leader are counseling with the people, being convivial in a Leninist manner, relying on the masses and utilizing their rich experience, persuading and explaining, and struggling passionately for that which is progressive.

Observance of the Leninist principle of collective leadership presupposes that any vitally important question in party organs be resolved collectively, taking into consideration the experience and opinion of the party masses. Examples were cited at the conference whereby certain leaders have tried to solve questions without the collective and have established a kind of "one man rule" in a party committee, which leads to serious mistakes. Thus, First Secretary V. K. Shishonkov of the Pavlodarskaya Oblast Party Committee introduced the practice of sending personal telegrams to rayons and kolkhozes, specifying the periods for conducting agricultural work, permitting serious mistakes in doing so. . . .

The development of public principles in party work were comprehensively discussed at the conference. The party line on expanding independent public principles reflects the natural (zakonomernyy) process of Soviet society's advance toward Communism. The 22d Party Congress posed the task of steadily reducing the paid party apparatus by broadly utilizing Communists as nonstaff [unpaid] officials in public activity.

As a result of the restoration and further development of Leninist norms of party life and principles of collective leadership, as well as the growth of Communists' activity, public principles have in recent years begun to enter into the work of party committees more and more steadily. There are now about 80,000 nonstaff instructors in party committees, almost 140,000 lecturers and speakers, more than 105,000 members of permanent commissions and councils, and more than 320,000 nonstaff officials in all. More than 10,000 Communists have been brought into such work on public principles in the Moscow City party organization. In the Ukraine, 10,000 nonstaff instructors, 157,000 nonstaff sections, and 1,940 public councils and commissions for various questions of party leadership are working in party committees. . . .

In accordance with a 13 December 1960 decree of the Central Committee CPSU, nonstaff party commissions for the preliminary examination of questions of acceptance into the party and personal cases of Communists were formed under the rayon party committees of Moscow and Leningrad and under the city and rayon party committees of Moskovskaya Oblast. This experiment has fully justified itself.

In all 11 January 62 decree, the Central Committee CPSU gave permission to union republic central committees and to kray and oblast party committees to form nonstaff party commissions for the preliminary examination of questions of acceptance into the party and personal cases of Communists under city and rayon party committees, using the experience of the party organizations of Moscow, Leningrad, and Moskovskaya Oblast. The decree stipulates that a city or rayon party committee secretary should be present at sessions of a nonstaff party commission. These and other commissions are auxiliary organs of party committees and their conclusions and proposals are subject to discussion and confirmation by the bureau of the party committee.

Several party committees still underrate the importance of the broad development of public principles in party work. This refers to a number of rayon and city party committees of Kurskaya, Ryazanskaya, and Kurganskaya oblasts. Until recently, there were no nonstaff instructors in the Andreyevskiy, Dzhambulskiy, and Kapal'skiy rayon party committees of Alma-Atinskaya Oblast. Until recently, rayon party committees in Kirgizia did not even attempt to form nonstaff sections.

Nonstaff work in the party committee is a fundamental and very important party commission (porucheniye), and those who fulfill it should not be overloaded with other tasks. Also, Communists must not be taken during working time for fulfillment of public duties.

The conference criticized party committees which do not always reason out their approach to the formation of commissions. For example, it is incomprehensible that commissions for assisting soviet control (komissii sodeystviya sovkontrol') were formed under several rayon and city party committees. Why was it necessary for the Gori City Party Committee of Georgia to form a permanent commission for housing distribution and a communal and medical commission when they already existed under the Gori Soviet?

On the initiative of the Lugansk City Party Committee, rayon and city councils of pensioners were formed; they try to act as independent organizations, assume the functions of party and soviet organs, and adopt their own decisions.

In comprehensively developing public principles, party commissions should be led strictly by Party Statutes and the Leninist norms of party life and principles of leadership which the Statutes contain. The conference emphasized that party organs must promote in every possible way the development of public principles in the work of soviet, trade-union, and Komsomol organizations.

The conference participants criticized the State Publishing House of Political Literature and the editorial boards of *Partiynaya Zhizn'* and newspapers and spoke of the need to elucidate more fully in the press the work of party committees under the new conditions. . . .

"The Cult of the Individual"

The troubles and complications recounted by the ancient legend of the opening of Pandora's box had a modern Soviet counterpart, figuratively speaking, in the troubles and complications which followed the downgrading of Stalin in 1956 and thereafter. By 1962, it was possible to distinguish three distinct stages in the process. The first stage, keynoted by the speeches of Mikoyan and Khrushchev at the Twentieth Party Congress, was marked by unrestrained, though not generally publicized attacks upon Stalin. Apparently the versions of these attacks which were gradually released to the Soviet people, or which reached the people by word of mouth, produced a reaction sufficiently adverse to require Khrushchev and his associates to modify their position. The modification, and this was the second stage, took the general form of acknowledging some of Stalin's contributions while insisting that he had been guilty of gross errors, not the least of which was his permitting the development of a "cult of the individual" centering upon himself. The Soviet people were told, in effect, "Stalin's undeniable errors must not blind us to the great things he accomplished." The third stage, dramatized by the removal of Stalin's body from the "Lenin Mausoleum" in Red Square, was marked by a partial reversion to the downgrading of Stalin and increased insistences that Khrushchev and his associates were the true continuers of Lenin's ideas and efforts.

The selections below were chosen to illustrate certain aspects of the downgrading of Stalin and its consequences. One task required by reason of these events was the "correction" of history. The first article, a slightly condensed translation of an article from *Izvestia* (14 February, 1962) continues the attack on Stalin. The second selection, an excerpt from an article by N. I. Shatagin, Deputy Director of the Institute of Marxism-Leninism, promises a new and "correct" history. The source is: *Sel'skaya Zhizn'* (*Country Life*), 21 January, 1962.

The editorial board of *Izvestia* has been receiving letters criticizing volumes 3, 4, and 5 of *Istoriia Grazhdanskoy Voyny v SSSR* (History of the Civil War in the USSR), which have been nominated for a Lenin Prize. Old Bolsheviks D. A. Sidorov, M. L. Sulimova, A. S. Rudenko, P. V. Petrovskiy, P. I. Vasilevskiy, V. N. Lapina, Yu. K. Milonov, I. P. Shmidt, and others consider that these editions bear a heavy burden of the consequences of the Stalin personality cult in the field of historical science. They write: "Many important events in the books have been distorted to magnify Stalin. His role during the Brest talks and at the Polish and Southern fronts have been elucidated incorrectly."

The authors of the collective letter note: "The activities of local Bolshevik organizations are insufficiently and often falsely outlined in *Istoriia Grazhdanskoy Voyny v SSSR* and in this way the history of the party's struggle is distorted."

In another letter Maj Gen V. F. Ryzhikov (ret) criticizes the book's description of military actions. He writes: "The reader gets the impression that the Civil War was unusually easy and that there were no mistakes or failures on the battlefields." Ryzhikov considers that many of the mistakes of the authors' and editorial collectives are explained by the fact that the advice and remarks of participants in the Civil War were not considered. Thus, there is a serious shortcoming in the book; many active fighters were not depicted in the book.

The writers of the letters agree that *Istoriia* . . . cannot be nominated for a Lenin Prize and that it needs substantial reworking.

* * * * *

The Communist Party and its Central Committee are constantly attentive to the collection and publication of the literature of Marx, Engels, and Lenin. Thanks to the efforts of the party, approximately 6,000 documents by Marx and Engels and more than 30,000 of Lenin's documents have been collected and are being preserved in original and photographed copies in the Institute of Marxism-Leninism.

The party has always been loyal to Leninism and has been guided by Leninist concepts in solving the complicated tasks of constructing socialism and Communism. During the period of the personality cult, the role of Lenin and his works was belittled; but no cult of personality can halt the progressive development of Soviet society or change the nature of socialist construction, the decisive, motivating force of which always was, is, and will be the mass of many millions of workers.

The elimination of the effects of the personality cult and the restoration of Leninist norms and principles of party life opened a wide area for the publication of Leninist documents which were previously unknown. After the 20th Party Congress, the Institute of Marxism-Leninism under the Central Committee CPSU published approximately 900 new Leninist documents.

According to a decision of the Central Committee, the fifth complete collection of *Sochineniia V. I. Lenina* (Works of V. I. Lenin) is being published. This edition includes works by V. I. Lenin included in the third and fourth editions as well as those published in collections of Lenin's works and in periodicals. A number of documents are being published for the first time in the *Sochineniia*.

In the complete collection of the *Sochineniia* of V. I. Lenin, the "Letter to the Congress," the latter "Concerning the Imparting of Legislative Functions to Gosplan," and "On the Question Concerning Nationalities or 'Autonomisation,' " dictated by Vladimir Il'ich in December 1922–January 1923, are also included. These important documents are a basic part of Lenin's final programmatic works. . . .

By decision of the Central Committee CPSU, work has begun on compiling a multivolume work on the history of the CPSU. The basic ideas for this historic work have been worked out. The first volume will be released in 1963, for the 60th anniversary of the Second Party Congress, which laid the foundation for our great Leninist party.

The multivolume history of the CPSU will be imbued with the spirit of Leninist concepts, the Leninist scientific method, and the decisions of the 20th and 22d party Congresses and the new Party Program. . . .

* * * * *

"Overcoming the harmful consequences of the Stalin cult" was obviously not without pitfalls. Party spokesmen explained repeatedly the need for party leadership, and the connection between party statutes and the cult of the individual. (The first excerpt below exemplifies such explanations.) Other party spokesmen warned against abusing the situation by attacking Marxist-Leninist theory under the guise of criticizing

Stalin's shortcomings. (The second excerpt, a condensed translation from a speech by Ye. Postovoy of the Moldavian SSR, illustrates this.) The source is: *Sovetskaya Moldaviya,* 31 January, 1962. And the Communist party bosses considered, among other instruments of control, the revival of the Workers' and Peasants' Inspectorates (*Rabkrin*) of the 1920's. Excerpts from an editorial in *Kommunist* (No. 2, 1962, pp. 4–12) and from an article by M. Mambetaliyev and A. Radvogin which was published in *Izvestia* on 16 February, 1962, deal with these matters.

. . . The Party Statutes are adopted on the basis of the Party Program; they issue from those political tasks and theoretical and organizational principles which the Program defines. In accord with the conditions and tasks of the period of the full-scale construction of Communism, the party formulated in the Program the theses which should be a guarantee against a revival of the cult of personality, advanced the principle of the systematic rejuvenation of leading party cadres, and pointed out measures for the further development of intraparty democracy. These important theses of the Program are expressed in concrete and developed form in the new Party Statutes which were adopted by the 22d Party Congress.

The Communist Party is the recognized and tested leader of the entire Soviet people and the leading force of the socialist state and of all mass organizations of workers. Therefore, the Party Program indicates the main direction, the general line, and the basic principles of the activity of all state and public organizations. In accord with the Party Program, each of these organizations in reorganizing its work according to the conditions and tasks of the full-scale construction of Communism.

* * * * *

Postovoy spoke further on the need to explain profoundly to Communists and all the toilers the party's measures in overcoming the harmful consequences of the Stalin cult. The personality cult caused a separation of theory from practice in ideological work in socialist construction and a contraction of the forms of ideological influence on the masses by the party. It is necessary to overcome these faults resolutely.

Postovoy pointed out the need to draw a precise line between the personality cult and all party activities. The personality cult hindered the initiative of the Central Committee and local party organizations, but it could not destroy all that which is alive and creative and which is by its very nature inherent in our party, and it could not remove the omnipotent Leninist spirit of creativity. The party acted as a living organism, and under its leadership our people achieved world-historic victories. That is why we must resolutely oppose those who try to use criticism of the personality cult for propaganda of bourgeois anarchy and to undermine the authority of the party and its leaders, and not permit a blow against the theory itself under the pretext of struggling against the consequences of the personality cult in the field of Marxist-Leninist theory.

In connection with the tasks for the final overcoming of the personality cult, particularly in ideological work, some comrades ask what shall be done with Stalin's works and which of his works can be used. The sole correct path is that of historical truth. The decisions of the 20th and 21st party congresses permitted establishment of this truth.

New textbooks on party history, political economy, and dialectical and historical materialism should be used widely in propaganda work. The publication of five volumes on the history of the Civil War in the USSR is complete. Three volumes of the history of the Great Patriotic War have appeared. Many consequences of the Stalin personality cult were overcome in the creation of these textbooks and scientific works. Now a multivolume history of the CPSU is being created, and it will permit full restoration of the historical truth. . . .

* * * * *

. . . The history of the Soviet socialist state is the history of a struggle for Leninist principles of state construction and against influences and tendencies which are alien to socialism, the history of a struggle against bureaucratic elements which took root in the riches of the Soviet state organization. Exceptionally important conclusions for theory and practice in state construction issue from the lessons of the cult of personality, which seriously damaged Soviet society and socialist democracy. The cult of Stalin's personality led to crude violation of socialist legality and of the democratic rights of Soviet citizens, limited the activity of democratic institutions, and infringed on the rights of union republics. Under conditions when exploiting classes had been liquidated and socialism had been victorious in the country and when the social, ideological, and political unity of Soviet society had formed and become strong, Stalin advanced the mistaken thesis on raising of the class struggle during the approach to socialism, and unjustified repressions against honest Soviet citizens increased; Stalin began to raise several limitations of Soviet democracy, which were unavoidable under the conditions of the fierce struggle against the class enemy, to a norm of state life, crudely violating Leninist principles of leadership. All this meant a serious distortion of the theory and practice of Leninism in questions of state.

Stalin's theoretical utterances and acts led to the hypertrophy of the executive, and primarily of the punitive, apparatus of the Soviet state and to a depreciation of the role of soviets as mass representative organizations. The Leninist thesis concerning soviets as schools of administration was to a considerable degree disparaged. Nevertheless, it is precisely the sovereign soviets, which resolve all state matters large and small, that should be, according to Lenin, a school of administration. The more complete the sovereignty of soviets, the better they will fulfill the tasks of instructing the masses in administration, for in this way alone are an economic attitude toward the matter, a feeling of high responsibility, and a taste for state work manifested and strengthened among people.

Obviously, the cult of personality could change neither the social and economic essence of the socialist system nor the democratic character of its political system. Precisely through the socialist nature of the social and state system which is alien to the cult of a "chosen personality" and the decisive force of the construction of socialism and Communism under all conditions, the working masses, led by the Communist Party which was tied closely to the people, substantially limited the harmful influence of the cult, and then overcame the cult and its consequences. However, it would be a crude mistake to underestimate the complete harm of the cult of personality for the development of socialist democracy, for it hampered —and did so increasingly—the progress of the Soviet system, as well as the growth of the activity and independence of builders of Communism. The criticism and unmasking of the cult of personality and the liquidation of its consequences are a truly great service of the CPSU and its historic 20th Party Congress. . . .

It is especially necessary to distinguish measures for intensifying state and public checking (kontrol'). Checking from above combined with checking from below on the activities of the state apparatus and all its links and all responsible persons is what is now primarily required successfully to rid ourselves of bureaucratism and other evils in the work of the state apparatus.

It is appropriate to recall the tremendous significance which V. I. Lenin attached to popular checking on the activities of the state apparatus. Defining the tasks of the Workers and Peasants Inspection (Rabkrin), Lenin emphasized that our goal is to have all the working masses, and especially women, participate in it. "The broad nonparty masses must check on all state matters and learn to administrate" Sochineniia (Works), Volume 30, p. 326.

In accord with these ideas of Lenin, the Party Program indicates that organs of control, which combine state checking with public inspection in the center and in the provinces, should function constantly. The party sees inspection by popular checking as an effective means for drawing the broad popular masses into the administration of matters of state and into the checking on strict observance of legality and as a means for improving the state apparatus, eliminating bureaucratism, and introducing in time the proposals of workers.

The socialist national state is in a condition to secure truly all-national checking on the activity of the state apparatus. And this is the reliable means of a timely suppression of bureaucratic arbitrariness and of the abuse of power by certain officials of state administration. This means that the apparatus of the socialist state in all its parts and links will fulfill with honor the great tasks of Communist construction. . . .

* * * * *

. . . In our view, all this happens because we do not have a general (yedinyy) checking agency. This permits certain economic workers to waste natural riches, often to expend thoughtlessly funds and raw materials, to permit localism, and to violate state discipline.

For this same reason, checking agencies do not genuinely rely on public checkers who are, essentially, not guided by anyone and whose rights and duties are not yet determined.

Practice shows that the need has matured for a basic reorganization of the whole system of checking (kontrol'). The direction of this reorganization is determined by the theses of the Party Program about the universal development and improvement of socialist democracy, enlisting all citizens in the administration of the state and leadership of economic and cultural construction, and improving the work of the state apparatus and intensifying popular checking on its activities.

Lenin repeatedly spoke of the need for participation by the broad masses in state checking. This Leninist idea was the foundation of the decision by the 12th Party Congress to organize the TsKK-RKI (Central Control Commission and Workers and Peasants Inspection). Lenin gave immense significance to the selection of cadres for the state checking apparatus. He demanded that this apparatus be staffed by people who were especially tested and conscientious and who knew the organization of labor in general and managerial and administrative work in particular.

The joint agency for state and party checking—TsKK-RKI—which was created at one time, played an exceptionally large role in strengthening the Soviet state apparatus and in improving its activities.

In our view, the reorganization of the state checking system must now be implemented with consideration of this experience as applicable to present conditions of Communist construction. It seems to us that a single agency of state and public checking should be created. This agency will meet the demands of the Party Program about combining state checking with a public inspectorate in the center and the local areas.

In our opinion, it is expedient to organize a single checking agency to which all present agencies of interdepartmental and departmental checking would be subordinated and which would lead the whole system of public inspectorates and checkers. The expediency of eliminating departmental checking in general may appear subsequently. The collegium of such an agency should include representatives of trade-union, cooperative, and Komsomol organizations, working on public principles in this collegium.

Participation of broad strata of the toilers in checks and audits will not only permit reduction of official staffs but will also provide more profound analysis of matters, disclosure of shortcomings, and elaboration of measures to eliminate them.

The activities of popular checking cannot be reduced merely to observing fulfillment of party and governmental decisions. The agencies for this checking must profoundly study administrative matters and not only disclose shortcomings but also disseminate positive experience, elaborate measures for the simplification and improvement of the Soviet state apparatus, achieving a genuinely scientific organization of its activities.

In our opinion, creation of a single agency of state and public checking would be a powerful means for fostering the further development of the national economy and improvement of the work of all levels of the state apparatus.

* * * * *

The final selection in this series is a translation of an article published in *Politicheskoye Samoobrazovanie* (*Political Self-Education*), no. 1 (1961), pp. 12–14. The author is A. Kosul'nikov, one-time Deputy Director (1957–1961) of the Propaganda and Agitation Section, RSFSR, and subsequently the editor-in-chief of *Voprosy istorii KPSS* (*Problems of History, Communist Party of the Soviet Union*). Kosul'nikov re-affirms the role of Marxism-Leninism and asserts the leadership of Khrushchev in the "creative" application of Marxism-Leninism to practice.

. . . The strength of our party is that it always marches in step with life, and life never stands still. By developing and changing, it creates new conditions and puts forth new tasks. The Communist Party approaches the solution of these tasks, which have been set forth by practice, from positions of creative Marxism and examines theory not as a code of dogmatic formulas and not as hardened canons given once and for all time but as militant guidance for action.

By devoting a thorough study to the processes and phenomena of life and by considering the given conditions and specific experience carefully and thoroughly, the party creatively develops Marxist-Leninist theory and enriches it with new conclusions and propositions. In this is seen the important condition of vitality and the growth of the transforming role of the ideas of Marxism-Leninism and of its powerful magnetic force.

The Communist Party invariably follows Marxism-Leninism and is faithful to this great and all-conquering teaching. But in the works of the founders of Marxism-Leninism we cannot find and shall not find detailed answers to all the questions arising in the field of economics, in the matter of managing the economy, in organizing public life, and in current international policies. Only inveterate dogmatists try to fit the living processes of reality to theoretical formulas which were correct for their time but which are now obsolescent. Only rigid persons and conservatives shut themselves in with blank fences of quotations away from the authoritative demands of life and from the persistent needs of modern development. Posing as the adherents of Marxism, in reality they are apostates from the eternally living and developing teachings of Marxism-Leninism.

The development of theory and practice in their organic unity is a clear distinctive trait of Soviet socialist society showing its great vital force. Marxism-Leninism teaches that theory without practice can become hardened and transformed into a dead scheme. Marxism-Leninism not only explains the world correctly but it also shows the working class and the working masses how to change it. It is their weapon in the struggle for the revolutionary transformation of society on Communist principles.

The Soviet people were fortunate to be the first to convert the ideas of Marxism-Leninism into reality—to build socialism and successfully to carry out the change toward Communism. The workers in the countries of the People's Democracies are successfully building socialism. This means that under modern conditions the theory of Marxism-Leninism has become a part of the everyday working life of more than one billion people and has merged with the practice of building socialism and Communism in the immense areas of Europe and Asia.

Marxism-Leninism recognizes the practice of scientific knowledge as its purpose and foundation and sees in it the criterion of truth, but this has nothing in common with narrow-minded practicalness of belittling of the significance of theory. The creative development of Marxism-Leninism has always been the subject of particular concern to the CPSU and to all fraternal Communist and workers parties. The period between the 20th and 22d party congresses is one of the richest periods in the development of theoretical thought. It shows that particularly in recent years attention to problems of Marxist-Leninist theory has grown among us. What is the explanation for this?

Firstly, the rapid and thorough development of our society and its entry into the period of full-scale building of Communism have produced vital new goals and problems which need a deep scientific analysis and theoretical generalization. Secondly, it has been necessary to explain theoretically the changes in the alignment of forces on the world scene and the experience of the development of the world socialist system and to determine new possibilities and tasks in strengthening peace in the whole world. Thirdly, we have had to expand the decisive and implacable ideological struggle against the attacks of modern revisionism, dogmatists, and sectarians and also increase the struggle against all manifestations of bourgeois ideology.

In our country the development of productive forces is proceeding at a furious pace, socialist production relations are improving, and science and culture are constantly reaching new boundaries. This is proof of the successful movement of a socialist society toward Communism. But it is natural that on the road to this great goal life puts forward new problems and such important questions to which theory, which moves hand in hand with the practice of building Communism, must find answers. N. S. Khrushchev said, "Each practical problem of socialist construction is simultaneously also a theoretical question which has a direct relationship to the creative development of Marxism-Leninism. It is impossible to separate one from the other." The Communist Party and its Leninist Central Committee are successfully solving the problems of immense practical and at the same time theoretical significance. The party does not hesitate at a daring break with obsolescent work methods and forms of leadership over the national economy and at replacing them with new ones which come closer to meeting the urgent modern demands of life.

In the decisions of the 20th and 21st party congresses, in the decrees of the plenums of the Central Committee CPSU, and in N. S. Khrushchev's speeches, Marxist-Leninist theory is receiving further creative development. An enormous collective contribution to the treasure house of Marxism-Leninism has been made by Communist and workers parties after having worked out and adopted the program documents at conferences of their representatives in 1957 and 1960. The Central Committee CPSU and its First Secretary N. S. Khrushchev played an enormous role in drawing up these outstanding documents in which the most vital and timely problems of our time received creative development.

The development of theory for Communists is not an end in itself but one of the most important means in the struggle for the revolutionary transformation of a society on the basis of socialism and Communism and for an improvement in the life of the people. N. S. Khrushchev said, "The main thing for us, the builders of Communism, is man. The struggle for Communism is a struggle for a better life for man. Everything is for man's happiness, everything is for him!"

Now all the efforts of the party and people are directed toward putting into practice the decisions of the 21st Party Congress and the Seven-Year Economic Plan. This is really putting Marxism-Leninism into action under modern conditions. This is a whole system of practical measures directed at creating the material and technical basis of Communism, at raising the well-being and cultural level of the workers, at strengthening the world socialist system, and at assuring a stable peace, friendship, and cooperation with the peoples of all countries.

Progressive and revolutionary ideas only play a transforming part in the life of a society when they take possession of the masses and when people put them into practice and convert them into specific deeds. Marx wrote, "Ideas in general cannot carry out anything. To carry out ideas we need people who must make use of practical effort." (K. Marx and F. Engels, Works, Vol. 2, p. 132.) . . .

"The Inevitability of War" and Intra-Party Politics

Khrushchev's pronouncement on the "inevitability of war"—made at the Twentieth Party Congress and elaborated at the next two party congresses—became entwined with the attacks upon Stalin ("the cult of personality") and with Khrushchev's power struggles against the "anti-party group." Three Soviet professors of international law—Ye. A. Korovin, F. I. Kozhevnikov, and G. P. Zadorozhny—wove these themes together in an article published in Izvestia on 18 April, 1962. A translation of their major points is printed below.

. . . Concerning the question of war and peace, I. V. Stalin advanced the thesis in Ekonomicheskiye Problemy Sotsializma v SSSR (Economic Problems of Socialism in the USSR) that the contemporary movement for peace can lead at the best only "to preventing the given war, to a temporary delay of it, to a temporary preservation of the given peace" in view of the "inevitability" of war in general, according to his assertion, as long as imperialism exists. The 20th, 21st, and 22d party congresses gave a different evaluation in principle. They drew precise, specific, universally based conclusions that as a result of the basic change in the relationship of forces in the international arena, war has now ceased to be a fatal inevitability and that the peace-loving forces cannot only forestall but even exclude world war from the life of society even before the complete victory of socialism on earth and with the preservation of capitalism in part of the world. . . .

V. I. Lenin is the creator of the thesis on peaceful coexistence of the two systems as an objective need of historical development after the Great October Socialist Revolution. He formulated precisely the idea of peaceful coexistence and he wrote of the "inescapability of agreement" of the capitalist system of ownership with the socialist "as equal with equal." However, I. V. Stalin allegedly said in a 1947 talk with H. Stassen that only the "thought of collaboration of the two systems" was first expressed by Lenin. In his letter to the 22d Party Congress, Molotov sank to the assertion that Lenin in general never spoke about peaceful coexistence.

It is no labor to restrain the hand of the bankrupt factionalist who for the benefit of his antiparty conceptions does not refrain from an improper attempt to stifle the well-known Leninist theses.

The 20th, 21st, and 22d party congresses affirmed with new force that the Leninist principle of peaceful coexistence was and remains the general line of Soviet foreign policy.

Great merit in the elaboration and justification of the principles of peaceful coexistence belongs to the consistent champion for peace and friendship among peoples, N. S. Khrushchev. His reports at party congresses and speeches at the UN and other speeches are the further development of the Leninist thesis on peaceful coexistence applicable to the contemporary, specific historical epoch. . . .

The underrating of the role of the popular masses in the science of international law is a consequence of the cult of personality, which was reflected in the definition of sovereignty and international law given by A. Ya. Vyshinskiy, which ignored the role of the people and their influence on international relations. Vyshinskiy gave a confused and harmful definition of the law in general and international law in particular. The basic harm of his determinations of sovereignty and international law is the obvious underrating of the Leninist idea of peaceful coexistence, the cornerstone of contemporary international law.

The struggle against every sort of deviation from the Leninist thesis of peaceful coexistence, manifestations of bourgeois ideology, revisionism, dogmatism, and sectarianism, just as against the harmful consequences of the cult of personality, is the vital task of the science of international law.

There is in the Leninist understanding of peaceful coexistence a specific form of class struggle, and not conciliation with capitalism, as the dogmatists and sectarians assert.

Where to Find More Information

There is a continuous improvement in quality as well as a vast increase in quantity and variety of materials dealing with the Soviet period. A complete bibliography would run to thousands of titles. Hundreds of selected titles may be readily found in the books by Professors Clarkson, Mazour, Wren, and myself —to mention only four of many possible sources of more information. In addition to this ready availability, most of the books on the Soviet period are specialized in theme or limited in chronological scope to the point that even a sampling would require an extensive list. For these reasons, the entries below are limited to the general works which have been cited in all the preceding sections.

CHARQUES, *Short History,* ch. 17.
CLARKSON, *History,* chs. 26–37.
HARCAVE, *Readings,* vol. 2, sections 12–22.
MAZOUR, *Russia,* chs. 29–38.
PARES, *History,* chs. 25–28.
WALSH, *Russia,* chs. 21–29.
WREN, *Course,* chs. 28–32.

From Ancient Times to Nicholas I

CONTENTS OF VOLUME I (cont.)